W9-BVY-550

BETTER BUSINESS

THIRD EDITION

Michael R. Solomon
Contributing Editor

Mary Anne Poatsy

Kendall Martin

6.3.19

PEARSON

Boston   Columbus   Indianapolis   New York   San Francisco   Upper Saddle
Amsterdam   Cape Town   Dubai   London   Madrid   Milan   Munich   Paris   Mon
Delhi   Mexico City   São Paulo   Sydney   Hong Kong   Seoul   Singapore   Taipe

Editor in Chief: Stephanie Wall
Acquisitions Editor: Sarah McCabe
Development Editor: Jennifer Lynn
Director of Editorial Services: Ashley Santora
Editorial Project Manager: Karin Williams
Editorial Assistant: Ashlee Bradbury
Director of Marketing: Maggie Moylan
Senior Managing Editor: Judy Leale
Production Project Manager: Jacqueline A. Martin
Operation Specialist: Cathleen Petersen
Senior Art Director: Kenny Beck

Cover and Interior Designer: LCI Design
Cover Image: Getty Images/Jose Luis Pelaez
Media Project Manager, Production: Lisa Rinaldi
Senior Media Project Manager, Editorial:
 Denise Vaughn
Full-Service Project Management and Composition:
 S4Carlisle Publishing Services
Printer/Binder: R.R. Donnelley/Willard
Cover Printer: Lehigh-Phoenix Color/Hagerstown
Text Font: Palatino LT Std, 10/12

Credits and acknowledgments borrowed from other sources and reproduced, with permission, in this textbook appear on the appropriate page within the text or in the reference notes (photo credits appear on page).

Microsoft and/or its respective suppliers make no representations about the suitability of the information contained in the documents and related graphics published as part of the services for any purpose. All such documents and related graphics are provided "as is" without warranty of any kind. Microsoft and/or its respective suppliers hereby disclaim all warranties and conditions with regard to this information, including all warranties and conditions of merchantability, whether express, implied or statutory, fitness for a particular purpose, title and non-infringement. In no event shall Microsoft and/or its respective suppliers be liable for any special, indirect or consequential damages or any damages whatsoever resulting from loss of use, data or profits, whether in an action of contract, negligence or other tortious action, arising out of or in connection with the use or performance of information available from the services.

The documents and related graphics contained herein could include technical inaccuracies or typographical errors. Changes are periodically added to the information herein. Microsoft and/or its respective suppliers may make improvements and/or changes in the product(s) and/or the program(s) described herein at any time. Partial screen shots may be viewed in full within the software version specified.

Microsoft® and Windows® are registered trademarks of the Microsoft Corporation in the U.S.A. and other countries. This book is not sponsored or endorsed by or affiliated with the Microsoft Corporation.

Copyright © 2014, 2012, 2010 Pearson Education, Inc., One Lake Street, Upper Saddle River, New Jersey 07458. All rights reserved. Manufactured in the United States of America. This publication is protected by Copyright, and permission should be obtained from the publisher prior to any prohibited reproduction, storage in a retrieval system, or transmission in any form or by any means, electronic, mechanical, photocopying, recording, or likewise. To obtain permission(s) to use material from this work, please submit a written request to Pearson Education, Inc., Permissions Department, One Lake Street, Upper Saddle River, New Jersey 07458.

Many of the designations by manufacturers and seller to distinguish their products are claimed as trademarks. Where those designations appear in this book, and the publisher was aware of a trademark claim, the designations have been printed in initial caps or all caps.

Library of Congress Cataloging-in-Publication Data

Solomon, Michael R.
 Better business / Michael R. Solomon, Mary Anne Poatsy, Kendall Martin. —
 3rd ed.
   p. cm.
  ISBN-13: 978-0-13-305904-5
  ISBN-10: 0-13-305904-9
 1. Business. 2. Entrepreneurship. 3. Commerce. I. Poatsy, Mary Anne.
 II. Martin, Kendall. III. Title.
  HD31.P555 2014
  658--dc23
                                              2012026331

**Notice:
This work is
protected by U.S.
copyright laws and
is provided solely
for the use of
college instructors
in reviewing
course materials
for classroom use.
Dissemination
or sale of this
work or any part
(including on the
World Wide Web)
is not permitted.**

9 8 7 6 5 4 3 2 1

ISBN 10: 0-13-305904-9
ISBN 13: 978-0-13-305904-5

DEDICATION

To Rose
Michael R. Solomon

For my husband, Ted, who unselfishly continues to take on more than his fair share to support me throughout this process; and for my children, Laura, Carolyn, and Teddy, whose encouragement and love have been inspiring.
Mary Anne Poatsy

For all the teachers, mentors, and gurus who have popped in and out of my life.
Kendall Martin

Brief Contents

Contents

PART 2
Starting and Structuring a Business   130

PART 3
Managing a Business and Employees 202

About the Authors

Michael R. Solomon, PhD, *Contributing Editor*

Michael R. Solomon is professor of marketing and director of the Center for Consumer Research in the Haub School of Business at Saint Joseph's University in Philadelphia. He also is professor of consumer behaviour at the Manchester School of Business, The University of Manchester, U.K. Michael's primary research and consulting interests include consumer behavior, branding, and marketing applications of virtual worlds. He has written several textbooks and trade books; his *Consumer Behavior* text is the most widely used in the world. Michael often speaks to business groups about new trends in consumer behavior and marketing strategy.

Mary Anne Poatsy, MBA, CFP

mpoatsy@mc3.edu

Mary Anne Poatsy is a senior adjunct faculty member at Montgomery County Community College, teaching various business, management, and computer application and concepts courses in face-to-face and online environments. She holds a BA in psychology and education from Mount Holyoke College and an MBA in finance from Northwestern University's J. L. Kellogg Graduate School of Management.

Mary Anne has been teaching since 1995 at a variety of elementary and secondary institutions, including Gwynedd Mercy College, Montgomery County Community College, Muhlenberg College, and Bucks County Community College, as well as training in the professional environment and presenting at several conferences. Before teaching, she was a vice president at Shearson Lehman Hutton in the Municipal Bond Investment Banking Department.

Kendall Martin, PhD

kmartin@mc3.edu

Kendall Martin has been teaching since 1988 at a number of institutions, including Villanova University, DeSales University, Arcadia University, Ursinus College, County College of Morris, and Montgomery County Community College, at both the undergraduate and graduate levels.

Kendall's education includes a BS in electrical engineering from the University of Rochester and an MS and a PhD in engineering from the University of Pennsylvania. She has industrial experience in research and development environments (AT&T Bell Laboratories) as well as experience with several start-up technology firms.

As an associate professor at Montgomery County Community College, she presents nationally on topics of entrepreneurship, student engagement, and technology in the classroom.

Acknowledgments

Like any good business, this project could not have been completed without the dedicated efforts of a talented group of people to whom we are eternally grateful. The authors would like to take this time to thank the many colleagues, friends, and students who have contributed toward our vision of an introductory textbook that excites and challenges students.

From the very conception of *Better Business*, 3rd edition, to the last page produced, a remarkable board of reviewers at schools across the nation has guided us with wise counsel. Our joy in working with such talented and student-centered faculty is deep. We extend our sincerest gratitude to our reviewers.

The division of Business Publishing at Pearson has been incredible in devoting time and resources to the creation of *Better Business*, 3rd edition, learning system. We are indebted to Jodi McPherson, our former executive editor, who had the vision for a new introduction to business textbook system that engages and excites students, and our acquisitions editor, James Heine, whose guidance provided the foundation for this edition. We also welcome our new acquisitions editor, Sarah McCabe, who has taken over where James left off. Without their vision, passion, dedication, and drive, this textbook would not exist. Our thanks also extend to our project manager, Karin Williams, who diligently kept us on track with only gentle threats when we went astray! Karin's fine management skills enabled this complex project to be completed on time—a feat not easily accomplished. Maggie Moylan, director of marketing, has been very instrumental in shaping the message of the book. We are so appreciative of her ardent attention to all the marketing details that are so important. We're also appreciative for the dedication of the media team of Cathi Profitko, Joan Waxman, and Denise Vaughn, who were instrumental in the development of all the multimedia products that make up **My*Biz*Lab**, and for their efforts to ensure that it works seamlessly with the textbook. Additionally, we would like to thank Kenny Beck, Judy Leale, and Jacqueline Martin for their efforts in the design and production of *Better Business*, 3rd edition. Lastly, our thanks to Paul Corey, president of business publishing, and Stephanie Wall, editor in chief, who have backed this project with the necessary financial and human resources to make our vision a reality.

We would be completely negligent if we did not acknowledge all the incredibly talented and devoted designers, permissions researchers, and others who contributed to the project and to whom we extend our sincerest thanks.

Additionally, we would like to thank the many supplement authors for this edition: Kate Demarest, Randy Gerber, Linda Hoffman, and Maureen Steddin.

Everything we do is inspired by the experiences we have in the classroom. We want to thank and encourage our students, whose experiences, struggles, victories, and honesty have shaped this project turn by turn. We strive for *Better Business*, 3rd edition, to serve our students as a stepping-stone to meaningful careers and lives.

Last, but not least, close to home, our families have sacrificed much to let us focus on the project. We appreciate their patience and support throughout the writing process.

Reviewers

Wendi Achey, *Northampton Community College*
Mustafa Akcadogan, *Pikes Peak Community College*
Joni Anderson, *Buena Vista University*
Lydia Anderson, *Fresno City College*
Natalie Andrews, *Sinclair Community College*
Sally Andrews, *Linn Benton Community College*
Roanne Angiello, *Bergen Community College*
Brenda Anthony, *Tallahassee Community College*
Maria Aria, *Camden County College*
Corinne Asher, *Henry Ford Community College*
Susan Athey, *Colorado State University*
Michael Aubry, *Grossmont College*
David Bader, *Columbus State Community College*
Mazen Badra, *Webster University*
Michael Baran, *South Puget Sound Community College*
Ruby Barker, *Tarleton State University*
William Barrett, *University of Wisconsin*
Denise Barton, *Wake Technical Community College*
Dick Barton, *El Camino College*
Crystal Bass, *Trinity Valley Community College*
Jeffrey Bauer, *University of Cincinnati*
Christine Bauer-Ramazani, *Saint Michael's College*
Leslie Beau, *Orange Coast College*
Gayona Beckford-Barclay, *Community College of Baltimore County*
Robert Bennett, *Delaware County Community College*
George Bernard, *Seminole Community College*
Patricia Bernson, *County College of Morris*
Rick Bialac, *Georgia College and State University*
Danielle Blesi, *Hudson Valley Community College*
Chuck Bowles, *Pikes Peak Community College*
Malcolm Bowyer, *Montgomery Community College*
Steven Bradley, *Austin Community College*
Charles Braun, *Marshall University*
Edwin Breazeale, *Midlands Technical College*
Sharon Breeding, *Bluegrass Community Technical College*
Richard Brennan, *North Virginia Community College*
Robert Bricker, *Pikes Peak Community College*
Lisa Briggs, *Columbus State Community College*
T. L. Brink, *Crafton Hills College*
Dennis Brode, *Sinclair Community College*
Katherine Broneck, *Pima Community College*
Harvey Bronstein, *Oakland Community College*
Deborah Brown, *North Carolina State University*
Sylvia Brown, *Midland College*
Janet Brown-Sederberg, *Massasoit Community College*
Lesley Buehler, *Ohlone College*
Barry Bunn, *Valencia Community College*
Carroll Burrell, *San Jacinto College*
Marian Canada, *Ivy Technical Community College*

Diana Carmel, *Golden West College*
John Carpenter, *Lake Land College*
Deborah Carter, *Coahoma Community College*
Tiffany Champagne, *Houston Community College*
Glen Chapuis, *St. Charles Community College*
Bonnie Chavez, *Santa Barbara City College*
Sudhir Chawla, *Angelo State University*
Lisa Cherivtch-Zingaro, *Oakton Community College*
Desmond Chun, *Chabot College*
John Cicero, *Shasta College*
Michael Cicero, *Highline Community College*
Subasree Cidambi, *Mount San Antonio College*
Joseph Cilia, *Delaware Technical & Community College*
Mark Clark, *Collin County Community College*
William Clark, *Leeward Community College*
Paul Coakley, *Community College of Baltimore County*
Ken Combs, *Del Mar College*
Jamie Commissaris, *Davenport University*
Rachna Condos, *American River College*
Charlie Cook, *University of West Alabama*
Solveg Cooper, *Cuesta College*
Douglas Copeland, *Johnson County Community College*
Julie Couturier, *Grand Rapids Community College*
Brad Cox, *Midlands Technical College*
Diane Coyle, *Montgomery County Community College*
Chad Creevy, *Davenport University*
Geoff Crosslin, *Kalamazoo Valley Community College*
Ebony Crump, *Kennedy-King College*
H. Perry Curtis, *Collin County Community College*
Dana D'Angelo, *Drexel University*
Mark Dannenberg, *Shasta College*
Jamey Darnell, *Durham Tech*
Amlan Datta, *Cisco College*
Shirley Davenport, *Prairie State College*
Helen Davis, *Jefferson Community Technical College*
Peter Dawson, *Collin County Community College*
David Dearman, *University of Arkansas*
Sherry Decuba, *Indian River Community College*
Andrew Delaney, *Truckee Meadows Community College*
Kate Demarest, *Carroll Community College*
Donna Devault, *Fayetteville Tech*
Susan Dik, *Kapiolani Community College*
Michael DiVecchio, *Central Pennsylvania College*
Gerard Dobson, *Waukesha County Technical College*
Kathleen Dominick, *Bucks County Community College and University of Phoenix Online*
Ron Dougherty, *Ivy Technical Community College*
Karen Drage, *Eastern Illinois University*
Nelson Driver, *University of Arkansas*

Allison Duesing, *Northeast Lakeview College*
Timothy Durfield, *Citrus College*
David Dusseau, *University of Oregon*
Dana Dye, *Gulf Coast Community College*
C. Russell Edwards, *Valencia Community College*
Karen Edwards, *Chemeketa Community College*
Stephen Edwards, *University of North Dakota*
Stewart Edwards, *North Virginia Community College*
Susan Ehrfurth, *Aims Community College*
Patrick Ellsberg, *Lower Columbia College*
Susan Emens, *Kent State University*
Karen Emerson, *Southeast Community College*
Theodore Emmanuel, *State University of New York Oswego*
Kellie Emrich, *Cuyahoga Community College*
Vince Enslein, *Clinton Community College*
Steven Ernest, *Baton Rouge Community College*
Mary Ewanechko, *Monroe County Community College*
Marie Farber-Lapidus, *Oakton Community College*
Geralyn Farley, *Purdue University*
Janice Feldbauer, *Schoolcraft College and Austin Community College*
Mary Felton-Kolstad, *Chippewa Valley Technical College*
Louis Ferracane, *University of Phoenix*
David Fitoussi, *University of California*
Joseph Flack, *Washtenaw Community College*
Jacalyn Flom, *University of Toledo*
Carla Flores, *Ball State University*
Carol Flowers, *Orange Coast College*
Jake Flyzik, *Lehigh Carbon Community College*
Thomas Foley, *Kent State University*
Craig Fontaine, *Northeastern University*
Joseph Fox, *Asheville-Buncombe Technical Community College*
Mark Fox, *Indiana University–South Bend*
Victoria Fox, *College of DuPage*
Charla Fraley, *Columbus State Community College*
John Frank, *Columbus State Community College*
Leatrice Freer, *Pitt Community College*
Paula Freston, *Merced College*
Fred Fry, *Bradley University*
Albert Fundaburk, *Bloomsburg University*
William Furrell, *Moorpark College*
Michael Gagnon, *Kellogg Community College*
Wayne Gawlik, *Joliet Junior College*
George Generas, *University of Hartford*
Vanessa Germeroth, *Ozarks Technical Community College*
Gerald GeRue, *Rock Valley College*
John Geubtner, *Tacoma Community College*
Katie Ghahramani, *Johnson County Community College*
David Gilliss, *San Jose State University*
Eric Glohr, *Lansing Community College*
Robert Goldberg, *Northeastern University*
Constance Golden, *Lakeland Community College*
Gayle Goldstone, *Santa Rosa Junior College*
Alfredo Gomez, *Broward Community College*

Phillip Gonsher, *Johnson County Community College*

Robert Googins, *Shasta College*

Karen Gore, *Ivy Technical Community College–Southwest*

Carol Gottuso, *Metropolitan Community College*

Gretchen Graham, *Community College of Allegheny County (Boyce campus)*

Selina Griswold, *University of Toledo*

John Guess, *Delgado Community College*

Kevin Gwinner, *Kansas State University*

Peggy Hager, *Winthrop University*

Lawrence Hahn, *Palomar College*

Semere Haile, *Grambling State University*

Lynn Halkowicz, *Bloomsburg University*

Clark Hallpike, *Elgin Community College*

Paula Hansen, *Des Moines Area Community College*

Frank Harber, *Indian River Community College*

LaShon Harley, *Durham Technical Community College*

Jeri Harper, *Western Illinois University*

Deborah Haseltine, *Southwest Tennessee Community College*

Carol Heeter, *Ivy Tech Community College*

Linda Hefferin, *Elgin Community College*

Debra Heimberger, *Columbus State Community College*

Dennis Heiner, *College of Southern Idaho*

Cheryl Heitz, *Lincoln Land Community College*

Charlane Held, *Onondaga Community College*

Rebecca Helms, *Ivy Tech Community College*

Heith Hennel, *Valencia Community College*

Dorothy Hetmer-Hinds, *Trinity Valley Community College*

Linda Hoffman, *Ivy Technical Community College–Fort Wayne*

Merrily Hoffman, *San Jacinto College*

Gene Holand, *Columbia Basin College*

Phillip Holleran, *Mitchell Community College*

Robert Hood, *Chattanooga State Technical Community College*

Sheila Hostetler, *Orange Coast College*

Larry Hottot, *North Virginia Community College*

William Huisking, *Bergen Community College*

Lynn Hunsaker, *Mission College*

Steven Huntley, *Florida Community College at Jacksonville*

Johnny Hurley, *Iowa Lakes Community College*

Kimberly Hurns, *Washtenaw Community College*

Holly Hutchins, *Central Oregon Community College*

Linda Isenhour, *Eastern Michigan University*

Katie Jackson, *Columbus State Community College*

Linda Jaeger, *Southeast Community College*

Dolores James, *University of Maryland University College*

Pam Janson, *Stark State College of Technology*

Larry Jarrell, *Louisiana Technical University*

Earlene Jefferson, *Kennedy-King College*

Joe Jenkins, *Tarrant County College*

Brandy Johnson, *Columbus State Community College*

Dennis Johnson, *Delaware County Community College*

Floyd Johnson, *Davenport University*

M. Gwen Johnson, *Black Hawk College*

Carroll Jones, *Tulsa Community College*

Jeffrey Jones, *The College of Southern Nevada*

Kenneth Jones, *Ivy Technical Community College–Central Indiana*

Gayla Jurevich, *Fresno City College*

Alex Kajstura, *Daytona Beach College*

Dmitriy Kalyagin, *Chabot College*

Radhika Kaula, *Missouri State University*

John Kavouras, *Ohio College of Massage Therapy*

Dan Keating, *Fox Valley Technical College*

Albert Keller, *Dixie State College of Utah*

Ann Kelly, *Georgia Southern University*

Jeffrey Kennedy, *Broward Community College*

Jeffrey Kennedy, *Palm Beach Atlantic University*

Daniel Kipley, *Azusa Pacific University*

William Kline, *Bucks County Community College*

Susan Kochenrath, *Ivy Technical Community College*

Linda Koffel, *Houston Community College Central*

Todd Korol, *Monroe County Community College*

Jack Kraettli, *Oklahoma City Community College*

Jim Kress, *Central Oregon Community College*

John Kurnik, *St. Petersburg College*

Paul Laesecke, *University of Denver*

Martha Laham, *Diablo Valley College*

Mary LaPann, *Adirondack Community College*

Deborah Lapointe, *Central New Mexico Community College*

Rob Leadbeater, *Mission College*

David Leapard, *Eastern Michigan University*

Denise Lefort, *Clemson University*

Ron Lennon, *Barry University*

Angela Leverett, *Georgia Southern University*

Sue Lewis, *Tarleton State University*

Kathleen Lorencz, *Oakland Community College*

Mark Lowenstein, *College of St. Joseph*

John Luke, *Delaware County Community College*

John Mago, *Anoka-Ramsey Community College*

Jan Mangos, *Valencia Community College*

Christine Marchese, *Nassau Community College*

James Marco, *Wake Technical Community College*

Suzanne Markow, *Des Moines Area Community College*

Gary Marrer, *Glendale Community College*

Calvin Martin, *Davenport University*

James Martin, *Washburn University*

Kathleen Martinez, *Red Rocks Community College*

Thomas Mason, *Brookdale Community College*

Marian Matthews, *Central New Mexico Community College*

Kelli Mayes-Denker, *Carl Sandburg College*

Kevin McCarthy, *Baker University*

Gina McConoughey, *Illinois Central College*

Lisa McCormick, *Community College of Allegheny*

Patrick L. McCormick, *Ivy Tech Community College*

Pamela McElligott, *Meramec Community College*

Edward McGee, *Rochester Institute of Technology*

Donna McGill-Cameron, *Yuba College*

Vince McGinnis, *Bucks County Community College*

Allison McGullion, *West Kentucky Community & Technical College*

Lorraine McKnight, *Eastern Michigan University*

Bruce McLaren, *Indiana State University*

Juan Meraz, *Missouri State University*

James Meyers, *Pikes Peak Community College*

Miriam Michael, *American River College*

Jeanette Milius, *Iowa Western Community College*

Carol Millard, *Scottsdale Community College*

John Miller, *Pima Community College*

Linda Miller, *Northeast Community College*

Pat Miller, *Grossmont College*

Morgan Milner, *Eastern Michigan University*

Diane Minger, *Cedar Valley College*

Susan Mitchell, *Des Moines Area Community College*

Theresa Mitchell, *Alabama A&M University*

Joseph Molina, *MiraCosta College*

Carol Moore, *California State University*

Wayne Moore, *Indiana University of Pennsylvania*

Richard Morris, *Northeastern State University*

Jennifer Morton, *Ivy Tech Community College of Indiana*

David Murphy, *Madisonville Community College*

Gary Murray, *Rose State College*

John Muzzo, *Harold Washington College*

Mark Nagel, *Normandale Community College*

Conrad Nankin, *Pace University*

Kristi Newton, *Chemeketa Community College*

Steven Nichols, *Metropolitan Community College*

Simon Nwaigwe, *Baltimore City Community College*

Mark Nygren, *Brigham Young University*

Asmelash Ogbasion, *Southwest Tennessee Community College*

Cynthia L. Olivarez Rooker, *Lansing Community College*

David Olson, *California State University*

Anthony O'Malley, *Baruch College*

Lori Oriatti, *College of Lake County*

Robert O'Toole, *Crafton Hills College*

Mary Padula, *Borough of Manhattan Community College*

Esther Page-Wood, *Western Michigan University*

Lauren Paisley, *Genesee Community College*

Dyan Pease, *Sacramento City College*

Jeffrey Pepper, *Chippewa Valley Technical College*

Clifford Perry, *Florida International University*

Melinda Phillabaum, *Indiana University–Purdue University*

Rose Pollard, *Southeast Community College*

Jackie (J. Robinson) Porter, *Eastfield College*

Kathleen Powers, *Henry Ford Community College*

Dan Powroznik, *Chesapeake College*

Sally Proffitt, *Tarrant County College*

Joe Puglisi, *Butler County Community College*

James Pullins, *Columbus State Community College*

Kathy Pullins, *Columbus State Community College*

Bobby Puryear, *North Carolina State University*

Martha Racine Taylor, *College of the Redwoods*

Anthony Racka, *Oakland Community College*

Robert Reck, *Western Michigan University*

Philip Regier, *Arizona State University*

Delores Reha, *Fullerton College*

David Reiman, *Monroe County Community College*

Robert Reinke, *University of South Dakota*

Gloria Rembert, *Mitchell Community College*
Reina Reynolds, *Valencia Community College*
John Ribezzo, *Community College of Rhode Island*
Cheri Rice, *Stark State College of Technology*
Carla Rich, *Pensacola Junior College*
Gayle Richardson, *Bakersfield College*
Dwight Riley, *Richland College*
Renee Ritts, *Cuyahoga Community College*
Susan Roach, *Georgia Southern University*
John Robertson, *Amarillo College*
Robert Robicheaux, *University of Alabama*
Tim Rogers, *Ozarks Technical Community College*
June Roux, *Delaware Technical & Community College*
Carol Rowey, *Community College of Rhode Island*
Mark Ryan, *Hawkeye Community College*
Ray Saenz, *Del Mar College*
Joanne Salas, *Olympic College*
Andy Saucedo, *New Mexico State University*
Jacqueline Scerbinski, *Kingsborough Community College*
David Schaefer, *Sacramento City College*
Elisabeth Scherff, *Alabama A&M University*
Glen M. Schmidt, *University of Utah*
Tobias Schoenherr, *Eastern Michigan University*
Marcianne Schusler, *Prairie State College*
James Scott, *Central Michigan University*
Carolyn Seefer, *Diablo Valley College*
Eugene Seeley, *Utah Valley State College*
Gary Selk, *University of Alaska*
Pat Setlik, *William Rainey Harper College*
Phyllis Shafer, *Brookdale Community College*
Dennis Shannon, *Southwestern Illinois College*
Richard Sherer, *Los Angeles Trade Technical College*
Lynette Shishido, *Santa Monica College*
Lance Shoemaker, *West Valley College*
Carole Shook, *University of Arkansas*
Dwight Shook, *Catawba Valley Community College*
Susan Sieloff, *Northeastern University*
William Silver, *University of Denver*

Denise Simmons, *North Virginia Community College*
Lakshmy Sivaratnam, *Johnson County Community College*
Steven Skaggs, *Waubonsee Community College*
Jacqueline Slifkin, *Monroe County Community College*
Kimberly Smith, *County College of Morris*
Anne Snell, *Pikes Peak Community College/Tulane University*
Fred Sole, *Youngstown State University*
Sandra Sousa, *Bristol Community College*
Ed Southeard, *Chattanooga State Technical Community College*
Ray Sparks, *Pima Community College*
Rieann Spence-Gale, *North Virginia Community College*
Cheryl Stansfield, *North Hennepin Community College*
Keith Starcher, *Indiana Wesleyan University*
Carol Steinhaus, *Northern Michigan University*
Jim Stemach, *College of the Redwoods*
John Stern, *Davenport University*
Richard Stewart, *Gulf Coast Community College*
Jack Stone, *Linn Benton Community College*
Connie Strain, *Arapahoe Community College*
John Striebich, *Monroe County Community College*
Chelakara Subbaraman, *Central Michigan University*
Dottie Sutherland, *Pima College*
Deanna Teel, *Houston Community College*
Rodney Thirion, *Pikes Peak Community College*
Carol Thole, *Hartnell College*
Michael Thomas, *Henry Ford Community College*
Alexis Thurman, *County College of Morris*
Frank Titlow, *St. Petersburg College*
Kathy Toler, *Asheville-Buncombe Technical Community College*
Edward Tolle, *Ivy Tech Community College*
Terry Tolliver, *Indiana University–Purdue University*

Francis Douglas Tuggle, *Chapman University*
Fran Ucci, *College of DuPage*
Shafi Ullah, *Broward Community College*
Dorothy Umans, *Montgomery College*
Robert Urell, *Irvine Valley College*
Richard Vaughan, *Durham Tech*
Sal Veas, *Santa Monica College*
Kam Vento, *Lassen Community College*
Victor Villarreal, *Austin Community College*
Richard Vobroucek, *State University of New York–Rockland*
Carol Vollmer-Pope, *Alverno College*
Randall Wade, *Rogue Community College*
Leatha Ware, *Waubonsee Community College*
Richard Warner, *Lehigh Carbon Community College*
Michael Washington, *Eastfield College*
Louis Watanabe, *Bellevue Community College*
Bill Waters, *Clackamas Community College*
Tom Watkins, *Solano Community College*
Barbara Joann Wayman, *Columbia College*
Sally Wells, *Columbia College*
Susan Wheeler, *Folsom Lake College*
Donald Wilke, *Okaloosa-Walton College*
Fred Williams, *University of Michigan*
George Williams, *Bergen Community College*
H. Brock Williams, *Metropolitan Community College*
Doug Wilson, *University of Oregon*
Marcus Wilson, *Fullerton College*
Mildred Wilson, *Georgia Southern University*
Colette Wolfson, *Ivy Technical Community College*
John Womble, *Cedar Valley College*
Dan Wubbena, *Western Iowa Technical Community College*
Merrill Yancey, *Ivy Technical Community College*
Sandra Yates, *University of District of Columbia*
Bernard Zannini, *Northern Essex Community College*
Charles Zellerbach, *Orange Coast College*

New to the Third Edition

We have invested a great deal of work creating the third edition of *Better Business* to give students and instructors a powerful learning and teaching tool that captures the evolving issues and opportunities of business. Enhancements for the third edition follow:

- We responded to reviewer requests for more content on the supply chain by devoting an entirely new section to the topic (Chapter 11). The financial chapters (Part 5) have also been heavily revised in response to instructor needs.

- Knowledge of the ever-changing laws governing today's business practices is essential. The third edition features a new mini chapter devoted to business law and its influence and impact on business, including important elements of contract law, intellectual property issues, environmental law, consumer protection laws, employment and bankruptcy law, and much more.

- One of the most significant shifts in the business environment since the first edition of *Better Business* is the explosive growth of social media in all parts of business. The third edition of *Better Business* continues to feature social media strategies and technologies in over 85% of its chapters, as well as significant updates to the technology chapter.

- All of the end-of-chapter materials have been reviewed, and we have modified up to 25% of these materials to include the most recent events and trends in the business environment. The third edition of *Better Business* provides instructors with wide-ranging choices for discussion topics, assessment questions, and group activities that cover the most current and timely topics in the business community, such as major economic shifts, changes in technologies, and ever-increasing globalization.

- All of the time-sensitive material has been updated. Stories and examples from the previous editions that have continued to evolve have been updated and placed in the most current context, and over 90% of the endnotes were replaced with current references. Timely examples have replaced older material, giving the third edition a more up-to-date feel that resonates with students.

- Feedback from the previous editions of *Better Business* indicated that the "Top Ten" lists not only interested students but also pushed them to go more deeply into the body of the text. For the third edition, we updated these lists—now simply called "The List"—and added new ones that reflect current market trends, with a focus on selecting topics that appeal to students.

Letter from the Authors

When we set out on this project, we had several goals in mind … and one guiding philosophy. We wanted to have a conversation with our students, not merely to write a book that we hoped they would read. We wanted to change the expectation that students will come to class unprepared. Why can't they come ready for class, with a desire to know about business? Why can't we have a little fun with the course while teaching students about the lighter side of business? We think we can.

To that end, we worked tirelessly on selecting our topics and our resources to help you, the student. We incorporated a Question & Answer format throughout to get you to want to know the answer and see more … and not simply because it will be on the test. We paid more attention to the details because that is where the course often comes together for you.

In each chapter, the *On Target* and *Off the Mark* features illustrate positive and negative outcomes of business ventures related to the chapter material. These features, along with "The List" found in each chapter, can fuel in-class dialogue.

Mini Chapters are five special sections in the book that give you additional information on key topics in business: Business Law, Constructing an Effective Business Plan, Business Communications, Finding a Job, and Personal Finance.

Better Business, 3rd edition, offers the content you need for a solid overview of business, but in a *better* way. By presenting the material in a stimulating way, *Better Business* encourages you to come to class prepared to have better conversations and a truly engaging classroom experience.

Prologue

The Ten Easy Steps for Better Business Success

Step 1: It's all up to you.

You've heard that before, right? You've bought textbooks, and read some of the materials, but maybe still haven't ended up with the grade you wanted. So the key to success is not just buying the book or simply reading it. Instead, your success depends on three skills:

1. • finding,
2. • understanding, and
3. • applying the information found within this textbook and all of its resources.

The following steps will help you succeed in this course, and if you apply some of these steps outside the classroom, you may also succeed in business and in life.

Step 2: Go to class with intent.

How do your classes go for you? Are you generally able to follow what the instructor and your classmates are saying in lecture and class discussions? Are you able to actively participate in a group discussion, or do you simply observe other group members? Your attitude and the plan you have for using class time can change the entire experience for you. Try these quick tips to make sure your classroom experience is as rich and fulfilling as possible:

> 66 *You should know the material so well you can explain it to others so that they understand it—even your mom.* 99
>
> —Brett Neslen, *student*

Review the Syllabus

If you have trouble speaking up in class, try this strategy. The syllabus is one of the most important documents in the course. It acts as a binding contract between you and the professor. Read the syllabus in detail as soon as it comes out. Then, in the next class, ask at least one question about it. It will show the professor you're serious about meeting your responsibilities in class—and will get you in the habit of speaking up in class.

Show Up!

As Woody Allen says, "Eighty percent of success is showing up." It's basic advice, but many students lose sight of how important it is to come to class. You should be punctual, if not early; be attentive; and be noticed. Sit near the front and ask good questions so that the professor gets to know your face and name. It's just as important that the professor knows you as it is that you know your professor (see Step 3).

Ask Questions

If you're confused during class, ask a question right then. Don't think, "I'll look really dumb if I ask this," or "I'll probably understand it after I read the text," or

"I'll wait to ask someone else, or go to office hours tomorrow." Asking now will save you time and effort and will probably help other students in the room. You'll learn so much more if you ask questions in class. If you do need to contact your instructor after class to clarify a point, stop by during office hours rather than asking the question electronically or over the phone. Keep in mind, face-to-face visits trump e-mail or voicemail. Now, aren't you glad you invested some time earlier to get to know your instructor (**Step 3**)? After all, it's easier to ask for help from someone with whom you already feel comfortable.

Write a One-Minute Review
Immediately at the end of class, take one minute and write all that you can recall from today's lecture. Try to identify what the main take-away points are by highlighting key ideas. Forcing yourself to be quick and brief helps you to capture the main ideas without the smaller details providing distraction.

Write Down Your "Muddiest" Point
When class is finished, also take a quick moment to write down two sentences that describe the most confusing part of today's lecture. Keep this in one specific part of your notebook—it's a great thing to bring along to your study group or to office hours. It will also work well in creating your own personalized study guide for the next exam.

Step 3: Connect with people.

Business is all about people. Right now, your business is getting a great grade in this class. As in any business, there are many people available to provide help: instructors, fellow students, and school staff. Look around for these people—and then enlist their help.

Get to Know Your Instructor: Go to Office Hours
Your teachers can be your most helpful contacts on campus. Not only can they become mentors, but as you near graduation, they can write job recommendations or references. They can't do that unless you get to know them beyond the focus of the course. So plan to make a couple of trips to office hours—even if you know everything.

> 66 *When studying for a test, I've found that it's very helpful to use a partner and a study guide. I like to come up with a study guide full of questions relating to every important topic that I think will be on the test and write the answers directly below them. Then, my partner and I go through the study guide and quiz each other. This way we can read aloud all of the main ideas and begin to remember key concepts. After we have gone through the study guide a couple times, we quiz each other from memory. Once we've memorized small concepts, it's easier to understand the bigger picture.* 99
>
> —Mallory Hensel, *student*

Create or Join a Study Group
Find study buddies early. In the first few days of class, try to get acquainted with at least two classmates in every course. Watch the people in your class to figure out who seems to know what's going on, who seems dependable, and who you could work well with. Approach those people and ask if they wouldn't mind forming a study group. You don't need to meet all the time—the group can be available on an "as needed" basis. But it's good to have a group of connected students who can help you prep for exams, confirm or clarify points made during class, and exchange notes if you miss a class. (Trust us: it's much better to have a buddy give you the information you missed than to ask the instructor, "Did I miss anything important?")

Use the People Around You
Do you know students who already took this class? Spend some time with them and ask the right questions. What sections of the course will demand more time out of your schedule? What tools in the library helped them out with their projects?

Be sure to look around the class for older students. Many colleges are seeing a large influx of people returning to college after successful careers. These people have that precious thing you may lack: real-world experience. Buy someone a cup of coffee and ask him or her for advice that helps you in the course or in finding a job.

Use All the Resources the School Provides

The faculty and staff at your school want you to succeed—we all take pride in our students' accomplishments! So be sure to investigate all the resources available to you at your school. Talk to your advisor about services such as the following:

Writing Support

Many schools provide special clinics that can help you with your writing. Some also provide writing labs where you can get assistance in editing and proofreading your work.

Support Services

Look for support services that offer help with note-taking techniques, strategies to combat stress in test taking, and workshops on helping you organize and manage your time. If you discover that you have a pattern of specific struggles (for example, you always underperform on tests), see if free screening for learning disabilities is offered. You may need specific testing accommodations (such as additional time or larger-print exams), or you may be eligible for help with an in-class notetaker. The key is to become your own best advocate. Be informed—know how your mind works and what conditions make you perform your best.

Step 4: Explore the world of business in real time.

While this text book intends to apply business concepts to current situations, the examples cannot be as current as those that are exposed in the business press. Until now, you may not have been interested in picking up the *Wall Street Journal*, *Financial Times, BusinessWeek,* or the *Economist* because you did not have the necessary background or interest. Try the following technique. Every day, go online and read the lead story in the *Wall Street Journal*. Keep a log that notes the theme of the article (e.g., the economic situation in the United States or some other part of the world, a government action that impacts business, an acquisition by a major company, trends in the workplace, the stock market, a new technology, etc.). Also, rate how easy it was for you to understand the article, with "1" being the easiest and "10" being the most difficult. Similarly, rate how interesting the article was, with "1" being absolutely fascinating and "10" being massively boring. Note any questions about the article, and how it relates to material being covered in class, or note from the syllabus or table of contents where it might apply to future class content. As the end of your course approaches, review your log. You should see that the articles are becoming easier to understand, and perhaps more interesting. Plus, you will also have created an informal study of the current business landscape, including the hottest business trends. For example, if you see that a significant percentage of the articles are about government actions, it is fair to assume that governments are taking a more active role in business and the economy for some reason. But, above all, this exercise will demonstrate that business—once you really understand it—is far more fascinating than you ever imagined, and it will also help you develop the exceedingly valuable habit of reading the business press regularly, a habit that will serve you well in both life and business.

Step 5: Experience business.

Business is about people. If you want to be a business success, leave your house and find someone who runs a small business (a restaurant, a print shop, a car wash, etc.) where you are a regular customer because you value the quality of their products. It doesn't matter if you don't have aspirations to work in this line of business, as you are just trying to understand the foundations of any small business that seems successful to you. Ask the owner or manager if you can interview them. Ask them how they spend their time, what is most important to the success of their business, and what their most troublesome problems are. Perhaps, you can even volunteer a few hours per week to do odd chores for them, so you can observe firsthand how they manage the business and continue to ask questions. It may start with meaningless errands, but one day you'll appreciate the foundation when a real opportunity arrives. Until that day, you'll be learning by watching a successful businessperson run a company.

Step 6: Know your learning style.

Determining what kind of learner you are will help you apply the most appropriate resources to create a successful learning program. Knowing your learning style can help you select and use the study strategies that best fit the way you learn. ■ **TABLE 1** will help you figure out whether you learn best by seeing (visual), hearing (auditory), or touching/doing (tactile and kinesthetic). Read the word in the far left column of the chart and then place a checkmark next to the statement

■ TABLE 1

What's Your Learning Style?

When you . . .	Visual	Auditory	Kinesthetic & Tactile
Spell	☐ You try to see the word.	☐ You sound out the word or use a phonetic approach.	☐ You write the word down to find if it looks right.
Listen	☐ You get easily distracted when asked to listen for a long time.	☐ You grasp the information quickly and easily.	☐ You find yourself doodling as you listen.
Talk	☐ You favor words such as see, picture, and imagine.	☐ You use words such as hear, tune, and think.	☐ You gesture and use expressive movements. You use words such as feel, touch, and hold.
Concentrate	☐ You become distracted by untidiness or movement.	☐ You become distracted by sounds or noises.	☐ You become distracted by activity around you.
Meet someone again	☐ You forget names but remember faces or remember where you met.	☐ You forget faces but remember names or remember what you talked about.	☐ You remember best what you did together.
Contact people for class or business	☐ You prefer direct, face-to-face, personal meetings.	☐ You prefer talking on the phone.	☐ You prefer talking with people while walking or participating in an activity.
Read	☐ You like descriptive scenes or pause to imagine the actions.	☐ You enjoy dialogue and conversation or imagine the characters talking.	☐ You prefer action stories or are not a keen reader.
Do something new at school or work	☐ You like to see demonstrations, diagrams, slides, or posters.	☐ You prefer verbal instructions or talking about it with someone else.	☐ You prefer to jump right in and try it.
Put something together	☐ You look at the directions and the pictures.	☐ You prefer verbal instructions or talking about it with someone else.	☐ You ignore the directions and figure it out as you go along.
Need help with a computer application	☐ You seek out pictures or diagrams.	☐ You call the help desk, ask a neighbor, or growl at the computer.	☐ You keep trying to do it or try it on another computer.
Total			

Source: Based on Colin Rose's Accelerated Learning (1987).

in one of the successive three columns to the right that best describes how you respond to each situation. Count the number of checkmarks in each column, placing the total at the bottom of the table. Your answers may fall into all three columns, but one column will likely contain the most answers, which indicates your primary learning style. If one of the remaining columns nears in the number of checkmarks to your primary learning style, that can be considered your secondary learning style.

After you've determined your primary—and perhaps, secondary—learning style, you can best match up the textbook, system, and resources from your instructor to help you achieve a better grade. And, if you can figure out how to succeed in this course, you can apply the same study strategies to succeed in other courses.

Note that your instructor also has a specific style of learning and teaching with which he or she is most comfortable. Watching how your instructor works can be a great clue to helping you succeed in the course. For example, does he or she talk without ever drawing a picture? Or does he or she use visuals to illustrate points? Figure out your instructor's learning style and use it to predict what kinds of interactions he or she wants in the classroom and on your assignments.

Step 7a: Read this book.

What is the best investment you can make in yourself right now? If there were something that could promise you an "A" in this course and that would help you to succeed in college in general, it would be worth paying for, right? There is: this book, plus your time. Really, all you need to succeed in this course is this book and its resources, plus some investment of your own time and energy. Doing well in this course is a good start at getting "A"s in follow-up business courses that you might take in the future. That leads to a great job after graduation, followed by huge wealth, fame, and fortune! (Well, maybe not those last three, but you get the picture.)

Step 7b: Use the system, not just the textbook.

Most likely, when you shelled out the cash to buy your textbook, you thought you were just getting a book, right? As it turns out, you actually bought a "system." ■ **TABLE 2** walks you through everything that comes with the purchase of this book. Remembering your learning style, consider how each of these resources can help you study and learn!

■ TABLE 2

Better Business Resource Guide

Resource	Where is it?	When does it help me?
BizSkills (interactive simulations that let you try out your skills in many common business situations)	On mybizlab.com	For test prep Concept reinforcement
PowerPoint Presentations	On mybizlab.com	Before the chapter starts For test prep
End of Chapter Exercises	On mybizlab.com At the end of each chapter	When you're on the go For test prep Concept reinforcement

Step 8: Take awesome notes.

Even if you're a strong auditory learner, you'll benefit from taking notes. Awesome notes are the key when you review and prepare for papers and exams. Take advantage of learning about different types of note-taking strategies. One will certainly work better for your learning style than another. Experiment and see which one best meets your needs. Three popular strategies are outlining, mind mapping, and the Cornell System.

Outlining

You might already use an outlining system. The main points are written down, and any supporting or additional points are indented and listed below the relevant main point. Outlining is a great system for taking notes from a book or PowerPoint presentation, because the material has already been organized for you. However, this system may not be as effective to record the points made in a lecture or class discussion, because the hierarchy structure of an outline is not very flexible, and this makes it hard to insert points that are made later on in a discussion but relate to something mentioned earlier.

Mindmapping

A mind map is a graphic representation of the content of a lecture or reading. It is a flexible system, and many visual learners find mindmapping beneficial because it organizes a lecture graphically. ■ FIGURE 1 shows one example.

Mind maps capture main and supporting ideas similar to an outline, but instead of a fixed hierarchy, the structure of a mind map is more fluid. The main points are captured in a box or circle in the middle of a page. Supporting points, or subtopics, are then drawn as smaller boxes or circles that radiate from the main circle. If later on another subtopics needs to be added, then a new branch can be

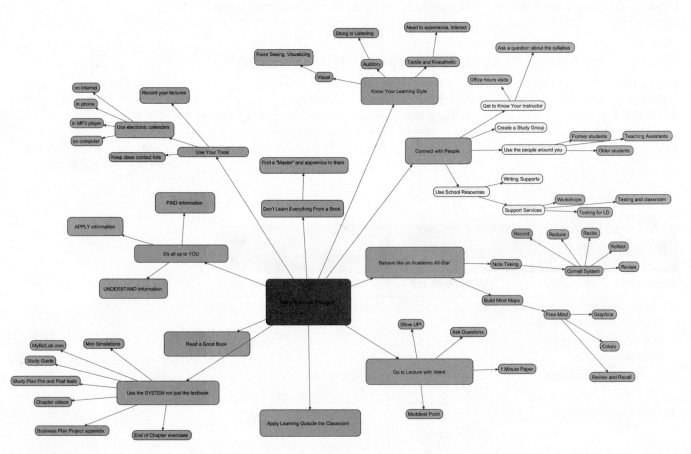

■ FIGURE 1
An Example of a Mind Map of This Prologue

drawn. If there is anything off-topic that should be noted, it can be recorded in a cloud or circle that is not connected to anything and sits outside the main concept area.

Later on, when reviewing, add colors to connect ideas or concepts that aren't necessarily connected by branches but do share the same theme (such as those topics that your instructor pointed out will be on the test, or that were from a PowerPoint presentation, or that should be further explored). As you review for a test or while preparing for a paper, you can use the boxes and colors to help you connect the main ideas of several lectures. Consider creating a *progressive mind map* (separate from individual lecture mind maps) that will express how specific topics relate to the course overall. Many free online resources, including software and templates, can help you begin to use mind maps. One such free product is FreeMind from SourceForge. Even if you just have paper and pencil, you can build useful mind maps.

> 66*I use a mind map to arrange the material before writing a paper. It helps me get all of my ideas on paper and makes the information easier to organize logically.*99
>
> —Laura Poatsy, *student*

The Cornell System

The Cornell System is a simple and powerful system that, if used correctly, can help with recall and increase the usefulness of your notes. When using the Cornell System, you don't need to rewrite or retype your notes. Instead, you use a specific set-up to define your notes. Begin by setting up your 8½ by 11 inch notepaper as shown in ■ **FIGURE 2**. Draw a vertical line 2½ inches from the left side of the page. Next, draw a horizontal line about an inch or so from the bottom of the page for a summary. You can also use a product such as Microsoft One Note, which comes preloaded with a Cornell Note System template (see Figure 2).

In the largest and main section of the paper, capture the main ideas of the lecture. You can use an outline or mind mapping system, whichever suites you best. Then, as soon as possible after the lecture, jot down in the skinny column ideas or key words that will define the main idea of the lecture. Lastly, in the bottom section of the page, summarize the key points in your own words. This forces you to process the information in a new way.

■ FIGURE 2
The One Note Template for the Cornell Note Taking System

THE List

Extra Tips for the Online Learner

Taking this class online? Here are some additional tips for success:

1. Purchase your textbook and any other course materials before class begins. If you're buying online, allow for delivery time.

2. Check your technology needs. Make sure your computer, software, and Internet connection are sufficient for the requirements of the course before the class starts. Faulty technology is not a good excuse for missing assignments in an online course. Have a backup computer you can use, just in case.

3. Establish a regular study time. Without specific classroom meeting times, it's easy to forget about the class. Time passes quickly and before you know it, your "other life" has taken precedent and you're playing catch-up to meet the requirements of the course. Set a regular study time—one that works with your schedule—when you can log into the class and do whatever work may be required.

4. Be proactive asking questions about assignments. If you have questions on an assignment, remember that sometimes getting answers is not immediate. You should always count on things taking more time than in a classroom.

5. Participate in discussions and ask questions. Your online instructor should provide a way for you to interact with other students and ask questions. Active participation will enable you to grasp the material better—and to know your classmates better.

6. Exchange contact information. Although it's harder to meet and interact with others in an online class, try to get contact information for at least one or two people with whom you can share information and questions.

7. Make sure the instructor knows who you are. Take the time in the first week or so to introduce yourself to the instructor via e-mail or through the class chat room. It's harder for an instructor to get to know you in an online course than in a traditional face-to-face class.

8. Know how to work your class Web site and course management software. Especially know how you can get and submit your assignments, check your grades, and communicate with your instructor, as well as with your classmates.

9. Be organized and don't procrastinate. Especially if the class is self-paced, make sure you know when the big assignments and tests are due. As soon as you get your syllabus, record all assignment due dates on your own personal calendar.

10. Become comfortable expressing your ideas in writing. You'll need to communicate in a professional way about both course content and your future career.

Review

With any of these systems, it will help you to vocalize the key points made as you review your notes. As dorky as it seems, reciting out loud is an effective way to learn, especially if you're an auditory learner, because hearing your thoughts helps you sharpen your thinking process, and stating ideas and facts in your own words challenges you to think about the meaning of the information.

Step 9: Use your tools: cell phone/tablet/ laptop.

Undoubtedly, you come to class armed with at least a cell phone—and may even have a tablet or a laptop. Here are a few ideas of how you can use these tools to get you to that "A."

Use a Calendar

Organization is a critical skill for success. Enter assignment deadlines into your cell phone's calendar. You also can use organizational tools such as Microsoft Outlook or Google Calendar to track key due dates and access them from your laptop.

Keep a Class Contact List

Collect the contact information for at least three classmates and for your professor in your cell phone or laptop contact list. Be sure to have it all—home phone, cell phone, IM identity, and e-mail address. This way, you'll have the information at your fingertips when you really need it and don't have your notebook with you. This habit will create all kinds of opportunities for you later in the real world. Successful folks call it "networking"!

Record Audio or Video of the Class

Smartphones and tablets are equipped to record audio, which can help in class. Note-taking applications allow you to write notes as the audio is being recorded. Then simply tapping on a note you jotted down takes you to that point of the audio recording.

Any cell phone that has a built-in camera can record video. Although the video may be low resolution, it will still be a useful review of what was said back on Tuesday. By adding a larger memory card (many phones now can use 8GB cards), you can record back-to-back lectures with no storage problems.

> **"***Take breaks during a study session—just be sure to come back to the work!***"**
>
> —Devin Kownurko, *student*

Laptops equipped with a camera can do the best job of video recording. Cameras such as the Logitech QuickCam Pro 5000 plug right into a USB port and actually track the voice of the lecturer, moving to keep him or her in focus even if he or she walks around the room while lecturing.

Many instructors are now beginning to create their own audio/video recordings of lectures and deliver them as podcasts to the class. If your instructor is not, ask for permission to record him or her and explain that you are happy to make the files available to him or her or willing to post them to the other students.

Step 10: Apply these rules outside the classroom.

All of these classroom tips also can apply to your career. For example, **Step 7** suggests you find, understand, and apply the information from this textbook system to meet the demands of your instructor. In your working life, you'll need to find out what your boss or client wants and figure out the best way to meet his or her needs. Likewise, **Step 6** encourages you to understand how you best learn. Revisit Table 1—many of the actions apply to a business context as well. Knowing your learning style will help you be successful in business as well as in the classroom.

Because business is all about people, think about how you can apply the strategies in **Step 3** to your job. If you can, get to know your boss or supervisor. They, too, can become your mentors and be instrumental in recommending you for advancement within the company. Bosses don't have office hours, but you can stop by their offices periodically to just say hello or ask to meet them for lunch or coffee every month or so. Get to know the people you work with and develop a contact list. You never know when you may need to contact someone in the office when you're not there, or vice versa. So, get a co-worker's e-mail, home or cell phone numbers, and maybe even his or her IM address. Again, it's much better to have someone in the office to ask, "What did I miss?" or "Can you help me?" than running to your boss (or not having anyone at all) to ask the same questions. Also, don't ignore the other people outside your immediate office. Get to know the cleaning staff, the elevator attendants, and the security guards in your building.

They can help you in a pinch and are more willing to do so if they know your face and name.

To get ahead, follow **Step 2**, and come to work with intent! Don't be afraid to ask questions; good questions indicate that you're thinking about the situation at work and trying to apply it to what you already know. If things don't make sense, or you don't understand something, ask for clarification.

Do you think you won't ever take notes again once you're out of the classroom? Think again. The workday includes attending lots of meetings, even when they occur over the phone. Use your college career and **Step 8** to perfect note taking so when you get to the business world, you'll have that skill down pat. And although you might occasionally get lucky with an instructor that ignores your absences in the classroom, such luck most likely will not follow you into the office. We also suggested ways you can use your cell phone, MP3 player, and laptop in the classroom in **Step 9**. These tools can also be used in the office as well. Again, you need to make sure people know about and agree to your taping/recording them, but having good records of meetings and discussions can be helpful to you and to your colleagues. And because many people are afraid of technology, establishing yourself as someone who is comfortable and innovative with technology can also be a good thing.

Don't stop learning and reading! In **Step 7** we encouraged you to read this book. When you find a career you're interested in pursuing, seek out books for advice and insight about that career. There is no end to learning—it's a lifetime activity, so embrace it. And by following the advice in **Step 4**, you should already have developed a love for reading real-time press. Knowing what is happening in the world around you helps anytime.

Finally, in **Step 5**, we encouraged you to interview a manager or owner of a business, or perhaps even volunteer some of your time. Becoming involved in a business, and learning it from the ground up, puts you in the position of better understanding any business in which you are involved. After all—as we say in **Step 1**: It's all up to you!

We hope you have found these steps to Better Business success helpful and hope you will be able to apply them to your academic and professional careers. Good luck in whatever endeavors you pursue!

Business Basics

The Business Landscape

The business landscape in the United States is vast and varied. Drew Houston and Arash Ferdowsi launched the file-sharing website Dropbox. Meanwhile, the Chang family opened a small Chinese restaurant. What do these seemingly unrelated businesses have in common?

Common Business Challenges and Opportunities

Leroy Washington is the owner of a local deli in Florida. When a Quiznos franchise moved in across the street, Washington had to think creatively to deal with the new competition. How did he manage to keep his small deli in business despite the major franchise nearby?

Types of Businesses

Wawa convenience stores are located in the mid-Atlantic region of the United States. Although the chain has over 500 stores, it is still considered a small, regional business. What would Wawa have to do to expand its business and become a national franchise?

Taking Business Personally

Do you run your life like a business? Managing a business requires many of the same financial and personal skills that you use in your daily life. Understanding how you use business concepts and methods in your life can help you understand how they are used in business.

MyBizLab®

⭐ **Improve Your Grade!**

Over 10 million students improved their results using the Pearson MyLabs.
Visit **mybizlab.com** for simulations, tutorials, and end-of-chapter problems.

The Business Landscape pp. 3–5

In 2007, Drew Houston and Arash Ferdowsi were MIT students who had the same problem—they kept losing their flash drives. It was such a hassle to have to keep e-mailing files to themselves from computer to computer. They started working on a software program, which eventually evolved into the software company Dropbox.com, to solve this once and forever.

Meanwhile, in a small town in Pennsylvania, the Chang family was developing a plan to open a restaurant. Over three decades ago, the Chang family emigrated from Hong Kong and set out to fulfill their goal of opening a Chinese restaurant. The Changs purchased an existing restaurant from an ad in the local newspaper. Although opening their new business was challenging, the Changs built a reputation for treating people like family and developed a loyal customer base. ■

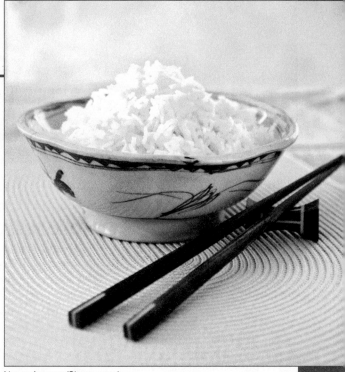

Noam Armonn/Shutterstock

What do a billion-dollar software company and a small-town family restaurant have in common? One is a software service that has over 50 million users, while the other is a family-run eatery in a small town. These organizations represent the varied spectrum of *business* in the United States. In this chapter, you'll learn about the basic skills it takes to run a successful business.

Business Defined

What exactly is a business? Both Dropbox and the Changs' Chinese restaurant are **businesses**—entities that offer products to their customers to earn a profit. A **profit** is earned when a company's **revenue** (the money it brings in) is greater than its **expenses** (the money it pays out). When expenses exceed revenue, the company posts a *loss*.

What kinds of products do businesses offer? A product can be either a *good* or a *service*. **Goods** are physical products a business sells. A roast beef sandwich at Arby's, a 42-inch LCD television at Best Buy, and a Honda Civic at your local car dealership are all considered goods because they are tangible items. Conveyer belts, pumps, and sundries sold to other businesses are also goods, even though they are not sold directly to consumers.

A **service** refers to an intangible product that is bought or sold. Services include haircuts, health care, car insurance, and theatrical productions. Unlike a polo shirt on the rack at Hollister, services cannot be physically handled.

Some companies offer products that are both goods *and* services. Take, for example, restaurant franchises like T.G.I. Friday's. When you order a sirloin steak

> **1** What is profit, and what is the difference between a good and a service?

3

Many not-for profit organizations, such as Amnesty International, operate like a business but do not pursue profits. Instead they seek to service their community through social, educational, and political means.

at T.G.I. Friday's, you're paying for the good (a fire-grilled sirloin) as well as the service of preparing, cooking, and serving the steak.

What do businesses do with their profits? More often than not, profit is the driving force behind a business's growth. As more profit is generated, a company can reward its employees, increase its productivity, or expand its business into new areas.

The proprietor of a business is not the only one who benefits from earned profits. A successful business benefits society by providing the goods and the services consumers need and want. Businesses also provide employment opportunities for members of the community. Because they offer desired goods and services, provide employment, and generate income and spending in the economy, successful businesses contribute to people's quality of life by creating higher standards of living for the entire society.

What about not-for-profits? Not-for-profits may operate like a business, but **not-for-profit organizations**, as their name suggests, do not go into business to pursue profits for their owners. Instead, a not-for-profit organization seeks to service its community through social, educational, or political means. Organizations such as universities, hospitals, environmental groups, and charities are examples of not-for-profit organizations, and any excess revenue is required to be used to further their stated mission.

2 How do for-profit businesses and not-for-profit organizations compare?

3 What are the factors of production?

The Factors of Production

What do businesses use to create the products they sell? To fully understand how a business operates, you have to consider its **factors of production**, or the resources it uses to produce goods and services. For years, businesses focused on the traditional factors of production: labor, natural resources, capital, intellectual property, and entrepreneurial talent. However, in our twenty-first-century economy, an additional factor has become increasingly important: technology.

- **Labor.** Needless to say, businesses need people to produce goods and provide services. **Labor** is a human resource that refers to any *physical* or *intellectual* work that people contribute to a business's production. Intellectual work refers to the ideas and knowledge contributed by the employees.

- **Natural resources.** **Natural resources** are the raw materials provided by nature that are used to produce goods and services. Soil used in agricultural production; trees used for lumber to build houses; and coal, oil, and natural gas used to create energy are all examples of natural resources.

- **Capital.** There are two types of capital: *real capital* and *financial capital*. **Real capital** essentially refers to the physical facilities used to produce goods and services, such as office buildings and factories. **Financial capital** refers to money used to facilitate a business enterprise. Financial capital can be acquired via business loans, from investors, through other forms of fund-raising, or by tapping into personal savings.

- **Entrepreneurial talent.** An **entrepreneur** is someone who assumes the risk of creating, organizing, and operating a business and directs all of a business's resources. Entrepreneurs are a human resource, just like labor, but what sets entrepreneurs apart from labor is not only their willingness to bear risks but also their ability to effectively manage an enterprise. Successful entrepreneurs are rewarded with profits for bearing risks and their managerial expertise.

NetPhotos/Alamy

- **Technology.** **Technology** refers to items and services such as computers, smartphones, software, and digital broadcasting that make businesses more efficient and productive. Successful companies are able to keep pace with technological progress and harness new knowledge, information, and strategies. Unsuccessful companies often fail because they have not kept pace with the latest technology.

- **Intellectual property.** In our modern economy, control of **intellectual property** through ownership of patents, copyrights and trademarks is a critical factor in the production of services and goods. Examples include a drug patent held by a pharmaceutical company or owning the copyright for a specific icon or slogan.

You will learn more about labor (Chapter 9), capital (Chapter 15), entrepreneurs (Chapter 5), and technology and knowledge factors (Chapter 10) as you continue to read the text.

Recall the examples of Dropbox and the Changs' Chinese restaurant. Dropbox provides a service to its users: the ability to instantly synchronize your files across multiple computers. The Changs provide goods to their customers in the form of the food they sell. They also provide a service in the form of the preparation and delivery of that food. Although the business models and products offered by these businesses vary considerably, the two businesses are similar because they were both started by creative entrepreneurs determined to make a profit. For Drew Houston and Arash Ferdowsi, their successful business is now valued well into the billions and generates over $240 million a year.[2] For the Chang family, the profits are much more modest; they make a solid living but are far from seeing a 10-figure profit. Although these two enterprises differ greatly in many ways, both the Changs and the founders of Dropbox have realized a dream by starting a successful business. ■

Common Business Challenges and Opportunities pp. 5–14

In 1998, Leroy Washington inherited his family's deli. The deli had a loyal clientele with a regular lunch crowd. However, a Quiznos franchise moved into a building directly across the street. As a national franchise, it has great name recognition from print ads and commercials. It also has a larger space, more workers and ovens, and a more extensive menu. Leroy found his lunch crowd dwindling as people switched to the national chain with its faster service and greater variety of sandwiches. To be competitive with Quiznos, Leroy had to become creative. Instead of just offering traditional deli choices, his deli expanded its menu to include Cuban pressed sandwiches and an "early bird special" light fare dinner menu. Leroy hoped that the changes would appeal to the large number of Cuban immigrants and senior citizens populating the area. ■

THE List

Ten Tech Entrepreneurs— Very young. Very successful.[1]

1. Arash Ferdowsi (25) and Drew Houston (28) Dropbox $4 billion
2. Mark Zuckerberg (27) Facebook $80 billion
3. Daniel Ek (28) Spotify $1 billion
4. Naveen Selvadurai (29) Foursquare $600 million
5. Kevin Systrom (27) and Mike Krieger (25) Instagram $100 million
6. Dave Gilboa (30) Warby Parker $120 million
7. Jennifer Hyman (31) and Jenny Fleiss (28) Rent the Runway $105 million
8. Ben Lerer (29) Thrilllist $150 million
9. Kim Kardashian (30) Shoedazzle $280 million
10. Danile Kafie (28) and Josh Kushner (26) Vostu $300 million

silver chopsticks/Fotolia

Dealing with competition is just one of the many challenges that business owners such as Leroy face in a twenty-first century economy. However, as Leroy found, confronting these challenges can sometimes lead to opportunities for growth as well. In this section, we'll discuss how competition, the social environment, globalization, and technological change manifest themselves as both challenges and opportunities in the business world.

> **4** How do competition, the social environment, globalization, and technological changes challenge and provide opportunities to business owners?

Competition

How does competition influence business? In a market-based economy, such as that in the United States, there is an emphasis on individual economic freedom and a limit on governmental intervention. In this type of market, competition is a fundamental force. **Competition** arises when two or more businesses contend with one another to attract customers and gain an advantage. The private enterprise system in the United States is predicated on the fact that competition benefits consumers because it motivates businesses to produce a wider variety of better and cheaper goods and services.

Competition in Today's Marketplace

A competitive environment is where a free-market economy thrives. Competition forces companies to improve their product offerings, lower their prices, aggressively promote their brands, and focus on customer satisfaction. Having to compete for a finite number of consumers usually weeds out less efficient companies and less desirable products from the marketplace. To win at the competitive game of business, today's companies need to deliver customer satisfaction, need to understand the power of social networking, and are finding they need to empower their employees.

CUSTOMER SATISFACTION AND BEYOND Because profit is the ultimate goal, it is the job of a successful business to convince customers that its product is either better or less expensive than that of its competitors. For example, consider the explosion in sales of Blu-ray players over the last few years. Because more manufacturers and retailers have jumped into the HDTV market, prices for HDTV sets have fallen dramatically over just a few years. This creates a market of people hungry for Blu-ray players to provide high-definition programming for the new sets. In fact, the sales of Blu-ray players—once the sole dominion of high-end retailers and manufacturers—are increasing dramatically as they become a staple in home entertainment systems. Because customers are able to find moderately priced Blu-ray players at such diverse retailers as Amazon.com, Costco, and Best Buy, prices have dropped. These companies are able to turn over merchandise quickly and in high volume, which allows them to narrow the margin between the

Nantucket Nectars: Tom and Tom's Partnership

ON TARGET

Tom First and Tom Scott were college buddies who did not want to climb the traditional corporate ladder. After graduating from Brown University, the friends moved to Nantucket, Massachusetts, and started a floating convenience store called Allserve. Based from Tom and Tom's red boat in Nantucket Harbor, the company provided delivery service of almost any item, from newspapers to laundry, to neighboring boats. While Allserve proved to be a modest success, the pair soon had another idea. They decided to sell their own natural juice blend, and Nantucket

Nectars was born. Popularity of the juice spread quickly in Nantucket, and Allserve purchased a distribution company to expand the reach of its products. While many national chains are now carrying their products, Tom and Tom maintained their local roots by starting the Juice Guys Juice Bar in Nantucket.[3] This partnership is an example of how a successful business can be started by two eager and driven people. Tom and Tom have come a long way since their days as floating delivery boys in Nantucket Harbor, and they are now running a nationally recognized corporation.

price they pay and the price the customer pays. At the same time, consumer electronics specialty stores, such as Audio Vision in San Francisco, compete by offering exceptional customer service and a more personalized buying experience. Audio Vision knows that keeping customers happy is a key to its success.

SOCIAL NETWORKING Sites like Facebook, Twitter, Ning, and many others are examples of social networking sites. **Social networking** describes a set of online services focused on building and supporting social relationships among people, for example, connecting old friends or people who share activities. People can quickly communicate with others by posting text, photos, and videos; they are automatically alerted when someone posts new information or comments on their site.

Facebook is probably the best-known social networking site, with over 800 million user accounts. Twitter is another popular social networking site. Users can choose to follow different Twitter accounts and are automatically alerted if a person they are following posts new information on their Twitter account.

What does social media have to do with business competition? Today more than ever, customers are connected to each other through a great variety of media—e-mail, texting, blogs, and social networking sites. Companies are therefore increasingly using social networking to connect to their customers. Through these sites, they can promote their products, offer discounts, and build relationships with people interested in their company. Individuals can use social networking sites to quickly spread the word about very good (or very bad) services or products. If a customer is dissatisfied, word can spread like the speed of light—very fast. Similarly, as is discussed later in the book, a happy customer base can be a powerful marketing tool for a company.

Other social networking sites are specialized for the needs of business. LinkedIn, for example, connects over 135 million professionals. LinkedIn users exchange résumés and build networking contacts by connecting with old acquaintances, former employers, and coworkers. When it made the move to a publicly held company with an Initial Public Offering (IPO) in 2011, its value was placed at $8.9 billion.[4]

EMPLOYEE EMPOWERMENT In a competitive environment, it is essential for a company to empower workers to feel free to deal with customer needs. This means employers seek workers who have interpersonal, communication, and

Biz CHAT

Apple: Taking a Bite Out of Microsoft?

Apple and Microsoft have a history of bitter rivalry revolving around the desire to dominate the personal computer (PC) market. The main point of contention between these companies was the graphical user interface (GUI), which is the user interface for the main program that runs PCs. Apple released the first GUI, which included folders and long file names, in 1983. When Microsoft released Windows 2.0 in 1988, Apple took Microsoft to court, complaining that the "look and feel" of the Windows interface was stolen from the Apple interface. This suit continued until 1992, when Apple finally lost.

Microsoft led the competition in the early 1990s. It became an industry standard to have Windows operating systems preinstalled on most PCs, which were dominating the computer market at the time. The 10-year battle finally ended when Apple announced an official alliance with Microsoft in 1997. Microsoft and Apple agreed to a five-year deal in which Microsoft would continue to develop Office software for Apple computers and Apple agreed to bundle Microsoft's Internet Explorer in all its operating systems.[5]

So competition can create new partnerships—strange ones at times. Today, Microsoft is actively wooing Apple, trying to place its search engine, Bing, as the default on the Apple iPhone.[6] This would replace the Google search engine the iPhone has always used. What's in it for Apple? Google has become one of Apple's main competitors in the mobile phone market with its Android phone platform. The element of competition between these rival high-tech companies drives them all to keep innovating and producing higher-quality products than if no one challenged them.

decision-making skills. Companies today need to be more reactive to customers' needs to retain their competitive advantage. Therefore, more companies are placing greater decision-making responsibilities on employees, rather than having decisions trickle down through layers of management. This also means greater employee satisfaction and more career advancement opportunities.

Social Environment

How does the social environment affect businesses? A social environment is an interconnected system of different demographic factors, such as race, ethnicity, gender, age, income distribution, sexual orientation, and other characteristics. Social, economic, and political movements and trends cause the social environment in the United States to constantly change. An influx of immigrants can change the racial demographic, or an economic slump can change the income distribution demographic. These changes affect where we live, what we buy, and how we choose to spend our money. To best serve their employees, customers, and the community, businesses must consider the shifts and changes in the social environment when making decisions. Let's discuss three specific issues surrounding the social environment that present potential challenges and opportunities for today's businesses.

AN AGING POPULATION Not only are older Americans living longer, healthier lives, but they are also better educated, are wealthier, and have achieved a higher standard of living than previous generations. *Baby boomers*, the generation born between 1946 and 1964, represent the majority of the aging population in the United States. Not only do the 78 million baby boomers make up the largest population group in the United States, but they are also the wealthiest. Baby boomers, who in 2011 were between the ages of 47 and 65, have an estimated spending power of over $2 trillion per year. This makes baby boomers a large and lucrative target for businesses. For example, the cosmetics company Garnier is eager to make a profit from the aging population by releasing an antiaging beauty line called UltraLift that is aimed at baby boomer women. Garnier is hoping this keeps its product offerings aligned with the shift in demographics—a change in the social environment.

Although an aging population presents many opportunities for businesses, it also presents challenges for the U.S. economy. Ben Bernanke, chairman of the Federal Reserve, has warned that the nation will be faced with difficult choices as baby boomers reach retirement age. Some potential problems include higher taxes, a reduction in government spending on entitlement programs such as Social Security and Medicare benefits, and a higher federal budget deficit. This is primarily because economic forecasters predict a shift in the demographics of the United States.

Why does this matter? As shown in ■ **FIGURE 1.1** in the year 2050, there will be over 80 million Americans age 65 or older. Today, almost 40 percent of the total personal income for senior citizens comes from Social Security payments. Together these trends imply that there will be a decrease in the number of workers and an increase in the demand for social services. Longevity is another aspect of this demographic shift; in 2005, there were 68,000 centenarians (people age 100 or older) in the United States.[7] Projections place that number at 580,000 by 2040. The health-care costs and services required to care for this population will need to be in place.

■ **FIGURE 1.1**
U.S. Population Age 65 and Over: 1990–2050
Source: Data from US Census Bureau.

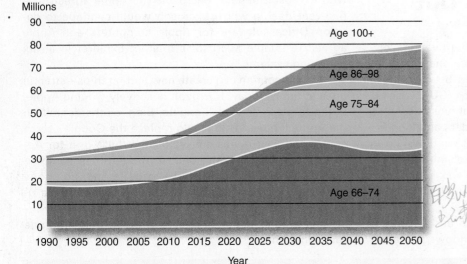

Along with these challenges, as we noted, caring for the needs of an older population will present businesses with opportunities for growth, especially for the health-care, pharmaceutical, and travel industries. After all, a bigger population translates to a larger market for these goods and services.

INCREASING WORKFORCE DIVERSITY   In business, there is no one-size-fits-all method to managing employees and appealing to customers because every person is different. As the United States becomes more diverse, it is important for businesses to mirror that diversity in their workforce. According to the latest data available, the U.S. Census Bureau reports that the minority population in the United States is about 35 percent, making one in three residents a minority. In some companies, minorities account for the majority of the workforce. At the hotel chain Four Seasons, for example, minorities represent 62 percent of the company's 12,400 employees.[8]

However, in today's business climate, increasing and managing a company's diversity involves more than just employing an ethnically diverse workforce. Companies must also develop a diversity initiative that outlines their goals and objectives for managing, retaining, and promoting a diverse workforce. A diversity initiative might include a nondiscrimination policy, a minority network, or diversity education. To increase diversity within a business the company must treat it as a business-critical goal.

Although the inclusion and advancement of racial minorities in the workplace is an important step in establishing a diverse workforce, it is only part of the process. Today, the term *minority* applies to more than just people of different ethnicities. Minority groups might represent a person's gender, culture, religion, sexual orientation, or disability. Companies must include these minority groups in their diversity initiative to ensure that all minority employees are treated fairly by management and coworkers.

THE GREEN MOVEMENT   In a study from the United Nations (UN), many of the world's most respected environmental scientists reported that the threat of global warming and climate change is real.[9] As environmental anxieties become prevalent throughout society, it is important for businesses to become involved in a **green economy**—one that factors ecological concerns into business decisions. Businesses that manufacture products that contribute to higher emissions of carbon dioxide and consume inordinate amounts of fossil fuels must adapt to this new environmental awareness if they want to be relevant in a green economy.

In the automotive industry, for example, hybrid vehicles, which run on a combination of electricity and gasoline, have become not only hot sellers but also are critical to meeting national objectives. President Barack Obama has proposed a new national fuel economy program. The program ultimately requires an average fuel economy standard from automobile manufacturers of 35.5 miles per gallon (mpg) of gas in 2016 (39 mpg for cars and 30 mpg for trucks), a jump from the current average for all vehicles of 25 mpg.

Almost every major car manufacturer—including Toyota, Honda, and BMW—now offers hybrid models. Hybrids have become part of our popular culture, with references on shows like *Curb Your Enthusiasm* and nightly comedy programming. Other alternative sources are appearing as well, such as the Nissan Leaf, a completely electric vehicle. The Leaf has a range of over 100 miles on a single charge . . . and not a tailpipe to be seen.

A focus on environmental issues also opens up a brand-new market that will be increasingly important in the future. The demand for more green products presents new opportunities for entrepreneurs to meet those needs. These "green-collar" jobs can revitalize large swathes of the U.S. manufacturing economy that have been decimated. Creating wind

Nissan Leaf electric cars are an example of how the automobile manufacturers are responding to changes in the social environment.

ZUMA Wire Service/Alamy

energy turbines, installing solar panels, and landscaping designs that make your microclimate (the climate immediately surrounding your home) energy efficient will be necessary businesses of the twenty-first century.

THE SOCIAL ENVIRONMENT AND YOU   As a prospective employee, any one of these social issues will probably affect the company for which you end up working. Because workers are increasingly retiring at later ages, competition for certain jobs and career advancement might be fiercer than in years past. On the other hand, the culture of business is constantly shifting to meet the ever-evolving needs of U.S. demographics. This means more opportunity for employees who can navigate a diverse environment. In addition, jobs aimed at responding to the needs of the growing green economy will also likely present new opportunities for job seekers. Entrepreneurial possibilities always exist for those who have the vision and desire to succeed and are willing to take risks.

Globalization

How has globalization affected businesses? You're probably familiar with multinational companies such as Nike, McDonald's, and Coca-Cola. **Multinational enterprises**—companies that have operations in more than one country—are among the leaders of a movement called globalization. **Globalization** is a movement toward a more interconnected and interdependent world economy. This means that economies around the world are merging as technology, goods and services, labor, and capital move back and forth across international borders. For example, FedEx, the world's largest express transportation company, conducts business in more than 220 countries and territories around the world.[10]

The effects of globalization on the business world vary widely, from economic transformation in India to the shutting down of major manufacturing plants in the United States. The Internet and modern technological advances are making it possible for a company of any size from anywhere in the world to compete globally. Lower tariffs and other trade restrictions give U.S. companies the option to export or import goods to and from other countries or conduct their business overseas. Instead of building their products in plants at home, a growing number of companies are relocating their production facilities overseas or subcontracting at least some of the components of their products to foreign companies around the world to achieve lower manufacturing costs. This is called **offshoring**. The low labor costs in countries such as China and India make these countries ideal locations for multinational companies seeking technology services and manufactured products at a low cost.

Although the concept of globalization is essential for many companies, it is still a highly controversial subject for many. Globalization presents both benefits and risks to the U.S. economy. For example, lowered production costs allow prices on consumer products to decrease, meaning that you as a consumer benefit by purchasing goods at lower prices. Yet concerns remain about workers in the United States who lose their jobs to workers overseas. Globalization poses other risks for U.S. companies, including the following:

- Increased competition from international companies
- Fluctuations in the value of the U.S. dollar
- Security and patent protection concerns
- Unstable political climates in foreign countries

Globalization has therefore sparked fierce debates among politicians, businesspeople, and the general public for the past few decades. We'll discuss the controversies surrounding globalization in greater depth in Chapter 4.

Benefits and risks aside, one thing is for sure: Globalization is here to stay. To stay competitive in the global market, companies must work to enhance quality and develop and implement innovative strategies for the long term. The increasingly global nature of business increases the demand for workers who can

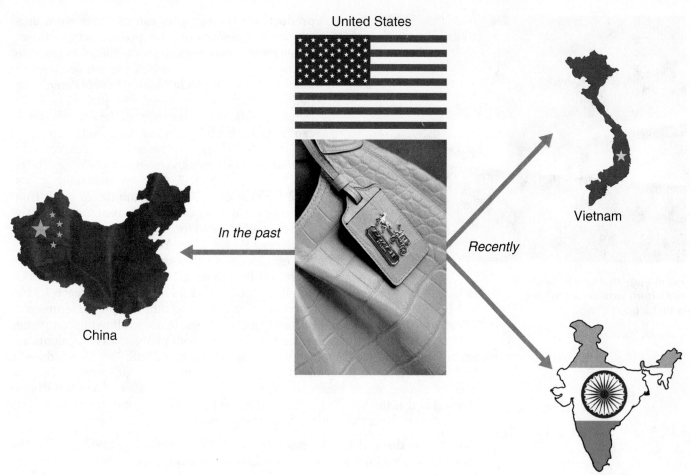

United States

Vietnam

China

India

In the past

Recently

Global outsourcing is always changing. Coach, the American handbag manufacturer, has out-sourced production to China in the past but now is moving to lower-wage countries like India and Vietnam.
Image Sources: China: Franck Thomasse/ Fotolia; US flag: Gino Santa Maria/ Fotolia; Coach bag: Lana Sundman/Alamy; Vietnam: Yahïa LOUKKAL/Fotolia; India: Speedfighter/Fotolia.

communicate with international business partners, have up-to-date technological talents, can demonstrate excellent communication and creative problem-solving skills, and possess leadership skills.

Technological Changes

Why does the pace of technological change present challenges to businesses today? Over the past 20 years, advancements in information technology (IT) have been revolutionary. In today's business world, companies must stay on the cutting edge of technology to remain competitive. No matter the business, technology can be used to keep a company flexible, organized, and well connected—either with customers or employees. There is no question that keeping up with the pace of technology is an expensive and time-consuming operation. The rapid pace of technological innovation means that computers are often outdated after three years and obsolete after five.[11] Add to that the cost of applicable software, training, and infrastructure, and it is no wonder that IT is often the single largest expense for many companies.[12] But cost isn't the only challenge to consider. In the same way that robotics completely revolutionized the automotive industry, advancements in computer and telecommunication technology are completely changing the foundation and focus of how many businesses are run.

What benefits does technology provide to business? Technology, when used and implemented effectively, can help streamline businesses and cut costs. For example, many new tools, such as Twitter and Facebook, have been created that promote better communications with customers. Companies can also use new technology systems to increase productivity. Giving employees what they need to get their work done more efficiently and effectively is the simplest way to increase

Technology makes it possible to work from virtually anywhere. Is that a good thing?

productivity. If employees can get more work done in a shorter amount of time, productivity increases. When employees are more productive, they are more valuable. This, in turn, makes the whole company more valuable. But technological benefits aren't limited to just helping employees; they streamline the internal operations of a business so the entire business can be more effective, efficient, and productive.

Thirty years ago, businesses were often centrally located, with all employees in one building. Today, this is less common. Technology is making it possible for employees to **telecommute**, or work from home or another location away from the office. The virtual global workforce, or telecommuters who work on a global scale, expands the pool of potential employees so that the right employee can be found for the job no matter where he or she works. In fact, the worldwide population of mobile workers is expected to reach 1.3 billion by 2015.[13] Teleconferencing is keeping CEOs and other corporate representatives from having to travel constantly for meetings. It is also allowing companies to communicate easily, no matter the distance. Both of these advancements are saving money on what used to be necessary expenses. With less travel, there is less money spent on plane tickets, hotel rooms, and food. With more employees telecommuting, many businesses can operate out of smaller offices, which are cheaper and easier to manage. The reduction in travel and other services also has an impact on the environment, consuming less energy and resources.

What role does the Internet play in technological growth? If IT is the tool that is changing the function of business, the Internet is the tool that is changing the scope of business. Although IT by itself would be extremely influential for the business world, the Internet makes it truly revolutionary. In 1995, the Internet was just starting to proliferate. Even though it had been commercially available for years at that point, the Internet had only recently become viable after the advent of the World Wide Web a few years before. Many people were intimidated by this new technology, and there weren't high hopes for companies that operated solely on the Internet. But this changed in 1995 when both eBay and Amazon.com launched. These companies showed that such an endeavor was not only possible but also potentially lucrative. Their high-profile success paved the way for the general acceptance of public e-commerce. As ■ **FIGURE 1.2** shows, people now are buying every type of product online. We'll discuss online business and technology in more detail in Chapter 10.

■ **FIGURE 1.2**
What Are People Buying Online?

E-COMMERCE   **E-commerce** consists of three different kinds of business: *business-to-consumer* (*B2C*), *business-to-business* (*B2B*), and *consumer to consumer* (*C2C*). B2C interactions are the ones you're probably most familiar with, such as buying books at Amazon.com or songs or movies from iTunes. B2C interactions take place between a business and a consumer. B2B interactions involve the sale of goods and services, such as personalized or proprietary software, from one business to another. Although both are fairly similar in many ways, the ways in which they differ are significant. B2B e-commerce often involves large transactions to few customers, customized products and pricing, and numerous managers from both businesses making sure that the transaction is beneficial to both parties. This process is obviously more involved than typical B2C transactions, such as downloading a new ringtone for your cell phone or buying an item from Amazon. C2C transactions have become possible through consumer-driven storefronts like Etsy, where individuals can offer their handmade crafts directly for sale to customers.

Every year, e-commerce becomes a more significant element of the overall economy. E-commerce has been growing rapidly since the new millennium, forcing many businesses to either adapt or be left in the dust. For example, the CEO of Procter & Gamble (P&G) Bob MacDonald, has announced plans to expand electronic sales of its products from $500 million to $4 billion annually, using Amazon.com and the firm's own websites.[14] As ■ **FIGURE 1.3** shows, almost 75% percent of all U.S. Internet users have made online purchases. So far this trend shows no sign of stopping. As it becomes easier for consumers to find even the most obscure items at competitive prices, e-commerce will continue to be a driving force in our economy.

It is important to note that the commercialization of the Internet has been around only less than two decades. The Internet, as a medium for sales, has yet to reach its full potential. As the Internet and its influence continue to grow, so will its economic importance and necessity for businesses. This growth will also affect the dangers and concerns that are associated with such prevalence.

ONLINE SECURITY The widespread access to information that the Internet affords affects businesses in a variety of ways. Personal information such as Social Security numbers, credit card numbers, addresses, and passwords are all accessible online. This sensitive information, even when it is secured, can be vulnerable to hackers. Because businesses often store this and other types of personal information, the responsibility is on them to take measures to protect the online security of all their customers. It's no coincidence that as the number of people and businesses who trade and store personal information online rises, so does the number of people who are victims of **identity theft**—the illegal gain and use of personal information. New forms of identity theft are emerging, like taking someone's identity for the purpose of getting medical care. In 2011 over 1.5 million people had their identity information misused in this way.[15] The need for more awareness of personal online security and better tools to ensure corporate online security is clear.

PRIVACY Privacy is another important issue for businesses. E-mails, internal documents, and chat transcripts all contain private information that is not intended for public viewing. Nevertheless, many of these documents can be accessed online because online storage has become a convenient alternative to hard drives. Web e-mail and Web-based documents are also becoming more common. Even gaining access to your desktop at work or at home from a remote location is a simple process that is becoming more popular. And with all this universal access, it is increasingly difficult to ensure that information remains private. Web-based storage and services offer many benefits to business. Yet privacy and security concerns cannot be overlooked. Over time, technology will continue to introduce challenges.

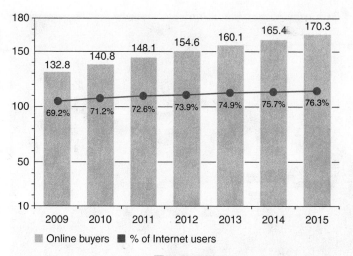

■ **FIGURE 1.3**
Online Buyers Among Internet Users
Source: Data taken from US Online Buyers and Penetration, 2009-2015. http://www.emarketer.com

Review the story about Leroy Washington. When competition from a national franchise threatened his business, Leroy confronted the challenge head-on. To capitalize on the diversity of the area—particularly the sizable populations of both Latinos and seniors—Leroy expanded his menu. His strategy was a success. The Cuban pressed sandwiches became a local favorite. Moreover, the deli was soon packed every day from 3:30 to 5:30 P.M., when the "early bird special" fare—consisting of sandwiches, soups, and salads at reasonable prices—was offered. As Leroy Washington demonstrated, challenges and opportunities abound and overlap in the business world. ■

Andre Jenny/Alamy

Types of Businesses pp. 14–17

In 1964, Grahame Wood opened a convenience store in Folsom, Pennsylvania. The business's focus was on providing fresh dairy products and produce and a full-service delicatessen. This marked the beginning of the Wawa chain of convenience stores, which serve the mid-Atlantic region of the United States. The chain now consists of over 570 stores in five states.[16] Although Wawa is certainly successful, it's still a regional company that does not currently serve a national or international market. Regional businesses, such as Wawa, face unique challenges that don't affect larger businesses, especially involving access to adequate funding and insurance. Wawa continues to expand in the mid-Atlantic region and may one day move into the category of a national business. Is that the best move for this regional chain? ■

What's the difference between a small business and a large corporation? What about everything in between? A small business has different goals and challenges than a large corporation. Small businesses such as a local dry cleaner often provide limited goods or services to a small population. A large multinational corporation, such as P&G, supplies a wide range of goods or services to many customers worldwide. A local or regional business will have very different needs and concerns. In this section, we'll look at the different types of businesses and what constitutes each.

5 | What are the four types of businesses?

Local and Regional Businesses

What defines local or regional businesses? Take a walk around your town or city, and you'll see a variety of local and regional businesses. Used bookstores, bakeries, shoe repair shops, boutiques, restaurants, and specialty shops are often local businesses. A **local business** is usually one of a kind, and it relies on local consumers to generate business. A company is local if it serves a limited surrounding area. A local catering company in Baltimore, for example, might have one kitchen and cater events in Baltimore and its surrounding suburbs. Local companies generally have a small number of employees and are associated with the town or city in which they are located. **Regional businesses** serve a wider area although, like local companies, they do not serve a national or international market. Wawa convenience store chain is an example of a regional business.

What special challenges do local and regional businesses face? The most common challenge for local and regional businesses is managing money. Poor financial planning, as well as unfavorable economic conditions, can lead to bankruptcy. **Undercapitalization** occurs when a business owner cannot gain access to adequate funding. When a business can no longer afford to produce goods or provide services, it goes out of business. The owner must anticipate the cost of doing business and estimate the revenue that the business will generate. To avoid going into debt, the owner should have enough projected revenue to cover expenses for at least the first year. So if the owner of a local catering company has $100,000 in expenses and expects to generate $75,000 in the first year of business, then the owner should have at least $25,000 to fund the company. Even with adequate funding, there is always a chance that the economy will not support the business. Many small businesses fail when the economy slows down because consumers are less likely to spend extra money.

Business owners also have to take taxes and insurance costs into consideration, such as a health insurance plan to cover employees. They also need liability insurance, which will protect the company in the event of stolen or damaged property or if an employee is injured on the job. If a local jewelry store is broken into and jewelry is stolen, liability insurance will cover the cost of the broken window and the stolen property. If the jewelry store is not insured, the business could go bankrupt if the owner can't afford to cover the loss and damages.

National Businesses

What defines national businesses in the United States? If you drive from New York to Los Angeles, you'll most likely encounter several CVS/pharmacies along the way. CVS/pharmacy has over 7,000 locations and can be found anywhere in the United States.[17] All CVS/pharmacy locations essentially look alike and carry similar merchandise—all within a similar price range. With companies such as this, the customer knows what to expect. A **national business** serves the country, but it does not serve an international market. It provides goods or services to virtually all U.S. residents, no matter where in the country they live. A car insurance company such as Allstate is another example of a national business. It has offices in 49 states and serves the entire country. National companies have become standard symbols of U.S. business.

What special challenges do national companies face? Like local and regional companies, national companies also have to worry about their budget and managing their finances. But they have other concerns that local businesses don't have. Because laws vary from state to state, national companies must be aware of state laws in every state in which they do business. For example, each state has its own tax laws. In most states, retail businesses are required to apply for a state sales tax permit to be able to collect sales tax from their customers. Every state imposes a corporate income tax, but the rate varies across states. And some states, such as New Jersey and Rhode Island, require businesses to pay for temporary disability insurance.[18] These laws can be difficult to keep up with and prevent companies from having standardized operational policies.

Another challenge that national companies face is a longer, more complex supply chain. The **supply chain** is the process by which products, information, and money move between supplier and consumer (see ■ **FIGURE 1.4**). The product flows from supplier to manufacturer to wholesaler to retailer to consumer. If the product is returned, it flows from the consumer back to the retailer. Information flow includes orders and delivery status, and financial flow includes manufacturing costs, payment, credit terms, and profit.

Businesses like CVS/pharmacy are national businesses in that they have locations throughout the United States but do not serve an international market.

Let's look at an example of a supply chain. When you go to Target to buy a bottle of Tide detergent, you are a part of the supply chain, as is the Target store itself. Target's stock of Tide was supplied by a distributor, whose supply of detergent came from its supplier, P&G. P&G has its own set of suppliers providing the chemicals and packaging materials required to manufacture the detergent.

The bigger a business is, the longer and more complicated its supply chain becomes. If not managed properly, long supply chains can be inefficient because products and materials have to pass through more warehouses and sustain more shipments. Products may get backed up in long supply chains, which can result in delayed shipments and late payments. A lack of communication among companies in the

© Ian Dagnall/Alamy

| Supplier | Manufacturer | Wholesaler | Retailer | Consumer |

■ **FIGURE 1.4**
The Supply Chain
Image Sources: left to right: Anita/
Shutterstock; Uwe Bumann/Shutterstock;
Nat Ulrich/Shutterstock; Supertrooper/
Shutterstock; Yuri Arcurs/Shutterstock.

chain can cause mix-ups and delays, especially if there is a sudden change in the process. A national company must therefore rely on the cooperation of all members of the supply chain to keep the business running smoothly.

Multinational (International) Businesses

What categorizes a company as multinational (or international)? As we discussed earlier, *multinational businesses* make and/or sell products in several countries. They are businesses that have expanded to provide goods or services to international consumers or serve only one country but have suppliers or production facilities in other countries. For example, you can now find a McDonald's restaurant in more than 119 countries, all serving distinctly U.S. food.[19] However, not every McDonald's restaurant is exactly the same. They have all been adapted to fit the culture of the country in which they are located. For example, if you enter a McDonald's restaurant in some parts of Canada, you'll see a McLobster on the menu. The McAloo Tikki Burger is a vegetarian sandwich made with potatoes, peas, and spices served in McDonald's restaurants in India. Because of the large Hindu population in India, beef is not used in any of their menu items.[20] This is the nature of multinational businesses.

What special challenges do multinational corporations face? Every country has different corporate laws and business practices, and multinational corporations must be familiar with the laws of the countries in which they operate. Laws concerning the import and export of goods vary greatly from one country to another. Things can get particularly complicated if a product is shipped to one country for assembly, another for packaging, and then yet another country for distribution. Often, several countries are involved in the manufacture of one product, in which case the laws and regulations of all those countries must be adhered to. It might be necessary for a U.S. company to work with the governments of foreign countries if there are strict importing restrictions or a multitude of taxes. Safety regulations, quality control, copyrights, and patent rights are just some of the laws that multinational corporations must keep in mind when doing business in foreign countries.

Cultural differences have as much impact as legal differences on international business. Some of these issues, which we'll discuss further in Chapter 4, include the following:

- Countries may have different business hours or workweek schedules. For example, in Spain, workers tend to take lunch from 1:30 to 3:30 P.M.
- Values and customs relating to business etiquette may vary. For example, timeliness is valued in Germany, but it is less important in Italy.
- Violating local taboos can be a concern, such as the preference for group harmony in many Asian countries.
- Multinational companies may have difficulty determining wages for foreign workers and pricing for international markets.
- The language barrier presents a challenge to businesses that are trying to establish themselves in foreign countries.

Multinational companies also must contend with many important economic differences among countries, such as the different levels of economic development, interest rates, and inflation rates that make international business more complicated than purely domestic business.

The move from being a regional business to a national, or even multinational, business is an exciting one, but it also brings a new set of challenges. Wawa currently deals with those issues that impact a regional company. In fact, the company has reached saturation in the five-state market (New Jersey, Maryland, Pennsylvania, Delaware, and Virginia) it controls. However, recent attempts to expand into nearby states, such as Connecticut, have proved challenging, as Wawa has had difficulty finding the right locations and replicating its focus on customer service and teamwork outside its regional base.[21] Instead of expanding toward being a national chain, Wawa has begun moving into gas retailing, creating superstores that combine the traditional Wawa convenience center with a gas station. Clearly, businesses must proceed carefully when making such decisions. ■

Taking Business Personally pp. 17–19

William Casey/Fotolia

Taylor Evans is a very organized and orderly person. He prides himself on being efficient and meticulous with his schoolwork, finances, and social life. His friends joke with him about this and tell him that he runs his life like a business. But Taylor doesn't take offense; why shouldn't he run his life like a business? His life is just as complicated. He has revenue, expenses, and assets. He participates in commerce. Taylor even likes to keep up with the latest technology to make sure he runs his life most efficiently. Taylor is always looking for cost-effective ways to operate his life, and any profits (or money he has left over after paying his bills) are set aside for future purchases. In many ways, his life *is* a business. Do you maintain your life like a well-run business? ■

Each of you probably has a different level of familiarity with the basics of business. Some of you may have witnessed the operations of a business firsthand while employed at a part-time job. For others, your business knowledge may be limited to what you've read or seen on television. Regardless of your prior work experience and business knowledge, you all have experience running a business, and that business is your life. Similar to a small company, your life requires careful planning, precise record keeping, and openness to change. To help you understand some of the business concepts discussed in this book, let's look at how you run your "business."

How do you receive funding? Regardless of whether you have a job or not, you're receiving money from somewhere. It could be from work, a family member, a student loan, or your own savings. You need these funds to secure the necessities of your life. Similarly, all businesses need funds to operate. Ideally, a business would produce revenue right away; however, some businesses may operate on funds received from a bank loan, investors, or their owners' capital.

What are your expenses? Rent, clothing, food, tuition—these are expenses whether they are paid for with cash, credit, or a loan. Ultimately, you will want to generate enough revenue, or income, to cover your expenses and have leftover cash.

6 How do life skills translate to the business environment?

The lives of some students operate a bit like a start-up business; you may have to pay for expenses with loans until you have enough experience to generate a profit.

How does the social environment affect your life? The social environment probably presents similar opportunities and challenges to you as it does to businesses. How do you deal with these opportunities and challenges? Are you open to learn from people who are different from you? Do you embrace diversity? How do you relate to people from an older generation? What about the green movement? Are you finding ways to make your lifestyle more eco-friendly? It is important to address these issues so you can live a more harmonious life and prepare yourself for the modern work environment.

How does globalization affect your life? Not only is the world getting smaller for businesses, but the world is also getting smaller for you. Your favorite music group may be a band from Germany. You might like to chat online about movies with a friend from Japan. Just as businesses now have the opportunity to work with other firms from all over the world, you have the ability to make friends or connections on any continent. You probably purchase items that are designed and/or manufactured in other countries. As the forces of globalization continue, the chances of you working in a foreign country for part of your career continue to climb.

How do you keep up with new technology? Whether or not you consider yourself to be tech-savvy, chances are you still use some sort of technology to run your life. Perhaps you use online banking, check your bank account via your smartphone, or buy things over the Internet. Similar to a business, if you don't keep up with new technology, you may find yourself in trouble.

What sort of e-commerce do you use? E-commerce is a popular form of purchasing goods. What sort of things do you buy online? There are many online clothing stores that let you design the products yourself, like the Sole Brother custom sneaker online store. Perhaps you even sell things over the Internet. Posting old clothing or other unwanted items on eBay might be your way of making a few extra dollars or gaining more room in your closet.

How do you keep your business secure? As businesses work to keep personal information secure, so also should customers. You can help keep your information secure by changing your online passwords on a regular basis, making sure your wireless connections are secure, switching to paperless mail, and removing personal information such as phone numbers or addresses from your Facebook account or other social networking sites. Keeping your personal information secure can help you avoid identity theft or other dangerous blows to your financial health.

Most e-commerce requires credit cards to complete transactions. How do you keep your online transactions secure?

Lev Dolgatsjov/Fotolia

What types of financial goals do you have? The goals of a business typically revolve around achieving financial success. You, too, might have certain financial goals that you would like to achieve in your life. To reach these goals, you'll need to make informed decisions about how you spend and save your money. Mini Chapter 5 (see p. 532) can help you manage your personal finances and plan for the future.

So when Taylor's friends say he runs his life like a business maybe that is a compliment! Many of the same concepts and strategies used to run a business can be used to monitor your day-to-day activities. As you learn new business concepts in upcoming chapters, you may find them easier to understand by applying them to your own life. However, not everything in the business world parallels your own life. The business world has its own unique issues and strategies that may not work for your personal life. Think about the material presented in this course carefully, as both a consumer of business goods and services and as a future business leader. ∎

CHAPTER 1
SUMMARY

MyBizLab
Go to **mybizlab.com** to complete the problems marked with this icon ⭐.

1 **What is profit, and what is the difference between a good and a service?** (pp. 3–4)

- **Profits** (p. 3) are earned when a company's **revenue** (p. 3) exceeds its **expenses** (p. 3).
- **Goods** (p. 3) are the physical products offered by a business. **Services** (p. 3) are intangible products, such as a haircut, health care, or car insurance.

2 **How do for-profit businesses and not-for-profit organizations compare?** (p. 4)

- A **business** (p. 3) is an entity that offers goods and services to its customers to earn a profit. A **not-for-profit organization** (p. 4) is an organization that does not pursue profits but instead seeks to service its community through social, educational, or political means.

3 **What are the factors of production?** (pp. 4-5)

- The **factors of production** (p. 4) are the resources used to create goods and services. The factors of production include **labor** (p. 4), **natural resources** (p. 4), **capital** (p. 4), **intellectual property** (p. 5), **entrepreneurial talent** (p. 5), and **technology** (p. 5).

4 **How do competition, the social environment, globalization, and technological growth challenge and provide opportunities to business owners?** (pp. 6–13)

- **Competition** (p. 6) arises when two or more businesses contend to attract customers and gain an advantage over one another. Competition forces companies to improve their product offerings, lower their prices, aggressively promote their brand, and focus on customer satisfaction.
- **Social environment** (p. 8) encompasses demographic factors such as race, ethnicity, gender, age, income distribution, sexual orientation, and other characteristics. An aging population, increasing diversity, and the green movement both challenge and pose opportunities to business owners.

- **Globalization** (p. 10) involves the merging of economies around the world as technology, goods and services, labor, and capital move back and forth across international borders. Although globalization provides profitable opportunities, such as increased markets and offshoring, it also leads to greater competition for U.S. businesses and workers.
- **Technology** (p. 11) items and services such as smartphones, computer software, and digital broadcasting make businesses more efficient and productive. E-commerce is well established and still growing, offering even small firms a chance to sell to a global market. At the same time, keeping up with the pace of technology is an expensive and time-consuming operation for many businesses.

5 **What are the four types of businesses?** (pp. 14–17)

- A **local business** (p. 14) relies on local consumers to generate business.
- **Regional businesses** (p. 15) are companies that serve a wider area than local businesses but do not serve national or international markets.
- A **national business** (p. 15) has several outlets throughout the country, but it does not serve an international market. It provides goods or services to all U.S. residents, no matter where in the country they live.
- **Multinational enterprises** (p. 16), also known as multinational companies or corporations, multinational businesses, or international businesses, are companies that have operations in more than one country. They are among the leaders of a movement called globalization.

6 **How do life skills translate to the business environment?** (pp. 17–19)

- You have income, expenses, and profits.
- You are affected by globalization and technology.
- You have concerns with security.

Key Terms

businesses (p. 3)
competition (p. 6)
e-commerce (p. 12)
entrepreneur (p. 4)
expenses (p. 3)
factors of production (p. 4)
financial capital (p. 4)
globalization (p. 10)
goods (p. 3)
green economy (p. 9)

identity theft (p. 13)
intellectual property (p. 5)
labor (p. 4)
local business (p. 14)
multinational enterprise (p. 10)
national business (p. 15)
natural resources (p. 4)
not-for-profit organization (p. 4)
offshoring (p. 10)
profit (p. 3)

real capital (p. 4)
regional business (p. 14)
revenue (p. 3)
service (p. 3)
social environment (p. 8)
social networking (p. 7)
supply chain (p. 15)
technology (p. 5)
telecommute (p. 12)
undercapitalization (p. 14)

Self-Test

Multiple Choice You can find the answers on the last page of this book.

1. Which of the following are the factors of production?
   a. Labor, natural resources, capital, entrepreneurs, technology, and intellectual property
   b. Labor, capital, entrepreneurs, motivation, and good ideas
   c. Natural resources, entrepreneurs, profits, and creativity
   d. Labor, profits, natural resources, technology, and motivation

2. Goods are products a business sells like
   a. haircuts.
   b. conveyer belts.
   c. car insurance.
   d. health care.

3. Which of the following is a current sociocultural trend?
   a. A decrease in the overall U.S. population
   b. An increase in the population of Americans ages 30 to 45 years old
   c. A decrease in the U.S. minority population
   d. An increase in the population of Americans ages 65 and over

4. Social networking makes it possible for
   a. companies to better manage their employees.
   b. customers to spread the word about great products.
   c. companies to keep network information secure.
   d. social gatherings to be monitored.

5. If a firm decides to shift the production of goods or services to an overseas company, this firm is
   a. diversifying.
   b. offshoring.
   c. telecommuting.
   d. forming a partnership.

6. Companies are placing greater decision-making responsibilities on
   a. new layers of management.
   b. the political leadership of foreign countries.
   c. the regulatory commissions of the federal government.
   d. employees directly.

7. B2B and B2C interactions are
   a. common now because of the explosive growth of e-commerce.
   b. important only for businesses, not consumers.
   c. two different names for the same thing.
   d. dominated by sole proprietorships.

8. To avoid debt, a new business owner should have enough projected revenue to cover expenses for the first
   a. six months.
   b. year.
   c. two years.
   d. five years.

9. Which of the following is NOT a common challenge facing most national companies?
   a. Undercapitalization
   b. A complex supply chain
   c. Complying with each state's different tax rates
   d. Differences in state laws

10. It is important to understand the challenges of business because
    a. everyone owns a business at some point in their lives.
    b. as online business opportunities grow you will be employed online.
    c. there are many ways your own life needs to be managed like a business.
    d. None of the above

True/False You can find the answers on the last page of this book.

1. Businesses are entities that offer goods and services to earn a profit.
   ☒ **True** or ☐ **False**

2. Identity theft is no longer a problem because of new Internet security protocols.
   ☐ **True** or ☒ **False**

3. The supply chain is the process by which products, information, and money move between a supplier and the consumer.
   ☐ **True** or ☒ **False**

4. Globalization poses risks to the U.S. economy because of security and patent protection concerns.
   ☐ **True** or ☐ **False**

5. A not-for-profit organization uses any revenue to reward the management team.
   ☐ **True** or ☐ **False**

Critical Thinking Questions

⭐ 1. Consider all the factors of production: labor, natural resources, capital, entrepreneurs, technology, and knowledge. Is each resource a vital part of the school you attend or the company for which you work? Which factors do you believe are most important to the goods and services provided by your organization?

⭐ 2. It is increasingly important to businesses to have green practices—reducing their carbon footprint, offering green options for consumers, and so on. What examples can you think of where a company's marketing campaign has highlighted its concern for the environment? What might the costs to a company be for going green? What consequences might a company face if it does not?

⭐ 3. Many businesses now maintain both an online presence and a bricks and mortar physical presence. Select a few specific companies and research the options for delivering product to customers. In what way does the online store compete with the physical store? How do the two storefronts support each other?

Team Time

THE COMPETITIVE EDGE

You now know that competition arises when two or more businesses contend to attract consumers and gain an advantage over one another. Divide into three groups: Company A, Company B, and Consumers.

Process

Step 1. Companies A and B: Collectively decide what type of business you want to represent, for example, sports apparel companies, beauty salons, or pet care agencies. Then choose a product or service applicable to that type of business. (Both groups should choose the same type of business and product or service.)

Step 2. Companies A and B: Decide how you will present your product to your customers. Focus on the following factors:
- Packaging/presentation
- Price/budget
- Quality

Consumers: Compile a list of what is important to you when choosing this product or service.

Team Time (continued)

Step 3. Companies A and B: Provide a brief presentation to your competition and consumers.

Consumers: Provide in-depth feedback to both companies as to how they could improve; consider your initial list.

Step 4. Companies A and B: Use the consumer feedback to alter your product or service to gain advantage over your competition.

Consumers: Discuss how the two companies compare to real-life companies offering similar products or services. Would you consider purchasing from either of these two companies? Why or why not?

Step 5. Companies A and B: Present your product again. Explain why your product or service surpasses that of your competition.

Consumers: Discuss the changes made by both companies and consider how they accommodated your needs. Did each company effectively incorporate your feedback into its revised presentation? Choose one company that you think gained the competitive advantage.

Entire Class: Openly discuss the factors real companies must face in competition. Were these factors considered in the challenge?

Ethics and Corporate Social Responsibility

CULTURAL AWARENESS: UNWRITTEN LAWS

There are many challenges facing multinational companies. Complete the following exercise to experience one challenge.

Process

Step 1. Divide into six groups, each representing one of the following countries: Hong Kong, France, Egypt, Japan, Mexico, and the United States. Examine the cultural practices, customs, and values of the country you will represent. This may be done in class, if you have Internet access, or as homework.

Step 2. Each group should pair together with a second group as follows: United States with Japan, Mexico with Egypt, and Hong Kong with France.

Step 3. Each group should produce one scenario of a business transaction that would be affected by cultural differences found in your research. Fabricate specific companies, characters, interactions, and resolutions.

Step 4. Answer these questions and discuss with the class:

- What were some challenges encountered in your business scenario, and how did you overcome them?
- Why is it important for multinational companies to research a foreign country with which they intend to conduct business?

Web Exercises

1. **Are You Savvy to Society?**
   Imagine you are starting a new business. To what demographic area would you market? Think about the following factors: race, ethnicity, gender, age, income, and sexual orientation. Visit www.census.gov to locate reports on the demographic area you are interested in. Do you believe your business can thrive in this area? If not, what area would be conducive to your future customers?

2. **The Languages of the Global Marketplace**
   As globalization increases and the world markets become more intertwined, language barriers become important. Investigate online resources for automated translation tools. How could you add a website translator gadget to your Web page? What happens if you want to read a Web page posted by a German firm? Can you make online purchases from a company based in Asia? What resources are there for translating telephone conversations in real time? Investigate Babelfish.com and personal interpreter services like LanguageLine.com.

3. **Business Technology On-the-Go**
   Mobile devices are evolving quickly and are setting the style of advertising and marketing. Using the site MobileBehavior.com, find one new trend appearing in modern advertising campaigns because of the prevalence of mobile devices. Write a brief summary.

4. **Budget Planning at Your Fingertips**
   What tools are available to help a business budget its finances? Type "business budget plans" into any search engine. Using online examples, write a brief budget plan for a start-up company of your choice.

5. **Comparing Companies**
   Consider two national companies discussed in this chapter—Allstate and CVS/pharmacy. In what states is each of these based? Go to www.sba.gov to research the laws applicable in the states in which these companies are based. How do the workers' compensation and tax laws differ for each company? Which company do you think was more difficult to establish based on state laws?

MyBizLab

Go to **mybizlab.com** for Auto-graded writing questions as well as the following Assisted-graded writing questions:

1-1. Most business owners agree that keeping up with the pace of technological change is a challenging task. Imagine you are the owner of a new business and must decide what technology would best suit your needs. From what types of technology would this business benefit? Consider the factors of production, organization, and communication in your decision.

1-2. Select a regional or local business in your area. Do you think the company would be successful in a national setting? As a multinational? Are there barriers keeping the company confined to a specific region?

1-3. MyBizLab Only – comprehensive writing assignment for this chapter.

Economics and Banking

The Basics of Economics

Why does water cost less than diamonds? It's a matter of supply and demand—a problem that Bryan Weirmoyer faces every day as a sales executive for a real estate development company. How can businesses use basic economic concepts to their advantage?

Determining Price: Supply and Demand

For many business owners, weathering shifts in supply and demand is like playing tug of war. The levels of supply and demand for a given good or service shift constantly, each influenced by a variety of factors. Consider, for example, the impact a more efficient oven has on a baker's ability to supply bread or the impact a low-carb diet craze has on the demand for a baker's muffins. From this dynamic economic landscape, a price for goods and services is determined.

Degrees of Competition

Once a player owns all the property of the same color in the famous board game, he or she has a monopoly and controls all that happens on that property. Although that's the goal of the board game, large monopolies are rarely allowed in the United States. Microsoft was investigated by the U.S. Department of Justice for illegally holding a monopoly. What is a monopoly? Why are there laws against it? And how does it differ from an oligopoly, monopolistic competition, and perfect competition?

Economic Indicators

Greg Johnson is managing the inventory of a large automobile dealership. Before the recession, ordering inventory was simple because the demand for new cars seemed constant. These days, he's not sure about his company's direction. The demand for new cars has been low over the past few years in his immediate area, but he's not sure if such low demand will continue. The economy seems to be improving, but is it really? Are there measurements of the economy that he can use to help him make his decision?

Government and the Economy

Nick and Jacinta Robertson are looking to buy their first home. What information do they need to make sure they stay within their budget? Can government actions have an effect on what Nick and Jacinta do?

MyBizLab®

⭐ **Improve Your Grade!**

Over 10 million students improved their results using the Pearson MyLabs.
Visit **mybizlab.com** for simulations, tutorials, and end-of-chapter problems.

The Basics of Economics pp. 25–28

I t was the third phone call this week, and Bryan Weirmoyer knew it wouldn't be the last. Bryan is the sales executive of a residential and commercial real estate developer in Oregon. As a sales executive, Bryan sells new properties to clients for commission. A couple of years ago, he enjoyed taking phone calls that generally ended by closing contracts for the construction of new homes. But now, the phone doesn't ring much, and when it does, it's generally a call to cancel contracts Bryan had worked hard to negotiate. Why were there so many sales a couple years ago and so few now? ■

Tomislav/Fotolia

Bryan's dilemma of diminishing sales is due to the economic concept of supply and demand. Have you ever wondered why water, a basic commodity that is critical to life, is priced so low, and diamonds, which aren't necessities, are expensive? It might seem that utility would have a large effect on price in that the more useful an item is, such as water, the greater its price. Instead, this paradoxical situation illustrates a different relationship, which is the fundamental concept of economics—*supply and demand*. Supply and demand determine how goods are priced and exchanged. The exchange of products and services between people, companies, and even countries is the very root of economics. In this chapter, we'll examine the laws of supply and demand, discuss economic indicators, and look at how government actions affect the economy. First, let's begin with a discussion of some basic economics concepts.

Economics Defined

So what is economics? Economics is the study of how individuals and businesses make decisions to best satisfy wants, needs, and desires with limited resources. It is about businesses making *goods* (such as books, pizza, or computers) or supplying *services* (such as giving haircuts, painting a house, or installing a home entertainment network) that we want or need to buy.

Because businesses don't have enough tools, money, or products to provide *all* the books, pizza, or haircuts that we want, they must decide what and how much to make. Not everyone will be able to have what he or she wants because of limited resources (such as money, space, or time) and supplies. Therefore, economists look at how resources are distributed in the marketplace and how equitably and efficiently those resources are disbursed. There are two basic studies of economics: *microeconomics* and *macroeconomics*.

> 1 What is economics, and what are the different types of economic systems?

MICROECONOMICS Microeconomics is the study of how individual businesses, households, and consumers make decisions to allocate their limited resources in the exchange of goods and services. When Bryan Weirmoyer tries to determine how a change in prices may help generate sales or analyzes the number of existing houses that are already for sale in the local market, he is using the microeconomic principles of supply and demand.

MACROECONOMICS Macroeconomics looks at the bigger picture. **Macroeconomics** is the study of the behavior of the overall economy. Economy-wide occurrences, such as changes in unemployment, interest rates, inflation, and price levels, are all part of the study of macroeconomics. Macroeconomists, for example, look at how a change in interest rates affects the demand for housing or how a change in the housing market affects the overall economy. The government and individuals in a society also affect the manner in which resources are allocated and define the economic system in which goods and services are allocated.

Different Types of Economic Systems

What are the different types of economic systems? An economy is a system that tries to balance the available resources of a country, such as land, capital, and labor, against the wants and needs of consumers. An economy deals with (1) what is produced, (2) how it is produced, and (3) who gets the finished product. Traditional economies found in earlier agrarian communities were primitive in nature and based on a strong social network. Very few traditional economies exist today. The world's different economies are classified into three basic economic systems:

- Planned (or controlled) economies
- Market economies
- Mixed economies

Although most economies today represent some form of a mixed economic system or a market economic system, some planned economies exist. ■ **TABLE 2.1** summarizes the features of the world's three contemporary economic systems.

Planned Economic Systems

In a **planned economic system**, the government plays a significant role in determining the goods and services that are provided and how they are produced and distributed. Communism and socialism are examples of planned economic systems.

Communism is an economic system in which a state's government makes all economic decisions and controls all the social services and many of the major resources required for the production of goods and services. Karl Marx, the originator of communist principles, envisioned in *The Communist Manifesto* that workers themselves would eventually take over the government's responsibilities to provide services. No country operating in a communist system has achieved this level of Marx's vision. Existing communist states, including North Korea and Cuba, are failing economically. This is a result of problems that have arisen with communist systems, such as shortages of goods and services. In fact, in the later years of the twentieth century, most former Soviet republic states and Eastern European countries turned from communism-based economies to market economies to combat these problems.

Socialism provides that the government owns or controls many basic businesses and services so that profits can be distributed evenly among the people. In socialist economic systems, governments traditionally run some of the social services, such as education, health care, retirement, and unemployment, as well

TABLE 2.1

World Economic Systems

Type of Economy	What to Produce	How to Produce	For Whom to Produce
Planned (Controlled): • Communism • Socialism	The government or other centralized group completely or partially determines what to produce.	The government or other centralized group completely or partially determines and controls the resources and means of production.	The government or other centralized group completely or partially determines wages and sets prices. Resources and products are distributed to the common group.
Market: • Capitalism	Individuals and businesses make decisions based on consumer needs and wants.	Individuals and businesses determine the production methods. The focus is on efficiency and profitability.	Individual income ultimately controls purchasing decisions.
Mixed	A blend of planned and market economies. Individuals and businesses determine what to produce, along with some level of government involvement.	Individuals, businesses, and the government control resources and determine production methods.	The government distributes some goods and services through selected social programs. Individual income determines purchasing decisions for other goods and services.

as other necessary businesses, such as utility companies (e.g., telephone, electric, water, and sewer). The government charges high tax rates to pay for the services it provides. For example, the highest *average* income tax rate in the United States in 2011 is 22 percent (marginal tax rate is 35 percent), while the Scandinavian countries of Denmark, Norway, and Sweden have average tax rates double that of the United States. Norway has the highest average tax rate of 59 percent; Denmark's and Sweden's are slightly less: 52.7 and 51.3 percent, respectively.[1] Although citizens of these countries pay higher tax rates, they benefit from social programs that tax proceeds are used to fund. For example, education at even the best universities in Denmark is free.[2] Recent studies have indicated that Scandinavians rank among the most satisfied people in the world.[3]

Although many feel government-controlled and government-supplied social services provide a fair and equitable distribution of such services, a concern with *true* socialism is the diminishing motivation for workers. In a true socialist system, workers turn over their earnings and profits to the state rather than keep their own earnings, so the incentive to work hard is reduced. Therefore, it is difficult to find purely socialist economies. Many socialist and communist countries are beginning to change their economies into free market economies through the practice of **privatization**—the conversion of government-owned production and services to privately owned, profit-seeking enterprises.

Market Economies

In a **market economy**, individuals are able to make their own economic decisions. For example, there may be several pizza parlors in your town, and each one may sell slices of pizza at different prices. No one is restricting the number of pizza parlors, and no one is controlling what prices they can charge. Similarly, you are free to buy any pizza you'd like. This freedom of choice for both the buyer and the seller defines a free market economy.

■ **FIGURE 2.1**
Continuum of Economic Systems: Degree of Government Control[4]

Planned Systems		Free Market Systems
High degree of government control		Low degree of government control
High level of social services		Low level of social services

North Korea	Russia	Italy	United Kingdom	Hong Kong
	China	South Africa	United States	
Cuba				Singapore
	India	Norway	Canada	

| COMMUNISM | SOCIALISM | CAPITALISM |

Capitalism is an economic system that allows such freedom of choice and encourages private ownership of the resources required to make and provide the goods and the services we enjoy. Capitalism has become a major influence in the Western world's economic system. In a capitalist economy, the production and pricing of goods and services is determined through the operation of a market—the mechanism by which buyers and sellers exchange goods and services.

Mixed Economies

Today, most economic systems are **mixed economies**, which are a blend of market and planned economies. Most Western European countries, for example, operate with a mixed economy of privately owned businesses and government control of selected social programs, such as health care. Although the United States is closest to a capitalist economy, there is still government intervention in many industries, with the potential for even greater intervention in the future. For example, a national health-care plan was passed into law in early 2010 and places the U.S. government in more control of health-care management. One provision of the bill mandates that most Americans will need to buy health insurance, and the government will provide financial assistance for those in need to pay the premiums. One way to think about the various economies and how they relate to each other is to place them on a continuum, as shown in ■ **FIGURE 2.1**.

Business and Economics

Why do business managers need to be concerned with economics?
It's important for business managers and owners to understand the principles of economics because the very nature of business is to provide items or services for purchase in exchange for something, generally money. Businesses need to know how much of their goods to produce or services to offer, as well as how much to charge for these goods and services. Additionally, business managers need to be aware of the potential impact that government decisions (such as changing interest rates) and the decisions of collective businesses (such as the general level of unemployment) can have on their individual business or industry. We will discuss how economics impacts business throughout this chapter.

One dilemma Bryan Weirmoyer faces as the need for new housing dwindles is whether or not he'll have customers to build houses for. His decisions affect other areas of the business, such as land acquisitions, inventory purchases, and staffing. Bryan watches the movement of interest rates carefully because he knows that even the smallest change in interest rates will influence a homebuyer's attitude toward mortgages, affecting Bryan's market directly. Understanding economics, how prices are determined, the relationship of supply and demand, and the involvement of government is instrumental to operating a successful business. ■

Determining Price: Supply and Demand pp. 29–35

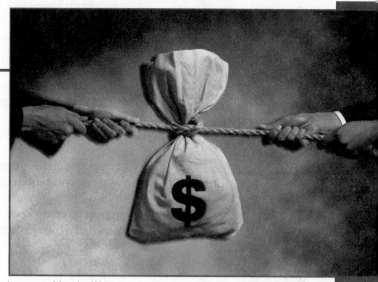

Lawrence Manning/Alamy

Rachelle Coleman has finally realized her dream of opening her own gourmet bakery. She successfully launched the business but never realized the ongoing demands of managing it. The line for her cakes and cookies sometimes wraps around the corner after a customer raved about her bakery on Facebook. Rachelle is concerned that the small, used oven she purchased when she started the bakery may not keep up with the increased demand. A new, bigger oven would definitely help, but would that added expense affect her prices? Similarly, the increase in cost of the quality ingredients she insists on using—such as real butter, fresh fruit, imported cocoa powder, and real vanilla beans—forced her to choose between raising her own prices or using less pricey and lower quality ingredients. What is the relationship between supply, demand, and prices? How can Rachelle use this information to better manage her bakery business? ■

In the days of bartering, when people traded goods or services without an exchange of money, the price of something was determined by the needs of each person in the bartering exchange and what they were willing to trade. For example, suppose you wanted milk but had no cow. Instead, you had chickens, and you were willing to exchange eggs for milk. Then, you would look for someone who wanted to trade his or her milk for your eggs. At the end of the trade, everyone was happy because you received the milk you needed and the other person received the eggs he or she needed. However, there are problems with this exchange system. Bartering can be inefficient and inconsistent. What if the person who had the cow didn't need eggs, or what if the cow owner thought his milk was worth a chicken, but the egg owner thought it was worth only a dozen eggs? To offset some of the difficulties of bartering, the concept of currency, or money, was developed. **Currency**, a unit of exchange for the transfer of goods and services, provides a consistent standard, the value of which is based on an underlying commodity, such as gold.

In a system using currency, items such as milk, eggs, cows, and chickens were assigned a price, or a value, based on how much the item was worth against a standard. Today, although we do have currency, ultimately the price for a good or service is determined by two fundamental concepts of economics: supply and demand.

Supply and demand is actually a very complicated process because many factors are involved, such as income levels and tastes, as well as the amount of competition in

Currency developed as a means to make the exchange of goods and services more consistent and equitable.

Brad Pict/Fotolia

the market. However, if we ignore those factors for the moment (and economists do this all the time—it's called "all else held constant") and examine the fundamentals only, we find that when the need and availability for an item are in balance, or in equilibrium, the **market price** for a good or a service is the price at which everyone who wants the item can get it without anyone wanting more or without any of the item being left over. The need for an item is *demand*, and the availability of that item is *supply*.

The closest real-world example of determining a market price that is based on pure supply and demand is the auction process, like that found on eBay. In an auction process, bidders state the price they are willing to pay for a particular item. The price increases depending on the demand: the greater the demand, the higher the price the bidders are willing to pay. Supply also affects price: If similar or identical items are available for auction, the price is lower. When a unique item is auctioned, prices tend to be higher because demand is higher and supply is lower. Eventually, the winning bid establishes the market price.

Supply

What is supply? Supply refers to how much of a good or a service is available for purchase at any given time. Supply is dependent on the resources that are required to produce the good or offer the service, such as land, labor, and capital (buildings and machinery), and the quantity of similar products that can easily be substituted for the product and that are competing for a customer's attention. However, if all these factors are ignored or held constant, then supply is directly affected by price.

Supply is derived from a producer's desire to maximize profits. The more money a business can get for its good or service, the more of its product it is willing to supply. In economic terms, the amount supplied will increase as the price increases; also, if the price is lower, less of the product is supplied. This is known as the **law of supply**.

Let's look at an example. If Eddie opens a coffee kiosk in the middle of a college campus, he will want to supply more cups of coffee at $2.00 per cup than at $0.50 per cup. The reason for this is obvious: Eddie has a greater incentive to supply more cups of coffee if he can sell them at $2.00 each rather than at $0.50 each because he'll generate more profit at the higher price. Notice in ■ **TABLE 2.2** that Eddie supplies only 10 cups of coffee at $0.50 per cup. However, if Eddie can charge $1.25, he has a greater incentive to supply more cups of coffee and produces 70 cups. Finally, at the price of $2.00, Eddie wants to supply even more cups of coffee, and his supply increases to 115 cups. We can illustrate this relationship between supply and price in a graph, which economists call a **supply curve**, like the one shown in ■ **FIGURE 2.2**. You can see that Eddie's desire to supply, or sell, more cups of coffee is affected by price. The more he can charge, the more he will want to supply. However, as you can imagine, the demand for coffee has a very different reaction to price.

Demand

What is demand? Demand refers to how much of a good or a service people want to buy at any given time. People are willing to buy as much as they need, but they have limited resources (money). Therefore, people will buy more of an item at a lower price than at a higher price. In our coffee example, as shown in ■ **TABLE 2.3**, students buy only 12 cups of coffee when Eddie charges $2.00 a cup, but they buy 120 cups at $0.50 a cup. In other words,

---

2 What are the principles of supply and demand and the factors that affect each principle?

■ TABLE 2.2

The Relationship Between Price and Supply

Price ($)	Coffee Supplied (cups)
0.50	10
0.75	30
1.00	50
1.25	70
1.50	85
1.75	100
2.00	115

■ **FIGURE 2.2**
The Supply Curve
The supply curve illustrates the incentive to supply more of an item as prices increase.

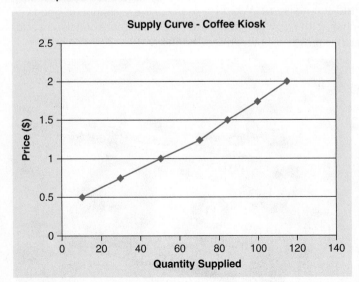

■ TABLE 2.3

The Relationship between Price and Demand

Price ($)	Coffee Demand (cups)
0.50	120
0.75	95
1.00	72
1.25	55
1.50	38
1.75	23
2.00	12

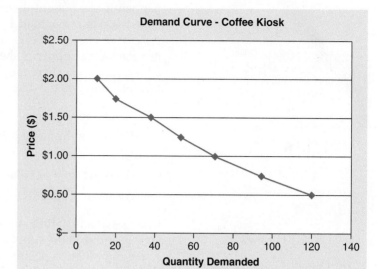

■ **FIGURE 2.3**
The Demand Curve
The demand curve illustrates that demand increases as prices decrease.

as price decreases, demand increases. Again, economists illustrate the relationship between demand and price with a graph that they call a **demand curve**, as shown in ■ **FIGURE 2.3**.

Factors That Determine Price

What factors determine price? As you've seen with Eddie's coffee kiosk, there is an obvious conflict when setting a price. As price increases, more product is likely to be supplied, but as price decreases, more product is likely to be demanded by customers. Because these two concepts of pricing are at odds with each other, what determines the final price?

Holding all other factors constant, prices are set at a point where supply equals demand. The supply-demand relationship is one of the fundamental concepts of economics. At Eddie's coffee kiosk, for example, at some point, supply and demand balance each other out. Although Eddie would love to sell coffee at $2.00 a cup (or even more), he realizes that not too many students are willing to buy coffee at that price. At $2.00 a cup, Eddie would not completely use up his entire supply, and he would end up with unsold product left over, creating a **surplus**.

As Eddie begins to lower his price, he finds that more students are willing to buy his coffee. However, if Eddie lowers his price too much, to $0.50 a cup, for example, then the demand would be so great that Eddie would run out before he was able to satisfy all the students who wanted coffee, creating a **shortage**.

Ideally, Eddie would strive to determine a price at which he is willing to supply the coffee and at which students are willing to buy (demand) the coffee without anyone wanting more or without any coffee being left over. As noted earlier, the price at which supply equals demand is the *market price*. The market price (or **equilibrium price**) is illustrated in a supply-and-demand curve, as shown in ■ **FIGURE 2.4**. In this case, 60 cups of coffee is equally demanded and supplied at a price of $1.15.

■ **FIGURE 2.4**
The Market Price
The market price is determined at the point where supply equals demand.

Factors That Shift Supply

What makes supply change? Think back to Rachelle's dilemma. What would happen if she bought a new modern industrial oven that could produce more baked goods faster than her old conventional oven? How does the increase in the cost of her ingredients impact her business? Both of these situations could affect Rachelle's supply, if she consequently needed to raise her prices to cover the added expenses. There are many factors that can create a change in supply. These factors, known as the **determinants of supply**, are as follows:

- Technology changes
- Changes in resource prices
- Price expectations
- The number of suppliers
- The price of substitute goods

Changes in any of these factors that help to create a good or a service can affect its supply and shift the supply curve to the left (have a negative impact on supply) or to the right (have a positive impact on supply). ■ **TABLE 2.4** summarizes the key determinants of supply and how they might affect business. Let's look at each in more detail.

TECHNOLOGY CHANGES Improvements in technology enable suppliers to produce their goods or services more efficiently and with fewer costs. For example, if Rachelle purchases a new modern oven, she would be able to make more fresh desserts in less time. Similarly, a sales force that uses iPads to connect immediately to inventory when placing an order would make the business run more efficiently than having to process a paper order.

CHANGES IN RESOURCE PRICES The price of the resources that are used to produce a good or a service affects the cost of production. An increase in resource prices increases the cost of production and reduces profits, thus lowering the incentive to supply a product. An increase in the cost of flour or butter would raise the price of fresh baked goods at Rachelle's bakery. Likewise, an increase in the price of gasoline could significantly reduce the profits of a transport or shipping service.

PRICE EXPECTATIONS Price expectations reflect the producer's best guess at the *future* price of a product. Current supply as well as the production schedule for

■ TABLE 2.4

Key Determinants of Supply

Determinants of Supply	Example
Technology changes	Continuing improvements in technology result in lower costs of production and create a higher level of productivity, which increases quantity and lowers price.
Changes in resource prices	A decrease in the cost of lumber may increase the number of new homes built.
Price expectations	An anticipated lowering of interest rates may indicate a future increase in new housing contracts.
The number of suppliers	An increase in homebuilders increases the supply of new homes and decreases the cost of new homes.
The price of substitute goods	The construction of townhouses is an alternate construction project to building new single-family residences.

future product may be increased or decreased depending on the expectations of future prices. If prices are expected to increase in the future, the supplier may reduce supply now to supply more at a later time when prices are higher. Similarly, if prices are expected to decrease in the future, the supplier may make every attempt to deplete supplies now at the higher price. From a buyer's perspective, the reverse can be true, as well. For example, if Rachelle is anticipating an increase in the price of sugar because of a blight that affected sugarcane crops, she may want to buy more sugar than she needs now at a lower price to continue to keep her prices low, or she will need to consider raising her prices to compensate for the increase in her costs.

NUMBER OF SUPPLIERS The supply of a good or a service increases as the number of competitors increases. It makes sense that the number of suppliers often increases in more profitable industries. Think about what Starbucks has done to the coffee business. Although Starbucks remains the leader in the retail coffee market, there are many companies, such as Dunkin' Donuts and McDonald's, that are marketing to coffee drinkers, thus increasing the availability of good, takeout coffee. Similarly, as an industry becomes less popular, due to a change in technology or other cause, the number of suppliers decreases. For example, when the digital camera became popular, the number of suppliers of film cameras decreased drastically. Eastman Kodak Co., once the leader in photographic supplies and equipment, filed for reorganization bankruptcy in early 2012, allowing the company to sell the photography division and related patents, and reemerge as a competitor in the digital industry.

PRICE OF SUBSTITUTE GOODS The price of comparable substitute goods also affects the supply of a product. If there are other equally comparable goods that are available at a lower price, the supply of goods will be affected. For example, if margarine, a substitute for butter, is priced lower than butter, then consumers switching from butter to margarine may affect the supply of butter. A change in any of these determinants of supply will affect the supply of a product and shift the demand curve. If the change is a positive effect, thereby increasing supply, the supply curve shifts to the right. Negative changes decrease supply and shift the supply curve to the left. Again, we are assuming that everything else is held constant.

Factors That Affect Demand

What factors affect demand? Just as there are factors that affect the supply of a product, there are also factors that affect the demand for a product. These factors, known as the **determinants of demand**, are as follows:

- Changes in income levels
- Population changes
- Consumer preferences
- Complementary goods
- Substitute goods

A positive change in any of these determinants of demand shifts the demand curve to the right, and negative changes shift the demand curve to the left. ■ **TABLE 2.5** summarizes the key determinants of demand. Let's look at each in more detail.

CHANGES IN INCOME LEVELS When income levels increase, people are able to buy more products. Conversely, when income levels decrease, most people cut back on spending and buy fewer products. Therefore, as we'll discuss later in this chapter, when the economy enters a recession and people begin to lose their jobs, the demand for some goods and services decreases. An improving economy will bring an increase in spending as more people find jobs and create an increase

■ TABLE 2.5

Key Determinants of Demand

Determinants of Demand	Examples
Changes in income levels	A job loss will reduce discretionary income and decrease the amount of coffee one buys. A promotion may allow a homeowner to buy a larger house or a house in a better neighborhood.
Population changes	An increase in young, working professionals in a neighborhood may increase the demand for coffee shops and single-family homes.
Consumer preferences	Needs and wants change based on fads and often manipulation by advertisers. A health alert concerning the negative effects of caffeine might reduce the demand for coffee.
Complementary goods	If the construction of new houses is in demand, complementary goods, such as appliances and other home goods, are also in demand. A reduction in new housing would negatively affect these complementary industries.
Substitute goods	Products or services that can be used in place of another. A purchase of a treadmill may substitute for a gym membership, or you could use Google Chrome as a Web browser instead of Internet Explorer or Firefox.

in demand for some goods and services. A change in income levels is one factor that affects the housing market, for example. With an increase in income, people can afford to buy a home for the first time or can afford to upgrade to a bigger, more expensive home if they already own a home. On the other hand, if people begin to lose their jobs, they may need to downsize into a smaller home and sell their more expensive home.

POPULATION CHANGES Businesses in resort communities experience an increase in demand during the "in" or "high" season. Increases in population create a greater demand for utilities (e.g., telephone, electric, sewer, and water) and public and consumer services (e.g., restaurants, banks, drugstores, and grocery stores). Demographic changes, such as the aging baby boomers, will also affect the demand for certain goods and services.

CONSUMER PREFERENCES Demand for a product can change based on what is popular at any given moment. Tickle Me Elmo dolls, Wii game systems, and the Apple iPad are all products that had high initial demand. As the demand for these items increases, there is a shift in the demand curve to the right. As demand begins to wane, the demand curve shifts to the left.

COMPLEMENTARY GOODS Products or services that go with each other and are consumed together, such as the iPod and iTunes, are considered **complementary goods**. The demand for iTunes is great as long as consumers are buying and using iPods and other portable media devices. If a new technology renders portable media devices obsolete, the demand for iTunes and the Apple store also decreases, shifting the demand curve for iTunes to the left. When the new iPad came out, the demand to download content from iTunes and the Apple store increased, shifting the demand curve for the online site to the right.

SUBSTITUTE GOODS Goods that can be used in place of other goods, such as Coke for Pepsi or McDonald's, Quarter Pounder for Burger King's Whopper, are **substitute goods**. Suppose, for example, someone reported getting violently ill after eating a McDonald's Quarter Pounder. The demand for the Burger King Whopper might increase, shifting the Whopper's demand curve to the right.

So how did Rachelle handle the increase in demand for her bakery goods and determine prices for her goods when her own costs rose? It is merely a factor of supply and demand. A higher demand provides an incentive to supply more baked goods and perhaps to increase prices. Higher costs may also force Rachelle to increase her prices, but this may lower demand for her goods. The simple solution for Rachelle is to set prices at a point at which supply equals demand. Ideally, Rachelle would determine a price at which she is willing to supply various baked goods and at which her customers are willing to purchase the goods without creating either a surplus or a shortage. ■

Degrees of Competition pp. 35–38

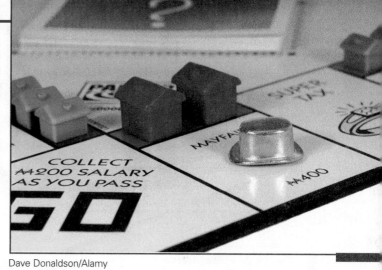
Dave Donaldson/Alamy

In 1996, Microsoft developed its own Web browser, Internet Explorer, and tried to pressure computer manufacturers and Internet service providers to carry it exclusively. As a result, the U.S. Department of Justice began investigating the corporation for attempting to establish a monopoly over the market. In 1999, a U.S. District Court found Microsoft to be in violation of the Sherman Antitrust Act and ordered the company to break up. In 2001, an appeals court overturned this order but maintained that Microsoft was illegally holding a monopoly. What exactly is a monopoly? And why doesn't the government allow large monopolies to exist in the United States? ■

Some products or services have no substitutes, whereas others share the market with many similar products. The number of substitutes for a certain good or service determines the *level of competition*. Various degrees of competition exist, from monopolies to perfect competition, as shown in ■ **FIGURE 2.5**.

Keep in mind that these degrees of competition are points on a continuum, not absolute measures. For example, many industries fall somewhere between a monopolistic competition and an oligopoly.

Monopolies

What is a monopoly? A monopoly occurs when there is only one provider of a service or a good and no substitutes exist. If one

■ **FIGURE 2.5**
Degrees of Business Competition

MONOPOLY
• One company dominates an entire industry; no substitutes exist

DUOPOLY
• Only two suppliers exist in an industry or have dominant control

OLIGOPOLY
• Only a few sellers exist, and each seller has a fairly large share of the market

MONOPOLISTIC COMPETITION
• Many buyers and sellers and little differentiation exists between the products, but there is a perceived difference among consumers

PERFECT COMPETITION
• Many buyers and sellers of virtually identical products; no barriers to market entry

bobhdeering/Alamy

ON TARGET

Apple iPad and Amazon Kindle

Apple's initial release of the iPad—a tablet device designed for media engagement and light content creation—in April 2010 was greeted by eager consumers and resulted in surging sales. Within a week of the launch of the basic model, an estimated 450,000 units were sold, and 3 million were sold within 3 months. By the end of 2010, nearly 15 million iPads were sold worldwide. After the iPad 2 was launched, Apple reported combined sales for all iPads of more than 15 million in just the last three months of 2011! Compare this to the initial sales for Amazon's e-book reader, the Kindle. The Kindle was first introduced to the market nearly 2.5 years earlier than the iPad and sold approximately 250,000 units in the first year. At the time, the Kindle was deemed a success in its own right.[5] Over the 2011 holiday season, generated sales of Kindle devices were reportedly over 1 million per week, but did not cut into iPad sales, indicating that there is plenty of room in the market for a range of tablet devices at varying price levels. Other companies have launched their competing products, including Motorola's ZOOM, Barnes & Noble's Nook, and the HP Slate. A market that was once thought of as a pure monopoly by Apple has now opened up to some interesting competition, or do you think Apple and Amazon have a lock in the tablet market?

---

3 What are the various degrees of competition?

company were the sole provider of automobile tires and no other tire manufacturers were available to the automobile industry, that company would be considered a monopoly. Monopolies can also happen in a local or a regional market. For example, if Eddie's coffee kiosk is the only place students can buy coffee on campus, then Eddie has a monopoly on campus coffee sales. In the United States, as well as in other countries, large monopolies are rarely allowed.

Why aren't there many monopolies? Without competition, the monopoly supplier can charge a higher price and may be less responsive to consumer needs. Monopolies can occur by combining companies that offer the same service or provide the same good and thus control the market. The U.S. Federal Trade Commission (FTC) and the Department of Justice must review mergers between large competitors to determine whether the combined firm would result in a monopolistic situation and thus thwart competition. For example, the FTC was involved when Gillette and Procter & Gamble (P&G) merged in 2005. Because these companies produced several similar personal hygiene products before the merger, P&G was required to sell certain product lines to other companies to avoid creating a near-monopoly by the newly merged company. Similarly, the Department of Justice has taken action to block the proposed merger between AT&T and T-Mobile on the grounds that the deal is anticompetitive.

In the United States, natural monopolies are an exception. Utility companies, such as those that sell natural gas or water to consumers, may be permitted to hold monopolies in an effort to conserve natural resources. However, the government regulates the prices for these goods and services, thus preventing the utility companies from overcharging for their products.

Duopolies and Oligopolies

What happens when one or two other companies enters a monopolistic market? In Eddie's situation, let's say that a bookstore on campus opens

Is Sirius XM Radio a Monopoly?

In 1992, the FCC established Digital Audio Radio Service and two licenses were awarded to American Mobile Radio and CD Radio to use the newly created frequencies. American Mobile Radio spun off XM Satellite Radio, which launched its first radio service officially in September 2001. CD Radio changed its name to Sirius Satellite Radio and went live nine months later. Since then, there have been no further entries into the satellite radio market. The appeal of satellite radio for some listeners is a wider variety of programs from a much larger geographic region with no or little advertisements. A subscription service is required to enjoy satellite radio.

The two companies competed fiercely with each other to grow their market share, causing each company to accumulate a heavy debt burden and to begin to operate unprofitably. It became apparent that to survive the two companies would need to merge. A merger would combine the exclusive contracts each service offered. A potential subscriber who wanted to listen to Howard Stern (offered by Sirius), but also receive play-by-play delivery of Major League Baseball games (offered by XM Radio) would not need to decide which to give up. The merger would clearly create a monopoly in satellite services, and yet the Justice Department in 2008 approved the merger. Why was the merger allowed to go through? Broadcasters and consumer groups feared that prices would increase, and attention to service and new programming options would decrease. The Justice Department's antitrust division felt otherwise, and also felt that while this would create a monopoly in satellite radio service, there were other options of music sources such as HD Radio and MP3 players that could be connected to car and home audio systems, and that the combined service would not negatively affect the consumer. In fact, the concern was that without the merger, the competition between the two companies would run each other into bankruptcy, thus eliminating a radio delivery option altogether. Since the combined company, Sirius XM Radio, was established, pricing has gone up. Although there has been some improvement of service delivery, the new company has begun to drop stations, and the playlists have been critiqued as diminishing and duplicative. What are your thoughts on satellite radio? Did the Justice Department make the right decision?

a café and sells coffee to students. Students now have a choice to buy coffee at two places—either at the bookstore or Eddie's coffee kiosk. The situation has now changed from a monopoly to a **duopoly**. A true duopoly is where only two suppliers exist, though in reality the definition is generally used to describe situations where only two firms have dominant control over a market. Examples of duopolies include PepsiCo and Coca-Cola in the soft drink market and Intel and AMD in the computer processor market.

However, if the campus cafeteria also begins to sell coffee, then an oligopoly is created. An **oligopoly** is a form of competition in which only a few sellers exist. When there are few sellers in a given market, each seller has a fairly large share of the market. Typically, oligopolies (and duopolies) occur in industries in which there is a high investment to enter, so oligopolies are often major corporations in certain areas such as the airline, automobile, high-tech, pharmaceutical, and tobacco industries. For example, the cellular phone market in the United States is controlled by an oligopoly of four companies, Verizon, AT&T, Sprint, and T-Mobile.

Because there is little differentiation between products, competition is strong in a duopoly and an oligopoly, and prices differ only slightly, if at all, between the few suppliers. If one company cuts prices, its action is usually matched quickly by the competition. Therefore, competition in duopolies and oligopolies is centered on product differentiation (making one product stand out from another) more than on price.

Monopolistic Competition

What happens when there isn't much differentiation between products? Let's assume that the coffee the cafeteria begins to offer is perceived among students to be superior to Eddie's and the bookstore's coffee. The added choice of a perceived superior product creates monopolistic competition. **Monopolistic competition** occurs when there are many buyers and sellers and little differentiation

Verizon, AT&T, Sprint and T-Mobile together control the majority of the U.S. cellular phone market, forming an oligopoly.

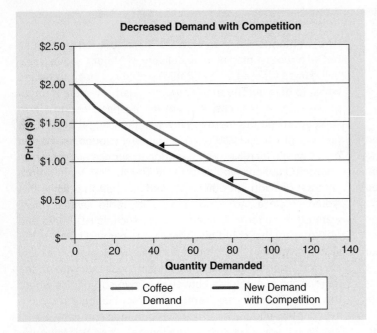

Decreased Demand with Competition

■ **FIGURE 2.6**
Demand and Competition
Increased competition negatively
changes coffee demand and moves
the demand curve to the left.

between the products themselves (coffee versus coffee), but there is a *perceived* difference among consumers, who thereby favor one product offering over another. Eddie's coffee kiosk faces new competition that is perceived to be better than his product, and demand for his coffee decreases, as shown in ■ **FIGURE 2.6**.

Monopolistic competition is everywhere. Think of the traditional strip mall or local shopping center in your neighborhood where most likely there is a pizza parlor, a dry cleaner, a hair or nail salon, a bank, and a dollar store. These mom and pop stores are traditional, monopolistic competitive businesses because there are many buyers and sellers and the products are similar but not identical. Often, the distinction between products is price.

Perfect Competition

What happens when products are almost identical? **Perfect competition** occurs when there are many buyers and sellers of products that are virtually identical and any seller can easily enter and exit the market. When these conditions exist, no single supplier can influence the price. In reality, there are very few, if any, examples of perfect competition. However, agricultural products such as grains, fruits, and vegetables come close. Many of these products appear to be identical, and, because there are many sellers in the market, no single seller can set the price for these products.

Competition encourages businesses to make creative decisions and gives customers options. Because of this need for competition, U.S. businesses face stiff penalties if they are found holding illegal monopolies. Microsoft was punished in 1999 and continued to face the effects of the legal battle years later, with the appeal court's ruling in 2001 and a $611 million fine in 2004 from the European Union (EU).[6] Stiff penalties such as these exist to discourage companies from creating monopolies. By keeping a close watch on monopolies, the U.S. government ensures that no single seller drastically influences the price of a certain service or good. ■

Economic Indicators pp. 38–43

Greg Johnson needs to decide how much inventory to purchase for his large automobile dealership. He has seen a decline in new car sales over the past year, but he knows that if certain conditions change, he could see an upswing in sales soon. The impact of the recession stalled new car purchases, but improved the sales of used cars on his lot, as well as the demand for his service department, because customers were choosing to fix their cars rather

Tatiana Belova/Fotolia

than trade them in. Greg found he needed to stock more parts than he had in the past. As a result of this shift in demand, both his staffing needs and inventory supply are affected. Does he continue to ramp up staff in his service area and decrease the number of salespeople? How many new models should he be buying for the upcoming sales season? Not knowing whether demand might pick up, how is Greg to decide how much inventory to hold or what staff to keep or let go? ■

The economy plays a big part in business. In Greg's situation, the economy has affected new car purchases, which in turn affects Greg's sales. Which aspects of the economy should Greg watch to help him make his business decisions? How can he tell how well or how poorly the economy is doing?

In the previous section, you learned about several factors that affect supply and demand. Another factor that affects supply and demand is the overall state of the economy. In a good economy, the demand for most consumer goods will be high, spurring business expansion. In a bad economy, the opposite generally will be the case (although there are always some products that are demanded, despite poor economic conditions). The economy is an indicator of how well or poorly businesses are doing in general. Because changes in the economy can affect a business, managers need to be aware of a number of key **economic indicators** and how they relate to business. Economists primarily use the following three economic indicators to determine how well businesses are performing overall:

- The gross domestic product (GDP)
- Consumer and producer price indices
- The unemployment rate

The Gross Domestic Product

How do we determine the health of an economy? The broadest measure of the health of any country's economy is its **gross domestic product (GDP)**. The GDP measures economic activity—that is, the overall market value of final goods and services produced in a country in a year.

It is important to note that only those goods that are actually *produced* in the country are counted in the country's GDP. (Hence the term *domestic* in *gross domestic product*.) For example, Toshiba Corporation, a Tokyo-based high-tech company, has a plant in Lebanon, Tennessee, that manufactures color television sets. The value of the television sets produced in the Tennessee plant is counted in the U.S. GDP, not in Japan's GDP.

What's the difference between GNP and GDP? Most countries outside the United States use GDP to measure their economic health. The United States formerly used the **gross national product (GNP)** as its economic yardstick, but in 1991 it changed to the GDP as the standard to allow for fairer comparisons between world economies. The GNP attributes earnings to the country where the company is owned, not where the product is manufactured. Therefore, those Toshiba television sets made in Tennessee would not be included in the U.S. GNP, whereas the Nike apparel and footwear produced outside the United States would be included. So the GNP measures the U.S. income resulting from production, whereas the GDP measures production in the United States, regardless of country of ownership.

How does the GDP act as an economic indicator? The GDP is the most widely used indicator of economic growth by countries worldwide. When the GDP goes up, the indication is that the economy is in a positive state. Goods and services are being produced, and businesses are doing well. A downward-moving GDP indicates problems with the economy because fewer goods are being

> **4** How do economic indicators—particularly the gross domestic product (GDP), price indices, the unemployment rate, and productivity—reflect economic health?

THE List

Countries by GDP, 2011[7]

Rank	Country	Millions of U.S. Dollars
1.	United States	15,040,000
2.	China	11,300,000
3.	India	4,463,000
4.	Japan	4,389,000
5.	Germany	3,085,000
6.	Russia	2,373,000
7.	Brazil	2,284,000
8.	United Kingdom	2,250,000
9.	France	2,214,000
10.	Italy	1,826,000

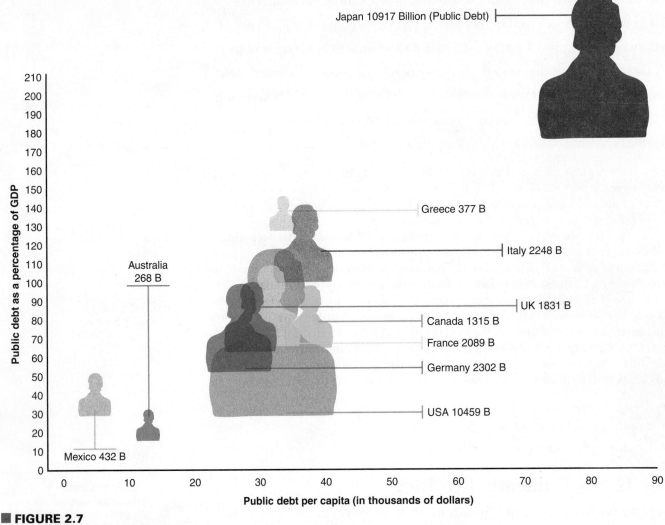

Japan 10917 Billion (Public Debt)

Public debt as a percentage of GDP

Australia 268 B

Greece 377 B

Italy 2248 B

UK 1831 B

Canada 1315 B

France 2089 B

Germany 2302 B

USA 10459 B

Mexico 432 B

Public debt per capita (in thousands of dollars)

■ **FIGURE 2.7**
Debt-to-GDP of World Economies
Source: Data from "The Global Debt Clock." The Economist. www.economist.com

produced, fewer services are being sold, and businesses are not doing as well and may have to lay off employees or shut their doors altogether. The GDP is often viewed in tandem with a country's debt level as an indicator of economic health. A low debt-to-GDP ratio indicates an economy that is healthy, while a high debt-to-GDP ratio indicates a country that is spending beyond its means. The debt-to-GDP ratio is calculated by dividing either the amount of government debt or total national debt by the country's GDP. As shown in ■ **FIGURE 2.7**, Japan's debt-to-GDP is the largest, nearing 200 percent, while the U.S. GDP in 2011 was about 70 percent. Business owners such as Greg use GDP data to forecast sales and adjust production and investment in inventory.

Consumer and Producer Price Indices

What else is used to gauge the health of an economy? There are two price indices used as economic indicators: the consumer price index (CPI) and the producer price index (PPI). You may not hear about these indicators often, but you've probably heard of inflation and deflation. A consistent increase in either indicator indicates inflation. **Inflation** is a rise in the general level of prices over time. A decrease in the rate of inflation is **disinflation**, and a continuous decrease in prices over time is **deflation**.

How are changes in the price of consumer products measured? The consumer price index (CPI) is a benchmark used to track changes over a period of time in the price of goods and services that consumers purchase. The CPI measures price changes by creating a "market basket" of a specified set of goods and services that represent the average buying pattern of urban households. The value of this market basket is determined by the combined prices of these goods and services and is compared to its value in a prior period (generally a month), and the change is noted.

What goods and services are included in the CPI? The basket of goods and services is evaluated by the U.S. Bureau of Labor Statistics to ensure that it reflects current consumer buying habits. The market basket as of December 2011 was determined by tracking the spending habits of about 7,000 families over 2007 and 2008.[8] The expenditure items are classified into 200 categories, which are further arranged into eight major groups[9] (see ■ **FIGURE 2.8**):

- Apparel
- Housing
- Food and beverages
- Recreation
- Medical care
- Education and communication
- Transportation
- Other goods and services (such as tobacco and smoking products, haircuts and other personal services, and funeral services)

■ **FIGURE 2.8**
CPI Components
Source: Data from "CPI Components" Bureau of Labor Statistics. www.bls.gov/cpi

Does the CPI measure the change in price of all goods? The CPI measures the change in prices of consumer goods only. It does not measure the change in prices of those resources that are used to create the goods. The **producer price index (PPI)** tracks the average change in prices at the wholesale level (that is, from the seller's perspective). Therefore, the PPI tracks the prices of goods sellers use to create products, such as raw materials, product components that require further processing, and finished goods sold to retailers. The PPI excludes energy prices and prices for services.

Why are price indices important? The CPI and PPI are important economic indicators because they measure purchasing power and consequently trigger some business decisions. During periods of increasing prices as reflected by the CPI, the purchasing power of a dollar decreases—meaning that less is bought with a dollar today than could have been purchased with the same dollar yesterday. To compensate for such price increases, wages eventually need to be increased to compensate employees for a higher cost of living (see the BizChat in this section). Businesses in turn must eventually increase the prices of their products to offset the higher cost of labor. Similarly, if the price to produce goods or services increases (as measured by the PPI), businesses may need to pass on those cost increases in the form of higher prices, again decreasing the consumer's purchasing power. Therefore, business leaders watch the CPI and the PPI to determine the rate at which consumer and wholesale prices, respectively, change.

The Unemployment Rate

What other indicators are used to measure the economy? The unemployment rate measures the number of workers who are at least 16 years old, who

How Much Money Do You Need to Get By?

The cost of living is the average monetary costs of the goods and services required to maintain a particular standard of living. It is closely related to the CPI. In fact, to keep up with inflation, the Social Security Administration calculates automatic cost of living adjustments to Social Security benefits based on annual percentage increases in the CPI. As you can imagine, the cost of living varies greatly by state and city. For example, the cost of living in New York City or San Francisco is much higher than in Topeka, Kansas, or Little Rock, Arkansas. Why do you think these differences exist? What factors account for the differences?

are not working, and who have been trying to find a job within the past four weeks and still haven't found one. Because there are different reasons why people are not working, there are several different measurements of unemployment:

- **Frictional unemployment** measures temporary unemployment in which workers move between jobs, careers, and locations.
- **Structural unemployment** measures permanent unemployment associated when an industry changes in such a way those jobs are terminated completely. Many steel workers and miners lost their jobs when there was a decline in those industries. Likewise, robots have replaced many automobile workers, and computers have replaced many newspaper typesetters. Workers displaced by these types of circumstances can hopefully learn new skills or receive additional training in an effort to keep their jobs or find new ones.
- **Cyclical unemployment** measures unemployment caused by a lack of demand for those who want to work. This generally follows the economy. Companies must cut back their workforce when there is a downturn in the business cycle. Once the demand for goods and services increases, companies begin to hire again.
- **Seasonal unemployment** measures those out of work during the off-season, such as those in snow- or beach-related industries, agriculture, and/or holiday activities. The shipping companies FedEx Corporation and UPS increase the number of part-time workers over the holidays. In 2011, UPS hired 55,000 additional workers and FedEx hired 20,000 to handle the surge in shipping needs.

Why is unemployment an important economic measure? Businesses, as well as government policy makers, pay close attention to unemployment rates. High unemployment results in an increase in unemployment benefits and government spending on social programs, such as Social Security, welfare (now called Temporary Assistance for Needy Families [TANF]), and Medicare. High unemployment can also result in increases in mental stresses and physical illnesses and can bring on increases in crime. It is costly for businesses to lay off workers and then, as the economy improves, hire and train new employees. In a declining economy, businesses prefer to reduce their workforce through retirement and natural attrition, which takes planning.

Ironically, if the unemployment rate drops too low, meaning the workforce is nearly fully staffed, the concern is that more workers have increased buying power and spend more, which ultimately causes prices to increase, resulting in increasing inflation. Therefore, the challenge is to keep both inflation and unemployment low—a difficult task because they seem to have an inverse relationship to each other.

The unemployment rate is an economic measure that businesses and the government watch carefully.

zimmytws/Fotolia

Productivity

How is the productivity of the workforce measured? In its broadest terms, **productivity** measures the quantity of goods and services that human and physical resources can produce in a given time period. It can be calculated as a physical measure or as a monetary measure. For example, measuring productivity for an automobile assembly plant may be either the total *number* of cars produced in a given period of time (week, month, or year) per worker-hours needed to produce them or as the total dollar *value* of cars produced in a given period per worker-hours needed to produce the cars. As you might expect, the calculation of productivity in the service sector may be slightly different, but it generally focuses on revenues generated per employee for a certain time period.

Why is measuring productivity important to businesses? No matter how it is measured, productivity is an indicator of a business's health. An increase in productivity indicates that workers are producing more goods or services in the same amount of time. Therefore, higher productivity numbers often result in lower costs and lower prices. Increasing productivity means that the existing resources are producing more, which generates more income and more profitability. Companies can reinvest the economic benefits of productivity growth by increasing wages and improving working conditions, by reducing prices for customers, by increasing shareholder value, and by increasing tax revenue to the government, thus improving the GDP. In aggregate, overall productivity is an important economic indicator of an economy's health.

So, how do all these indicators help Greg and his inventory decision? After ensuring there is inventory to fill current needs, Greg keeps a close eye on all economic indicators, especially the CPI and the unemployment rate to help guide his future buying decisions. He knows that movements in the CPI determine the trend of current prices. Such trends can help Greg determine whether it is better to stock up now or wait to buy later.

Equally important is the unemployment rate. Unfortunately, Greg is feeling the pressures of a declining economy. He is hoping that he can get by with his current staffing arrangement, both in his sales force and service department. A lack of improvement in the economy will continue to have a negative effect on the unemployment rate, an indicator for Greg that his new car inventory might not move quickly. Although none of the indicators can guide Greg's decisions precisely, watching the indicators over time allows Greg to get a feel for future expectations and helps him make better business decisions. ■

Government and the Economy pp. 43–49

Nick and Jacinta Robertson have been saving for years to buy their first house. Over the past several years, the interest rate that banks charge for home loans has been at historically low levels. Recently, however, all Nick and Jacinta hear is news about the rapid changes in the stock market, reports from the chairman of the Federal Reserve Board about changes

SeanPavonePhoto/Fotolia

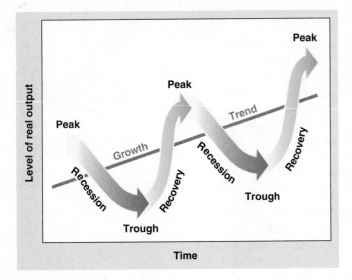

■ FIGURE 2.9
The Business Cycle

in interest rates, and debates on how the government might change its tax policies to control the economy. They aren't sure what effects all of this will have on their ability to be approved for a mortgage loan and buy a home. Is now the best time to buy a house? ■

If you or someone you know has tried to buy a house or if you know a small business owner who needs to make a big investment, you may have realized that the state of the economy can have a big impact on that decision. What makes the economy change? How does the government help control the economy? What do you need to be aware of when making decisions on large investments?

Economic Policies

Why does the state of the economy change? In 1980, the rate of inflation was at its highest level—nearly 15 percent.[10] Only eight years before and six years after that high inflationary period (1972 and 1986), inflation was hovering around 2 percent.[11] Over time, the economy naturally goes through periodic increases and decreases. Economists refer to these increases and decreases as the **business cycle**.

There are four stages of the business cycle, as illustrated in **■ FIGURE 2.9**.

5 What are the four stages of the business cycle?

- **Peak:** The peak occurs when an expansion ends and a recession begins, and when the economy is at its most robust point.
- **Recession:** By definition, a **recession** is a decline in the GDP for two or more successive quarters of a year. In recessionary times, corporate profits decline, unemployment increases, and the stock market reacts with large selling sessions that result in decreasing stock prices. The U.S. economy has experienced seven recessions over the past 40 years; the most recent recession began in late 2007 and ended in the fall of 2009. This was the country's worst and longest recession since the Great Depression. A very severe or long recession is a **depression**. Depressions are usually associated with falling prices (deflation). After the onset of the Great Depression in 1929, the government used policies to control the economy to avoid another such depression.
- **Trough:** A trough occurs when the recession hits bottom and the economy begins to expand again.
- **Expansion or recovery:** Eventually, after a recession or even a depression, the economy hits a trough and begins to grow again and therefore enters into an expansionary or recovery phase. Eventually, the recovery will hit a peak, and the cycle begins again.

How does the government control swings in the business cycle? Ideally, the economy should stay near its peak all the time. But left to its own forces and in reaction to external actions on the economic system, such as wars and variations in the weather, it is inevitable that the economy cycles through recession and recovery. To smooth out the swings in the business cycle, the government influences the economy through its **fiscal policy**, in which the government determines the appropriate level of taxes and spending, and its **monetary policy**, in which the government manages the supply of money.

6 How does the government use both fiscal policy and monetary policy to control swings in the business cycle?

Fiscal Policy

Why does the government increase taxes to influence the economy? Threats of increasing taxes are a concern to Nick and Jacinta. They feel they pay

U.S. Consumer and Business Debt Levels Cause Bankruptcy

The U.S. has recently suffered a serious recession—the most serious since 1930. As a result, huge and steadfast companies filed bankruptcy and even permanently closed their doors due to receding revenues that could not cover staggering debt levels. Lehman Brothers closed its doors with over $600 billion of debt, creating the largest bankruptcy in U.S. history.[12] General Motors filed the fourth largest bankruptcy proceedings with over $170 billion of debt,[13] and Chrysler followed suit shortly thereafter with a much smaller but nonetheless significant bankruptcy.

The recession hit individuals with similarly severe results. Prior to the recession, consumers were carrying significant levels of personal debt in the form of credit cards, mortgages, auto loans, and home equity loans. The amount of accumulated personal debt became unmanageable as wage increases began to slow down and layoffs began to rise. Personal bankruptcies rose over 30 percent in 2008 and 2009 from the previous year. The average bankruptcy profile reflects those who have lost jobs or have experienced a serious health problem.[14] In a bad economy, workers find it tougher to pay their bills. Unpaid bills reduce a company's revenues, causing greater negative pressure on an already struggling economy. It's a vicious cycle.

A surprising light in this gloomy situation are the third-party debt collectors: those individuals and companies that continue to pursue payment on outstanding consumer obligations that would otherwise go uncollected. In 2010, nearly $55 billion in total debt was collected, giving back nearly $45 billion to the economy after commissions were paid. In addition, this industry segment employs approximately 148,300 workers who add additional positive contributions by paying taxes and making charitable contributions.

too much already and need as much of their paychecks as possible to make their anticipated mortgage payments. However, they are told that an increase in taxes is necessary to offset rising inflation. Higher taxes translate into consumers spending less money, which in turn slows the growth of businesses and consequently slows down the economy by reducing the amount of money in the system. Decreasing taxes does not have quite the opposite effect on the economy as increasing taxes. It would seem that if increasing taxes would slow down an economy, a tax cut would help stimulate the economy. Although that is partially true, the amount of money entering into the system is dependent on how much of the reduction in taxes consumers spend and how much of the tax cut consumers put into savings. Money put into savings does not help stimulate the economy immediately. To stimulate the economy more quickly, the government uses another form of fiscal policy: government spending.

How does government spending help stimulate the economy? The government spends money on a wide variety of projects, such as infrastructure improvements and projects that benefit the military, education, and health care. Government spending increases cash flow to the economy faster than decreasing taxes because it is an immediate injection of funds into the system. Often, government spending creates additional jobs, which also helps stimulate the economy. The huge stimulus plan President Obama introduced in 2009 included government spending for infrastructure, education, and health-care improvements. During periods of high economic growth, the government may decrease its spending. But, reducing government spending is more easily said than done. There always seem to be government programs that are essential and cannot be cut, regardless of the state of the economy. This is always a debate around election time, and there really isn't one right answer to this issue.

The American Recovery and Reinvestment Act was implemented by President Obama in 2009 to help stimulate a failing economy.

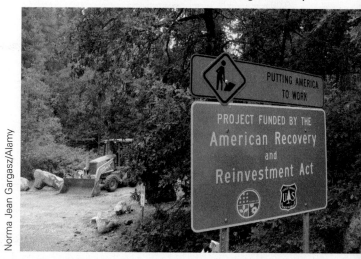

Norma Jean Gargasz/Alamy

■ **FIGURE 2.10**
**The 12 Federal
Reserve Districts**
Source: the Federal Reserve

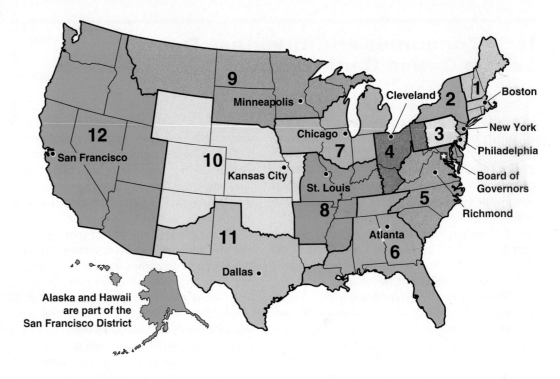

Monetary Policy

What else can be done to control the economy? The second tool the government uses to manage the economy is through its monetary policy. The **Federal Reserve System (the Fed)** is the central banking system of the United States. Created by Congress as an independent governmental entity, it includes 12 regional Federal Reserve Banks (see ■ **FIGURE 2.10**) and a Board of Governors based in Washington, D.C. The Federal Reserve Banks carry out most of the activities of the Fed. The Fed also includes the **Federal Open Market Committee (FOMC)**, which sets the policies of the Fed, including monetary policies. Through its monetary policy, the Federal Reserve affects the nation's money supply and helps shape the direction of the economy.

■ **FIGURE 2.11**
**Money Supply Measures
for M-1 and M-2**
**Surprisingly, currency is not the
biggest component of the U.S.
money supply. Savings and other
deposits represent the largest
components of the money supply.**
(From Money Stock Measures, released
April 1, 2010. Federal Reserve. www
.federalreserve.gov)

What is the money supply? When determining the amount of money in our system, it is natural to think of all the coins and bills held by people, businesses, and banks. However, that would represent only a portion of the money supply. **Money supply** is the combined amount of money available within an economy, but there are different components to the money supply (see ■ **FIGURE 2.11**):

- **M-1:** Coins and bills (currency), traveler's checks, and checking accounts constitute the narrowest measure of our money supply, which is referred to as **M-1**. M-1 assets are the most liquid in that they are already in the form of cash or are the easiest to change into cash.

- **M-2:** Another part of the money supply is that which is available for banks to lend out, such as savings deposits, money market accounts, and certificates of deposit (CDs)

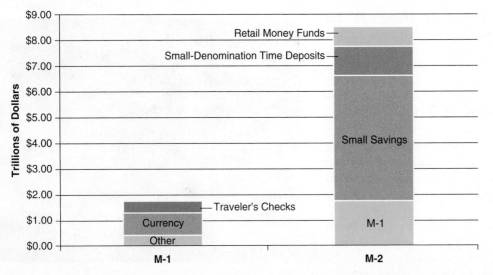

less than $100,000. This layer of the money supply, in addition to the M-1 layer, constitutes **M-2**.

- **M-3:** The third layer of the money supply is **M-3**. M-1 and M-2 plus less liquid funds, such as larger CDs (greater than $100,000), money market accounts held by large banks and corporations, and deposits of Eurodollars (U.S. dollars deposited in banks outside the United States) make up M-3. The Federal Reserve Board of Governors stopped publishing M3 data after March 2006.

Why is the money supply important? Money has a direct effect on the economy. The more money we have, the more we tend to spend. When we as consumers spend more, businesses do better. Demand increases for resources, labor, and capital due to the stimulated business activity, and, in general, the economy improves. However, there can be too much of a good thing. When the money supply continues to expand, eventually there may not be enough goods and services to satisfy demand, and, as was previously discussed, when demand is high, prices will rise. (Remember the demand curve? It shifts to the right.) Inflation results from an increase in overall prices. Economists carefully watch the CPI to monitor inflation, especially because they don't want inflation to go too high.

An opposite effect can happen when the supply of money becomes limited following a decrease in economic activity. When the economy begins to slow down due to decreased spending, either disinflation (reduced inflation) or deflation (falling prices) results. To help manage the economy from being in the extreme economic states of inflation or deflation, the Fed uses three tools to affect money supply (see ■ **TABLE 2.6**):

- Reserve requirements
- Short-term interest rates
- Open market operations

Reserve Requirements

What are reserve requirements? The reserve requirement, determined by the Federal Reserve Bank, is the minimum amount of money banks must hold in reserve to cover deposits. When you deposit money into a bank, the money does not sit in a vault waiting for the time when you want to withdraw it. Instead, banks use your deposited money to make loans to others: people, small businesses, corporations, and other banks. Banks make money by the interest charged on those loans; however, a bank must be able to give you back your money when you demand it. Therefore, banks do not lend out the entire balance of deposits. The Fed requires banks to retain a certain reserve requirement that is sufficient to cover any demands by their customers for funds on any given day. This includes trips to automatic teller machines

TABLE 2.6

Federal Reserve Bank Monetary Policy

Federal Reserve System Action	Increase Supply of Money to Stimulate Economy and Offset Potential Deflation/Recession	Decrease Supply of Money to "Cool" Economy and Tame Concerns of Inflation
Reserve requirements	Lower reserve requirement	Increase reserve requirement
Short-term interest rates	Lower discount rate	Increase discount rate
Open market operations	Buy securities	Sell securities

Based on data from "Historical Changes of the Target Federal Funds and Discount Rates 1971-Present." Federal Reserve Bank of New York. http://www.ny.frb.org

(ATMs), the use of debit cards, requests for loans, and the payment of checks that you write. If banks don't have enough funds to cover daily demands, customers might get nervous that they may eventually not have access to their money, and so they will withdraw all their funds. In fact, this concern is what contributed to the bank run in 1929 at the beginning of the Great Depression. At that time, people were so nervous about banks not being able to cover their deposits that the massive withdrawals forced many banks to close. The Fed can ease or tighten the money supply by increasing or decreasing the reserve requirement. For example, if the Fed decreases the money supply, it forces banks to hold onto money rather than putting it into the marketplace as loans to people and businesses. This slows down economic activity. However, the Fed rarely uses the reserve requirement as a means of monetary policy as these actions would be very disruptive to the banking industry.

Short-Term Interest Rates

What is the discount rate? The Federal Reserve Bank is the bank's banker, and sometimes the "lender of last resorts." Occasionally, commercial banks have unexpected draws on their funds that might put them near their reserve requirements. In those instances, banks may turn to the Federal Reserve Bank for short-term loans. When these banks borrow emergency funds from the Fed, they are charged an interest rate, called the **discount rate**. The Federal Reserve has the power to increase or decrease the discount rate in its efforts to control monetary supply. When the Fed lowers the discount rate, commercial banks are encouraged to obtain additional reserves by borrowing funds from the Fed. Commercial banks then lend out the reserves to businesses, thereby stimulating the economy by adding funds into the economic system. However, if the economy is too robust, the Fed can increase the discount rate, which discourages banks from borrowing additional reserves. Businesses are then discouraged from borrowing because of the higher interest rates that the banks charge on their loans.

Is the discount rate the same as the Fed Funds rate? The Fed Funds rate is not the same as the discount rate. It is often reported in the news that the Fed intends to change the Fed Funds rate in its efforts to stabilize the economy. The **Fed Funds rate** is the interest rate that banks charge other banks when they borrow funds overnight from one another. (As mentioned above, the Fed requires banks to have so much money on reserve depending on the deposits in the bank and the other assets and liabilities held by each bank. Banks avoid dipping below their required reserves by borrowing from each other.) Despite news reports, the Fed does not control the Fed Funds rate directly. Instead, the Fed Funds rate is the equilibrium price created through the Fed's open market operations and the exchange of securities.

The excess reserves that are available to lend between banks come from securities that the Fed buys and sells through its open market operations. If there are many excess reserves on hand, banks have adequate funds to lend to other banks. On the other hand, if excess reserves are not as plentiful, banks lend funds to one another more sparingly. To increase the Fed Funds rate, the Fed sells bonds in the open market. Banks buy the securities, thus reducing their excess reserves available for loans. The decrease in excess reserves increases the Fed Funds rate.

The opposite holds true as well. To decrease the Fed Funds rate, the Fed will buy bonds in the open market. Buying securities from banks increases the banks' excess reserves, making money supply more available, which decreases the Fed Funds rate and helps stimulate the economy. ■ **FIGURE 2.12** shows the trend of Fed Funds rates over the past several decades.

Open Market Operations

What are open market operations? The primary tool the Fed uses in its monetary policy is **open market operations**, buying and selling U.S. Treasury and

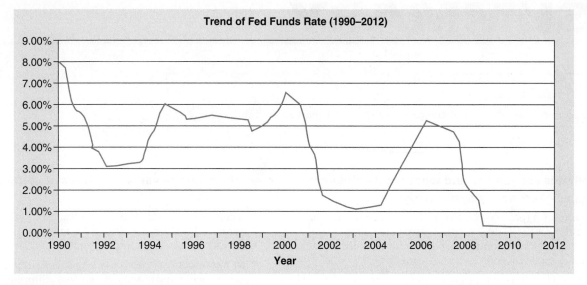

■ **FIGURE 2.12**
Trend of Fed Funds Rate (1990–2012)[15]

federal agency bonds on the "open market." The Fed does not place transactions with any particular security dealer; rather, securities dealers compete for federal transactions in an open market. When the Fed buys or sells U.S. securities, it is changing the level of monetary reserves in the banking system by adding or taking away money from the system. When the Fed sells securities, reserves are reduced to pay for the securities (money is said to be "tight"), and interest rates rise. However, when the Fed buys securities, it adds reserves to the system (money is said to be "easy"), and interest rates drop. Lower interest rates help stimulate the economy by decreasing the desire to save and increasing the demand for loans such as home mortgages. Because Nick and Jacinta would benefit by obtaining a mortgage with the lowest interest rate possible, they should watch for reports that would indicate what the Fed intends to do with its open market operations. Using open market operations is probably the most influential tool the Fed has to alter money supply.

I t is important to be aware of the overall state of the economy when making decisions on large investments. Because the government's actions affect the economy, it's also important to be aware of what these actions are and their effects. In making their decision about whether to buy a home, Nick and Jacinta would benefit from paying attention to the Fed's monetary policies. Through open market operations, if the Fed buys securities, it's likely that interest rates for mortgage loans will decrease. Additionally, Nick and Jacinta can look to the discount rate and the Fed Funds rate. News about the lowering of the discount rate will signal that banks might have funds available to lend out, at potentially lower rates. And, while the Fed Funds rate does not have a direct impact on mortgage rates, it does have an indirect effect because interest rates respond to economic growth and inflation. Reports on the news that the Fed is striving to change the Fed Funds rate will indicate to Nick and Jacinta whether it's likely that interest rates will increase or decrease in the near future. These Federal Reserve tools can help them determine the best time to buy a home. ■

CHAPTER 2
SUMMARY

MyBizLab

Go to **mybizlab.com** to complete the problems marked with this icon ⭐.

1 **What is economics, and what are the different types of economic systems?** (pp. 25–28)

- **Economics** (p. 25) is the study of how individuals and businesses make decisions to best satisfy wants, needs, and desires with limited resources and how efficiently and equitably resources are allocated.
- There are different types of economic systems.
  - **A planned economic system** (p. 26) is a type of economy in which the government has more control over what is produced, the resources to produce the goods and services, and the distribution of the goods and services. **Communism** (p. 26) and **socialism** (p. 26) are planned economic systems.
  - **Market economies** (p. 27), represented by **capitalism** (p. 28), give control of economic decisions to individuals and private firms.
  - Most modern economies in the Western world are **mixed economies** (p. 28), which are a blend of market and planned economies.

2 **What are the principles of supply and demand and the factors that affect each principle?** (pp. 30–34)

- **Supply** (p. 30) refers to how much of a good or service is available. The amount supplied will increase as price increases. Supply is affected by five factors:
  - Technology changes
  - Changes in resource prices
  - Price expectations
  - The price of substitute goods
  - The number of suppliers
- **Demand** (p. 30) refers to how much people want to buy at any given time. The amount demanded increases as price declines. Demand is affected by five factors:
  - Changes in income levels
  - Consumer preferences
  - Changes in population
  - Changes in the prices of substitute or complementary goods
  - Changes in expectations

3 **What are the various degrees of competition?** (pp. 36–38)

- There are several degrees of competition, including **monopoly**, **oligopoly**, **duopoly**, **monopolistic competition**, and **perfect competition** (pp. 35–38).
- In a monopoly, where only one seller supplies a good or service, supply may be limited. Supplies may increase with a duopoly, or an oligopoly, in which two or a few sellers exist, respectively. Monopolistic competition allows for many sellers, increasing the supply and choices for consumers. Similarly, there are many sellers in perfect competition, which also increases the supply of a good or service.

4 **How do economic indicators—particularly the gross domestic product GDP, price indices, the unemployment rate, and productivity—reflect economic health?** (pp. 39–43)

- The **gross domestic product (GDP)** (p. 39) measures the overall market value of final goods and services produced in a country in a year. When the GDP goes up, the indication is that the economy is moving in a positive direction.
- The **consumer price index (CPI)** and **producer price index (PPI)** (p. 41) are indicators of **inflation** (p. 40) or **deflation** (p. 40).
  - The CPI tracks changes in prices over time by measuring changes in the prices of goods and services that represent the average buying pattern of urban households.
  - The PPI tracks the average change in prices of those goods the seller uses to create products, such as raw materials, product components that require further processing, and finished goods sold to retailers.
- The **unemployment rate** (p. 41) is watched as an indicator of how productive the workforce is. An increasing unemployment rate generally has a corresponding increase in government spending on social policies (such as welfare and unemployment payments).
- Increasing **productivity** (p. 43) means that the existing resources are producing more, which generates more income and more profitability. Overall productivity is an important economic indicator of the economy's health.

5 **What are the four stages of the business cycle?** (p. 44)

- The four stages of the **business cycle** (p. 44) are peak, **recession** (p. 44), trough, and expansion or recovery.

6 **How does the government use both fiscal policy and monetary policy to control swings in the business cycle?** (pp. 44–47)

- The government's **fiscal policy** (p. 44) determines the appropriate level of taxes and government spending. An increase in taxes translates into lower consumer spending and helps contain an economy that is growing too quickly. Lowering taxes will stimulate spending and help boost a lagging economy.

- The government's **monetary policy** (p. 44) manages the **money supply** (p. 46) to control inflation by changing interest rates, buying and selling government securities, and/or trading in foreign exchange markets.

- The **Federal Reserve System** (p. 46) is responsible for the monetary policy and uses manipulations of the **reserve requirements** (p. 48), changes in the **discount rate** (p. 48), and **open market operations** (p. 48) to help keep the economy from experiencing severe negative or positive swings.

Key Terms

business cycle (p. 44)
capitalism (p. 28)
communism (p. 26)
complementary goods (p. 34)
consumer price index (CPI) (p. 41)
currency (p. 29)
cyclical unemployment (p. 42)
deflation (p. 40)
demand (p. 30)
demand curve (p. 31)
depression (p. 44)
determinants of demand (p. 33)
determinants of supply (p. 32)
discount rate (p. 48)
disinflation (p. 40)
duopoly (p. 37)
economic indicators (p. 39)
economics (p. 25)
economy (p. 26)
equilibrium price (p. 31)
Fed Funds rate (p. 48)

Federal Open Market Committee (FOMC) (p. 46)
Federal Reserve System (the Fed) (p. 46)
fiscal policy (p. 44)
frictional unemployment (p. 42)
gross domestic product (GDP) (p. 39)
gross national product (GNP) (p. 39)
inflation (p. 40)
law of supply (p. 30)
M-1 (p. 46)
M-2 (p. 47)
M-3 (p. 47)
macroeconomics (p. 26)
market (p. 28)
market economy (p. 27)
market price (p. 30)
microeconomics (p. 26)
mixed economy (p. 28)
monetary policy (p. 44)

money supply (p. 46)
monopolistic competition (p. 37)
monopoly (p. 35)
oligopoly (p. 37)
open market operations (p. 48)
perfect competition (p. 38)
planned economic system (p. 26)
privatization (p. 27)
producer price index (PPI) (p. 41)
productivity (p. 43)
recession (p. 44)
reserve requirement (p. 47)
seasonal unemployment (p. 42)
shortage (p. 31)
socialism (p. 26)
structural unemployment (p. 42)
substitute goods (p. 34)
supply (p. 30)
supply curve (p. 30)
surplus (p. 31)
unemployment rate (p. 41)

Self-Test

Multiple Choice   You can find the answers on the last page of this book.

1. Which of the following is a good example of microeconomics?
   a. How a specific company would maximize its production and capacity so it could better compete in its industry
   b. How an increase in the unemployment rate would affect a country's GDP
   c. How a decrease in taxation affects consumer spending
   d. All of the above

2. There are four pizza parlors in your town. You can choose to buy pizza from whichever shop you want, and the restaurants can charge whatever price they feel is best. This situation defines what kind of economic system?
   a. Communism   c. Market economy
   b. Planned economy   d. Socialism

3. DeJean has a successful landscaping business in which he mows lawns, weeds flower beds, and trims hedges. Last summer, he bought a brand new mower and hired a helper. The supply curve for DeJean's business would shift in which direction?
   a. To the right
   b. To the left
   c. No change would occur
   d. There is a shift along the demand curve only.

4. Which of the following is a determinant of demand?
   a. Technology changes
   b. Changes in income levels
   c. Price of substitute goods
   d. Change in the price of resources

5. Racerback Swimwear, an Australian company, opens a factory near Tallahassee, Florida. The value of the swimsuits produced in the new Florida factory is included in which country's GDP?
   a. Australia
   b. United States
   c. Both Australia and the United States
   d. It is not included in the GDP at all.

6. Which of the following tracks the prices of goods and resources sellers use to create their products?
   a. GDP
   b. CPI
   c. PPI
   d. GNP

7. Jackson Paulson works as a waterskiing instructor at Migis Lodge on Sebago Lake. He claims unemployment from October through April. Jackson experiences which type of unemployment?
   a. Frictional
   b. Seasonal
   c. Cyclical
   d. Structural

8. Which of the following is an example of the government's fiscal policy to stimulate an economy?
   a. Increase government spending
   b. Increase taxes
   c. Decrease the discount rate
   d. Sell government securities in open markets

9. What results when the economy begins to slow down due to decreased spending?
   a. Inflation
   b. Deflation
   c. Expansion
   d. Recession

10. The tobacco industry is represented by five companies in the international market. This represents
    a. perfect competition.
    b. monopolistic competition.
    c. oligopoly.
    d. None of the above

True/False   You can find the answers on the last page of this book.

1. Macroeconomics is the study of the behavior of the overall economy.
   ☒ **True** or ☐ **False**

2. The discount rate is what is charged when banks borrow emergency funds from each other.
   ☐ **True** or ☒ **False**

3. Sweden, with its high taxes and widespread government programs, is an example of a market economy.
   ☐ **True** or ☒ **False**

4. An unexpected early snowstorm in the Pocono Mountains will most likely shift the demand curve for ski rentals to the right.
   ☒ True or ☐ False

5. The money supply is strictly cash and cash equivalents deposited in banks throughout the United States.
   ☐ True or ☒ False

Critical Thinking Questions

1. Look in the newspaper or on the Internet for economic indicators, such as the unemployment rate and the CPI for the past several years. Determine by these factors whether the economic state in the United States is improving or deteriorating. Explain your decision. *AS BOTH IMPROVED.*

2. Discuss whether you think the National Football League (NFL) or Major League Baseball (MLB) is a monopoly. *BOTH MONOPOLIES— CONTROLLED BY CLOSED GROUP*

3. The text defines the GDP as a measurement of economic activity. Think about other things that may "help" the GDP that are really not good for our society in general, such as the economic activity required to clean up oil spills or increases in consumer debt to buy more goods. In addition, there are other situations that may "hurt" the GDP by limiting expenditures on items but help the overall good of society, such as reusing plastic bags or installing solar water heaters (thus limiting spending on oil, gas, or electricity). Does the definition of GDP need to be revised?

Team Time

THE GREAT DEBATE

Your instructor will divide the class into three groups and assign each group one of the following debate topics. Once in your group, divide the group into two smaller groups to prepare stances on your assigned debate issues.

Debate Topics

1. In 2009, the government bailed out several large banks and automotive and insurance firms in an effort to thwart a huge financial crisis. Were the government's actions successful?

2. Minimum wage laws were introduced in the 1930s to protect workers after the Great Depression. In the 2008 presidential election, minimum wage increases were a topic of discussion. What impact does increasing the minimum wage have on unemployment? Does increasing the minimum wage benefit the worker, or does it ultimately result in higher unemployment?

3. Taxation and tax cuts are fodder for volatile debate among political leaders. Many propose that tax cuts help strengthen the economy by freeing money to increase spending. Others propose that past tax cuts have not had a positive effect on the economy and have caused greater stress on the government budget and reduced the government's ability to spend on important public needs. Do tax cuts benefit the economy?

Team Time (continued)

Process

Step 1. After dividing your group into two debate sides, meet separately to discuss the issues of the debate.

Step 2. Group members should then individually prepare their responses to their side of the debate issue.

Step 3. Gather your smaller groups and discuss the responses provided by each group member. Develop a single list of responses.

Step 4. Determine who will be the group's primary spokesperson for the debate.

Step 5. Each group will be given five minutes to present its side of the issue. After each group has presented its argument, each team will be given five minutes to prepare a rebuttal and then three minutes to present the rebuttal.

Step 6. Repeat this process with the other groups.

Ethics and Corporate Social Responsibility

ECONOMIC INEQUALITY

Economic inequality refers to the differences of assets and income among groups. It has long been the subject for great discussion and can refer to the inequality among individuals, city/rural areas, countries, or economic structures.

Questions for Discussion

1. How do you define economic equality? For example, is economic equality simply making sure everyone has equal income, or is it enough to provide all equal opportunity to earn income?

2. Is economic equality feasible? Would other problems result from economic equality?

3. One method used to measure differences in national income equality around the world is the national Gini coefficient. Research the Gini coefficient. Which countries have the most equality? Which have greater inequality?

4. What other methods could be used to measure economic equality?

Web Exercises

1. **Getting Acquainted with Your Local Federal Reserve Bank**
   What Federal Reserve Bank branch is nearest your home or school? Go to the website of your local Federal Reserve Bank and outline its latest policies. What kind of information does the website give you?

2. **AT&T and Antitrust Regulations**
   Watch the video by Stephen Colbert on AT&T History on YouTube. Then, look at a more complete diagram of the outcomes of the forced breakup of AT&T in 1984 on the Quest Communications page on Wikinvest. Briefly describe the government's rationale for forcing the break-up of AT&T in 1984 and then comment on the subsequent corporate actions by AT&T and the "Baby-Bells." How have these corporate actions impacted the communications industry?

3. **Learning More About Supply and Demand**
   Search on Google to find The Lemonade Stand Game and play a round or two. Using information you learned from this chapter, write a brief paper about your experience. How much money did you make each time you played the game? What are the important variables? How does this game illustrate the effects of supply and demand?

4. **Pro Sports and the Economy**
   How do professional sports and the economy interact? Play Peanuts and Crackerjacks on the Boston Federal Reserve Bank's website (under Education Resources: Games and Online Learning) and test your knowledge of basic economic principles in the context of professional sports. Write a brief summary of your experience. What did you learn from playing the game?

5. **Monetary Policy: You're in Control**
   How would it feel to be in control of the monetary policy for a country? Go to the Federal Reserve Bank of San Francisco website, and under Student Activities, find the Fed Chairman Game. In this game, you act out the role of a fictitious central bank by implementing monetary policy in a simple virtual economy so you can get a feel for the options and limitations of monetary policy. Write a brief summary of your experience. What did you learn from playing the game?

MyBizLab

Go to **mybizlab.com** for Auto-graded writing questions as well as the following Assisted-graded writing questions:

2-1. How have the Kindle and the iPad affected the supply and demand for newspapers and other printed material (such as textbooks)? Discuss the impact of technology on those industries that produce printed information.

2-2. The text discusses the unemployment rate as a measure of economic performance. While the U.S. unemployment rate has reached historically high levels, ranging between 8.5 and 10.2 percent in 2009–2011, consider the dire unemployment situation in Spain, where the jobless rate has reached over 20 percent! What happened in that European country to provoke such drastic employment consequences? What actions might be taken to begin to increase jobs in Spain?

2-3. MyBizLab Only – comprehensive writing assignment for this chapter.

Ethics in Business

Ethics: The Basics

Ethics and business—many people consider these terms to be unrelated. How can you maintain your own personal integrity while still fulfilling your business responsibilities? Examining your own personal ethical code is the first step in successfully navigating this potentially tricky terrain.

Personal Ethics Meets Business Ethics

Randy Marks had a recipe for success with his pottery business, but it went against his personal beliefs. What do you do if your own ethics conflict with success in business?

Corporate Social Responsibility

Although the primary focus in business seems to be on making money, many businesses also make meaningful contributions to the social, environmental, and economic development of the world. CEO Howard Schulz runs Starbucks with a mission to be a company with values and guiding principles that his employees could be proud of. How can such a lofty goal lead to amazing profits and growth?

Dangers of a Weak Ethical Focus

Of course DVDs are copyrighted, but with a big trade show coming up, Lana's project team needed to rip some videos to hard drives for testing. Who would it hurt, after all? Sometimes it seems that if you break ethical standards just a bit, you'll come out ahead. But does it really pay in business to ignore ethics? Or do good guys come out ahead?

Business Opportunities Created by Ethical Needs

Richard Stephenson saw a need—more compassionate medical care that was still state of the art in quality. By creating new markets based on ethical needs, many companies like Stephenson's reap financial rewards, improve employee morale, and make valuable contributions to the world.

How Businesses Develop an Ethical Environment

Unbelievable. There they were—the once-frozen test tubes of samples, leaking all over the back delivery dock. Rashid Divecha's heart sank. He needed to manage his client—and his bosses—in an ethical way. But what did that mean exactly?

MyBizLab®

⭐ **Improve Your Grade!**

Over 10 million students improved their results using the Pearson MyLabs.
Visit **mybizlab.com** for simulations, tutorials, and end-of-chapter problems.

Ethics:
The Basics pp. 57–60

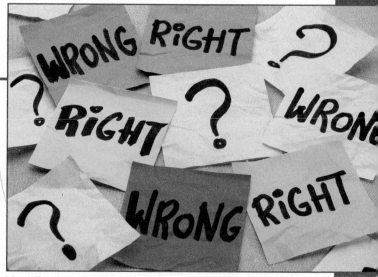

Marek/Fotolia

When Tracy Bingham gets up each morning, he turns on SiriusXM Radio to listen to the Howard Stern broadcast, laughing along with the quips and jokes about stereotypes. He grabs his keys and heads out the door to school. As he leaves the line in the school cafeteria, he realizes that he received $20 in change instead of $1 and just keeps on walking. He then heads into the photocopy room to duplicate his homework but discovers the answer key to his next exam was left on the machine. He shoves the answer key into his backpack, not sure what, if anything, he'll do with it. Before the end of class, the professor compliments him in front of everyone for outstanding writing on his last paper. Tracy knows the writing came from a friend in class but just nods in thanks. That night, he thinks over the day, reviewing the choices he made along the way as he drifts off to sleep. What would you have done if you were in Tracy's shoes? ■

Like Tracy, we all make ethical decisions every day. We decide how we will act, which thoughts we will feed, and which we will dispel. We make these decisions based on a set of beliefs about how the world works and what kinds of behaviors are rewarded. These beliefs can be classified as our set of values. In this chapter, we'll see that businesses are similar in that they also have a set of values that guide their actions. Let's examine how values and beliefs about how the world operates influence our personal and business lives.

Ethics Defined

What exactly *is* ethics? Ethics is the study of the general nature of morals and the specific moral choices a person makes.[1] In effect, ethics represents the guidelines you use to make decisions every day. But not all people share the same ethics. Many systems of ethical conduct exist. Some are based on religious systems, some are cultural or national, and some have been passed from generation to generation within a specific ethnic group.

1 **What are ethics and different ethical systems?**

Systems of Ethical Conduct

What are the different systems of ethical conduct? One ethical system is **moral relativism**, a perspective that holds that there is no universal moral truth; instead, there are only people's individual beliefs, perspectives, and values. This means that there is no single view that is more valid than any other; thus, no single standard exists to assess ethical truth. According to moral relativists, each person has his or her own ideas of right and wrong, so no one should judge anyone else. Imagine trying to organize any group of people—a family, a company, or a country—according to this ethical system.

Another ethical system is **situational ethics**, in which people make decisions based on a specific situation instead of universal laws. Joseph Fletcher, a Harvard Divinity School professor, developed situational ethics because he believed that applying the Golden Rule—treating others as you would like to be treated—was more important in making ethical decisions than applying complex sets of moral rules. Because it challenged the idea that universal rules exist and can be applied to every situation, Fletcher's ethical system was considered very controversial.

Many other ethical systems exist, some of which are defined by religious traditions. For example, **Judeo-Christian ethics** refers to the common set of basic values shared across both Jewish and Christian religious traditions. These include respecting property and relationships, respecting one's parents, and being kind to others.

Of course, people sometimes act in a manner that violates the beliefs they hold or the beliefs of the ethical system they say they follow. **Unethical behavior** is defined as behavior that does not conform to a set of approved standards of social or professional behavior. This is different from **amoral behavior**, in which a person has no sense of right and wrong and no interest in the moral consequences of his or her actions.

Personal Ethics

What are personal ethics? Every day you have thoughts that lead you to say and do certain things. As you choose your words and actions, you're following a set of **personal ethics**, the principles that guide the decisions you make in your life. Sometimes, people have a very clear, well-defined set of principles that they follow. Other times, a person's ethics are inconsistent or are not applied the same way in every situation. Still other times, people have not taken the time to clarify what they value most.

Sometimes, it seems clear that making an unethical decision will produce an immediate benefit. This is when it is most challenging to adhere to your own ethical system. Consider this example: When applying for a dream job, a college senior exaggerates a bit on her résumé about her experiences and responsibilities during an internship to seem more qualified. Is this lying, or is it justified behavior?

Now consider how you treat property. Say you bring home a few pads of paper, some pens, and a stack of blank CDs from the supply closet at work. Is this stealing? What if it were just one piece of paper you brought home? Some would say it depends on whether you use the material to do work at home. What if you used some of it on work projects and some on personal projects? What if it wasn't you who was taking office supplies but someone else with whom you work? It's often easy to have one view when you're taking the supplies and another when it's the person you like least in the office.

| 2 | How does someone create a personal code of ethics? |

How can I clarify what my personal ethics are? Taking the time to examine your personal ethical code is of great value. If you have a clear idea of which values are most important to you, it will be easier to handle situations in your personal and professional life that require you to make complex ethical decisions. ■ **TABLE 3.1** outlines one way to analyze your own ethical system. Let's look at each step in the process:

1. Write down what kind of person you are. What is your *character*? Would a friend describe you as honest and kind? Ambitious and self-serving? Interested in others' well-being? Be honest in your assessment of yourself.

■ TABLE 3.1

Determining Your Code of Personal Ethics

	Questions	Examples
Base Character	What characteristics would others use to describe you?	Honest, reliable, kind, self-centered, aggressive
Beliefs	What are the most important beliefs you hold and use to make decisions in your life?	"Nice guys finish last." "Hard work always pays off."
Belief Origins	Where did your beliefs and your view of your character come from?	Family, religion, movies, personal experiences, people you admire
Behavior	How do your relationships reflect your character and beliefs?	"I have mostly shallow relationships because I tend not to follow through on my commitments." "I have many deep, long-lasting friendships because I value friendship and work to take care of my friends."

2. List the *beliefs* that influence your decision making. For example, would you feel comfortable working in a lab that uses animal testing for medical research purposes? Do you think it is okay to lie? If so, which kinds of lies are acceptable to you and which kinds are not acceptable? Are your answers inflexible—that is, are you committed to adhering strictly to your ethical positions?

3. Now that you have your beliefs written down, think about *how you came to believe them*. Life experiences offer all of us opportunities to develop our personal ethics. We also are taught about ethical behavior by our families, places of worship, first-grade teachers, and so on. Sometimes, our experiences lead us to abandon some ethical rules and adopt others. And for some of us, our ethical rules are modified depending on what is at stake. Have you accepted your ethical beliefs without investigation, or do they stand up to the test of real-world experiences in your life?

4. Consider your *behavior* with regard to the places you work, study, and live and how you relate to people around you. Would you like to change anything about your behavior? For example, do you ever find yourself gossiping or speaking in a way that creates a more divisive atmosphere? You may feel justified in the comments you're making, but is your ethical position on gossiping creating the kind of environment you ultimately want?

How can an ethical life get me ahead? Sometimes, ethics feels like an abstract ideal—ideas that would be nice in a utopian world but have no real impact on your life in the here and now. Yet there are some clear benefits from living ethically.

First, society has established its own set of rules of conduct as *laws*. It's no surprise that ignoring or being inconsistent in following laws can have an immediate impact on your life. Because we live in a society of many different cultures, religions, and ethical systems, the laws do not always reflect our personal ethics. Acts of civil disobedience occur when people choose to nonviolently follow their own beliefs even when they go counter to current laws. Whether it is complying with a law about the way you run your business or following laws that affect your personal life, deciding how your own ethics align with a society's laws is critical.

Living ethically may even be good for your health. When your day-to-day decisions are in conflict with the values that you consider most important, you often feel stressed and angry. In situations where constant conflict exists between what you value and what actions you take, a variety of types of mental and physical damage may follow.

Can Living Ethically Make You Happy?

Research suggests that happiness itself is a result of living ethically. Psychology has established this as a new focus with the emergence of an area of psychology known as *positive psychology*. Dr. Martin Seligman of the University of Pennsylvania's Positive Psychology Center[3] pioneered this field. He and his colleagues have worked to discover the causes of happiness instead of addressing the treatment of mental dysfunctions. Seligman's research has shown that by identifying your personal strengths and virtues (things like having empathy or a sense of justice) and aligning your life so you can apply your personal strengths and values every day, you will see an increase in happiness (and a decrease in depression) equivalent to the effects of antidepressant medication and therapy. Finding a way to identify and then apply your ethics and virtues to your daily life does indeed have an impact on your happiness.

For example, Renate Schulster was a vice president for the human resources department at a financial services firm.[2] She was asked to investigate an employee's allegation of sexual harassment. Schulster's investigation led her to believe that the CEO of the corporation was guilty of the offense. Her personal ethics dictated following through with the employee's claim, which put her at odds with the company. As pressure from the conflict between her own values and those of the CEO grew, she sought psychological counseling for the emotional impact of the stress. She was eventually able to recover her medical and legal expenses from the employer and left the position. Renate held onto her integrity; however, the battle was not an easy one.*

Personal ethics are a large part of how people define themselves, their roles in society, and their business conduct. Remember Tracy? Like all of us, Tracy will continue to face ethical decisions throughout his life. By truly thinking about his thoughts and actions—that is, by developing a code of personal ethics—he will be in a better position to see what his options are in complex and challenging situations. ■

Personal Ethics Meets Business Ethics pp. 60–63

Irina MANSIEUX/Fotolia

"It was a beautiful glaze," Randy Marks says with a sigh. His small pottery shop depends on orders from individuals and small architecture firms who are looking for authentic, custom pieces of tile to adorn their kitchens, floors, or fountains. "I used copper and a special firing method to give the glaze a stunning crimson color," Randy explains. "It was our best-selling item." An architect in New York City quickly signed the shop to produce a much larger number of tiles for his clients. This meant more hours

*The character's name in this story was changed from the name used in the original article.

and more employees hired at the shop to handle this boom. However, part of the production process entailed the introduction of additional copper during firing, producing a thick black smoke laced with toxic copper. As the orders increased, more often than not, the kiln in the back of the workshop spewed this smoke into the air, in contrast to the clean white smoke produced by normal glazes.

Randy had been part of environmental groups in his community for years, so he knew how detrimental to the environment this process was. How could he find a way to stay true to his ethical standards and still be mindful of his responsibilities to his employees and customers? ■

We often find ourselves torn between several choices, and finding a path that works for both you and the company you work for can be challenging. In some settings, the line between right and wrong is difficult to see. Other times, your own personal values just won't align with the company's, and you may wish you had better understood the company's sense of ethical culture early in your career—before you invested your time and effort. Let's review some examples, resources, and techniques to help you navigate ethical conflict in the workplace.

You as a Person and as an Employee

What role do personal ethics have in a business environment? Our personal ideas of right and wrong influence our actions, words, and thoughts. But how does that carry over into the work environment? After all, our employer is purchasing our time and energy. As employees, we feel a responsibility to follow the ethics that the owner or director has established for the business. However, a business owner has no control over or even input into your conduct outside the office.

But is this really true? Perhaps at one time this model applied to life in the United States, but the modern workplace is more complex. Today, off-the-job behavior, integrity, and honesty relate to on-the-job performance. For example, in the modern workplace, workers telecommute, working from home using technologies to connect electronically to office documents and meetings. In this newly expanded workplace, an employer may indeed care if an employee drinks at home during the workday or experiments with drugs recreationally after hours. The business environment is a changing landscape, and the lines of privacy laws are becoming blurred. Do employers really have a say over employees' behavior outside the office if that behavior may affect the company for which he or she works?

Likewise, stockholders (people who own stock in a company) and employees sometimes have a say over the behavior of management outside the office. A classic example is seen when Boeing was recovering from a set of scandals involving how it obtained military contracts.[4] The aerospace leader fired its current CEO and hired a former Boeing employee, Harry C. Stonecipher, to lead the company back to stability. Fifteen months later, Stonecipher, who was married, was discovered having an affair with a female employee. The very same code of ethical conduct that Stonecipher had created and pointed to as a sign of the return of ethical conduct at Boeing was used to force his resignation. There were no charges of sexual

3 | **How might personal ethics play a role in the workplace?**

Boeing fired its CEO Harry Stonecipher for unethical conduct. Ironically, Stonecipher had been hired to lead Boeing back to stability after a number of scandals had rocked the aerospace company.

Richard Ellis/Alamy

Ken Schles/Getty

ADM was at the center of an international price-fixing scandal, meeting with its own competitors to set the price and amount of product it sold. ADM employee Marc Whitacre became an FBI informant for two years to expose the scandal. He was portrayed by Matt Damon in The Informant, a dark comedy about these events.

harassment, and the woman did not work directly for Stonecipher. He never showed her any favored treatment within Boeing. But there still was a conflict between his personal ethics and his role in the business. It took a great toll on him personally as well as the company he was working to restore.

What if you are asked to do something that is outside your understanding of ethical behavior? It can be challenging to decide whose ethics to follow, yours or your company's, and each path has legal and moral consequences. For example, Andrea Malone[5] was ordered by the president of her company to fire an employee who had a brain tumor because the tumor had lowered the employee's productivity. Andrea knew the Americans with Disabilities Act (ADA) covered such situations and that it was a violation of federal law to fire the employee under these conditions. However, her company insisted she fire the employee and say that it was for other reasons, not the tumor. Andrea chose to leave the company rather than fire the person unfairly, but she has since had difficulty finding other employment. Andrea held to her personal ethics but was not properly prepared for the short-term consequences.*

What if you find you are taking part in unethical activity without realizing that you were doing so? Before Bruce Forest accepted a job offer as a human resources director, he asked the firm about rumors that they hired undocumented immigrants. He was assured that was no longer the case. However, soon after Bruce started to work for the company, reports began arriving that such illegal hiring was a continuing practice. His boss ordered Bruce to stop investigating the situation, saying that the company would prefer the risk of being fined by U.S. Citizenship and Immigration Services. The fine the company would have to pay was "an acceptable business expense,"[6] according to Bruce's boss. So now Bruce was complicit in an illegal activity and had to make some tough decisions. Should he move his family, take a pay cut, and lose his promised bonus or stay, knowing he's now a party to this deception?*

To stumble unknowingly into unethical and even illegal activity brings the consideration of our own ethics to the forefront. Both inside and outside the office, people can find themselves involved in situations that are difficult for them ethically, but it is especially difficult when your job is on the line.

Consider Mark Whitacre, a senior executive with the agricultural giant Archer Daniels Midland (ADM). ADM was involved for years in a multinational price-fixing scheme. **Price fixing** occurs when a group of companies agree among themselves to set a product's prices, independent of market demand or supply. Based on such price fixing, ADM stole millions of dollars from its customers by agreeing with its own competitors to set a product's price. Whitacre was a participant in the illegal activities and was set to rise to the very top of the organization. His wife, however, became increasingly conflicted with what was happening at ADM and with her own ethical values. She finally threatened to divorce Whitacre unless he found a way to end his involvement. Whitacre then went to the FBI and agreed to record secret meetings at ADM, ultimately capturing over 250 hours of incriminating audiotape and videotape.[7] Whitacre himself ended up spending almost nine years in prison and is now the chief operating officer (COO) of a biotech firm in California. The story is so compelling that it was made into a film starring Matt Damon—*The Informant*.

Although some people decide they will be flexible with their own ethical standards in the workplace, it can often take a toll on their mental state, relationships, and physical health.

---

*The character's name in this story was changed from the name used in the original article.

Identifying a Company's Ethics

How do I examine a company's ethics? Some companies may have a written **code of ethics**, or a statement of their commitment to certain ethical practices. Also called a *code of conduct*, it is meant to give employees guidance on how to handle themselves in challenging ethical situations. Additionally, many companies have a public **mission statement** that defines the core purpose of the organization—why it exists—and often describes its values, goals, and aspirations. Consider the following mission statement of Fetzer Vineyards:

> Enhance the quality of life for our consumers, community, stakeholders, and employees in ways that build great brands thereby giving us a competitive advantage in the wine business.[8]

This mission statement has led to 100 percent organic wine production, awards for the conservation of energy, and a companywide English as a Second Language training program offered as part of its education package to employees.

How can I find out the best and worst aspects of a company's ethical conduct? In addition to a company's code of ethics and mission statement, other resources allow you to evaluate the acts of responsibility and legal violations by any given company. For example, you can check the legal compliance of a corporation by researching actual charges that have been filed or cases that have been adjudicated against a company. Websites such as **lawcrawler.findlaw.com** help you find relevant case law generated by lawsuits filed by or against many corporations.

There are also organizations, such as the Boston College Center for Corporate Citizenship, that work with corporations to help them define, plan, and institute their corporate citizenship. This center also highlights companies that act in positive ways by publicizing responsible corporate activities and listing on its website reports in the general media of ethical issues in business. By doing so, the center works with companies to "leverage their assets to ensure both the company's success and a more just and sustainable world."[9] We'll discuss other ways you can assess a company's ethics and sense of corporate responsibility in the next section.

What did Randy Marks decide to do when his personal ethics and business ethics collided with the production of the special pottery glaze? No one was "watching"; there was no censure from any environmental authority, and no laws were being broken. But the conflict for Randy was too much. "I had campaigned against factory emissions of air pollution for years," Randy said. "The ethical conflict was too great; I had to stop making the glaze." Randy's decision led to difficult times for the shop. The New York architect cancelled his order—the glaze had been the winning factor for his business. The workers in the shop were also frustrated. They loved producing interesting, beautiful pieces, and the new orders meant extra hours and extra earnings. Their shop was so small, they argued, how could a little smoke possibly matter in the big scheme of things?

Although Randy's pottery shop does not have a formal written mission statement, his behavior and willingness to discuss his decision behind discontinuing the popular glaze let each employee see clearly the priorities Randy held for the business. Randy had to be firm, repeatedly explaining that his personal ethics had to be consistent with his workplace ethics and that he was sure that, in the long run, the shop would benefit from his decision. Even though Randy's employees did not easily accept his decision, they felt the larger mission of the business was well defined and respected. ∎

4 How can you evaluate a company's ethical code using available resources, such as a mission statement?

Ian Dagnall/Alamy

Corporate Social Responsibility pp. 64–71

Howard Schulz purchased Starbucks, a Seattle storefront that sold fresh-roasted whole bean coffee, in 1987 with the lofty mission to become a national company with values and guiding principles that his employees could be proud of. Since then, Starbucks has become an entrepreneurial dream business, with over 16,000 stores in over 50 countries. How are the goals of helping communities, protecting the environment, and inspiring employees related to the bottom line of business—profit and growth? ■

Corporate decisions reflect a company's desire to fulfill a sense of corporate social responsibility. Every day, large companies like Gap, Disney, and Shell, as well as medium-sized firms and small local businesses, must make decisions regarding corporate social responsibility. Let's look at what it means, who it affects, and how companies can achieve it.

The Five Pillars of CSR

> **5** How do a company's policies and decisions affect its achievement of corporate social responsibility (CSR)?

What is corporate social responsibility? Corporate social responsibility (CSR) is defined as a company's obligation to conduct its activities with the aim of achieving social, environmental, and economic development. All business organizations, regardless of their size, have a corporate responsibility. By being socially responsible, a company makes decisions in five major areas (see ■ **FIGURE 3.1**):[10]

1. Human rights and employment standards in the workplace
2. Ethical sourcing and procurement
3. Marketing and consumer issues
4. Environmental, health, and safety concerns
5. Community and good neighbor policies

Let's look at each of these areas.

Human Rights and Employment Standards in the Workplace

CSR concerns affect the world outside the office in both local and global communities. For example, employment standards—how a company respects and cares for

---

OFF THE MARK

Marketing Campaign Meets Ethics

The new marketing campaign had just begun for Cathay Pacific airlines. The catchy new slogan that emphasized the company's willingness to do "a little extra" to make their passengers' flight experience special was ready to go.

But then a photograph made its way onto the Internet showing a Cathay pilot and a flight attendant on board a plane in a compromising position. Knowing the rate at which the image could go viral over social networking, Cathay's CEO John Slosar pulled the campaign.

Could Cathay Pacific airlines have dealt with the problem differently?

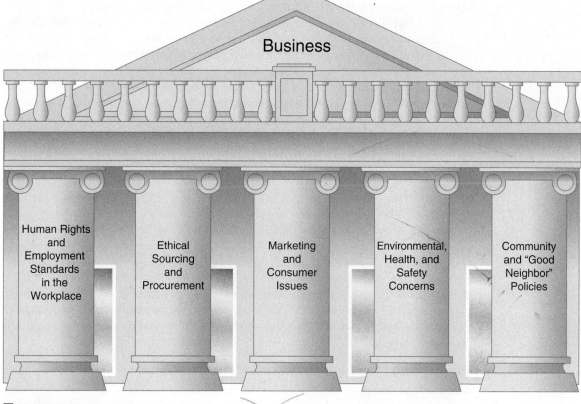

Business

Human Rights and Employment Standards in the Workplace

Ethical Sourcing and Procurement

Marketing and Consumer Issues

Environmental, Health, and Safety Concerns

Community and "Good Neighbor" Policies

■ **FIGURE 3.1**
The Five Pillars of CSR

profit & growth

Corporate social responsibility is the collection of policies covering five major areas and can be the foundation of a business.

its employees—are reflected locally in the policies a company sets and the impact a company has on the community. As a business interacts more with the global marketplace, a company will have to make decisions about ethical standards on tough issues such as child labor, pollution, fair wages, and human rights. Consider the case of the Vadanta Resources, a mining and aluminum refining company based in the United Kingdom. When Vadanta came into the Indian community of Orissa, it promised great gains in the quality of life for its employees and the entire region. Such gains have not appeared, however, and, because of the refining company's practices, the air is hard to breathe. Meanwhile, the river, the main source of drinking water, is so polluted that bathing in it causes rashes and blisters.[11] What responsibility does Vadanta have to its employees, the people of the area, and company stockholders?

Ethical Sourcing and Procurement

Finding a source for raw materials and making agreements with suppliers is an aspect of many businesses. In today's global marketplace, many companies find themselves working with international suppliers. Once a business considers purchasing materials from a supplier in a different country or even a different region of their home country, the company is tied to environmental and social concerns in that area. Consider a company that has an assembly plant in a different country. That company is now tied to the social conditions there. To keep its supplier operating or keep an assembly plant running smoothly, the company has a vested interest in the quality of the schools in that area so that the local workforce is educated.

The banana supplier Chiquita, for example, has a vested interest in other parts of the world where they get their product—bananas. Chiquita has had a decades-long reputation of allowing dangerous conditions for its farm workers, contaminating water, and clear-cutting tropical forests. With the threat of these environmental and workers' rights issues endangering the brand, Chiquita began to improve conditions. It constructed housing and schools for employees' families, and now the environmental group Rainforest Alliance certifies all of Chiquita's farms.[12] A commitment to CSR means that companies must be aware of the ethical impact of their behavior—both at home and in communities far from their shores.

Many people have purchased the Apple iPhone but few were aware of the working conditions of Apple suppliers. Apple was forced to take a serious look at ethical sourcing with increased production of the iPhone, iPad, and iTouch. An audit of supplier factories in China revealed the use of underage workers, environmental violations, and unsafe worker conditions sometimes so severe that there were suicide attempts by workers. Apple disclosed the results of this audit publicly in their Apple Supplier Responsibility Progress Report, but it is not clear how the company will move to correct conditions.

Marketing and Consumer Issues

Marketing can often present ethical challenges. In addition to issues regarding truth in advertising, marketers must consider messages that may be manipulative even if they are not outright lies. For example, several major fashion labels like Prada, Versace, and Armani have agreed to ban size-zero models from their fashion shows. As more medical authorities have linked the viewing of these images with an increase in eating disorders, the fashion industry is faced with a decision. There are many marketing and consumer issues that companies must consider if they are to behave in a socially responsible way. What do you think? Is the use of size-zero professional models socially irresponsible? How do we judge when responsible behavior turns into irresponsible behavior?

Environmental, Health, and Safety Concerns

Many industries, even small companies, make decisions every day that affect the environment and the safety of their workers or neighbors. From multinational manufacturing giants to the local auto body shop, any industry involved with processes that produce toxic waste must make decisions that directly affect the environment. Meanwhile, the production of toxic materials is moving at a far faster pace than the growth of proper storage and disposal facilities and techniques, so disposal becomes more and more expensive. One of the most infamous cases was documented in the award-winning book *A Civil Action* (Vintage, 1996). A high incidence of childhood leukemia appeared in a small Massachusetts town. A civil action lawsuit filed by one boy's mother ultimately found that the town water supply had been poisoned by trichloroethylene dumped by two local businesses. What are the short- and long-term costs of ignoring these concerns? Companies that have a CSR focus concentrate on ways to make such decisions in a socially sound way.

Community and "Good Neighbor" Policies

Finally, CSR is concerned with how a company affects the community, particularly the surrounding neighborhood. This issue has been a challenge for Walmart for years. In the documentary *Wal-Mart: The High Cost of Low Price*, film director Robert Greenwald argues that Walmart pays its associates so little that the arrival of a Walmart outlet in a community actually costs the community.[13] Because workers are paid poorly and are not offered medical benefits to cover their children, Medicaid expenditures increase. In addition, Greenwald argues that many local and smaller businesses cannot compete with the giant and are forced to close. Adding insult to injury, often a community has given Walmart subsidies to attract them to the area. Finding a way to be a good corporate neighbor is important to avoid the tensions and bad publicity that Walmart has struggled against.

The Conflict of CSR in the Business Environment

Can a corporation really be socially responsible? The Nobel Prize–winning economist Milton Friedman said, "Asking a corporation to be socially responsible makes no more sense than asking a building to be."[14] He argued that an abstract idea, like a corporation, cannot perform human functions, such as meeting

Nine Causes Americans Think Charities Should Focus On

Education

Youth and Families

Medical Research

Human Rights

Environment

Disaster Relief

Global Health

Animal Rights

Arts

6

What challenges does a company face in balancing the demands of social responsibility with successful business practices?

responsibilities. There has long been debate around these ideas. The Citizen United decision of the Supreme Court in 2010 ruled that corporations have the same constitutional rights as people to choose elected officials—and therefore have the ability to make unlimited political contributions.

A company has a unique responsibility to its stockholders: to deliver a profit at the end of the year. It is difficult to measure how that responsibility interacts with a long-term responsibility to the community or the planet. There can be a conflict between a company's need to produce profit for its shareholders and the demands of quality in the product it delivers to its customers. With so many competing interests, companies must carefully analyze the idea of appropriate social and corporate responsibility.

Walmart's impact on a community has been hotly debated.

The Benefits of CSR

What are the benefits of CSR? Having a strong and clear ethical policy helps a business in a number of ways:[15]

- A company develops a positive reputation in the marketplace with consumers as well as with its suppliers and vendors.
- A company enjoys strong recruitment and retention of the best available talent.
- Efficiency increases when companies use materials resourcefully and minimize waste.
- Sales increase through new product innovations and environmentally and ethically conscious labeling.

Although businesses reap benefits while being socially responsible, management at very high strategic levels must have a common vision of how the interests of the business can be supported by an effective CSR policy.

Measuring CSR

Is it possible to measure a company's CSR level? It may seem impossible to measure something as complex as CSR, but there are reports that present a useful picture of the overall strength of a company's CSR effort.

Social Audits

A **social audit** is a study of how well a company is meeting its social responsibilities. It is an internal and systematic examination that measures and monitors what

Corporations as People

In the famed Citizen United case, the Supreme Court ruled that corporations, which are made up of individuals, have the same constitutional rights as people to choose elected officials and so can make unlimited contributions to political campaigns. It opened the door to a discussion of the state of democracy in America. Does this decision allow corporations, and a small collection of the ultra-rich, to overpower the voice of the individual in American politics?

Should a corporation have all the same rights as an individual? Could a company plead the fifth and avoid self-incrimination in criminal proceedings? In what sense do we want corporations to be legal entities with rights and responsibilities? Should corporations be measured to the same standard of ethical conduct and compassion that we hold for the people we admire?

Mark Scheuern/Alamy

JON HRUSA/EPA/Newscom

The Bill and Melinda Gates Foundation commits more than $1.5 billion a year in grants to global health and development projects, such as funding the search for a vaccine to prevent malaria.

goals a company has set, what progress it has made, and how resources such as funding and labor have been applied to the CSR goals.

Ratings and Rankings

In addition to social audits, organizations like the Boston College Center for Corporate Citizenship assess corporate responsibility and publish their findings. And companies like the Calvert Investment Company provide corporate responsibility ratings and reports to consumers. The Calvert Investment Company assigns companies a score based on performance in the categories of environment, workplace, business practices, human rights, and community relations. Investors can use the "Know What You Own®" tool to investigate a fund and check the environmental and social performance of the companies in the fund.

In addition to social audits and the Calvert ratings, various magazines, such as *Fortune*, publish lists of admired companies each year. Other organizations award businesses for superior CSR. For example, as a recipient of the WorldBlu Most Democratic Workplaces award, Chroma Technology Corp., a manufacturer of optical filters, has many innovative practices.[16] In this global company, employees hold all the seats on the board of directors. In addition, the salary structure heavily rewards loyalty, with each employee making a base salary based on occupation that then increases based on seniority.[17]

Another often-cited CSR award winner is Clif Bar, Inc., a manufacturer of organic energy bars. Gary Erickson started the company in his kitchen with $1,000. After 10 years of consistent growth, he was about to accept an offer of $120 million for the company. At the last minute, he learned that the purchasers were planning to move Clif Bar out of state and lay off all the current employees. He felt his integrity and vision were at stake, so he canceled the deal and took over the company again.

Self-Reporting

The practice of companies self-reporting their own efforts in addressing ethically complex issues and issues of social responsibility is also becoming more prevalent. For example, every year, Time Warner presents to its stockholders a CSR report that discusses its advances in corporate citizenship, including its focus on journalistic integrity, socially responsible programming (including such issues as the depiction of smoking in films), content accessibility, consumer privacy, content diversity, and child protection.[18]

Corporate Philanthropy

Many companies participate in **corporate philanthropy**, donating some of their profits or resources to charitable organizations. Often companies view such charitable activity as a marketing investment that builds a stronger relationship with the community and their own employees. Consider the Target store chain. The retailer donates 5 percent of its pretax profits to charity, which is about $3 million a week.[19] This is more than twice the average of other American corporations.

Another example is the Bill and Melinda Gates Foundation, started by Microsoft chairman Bill Gates. With an endowment of $33 billion, the Gates Foundation has tackled issues like global infant survival rates, began an initiative for a malaria vaccine, and is working to upgrade public access to technology. Even though the foundation is not directly associated with Microsoft, it has had a positive impact on the public perception of Microsoft.

CSR and Social Networking

What does social networking have to do with CSR? As is the case with many aspects of business, social networking is changing the face of CSR. Wendy's used Twitter to fundraise for the Dave Thomas Foundation for Adoption. Each retweet of their message #TreatItFwd meant they would contribute 50 cents to help kids in foster care. The Father's Day promotion raised $1.8 million.[20] Pepsi has passed up on many traditional marketing opportunities, like Super Bowl ads, in favor of funding its Pepsi Refresh Project website. At refresheverything. com, people from across the country can post their project proposals in different categories of need—$5,000, $25,000, and so on up to $250,000. Over 1,000 ideas per month are accepted at the site, and visitors to the site then vote and comment on the projects. PepsiCo funds the 10 most popular ideas in each category for that month. PepsiCo has given away over 1,000 grants and impacted over 1.4 million people through this initiative. After funding, the winning projects continue to update the site with their results, keeping voters engaged in the final outcome. Project winners included an autism classroom in New York, science classrooms in a Wisconsin middle school, and an animal shelter in South Carolina. Besides the main Web page, the Refresh project also maintains a Facebook site and a Twitter channel.

What does PepsiCo get in return for its shifted focus from Super Bowl ads to corporate philanthropy? Perhaps a more positive reputation and increased engagement by its customers. As you can see, the look of CSR is changing as the current tools of social media are incorporated.

The Challenges of CSR

What challenges does CSR pose? It's clear that the many conflicting demands facing businesses today pose numerous ethical challenges. Consider the dilemma facing companies that produce unique products, such as pharmaceutical companies that develop medications to treat AIDS. What is their exact moral and ethical obligation with regard to the AIDS pandemic in sub-Saharan Africa? Over 33 million people are living with HIV in Africa and there are over 2 million deaths a year.[21] Tuberculosis kills approximately 550,000 a year, and at least 1 million people die from malaria each year, mostly children.[22] Meanwhile, 70 percent of the population exists on less than $2 a day and is unable to pay for the medications at a price point that would reimburse pharmaceutical companies for their research investment. It is a challenge for modern business leaders to balance their need to respond to investors and produce a profit with their desire to alleviate human suffering. There is no fixed training that prepares and equips business decision makers to navigate such difficult decisions.

As noted, some corporations manage to consistently balance the demands of social responsibility and successful business practices. For example, Intel scores high as an industry leader in its commitment to strong CSR practices.[23] Environmentally, it has decreased the emissions from its operations over the past four years, mitigating its impact on global warming. It has shown a strong commitment to its employees by providing benefits for domestic partners as well as carefully monitoring workers for exposure to hazardous chemicals. The company also has human rights policies in place in each country in which it operates; it donates computer equipment to many organizations, supports many charitable organizations through monetary donations, and is responsive to community needs.

The Effects of CSR on Society

How does CSR affect society as a whole? Businesses do not operate separately from society as a whole, so CSR affects us all in many ways.

Environmental Effects

Environmentally, how businesses operate has both local and global effects. For example, people living in the Silicon Valley area near San Francisco rely on groundwater for their main supply of water. This leaves the entire Silicon Valley area dependent on proper industry practices by the many semiconductor manufacturers in the area. If these companies allow chemical contaminants to enter the groundwater system, the entire region suffers.

Businesses raise troubling environmental questions on a global scale as well. Some say that allowing free trade—in which countries produce and sell products anywhere in the world—will export pollution to less developed countries. Would companies move "dirty industries"—those that have a high risk of pollution, danger to workers, or toxic damage of the environment—to a country where environmental regulations are lacking? It is increasingly important for industry leaders to have some structured ethical system to make such complex, long-reaching decisions.

Economic Effects

As an individual, CSR affects you as well. Financially, the long-term consequences of businesses implementing a strong CSR plan have an impact on the prices you pay for products, the products that are available, and the quality of those products. Both short-term savings and long-term investments rely on interest rates that are related to the perception of how stable a business is. Industries that act in ways that jeopardize their own long-term sustainability can create economic ripples that affect the bottom line of individual consumers.

Effects on Employee Morale

Think of your own career. Your potential for advancement, day-to-day work environment, and overall sense of purpose and value are affected by the degree to which the company you work for practices sound CSR. The ethical culture of a company and its leadership has effects on its workers every day. Sometimes, this effect is a positive one. Consider the Kaplan Thaler advertising agency, the fastest-growing advertising firm in the country, started by Linda Kaplan Thaler and Robin Koval.[24] The company, which began as a one-client start-up in 1997 and has reached billings of more than $1 billion, prides itself on creating unique ad campaigns—like the Aflac duck campaign—that grab viewers' attention.

Yet with all of its success, the core philosophy of the company is that it pays to be nice, described in Thaler and Koval's book, *The Power of Nice*. After spending years at high-powered, high-pressure firms where "those who eat their young get raises,"[25] Thaler and Koval founded a firm dedicated to the principles of being empathetic. They assume that the people you work with are there to help you, and remember that emotionally, well-adjusted people earn higher incomes, live longer, and have more satisfying lives.[26] The company founders' beliefs affect the employees at Kaplan Thaler each and every day.

Even from the initial interview, aspects of a company's CSR plan may be apparent. Some companies find that personality testing of job candidates helps them find employees who match their own corporate values. Tools like the Hogan Personality Inventory assess a candidate in areas such as interpersonal sensitivity, stress tolerance, and learning approach. As a job seeker, you'll want to decide whether you value a company for using these tools or if their use violates your sense of appropriate business and personal privacy boundaries.

The Effects of Individuals on CSR

How can I affect how businesses operate ethically? There are many ways that individuals can work toward a more ethical world filled with more ethical businesses. In addition to contributing by means of your own personal conduct, both at the workplace and outside it, your choices about where and on what to spend your money greatly influence corporate behavior. Companies survive only because consumers buy their products or use their services. If you don't believe in a company's ethics, you can take your business elsewhere.

Meanwhile, if you choose to invest money in mutual funds and the stock market, you have another opportunity to make a statement about corporate ethics. **Socially responsible investing (SRI)** is investing only in companies that have met a certain standard of CSR. This means that fund managers look at the social and environmental behavior of companies to decide which companies to include and exclude from the investment fund portfolio. As a shareholder, you can also use your voice to encourage a company to improve or maintain a high standard of ethics.

Finally, when you choose an employer, you're making a clear statement on ethical conduct by offering the company your valuable time and energy. By agreeing to work for a company, you're saying that you agree with its mission and ethics.

As a boy, Starbucks founder Howard Schulz saw his family lose their home and be driven into public housing because of the financial consequences of his father's illness. He was determined that any company he ran would never let such a thing happen to an employee. When he bought Starbucks in 1987, he immediately extended a company-subsidized health-care package to all full- and part-time employees and their dependents. The deductibles, co-pays, and benefits are the same for all employees. The incredible success of Starbucks could be an accident that happened in spite of the company's commitment to ethics and social responsibility, but Howard Schulz would tell you something different. ■

Dangers of a Weak Ethical Focus pp. 71–74

Ken Mellott/Fotolia

"To me, it was stealing, and, bottom line, stealing is wrong." The software firm that Lana Phillips worked for had finished developing a program to deliver movie content on-demand to home cable subscribers. Before it could break into the market, however, it needed to test its product and make appearances at big electronics trade shows. To test the program, the company needed data—that is, DVD movies. But DVD movies are copyrighted and protected with specific software encoding schemes so they cannot be copied onto a computer hard drive. As the testing phase approached, word came down from management: purchase some DVDs, break the encoding scheme, and rip them to hard drives to use as testing. After all, the managers reasoned, the company was not going to make money from violating DVD copyrights; it was just using it to test its software. And if it worked well, it would then run demos for clients and at trade shows using those DVDs. What was the harm?

The company consulted its attorneys, and half felt the use of the DVDs might be illegal and half felt it could be defended. Lana suggested some other solutions: The company could use Hollywood films that were older and not covered by copyright protection or public domain documentaries, which were freely available for public use. Company managers worried what the impact on business would be. Would a product shown running a 30-year-old movie or an unknown documentary grab the attention of buyers on a busy Vegas trade-show floor? The danger on the other side was that a successful product launch by the company might not save it from facing future legal action for copyright infringement. How could Lana and her boss resolve the issue when it wasn't even clear what the correct legal path was? ■

Depending on the industry, there may be significant legal consequences to business behavior that ignores agreed-on ethical standards. Companies are responsible for following complex sets of laws, and if they violate them, even unknowingly, their businesses may be in jeopardy. Violating the law deliberately may be the result of a lapse in emphasis and an understanding of ethics, and will have a serious impact on the future of the people inside the company and the entire business community. In this section, we'll examine some of the business dangers of ignoring ethical conduct.

Legal Regulations and Legal Compliance

7 What is legal compliance, and how does it affect ethical conduct?

How is a company regulated legally? Legal regulations are the specific laws governing the products or processes of a specific industry. When enough people feel that a particular ethical standard is important, it eventually becomes law. For example, in 1962, the Consumer Bill of Rights was passed in Congress. This bill made the following ethical standards legal rights: the right to safety, the consumer's right to choose, their right to information, and their right to be heard.[27]

Another example is the Organic Seal of the U.S. Department of Agriculture (USDA), which assures consumers of the quality and integrity of organic products. To certify a product as organic, a company must meet stringent conditions set by the USDA, including annual and random inspections to check on standards.

Legal compliance refers to conducting a business within the boundaries of all the legal regulations of that industry. Various government agencies, such as the Equal Employment Opportunity Commission (EEOC) and the Securities and Exchange Commission (SEC), provide guidance to companies to help them maintain legal compliance. The EEOC monitors compliance by investigating complaints of federal law violations on issues such as discrimination, sexual harassment, or violations of the ADA. The ADA of 1990 requires companies to make a reasonable accommodation to the known disabilities of an applicant or employee, as long as it doesn't require undue hardship for the employer. The SEC governs the securities industry, making sure that all investors have the same access to information about companies.

Violations of federal laws can severely damage a company. We mentioned earlier how ADM, the agriculture giant, was involved in a large price fixing scheme in which it bilked its own customers out of millions of dollars. The company was later fined $100 million for its role in the price fixing. Likewise, in 2010, British Petroleum (BP) agreed to establish a fund of $20 billion to begin to meet claims of damage resulting from the Deepwater Horizon oil spill.[28]

Don't companies often break the law and still make money? There are plenty of cases in which companies have broken the law and seemed to benefit for a time. Take the case of Enron. With 21,000 staff members in more than 40 countries, Enron had grown to become the seventh largest company in the United States. The company was lauded by *Fortune* magazine as the Most Innovative Company in America many times and was in the top 25 of *Fortune*'s 100 Best Companies to Work For. Enron had published its social and environmental positions, noting that the company made decisions based on three values:[29]

- *Respect:* mutual respect with communities and stakeholders affected by the company's operations
- *Integrity:* examining the impacts, positive and negative, of the business on the environment and society and integrating human health, social, and environmental considerations into the company's management and value system
- *Excellence:* continuing to improve performance and encouraging business partners and suppliers to adhere to the same standards

However, by October 2001, a series of scandals began to emerge when it was discovered that Enron's success had been largely based on fraudulent activities. The company had hidden debts totaling more than $1 billion to inflate its own stock price; manipulated the Texas and California power markets, causing enormous hardship; and bribed foreign governments to win contracts abroad. A few months later, the company dissolved in bankruptcy, and founder Kenneth Lay was convicted on 10 counts of fraud and conspiracy. He later died while awaiting sentencing. CEO Jeffrey Skilling was convicted of 18 counts of fraud and is serving a 24-year prison term.

Even the famous accounting firm Arthur Andersen that Enron had hired collapsed as a result of its involvement. Arthur Andersen was convicted of obstruction of justice for destroying thousands of documents relating to its work with Enron and its knowledge of the criminal fraud at Enron. For both Enron and Arthur Andersen, the flagrant violations of ethical conduct led to outside agencies levying huge penalties. It also led to the internal collapse of both companies, with the subsequent loss of each company's management and employees within the firms. Most sadly, it led to the loss of pensions for thousands of employees who had dedicated their lives to the companies, not knowing management was participating in such illegal activities.

To avoid future occurrences such as these, the Sarbanes-Oxley Act of 2002 was enacted. Under this act, CEOs are required to verify their companies' financial statements and vouch for their accuracy with the SEC.

Still, in 2008, one of the largest financial scandals of all time was exposed. Bernie Madoff owned and ran a large investment firm, managing the funds of many clients, including pensions and not-for-profit charities. In December 2008, it was revealed that over $65 billion was missing from client accounts. For years Madoff had been running a massive Ponzi scheme, defined as an investment swindle in which some early investors are paid off with money put up by later investors to encourage more and bigger risks.[30] Madoff was convicted and sentenced to a 150-year prison sentence and a $170 billion fine.

Recovering from Weak Ethical Conduct

> **8** What strategies can a company use to recover from ethical lapses?

What if your company is breaking the law and you want it to stop? Some people risk their positions and future careers to stop corporate abuse when they see it in the workplace. A **whistle-blower** is an employee who reports misconduct, most often to an authority outside the firm. Famous examples include Jeffrey Wigand, a vice president of a tobacco company who revealed on *60 Minutes* in February 1996 that his company was deliberately manipulating the effect of the nicotine in its cigarettes to promote addiction. Another example is Sergeant Joseph Darby, who sent to the U.S. Army Criminal Investigation Command an anonymous note and a set of images of the abuse that was taking place at Abu Ghraib prison in Iraq. It sparked an investigation that eventually revealed to the public the abuses at Abu Ghraib. Darby later received a John F. Kennedy Profile in Courage award, but he and his wife were forced to live in protective custody in an undisclosed location because of threats made against them.

Legal protection for whistle-blowers varies from state to state and industry to industry. For the people who take such a step, the pressure of the conflict between what they see and their own ethical standards forces them to make sacrifices.

Can a company really recover from an ethical lapse? Companies seeking to recover from publicized ethical lapses often face long battles once customer loyalty and a company's reputation have been lost. Recovery almost certainly requires pervasive change, and usually people who were not involved in the wrongdoing work to forge a new image. For example, a major scandal broke at Tyco International in 2003. An SEC investigation had found that company president Dennis Kozlowski and chief financial officer (CFO) Mark Swartz had swindled more than $170 million in illegal corporate loans and another $430 million by manipulating the company's stock price. Both Kozlowski and Swartz were convicted of fraud and later sentenced up to 25 years in prison. Within a few months of being named the new CEO of Tyco, Edward Breen replaced the entire Tyco board and 290 employees.

Companies that are attempting to recover from scandal often follow some common strategies:

- They work to find a leader who will set an example of the new ethical image of the company.

- They restructure their internal operation to empower all employees to consider ethical implications of decisions and feel free to speak up when they spot a concern.

- They redesign internal rewards—for example, restructuring the incentive package for a sales department so that there is a financial reward for building an ongoing relationship with a client rather than just closing a sale one time.

By using creative thinking and adhering to clearly stated ethical principles, a company can actually turn a scandal into something good. For example, in 2004, many shoppers boycotted Target because the chain had a policy of not allowing solicitors to collect money outside its doors, including volunteers collecting for the Salvation Army. In fact, the Salvation Army claimed the ban cost them more than $9 million in possible donations. Target could have responded with a defensive attack on the Salvation Army. They could have defensively pointed to the 5 percent of their income they had invested in local communities since 1946. Instead, the company chose to work with the Salvation Army, first donating the lost $9 million directly and then by creating an online "wish list" that shoppers could use to donate toys, clothes, and household items to needy families during the holiday season. By acting together with the Salvation Army in new ways, Target was able to turn a negative situation into something beneficial for both Target and the community.

Think back to Lana Phillips' company and their work of digitally ripping movies from DVDs into electronic files. Even though Lana's firm was not knowingly committing fraud on the scale of the Enron scandal, many of the same principles were at play. The temptation to ignore existing laws to make a profit, or even the chance for profit, was at the heart of both stories. For Enron officials, the penalties they paid for their unethical actions were devastating to thousands, if not millions, of people. At Lana's firm, future penalties could cripple the company, but the immediate penalty of knowingly violating her own personal code of ethics was the driving force for Lana. She was forced to decide whether she would refuse to work on the project and potentially lose her job, knowing that her manager would assign the work to another employee who would then be breaking the law. Lana decided to make her case to the company, urging it to not use the copyrighted DVDs. Ultimately, the company executives agreed with Lana's argument. They felt that the risk of future copyright infringement lawsuits was too great. Lana's persistence paid off, and she was able to maintain both job security and a personal code of ethics. ■

Business Opportunities Created By Ethical Needs pp. 75–77

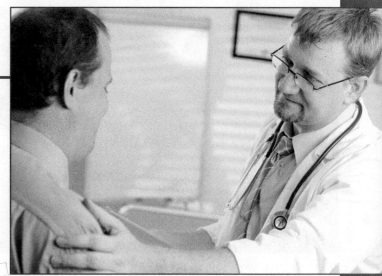

nyul/Fotolia

I n the early 1980s, Mary Stephenson lost her battle with cancer. After her death, her son, Richard Stephenson, tried to explore what options the family might have pursued that would have made his mother's final days with her family of higher quality. He found facilities that were equipped to provide top-notch technical care, but none that provided compassion and nurturing for the whole person who was ill, as well as for his or her entire family. How could he give his mother's death meaning and positively affect the lives of others? Was there a way that the business of health care could be both successful and compassionate? ■

So far we've addressed the extra work and the difficult decisions that are required for conducting business ethically. But there are also opportunities and the potential for gain by understanding and applying ethical standards to a business. Some companies focus on creating new markets with an ethical focus. Others redesign their businesses so that they no longer have a negative impact on the environment. Still others use ethical challenges as a tool to unite and empower employees.

Creating New Markets with an Ethical Focus

How can firms create business by acting ethically? By examining the world with an eye toward social responsibility, many firms have created opportunities with new types of products and services. Let's examine a few examples.

> **9** How can companies apply ethical standards to create new business opportunities?

Offering Clean Fuel

Topia Energy, an energy company in Canada, has opened the first chain of alternative fuel stations, named GreenStop, which offer only renewable fuel blends, such as gasoline combined with corn ethanol. The gasoline products can be used in regular cars, and the stations themselves are constructed from renewable, chemical-free products. Inside you won't see the same lineup of cigarettes and candy, but you will have your choice of organic veggie wraps and coffee roasted using solar energy.[31]

Creating Medical Vaccines

Other companies have created business opportunities by addressing the world's most serious medical needs. Malaria kills up to three million people a year, mostly children, and is the leading cause of death in children worldwide, mostly in Africa. The disease is transmitted very easily, whereas the drugs currently used to treat it are becoming increasingly ineffective. Many businesses haven't found a way to balance the tremendous cost of research for creating a malaria vaccine with the anticipated meager profits. Enter Sanaria, a new pharmaceutical company founded by Dr. Stephen Hoffman, whose mission is to create a malaria vaccine. Hoffman remarks, "I haven't spent 25 years working on diseases of the most disadvantaged and neglected people in the world to start a company that's just here to make

Mosquito nets work to reduce the risk of malaria, but the discovery of a malaria vaccine would benefit millions.

money."[32] Already the company has secured government grants and a $29.3 million Gates Foundation grant. A malaria vaccine, long considered to be impossible, is now about to enter clinical trials.[33]

Fighting Censorship

Still other companies are creating business opportunities by fighting censorship. The Chinese government maintains a tight rein on the flow of information to its citizens, including controlling the accessibility of certain Internet sites. This policy of censorship garnered the attention of the international business community when, in 2010, after four years of complying with China's system of censorship so that search results were edited before being presented to users, Google did an about-face and announced it would no longer censor search results for China.[34] Google's announcement was met by an announcement from Microsoft that its Bing search engine would continue to abide by Chinese censorship laws.

This censorship left Dynamic Internet Technology (DIT) company founder Bill Xia with a very skewed view of the world when he arrived in the United States from China. "I was a believer of the propaganda," he says.[35] DIT and similar companies provide a service to their clients in an effort to counteract the impact of censorship. When a site is placed on the list of censored sites by the Chinese government, DIT quickly creates a new, uncensored Web address that points users to the same material. A list of the new accessible sites is then e-mailed to Web surfers who want full Internet access. Chinese censors often stamp out the new site within a few days, at which point DIT starts the process again, determined to override government censorship. DIT and other companies are showing there are ways to fight censorship and profit from it. This lesson may continue to be important as other countries, like India, are now requesting Google to restrict content the government feels is "antisocial" or "anti-religious."[36]

Businesses Going Green

How can businesses benefit by going green? While some businesses are tackling ethical issues and offering consumers more ethical choices through their businesses, others are attempting to reduce the impact they have on the environment. Take Interface, Inc., the world's largest commercial carpet manufacturer. The company was careful to follow all laws and regulations relating to its industry in its first 21 years of business, but it made no special commitment to stewardship of the environment beyond that. Then CEO Ray Anderson read *The Ecology of Commerce* (HarperBusiness, 1994).[37] He was so inspired by the book's message that he began the process of reorganizing his $1.4 billion company using the principles of **sustainability**—the process of working to improve the quality of life in ways that simultaneously protect and enhance the earth's life support systems.[38] Interface has a mission statement, nicknamed Mission Zero, that reads: "Our promise is to eliminate any negative impact Interface has on the environment by 2020."[39]

Interface is considering all aspects of its business in its goal to run its business without having a negative impact on the planet. It is eliminating waste and toxic substances from its products, using renewable energy, and finding how to route its trucks for more efficient transportation routes. The grand goal of Mission Zero has resulted in a shift in the company's principles and the goals and expectations of shareholders.[40]

Cool Carpet is one product that demonstrates how Interface now operates. The "cool" part of Cool Carpet is that it allows customers to choose to have an impact on global warming. Interface makes sure that all carbon dioxide emissions over the full life cycle of Cool Carpet—from its manufacture through its delivery—are offset.

Actions like purchasing energy from wind farms and choosing suppliers that are ecologically friendly balance out the necessary carbon dioxide produced in other stages of carpet production. For example, Interface purchases carbon offsets by buying energy from family-owned dairy farms in Pennsylvania and Wisconsin.[41] These farms generate electricity by processing their manure differently, preventing the release of methane, a powerful greenhouse gas. Anderson recognized the choices Interface makes today will ultimately affect future generations and hoped his customers would see the value in these choices and go green themselves.

Another large international company that has worked for over a decade to reduce its environmental footprint is Starbucks. Their corporate Shared Planet progress plan sets clear objectives for the company in recycling, energy and water usage, building, and climate change.[42] Starbucks convened a summit with local governments, cup manufacturers, and recyclers to identify the steps required to make its cups recyclable. Stores are being designed to have recycling locations in the front, and customers are given $0.10 off each cup of coffee served in a reusable tumbler. The company has set a goal of 25 percent of all beverages being served in recyclable cups by 2015.

As we have seen, companies can create opportunities based on ethical challenges in a variety of different ways. New businesses are appearing, focused on addressing the ethical issues of our times. For example, a newly diagnosed cancer patient has more options today than ever before. Richard Stephenson responded to his mother's death by founding a network of hospitals called the Cancer Treatment Centers of America (CTCA). At CTCA, providers are guided to treat patients with the "Mother Standard of care," the level of compassion and support that you would want for your own family members. In four hospitals spread across the United States, CTCA treats patients with the latest conventional therapies but also provides a full range of complementary treatment options and access to multidisciplinary team support. Hospital staff members are available for nutritional consults; spiritual support; mind-body counseling; and the latest treatments in chemotherapy, radiation, and surgery. The hospital policies are centered on a model called "Patient Empowerment Medicine,"[43] in which both the patient and caregivers play an active role in treatment options. From the pain of his mother's illness and the lack of compassionate, integrated care available for her, Richard Stephenson recognized the opportunity for a more ethical, humane medical system. ∎

Realimage/Alamy

Starbucks discounts coffee if customers bring their own recyclable tumblers. The company has set a goal of 25% of all beverages being served in recyclable cups by 2015.

How Businesses Develop an Ethical Environment pp. 77–79

Rashid Divecha has seen it all as a project manager at a major clinical laboratory—samples left on the dock over the 4th of July weekend (thawed beyond repair), tests done with old

mario beauregard/Fotolia

chemicals, and reports delivered late and incomplete. But he knew he'd really be on the hot spot with a client when a lab technician walked in on Friday and announced that three key samples from the testing for a major client were missing. The results for those samples were critical to the report that was being delivered to that client on Monday . . . but now there was no proof for the Food and Drug Administration (FDA) that those data points had ever really existed. As Rashid pondered how to handle the situation, his e-mail inbox was filling up with demands from his supervisors not to say anything to the client until a complete "story" had been developed that would make the lab appear blameless. Some even suggested covering up the whole episode with false data. What would Rashid do? ■

Almost every business wants to promote an ethical environment, but sometimes managers find it difficult to know how to implement this successfully. Let's look at some different approaches being used by businesses to help their employees and the company decision-making processes become attuned to an emphasis on ethical conduct.

Ethical Focus from the Start

How can a business improve its own culture of ethical and responsible conduct? There are steps that businesses can take to make sure employees get off to an ethical start:

- Managers can make sure a strict code of ethics and a meaningful and current mission statement is in place and that both are clearly communicated to employees when they start working at an organization. The code of ethics and mission statement should be posted throughout the workplace.

- A company can offer orientation programs to new employees to inform them of the ethical standards in place and the conduct expected of them from the beginning of their careers at a company.

Companies should set the right tone at the beginning—show how serious they are about ethics and act with the highest regard to ethical behavior.

Ethical Focus Every Day

How can a business maintain its policy of ethical conduct in the workplace? When employees are faced with unethical situations on a daily

> **10** What approaches can a company use to develop and maintain an ethical environment?

ON TARGET

Playing the Ethics Game

A unique approach to ethics training is emerging in the corporate world: games. For example, Cadbury Schweppes, an international confectionery and beverage company, has created a board game called "Ethical Risk" that its employees play to help bridge the gap between the values the company wants to achieve and the day-to-day decision making and practices of its managers.[44] Lockheed Martin uses a computer game called "Gray Matters," which presents a series of ethical dilemmas. Group discussion with a facilitator leads to a better understanding of how to resolve complex ethical issues.[45] Many other companies offer self-paced online training in ethics awareness issues. The use of multimedia and a gaming environment promotes a stronger dialogue and builds insight into the practical ways to address the complex issues of corporate ethics and social responsibility.

basis, adhering to a company's code of ethics can be very difficult. Business leaders must take steps to make sure that all employees are making ethical decisions. This becomes even more of a challenge during tough economic times, such as has been experienced recently in the United States. In recent surveys, however, the majority of U.S. employers say they are keeping their budgets for ethics training and compliance monitoring at the same level or increasing them, despite the economic downturn.[46]

Companies often report trying many things to support ethical conduct. Managers communicate regularly with employees about acceptable and unacceptable business practices. They check to determine that the code of ethics is being followed. Good managers focus on ethics themselves, setting clear examples for the behavior expected at all levels of the organization. Often companies create a hotline for employees to anonymously report violations of the ethics code and make sure the allegations are followed up.

Companies also employ ongoing **ethics training programs** designed to boost the awareness of their employees about ethics issues. Such training occurs at all levels of the organization. From top management that makes strategic and far-reaching decisions, to frontline managers who use their decision-making skills to put out fires, to salespeople who work with vendors and must navigate ethics questions, to lower-level employees who make decisions regarding whether to follow the advice of their leaders, all levels of employees are involved in ethics training.

Of course, private-sector businesses are not alone in wanting ethics training programs for their employees. State and government organizations face similar challenges. Many law enforcement agencies—including local police, state police, and the FBI—have ethics training programs to help officers deal with cases in which there may be no clear response.[47] For example, when an officer responds to a domestic disturbance call but decides no crime has been committed, does he or she have a responsibility to try to prevent a potential escalation into a future criminal incident? By discussing, role-playing, and writing about these scenarios, the officers are more prepared for the ethical dilemmas facing them on the job.

Developing an ethical environment involves several components and often requires a concentrated investment of time and resources; however, it remains a priority for most businesses. Think back at Rashid's story. What did Rashid decide to do? Although he was pressured by his supervisors not to say anything to the client until a complete "story" had been developed, Rashid knew how he would want to be treated and was willing to live up to his personal ethical beliefs even in this crisis. In doing so, he set an example for his own employees to emulate.

Next he went looking for the company's stated procedure for the ethical handling of a corrective action like this. It turned out there was no such document at his facility, but the company's Salt Lake City lab had a corrective procedures document, so Rashid obtained a copy of it. He then began a series of interviews with all the employees involved, not as a hunt for blame but with a clear message of improving lab performance. Some practices were identified that needed to be changed—for example, scientists often just walked into the lab and took samples they wanted for their own research. It also became clear there was one employee who had been involved in several instances of sample mishandling. It was never proven whether this was due to incompetence or unethical conduct, but the employee was given a "performance improvement plan" to help train him and monitor and improve the situation. As these results were communicated to the client, their trust in the lab began to grow again. Rashid's supervisors begrudgingly saw the value of having made early contact with the client, and the corporate policies were modified formally. ■

CHAPTER 3
SUMMARY

MyBizLab

Go to **mybizlab.com** to complete the problems marked with this icon ⭐.

1 **What are ethics and different ethical systems?** (pp. 57–58)

- **Ethics** (p. 57) are the moral choices people make.
- Ethical systems include the following:
  - **Moral relativism** (p. 58), a perspective that holds that there is no universal moral truth but instead only individuals' beliefs, perspectives, and values
  - **Situational ethics** (p. 58), which encourages people to make ethical decisions based on the circumstances of a particular situation, not on fixed laws
  - Systems defined by religious traditions, such as **Judeo-Christian ethics** (p.58), which refers to the common set of basic values shared across both Jewish and Christian religious traditions

2 **How does someone create a personal code of ethics?** (pp. 58–59)

- Determine your base character.
- List all the beliefs that influence your decision making.
- Think about how your behavior reflects these beliefs.
- Now think about where your beliefs and view of your character come from. Why do you hold these beliefs?

3 **How might personal ethics play a role in the workplace?** (pp. 60–63)

- Having a strong ethical foundation can help you achieve success in business and greater happiness in life.
- In the modern workplace, there is less distinction made between how you conduct yourself inside and outside the office. Telecommuting is one instance when a person's employer may influence how an employee behaves at home.
- Conflicts can emerge when your **personal ethics** (p. 58) are different from those of your company.

4 **How can you evaluate a company's ethical code using available resources, such as a mission statement?** (p. 63)

- Some companies may have a written **code of ethics** (p. 63), or a statement of their commitment to certain ethical practices.
- Many companies have a public **mission statement** (p. 63) that defines the core purpose of the organization and often describes its values, goals, and aspirations.

5 **How do a company's policies and decisions affect its achievement of corporate social responsibility (CSR)?** (pp. 64–66)

- **Corporate social responsibility (CSR)** (p. 64) consists of five major areas: employment standards, ethical sourcing, marketing issues, environmental concerns, and community policies.
- A strong CSR plan allows a company to serve its local and global communities well. It also benefits a corporation in direct and indirect ways.

6 **What challenges does a company face in balancing the demands of social responsibility with successful business practices?** (pp. 66–69)

- Companies must balance their moral and ethical obligations to consumers with their need to respond to investors and produce a profit.
- It's also important for companies to show a strong commitment to their employees (by ensuring workplace safety), the local community (by responding to community needs, for example), and all the countries in which they operate (by upholding human rights policies). At times, it can be difficult to balance these commitments with the need to ensure that the business remains financially successful.

7 **What is legal compliance, and how does it affect ethical conduct?** (pp. 72–73)

- **Legal compliance** (p. 72) refers to conducting a business within the boundaries of all the legal regulations of that industry.
- Companies that establish and adhere to high ethical standards are more likely to maintain legal compliance.

8 **What strategies can a company use to recover from ethical lapses?** (pp. 73–74)

- A company can work to find a leader who will set an example of the new ethical image of the company.
- A company can restructure its internal operations to empower all employees to consider the ethical implications of decisions and feel free to speak up when they have concerns.
- A company can redesign internal rewards.

9 **How can companies apply ethical standards to create new business opportunities?** (pp. 75–77)

- While some businesses are tackling ethical issues and offering consumers more ethical choices through their businesses, others are attempting to reduce the impact they have on the environment.

10 **What approaches can a company use to develop and maintain an ethical environment?** (pp. 77–79)

- Managers can make sure a mission statement is in place and set clear examples for the standards of behavior expected at all levels of the organization.
- Companies can offer orientation programs to new employees to inform them of the ethical standards in place.
- **Ethics training programs** (p. 79) can boost the awareness of employees about ethics issues.

Key Terms

amoral behavior   (p. 58)
code of ethics   (p. 63)
corporate philanthropy   (p. 68)
corporate social responsibility (CSR)   (p. 64)
ethics   (p. 57)
ethics training program   (p. 79)

Judeo-Christian ethics   (p. 58)
legal compliance   (p. 72)
legal regulations   (p. 72)
mission statement   (p. 63)
moral relativism   (p. 58)
personal ethics   (p. 58)
price fixing   (p. 62)

situational ethics   (p. 58)
social audit   (p. 67)
socially responsible investing (SRI)   (p. 70)
sustainability   (p. 76)
unethical behavior   (p. 58)
whistle-blower   (p. 73)

Self-Test

Multiple Choice   You can find the answers on the last page of this book.

1. Ethics are based on
- a. the current popular culture.
- b. religious, cultural, or ethnic systems.
- c. society's legal system.
- d. each situation and the moral consequences of an action.

2. A corporation can behave in a socially responsible way by
- a. having strong policies in place to help the community.
- b. acting to reduce the negative impact a company has on the environment.
- c. being truthful with consumers in its market.
- d. All of the above

3. Personal ethics collide with business ethics
- a. whenever there is a claim of sexual harassment.
- b. when a business owner tries to control employees' behavior outside of work.
- c. if employees try to dictate corporate policies.
- d. None of the above

4. CSR can be measured by
- a. a company's rate of growth.
- b. organizations that monitor and rank performance on social issues.
- c. the happiness level of employees in a company.
- d. businesses that have a high profit margin and gross sales.

5. A business is in legal compliance if
- a. it follows all the laws of which it is aware.
- b. it cannot be proven guilty of violating any laws.
- c. it meets all local, state, and federal regulations.
- d. it hires only employees who do not have criminal records.

6. A company's ethics can be examined by
- a. following its stock price.
- b. interviewing employees.
- c. checking documents filed when it was incorporated.
- d. reviewing its code of ethics and mission statement.

Self-Test (continued)

7. **A social audit**

   a. defines the marketing direction for a business.

   b. is a set of principles that defines how to measure the success of a business.

   c. indicates how well a company is doing at keeping good relationships with its neighbors.

   d. is a study of how well a company is meeting its social responsibilities.

8. **Ethical sourcing means that**

   a. people should make ethical decisions based on a particular situation.

   b. there is one accepted source for guiding ethical decision making.

   c. a company follows accepted conduct when acquiring raw materials from suppliers.

   d. companies will not work with international suppliers.

9. **Which of the following strategies is *not* designed to help a company recover from an ethical lapse?**

   a. Ensuring that the whistle-blower faces legal consequences

   b. Working to find a leader who will set an example of the new ethical image of the company

   c. Restructuring internal operations to empower all employees to consider ethical implications of decisions and allowing them to feel free to speak up when they have concerns

   d. Redesigning internal rewards—for example, restructuring the incentive package for a sales department so that there is a financial reward for building a relationship with a client rather than just closing a sale

10. **The practice of corporate philanthropy**

    a. is only a marketing strategy.

    b. can build stronger relationships with employees and the community at large.

    c. states that success can be found by competing fiercely to provide lowest price.

    d. is a strategy that works only in certain segments of industry where there is a lot of media attention.

True/False   You can find the answers on the last page of this book.

1. **A mission statement details the plans of how a company will achieve profitability.**
   ☐ **True** or ☒ **False**

2. **Minimizing a company's carbon footprint is part of a plan to increase corporate philanthropy.**
   ☐ **True** or ☒ **False**

3. **Ethics is the study of the general nature of morals and the specific moral choices a person makes.**
   ☒ **True** or ☐ **False**

4. **When a company follows a strong CSR program, it will restrict opportunities for growth.**
   ☐ **True** or ☒ **False**

5. **Employee morale is the responsibility of only individual employees.**
   ☐ **True** or ☒ **False**

Critical Thinking Questions

1. Do you believe being ethical will lead to a better quality of life for you? Do cheaters win in the real world, or does ethical conduct lead to a more satisfying outcome? Are there times you would be willing to compromise your ethics for business gain?

2. Which of the five pillars of CSR seems the most important to you? How do the five areas relate to each other?

3. How should the online companies Google and Facebook react to requests for censorship? Does a government have the right to exercise a filtering of the information available if they feel it protects and increases the safety of its citizens?

Team Time

ONE ISSUE, THREE SIDES

Divide into three teams, one to represent each of the following:

a. Pharmaceutical company executives

b. People with a catastrophic but treatable illness

c. People identified as having "unique" DNA

Scenario

Are there some things that can't be owned? Leukemia patient John Moore would answer yes. After Moore had his cancerous spleen removed at the University of California at Los Angeles, the university kept the spleen and was eventually granted a patent for DNA removed from the organ. The value of the DNA was estimated to be more than $1 billion. When Moore demanded that his cells be returned, the California Supreme Court ruled against him, saying that he had no right to his own cells after they had been removed from his body. Pharmaceutical researchers, like those at the University of California, often hope to later license the DNA patterns or sell them to other companies so they may use them to develop drugs or tests for the presence of disease. In March 2010, a Maryland state judge ruled that patents on two other genes, BCRA1 and BCRA2, breast cancer markers claimed by the University of Maryland and Myriad Genetics, were invalid. However, the judge chose not to rule on the larger issue of whether people own the genetic information their cells carry.[48]

Does a person or a group of people who have that specific, perhaps unique, gene have ownership? Do they deserve payment? Do they have a right to a voice in the use of their genetic material? Or are their interests trumped by the value of such discoveries to the greater good?

Process

Step 1. Record your ideas and opinions about the issue presented in this scenario. Be sure to consider the issue from your assigned perspective.

Step 2. Meet as a team and review the issue from multiple perspectives. Discuss together what one best policy could be developed to address the concerns of all three groups.

Ethics and Corporate Social Responsibility

PERSONAL AND BUSINESS ETHICS

As you've learned, sometimes a person's personal code of ethics does not fall within the code of ethics used in his or her profession. What is your personal code of ethics? What profession do you hope to have in the future? How does your personal code of ethics match the code of ethics used in that profession? Would you be willing to ignore your personal ethical code for business?

Process

Step 1. Draft your personal code of ethics. Use the steps for analyzing one's own ethical system outlined at the beginning of this chapter.

Step 2. Think about a profession you'd like to have in the future. Visit ethics.iit.edu/codes/codes_index.html to find the code of ethics employed in this profession.

Step 3. Compare your personal code of ethics to the profession's code of ethics. Then write a paragraph explaining how the two codes compare.

Web Exercises

1. **Government's Role in Happiness**
   The country of Bhutan is the only country that measures its progress by the level of happiness of its citizens, a metric named the Gross National Happiness (GNH). Examine grossnationalhappiness.com and see if you think the idea of a Gross National Happiness measurement can be incorporated into organizational decision making.

2. **Identifying Your Strengths**
   Visit Martin Seligman's website, found at authentichappiness.sas.upenn.edu/Default.aspx, a psychologist who promotes the field of positive psychology. Complete the VIA Survey of Character Strengths. Consider how you can use your strengths each day in the work schedule you have right now.

3. **Socially Conscious: How Do Your Investments Measure Up?**
   When you invest in mutual funds, you can make decisions in different ways. You may want to just put money into funds that had the greatest gain last year or you may want to invest in funds that are collections of socially responsible companies. Find several socially conscious mutual funds. What restrictions do they make on the companies they include? What is their average rate of return?

4. **Corporate Scandal for a Scandal Sheet**
   The London tabloid *News of the World* specialized in scandalous stories until it was shut down amid its own scandal. How did the ethical conduct within the company contribute to its demise? Was the decision to close the paper enough to restore integrity to the Murdoch publishing empire?

5. **Corporate Social Responsibility with Your Java**
   Visit the responsibility page of Starbucks' website. Discuss three different strategies supported by Starbucks to "have a positive impact on the communities we serve." Do any of these cost Starbucks profits? Do you think these policies attract more customers to the store?

MyBizLab

Go to **mybizlab.com** for Auto-graded writing questions as well as the following Assisted-graded writing questions:

3-1. How can a person determine his or her personal ethical code? What is your personal ethical code? What forces have helped build your personal code of ethics?

3-2. How does a corporation's responsibility to shareholders to produce a profit interact with its social responsibility? Name several areas of possible conflict and analyze them from both a short-term view and a long-term view.

3-3. MyBizLab Only – comprehensive writing assignment for this chapter.

Business in a Global Economy

What Is Globalization?

Devin Kay always "buys American"—but what does that mean in the new global marketplace?

International Trade

As foreign companies begin to compete in U.S. markets, there is more competition and more pressure on American businesses. What are the benefits of international trade? What are the costs?

Free Trade and Protectionism

Trying to compete in the world marketplace means using every means available. So when the Miller farm found genetically modified organisms (GMOs) helped to boost their yield, they were thrilled. Now they have discovered they can't sell in 27 countries because they used GMOs. How do free trade agreements affect businesses and members of a community?

Conducting Business Internationally

When conducting international business, many factors come into play. What are the strategies of international business? How can you enter a foreign market? Which entry mode is best? Hachimo Isu needs some answers before he expands his business.

International Business: Economic Factors and Challenges

Exchange rates both encourage and deter countries from trading with one another, and other economic factors affect what products are exported overseas. Business owners like Rachel Gao are turning to countries with favorable exchange rates to import goods. How do exchange rates impact a nation's economy? How do exchange rates impact the bottom line for Rachel's jewelry business?

Creating Successful International Businesses

How would you feel if a potential client from Venezuela wouldn't sign with you because you didn't pat him on the shoulder when you first met? Joe Fox lost one account that way. He now thinks he's done something wrong again when he received a gift from his client from India. What challenges does he face there? Is there a problem opening a gift when it's received? Knowing the answers to such questions is vital to running a successful global business.

MyBizLab®

⭐ **Improve Your Grade!**

Over 10 million students improved their results using the Pearson MyLabs.

Visit **mybizlab.com** for simulations, tutorials, and end-of-chapter problems.

What Is Globalization? pp. 87–91

Feng Yu/Shutterstock

Devin Kay is a worldly guy who has traveled globally, including camping in Canada as a child and taking a spring break vacation in Mexico one year. But he is very loyal to American products and tries to buy American whenever he can. So he doesn't even dream of a fancy Italian Maserati. "Italian car? Never! I'd rather buy a good ol' American Jeep," he says. When it comes to vacationing now, he chooses a weekend in Manhattan over spending money abroad that would go to a foreign company. Politically, he favors high tariffs to make foreign beer sold here more expensive so that American products sell better. "The world is a tough place, and we should do whatever we can to give American companies an edge," he tells his friends. ■

Former President Bill Clinton once said, "Globalization is not something we can hold off or turn off . . . it is the economic equivalent of a force of nature—like wind or water."[1] In recent years, the rise of globalization has made a dramatic impact on the lives of people around the world. People from the United States to Taiwan to Argentina are interconnected and dependent on one another for a variety of goods and services. The United States and other nations are increasingly **importing**, or buying products from other countries, and **exporting**, or selling domestically produced products to other countries. Many products we own were made in countries other than the United States. Globalization has affected the way companies conduct business around the world.

What can people do to enhance their country's ability to compete in the global economy? What can a country do to provide good-paying jobs for its citizens? How can U.S. companies increase their profitability in the face of foreign competition at home or enhance their market share overseas? When the U.S. dollar is stronger or weaker than the currencies of other countries, how does it affect business in the United States? After studying this chapter, you'll be able to answer these and other questions.

The Effects of Globalization

How does globalization affect the United States? The old saying "No man is an island" can be used to describe globalization. **Globalization**, the movement toward a more interconnected and interdependent world economy, may be one of the most profound factors affecting people in the United States and around the globe.[2] Why is this? Whatever happens today in the U.S. economy— the world's largest economy—will have a significant impact on people not only in the Unites States but also worldwide. Meanwhile, economic conditions in other

THE List

Powerful People to Know

Do you know every name on this list?

1. Hu Jintao
2. Angela Merkel
3. Ben S. Bernanke
4. Sergey Brin and Larry Page
5. Carlos Slim Helu
6. Dilma Rousseff
7. Abdullah bin Abdu Aziz al Saud
8. Tenzin Gyatso
9. Manmohan Singh
10. Christine Lagarde

1 What are the implications of the globalization of markets and the globalization of production?

Stereo and other key electrical components manufactured in Japan

Engine made in Detroit, Michigan

Ford car assembled in Canada

Transmission produced in Mexico

Dash and other plastic components manufactured in China

Seats made in Great Britain

■ **FIGURE 4.1**
Made in the USA?
Many brand-name products are composites of components manufactured around the world. For example, most people think that Ford cars are made in the United States. But is it really "made in the USA" if most of its components are manufactured in other countries or it is assembled outside the United States?
Image Sources: US, Japan, Canada, China, Great Britain flags: daboost/Fotolia; Mexico flag: michanolimit/Fotolia.

countries also affect the U.S. economy, producing changes and challenges for U.S. consumers, businesses, and workers.

One example of this can be seen in the booming economies of India and China. Their growth is a major reason for the increasing global demand for energy. Increased energy demand is a major cause of the world's rising oil prices, which have created higher prices at the gas pump for people around the world. As a result, people have less money to spend on other things, such as eating out. Local restaurants and other local businesses feel the pinch, and their sales fall. In response to lower demand, businesses curtail production and lay off employees. Higher energy prices can also drive up production costs, which, in turn, drive up the prices businesses must charge consumers.

So globalization means that the behavior of each country has an impact on other countries of the world. Of course, markets have not only become more interconnected but also more reliant on one another. If you inspect the packaging of items you buy, you'll see that many products consumed in the United States, such as laptop computers and cars, are made from parts that are manufactured in other countries. ■ **FIGURE 4.1** shows how Ford cars, which many people think are made in the United States, are comprised of components manufactured in other countries or are assembled outside the United States.

How does globalization offer more marketing opportunities to businesses? Globalization has two main components:

- the globalization of markets
- the globalization of production[3]

The **globalization of markets** refers to the movement away from thinking of the market as being the local market or the national market to thinking of the market as being the entire world. This offers incredible new opportunities for businesses. Companies such as General Electric (GE), Dell, and Toyota are not just selling to customers in Dallas or Atlanta, California or Vermont, or Japan or Europe; they're selling to customers all over the globe. ■ **FIGURE 4.2** shows that for Ford Motor Company, the overseas markets are the dominant markets in which sales are increasing. People in China purchased over 18 million cars last year (compared to just 13 million in the United States), so all auto manufacturers are looking to establish more of a presence there.[4] Other U.S. corporations are recognizing the same trend and are benefiting from increased international sales, and even some relatively small companies find it profitable to sell their products abroad.

The globalization of markets has become so widespread that more and more businesses are finding that they must "think globally and act locally." Companies often need to adjust their products or marketing campaigns to suit the unique tastes and preferences of their local customers, wherever they may be. For example, Coca-Cola often must tweak its recipes to appeal to the tastes of consumers in different parts of the world. In India, Coca-Cola adapted its Minute Maid orange soda recipe to suit the taste of the majority of the Indian population, who prefer a sweeter version of the drink than the version sold in the United States.[5] Similarly,

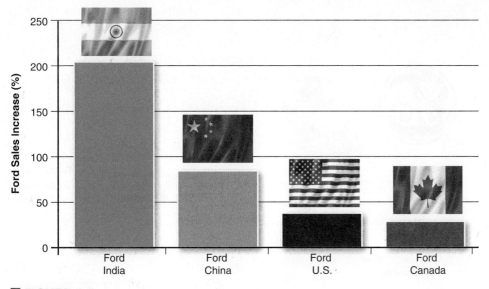

■ FIGURE 4.2
Help from Overseas
Markets are becoming increasingly global. For example, Ford auto sales in foreign markets are growing at very strong rates.
Image Source: all flags from: daboost/Fotolia. Created from data in "Ford Sales Grow by Double Digits in China, Canada." 2 April 2010. Channelnewsasia.com

many foreign-owned companies advertise or adapt their products for sale in the United States to attract consumers.

How does globalization make it easier to manufacture products? The **globalization of production** refers to the trend of individual firms moving production to different locations around the globe to take advantage of lower costs or enhance quality. Globalization of production often involves *outsourcing*. **Outsourcing** is the assignment of certain tasks, such as production or accounting, to an outside company or organization. Currently, much outsourcing is **offshore outsourcing** (or **offshoring**), moving production from a domestic site to a foreign location. In addition, companies may decide to relocate at least some of their own production facilities to another country to realize lower costs so they can offer customers lower prices.

Reasons for the Rise in Globalization

> 2   **Why has globalization accelerated so rapidly?**

Why has globalization accelerated so rapidly? Two main factors underlie the trend toward greater globalization:[6]

- **A dramatic decline in trade and investment barriers.** Trade and investment barriers are government restrictions that prevent the flow of goods, services, and financial capital across national boundaries. The lowering of trade barriers makes global business much cheaper and easier. It also allows international firms to move their production facilities to the least-cost location for that activity. A firm might design its product in one country, produce component parts in two or three other countries, assemble the product in yet another country, and then export it around the world.

- **Technological innovations.** Advances in technology have made it possible to manage the global production and marketing of products. There have been dramatic breakthroughs in communications, transportation, and IT in the last decade. Using Web conferencing tools, a business manager in New York can meet with contacts at a firm's European and Asian operations centers without ever leaving the office. This has significantly reduced the cost of doing business. Technological advancements are a great equalizer for small companies, enabling them to access customers worldwide through their websites at negligible expense, so they can more effectively compete with huge global corporations.

■ **FIGURE 4.3**
Company Revenue Versus National Incomes
Today, many international businesses are larger than entire countries in terms of the economic activity generated.
Data from Vincent Trivett, "25 Mega Corporations: Where They Rank If They Were Countries." Business Insider. June 27, 2011. www.businessinsider.com

GE is larger than New Zealand

Costco is bigger than the Sudan

Apple is bigger than Ecuador

Walmart outperforms Norway

Based on these and other factors, the globalization of markets and the globalization of production have resulted in some international firms becoming so large that they actually generate more revenue than the GDP of many nations. As you can see in ■ **FIGURE 4.3**, several American companies rank above many countries in the world in terms of the total revenue they generate.

Global Business Trends

Where will trends in global business take us? Four noteworthy global business trends will continue to impact our future:[8]

1. **A growing role for developing nations.** Over the last several decades, U.S. dominance of world output and world exports has declined in relative terms due to the rapid economic growth of several other countries, most notably Japan, China, and India. This trend is expected to continue as developing nations, such as Indonesia, Thailand, and many Latin American nations, continue to increase their presence on the world economic stage.

2. **A rise in non-U.S. foreign direct investment.** Over the previous 30 years, U.S. dominance in **foreign direct investment**, which is the purchasing of property and businesses in foreign nations, has declined. The direction of investment has switched and now many other countries have begun to undertake foreign direct investment. Other countries have invested much of their money in companies in the United States. Not only is more foreign direct investment flowing into the United States than ever before, but also more and more foreign direct investment is flowing into developing nations.

3. **A rise in multinational enterprises.** Over the last several decades, there has been a rise in the importance of **multinational enterprises**, businesses that manufacture and market products in two or more countries. Moreover, *mini-multinationals* (small- and medium-sized multinational enterprises) have become prominent on the world stage. There is an increase in the number of

Countries Where It Is Easy to Do Business, 2011[7]

1. Singapore
2. Hong Kong SAR, China
3. New Zealand
4. United States
5. Denmark
6. Norway
7. United Kingdom
8. Republic of Korea
9. Iceland
10. Finland

companies that can grow into an international presence. Consider Tekelec of North Carolina, a $400 million company that has expanded into 20 countries in less than a decade. They now have 60 percent of their sales of mobile broadband software outside of the United States.[9]

4. **Increasing democratization.** With the movement toward democratization and the adoption of free-market economies around the globe, many more nations are becoming involved in the global economy. If this trend continues, the opportunities for international business will be enormous as the global marketplace expands and more locations open as potential production sites.

Remember Devin? Devin has a U.S.-centric worldview that was common a generation ago but is difficult to maintain with the rapid growth of globalization. The Maserati car he would never buy is owned by Fiat, which owns 20 percent of Jeep. And his vacation in New York City? More than one-tenth of all the goods and services produced in New York and 1 in 20 jobs are supplied by companies controlled by foreign investors.[10] And although Devin argues that tariffs will protect U.S. products, most economists believe that in the modern global marketplace, using tariffs to protect a country's trade borders actually reduces domestic jobs and economic health. Devin's view of how the world works has the advantage of being simple, but it no longer reflects the reality that globalization has brought us. ■

International Trade pp. 91–94

Paper Boat Creative/Getty Images

Thom McGovern runs a successful textile manufacturing firm. The business was started by his father and has grown every year since Thom took over. He creates high-quality clothing products that his company sells to retail stores. He is a dependable supplier with many satisfied customers who trust his prices and advice on textile products. Over the past several years, though, there have been increasing business pressures on Thom. Foreign textiles are showing up on the market in greater numbers, selling at prices far below anything Thom can match. His customers have appreciated doing business with him over the years, but are slowly moving to other suppliers. Thom could drop prices to his customers and increase his company's profits if he bought from the foreign suppliers. Thom is angry and frustrated, unsure of how to protect his business and employees. What should he do? ■

Economists argue that international trade flourishes because it is in the best interest of the country as a whole. However, competition in the international market often puts new pressures on domestic businesses like Thom McGovern's firm unless they find ways to keep up with the high-quality and low-cost products that international trade provides. Let's take a closer look at why countries participate in international trade, how trade affects competitiveness, and what costs and benefits are associated with international trade.

International Competition

What is the theory of comparative advantage? Many theories apply to international trade. The most popular theory is the **theory of comparative advantage,** which states that specialization and trade between countries benefit all who are involved. The theory of comparative advantage suggests that a country should sell to other countries the goods that it manufactures most efficiently and effectively and buy from other countries the goods it cannot manufacture as efficiently or effectively. If this method is practiced, each nation will have a greater quantity and variety of higher-quality products to consume at lower prices.

For this mutually beneficial system to work, each country must specialize in the production of those products for which it possesses a comparative advantage. To possess a **comparative advantage** means that a country can produce a good or a service relatively more efficiently compared to other countries. A comparative advantage should not be confused with an **absolute advantage**, which is the ability to produce *more* of a good or a service than any other country. Just because a large country can produce more of a good than a small country can doesn't necessarily mean it is relatively more efficient at producing that good. What matters is relative efficiency, or comparative advantage—not absolute advantage.

When all countries focus on producing products for which they have a comparative advantage, collectively they all have more production to share. This, in turn, creates higher standards of living for these countries. As you've probably guessed, countries export products for which they have a comparative advantage and import products for which they do not have a comparative advantage.

Fostering Competitiveness

What can a country do to have an edge in world markets? In many nations, governments focus on improving a nation's resources—natural resources, labor, capital (plant, equipment, and infrastructure), technology, innovation, and entrepreneurialism—to improve competitiveness.

Governments can't do much to improve a nation's natural resources; they have to work with what they have. Nations with abundant natural resources will likely have a comparative advantage in the production of goods that require these raw materials. For example, big-leaf mahogany trees are found in only a few countries, including Mexico and Belize. So these countries have a comparative advantage in the production of mahogany furniture and musical instruments.

However, governments can and do invest in health, education, and training designed to increase the productivity of their labor forces. All international businesses are constantly looking for good workers, and each country wants to attract businesses to enhance employment opportunities for its citizens. For example, officials in Queensland, Australia, have recently budgeted a massive $9.5 billion in education and training, including vocational training and apprenticeships, in the hopes of building a strong employment force for the country.[11]

Many governments try to create incentives for private company investments in capital (plant and equipment). For example, governments may try to keep interest rates low so that private companies will invest in the latest state-of-the art equipment, thereby giving them an edge over foreign competition. Governments also invest in *public capital*, which is sometimes called *infrastructure*. Infrastructure includes roads, bridges, dams, electric grid lines, and telecommunication satellites that enhance productivity.

Governments also try to promote technological advances to give their nations a competitive edge. This can include investments in basic and applied research at state-funded higher education institutions. Finally, governments might also promote innovation and entrepreneurialism. Many studies have documented a gender gap in entrepreneurship, that in most countries men are more likely than women to be entrepreneurs. In countries like Korea, France and Norway, the gender gap is very large.[12]

The Norwegian government has therefore created an action plan to increase grant accessibility for female entrepreneurs. The objective is to have women representing at least 40 percent of entrepreneurial businesses.[13] On the flip side, sometimes governments use trade restrictions and added tariffs on goods from other countries to create an artificial competitive advantage. We'll discuss these practices later in the chapter.

What can businesses do to be more competitive? To be competitive, businesses must grapple with many of the same issues as nations do to be more competitive. That is, successful companies try to gain access to cheap raw materials, invest in their workers' training and productivity, and purchase state-of-the-art plants and equipment that will give them an edge. Successful companies also invest in cutting-edge technology in their research and development (R&D) departments. Finally, they promote innovativeness throughout their organizations.

Conversely, if a company, an entire industry, or even a nation has lost its **competitive advantage**, then it probably failed in one or more of these areas. For example, at one time, the U.S. steel and textile industries had a competitive advantage in the world. Today, however, those industries have fallen behind their international competitors. It is the joint job of government and private business to determine the ways to improve to compete more effectively.

The Benefits and Costs of International Trade

What are the benefits and costs of international trade? The theory of comparative advantage indicates that countries that participate in international trade will experience higher standards of living because of the greater quantity and variety of higher-quality products offered at lower prices. These results stem from the increased competition associated with more open trade. But these benefits are not without their costs.

The costs of international trade are borne by those businesses and their workers whose livelihoods are threatened by foreign competition. Some domestic businesses may lose market share to foreign companies, stunting their profitability and ability to create jobs. Other firms may face so much foreign competition that they're driven out of business entirely.

Do the benefits of international trade outweigh the costs? This is a difficult question to answer. The costs of increased international trade—including lost jobs to foreign competitors—are often easy to identify. The benefits are not always easily seen, however, as they are spread out among millions of consumers. For example, a greater quantity and variety of higher-quality products to purchase may not be easily traced to increased international trade because these benefits are often slow and subtle. People benefit from lower-priced products, although price reductions may save people only a nickel here and a dime there. But the sum of these lower prices for the public at large can be dramatic—especially over time. As we'll see in the next section, governments play a large role in determining how much international trade they will support, for example, by choosing to impose restrictions on the quantity and types of goods that can cross their nation's borders.

3 | What are the costs and benefits of international trade?

mbolina/Fotolia

When foreign imports arrive in the United States, they increase the supply of a product, pushing its price down. Consumers welcome competition and lower prices, but domestic competitors are displeased.

We started this section by discussing Thom McGovern's textile business, which was struggling in the midst of increased international competition. Did Thom just close up shop, or did he adapt to the pressures and take advantages of the opportunities of globalization? As company president, Thom chose to invest in new equipment and training for his workers to try to gain a competitive advantage. He also began to explore acquiring raw materials from foreign suppliers, a process that is easier to coordinate and arrange than ever before. Finally, he has begun to investigate new markets for his specialty products, expanding into countries like India and China. Thom is not sure what his company will look like in five years, but he is sure that the globalization of the world marketplace will bring him both challenges and opportunities. ■

FikMik/Fotolia

Free Trade and Protectionism pp. 94–100

Farming has changed, and the Miller farm has always changed with the times. As the pressure to produce more from the same size farm has grown, the Millers have begun to use genetically modified organisms (GMOs) to grow crops that are more resistant to frost. Using GMOs has boosted their yield each year, and the farm has never had more output. But, recently, news came out that the EU (the European Union)—a block of 27 countries—had released a new health directive: To be eligible for sale in the EU, any product meant for human consumption could not contain any GMOs. The Millers worry this means that the manufacturers they sell to will be dropping their orders because now the entire block of EU business will be closed to them. ■

Countries implement trade barriers for a variety of reasons. Sometimes, as in the case of the Millers, trade barriers may be implemented to protect consumers. Other times, trade barriers are established to protect domestic businesses from international competition that could put them out of business. Many people believe that such protectionist trade barriers are the best way to defend a nation's economy; others are in favor of free trade. **Free trade** refers to the unencumbered flow of goods and services across national borders. That is, free trade is free from government intervention or other impediments that can block the flow of goods across borders. Virtually all economists are free-trade advocates because they argue that, over time, the benefits far outweigh the costs for a nation as a whole. However, some people—especially those who feel their livelihoods are threatened by free trade—are not convinced. In this section, we'll examine both sides of this debate.

Types of Trade Barriers

What trade barriers can governments put in place? As shown in ■ **FIGURE 4.4**, there are three types of trade barriers:

4 What are the different types of trade barriers?

- **Tariffs and subsidies.** The most common trade barrier is the **tariff**, a tax imposed on an imported good or service, such as a U.S. tariff on imported French wine. Governments prefer to impose tariffs because they raise tax revenues. The opposite of a tariff is a **subsidy**, in which governments make payments to *domestic* producers, such as California wine growers. A subsidy can take many forms. It can be a direct cash grant or a payment in-kind that could include tax concessions or a low-interest loan.

- **Quotas and embargoes.** A **quota** is a limitation on the amount of an import allowed to enter a country. For example, a U.S.-imposed quota on French wine might limit the quantity to 10,000 cases per day. The most heavy-handed government trade barrier is an **embargo**, a total restriction on an import (or an export). Since the 1960s, for example, the United States has imposed an embargo on most goods traded with Cuba. Embargoes are usually tools designed to achieve a political goal. In the case of Cuba, the U.S. embargo began when Fidel Castro moved the country to a one-party communist system. The embargo has been used as a tool to apply pressure for change toward a more democratic system.[14]

- **Administrative trade barriers.** Several other types of trade barriers can be lumped under the heading of *administrative trade barriers*—government rules designed to limit imports. One example is a **local content requirement**, which is a requirement that some portion of a good be produced domestically. This usually drives up the cost of an import. Administrative trade barriers may also require an import to meet some technical standard or bureaucratic rule, effectively shutting out the import from a domestic market. For example, the EU has banned the importation of all animal meats in which steroids were used to stimulate growth. This decision heavily impacted the U.S. beef and dairy industries. Although administrative trade barriers can be legitimate, they may be designed purely to protect domestic producers from international competition.

■ **FIGURE 4.4**
Trade Barriers
Countries use these strategies to make it more difficult for foreign firms to sell their products competitively.

Trade Barriers: Winners and Losers

Who benefits and who suffers from trade barriers? Without a doubt, trade barriers benefit domestic producers and their workers but hurt domestic consumers. Trade barriers increase costs to foreign companies or restrict the supply of imports, driving up prices and reducing sales in the domestic market. As a result, higher-priced imports increase the demand for domestically produced substitute goods or services. This higher demand also increases the domestically produced product's price, although it simultaneously increases domestic sales. And this is exactly what trade barriers are designed to do—restrict sales of imports while stimulating sales for domestic firms. Because domestic firms are selling more at higher prices, they are more profitable. This profitability also creates more job security for their employees. The undesirable outcome, however, is that both imports and domestically produced substitute products are now more expensive. Domestic consumers lose while domestic producers and their workers gain. Trade barriers also hurt consumers because the overall quantity, variety, and quality of products are lower as a result of curtailing foreign competition.

What are common arguments in favor of protectionist trade barriers? Four main arguments exist for implementing protectionist trade barriers:

- **National security.** The *national security argument* states that certain industries critical to national security should be protected from foreign competition. For example, the United States wouldn't want to become dependent on another nation for a critical component of national defense. If all the manufacturers of the targeting systems for Air Force fighter planes were Chinese companies and hostilities increased between the two countries, the interests of the United States might be compromised. However, critics argue that rarely have protected industries used this argument in terms of national defense.

- **Infant-industry.** The *infant-industry argument* states that an undeveloped domestic industry needs time to grow and develop to acquire a comparative advantage in the global economy. The protected time to grow allows opportunities for an industry to make the needed investments to become innovative. Once comparative advantage is captured, the argument goes, then protection from foreign competition will no longer be necessary. Opponents of this view argue that, in practice, it can be very difficult to determine whether an industry legitimately holds promise of developing a comparative advantage. In addition, they argue that rarely do infant industries ever grow up; thus government protection becomes addictive.

- **Cheap foreign labor.** The *cheap foreign labor argument* centers on lower wages paid to workers of foreign companies. How can domestic companies compete with these low wages? The issue of balancing wages and worker productivity is complex and has become much more critical with increased globalization. The relevancy for costs of production is not only wages but also productivity in relation to wages. A company's costs of production can be lower even when it pays its workers twice as much if the productivity of workers is at least twice as high. If a country wants to maintain high wages in a global marketplace, it needs to find a way to increase the productivity of its labor force. Opponents of such protectionist policies argue that trying to protect jobs at the current wage structure might create still higher costs for a nation in the form of higher prices and reduced quantity, quality, and variety of products from which to choose.

- **Threat of retaliation.** The *threat of retaliation* (or the *bargaining chip*) *argument* says that if a trading partner increases its trade barriers on your exports or fails to reduce trade barriers as you reduce yours, then an uneven, unfair playing field is created. Domestic companies may also be put at a disadvantage if a foreign firm is dumping its product. **Dumping** refers to selling a product at a price below the price charged in the producing country; although it is illegal, it can be difficult to prove. The intent of dumping is to dominate an industry and then control it. The threat of higher trade barriers can be a bargaining chip in retaliation for dumping or negotiating lower trade barriers for exports. The risk of that policy is that if it fails, the result can be a trade war; nations would implement higher trade barriers and leave everyone at a disadvantage.

How do economists feel about protectionist trade barriers? As noted earlier, most economists are free-trade advocates because they believe that the economic benefits of free trade outweigh the economic costs. Economists insist that the best way to address the concerns of those industries and their workers whose livelihoods are threatened by foreign competition is *not* to impose protectionist trade barriers. Instead, these displaced individuals need to be equipped with the education, training, and skills necessary to smooth their transition into a line of business or work in which the nation has a comparative advantage and demand is rising. Although all governments have protectionist trade barriers in place, they have been working to reduce them because they believe the economic benefits of doing so generally outweigh the costs. This political position explains the recent trend toward reduced trade and investment barriers that have fueled globalization. ■ **TABLE 4.1** summarizes the economic benefits and costs of free trade and protectionism for a nation.

International Organizations Promoting Free Trade

What groups are working to promote free trade? Countries realize that unilaterally reducing their trade barriers puts their businesses at an unfair

■ TABLE 4.1

Economic Benefits and Costs of Free Trade and Protectionism for a Nation

	Free Trade	Protectionism
Economic Benefits	A **greater quantity** and variety of **higher-quality** products at **lower prices**	**Increased sales** at **higher prices** improves the profitability of protected domestic companies, creating **greater job security** for their workers
Economic Costs	**Reduced sales** and **lower prices** for domestic firms that find it difficult to compete internationally, which **reduces their profitability** and **lowers job security** for their workers	A **lower quantity** and variety of **lower-quality** products at **higher prices**

disadvantage. The key for realizing the mutual benefits of international trade is to get all countries to lower their trade barriers simultaneously, which was the reason for creating organizations such as GATT and the WTO.

The **General Agreement on Tariffs and Trade (GATT)** was created in 1948 with 23 member nations and grew to 123 member nations by 1994. Although GATT was not an organization with any real enforcement powers, its eight rounds of negotiated agreements or treaties were very successful in reducing tariffs and other obstacles to free trade on goods. This, in turn, spurred significant world economic growth.[15] However, GATT was not as successful in reducing trade barriers on services, protecting intellectual property rights, or enforcing agreements among member nations. As a result, the **World Trade Organization (WTO)** replaced GATT in 1995 during the eighth and final round of negotiations (called the Uruguay Round because it was launched in Punta del Este, Uruguay).

The WTO has strengthened the world trading system by extending GATT rules to services and increasing protection for intellectual property rights. But, perhaps most significantly, the WTO has taken on the responsibility for arbitrating trade disputes and monitoring the trade policies of member countries.[16] The WTO operates as GATT did—on the basis of consensus—when settling disputes. However, unlike GATT, the WTO doesn't allow losing parties to ignore the arbitration reports of the WTO. The WTO has the power to enforce decisions, which is something that GATT did not have. ■ **FIGURE 4.5** shows which countries are members of the WTO.

Is there more that can be done to promote free trade? Advocates of free trade argue that much remains to be done to reduce trade barriers in the global economy. The first round of talks under the umbrella of the WTO was launched in Seattle in 1999, but antiglobalization protestors disrupted and derailed these talks. The meetings were relaunched in 2001 in Doha, Qatar, in the Persian Gulf, with an agenda to curtail dumping, reduce protectionist trade barriers, protect intellectual property rights, and reduce government barriers on foreign direct investment.[17] The Doha Round was slated to last three years but had not yet concluded as of the publication of this text.

What are some problems that may come from free trade? The 1999 demonstration in Seattle reflects an ongoing concern that free trade may encourage

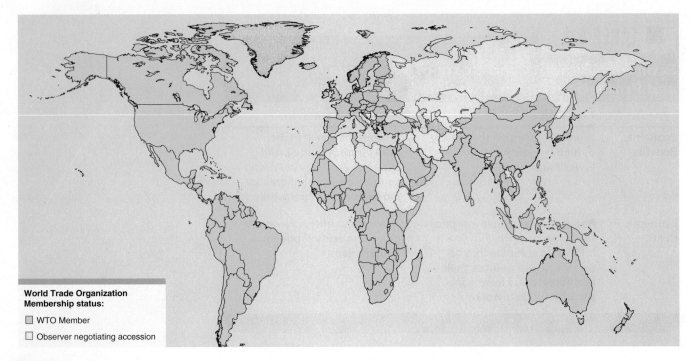

**World Trade Organization
Membership status:**

☐ WTO Member

☐ Observer negotiating accession

◼ FIGURE 4.5
Countries in the WTO
Based on from "Members and observers
of the WTO," World Trade Organization.
http://www.wto.org/

firms to shift their production to countries with low wages and lax labor standards. Critics argue that the exploitation of workers can contribute to the gap between the rich and the poor. Environmentalists have also expressed a growing concern that expanded international trade encourages companies to move production to countries in which they are freer to pollute and degrade the environment, which contributes to global climate change and all the problems that may stem from global warming. These concerns highlight the fact that the *economic* perspective on the benefits and costs of free trade is not the only perspective. Important social, ethical, political, and environmental concerns also need to be considered.

Regional Free Trade Agreements

What are regional free trade agreements? Many nations have been so eager to achieve the higher standards of living associated with free trade that they have struck out on their own by creating **free trade agreements**, or compacts abolishing trade barriers among member countries. Although all current free trade agreements still have some obstacles to free trade among their members, many have made considerable headway in reducing these barriers. Let's look at some of the most powerful regional free trade agreements.

The European Union

The greatest free trade area exists among member nations of the EU, which is the oldest and largest free trade area. The EU can trace its roots to 1957 with the creation of the European Economic Community (or Common Market), which consisted of six founding countries. (In 1960 the European Free Trade Association (EFTA) was established for countries that could not or did not want to be part of the EU.)

Although many obstacles had to be overcome, such as the concern over the potential loss of national sovereignty, the EU has grown to its current membership of 27 independent states, as shown in ◼ **FIGURE 4.6**. The EU's success is due in large part to its demonstrated commitment to the free flow of goods, services, capital, and people across borders in Europe.

The EU is currently the world's largest single market, surpassing the United States. It accounts for approximately one-third of the world's total production. The EU is the largest exporter in the world and the second largest importer.[18]

The European Union (EU-25)

EU countries shaded in blue

■ **FIGURE 4.6**
The European Union
As of 2012 the EU has 27 member countries. It is the most economically integrated free trade area in the world.

In 1999, the EU also surpassed all other free trade areas with respect to economic integration by adopting a common currency—the euro. The euro is currently used by 16 of the 27 member states and has become a major currency in global financial markets.[19] The EU has a population of over 500 million people and is likely to continue to grow as other countries—such as Albania and Turkey—apply to join the EU.

The EU's economic power and political clout has a huge influence on international businesses worldwide. For example, some international businesses have been motivated to invest in production facilities within the EU to hedge against any potential trade barriers. The EU has also established many legal, regulatory, and technical standards for imports to the EU market. In addition, the EU's antitrust rulings have significantly affected U.S. businesses. For example, the EU found Microsoft guilty of anticompetitive practices and levied a fine of $613 million on the company.[20]

The North American Free Trade Agreement

The **North American Free Trade Agreement (NAFTA)** is an ongoing agreement to move the United States, Mexico, and Canada closer to true free trade. NAFTA was established on January 1, 1994, after considerable political opposition. One big issue confronting NAFTA is the proposal to expand into a greater Free Trade Area of the Americas (FTAA) that would include most countries in the Western Hemisphere. Although meetings are being held for a workable FTAA, some countries, such as Brazil and Venezuela, stand in opposition to this agreement. As a result, significant progress in the near future toward more free trade within the framework of FTAA is unlikely.

Other Noteworthy Free Trade Areas

Many other free trade areas exist in the world. The following are some of the more noteworthy examples:

- The *Andean Group* was formed in 1969 between Bolivia, Chile, Ecuador, Colombia, and Peru. Another free trade pact was formed in 1988 named *MERCOSUR* between Brazil and Argentina, and it was expanded in 1990 to include Paraguay and Uruguay. In 1999, these two organizations began negotiating a merger that culminated in 2004 with a signed agreement to move toward integrating all of South America based on the EU model. However, not much progress has been made to date. At the time of this writing, the only full members of MERCOSUR are the original four countries: Brazil, Argentina, Paraguay, and Uruguay.[21]

- The *Association of Southeast Asian Nations (ASEAN)* includes Indonesia, Malaysia, the Philippines, Singapore, Thailand, Brunei, Vietnam, Laos, Myanmar, and Cambodia. Progress toward integration has been limited, but ASEAN has negotiated free trade agreements with China, Korea, Japan, Australia, New Zealand, and India and is working to create a free trade agreement with the EU.

- The *Asia-Pacific Economic Cooperation (APEC)* was founded in 1989 at the suggestion of Australia and currently has 21 member countries, including economic powerhouses such as the United States, Japan, and China. The member economies of APEC account for approximately 40 percent of the world's population, approximately 54 percent of world GDP, and about 44 percent of world trade.[22]

Most free trade areas haven't had the kind of success that the EU and NAFTA have had in reducing their trade barriers. However, it is clear that most countries are eager to come together to reduce trade barriers in an attempt to realize the economic benefits of greater free trade.

We started this section with a story about the Miller farm and its struggles to determine what to do in light of a EU decision to disallow GMO products in its member countries. Regional free trade agreements create powerful negotiating bodies, and, as the Millers have found, the EU can make decisions that ripple through many levels of government, all the way to impacting the Miller's farm management.

Now that you have reviewed both sides of the issues concerning protectionism and free trade, what is your opinion? Can a balance be struck between protecting domestic businesses and consumers and opening markets up to more free trade? ■

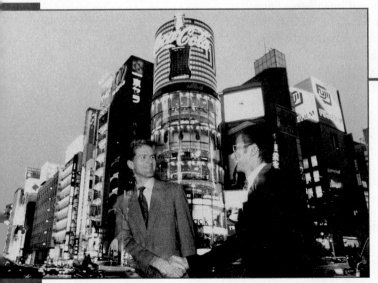

Karin Slade/Getty Images

Conducting Business Internationally pp. 100–105

Hachimo Isu worked as a professional translator for many years before opening his own consulting business. The company made its mark by offering personalized translation services of spoken languages and written materials with great speed and accuracy. As business grew, Hachimo hired more translators and began to look to expand to more offices. As Hachimo thinks of taking his company to new countries and offering expanded services, he needs to determine which country would be the best starting place. How can he prepare himself for the changes that will come from expanding his business internationally? ■

All business operations are undertaken within economic, sociocultural, political, and legal environments. When doing purely domestic business, keeping up with environmental forces can be a huge challenge, even for the savviest manager. However, managing an international business is even more complex because different economic, sociocultural, political, and legal environments must be considered. The rest of this chapter will explore some of the numerous important economic, sociocultural, political, and legal differences among nations. An understanding of these differences is critical for successfully conducting global business. First we'll discuss the strategies of international businesses and how firms enter foreign markets.

Strategies of International Business

What types of strategies can an international business follow? Every international business needs to determine which strategy it will pursue.

5 What are the three basic strategies of international business?

1. **Global strategy.** Companies that pursue a **global strategy** sell a standardized (or homogeneous) product across the globe. Standardized products are basic products that meet universal needs. Examples of standardized products include agricultural products, oil, and raw material commodities. These goods are essentially the same from company to company—they are homogeneous—because they are universally recognized and appeal to consumers across many cultures. When selling standardized products, firms compete aggressively on the basis of price. The company with the lowest price captures the most market share.

2. **Multidomestic strategy.** Companies that pursue a **multidomestic strategy** customize or differentiate their products to meet unique local needs, tastes, or preferences. For example, in Asian countries McDonald's offers a seaweed-flavored seasoning for their French fries. Firms pursuing a multidomestic strategy face relatively low pressures for cost reduction because price is often of secondary concern to buyers. Instead, what is important to customers is whether a product meets their needs or is distinct from a competitor's product. Companies that pursue a multidomestic strategy work to make their respective products appeal to different customers around the globe.

3. **Transnational strategy.** Companies that pursue a **transnational strategy** offer a customized product while simultaneously selling it at the lowest possible price. The strong cost pressures *and* strong pressures for differentiation that motivate this type of strategy are typically at odds. Therefore, a successful pursuit of this type of strategy is difficult in practice.

Entering Foreign Markets

6 How can international firms successfully enter foreign markets?

How do international firms enter foreign markets? In addition to determining a business strategy, international businesses must determine how they will serve foreign customers. Companies may undertake one of six strategies:

- Export their product
- Implement a turnkey project
- Undertake franchising
- Enter into a licensing agreement, a joint venture, or a strategic alliance
- Undertake contract manufacturing
- Establish a wholly owned subsidiary

Let's look briefly at each strategy.

Exporting

As noted earlier, *exporting* is the sale of a domestically produced good in a foreign market. Some businesses begin serving a foreign market by exporting and only later switch to another mode to expand sales abroad. Exporting is relatively easy and inexpensive compared with establishing a physical presence in a foreign market. In addition, exporting may help a firm realize lower costs because companies can move production to an inexpensive location and then export its product from that location around the world. Exporting also has a few disadvantages. It is not economical for heavy or bulky products with high transportation costs. Exporting may also become uneconomical if foreign trade barriers are unexpectedly imposed.

Turnkey Projects

When firms export their technological know-how in exchange for a fee, they have implemented a **turnkey project**. Turnkey projects are common in the production of sophisticated and complex manufacturing facilities, such as those involved in petroleum refining, steel, and hydroelectric energy production. Once a facility is up and running and the locals are trained, the keys are turned over to the new foreign owners. For example, the largest traffic control system in China is the Wuhan Urban traffic control system, delivered by the German electronics firm Siemens.[23] Turnkey projects allow firms with specialized know-how, like Siemens, to earn higher profits from their technical expertise. The drawback is that a firm may create a viable competitor if their technological expertise is easily accessible.

Franchising

Franchising involves selling a well-known brand name or a proven method of doing business to an investor in exchange for a fee and a percentage of sales or profits. The seller is the *franchisor*, and the buyer is the *franchisee*. Franchising is popular both domestically and internationally. Examples of franchising abound in the fast-food and entertainment industries. McDonald's and Kentucky Fried Chicken (KFC) restaurants are now found all over the world. Subway sandwiches can be purchased in over 83 countries.[24] Walt Disney has recently franchised 150 stores in India.[25] Undoubtedly, all of these franchises must be careful to adapt their goods and services to appeal to their different global customers.

The main advantage of franchising is that the franchisor shifts to the franchisee the costs and risks of opening a foreign market. The disadvantages include enforcing franchise contracts that ensure quality control over distant franchisees and ensuring that the product is properly adapted to appeal to customers.

Licensing

Licensing is an agreement in which the licensor's *intangible property*—patents, trademarks, service marks, copyrights, trade secrets, or other intellectual property—may be sold or made available to a licensee in exchange for a royalty fee. The *licensor* holds the original patent or copyright, and the *licensee* is paying a fee to be allowed to use that property. The advantage of licensing is the speed with which the *licensor* can enter a foreign market and the assumption of risks and costs by the *licensee*. The disadvantage is the loss of technological expertise to the licensee and the creation of a potential competitor. SRI International is a company that holds patents in the areas of biosciences, computing, and chemistry-related materials.[26] They license their vast array of intellectual property around the world.

Joint Ventures

Joint ventures involve shared ownership in a subsidiary firm. International joint venture partners involve an international business teaming up with a local partner. The advantages of a joint venture include gaining local knowledge of the economic, social, and political landscape while sharing the costs and risks of accessing a foreign market. For example, Walmart would love to be a big presence in India.

With 1.1 billion people, the market for consumer goods, such as soap, detergent, and shampoos in India is huge. India, however, has many restrictions on foreign business in order to protect small Indian businesses. So Walmart had to enter India through a joint venture with the Indian company Bharti Enterprises. This may change over time, since recently the government has pushed to allow companies like Walmart to be able to open retail stores themselves, to the cheers of some Indian farmers who could sell to Walmart and to the opposition of small shopkeepers.[27]

Entering into a joint venture, like entering into a marriage, requires considerable thought in the selection of a complementary partner. The disadvantage of joint ventures is losing control over a company because compromise with the partner is inevitable. The risk of losing proprietary technology in the event of dissolution or divorce of the joint venture is also a major drawback.

Strategic Alliances

Strategic alliances are cooperative arrangements between actual or potential competitors. Unlike a joint venture, in a strategic alliance each partner retains its business independence. Typically strategic alliances are agreements for a specific period of time or the duration of a particular project. The advantages of strategic alliances include the pooling of unique talents and expertise and the sharing of the costs and risks of a project for mutual benefit. The disadvantages include a loss of technology and initial difficulty in finding a compatible partner.

Microsoft has a strategic alliance with Japanese mobile phone manufacturer Nokia. The companies work together to optimize the mobile phone experience for Microsoft's Windows Phone software and Nokia hardware. Together they joined their workforces of talented engineers and their financial clout; now they have the power to compete more effectively.[28]

Contract Manufacturing

Contract manufacturing occurs when a firm subcontracts part or all of its goods to an outside firm as an alternative to owning and operating its own production facility. When doing international business, the subcontractor is a foreign firm. Therefore, contract manufacturing is really a form of offshore outsourcing. For example, Hewlett-Packard (HP) uses contract manufacturing in the production of its calculator products. Although the design for its calculators is done in the United States, the manufacturing is done in Taiwan.[29] Contract manufacturing allows business to enter a foreign market by placing its label on the good and selling it in the foreign market where it was produced. Contract manufacturing also enables a firm to test-market its product in a foreign market with very little expense compared with the high start-up costs of building its own facility on foreign shores. The disadvantage centers on the lack of quality control over the subcontractor.

International franchising means you can get Kentucky Fried Chicken in Lebanon, China, and Egypt.
Source: Bloomberg/Contributor/ Getty Images (top), STEPHEN SHAVER/Staff/ Getty Images (middle), Courtney Kealy/ Stringer/Getty Images (bottom).

When toy maker Mattel used a contract manufacturer in China to produce their Hot Wheels cars and Barbie dolls, they ended up paying millions in fines. The toys had been painted with a paint that had lead levels illegal in the United States. The Consumer Product Safety Commission forced Mattel to recall nearly a million toys and fined the company over $2.3 million.[30]

Wholly Owned Subsidiaries

A **wholly owned subsidiary** involves establishing a foreign facility that is owned entirely by the investing firm. For example, Hyundai is a South Korean automotive manufacturer. It entered the Russian market by establishing Hyundai Motor Manufacturing Russia, a wholly owned subsidiary of Hyundai Motor Company. This is Hyundai's sixth venture into expanding its foreign manufacturing base.[31] The advantages of this entry choice include total control over foreign operations and technological know-how. The disadvantage is that the parent company must bear all the costs and risks of entering a foreign market.

The Advantages and Disadvantages of Each Entry Mode

Which mode of entering foreign markets is optimal? The optimal entry mode depends on many factors, including a firm's strategy. ■ TABLE 4.2 summarizes the advantages and disadvantages of the various entry modes.

■ TABLE 4.2

Advantages and Disadvantages of Foreign Market Entry Modes

	Advantages	Disadvantages
Exporting	• **Speed** of entry • Production site in **lowest-cost** location	• High **transportation** costs • Threat of trade barriers such as **tariffs** • Lack of **access** to local information
Turnkey project	• Increased **profits** for high-tech firms	• Loss of technical **know-how** to potential competitors
Franchising	• Costs and **risks** of opening the foreign market fall on the **franchisee**	• Difficulty in maintaining **quality** control over distant franchises
Licensing	• **Speed** of entry	• Licensee may become **competitor** • Loss of **knowledge** to potential competitor
Joint venture	• High potential for **learning** • Benefit of **combined** resources	• **Shared** control of business • Risk of losing **specialized** technology to partner
Strategic alliance	• **Pooled** talents and expertise • **Shared** costs and risks	• Risk of losing **specialized** technology to partner • Difficulty in finding a **compatible** partner
Contract manufacturing	• **Speed** of entry • Low **test-marketing** costs	• Lack of **quality control** over distant subcontractor
Wholly owned subsidiary	• Total **control** over all operations • Preservation of **proprietary** technology	• **Risks** and costs of entering a foreign market

We started this section with a story about Hachimo Isu, who was considering expanding his business overseas. After spending more time reviewing the idea of going global, he is thinking of two different target countries: Saudi Arabia or Belgium. For each he needs to consider how he would modify the services he offers to reflect the needs of the local area. For example, Brussels, Belgium, is the headquarters of the EU and has very specific political and legal translation needs. Saudi Arabia is experiencing a construction boom and requires the translation of engineering and legal documents. Hachimo needs to investigate the differences in available networking and computer technology supports because these are so critical to his business. He also needs to review the different entry modes into an international market and decide which mode has the most benefits for his company. It is an exciting time, and there are a lot of frequent flyer miles in his immediate future! ■

International Business: Economic Factors and Challenges pp. 105–109

When Rachel Gao decided to expand her jewelry business to include handbags, she thought importing goods would be cheaper than purchasing them from a domestic company. Her initial thought was to go with a small European designer, but after she saw the exchange rate for the euro, she changed her mind. To make a profit, the retail price would be extremely expensive, and she didn't think her customers would pay such a high price. What other options would still allow her to expand? ■

Rafael Ben-Ari/Fotolia

Businesses are impacted by fluctuating exchange rates every day. Transactions between international companies not only have to specify what each side will be paid but also in which currency. In addition, multinational enterprises use foreign currency to pay foreign workers or to invest spare cash in other nations where interest rates may be more attractive. In this section, we'll look at exchange rates and how fluctuations in the value of currency affect the global economy. We'll also explore other economic factors and challenges that affect global business.

The Role of Exchange Rates

What are exchange rates? Foreign exchange markets determine **exchange rates**, the rates at which currencies are converted into another country's currency. A *strong dollar* means that the U.S. dollar exchanges for a relatively large amount of foreign currency. A *weak dollar* does not, and you will get many fewer Mexican pesos for a dollar, for example. Depending on a firm's perspective, it may prefer

7 What are exchange rates, and how do they affect international business?

a strong dollar or a weak dollar. U.S. exporters prefer a weak dollar because their products will be more affordable to foreigners. However, U.S. importers prefer a strong dollar because the cost of importing foreign goods is cheaper. If goods are imported cheaply, then those savings can be either passed on to the consumer or kept as higher profits.

How do exchange rates affect international business? Changes in exchange rates can have important implications for international businesses.

Export and Import Prices

Suppose that the value of the dollar rises or gets stronger against the yen (the currency of Japan). What impact will this have on U.S. and Japanese businesses? Goods exported from the United States will become more expensive because the Japanese will now need more yen to purchase each dollar. This means, for example, that the cost of a $40 pair of jeans made in the United States will increase in price for the Japanese consumer. Japanese consumers will buy fewer U.S. goods, like jeans, and exports to Japan will fall. U.S. businesses selling to the Japanese will be hurt.

At the same time, this stronger dollar will cause a decline in the relative price of Japanese goods for U.S. consumers because fewer dollars are required to purchase each yen. Thus, due to the change in currency exchange rate, the United States will import more Japanese goods, and U.S. businesses will lose market share to Japanese companies.

This example of Japanese and U.S. trade illustrates that **currency appreciation**, an increase in the exchange rate value of a nation's currency, causes the relative price of imports to fall as the relative price of exports rises. When currency appreciates, the currency becomes stronger. **Currency depreciation**, a decrease in the exchange rate value of a nation's currency, has the opposite effect on the relative prices of exports and imports. A weak currency causes exports to become cheaper and imports to become more expensive.

Changing exchange rates also affect multinational firms in other ways. Many companies feel competitive pressure to shift production to countries with weak or low-valued currencies to take advantage of lower costs of production. For example, a weak Chinese currency reduces labor costs in China. If a firm doesn't shift more of its production to China but its competitors do, then its costs will be higher, and the company will lose global market share.[32]

Trade Deficits and Trade Surpluses

Exchange rate changes can also create *trade deficits* and *trade surpluses* for a country. A **trade deficit** exists when the value of a country's imports exceeds the value of its exports. For example, a stronger dollar will create a trade deficit for the United States because a strong dollar can cause export prices to rise as import prices fall.

The United States has experienced significant trade deficits every year since the early 1980s. The advantage of the trade deficit is that it enables the United States to consume more than it produces. However, the disadvantage is that domestic assets, such as real estate or stocks and bonds, must be sold to foreigners to pay for the trade deficit. This is similar to an individual who spends more money than he or she makes. The individual will go into debt and eventually have to sell off assets to continue to live beyond his or her means. The United States' experience with trade deficits helps explain the dramatic, news-making purchase of U.S. assets, such as U.S. businesses and real estate by foreigners.

A **trade surplus** occurs when the value of a country's exports exceeds the value of its imports. What do countries do when they experience a trade surplus? Often countries that trade in raw materials, such as oil or diamonds, find the commodity price fluctuates a great amount from year to year. So, taking the pool of money that exists in the year of a trade surplus and investing it would be a good strategy. **Sovereign wealth funds (SWFs)** are government investment funds that do just that. They are managed separately from the official currency

U.S. Trading Partners, 2012

Rank, Country, Percent of Total Trade

1. Canada 16.5%
2. China 13.1%
3. Mexico 12.6%
4. Japan 5.6%
5. Federal Republic of Germany 4.1%
6. United Kingdom 2.9%
7. Saudi Arabia 2.3%
8. Brazil 2.1%
9. France 1.9%
10. Taiwan 1.7%

"Foreign Trade." U.S. Top Trading Partners. U. S., Department of Commerce, 1 Apr. 2012. Web. 10 June 2012. http://www .census.gov reserves of the country. In 1953, Kuwait established the first SWF, which is now worth almost $300 billion. Many countries now have SWFs, including Norway, China, Saudi Arabia, and Singapore. The amount held by all SWFs is currently over $5 trillion.[33]

SWFs can invest in anything they want, and sometimes the investments of SWFs stabilize and allow foreign companies to expand. But during the recent credit crisis, many SWFs invested in collapsing banks in Europe and the United States. In fact, more than $69 billion was invested in a range of struggling banks and financial institutions.[34] The oil-rich emirate of Abu Dhabi made a $7.5 billion investment in the U.S. banking firm Citigroup. The political implications of this level of investment make some uneasy about the rapid growth of SWFs. China's fund has made significant investments in major U.S. financial firms. How might that impact the political tensions between the two countries? What if an Arabian SWF invested in a shipping company, giving it control of U.S. ports?

Fixed and Freely Floating Exchange Rate Systems

Exchange rates can be manipulated or fixed by governments. For example, China has fixed its currency to a rate that is weak compared to the dollar. This means Chinese exports to the United States are cheap, and imports from the United States to China are expensive. As a result, the United States faces a huge trade deficit with China. The U.S. government is now calling on the Chinese to allow their currency to "float," or change in response to changing market conditions. Indeed, most countries operate under a *freely floating* (or *flexible*) *exchange rate system*, a system in which the global supply and demand for currencies determines exchange rates. Many specific factors affect the demand and supply of a nation's currency, such as changing interest rates, tax rates, and inflation rates. Generally, however, changes in exchange rates in a freely floating exchange rate system reflect a country's current economic health and its outlook for growth and investment potential.

The problems with floating exchange rates are that they can create relative price changes outside the control of international businesses and engender risks of losses due to rapid and unexpected changes in exchange rates. For example, in the 1980s, Japan Airlines purchased several 747 airplanes from Boeing and agreed to pay in U.S. dollars. In the interim period between signing the contract and the delivery of the planes for payment, the value of the dollar rose dramatically. The airline company had to pay a lot more money than anticipated for the airplanes, and it almost went bankrupt. This example illustrates that unanticipated exchange rate changes can pose huge risks for international businesses.

Nonconvertible Currency and Countertrade

Governments also reserve the right to restrict the convertibility of their currency. Many developing countries have a *nonconvertible currency*, a currency that can't be converted into another currency in the foreign exchange market. For example, the national currency in Morocco is the dirham. It cannot be converted outside the Kingdom's borders, so visitors want to spend every dirham they have before ending their Moroccan vacations. Governments with nonconvertible currencies often fear that allowing convertibility will result in *capital flight*, the transfer of domestic funds into a foreign currency held outside the country. Capital flight would deprive the nation of much-needed funds for investment and development.

Global companies can still do business with countries that have nonconvertible currencies through the use of countertrade. *Countertrade* is a form of international barter, the swapping of goods and services for other goods and services. Currently, countertrade may account for as much as 10–15 percent of total world trade. Companies engage in countertrade because of necessity and profitability. Examples of companies that have undertaken countertrade include General Foods, Goodyear, GE, Westinghouse, 3M, General Motors (GM), Ford Motor Company, Coca-Cola, and PepsiCo.[35]

Which Is Better—A Strong Dollar or a Weak Dollar?

The answer to this question depends on the type of business a firm undertakes. Companies that do a lot of exporting—such as vehicle manufacturers, chemical manufacturers, and farmers—prefer a weak dollar because their product's price is lower in the global marketplace, so their sales and profits will be higher. However, companies that import components or finished goods for resale in the domestic market prefer a strong dollar because the relative price of their imports is lower.

From a consumer's perspective, a strong dollar is typically preferred because import prices are lower, which has a tendency to keep domestic competitors' prices low as well. As an employee, if you work for a company that exports much of its product, you would prefer a weak dollar to stimulate sales and ensure your job security.

The benefits of a strong dollar for a nation as a whole are lower-priced imports, such as oil, lower prices, and a lower inflation rate in general. However, a strong dollar creates a trade deficit. A weak dollar, on the other hand, is good for domestic international businesses because it stimulates employment and raises standards of living. The drawback of a weak dollar is the higher costs of energy and other imports that create higher rates of inflation. So, which is better—a strong dollar or a weak dollar? Like most real-world issues, the answer depends on your perspective.

> **8** What economic factors and challenges play a role in conducting business on a global scale?

Other Economic Challenges to Conducting International Business

What are some other economic challenges to conducting international business? Changing exchange rates and nonconvertible currencies are not the only economic challenges to conducting international business. Companies must also consider how to adapt their products for sale in developing nations, how certain government policies might affect their business, and how the socioeconomic factors of an area impact the types of products they sell.

Economic Growth and Development

Many developing countries are experiencing more rapid growth than advanced economies are, and they have hundreds of millions of eager new customers ready to put their money into the global market. However, some developing countries still lack the basic infrastructure necessary for the effective transportation of goods and/or lack access to dependable electricity. They may also be lacking in modern communication systems. The implications for companies doing business with these nations are clear. For example, the types of food products offered for sale would have to be altered and packaged differently. The modes of advertising would shift from television to radio, and marketing a product via the Internet wouldn't be effective because few customers would own a computer. It would be important for a business entering India, for example, to know the explosive growth there is not as much toward computer ownership as it is toward mobile phone ownership. Today there are 1.2 billion people in India and 900 million mobile cell phones.[36] Advertising delivered via mobile phones would be critical in that setting.

Government Economic Policies

The degree to which markets are allowed to operate freely from government intervention is another important economic consideration. International businesses prefer free market economies to state-run or socialized economies because the bureaucratic hassles associated with government intervention drive costs up. Other economic factors include the debt load of a nation (the amount of debt a country has), its unemployment and inflation rates, and its fiscal and monetary policies. *Unit labor cost*—a measure that divides a worker's wages by the average productivity of that worker—is also important. Global companies are concerned with labor costs when looking for lowest-cost locations to establish production facilities.

In addition, the degree of competition that exists in a nation is important because it's more attractive to relocate to places with fewer competitors.

Socioeconomic Factors

Several socioeconomic factors also need to be taken into account, such as the demographics of population density and age distribution. The birthrates of many developing countries are high and offer exciting opportunities to toy manufacturers such as Mattel. Other socioeconomic factors that firms must consider include income distribution, ethnicity, and the cultural behaviors of a community.

Remember Rachel Gao? She decided to expand her jewelry business to include handbags and thought importing goods would be cheaper than purchasing them from a domestic company. Although she wanted to buy from a small European designer, she quickly realized that based on the exchange rate for the euro, the goods would be too expensive. So, she kept looking and found that many other business owners were importing products from China. She investigated the exchange rate for the Chinese yuan against the dollar and found she would be able to import a variety of handbags at an inexpensive price. Not only would her customers appreciate the price point, she would also be able to make a strong profit on her handbag line. Do you see any risks with her decision? ■

Creating Successful International Businesses pp. 109–112

JUPITERIMAGES/ BananaStock\Alamy ImagesRoyalty Free

International sales is the dream job for Joe Stein. He loves travel and is fluent in several languages. He prides himself on being good with people and loves to negotiate. The part of the job that is the most challenging for him is to understand the unwritten rules that are so different from country to country. In Venezuela, he needs to remember that business partners want a firm handshake and a pat on the shoulder when they first meet. In Japan, he needs to be sure to read a new business card carefully on the spot and not just put it in his pocket. Recently, he traveled to India and was given a gift by an Indian business partner. After opening the gift, Joe thanked him profusely, but he sensed that he had done something wrong. Was this going to cost him the deal? What should he have done differently? ■

When a business expands into an international market and lacks cross-cultural awareness, it is destined to fail. Along with cultural norms, political, legal, and ethical ideals vary from country to country. The role of government involvement in business is not universal, so knowing how specific government policies govern business activity is also critical for business success. And because there is no global court to settle differences and disputes, businesses need to thoroughly study what is acceptable legally and ethically in each country. In this section, we'll review the sociocultural, political, legal, and ethical concerns that can make or break a company working in the global marketplace.

Sociocultural Challenges

9 What are the sociocultural, political, legal, and ethical challenges to conducting business in a global marketplace?

How does culture affect business? *Culture* is the complex set of values, behaviors, lifestyles, arts, beliefs, and institutions of a population that are passed on from generation to generation. Culture impacts all aspects of business, from managing workers and production techniques to marketing and beyond. Most international businesses fail because they suffer from a lack of cross-cultural awareness. *Cross-cultural awareness* is an understanding, appreciation, and sensitivity to foreign culture. **Ethnocentrism**, a belief that one's own culture is superior to all other cultures, makes succeeding in international business very difficult.

Why do aesthetics matter when it comes to international business? *Aesthetics* refers to what is considered beautiful or in good taste. Aesthetics encompasses etiquette, customs, and protocol. Few things are more embarrassing than violating a sense of good taste. For example, a company advertised eyeglasses in Thailand by featuring a variety of cute animals wearing glasses. The ad was a poor choice in Thailand because animals are considered a low form of life there, so no self-respecting Thai would wear anything worn by animals. Likewise, when former president George H. W. Bush went to Japan with the former chairman of Chrysler, Lee Iacocca, and other U.S. business magnates to make explicit and direct demands on Japanese leaders, they violated Japanese etiquette. The Japanese considered this assertiveness rude and a sign of ignorance or desperation. Japanese businessmen don't condone lowering themselves to make direct demands. Some analysts believe this violation of cultural aesthetics severely damaged the negotiations and confirmed to the Japanese that U.S. citizens are barbarians.[37]

What other cultural prejudices must be examined for success in other countries? Attitudes toward time vary considerably across the world. Time is paramount to those in the United States, where people in general expect promptness and directness. Some cultures view this as pushy and impersonal. In addition, the U.S. time horizon differs markedly from, for example, the Japanese perspective. A long-term view to a U.S. citizen may be four to seven years

OFF THE MARK

International Business Blunders

When selling products in the global marketplace, companies must research the cultural norms and language of the location in which they plan to sell. If not, the results could be disastrous, as illustrated by the examples below.[38]

- Translation difficulties can cause a fine slogan to fail miserably in another language. The Pepsi slogan "Come alive with the Pepsi Generation!" was translated into Mandarin Chinese as "Pepsi will bring your ancestors back from the dead!"

- In many Latin American cultures, women do not order their husbands around, and people are not usually very concerned with punctuality. A popular U.S. telephone company didn't know this. When the company showed a commercial in which a Latino wife tells her husband to call a friend and tell her they would be late for dinner, the commercial bombed.

- P&G could not imagine the backlash it would receive when it used a popular European television commercial in Japan. The ad showed a man entering a bathroom and touching his wife while she bathed. The Japanese disapproved of this ad because the man's behavior did not adhere to the nation's cultural norms.

- When a golf ball manufacturing company tried selling its golf balls in packs of four in Japan, the campaign was unsuccessful. That's because pronunciation of the word for "four" in Japanese sounds like the word for "death," so items packaged in fours are unpopular.

in the future, while the Japanese approach is often to prepare for decades in the future. Attitudes toward work also vary. For example, the Germans argue that people in the United States live to work, while Germans work to live. Germans and other Europeans expect four to six weeks of vacation per year. Compare this to the two weeks on average a person in the United States gets and it is clear which country values vacation time more.[39]

Religion plays a profound role in shaping a culture. International businesses are well advised to educate themselves on varying religious value systems, customs, and practices if they don't wish to offend customers in marketing campaigns. For example, a soft drink was introduced into Arab countries with an attractive label that had stars on it—six-pointed stars. The Arabs interpreted this as pro-Israeli and refused to buy it. Another label was printed in 10 languages, one of which was Hebrew; again, Arabs largely did not buy the product.[40]

Why is knowing the native language not enough?
Language, both spoken *and* unspoken, is extremely important. Consider a few more examples of international business blunders due to a lack of cross-cultural awareness.[41] A U.S. oil rig supervisor in Indonesia shouted at an employee to take a boat to shore. Because berating a person in public is abhorred in Indonesia, a mob of outraged workers chased the supervisor with axes.

Unspoken language, or body language, also differs significantly around the world. Mountain Bell Company tried to promote its telephone services to Saudi Arabia. Its ad portrayed an executive talking on the phone with his feet propped up on the desk, showing the soles of his shoes—something an Arab would never do.

Although the world is getting smaller and a global culture is emerging, there are still profound and significant cultural differences. Cross-cultural awareness is a prerequisite to successful international business.

Should you bow or shake hands when you visit a Japanese client in Japan?

Image Source IS2/Fotolia

Political Challenges

What are the political challenges to conducting international business? International businesses look for nations that have a stable government, a well-established educational system, and a well-maintained infrastructure. Political changes can create disruptive environments that impact business concerns. The political differences among nations can also pose a challenge when conducting international business.

In today's global economy, companies often do business in government-controlled socialist economies, such as China, Cuba, and North Korea. The differences in political systems can cause tensions. One example is the experience of Google in China. China has a questionable record on human rights issues and privacy. When Google wanted to enter China, the government demanded Google comply with Internet censorship laws so the results Google's search engine returned to Chinese citizens were controlled and filtered. Google agreed and became an established presence in mainland China, rising to become the number-two search engine.

Then Google experienced a cyber attack originating from China that targeted the Gmail accounts of dozens of human rights activists in China. That action, along with an increase in the government blocking of sites such as Facebook, Twitter, and Google Docs, led Google to reverse its decision. It decided to stop censoring results, forcing a standoff with the Chinese government. Ultimately, China did renew Google's license to operate in the country, but this is an example of how the pressure from an international business giant can be at odds with political forces in a foreign country.

Government intervention in the process of determining which goods are undesirable and whether goods should be regulated, taxed, or banned also varies from country to country. Many products that pollute the environment are deemed undesirable and have been regulated in one form or another by most governments around the world. The differences in these regulatory standards can impose big differences in costs of production for global businesses. There are also growing pressures on governments to address global climate change issues that will affect international business.

Legal Challenges

What are the legal challenges to conducting international business?

Laws, regulatory standards, and access to unbiased judicial systems based on a rule of law differ considerably around the world. No universal laws, regulatory standards, or global courts exist to settle disputes in the global economy. The different laws governing contracts, product safety and liability standards, and property rights are of particular importance when conducting global business. Property rights violations, including violations of patents and copyrights in the software, music, and publishing businesses, have cost businesses billions of dollars a year. Without adequate protection of intellectual property, technological developments would be too expensive and risky for companies to continue to fund long-term R&D.

Different laws also govern the use of bribery throughout the world. The United States passed the Foreign Corrupt Practice Act in the 1970s in response to questionable or illegal payments to foreign government officials to secure contracts or other favors. The act was designed to restore public confidence in the business community in the United States. But Congress became concerned that U.S. businesses were put at a disadvantage. Many foreign companies routinely paid bribes and were even able to deduct the cost of bribes from their taxes as legitimate business expenses. The United States therefore pushed for the creation of the Organisation of Economic Co-operation and Development (OECD) in 1988, which currently consists of 30 member nations committed to combating bribery. In many places in the world, however, bribes are common and may even be necessary for doing business.[42]

Ethical Challenges

What are some ethical challenges faced by international business?

Bribery is just one of the many ethical dilemmas surrounding global business. Unique differences in economic conditions and cultural values give rise to many ethical dilemmas surrounding global business. For example, should a firm conform to its home country's environmental, workplace, and product safety standards—even though it's not legally required to do so—while operating in another country? Should a company do business with a repressive totalitarian regime? When conducting international business, companies must determine whether they are willing to defy ethical codes to make a larger profit.

We started this section by introducing Joe Stein, who works in international sales and must deal with a variety of cultures. Joe has learned a lot about the world and about himself by working in international sales. When his Indian business supplier offered him that gift, he politely said thank-you and opened it. But he saw Sheshadri's face wince, and others in the group began to look uncomfortable. Joe quickly apologized and asked Sheshadri privately whether he had done something inappropriate. "In India you should never open a gift before the person has left. It shocked a few of us that you would be so rude." Joe thanked him for the insight and made sure to apologize to the people there. Understanding and respecting the differences in cultures around the world will help Joe succeed in international business. ■

CHAPTER 4
SUMMARY

MyBizLab

Go to **mybizlab.com** to complete the problems marked with this icon ⭐.

1 **What are the implications of the globalization of markets and the globalization of production?** (pp. 87–89)

- The **globalization of markets** (p. 88) refers to the movement away from thinking of the market as being the local market or the national market to the market being the entire world. Businesses need to "think globally but act locally," which means that companies must market their products so that they appeal to their local customers.

- The **globalization of production** (p. 89) refers to the trend of individual firms to disperse parts of their productive process to different locations around the world to take advantage of lower costs or enhance quality. The globalization of production often involves **outsourcing** (p. 89), which is contracting with another firm to produce part of a product that formerly was produced in-house. **Offshore outsourcing** (p. 89) has become a significant concern for U.S. workers.

2 **Why has globalization accelerated so rapidly?** (pp. 89–90)

- The decline in trade and investment barriers, which are government barriers that inhibit the free flow of goods, services, and financial capital across national boundaries, is one factor that has led to increased globalization. This decline has encouraged developing nations to become involved in international trade and allowed companies to base production facilities at the lowest-cost location.

- Technological changes that have also contributed to the rise in globalization include the following:
  - Teleconferencing, which allows businesspeople to conduct meetings with contacts around the world
  - IT, such as the Internet and cable and satellite television systems, which allow companies to advertise and sell products on a global scale

3 **What are the costs and benefits of international trade?** (p. 93)

- The **theory of comparative advantage** (p. 92) states that specialization and trade between countries benefits all who are involved. This is true because countries that participate in international trade experience higher standards of living due to the greater quantity and variety of higher-quality products at lower prices.

- The costs of international trade are borne by those businesses and their workers whose livelihoods are threatened by foreign competition. Businesses may lose their market shares to foreign companies, which in turn force businesses to lay off workers.

4 **What are the different types of trade barriers?** (pp. 94–95)

- The different types of trade barriers are **tariffs**, **subsidies**, **quotas**, and **administrative trade barriers** (pp. 94–95):
  - Tariffs are taxes imposed on a foreign good or service.
  - Subsidies are government payments to domestic producers in the form of a direct cash grant or a payment in kind.
  - Quotas are quantity limitations on the amount of an export allowed to enter a country.
  - Administrative trade barriers are government bureaucratic rules designed to limit imports. One example is a **local content requirement** (p. 95), which is a requirement that some portion of a good be produced domestically.

5 **What are the three basic strategies of international business?** (p. 101)

- The three basic strategies of international business are the **global strategy**, the **multidomestic strategy**, and the **transnational strategy** (p. 101).

6 **How can international firms successfully enter foreign markets?** (pp. 101–104)

- There are eight common ways for a company to enter foreign markets, as follows:
  - **Exporting** (p. 102), the sale of domestically produced goods in a foreign market
  - **Turnkey projects** (p. 102), firms export their technological know-how in exchange for a fee
  - **Franchising** (p. 102), selling a well-known brand name or business method in exchange for a fee and percentage of the profits

- **Licensing** (p. 102), an agreement in which the licensor's intangible property may be sold or made available to a licensee for a fee
- **Joint ventures** (p. 102), the shared ownership in a subsidiary firm
- **Strategic alliances** (p. 103), cooperative agreements between competitors
- **Contract manufacturing** (p. 103), a firm subcontracts part or all of its goods to an outside firm
- **Wholly owned subsidiary** (p. 104), establishing a foreign facility that is owned entirely by the investing firm

7 What are exchange rates, and how do they affect international business? (pp. 105–107)

- An **exchange rate** (p. 105) is the rate at which one currency is converted into another.
- **Currency appreciation** (p. 106), the increase in the exchange rate value of a nation's currency, causes the price of imports to fall and the cost of exports to rise. **Currency depreciation** (p. 106), the decrease in the exchange rate value of a nation's currency, creates the opposite effect.

8 What economic factors and challenges play a role in conducting business on a global scale? (p. 108–109)

- Economic growth and development present a challenge because some countries lack the infrastructure necessary to transport goods effectively.

9 What are the sociocultural, political, legal, and ethical challenges to conducting business in a global marketplace? (pp. 109–112)

- **Ethnocentrism** (p. 110), the belief that one's own culture is superior to all others, can lead to conflict when conducting business globally. Other sociocultural challenges include differences in aesthetics, religion, and attitudes toward time and work.
- International businesses prefer stable governments with a strong infrastructure. However, many countries do not offer this kind of political and economic environment. Government decisions about taxation, infrastructure investments, and antitrust law enforcement can all affect global business.
- From a legal standpoint, the differences in laws and regulations around the world provide challenges for conducting business. There are no universal laws or policies for governing contracts, product safety and liability standards, or property rights.
- Bribery is an ethical challenge facing international business. Decisions about whether to conform to a home country's environmental, workplace, and product-safety standards while operating in a foreign country are other ethical dilemmas.

Key Terms

Self-Test

Multiple Choice You can find the answers on the last page of this book.

1. **Governments with nonconvertible currency are**
   a. often developing countries that are trying to protect themselves from capital flight.
   b. countries that have strong economic health and prospects of growth.
   c. are planning to move toward a floating exchange rate system.
   d. developed countries that are protecting the value of their currency.

2. **The globalization of markets and the globalization of production means that**
   a. people are no longer in control of their own lives.
   b. we are all connected by the Web.
   c. companies can take one product to international markets without having to adapt it.
   d. companies design products for global markets and can produce them offshore.

3. **The theory that states that specialization and trade are mutually beneficial to all economies involved in trade is called the**
   a. theory of comparative advantage.
   b. theory of beneficial trade.
   c. theory of absolute advantage.
   d. theory of relative trade.

4. **Which of the following are global business trends?**
   a. A growing role for developing nations in importing and exporting
   b. A rise in multinational enterprises
   c. Increased adoption of the free-market economy model
   d. All of the above

5. **The theory of comparative advantage indicates that**
   a. a country should sell to other countries the products it produces most efficiently and buy from other countries the products that it cannot produce as efficiently.
   b. international trade will force domestic businesses to lose market share to foreign competitors.
   c. countries that participate in international trade will have a higher standard of living.
   d. a limit is placed on the amount of goods and services that can be traded.

6. **Which of the following international organizations promote free trade?**
   a. GATT
   b. The euro
   c. The IMF
   d. All of the above

7. **If an international business is selling a standardized product and competing chiefly on price, the business is initiating a**
   a. transnational strategy.
   b. multidomestic strategy.
   c. standard-price strategy.
   d. global strategy.

8. **Exchange rates affect international businesses because**
   a. nonconvertible currency is worthless.
   b. currency depreciation and appreciation changes the relative price of imports and exports.
   c. U.S. exporters prefer a strong dollar.
   d. exchange rates fluctuate after the G20 meeting each year.

9. **Which method of entering foreign markets has the advantage of allowing for test-marketing a product in a foreign market at the lowest cost?**
   a. Joint ventures
   b. Wholly owned subsidiaries
   c. Exporting
   d. Contract manufacturing

10. **Doing business in countries with socialist economies that are government controlled**
    a. is not legal for businesses headquartered in the United States.
    b. happens often today despite political tension.
    c. almost ensures profit because socialist economies have lower costs of production.
    d. is unprofitable because of embargo sanctions.

Self-Test (continued)

True/False   You can find the answers on the last page of this book.

1. A free-floating exchange rate system uses global supply and demand to set exchange rates.

   ☑ **True** or ☐ **False**

2. Outsourcing sometimes involves moving the production of a product from a domestic location to a foreign location.

   ☑ **True** or ☐ **False**

3. Increasing U.S. dominance of foreign direct investments has helped accelerate globalization.

   ☑ **True** or ☐ **False**

4. Entering a foreign market through a strategic alliance does mean your business loses its independence

   ☑ **True** or ☐ **False**

5. Trade barriers include tools like embargos, quotas, and local content requirements.

   ☑ **True** or ☐ **False**

Critical Thinking Questions

1. When governments invest in education and training for its citizens, they hope to build a competitive advantage in world markets. Could a government invest too much in education? Are there other technologies or services that would give a country more of a competitive advantage in today's markets?

2. Review the three basic strategies of international business. Discuss the type of companies that would most likely pursue a global strategy, a multidomestic strategy, and a transnational strategy.

3. Organizations to promote free trade, like the EU, have had difficulty creating a common currency. Why do you think not all EU countries use the euro? Why do some countries that are not part of the EU choose to use the euro?

Team Time

THE DEVIL'S ADVOCATE

Read the following issues and questions. Which side of the issue do you believe is correct? Form a group with other students in the class who share your belief. As a group, play devil's advocate by creating a case for the opposing side of the issue. Now that you've considered both sides, you're ready to debate the opposition.

1. In the recent wave of globalization, developing countries have become the focus for many international businesses. Is this process of globalization the best way to strengthen developing countries and establish a level playing field, or does it keep them under the control of wealthy industries and drive income inequality?

2. Free trade versus protectionism is a heated debate in today's fragile economy. Which is better for the health of the U.S. economy over the next 10 years—free trade or protectionism?

3. Currently, the minimum age for a child to work in Indonesia is 12 years old. The minimum age for a child to work in the United States is 14 years old. If a garment company from the United States decides to outsource production to Indonesia, would it be ethical for the company to hire 12- or 13-year-old workers in the factory?

Process

Step 1. Meet as a group to discuss the issue. Remember that you must build a case for the side you chose. Look for problems with your own personal beliefs to develop a case for your side.

Step 2. Prepare an individual response that supports your side of the issue.

Step 3. Share your response with your group. Think of possible rebuttals for each response. Then alter any responses that can produce a strong rebuttal.

Step 4. Determine who will be the group's primary spokesperson for the debate.

Step 5. Each group will be given five minutes to present its side of the issue. After each group has presented its argument, each team will be given five minutes to prepare a rebuttal and then three minutes to present the rebuttal.

Step 6. Repeat with other groups.

Step 7. After each group has debated, discuss whether anyone's personal views have changed after this assignment.

Ethics and Corporate Social Responsibility

OFFSHORE OUTSOURCING

Workers in the United States often view offshore outsourcing in a negative light. Many people believe that this practice is a way for companies to make more money by eliminating U.S. jobs. However, offshore outsourcing sometimes seems necessary for the survival of a company. Review the following scenario.

Scenario

You are the owner of a company that makes industrial sewing machines. Currently, your company's profits are decreasing because your competitors have lower prices. You cannot lower the price of your machines without losing a significant amount of money. The majority of your costs come from labor. You have 2,000 employees in your factory, and your company is the primary employer in the region. You could sell your product for a third of the price if you outsourced half your production to a foreign country. However, this would eliminate 1,000 jobs and devastate a community. Also, the country that you would be outsourcing to has a reputation for unsafe working conditions and practices. If you don't outsource some of your production, over time your company may be unable to compete, possibly forcing you to shut down your company.

Questions for Discussion

1. As a business owner, what are the costs and benefits of moving half your production overseas?

2. Do the benefits of offshore outsourcing outweigh the costs? Why or why not?

3. Are there any possible alternatives to consider? What other decision could you make so that each side (domestic and international) benefits?

Web Exercises

1. **A Euro for Greece?**
   At the time of this writing, the political elections in Greece have been dominated by discussion of how to handle Greece's financial instability. As a member of the European Union, other EU countries like Germany have a vested interest in the outcome of the Greek elections. Is membership in the EU helping Greece through difficult times or not? What are the arguments both for and against Greece staying with the euro?

2. **Same Company, Different Products**
   Go to the website of the Swedish furniture maker IKEA (ikea.com). Under the "select a location" option, choose the United States. Review the site and note the products and the design of the page. Then go back to the homepage and choose a different country. Look for differences in the appearance of the website and the products offered. Why do you think these sites are different for each county?

3. **Go State!**
   Have you ever considered a career with the U.S. State department? At state.gov, under Youth and Education, select Student Career Programs. What aspects of these careers appeal to you? Visit the Fulbright Scholar program. What information in the Fulbright Fellow Orientation Handbook is new to you?

4. **Cultural Guidelines**
   Knowing how to behave in a variety of countries is critical with increased globalization. Using the materials at www.kwintessential.co.uk/etiquette/doing-business-in .html, select three different countries from very different regions of the world. Review the "Doing Business In?" guides for each country. Create a pamphlet for business travelers on the business dos and don'ts for each country.

5. **You're the Trader**
   Imagine you're in charge of trading goods for a country. Would you focus on building wealth by selling commodities or on developing an industry by purchasing raw materials? Visit www.imf.org/external/np/exr/center/students/ trade/index.htm and become the trader. Measure your success on the global economics conditions scale.

MyBizLab

Go to **mybizlab.com** for Auto-graded writing questions as well as the following Assisted-graded writing questions:

4-1. Sometimes an international business needs to modify its product to adjust to the specific needs or tastes of the local market. How might a company like Trek modify the design of its line of bicycles for sale in Ghana, China, and England?

4-2. What are the advantages of increased competition in the global market? What are the disadvantages? Is foreign competition *always* good for the consumer? Is foreign competition *always* bad for local businesses?

4-3. MyBizLab Only – comprehensive writing assignment for this chapter.

Business Law

Every business, whether it is a large multinational corporation, or a small, simple sole proprietorship, must comply with laws and regulations that govern how businesses operate. Large or complex business entities have lawyers and legal counsel to help ensure that the corporation is running legally. Small business owners, whether they intend to stay small or are planning to grow, generally hire lawyers only on an as-needed basis. Therefore, they should have a good understanding of the United States legal system, and the laws that govern businesses so they can ensure that their small operation is functioning within the law.

The Legal System

The United States is a federalist system, meaning there is government authority at both the national and state levels. The national government has specific powers, and the 50 states retain substantial autonomy and authority. United States government and each of the 50 state governments are divided into executive, legislative, and judicial branches. Written constitutions, both federal and state, form a system of separated powers, checks, and balances among the branches (see ■ FIGURE 1).

■ FIGURE 1
The Legislative System

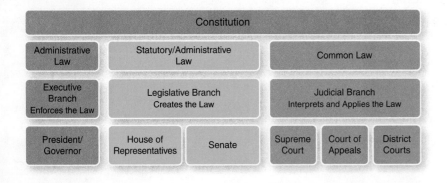

Sources of Law

There are four sources of law: constitutional law, statutory law, administrative regulations, and common law. **Constitutional law**, the written text of the U.S. Constitution and the Bill of Rights, is the foundation of United States law. All laws fall subordinate to the laws of the U.S. Constitution. **Statutory law** is written law determined by the legislative branch of the government. The executive and legislative branches of the federal or state government also establish regulatory bodies (such as the Securities and Exchange Commission [SEC], the Federal Trade Commission [FTC], and the Food and Drug Administration [FDA]). These regulatory bodies have the power to pass **administrative laws**—rules and regulations within their area of authority. The judicial branch of the government not only applies established constitutional and statutory laws, but also creates law when their decisions become precedent for decisions in future cases. This type of unwritten but applied law is considered **common law**, also known as **case law**.

How Laws Affect Businesses

In addition to the laws that govern all citizens of the United States, there are specific laws that pertain more directly to businesses. **Business law**, those laws that directly affect every aspect of business activity, begin from the moment a business is formed. Once a legal business structure is determined (see Chapter 6), a wide variety of laws affect how a business is run, as well as how the business treats its employees and consumers. Finally, there are laws that determine what happens when a business needs to stop operating.

Running a Business—Essential Concepts of Business Law

Once a business opens its doors, some sort of business law affects it. There are laws that regulate how businesses interact with each other and with customers in contractual arrangements, as well as laws that dictate the consequences when a wrongful act occurs, causing injury or damages. Laws are in place to govern commercial transactions, and laws exist to help protect ideas, inventions, and literary artistic works, as well as designs and images used in business. In addition, laws are in place to ensure that competition between businesses remains vibrant as well as to protect the consumer from fraud or deceit. Lastly, laws are in place to ensure that businesses operate in such a manner that do not threaten the environment. Let's look at these laws in greater detail.

Contract Law

Contracts form the basis for much personal and business interaction. A **contract** is an agreement between two parties. In our personal lives, contracts are used in marriage and divorce, for example. In business, contracts are used when a company hires another company or individual to do work for them, when property is bought or sold, and when services are exchanged. See ■ **FIGURE 2**.

ELEMENTS OF A CONTRACT   In order for a contract to be valid an offer must be made, the parties must understand and agree on the terms of the contract, consideration must be given, and the offer must be accepted.

- **An offer is made and accepted by competent parties.** The offer (what is given in exchange for goods or services, generally a price) can be spoken or in writing, and must be accepted (generally by signing a written contact, or it can be done through a simple handshake). Offers can also be made to the general public, as in the form of an advertisement. In addition, all parties entering into the contract must have the capacity of doing so, so they understand the terms and conditions of the contract. Therefore, minors, mentally incompetent individuals, and those who are under the influence of drugs or alcohol do not have the capacity to execute valid contracts. Lastly, all parties involved must enter into the contractual agreement voluntarily without duress, fraud, or undue influence.

- **Terms of offer must be defined and understood and of legal purpose.** Although contracts can be casually created—either orally or even on a napkin or on the back of an envelope—most are formally drafted. In any contract, however, the terms of the offer must be clearly defined and understood. The underlying purpose of the contract must be legal; otherwise the contract is void.

- **Consideration is defined and exchanged.** Something of real value must be exchanged in any valid contract, whether it is an exchange of services or goods (trading or bartering) or payment for services or goods.

Green Thumb Landscape Services
3156 Funks Road * Lansdale, PA 19464 * 610-555-4326

An offer is made.

THIS AGREEMENT made **April 12, 2013** by and between Green Thumb Lawn Services and **Mr. and Mrs. Charles Moyer** at **1032 Skippack Lane, Lansdale, PA 19464.**

Work to be done is legal.

Scope of Work

Green Thumb Lawn Services shall furnish all materials and perform all of the work on the property at **1032 Skippack Lane, Lansdale, PA 19464** as specified below:

Terms of offer outlined.

Work to be Performed

1. Remove all existing plant material as specified on plan provided.
2. Install landscape rock accent wall as per design provided.
3. Install new plant material as per design provided with fertilizer and a one (1) year warranty upon completion of work.
4. Install brown bark mulch throughout to completion.
5. Return any areas disturbed during the installation to acceptable standard, with grass seed, starter fertilizer, lime and mulch, as needed.

Consideration determined: services in exchange for payment.

Contract Price

The Owner shall pay the contractor for material and labor to be performed under the **sum of $4,500**

Progress Payments

Payments of Contract Price shall be made as follows:
1/3 of contract price ($1,500) upon acceptance of proposal,
2/3 of contract price ($3,000) upon completion of project.
Net 10 days, interest charged after 30 days.

Signatures imply offer is accepted and valid. Signers are deemed competent.

Owner Signature _Charles Moyer_   Date _4/12/13_

Contractor Signature _Justin Clark, Green Thumb_   Date _4/12/13_

■ **FIGURE 2**
A Valid Contract

BREACH OF CONTRACT Most contractual arrangements are fulfilled to completion, with the terms of the contract being satisfactorily met. However, there are situations in which a party will fail to uphold his or her stated obligation, whether it's because of a dispute over the quality of goods or services provided, or a failure to complete the contractual obligation. In these instances when a contract is not fulfilled, a **breach of contract** occurs. Some breaches are resolved in lawsuits, but many can be resolved in a less formal manner.

Tort Law

Another common business law concept is that of torts. A **tort** is a wrongful act, resulting in injury or damages. A tort differs from a breach of contract in that a tort is a violation of a right given by law, whereas a breach of contract occurs when there has been a violation of a right acquired by contract. In some instances, a circumstance can be both a tort and a breach of contract. There are different types of torts: intentional, negligence, and strict liability.

- **Intentional torts** are actions designed to injure another person or person's property such as battery, assault, fraud, misrepresentation, trespass, slander, and defamation by computer.
- **Negligence** is a failure to exercise reasonable care to avoid causing harm to others. Negligence is not intentional, and is thereby distinguishable from intentional tort. Negligence occurs when a person or entity is not reasonably careful, and someone was injured as a result of the carelessness.
- **Strict liability (or absolute liability)** is the legal responsibility for damages, or injury, even if the person found strictly liable was not at fault or negligent.

Strict liability is usually associated with defectively manufactured products, known as **product liability**. In these situations, the injured party needs to prove only that the item was defective, and that the defect caused some type of harm. Product liability is most often associated with manufacturing defects, design or marketing defects, and a failure to warn.

The McDonald's coffee case, in which a 79-year old woman spilled McDonald's coffee on her lap, causing third-degree burns, is a classic example of not only a failure to warn, but also a manufacturing defect. The woman sued McDonald's for knowingly serving coffee that could cause third-degree burns in two to seven seconds if spilled. Additionally, the warning on the cup was deemed too small to be of use. The case went to trial, and was settled in the woman's favor. McDonald's subsequently has reduced the serving temperature of their coffee and has increased the size of the warning. Bridgestone/Firestone recalled nearly 6.5 million Firestone tires after defective products caused death and serious injuries to owners of Ford Explorers. Mattel settled product liability claims for toys made in China containing high levels of lead paint. And more recently, Toyota recalled 10 million automobiles in response to product liability claims of unintended acceleration and braking problems. No doubt you can think of many other cases where companies were held liable for damages associated with faulty products.

Tort reform—proposals to limit tort filings and proceedings and to cap damage awards—is an ongoing source of debate and discussion. The economic effects of the current tort system are the biggest driver of the debate. Some argue that the cost of litigation and the multibillion-dollar awards raise the cost of insurance and/or product cost to the consumer. Some feel that our society is too litigious and that frivolous lawsuits have escalated out of control. Others argue that tort reform would make it more difficult for the injured to file a lawsuit and/or to be fairly compensated. What are your thoughts?

Intellectual Property Laws

Intellectual property laws are put in place to protect **intellectual property**—creations of the mind such as ideas, inventions, literary and artistic works, as well as symbols, names images, and designs used in commerce. Intellectual property laws include patents, trademarks, copyright, trade secrets, and digital rights. The concept behind protecting intellectual property is to encourage "innovation incentive" by preserving the incentive for authors and inventors to create by removing the worry that they will not be able to recoup the costs associated with developing their product.

- **Patents.** A patent is a property right granted by the U.S. Patent and Trademark Office (USPTO) on a new and useful invention. A patent grants the patent holder the exclusive right to his or her invention, excluding others from using, making, or selling the same invention for 14 or 20 years, depending on the type of patent issued. There are three types of patents: utility patents, design patents, and plant patents. Utility patents protect inventions for processes, machinery, manufactures, or composites of matter, or an improvement on a previous invention. Design patents protect the appearance of an object rather than its functionality (which is covered by the utility patent). Plant patents protect new, reproducible plants (organic matter). Patents can be assigned (sold) for a lump sum payment, but most often are licensed to a company that will develop the invention. The inventor will receive a license fee and royalty payments based on the revenues generated from the invention.
- **Trademarks.** A trademark is any word, name, symbol, or device (or any combination of these) that is used to identify and distinguish a good. A service mark is a similar concept, used to identify a service. Trademarks and service marks are often referred to as "brands" or "brand names." Generally,

■ **FIGURE 3**
Can you identify these corporate logos?
Image sources, from top, left to right: vQ-Images/Alamy; Maurice Savage/Alamy; Matt Rourke/AP Photo; Alistair Laming/Alamy; Caro/Alamy; Howard Harrison/Alamy; Barrie Harwood/Alamy; PhotoStock-Israel/Alamy; Bruce McGowan/Alamy

consumers identify products bearing the trademark with a certain standard of quality (see ■ **FIGURE 3**). What reactions do you have when you see the Nike swoosh, McDonald's, golden arches, or Apple's apple? Trademark rights exclude others from using a similar mark, thus protecting the owner of the trademark against any potential fraud. Only those trademarks registered with the USPTO bear the symbol ®, but anyone can use the ™ or ℠ to identify a mark, even though it might not be registered with the USPTO. Trademarks can be licensed, which is generally the case with franchising arrangements.

- **Copyrights.** A copyright is a form of protection provided to authors of original works of authorship for a limited period of time. Copyrights protect works such as books, music, photographs, works of art, movies, and computer programs and apply to both published and unpublished works. A copyright provides protection of reproducing the copyrighted work, making a derivative work (such as a movie from a novel), distributing copyrighted works to the public, performing publicly certain works (i.e., music), and displaying publicly certain works (i.e., paintings).

- **Trade secrets.** A trade secret is information that companies keep secret to give them a competitive advantage. Trade secrets can be any formula, pattern, physical device, idea, process, or compilation of information. Unlike trademarks and patents, trade secrets are not protected under federal statutes, and are protected only under state laws. Another distinction from trademarks and patents is that trade secrets are protected only when the secret is NOT disclosed. Employees of companies who, by the nature of their position within the company, have firsthand knowledge of the trade secret usually are asked to sign a nondisclosure agreement (NDA), an agreement not to reveal his or her employer's proprietary information if the employee leaves the company. Violation of such an agreement can lead to imprisonment. For example, two employees of Coca-Cola were sentenced to five- and eight-year federal prison terms for conspiring to steal and sell company trade secrets to Pepsi.

- **Digital rights.** Digital intellectual property is the digital (or electronic) representation of an individual's intellect that holds value on the commercial market. Unlike other intellectual properties that are protected by patents, trademarks, and copyrights, protecting digital intellectual property is much more difficult because of the very nature of digital media. The biggest issues with protecting digital works are that a copy is virtually an exact replica of the original, and it is extremely easy to distribute digital works very quickly and inexpensively to a vast number of individuals. Although the individual works (books, music, film, art) are technically covered under traditional copyright laws, the ability for those laws to protect digital works was questioned by the film and music industry, and subsequently by publishers. As a means to strengthen the legal protection of intellectual property rights in the new digital age, and to comply with the World Intellectual Property Organization Copyright Treaty, the **Digital Millennium Copyright Act (DMCA)** was signed into law in 1998. The DMCA further protects copyrighted material from unauthorized digital reproduction and distribution. The DMCA extends the reach of a copyright by criminalizing the creation and distribution of technology, devices, or services that control access to copyrighted works, and tightening the penalties for copyright infringement in the digital environment. Some believe, however, that DMCA does little to really reduce the confusion that still surrounds the protection of digital works. There are still ongoing debates as to whether or not the works are indeed protected, or whether the current copyright laws, as they apply to digital media, become a detriment to consumers and impair the evolution of the technology.[1]

Sales Law

Businesses sell goods or services. There are laws in place that govern the sales of goods. The most comprehensive of these laws is the **Uniform Commercial Code (UCC)**, a set of model laws that govern businesses selling goods within the United States and its territories. Such transactions include borrowing money, leases, contracts, and the sale of goods. The UCC laws are "model laws" because they first must be adopted by the state—either verbatim or modified; once adopted, they become state law. All 50 states and territories have adopted some version of the UCC. ■ **TABLE 1** outlines the articles and general provisions of each article in the UCC. Everyday business transactions involve provisions in Articles 3, 4, and 5. Article 3 involves negotiable instruments, such as checks, paper money, and commercial paper (short-term debt issued to finance short-term credit needs). The debt is unsecured, issued without any form of collateral. Article 4 pertains to banking matters, and Article 5 applies to letters of credit. A letter of credit is a letter from a bank that guarantees a buyer's payment to a seller will be made, regardless of the buyer's current financial situation.

Antitrust Laws

A healthy economy depends on businesses being able to compete with each other in free and open markets. Competition between sellers benefits consumers by keeping prices low, maintaining higher quality products, offering greater choices, and improving innovation. In order to oppose or regulate business monopolies and to maintain healthy competition between businesses, **antitrust laws** are in place. The first American antitrust law, the **Sherman Act of 1890**, was created to prevent large, powerful companies from coming together as "trusts" and dominate industries, and the **Clayton Antitrust Act of 1914** added further substance to antitrust legislation. Today, the Federal Trade Commission's Bureau of Competition reviews and analyzes potential mergers and other agreements between businesses to prevent anticompetitive conduct and to ensure that competition is maintained.

- **Mergers.** The FTC monitors mergers to ensure that a combination of two or more businesses will not result in market dominance by the newly formed bigger company. Not all mergers result in monopolies. Some mergers result in new efficiencies by combining operations such as when Kmart and Sears

TABLE 1

Description of Articles in the Uniform Commercial Code

Article	Title	Contents
1	General Provisions	Principles of interpretation, general definitions
2 and 2A	Sales and Leases	Applies to all contracts for the sale and lease of goods
3	Negotiable Instruments	Checks, banknotes (paper money), and commercial paper
4	Bank Deposits	Bank collections, deposits, and customer relations
4A	Funds Transfers	Corporate to corporate electronic fund transfers and payments such as wire transfers and automated clearinghouse credit transfers
5	Letters of Credit	Laws that address promises by a bank to pay the purchases of a buyer quickly and without reference to the buyer's financial condition
6	Bulk Transfers and Bulk Sales	Imposes an obligation on buyers who order the major part of the inventory for certain types of businesses
7	Warehouse Receipts, Bills of Lading, and Other Documents of Title	Applies generally to trucking companies; includes rules on the relationships between buyers and sellers and any transporters of goods
8	Investment Securities	Rules pertaining to the issuance of stocks, bonds, and other investment securities
9	Secured Transactions	Security interests in real property

Roebuck Co. came together to create the third largest retail chain. However, when Staples, Inc., proposed to buy Office Depot, the FTC blocked the merger of the two large office supply retail stores, stating that the merger would reduce the number of competing stores in some parts of the country, and thus allow for higher pricing. It is estimated that by blocking the merger, consumers were saved millions of dollars.[2]

- **Price collusion.** The FTC also watches out for companies that collude on price-related matters that then might either make it difficult for others to enter a market or would artificially raise prices to the consumer. In 2002, a group of large music companies and retailers that included Sony Music, Warner Music,

The FTC blocked the proposed merger between Staples and Office Depot, stating that such a merger would allow for higher pricing.

tom carter/Alamy

Ian Dagnall/Alamy

Musicland Stores, and Tower Records were investigated for coming together and artificially inflating CD prices over a five-year period. The companies settled the case, paying $143 million in lieu of continuing litigation.[3]

- **Manufacturer/dealer agreements.** Similarly, the FTC monitors any agreements between manufacturers and product dealers. Often these agreements make sense and benefit the consumer, such as when a computer manufacturer arranges to include a specific software application in their computers. But, the FTC watches for instances when a manufacturer forces an unwanted associated product onto a dealer. Thus was the case when Microsoft bundled their Web browser, Internet Explorer, with the Windows operating system, enabling Microsoft to have a significant advantage in the Web browser market. Today, as you may know, we have the choice of installing Internet Explorer or another Web browser such as Google Chrome, Safari, and Firefox.

The EPA is responsible for maintaining and enforcing environmental standards, and controlling air and water pollution, among other things.

Through such scrutiny of competitive business practices, the FTC strives to ensure that consumers have choices in price, selection, quality, and innovation.

Environmental Laws

The rapid growth of business and industry through the mid-20th century had a significantly negative impact on the environment. As a result, to protect the environment for future generations several laws were passed in the 1960s and 1970s that regulated air and water quality, and additional regulations have been passed to control the disposal of hazardous waste. The Environmental Protection Agency (EPA) was formed in 1970 to "protect human health and the environment."* The EPA is responsible for maintaining and enforcing national environmental standards, as well as conducting research and providing education on environmental issues. Most recently, environmental attention is being directed to modify the United States energy policy in response to global warming concerns.

Laws for Consumers and Employees

Various regulatory schemes control how commerce is conducted, particularly with regard to employees and customers. Advertising laws, employee safety laws, and food and drug laws are examples.

Advertising Laws

Consumers are inundated with advertisements that tout product features and benefits. Companies engage in advertising, some of which is very expensive, with the hopes of enticing us to purchase their products. In 2010, U.S. businesses spent $279 billion on advertising.[4] The FTC regulates all forms of business advertising.

- **Truth-in-advertising** rules help to ensure that advertisements are truthful and nondeceptive, that there is sufficient evidence to support claims made in advertisements, and that the advertisements are not unfair (and subsequently cause unavoidable consumer injury that is not outweighed by the benefit).

- **Product labeling** laws include laws that mandate that food products have specific nutritional and product information on their labels, cigarette packages must include a warning label, and any products that might be hazardous to children must contain warnings.

*Source: From "Our Mission and What We Do." Environmental Protection Agency. www.epa.gov

Truth-in-advertising laws ensure that advertisements are not deceptive and support the claims made in the advertisement.

In addition, there are specific product advertisements that the government regulates, including alcoholic beverages, automobiles, Internet services, health and fitness products, housing and real estate, and telephone services.

Employment and Labor Law

There are hundreds of laws in place that regulate how companies hire and treat employees. **Employment laws** mandate that companies in their hiring practices do not discriminate against candidates based on disabilities, age, race, religion, sexual orientation, or nationality. These laws include Equal Employment Opportunity Laws, Civil Rights Act, Americans with Disabilities Act, and Age Discrimination in Employment Act. See Chapter 9 for more details on employment laws.

Employee laws ensure that all workers and employees are treated fairly with respect to wages, workplace conditions, medical care due to a workplace injury, and employee benefits, to name a few. ■ **TABLE 2** lists some of the major employee laws.

Laws That Govern Closing a Business

At some point, businesses close their doors and cease operating. Sometimes, especially with family-owned businesses, sole proprietorships, or partnerships, businesses close because the current head of the business leaves and there is no further succession in business ownership. Sometimes, through a merger or acquisition, a business is incorporated into another business. In those instances, regulations and processes ensure that all financial obligations (taxes and business debts) have been successfully met, that employees have been notified and paid appropriately, and that all aspects of the business operations, including permits, licenses, and trade names are cancelled. In some instances, businesses are forced to file for bankruptcy because they can no longer meet their financial obligations.

■ TABLE 2

Examples of Laws That Govern How Businesses Need to Treat Their Employees

Law/Regulation	Description
Fair Labor Standards Act	Regulates standards for wages and overtime pay.
Occupational Safety and Health Act (OSHA)	Regulates safety and health conditions for employees.
Workers Compensation	Provides for compensation and medical care for employees of specific industries that put employees at greater risk for harm on the job, or contracting a life-threatening disease as a result of performing their job, including longshore and harbor workers, energy employees, and miners, and federal employees.
Employee Retirement Income Security Act (ERISA)	Regulates the administration of retirement, pension, and welfare benefits.
Labor-Management Reporting and Disclosure Act	Regulates the fiduciary responsibilities of unions to its members.
Family and Medical Leave Act	Regulates the amount of leave employers must give their employees upon the birth or adoption of a child, or for the serious illness of a direct family member.

Bankruptcy

Bankruptcy is the legal status of an insolvent person or organization, by which their debts are relieved through court action. Bankruptcy can be filed voluntarily or involuntarily; and after all debts have been paid, the debtor is free to begin anew. The source of funds from which creditors can collect is first determined by how the business is structured. For example, when a sole proprietorship needs to file for bankruptcy, business assets are first used, but then all personal assets of the business owner (such as a homes, retirement accounts, cars) can also be used to pay off any remaining business debts. Corporations, limited liability corporations (LLCs), and some forms of partnerships protect personal assets, allowing only business assets to be used to pay off debts incurred by the entity.

There are three types of bankruptcy, and they are named for the specific chapter of the U.S. Bankruptcy Code:

- **Chapter 7.** All business (and sometimes personal) assets are liquidated, and outstanding debts are paid off in a Chapter 7 bankruptcy. Any outstanding debts remaining after all assets are used are discharged. The business ceases operation.

- **Chapter 11.** A business applying for Chapter 11 bankruptcy is allowed to continue operations, but proposes a plan of reorganization to keep its business alive and pay creditors over time.

- **Chapter 13.** Chapter 13 is the most common form of bankruptcy for individuals. Chapter 13 allows an individual to use proceeds from the sale of some assets, and pay off remaining debts with operating income through a 3–5 year repayment plan. This enables an individual to keep his or her home and potentially a car and other productive assets.

Bankruptcy resolves a current situation of insolvency; however, it should be looked upon as a last resort action. For companies and individuals who survive bankruptcy, lingering issues remain that involve establishing a new credit rating. Until a good credit rating can be reestablished, banks and other lenders may not extend credit at all, or will offer loans with higher interest rates.

Small Business and the Entrepreneur

Small Business: The Mainstream of the American Economy

Allison Juarez left a secure position in a good company to start her own personal organizing business. For Allison, the financial risk of leaving a set salary and retirement plan was offset by independence and flexibility. What exactly is a small business? And why are they so important to the American economy?

Entrepreneurs and the American Dream

The Wahoo brothers took the concept of a fish taco and created a multimillion-dollar business with several locations. Their success is not just based on their delicious food. What else about these brothers, and their business, makes them successful entrepreneurs? Do you have what it takes to be an entrepreneur?

Buying Franchises and Existing Businesses

Have you ever thought of owning your own business but didn't know where to start? Aisha Lawrence had always dreamed of running a restaurant. Should she start her own from scratch? Or would buying a franchise or an established restaurant be the right move for her?

The Risks of Small Businesses and Where to Get Help

There's a good reason why entrepreneurs are known for being risk takers: Starting a small business is risky! Roger Sherman knew the pressures and risks of business as he left a failing company to start his own. After making a good start, Roger needed some assistance. Where can Roger go for advice and some minor short-term financial assistance?

Financing Considerations

All that stands between many would-be entrepreneurs and their pot of gold at the end of the rainbow is a way to finance their dream business. Although operating a sandwich shop was not Fred DeLuca's dream, it did become his pot of gold as it turned into one of the world's top franchise opportunities and largest privately held businesses. And it all started with a $1,000 investment from a friend. How do small businesses obtain financing? What are the considerations between all the options?

MyBizLab®

⭐ **Improve Your Grade!**

Over 10 million students improved their results using the Pearson MyLabs.

Visit **mybizlab.com** for simulations, tutorials, and end-of-chapter problems.

Small Business: The Mainstream of the American Economy pp. 131–137

Allison Juarez thought she had landed the job of a lifetime when the offer came a month before graduation. She worked for a large, secure company; she received a regular paycheck, had a 401(k) plan, and had already been promoted twice. By others' standards, life was good.

tiero/Fotolia

But still, Allison felt something was missing. She fantasized about owning her own business, of making her own decisions, having some flexibility in her schedule, and hopefully not having someone else set her earning potential. But she never could gather enough courage to leave the stable paycheck. Finally, with the threat of a potential downsizing ahead of her, Allison jumped the corporate ship and started her own professional organizing business. She had helped to organize many garages, basements, and offices for friends and family, but she had never considered charging for her time. It was just fun for her. Now, she was actively seeking clients, marketing her services, and enjoying the results. Business has been steady but not overwhelming, so Allison is glad that she has a nest egg to rely on during slow times, but she has not regretted her decision one bit. ■

Although starting your own small business might not be the answer to all your problems, it can mean independence, control, and flexibility, as it did for Allison. For many people seeking a new opportunity, it's a promising and attractive option. Many new small businesses today are founded to solve a unique problem with an innovative solution. Many provide a specialized product to other corporations. Small businesses often fill a niche that large companies do not. As a whole, small businesses in the United States play a major role in the economy.

Small Business and the Economy

What is a small business? The **Small Business Administration (SBA)** is an independent agency of the federal government that was formed to aid, counsel, assist, and protect the interests of small businesses. The SBA defines a **small business** as one that is independently owned and operated and not dominant in its field of operation.[1] To qualify for governmental programs and benefits specifically targeted for small businesses, a small business must also meet employee and sales standards established by the SBA. In general, most small businesses must have fewer than 500 employees, though, as shown in ■ **FIGURE 5.1**, nearly 90 percent of all small businesses have 20 or fewer employees.[2] Also, to qualify as a small business, the SBA places restrictions on how much annual revenue a small business can earn. The limits on average annual revenue vary significantly by industry, but in the retail and service industries, which account for the

> 1 What is the role and structure of the small business within the U.S. economy?

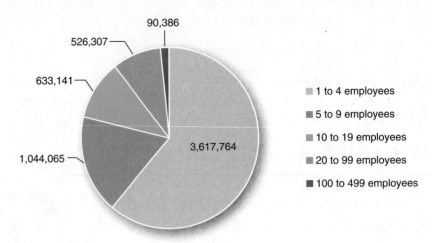

■ **FIGURE 5.1**
U.S. Small Businesses by Employees
(Source: Data from "Statistics about Small Business from the Census Bureau." U. S. Census Bureau. Web. 06 Feb. 2012. http://www.census.gov)

majority of small businesses, the standard annual revenue for a small business is $7.5 million.[3]

Why are small businesses important to the economy? Because there are so many small businesses, they are very important to the economy and the job market. In fact, they generate about 65 percent of net new jobs and create more than one-half of the U.S. gross domestic product.[4] This makes U.S. small businesses the world's second largest economy, preceded only by the entire U.S. economy, putting them ahead of China, Japan, and Germany, as shown in ■ **FIGURE 5.2**.[5,6] Small businesses also export about one-third of total U.S. exported goods and services, valuing nearly $308 billion.[7]

How do small businesses foster innovation? Small companies often introduce new products or procedures that many large businesses do not have the flexibility, the time, the resources, or the inclination to offer. Smaller companies often are better poised to take risks, more flexible to explore innovative techniques, and better equipped to push through inventions than are larger firms. In fact, small businesses create more patents per employee than do large firms.[8]

The impact of small business innovations is well known in the computer, IT, and communications industries. Legendary entrepreneurs include Mark Zuckerberg, who created Facebook from his Harvard dorm room at the age of 19, and two Stanford students, Larry Page and Sergey Brin, who began Google as part of a graduate project. Many years earlier, Michael Dell shook up the computer retail industry by being the first to market computers directly to customers via the Internet rather than through retail stores. Today, Dell's competitors, Hewlett-Packard, Toshiba, and Sony, all have online, customized shopping options.

Other industries besides the technology field also have benefited from the innovative contributions of small businesses. For example, in the biotechnology industry, many small businesses have found innovative solutions to medical issues. One such company is the Insulet Corporation, which received an innovation award from the Smaller Business Association of New England for developing the OmniPod. This tiny instrument, weighing a little more than an ounce, sticks to the skin and delivers insulin at a constant rate based on instructions programmed into its wireless

■ **FIGURE 5.2**
U.S. Small Businesses versus World Economies
(*Sources:* "NFIB's Small Business Growth Agenda for the 112th Congress | NFIB." NIFB.com. National Federation of Independent Business. Feb. 7 2012. http://www.nfib.com)

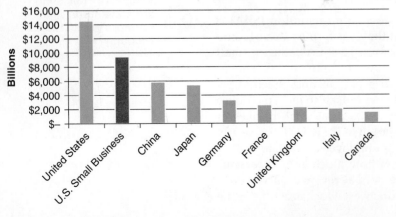

companion.[9] The flexibility inherent in small businesses such as the Insulet Corporation allows them to react more quickly than larger companies to changing market trends and needs. As such, small businesses play an important role in maintaining a healthy economy.

The "green industry"—businesses that provide environmentally friendly products and services—are a hotbed for entrepreneurial activity. Entrepreneurs in this new industry seem to be one of two types: either someone who takes an existing product and sees how that business can be made green, or someone who sees a new green idea and creates a business from the idea. Wind turbines, solar panels, and recycling products have spurred many business initiatives. Patagonia, for example, was the first company to use recycled plastic bottles to create Polartec fleece and now also incorporates recycled polyester as well.[10] Shai Agassi started a company called Better Place that was inspired by developments in the electric car industry. Agassi's inspiration sprung from a problem with electric cars, namely the limited capacity of the car batteries. When the electric battery power is exhausted while driving, a different form of power—usually gasoline—takes over. However, Better Place created an electric vehicle network of changing stations (similar to gas stations) where someone can drive their electric car up to a battery changing station and in a few minutes, the car has a new battery and the person drives away. It's an aggressive idea that requires not only a changing station infrastructure to be deployed, but also a change in current designs of electric cars to allow for a swapping of batteries.

How do small businesses help bigger companies? Small businesses often operate in cooperative relationships with bigger businesses. In the automotive industry, for example, small businesses are important because they make and supply parts that are required in large manufacturing processes. In fact, parts that go into a single automobile, such as seats, engine blocks, and bumpers, are provided by independent suppliers.[11] Using small businesses to provide small and specialized parts not only helps large manufacturers, such as General Motors Corporation, reduce their costs, but also helps with product design and innovation. Many of the features in cars, such as heated seats and intermittent windshield wipers, were first developed by small companies and later sold to large automotive manufacturers. Auto-parts suppliers help U.S. auto makers meet the new government safety and emission standards. It is estimated that small business suppliers now provide two-thirds of the value added in the production of a vehicle through their increase in research and development.[12]

How do small businesses help consumers? Small businesses directly provide us with many of the specialized products and services we use every day. Service businesses, such as hair salons, landscapers, and dry cleaners, as well as local restaurants, auto repair, and many other "mom and pop" stores, provide the services and goods larger businesses can't or don't want to provide.

Small Business and the Workforce

What kind of workers do small businesses employ? Almost all new businesses are small; therefore, they account for a substantial portion of the newly created jobs in the United States. In fact, small businesses create over 65 percent of net new jobs every year.[13] In addition, small businesses hire a larger proportion of younger workers, older workers, and part-time workers, so they help employ millions who do not fit into a traditional corporate structure.[14]

Do small businesses provide opportunities for minorities? Many individuals see owning and operating their own business as a means of achieving the American dream. To that end, women, minorities, and immigrants are becoming more important players in the small business arena. According to an SBA report, approximately one-fifth of all U.S. small businesses are owned by minorities. African American- and Asian American- and American Indian-owned businesses account for approximately 5 percent each of all U.S. firms, and Hispanic-owned

Asian/American Indian
5%

Black
5%

Hispanic
9%

Multiple
1%

White
80%

■ FIGURE 5.3
Small Business Ethnic Ownership
(*Source:* Created with data from Table A.13 Characteristics of Self-employed Individuals, 2000-2007. "The Small Business Economy." (2009). U.S. Small Business Economy. http://archive.sba.gov)

Zappos.com quickly became a billion dollar online shoe merchant when founder Nick Swinmurn created a new solution to buying shoes.

Karen Bleier/Newscom

businesses account for 10 percent of all U.S. firms (see **■ FIGURE 5.3**). Women own 5.3 million businesses, representing approximately one-third of all small businesses. The number of minority-owned businesses is increasing. Between 2000 and 2008, the number of Hispanic-owned businesses grew an amazing 80 percent, women-owned businesses increased by nearly 10 percent, and firms owned by Asian Americans and American Indians increased by nearly 50 percent.[15] Unfortunately, the recession that impacted the United States in 2008–2010 saw a reverse trend. At the peak of the recession, small businesses accounted for nearly 60 percent of job losses. However, the downward trends have shown improvement as the economy has improved.

The infusion of foreign nationals and ethnic cultures in America has spawned more small business opportunities to provide goods and services that cater to new needs and tastes. For example, Rajbhog Foods, Inc., which started as a small, family-owned Indian sweets shop in Queens, New York, provides the local Indian community with authentic Indian sweets and snacks. As the Indian population increased, so did the volume of items made and sold by Rajbhog Foods. The company has expanded its operations to sell to 41 states and Canada and also caters to large weddings and conventions. There are also franchise operations in other East Coast locations where large populations of Indians have settled.

The Impact of Technology on Small Businesses

How has technology affected small businesses? Entrepreneurial success stories, such as YouTube, Facebook, and Google, illustrate the vast opportunities that technology creates for new business start-ups. Evolution of mobile devices, faster access to the Internet, and the infusion of social media impact small businesses. Technology brings new business opportunities, new ways to conduct business, as well as new ways to access and communicate with customers.

Mobile Devices

Mobile devices have brought new ways for customers to shop. With the introduction of mobile apps, consumers can use the phone's camera to scan QR and bar codes to find product information and to make price comparisons immediately in the retail location. Through location apps such as Foursquare and Gowalla, consumers can have access to coupons, discounts, and special offers. There are even devices that fit onto smartphones to process credit cards, which is a perfect solution for businesses that primarily do transactions at tradeshows, flea markets, and craft shows. The UniMag from ID Tech is a magnetic card reader that clips into the headphone jack of many mobile devices.

The Internet

In addition to creating entirely new business opportunities, the PC and the Internet have made starting a new business much easier. Small businesses can flourish with an Internet connection; a modest website for marketing and communication; and a computer for financial, database, and research needs. Entrepreneur Nick Swinmurn, for example, went on a search for a new pair of his favorite boots one fateful day in 1999 and had a complete lack of success. He decided to form an Internet shoe store. The site started small, but after Swinmurn realized the potential for advancement, with the help of CEO Tony Hsieh, he expanded the selection and shipping capacity of the site, and Zappos.com quickly became a billion-dollar success.

In addition, sites such as Alibaba.com and Elance .com help with locating product designers, manufacturers, and freelance professionals. Knowing about these sites helped Bill McNeely create a new product and build a business from Kunduz, a northern Afghanistan city in which he was working as the manager of logistics operations at a training camp for the Afghan National Police.[16]

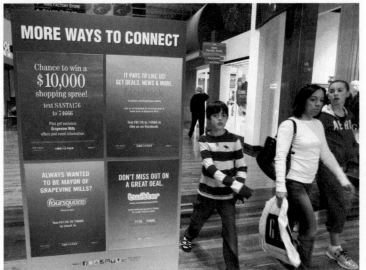

Social Media and Beyond

Technology advances and innovations are also creating new ways for small businesses to interact with, market to, and keep abreast of their customers through services, such as blogs, social networks, smartphone apps, and podcasts. These new advancements can be beneficial to small businesses because they are generally low-cost means of marketing. For example, Sprinkles Cupcakes, a cupcake bakery based in Beverly Hills, California, has used Facebook to its advantage. Each day a secret word is posted on Sprinkles' Facebook page. Customers who retrieve the word and mention it at any one of the locations get a free cupcake. This strategy has caused many to "Like" the company on Facebook. In fact, Sprinkles launched a contest for a trip to the Sprinkles Hollywood store for a randomly chosen "BFF" (Best Friend Forever) when they reached 100,000 Facebook fans. In addition, the company also uses Facebook to pretest flavor ideas and upcoming promotions in an effort to increase interaction with customers. Facebook is not the only social media tool used by small businesses. Twitter, Foursquare, and LinkedIn are also popular ways to connect with customers and prospective employees. Over the holiday season, to help visitors with their holiday shopping, the Grapevine Mall in Grapevine, Texas, posted signs throughout the mall to remind shoppers how to use social media to stay connected.

Social media is being used by businesses, even this mall in Grapevine, Texas, to stay connected with customers.

However, social media can also become problematic if not managed well. Creating a fan page on Facebook without monitoring what people are saying about your business may not be useful. Although most consumers report that they use social media to communicate with businesses, only 8 percent are satisfied with businesses' responsiveness on social media. Nearly one-third felt their complaints were ignored, and nearly 9 out of 10 customers felt that if they see their complaint or even another's complaint being ignored, they'd be less likely to buy from that company.[17] Similarly, writing a blog may help get out your message, but if no one reads the blog, it's not effective. A well-thought-out technology plan is an important aspect of any business's overall strategy.

Reasons for Starting a Small Business

Why would I want to start my own business? Bill McNeely, a logistics operations manager at a training camp for the Afghan National Police, hopes starting a business will enable him to leave his current job that keeps him so far away from his family in Texas. But people start small businesses for many different reasons (see ■ FIGURE 5.4):

1. **Opportunity knocks.** An idea for a new company often starts when someone envisions a product or a service that isn't being offered yet. Other people create opportunities from their own obstacles. For example, a father frustrated at watching his autistic child try to communicate with others founded the Animated Speech Corporation, a company that develops software-based conversational language learning systems to help autistic children communicate.[18]

THE List

The Ten Best Industries for Starting a Business

1. Home health care
2. Wellness and self-improvement
3. Elder care
4. Mobile apps and software as a service
5. Education and education technology
6. Employment and temporary staffing services
7. Green construction
8. Consulting—business, technical, niche
9. Debt settlement/personal financial advisory services
10. Motion picture/video/ entertainment

Opportunity & Innovation
New ideas and needs bring
new businesses.

Control
More control of business decisions;
do not want to work for someone else.

Financial Independence
Owners feel they can make more
money operating their own business.

Schedule Flexibility
Looking for a better
work/life balance.

Unemployment
Seeking income due to job loss.

■ **FIGURE 5.4**
Reasons to Start a Small Business
Image Sources: top to bottom, left to right: Carsten Reisinger/Fotolia; alphaspirit/Fotolia; tiero/Fotolia; almagami/Fotolia; alphaspirit/Fotolia

2. **Financial independence.** Many people begin a small business because they want financial independence, though this should not be the sole reason. Most small businesses don't start out as profitable ventures. Traditionally, it takes three to five years for new businesses to become profitable.

3. **Control.** Many people starting their own business state that they want to take more control of business decisions than their current position allows. Others know that they aren't satisfied working for someone else.

4. **Flexibility.** Many small business owners appreciate the work/life balance that owning their own business affords. Many also feel working in a small business is more rewarding than working for a larger company. Small business owners believe their companies offer less bureaucracy and more flexibility than larger firms. With fewer channels to go through when decisions need to be made, small business owners can react more quickly to take advantage of immediate opportunities. In addition, small business owners say running their own business allows them the flexibility to adjust their work to their particular situations.

5. **Unemployment.** Whereas most individuals start their own businesses for the reasons mentioned previously, some are pushed into starting their own businesses because they have no other employment opportunities. "Life begins when you get fired," was exactly the case for Bruce Freeman, owner of ProLine Communications, Inc. Three months after being fired, he couldn't think of what to do next. Then, encouraged by a friend, Bruce started his own business. His first client was a company he worked with in his previous job. Now, over 10 years later, he's making more money than he ever could have in his old job.[19]

OFF THE MARK

iSmell

The dot-com era produced many businesses that just couldn't get off the ground. One example was the iSmell, a product that plugged into a computer's USB port and promised to enhance a user's Web surfing experience by generating different scents. Using the iSmell, you could smell a new perfume before buying it or conjure up the smell of a ballpark while playing a baseball videogame. Unfortunately, iSmell never made it beyond the prototype stage. Its parent company, DigiScents, shut its doors in 2001.[20]

$\int$ tarting a small business is a sizable challenge, as Allison can attest to. It didn't solve all her problems; in fact, it might have created a few more, but she is glad to be in control of her own situation. It is a challenge to which many entrepreneurs, looking for their piece of the American dream, enthusiastically rise. For Allison, having a flexible schedule, doing what she loves to do, and making money doing it made the risks of starting her home organizing business worth taking. ■

Entrepreneurs and the American Dream pp. 137–143

W ho would ever have thought that blending Mexican, Brazilian, and Asian cuisines and $30,000 would lead to 50 restaurants in four states 20 years later? Certainly not the Wahoo brothers. If you ask them, it just kind of happened. The Wahoo brothers—Wing, Ed, and Mingo—were raised above their parents' Chinese restaurant. They took the concept of a fish taco—a staple they had grown to love while surfing in Mexico—and enhanced it with their favorite Brazilian and Asian dishes. Combined with a casual, surf-inspired decor, their concept was well received by the local southern California crowd. The brothers brought in another partner to help manage their second location, and the business quickly took off from there.[21] So, what qualities do the Wahoo brothers have to take their small fish taco eatery and turn it into a multimillion-dollar business? What makes them entrepreneurs? ■

Massey/Newscom

We've all heard of Starbucks, Nike, and Microsoft, but you probably don't associate these big-name companies with small business. At one point, however, each of these companies originated as a small business. They were all started by **entrepreneurs**—people who assume the risk of creating, organizing, and operating a business. Not all small businesses are entrepreneurial. What makes a new venture entrepreneurial is that the idea behind the business is innovative or change oriented. Entrepreneurs most often start a business to satisfy a need in the market that is not being adequately fulfilled. This area of need is called an **opportunity niche.**

Like the Wahoo brothers, the McDonald brothers who started the famous fast-food restaurant spotted an opportunity niche. Realizing that the hamburger was the best seller in their California restaurant, they created an assembly line that allowed them to produce burgers quickly and inexpensively, and business boomed. It expanded even more when businessman and entrepreneur Ray Kroc, who was selling milkshake machines in California, convinced the brothers not only to use his milkshake machines but also to let him open another McDonald's restaurant in Chicago. Seeing the opportunity niche in fast food franchising, Kroc later bought the McDonald's restaurants from the McDonald brothers. The company now operates over 32,000 restaurants in 117 countries, generating more than $27 billion in revenue annually.[22]

2 What are the traits of an effective entrepreneur, and what are the different types of entrepreneurs?

The Traits of Successful Entrepreneurs

What are the traits of successful entrepreneurs? Businessman Wayne Huizenga started Waste Management, Inc., a leader in the waste and environmental services industry, by buying a single garbage truck in 1968. He expanded the company by buying other trash collection services, and by 1983 the company had grown into the largest of its kind in the United States. But Huizenga didn't stop there. He also started Blockbuster Video, the video rental company, as well as AutoNation, the behemoth automotive dealer.[23] How can some entrepreneurs like Wayne Huizenga begin successful businesses, while others have a difficult time getting their ideas off the ground? How do successful entrepreneurs see an opportunity niche and know exactly what they need to do to seize the opportunity and succeed?

Although luck and timing play a large role in entrepreneurial success, research has also shown that successful entrepreneurs have the following characteristics:

1. Are innovative to realize a vision
2. Take risks
3. Are motivated to succeed
4. Are flexible and self-directed
5. Work well with others and possess good leadership skills
6. Are "system thinkers"—view the whole process rather than just its individual pieces

How are entrepreneurs innovative? Successful entrepreneurs see problems to be solved or opportunities that aren't being addressed in the marketplace; they recognize opportunity niches. They also make improvements to existing products or systems, or they introduce something new and make profitable solutions out of problems. Renowned management and business thinker Peter Drucker noted that successful entrepreneurs "exploit change as an opportunity for a different business or a different service."[24] For example, Henry Ford turned his knowledge of engines into the first "horseless carriage," which he later improved to become the Model T.[25] His improvement was not only in creating a new machine but also in developing an assembly-line process by which his company could make multiple automobiles more efficiently. Ford's innovative assembly process became the standard for efficient manufacturing.

Think about other entrepreneurs and the innovation behind their success. Mark Zuckerberg changed how we communicate and network with others by launching Facebook. Steve Jobs, arguably one of the greatest innovators of modern times, helped to bring personal computing to the home with the introduction of the Apple computer, and more recently changed how we listen to music with the iPod and iTunes, how we use a mobile phone with the iPhone and mobile apps, and how we access media information and entertainment with the iPad. Entrepreneurial doesn't just mean that you start from scratch. Obviously, Jobs had the powerful resources of Apple behind him when he launched his most recent innovations, but nonetheless his products were innovative and radically changed very traditional processes. ■ **FIGURE 5.5** lists some other important innovations by entrepreneurs in the twentieth century.[26]

■ **FIGURE 5.5**
Entrepreneurial Innovations

FM radio	Polaroid camera	Super computer	Portable computer	Digital X-ray	Portable MP3 player	Consumer GPS devices	Apple iPhone
1933	1947	1958	1981	1983	1998	2000	2007

How do entrepreneurs take risks? Being an entrepreneur involves risk: the risk of failure, the risk of losing one's career or reputation, and, of course, financial risks. Because entrepreneurs are often creating new and innovative products, the processes they develop often are untried and therefore involve risk. Successful entrepreneurs are aware of these risks, recognize that they can influence events but do not have complete control over them, and are willing to accept the knowledge that they may fail. Successful entrepreneurs therefore take calculated risks—that is, they consider the likelihood of success before deciding whether to take a particular risk.

What makes entrepreneurs motivated to succeed? Entrepreneurs are motivated by many different factors. Some entrepreneurs are motivated to provide for themselves or their families. These individuals may be driven to pursue multiple ventures before uncovering a successful idea. Other entrepreneurs are motivated to succeed by the personal fulfillment they feel after successfully launching a business.

The entrepreneur's keen desire to tackle challenges and obtain success has led one entrepreneur, Ted Kennedy (not the former Massachusetts senator), to start a company rooted in this notion. Kennedy noticed that many participants in the Ironman Triathlon Challenge were corporate executives. He also noticed that these executive triathletes sought above-average accommodations, as well as enjoyed meeting and socializing with other CEOs prior to and during their competition. So Kennedy formed CEO Challenges, providing sporting competitions specifically for the CEO. Although Kennedy began his company focusing on triathlons, he has since expanded it to offer cycling, hockey, fishing, golf, sailing, tennis, and other competitive adventures to executives. The company has also expanded to hold challenges in Canada and Europe.

Why do successful entrepreneurs need to be flexible and self-directed? Because entrepreneurial ventures are subject to uncertainty and risk, entrepreneurs need to be able to react quickly to new and unexpected situations, such as the sudden and unexpected downturn in the financial markets in 2009. Jason Hogg, co-founder and CEO of Revolution Money, Inc., a financial services company (now a part of American Express), credits his company's success during the unsettled economic times to being "flexible and creative." He had to quickly reevaluate his business plan and develop new partnerships to continue to grow his business during the recession.[27] And because entrepreneurs are their own bosses, they need to be able to make their own decisions, such as the decision to sell to American Express in 2009. An entrepreneur must be able to wear many hats, acting not only as executive but also sales manager, financial director, secretary, and mailroom person.

Why are people skills and leadership skills important to entrepreneurs? They may come up with the initial idea behind their businesses, but entrepreneurs rarely work by themselves. As much as they have the capacity to wear many hats, at some point most entrepreneurs need other people with complementary skills to join them in their ventures. If their businesses expand, they must hire employees and other managers to help them run it. Leadership and communication skills are therefore important traits of successful entrepreneurs who must motivate others to feel as passionately about the entrepreneurial enterprise as they do.

What does it mean for entrepreneurs to be "system" thinkers? Although entrepreneurs develop companies from an idea, they must focus on the entire process of turning their idea into a business to succeed. Successful entrepreneurs are able to see the whole picture when they establish their businesses. They determine how to resolve a problem or capitalize on an opportunity by developing a solid plan, including producing, financing, marketing, and distributing the service or the product. For example, Pete Slosberg, founder of Pete's Brewing Company, recognized the rise in popularity of microbreweries and brewpubs around the country. Slosberg saw the opportunity and began the process of creating his company with not only an idea but also a system: create a to create a fantastic-tasting beer, an eye-catching label, and a name that sticks in people's minds. Slosberg wanted to have the name and label encourage folks to try the beer once, and the taste of the beer be good enough so people would continue to buy the beer.[28] In 1998, Pete's Brewing Company had $19 million in sales before being sold to the Gambrinus Company.

Types of Entrepreneurs

Are there different types of entrepreneurs? Beyond traditional entrepreneurs described in the previous sections, other entrepreneurial categories have begun to crop up:

1. Lifestyle entrepreneurs
2. Micropreneurs
3. Home-based entrepreneurs
4. Internet entrepreneurs
5. Growth entrepreneurs
6. Intrapreneurs
7. Social entrepreneurs and social intrapreneurs

Let's take a look at each of these types.

What are lifestyle entrepreneurs? Lifestyle entrepreneurs look for more than profit potential when they begin their businesses. Some lifestyle entrepreneurs are looking for freedom from corporate bureaucracy or the opportunity to work at home or in a location other than an office. Others are looking for more flexibility in work hours or travel schedules. Take Richard Dahl, for example. He is traveling around the country in a travel trailer selling more than 300 items, including his flagship water filter system at trailer parks, campgrounds, and motor home shows.[29] His business, the RV Water Filter Store, allows him to fulfill his passion of traveling around the country with this wife.

What are micropreneurs? Micropreneurs start their own businesses but are satisfied with keeping their businesses small in an effort to achieve a balanced lifestyle. For example, a micropreneur might open a single restaurant and be satisfied with running only that one restaurant, instead of expanding as Ray Kroc did with the McDonald brothers' restaurant. Micropreneurs have no aspirations of growing large and/or hiring hundreds or thousands of employees. Businesses such as dog-walking services, painters, and special-occasion cake bakers would all be considered micropreneurial opportunities.

What are home-based entrepreneurs? As the name suggests, **home-based entrepreneurs** are entrepreneurs who run their businesses out of their homes. Home-based entrepreneurs are often parents who like being able to stay home with their children and run a business. Sheena Edwards was a stay-at-home mom who was looking for a creative outlet. Sheena decided to start making crystal-embellished women's flip-flops and now runs Lizzie Lou Shoes from her home. Production of the shoes is managed by Sheena's cousin in New Delhi, India. "I love owning my own business, as it gives me the creative outlet I crave while still allowing me to be home with my kids and not miss a thing (with the exception of sleep!)," says Sheena.[30] Lizzie Lou Shoes is one of the top 100 winners of Startup Nation's 2011 Leading Moms in Business competition. In addition to offering lifestyle advantages, such as being able to stay at home with children, home-based businesses offer several financial advantages. Staying at home eliminates commuting time and costs, as well as office rent and other overhead expenses. Also home-based entrepreneurs can take advantage of deducting from their taxes a part of their rent or mortgage payment, depreciation, property taxes, insurance, utilities, household maintenance, and home repairs and improvements.

What are Internet entrepreneurs? Advances in technology have spawned another type of entrepreneur, the **Internet entrepreneur**, who creates businesses that operate solely online. The early 1990s saw the first group of Internet entrepreneurs, but most did not survive the dot-com era. Now, however, with the advent of Web 2.0 technologies (such as blogging and social networking), smartphone apps, contextual Web-based advertising (such as Google Ads) that help to provide revenue, along with faster broadband connections, a greater number of successful online businesses are being established. Some of the most famous Internet entrepreneurs include Mark Zuckerberg (Facebook), Jeff Bezos (Amazon), Pierre Omidyar and John Donahoe (eBay), Sergey Brin and Larry Page (Google), and Jimmy Wales (Wikipedia).

Youth may have an advantage in this entrepreneurial genre because success requires little investment, some spare time, and a good understanding of what their peers are looking for. For example, David and Catherine Cook and their older brother Geoff started MeetMe (formerly myYearbook.com) over spring break in 2005. The social networking site invites members to meet new people through playing games, chatting, and sending virtual gifts purchased with Lunch Money, the site's virtual currency. Members are also given the opportunity to donate Lunch Money to their favorite charity through their charity application. MeetMe has over 1 billion page views on mobile devices, and 1.2 billion page views on the Web each month. In 2010, the social networking company had revenue of $23.7 million.[31]

A simple homework assignment for a class at Stanford University in 2007, now known as the "Facebook Class," spawned many successful companies and ideas. By just asking student teams to create applications for the popular social networking site, the class of 75 students created apps that engaged a total of 16 million users in just 10 weeks.[32] Many of the apps had a short lifespan, but their creators went on to create other apps for the newly released iPhone, or to begin other Internet businesses such as the social networking site Friend.ly, or have sold their businesses to companies like Zynga.

What are growth entrepreneurs? **Growth entrepreneurs** strive to create fast-growing businesses and look forward to expansion. The companies that these types of entrepreneurs create are known as *gazelles*. Typically, a gazelle business has at least 20 percent sales growth every year for five years, starting with a base of at least $100,000.[33] It is hard to recognize a gazelle business during its rapid growth period, though companies such as eBay and Google can clearly be identified in retrospect as having been gazelles in their early years. Gazelle companies also help the economy. Although they only represent approximately 1 percent of all businesses, they generate about 10 percent of all new jobs.[34]

Catherine Cook, at the age of 17, co-created the wildly successful website MeetMe with her older brothers Dave and Geoff during spring break.

What are intrapreneurs? You don't necessarily have to leave your company to have an entrepreneurial experience. Some companies are fostering **intrapreneurs**—employees who work in an entrepreneurial way within an organizational environment. At the home appliance company Whirlpool, for example, developing intrapreneurs is an important part of corporate success. The company's success depends on producing creative solutions to household problems. Instead of relying solely on the traditional research and development (R&D) process, Whirlpool management is tapping the creative

Catherine Cook/Newscom

juices of their employees by encouraging them to generate ideas that will enhance the company's existing products. Although employees are not separately compensated for their ideas, they are pleased that the company asks for their ideas and have responded enthusiastically. By the end of the first year of the program, 60 ideas were in the prototype stage, and 190 were close to entering the marketplace.[35,36] Other examples of products generated from employee innovation include Post-it Notes, the Sony PlayStation, the Java programming language, and ELIXIR guitar strings.[37]

What are social entrepreneurs and social intrapreneurs? Just as a business entrepreneur seeks to create innovative solutions that satisfy an unfulfilled corporate or consumer need, the idea can be extended to society at large. **Social entrepreneurs** set out to create innovative solutions in the social sector; they are entrepreneurs with a social mission.[38] For example, Mimi Silbert founded Delancey Street Foundation, a residential education center that teaches substance abusers, former felons, and the homeless the necessary skills to enable them to lead productive lives. The foundation runs on income generated by businesses created by the foundation that act as the training ground for program participants. It has been called the most successful rehabilitation project in the United States.[39]

Similarly, **social intrapreneurs** build and develop ventures within a company that are designed to identify and solve large-scale social problems.[40] In an effort to create a "social corporate enterprise," eBay, for example, gathered 40 employees to discuss ways to make eBay a more environmentally aware company. What resulted was a myriad of projects, ranging from rideshare programs and community gardens to the largest solar installation in San Jose, California, at their corporate headquarters.[41]

Entrepreneurial Teams

What if I don't have all the skills to be an entrepreneur? Look at the list of entrepreneurial traits described earlier in this section. In addition to being innovative, motivated, and self-directed, an entrepreneur initially may need to fill the role of executive, sales manager, financial director, secretary, and mailroom person. If you don't possess all of these traits, it doesn't preclude you from starting your own business and becoming a successful entrepreneur. If you have an idea and really want to make it happen, you might want to reach out to others who can do what you can't or don't want to do and assemble an entrepreneurial team.

What is an entrepreneurial team? An **entrepreneurial team** is a group of qualified individuals with varied experiences and skills that come together to form a new venture. The skills of the entrepreneurial team members complement one another so that as a group, the team has the necessary skills and traits to manage a successful project. For example, Lin Miao, Andrew Bachman, Lucas Brown, and Lee Brown came together to form Tatto Media, an Internet marketing company that "changes how advertisers pay for display advertising." The company's success is in part due to the "genius of Lin, and the design and engineering skills of Luc and Lee." Andrew Bachman, the president, confesses, "I never would have had a product to sell because I can't see it like Lin sees it, and I can't build it like Luc and Lee build it."[42]

Entrepreneurial teams are also great for those who want to run their own businesses but perhaps lack the personal experience. For example, many college and business school students form entrepreneurial teams to get their first project launched. There are several examples of students who met in college and began to work on projects together that turned out to be successful businesses. Students from Stanford University have come together to create well-known companies such as Google, HP, Cisco, Imagen, and Yahoo!. Many schools run entrepreneurial challenges, such as the Big Bang competition at the University of California at Davis. In this year-long program, UC Davis students, alumni, staff, and faculty join forces to construct and test their business plans, which serve as the springboards for new companies. Advanced Enological Closures, is a competition winner that designs a "breathing screw cap" for wine that makes the wine more consistent

Threadless

ON
TARGET

Like many successful entrepreneurs of the twenty-first century, Jack Nickell began his venture when he was a design student. After winning a T-shirt design contest, Nickell invited other artists to submit their designs online to his new website, Threadless.com, and using a social voting system, Nickell printed the best designs on T-shirts. Initially, it took several months for a batch of T-shirts to sell out, but within four years, Threadless was printing out new batches every week and annual sales were reaching $5 million. In 2008, Threadless was featured on the cover of *Inc. Magazine* as "The Most Innovative Small Company in America," and touted as a "perfect example" of an innovative business model called crowdsourcing—new products and ideas generated by those who use the products.

after the bottle has been opened because of the amount of oxygen traditional or synthetic corks allow into a wine bottle.[43]

Perhaps you're part of an entrepreneurial team, an employee in an intrapreneurial company, or prefer to go it alone. Maybe you want to keep your business small or expand it like the Wahoo brothers or McDonald's. Whatever the case, being an entrepreneur is more than just being in business for yourself. Taking advantage of an opportunity niche, riding the bumps along the way with creative solutions, and being a system thinker all describe successful entrepreneurs. Do you have what it takes to be an entrepreneur? Entrepreneurial opportunities exist if you're up to the challenge. ■

Buying Franchises and Existing Businesses pp. 143–149

It was a desired change in lifestyle that prompted Aisha Lawrence to think about starting her own business. She had always dreamed of running her own restaurant, but she didn't have much business background or restaurant experience. What she did have was a lot of tenacity and knowledge of marketing. Additionally, she was a people person—a necessity for restaurant owners. Still, she was unsure of where to begin. Aisha was uncomfortable starting from scratch, as she knew that the risks were way too high to start a restaurant on her own. She felt that she needed the support of someone who had been through the process before. What are her options? Which would be the best route for Aisha to take? ■

© Lon C. Diehl/PhotoEdit

For those who want the opportunity of owning their own business but want to avoid the stress of starting a business completely from scratch, buying an existing business or purchasing a franchise may be a viable alternative. For some, these choices seem like less of a gamble. Franchises are a popular way for people like Aisha to enter the world of small business. Alternatively, there are definite advantages to buying an existing business, especially if it has previously enjoyed a good reputation and has an existing customer base. In this section, we'll look at what it means to buy a franchise. We'll also discuss buying an existing business and molding it into your own.

Franchising Basics

What is a franchise? Franchises have been around a long time. In the United States, Singer Sewing Machines, one of the first franchises, started in 1851. A **franchise** is a method of doing business whereby the business (the **franchisor**) sells its products or services under the company's name to independent third-party operators (the **franchisees**).[44] Aisha would be a franchisee using a franchisor's marketing methods and trademarked goods under the name of the business. In exchange, she would make monthly payments to the franchise.

What kinds of business opportunities are available as franchises? Franchises play an important role in our economy. Over 760,000 franchised businesses are in operation, employing approximately 7.6 million people, with an output of nearly $700 billion.[45] Franchises in the automotive, lodging, and retail products and service industries are forecasted to have the greatest opportunities in growth of number of new establishments and employment opportunities.[46] But franchise opportunities exist in nearly every industry, and many can be run from your home, which lowers the start-up costs because there is no need to purchase or rent real estate. Most can be purchased for less than $100,000.[47] Home-based franchises, such as ServPro, Stratus Building Solutions, Jazzercise, and Matco Tools are among today's top home-based franchises. Additionally, as we discussed in Chapter 4, franchising provides a great opportunity for doing business internationally. For example, the European Franchise Federation estimates that there are over 8,500 distinct franchise brands operating in the EU, nearly three-and-a-half times the number of franchise brands in the United States, and about one-third of U.S. franchisors would consider expanding into the EU.[48]

If you are thinking of purchasing a franchise, you will need to do your homework. There are several sources of helpful information about franchises that you should study before taking the leap. ■ **TABLE 5.1** lists several helpful Web-based resources that you can begin with.

■ TABLE 5.1

Web-Based Resources for Potential Franchisees

The **SBA** and **FranNet** sponsor a site that features a video that explains what franchising is, how to determine if franchising is right for you, and how to select the right franchise.

The **American Franchisee Association** offers advice on buying a franchise, legal resources, and opportunities to network with other franchisees.

The **Federal Trade Commission** provides consumer information on franchise and business opportunities. The publication *Buying a Franchise: A Consumer Guide* outlines the steps to take before selecting a particular franchise, how to shop at a franchise exhibition, and what you should know before signing the franchisor's disclosure document.

Entrepreneur.com's **Franchise Zone** allows users to search a directory of franchising opportunities and provides tips on buying a franchise. This site also ranks the top franchises in terms of growth, cost, global appeal, and other aspects.

The **International Franchise Association** provides answers to frequently asked questions about franchising and resources for potential and current franchisees. This website also hosts a directory of franchising opportunities in various industries.

Source: SBDCNet.org and "Buy a Franchise" from U.S. Small Business Administration. www.sba.gov

Pros and Cons of Franchising

3 What are the advantages and disadvantages of franchising?

What are the advantages of franchising? For many, franchising is an easier, less risky means of starting a business because of the immediate effects of owning a business with an established brand and name. In addition, since the franchisor provides much of the marketing and financial tools needed to run a business, all the franchisee is expected to bring to the table is management and marketing skills, time, and money. There are many other advantages of owning a franchise.

- **It is a proven system of operation.** Instead of wading through the muddy waters of new business ownership by themselves, franchisees benefit from the *collective experience* of the franchise company. The franchisor has determined, through trial and error, the best system of daily operations for the established business. New franchisees can therefore avoid many of the common start-up mistakes made by new business owners because they will be working with standardized products, systems, and financial and accounting systems.
- **There is strength in numbers.** You are not alone when you buy a franchise. Because you belong to a group, you might benefit from economies of scale achieved by purchasing materials, supplies, and services at discounted group rates. In addition, it is often easier to get approved for business loans when running a franchise, as lending institutions often view that there is less risk associated with franchises.
- **Initial training is part of the deal.** The beauty of franchising is that you're in business *for* yourself but not *by* yourself. The franchisor offers initial training to ensure that you have a successful opening. They might offer ongoing training if new products or services are being incorporated into the franchise line.
- **Marketing support is provided.** As a franchisee, you are often given marketing materials generated at the corporate level and have the benefit of any national advertising programs that are created. Although you are expected to run your own local marketing efforts, you have the support of other franchisees in the area to help you in your efforts.
- **Market research is often provided.** Good franchisors do considerable market research and can generally conclude whether there is demand for the product or service in the area before selling the franchisee a franchise. The franchisor should also help to identify the competition and offer strategies to differentiate the franchise from them.

What are the disadvantages of franchising? Although buying a franchise provides the franchisee with many benefits, there are some disadvantages too (see ■ FIGURE 5.6).

- **Lack of control.** There is not much opportunity to contribute creatively to the franchise because the franchisor often controls the look of the store and the product or the service. The franchisee, however, is expected to bring the necessary drive and spirit to make the franchise a success.
- **Start-up and ongoing costs.** Most franchises require an initial investment (see ■ FIGURE 5.7). For example, the initial franchise fee for the very popular Subway is $15,000. Jan-Pro, a commercial

■ **FIGURE 5.6**
Pros and Cons of Franchising

Total Investment: $3,000–$75,500
• Initial Franchise Fee: $500–$1,000
• Royalty Fee: Up to 20%
• Term of Agreement: 5 years
• Renewal Fee: None

Total Investment: $78,600–$238,300
• Initial Franchise Fee: $15,000
• Royalty Fee: 8%
• Term of Agreement: 20 years
• Renewal Fee: None

Total Investment: $950,200–$1,800,000
• Initial Franchise Fee: $45,000
• Royalty Fee: 12.5%
• Term of Agreement: 20 years
• Renewal Fee: $45,000

■ **FIGURE 5.7**
Franchise Costs and Fees
Image Sources: PETER FOLEY/EPA/
Newscom; Finnbarr Webster/Alamy; Ian
Dagnall/Alamy

cleaning franchise company and the fastest growing franchise in the United States, requires just $3,000 to start a unit franchise. Other franchises, such as H&R Block, Jani-King, and Jazzercise, can also be purchased with less than $50,000.[49] Additional start-up costs the franchisee might incur include real estate purchase or rental, equipment purchase or rental, extra signage, and opening inventory. In addition, franchisees must pay a monthly royalty fee to the franchisor, which is typically 6–10 percent. The royalty fees are usually reinvested into the growth of the franchise corporation and are due regardless of how the business is doing. Royalty fees can be a huge overhead expense.

• **Workload.** As with any new business, new franchisees shouldn't expect easy hours. Aisha Lawrence admits that she spends a lot more time running her franchise than she thought she would. However, because she can hire employees to run the day-to-day operations, her time is spent more on the business development and management end of the business.

• **Competition.** Some franchises do not restrict the location or number of their franchise locations. In those instances, franchisees could experience serious competition not only from another company but also from other franchisees in the same franchise organization. In addition, some franchises do not offer geographic or demographic studies of the best location to open a new store and instead may expect the franchisee to have completed a good market analysis and be familiar with the surrounding competition.

• **Share common problems.** If the franchisor or another franchisee is having problems, all franchisees will feel its pain. For example, when a Wendy's restaurant was falsely accused of serving chili with a human thumb mixed in, business in all Wendy's restaurants plummeted.

Franchising Considerations

What are things to watch out for when considering buying a franchise? The most common piece of advice offered to anyone interested in buying a franchise is to do homework up front. Although much of the start-up process is done for you, you are still buying a business that will require your time and money, and it is not guaranteed to succeed. ■ **TABLE 5.2** shows suggested questions to ask the company that you are buying the franchise from and other people who have bought franchises from the company before you take the plunge.

Buying an Existing Business

Are there other ways to start a business besides starting new or buying a franchise? Although buying a franchise is a popular way to begin a business without starting from scratch, another option is to buy an existing business. Just like buying a franchise or starting from scratch, the decision must be well thought-out.

What are the advantages of buying an existing business? Just as with buying a franchise, buying an existing business has certain advantages:

• **Ease of start-up.** It's often simpler to buy an existing business than to start one from scratch. For example, there is a reduction in start-up time and energy if you are purchasing a business that is operational and without serious problems. This means that suppliers, existing staff and management, and equipment and inventory are all in place to help facilitate the transition.

■ **TABLE 5.2**

Questions to Ask Before Buying a Franchise

	Questions to Ask the Franchisor	Questions to Ask Other Franchisees
Competition	• What is the competitive advantage of the good/ service? • What makes the business more attractive to an owner and more attractive to a customer?	• How is your system better than competitors'? • How does your business match up? • Who are your competitors?
Franchise System	• How time tested and standardized is the franchise system? • What franchise system is used, and how does it work? • How long has the franchise been in business, and what improvements have the franchise company made recently?	• How long have you been in business? • Does your location meet your customers' needs? • Who selected the site?
Support and Training	• How much support does the franchisor give the franchisee? • What is the initial and ongoing training? • Are there toll-free help lines, field support, annual meetings, local meetings, purchasing programs, and marketing promotion?	• How is the relationship with the franchisor? • How were the initial and ongoing training, and ongoing support? • How are the marketing, advertising, and promotional programs handled?
Financial Strength	• What are the financial strengths of the company and the experience of management? • How much revenue comes from franchise fees, and how much revenue comes from royalties? • How has the stock performed?	• Are you pleased with earnings? • Is volume growing?
Franchise Relationships	• How important is the franchisee to the franchise? • How can they describe the relationship with the franchisor?	• Have there been lawsuits and/or arbitration? • If so, how have they been resolved? • Do you have second thoughts (would you do this again)? • Would you own more units?

Source: Based on "A Checklist of Questions to Answer Before You Buy a Franchise," PowerHomeBiz.com.

• **Existing customer base.** An operating business may have a satisfied customer base already in place. If no significant changes are made to drive away current customers, the business can continue to run and provide immediate cash flow.

• **Financing opportunities.** If the business has had a positive track record, it might be easier to obtain financing to purchase the existing business.

What are the disadvantages of buying an existing business? There are also disadvantages to buying an existing business:

• **High purchase price.** Because you may need to buy the owner out of the business, the initial purchase price may be high. This can be more than the immediate up-front costs associated with a start-up but not necessarily any different from a franchise. Although you can determine the value of the physical business and its assets, it is more difficult to determine the true value of the previous owner's **goodwill**—the intangible assets represented by a business's name, customer service, employee morale, and other factors—that might be lost with a change in ownership. Often the intangible assets are overvalued, making the business cost more than it is worth.

- **Inheriting the previous owner's mistakes.** In addition, with a preexisting business, you are sometimes stuck with the previous owner's mistakes. This means you might inherit dissatisfied customers, bad debt, and unhappy distributors or purchasing agents. You'll need to work to change the minds of people who have had a bad experience with the previous ownership.

- **Unknowns in transition.** There is no guarantee that existing employees, management, customers, suppliers, or distributors will continue to work with the business once new ownership takes over. If the staff does stay, you might be inheriting unanticipated problems.

What do I need to do before I buy a business? Existing businesses are sold for many reasons. Before buying an existing business, make sure you perform **due diligence**—which is conducting a reasonable investigation into the business history, operating and financial records, contracts, and valuation of the business so that a complete and full understanding of the business is achieved. You want to avoid buying a company with a dissatisfied customer base or with a large amount of unpaid bills or with unfavorable contracts that cannot be renegotiated. ■ **TABLE 5.3** provides a brief checklist of things you should look into before buying a business.

Not all businesses are put up for sale because there are problems. For example, some family-owned businesses run out of family members who want to continue to operate the business. This was the situation that Dan Ratto, a business consultant in Texas, and Chris, his godson in California, came across. Chris knew of a restaurant near his home that was up for sale. The restaurant had been part of a family business for many years, but no one in the family wanted to continue the business, so it was put up for sale. Dan and Chris did their due diligence and came up with an estimate of the restaurant's value. The owner's price was much less than Dan and Chris's estimate, so they scooped up the business. With only a few minor improvements, Dan and his godson exceeded initial sales expectations within the first year of ownership. They have since opened a few other locations and are considering the possibility of franchising the operation in other states.

We started this section with a story about Aisha Lawrence, who had a dream of owning a restaurant. What did she decide? Aisha knew that the risks were way too high to start a restaurant on her own. She considered buying an existing restaurant, but still felt that she didn't have enough experience to handle the demands of a full-service restaurant. Instead, she felt that she could run a small, single-product food business, such as a coffee bar or an ice cream shop, to give her the experience she would need to run her own full-service restaurant someday. Ultimately, Aisha decided that she wanted to open an ice cream franchise. There were many to choose from, so she spent months doing product research, visiting and tasting the various frozen treats offered by most of the ice cream franchises.

■ TABLE 5.3

Things to Consider Before Buying a Business

Initial Questions to Ask

- Why is the business for sale?
- What do current customers say?
- Are there opportunities for growth? How much time does the current owner put into the business?
- Who is the competition?

Due Diligence Checklist

- Get an independent valuation of inventory and equipment.
- Have an accountant review the financial statements for the past three years.
- Have a lawyer analyze pertinent business documents—property leases, employment contracts, and so on.
- Talk to suppliers to see if they will continue to supply the business when ownership changes hands.
- Check for lingering or festering hazardous waste problems. They'll become your responsibility as the new owner.

What's in a Name?

Naming a business should be fun, but it can be stressful, especially if you make some of the more common mistakes:

Mistake 1 Involving friends, family, employees, or clients in the naming decision. The name should communicate the key elements of your business, not the combined efforts of your friends and family.

Mistake 2 Description + Product = Name. Although it might seem catchy at the time, the result of company names that try to marry description with product is forced and often trite. A service franchise named QualiServe or a day spa named TranquiSpa ultimately aren't the right choices.

Mistake 3 Using generic names. Gone are the days when ACME Foods works as a corporate name. Similarly, using names such as Joe's Bar or Smith's Hardware is inadequate. In such highly competitive times, when new products or services are fighting for attention, it is best to choose a more unique name.

Mistake 4 Making up a name. Although using generic names may not be good, be careful to avoid names that are obscure, hard to pronounce, or hard to spell unless there is solid market research behind it.

Mistake 5 Using geographic names. Unless you plan to stay local, including a specific geographic name may imply that you won't go beyond that regional territory.

TIP: You might need to hire a company to create a name for you. Acura, Flixx, and Compaq are all names that were created by experts.

Whether you buy an existing business or franchise or begin a business of your own, you'll be joining a large group of small business owners who make a significant contribution to the U.S. economy. ∎

The Risks of Small Businesses and Where to Get Help pp. 149–154

When Roger Sherman heard rumors that the company he was working for was considering filing bankruptcy, he felt he would be better off on his own. Roger took advantage of an early retirement package and, together with his life savings, began to fiddle around with energy-efficient, solar-powered scooters and bicycles. But even Roger's well-thought-out business plan couldn't predict

alphaspirit/Fotolia

the sudden and massive downturn in the economy that has kept his business from really taking off. Roger was concerned he might not be able to make payroll or keep all his employees. What should he do? ∎

In this section, we'll talk about the risks facing small businesses and where owners can go for help.

Why So Many Small Businesses Fail

What are the risks of owning my own business? Starting a business is a lot of hard work and comes with no guarantee for success. As shown in ∎ **FIGURE 5.8**,

> **4** Why is a business plan crucial to small business success, and what factors lead to small business failure?

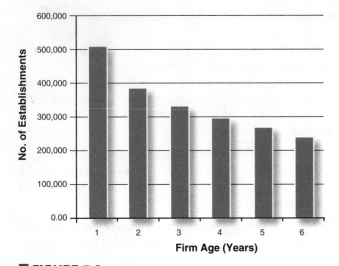

■ FIGURE 5.8
Average Survival Rate of
Small Business Start-ups

nearly one-fourth of all start-ups fail in the first year, and two-thirds survive only two years, with just over one-half surviving after five years of operation.[50]

While many feel the benefits of owning their own businesses are worth the risks, it is important to be aware of the situations that potentially can be fatal to a new business. Reasons for failure include the following:

- Accumulating too much debt
- Inadequate management
- Poor planning
- Unanticipated personal sacrifices

Let's examine each risk in more detail.

What causes excessive debt accumulation? One reason many new businesses fail is that they accumulate too much debt too soon. Most begin a new business by borrowing funds. Regardless of whether the loan comes from a bank, an outside investor, or a credit card company, if the new business does not generate revenue quickly enough to begin to pay back the loans, the burden of paying the debt balance plus additional interest as well as normal operating expenses can cause an owner to become further entrenched in a potentially unrecoverable situation. The situation might also tempt the owner to take out more loans to keep the business running. What's worse is that some business owners borrow against their personal assets, putting them at risk of not only losing their business, but potentially forcing them to file personal bankruptcy as well.

How does poor fiscal management lead to failure? Although entrepreneurs and small business owners are good at coming up with ideas, they may not be great at managing the books. The fact that so many businesses fail due to high levels of debt can be a sign of poor financial and business management. It is important that financial statements and budgets are created and adhered to honestly and accurately each month, accounts receivable are religiously collected, and accounts payable are aggressively managed. Take Jodi Gallagher, for example. Jodi owns a business that designs and creates lingerie. In an effort to get her product into as many stores as possible, Jodi was lenient on the terms of collection. Rather than insisting on immediate payment, she extended stores at least 30 days credit, and, as a result, it took her months to collect. Realizing that her mistake almost cost her business, Jodi no longer extends credit.[51]

What other types of improper management lead to failure? For some new owners, an early surge in sales proves to be overwhelming. This was a large part of many dot-com busts in the late 1990s. Many successful e-commerce businesses did not plan for rapid growth and therefore did not have sufficient inventory to fulfill orders when they came in. They also didn't take into consideration the subsequent impact this would have on dealers and retailers who were a part of their distribution channels.

Many business owners ignore the signs of a business beginning to fail or attribute the failure to the wrong reasons. Good management stays on top of all aspects of the business, remains objective, and makes the tough decisions when necessary.

How important is planning to a business's success or failure? Large debt accumulation and poor business management happen after the business is up and running. One of the biggest reasons businesses fail is that there was no formal plan in place to begin with. The old adage "failing to plan is planning to fail" certainly applies to starting a business. Many budding business owners, in the excitement of starting something new, neglect to take the boring and difficult but necessary steps

■ **FIGURE 5.9**
A Business Plan Outlines a Company's Goals and Strategies

of building an effective business plan. A **business plan** is a formal document that states the goals of the business as well as the plan for reaching those goals.

As shown in ■ **FIGURE 5.9**, the plan includes the company's mission statement, history, and the qualifications of the owners and management team and any resources they might have to contribute to the business. It includes a marketing plan, an operational plan, a financial plan, and a risk analysis, as well as identifies the competition and highlights opportunities for success. (You'll learn more about creating successful business plans in Mini Chapter 2.)

Neglecting to consider any of these factors can doom a business from the start; writing a business plan forces you to think through some of the more difficult aspects of the business up front. Poor planning can lead to unnecessary spending. Equally, a well-written and thought-out business plan can lead to greater financing options. Success is a lot more difficult without adequate funding.

New businesses also may fail when owners do not adequately anticipate the many personal sacrifices—financial, time, and otherwise—that new business owners are forced to make. For example, the cost of health insurance and retirement accounts for the owner and employees falls solely on the shoulders of the new business owner. Sometimes, in order to keep the business running, the expense of health insurance and long-term retirement funding gets postponed. Additionally, the amount of time and effort owners must invest in the business, as well as the necessity to take on multiple responsibilities, makes running your own business not for the faint of heart.

Getting Help

Where do small business owners go for advice? Most new business owners are just that—new. Because they haven't experienced much of what they will encounter, knowing when and where to go for help, a second opinion, or just advice can make all the difference. There are several sources of help and advice that a small business owner can turn to (see ■ **FIGURE 5.10**).

5 What resources are available to provide assistance and guidance to small business owners?

- **The Small Business Administration.** As noted earlier, the SBA is an independent agency of the U.S. government. Its sole purpose is to cater to the

SBA

- www.sba.org
- Sole purpose is to cater to the needs of small businesses. Provides counseling, workshops, small loans.

SCORE

- www.score.org
- Volunteer organization of retired executives who offer workshops and counseling to small businesses at no cost.

Entrepreneurs Organization

- www.eonetwork.org
- Offers industry-related conferences and seminars, and help to connect business owners with industry experts for individual mentoring.

National Business Incubators Association

- www.nbia.org
- Provides start-ups with information, education, advocacy, and networking resources.

■ **FIGURE 5.10**
Small Business Support Websites

needs of small businesses. The SBA offers assistance in the legalities associated with beginning and operating a business as well as education and training, financial assistance, disaster assistance, and counseling. The SBA holds events in major cities in all states, such as workshops in financial analysis, creating a business plan, and launching a business. It also offers free online courses and coordinates links to academic institutions that offer private online training. The SBA also acts as an advocate for small business owners to national and state policymakers. It works to reduce regulatory requirements and maximize benefits that small businesses receive from the government.

- **SCORE.** The nearly 11,000 volunteers who comprise the SBA's **Service Corps of Retired Executives (SCORE)** offer workshops and counseling to small businesses at no cost. The volunteers are currently working in or have been in the field and can therefore provide advice to new or existing small business owners. They review business plans, help with tax planning, and offer new ideas and fresh insights. Some SCORE success stories include Vermont Teddy Bear, Vera Bradley Designs, and Jelly Belly Candy.

- **Other mentoring sources.** SCORE is not the only resource new business owners can turn to for mentors. Industry-related conferences or seminars often present new business owners with opportunities to find others who can serve as sounding boards and guides. In addition, other organizations, such as the Entrepreneurs Organization (EO), connect business owners with experts in their industry for individual mentoring. Although EO is for those who are currently in a viable operation (its requirements are that you must be a founder, cofounder, owner, or controlling shareholder of a business with a minimum of $1 million in annual gross sales and younger than 50 years old), such mentoring services can be helpful to second-stage small-business owners.

What kind of training is appropriate for small business owners?

Before jumping into any endeavor, it's always good to have some experience or training. Although many entrepreneurs have advanced degrees in business, that level of formal education is often not necessary. If you are currently in college, look for internship opportunities in your industry of interest. Some internships are with big, well-known companies, but smaller companies are beginning to realize that hiring interns can be a cost-effective way to get some help. Internships can be seen as an extended "dating period" between employer and candidate, reducing the risk on both sides of making the wrong long-term decision.

Most community colleges offer business classes for credit, or noncredit community education classes that are taught by industry professionals. Trisha Wosny had been an elementary education teacher for many years but had always wanted to own her own business. Because she didn't know where to start, a friend told her about programs offered at her local community college for women business owners, small business start-ups, and management. A year later, she opened Adornment Expressive Accessories, a specialty retail shop offering unique purses and women's accessories. In addition to formal classroom training, you can also obtain hands-on experience by interning or working part-time for a company in a related field; if no opportunities exist in a related field, working for any start-up company can give you experience on running a small company.

Where can small business owners go for support services? One of the biggest overhead costs for many new businesses is the support services required to run the business. **Business incubators** are organizations that support start-up businesses by offering administrative services, technical support, business networking, sources of financing, and more that a group of start-up companies share. Business incubators are often run by two- and four-year colleges, universities, and technical schools, and many are sponsored by economic development organizations, cities, or counties.

There are several benefits to incubation beyond sharing a receptionist and a photocopy machine. Incubators offer the support and advice that many start-ups lack when operating on their own. Eventually, participants must leave the incubator, but beginning in an incubation program increases the success rate of a start-up company by as much as 90 percent.[52] The primary goal of a business incubator is to produce successful businesses that are able to operate independently and become financially viable in the early years when they are most vulnerable to failure. Incubators create a synergistic environment where companies can act as peer-to-peer mentors, sharing both successes and failures. Incubators also lend legitimacy to a beginning company as well as a more professional atmosphere than someone's home office. The success rate suggests that incubators are meeting their goal.

Incubators can be either private organizations or public services. Over the past few decades, many cities as well as developed and developing countries have started public business incubators, often in conjunction with universities and research institutions, to promote new business development. For example, the National Science Foundation has created Innovation Corps—a $5 million incubator for student entrepreneurs—and Rensselaer Polytechnic Institute runs one of the oldest incubator programs in the country.

What other options exist for small business advice and assistance? As noted earlier, starting up a small business requires owners to take on multiple roles, acting not only as the CEO but also the COO, the CFO, and any other position that may need to be filled. Many owners quickly realize that their strengths lie in only one or a few of these areas and therefore seek assistance from others. One option is to team up with *partners* who offer the company strengths that the new owner does not possess, who in turn share in its profits and liabilities. Forming an advisory board is another option. An **advisory board** is a group of individuals who offer guidance to the new business owner. Such boards are similar to boards of directors in publicly held companies except that they generally do not have the authority to make decisions.

Does where I locate my business make a difference in the type of help I can get? In most cases, new business owners look for a location that is suitable for their business, has good traffic flow, is safe, and so on. However, in an effort to build up and even resuscitate communities throughout the United States, federal and state governments have established **enterprise zones**, geographic areas targeted for economic revitalizing. Almost every state has some form of enterprise zone program. In addition, the federal government has so far designated a total of 172 enterprise communities and empowerment zones across the United States. These designations are based on various criteria, including population, poverty rates, and economic distress. Businesses receive generous tax benefits for locating and hiring in these enterprise zones. Given the success of many businesses established in enterprise zones, the economic benefits companies receive when they locate in an enterprise zone outweigh the risk of locating in a distressed area. And the state also wins with the creation of new jobs and new businesses.

Remember Roger Sherman? When he found he had troubles with his small business, Roger decided to consult with a SCORE volunteer and took advantage of SBA services. Many new business owners think they can't afford professional advice, so they rely on their own efforts, advice from friends and family, and trial and error. Often, they find that it takes more than a good idea and hard work to make a business successful. Knowing all the resources available to fledgling businesses can help entrepreneurs avoid making the mistakes that eventually lead to the demise of their businesses. Careful financial decision making, savvy management, meticulous planning, and the willingness to make significant personal sacrifices all play key roles in creating a successful business. Knowing when, where, and how to ask for help is also a critical factor to success. ■

Financing Considerations pp. 154–157

Fred DeLuca began his sandwich shop in 1965 when he was 17. He had just graduated from high school and was worried about how he was going to pay for college with his $1.25 per hour minimum wage job at a local hardware store. A family friend, Dr. Peter Buck, suggested that Fred open a sandwich shop. All he needed to do was to rent a shop, build a counter, buy some food, and make the sandwiches. Customers would come in and pay; then Fred could pay his suppliers and still have enough money to pay for college. Dr. Buck was so sure this would work that he gave Fred $1,000 to begin. Four decades later, Subway is one of the largest privately held businesses, with restaurants around the world.[53] ■

Although Fred started with a loan from a family friend, there are other means for entrepreneurs to finance their new ventures before going to more formal financing arrangements. In this section, we'll present the many sources of funding available to small business owners, and we'll discuss the problems associated with some of them.

Eric Piermont/Newscom

Cash and Credit

Where can I get the money to start a business? Most new ventures need capital to purchase inventory, secure a physical location, and begin some modest marketing efforts. Often, new business owners must make do with whatever sources of financing are available, sometimes just what is in his or her own pocket. When entrepreneurs start a business with little capital, they are said to be using **bootstrap financing.** This includes financing with using your own money, borrowing funds from family and friends, and possibly trading services and products with vendors or clients. These informal funding options may be enough to start the business.

Is it reasonable to use crowdfunding sites to raise capital? Sites like Kickstarter and Indiegogo have popularized a new type of start-up funding known

6 What are the potential benefits and drawbacks of each major source of small business financing?

as *crowdfunding*. Entrepreneurs put togther a detailed explanation of their project or business and ask for funding from the Internet community. Typically, specialty products are offered as thank you's for different levels of contribution, for example the chance to purchase the product in a special edition color or even a meeting with the designer. People supporting a Kickstarter business do not own any part of the new business and are not guaranteed that it will be successful—they are simply making a donation. The Pebble Watch is a famous example. The Kickstarter site for this digital watch was looking to raise $100,000 in one month and ended up with over $10 million.

Friends and family are generally go-to financing options for new business owners because, unlike banks, they often do not require a high rate of return or generally do not demand that the business turn a quick profit. However, it is important when borrowing from friends and family that you treat them as professionally as possible. Make sure you give them a document with an indication of how you intend to pay them back and some sort of a contingency plan if things go wrong. In addition, they should be kept informed of any risks of the venture—up front and ongoing. Other means of bootstrap financing include using *trade credit*, *factoring*, and *leasing*. We will discuss these options in Chapter 15.

Should I use credit cards to finance my business? Credit cards offer a convenient way to obtain funds quickly, especially with some of the zero percent financing options available. If used wisely, credit cards are a convenient means of financing short-term needs. However, credit cards should be used only if you can pay the balance *completely* every month. If the balance is not paid off completely every month, the interest charged on unpaid balances can grow quickly due to interest rates ranging from 18 to 25 percent. Over time, you're paying interest on any unpaid balances as well as interest on any carry-over interest, which quickly can become a huge financial burden.

Small Business Loans and Grants

What if I need more money than what I can provide myself? For larger amounts, new business owners sometimes borrow against their own assets, such as the equity in their homes or against their retirement accounts. However, this is a risky practice since the consequences of the business failing are personally devastating. Bailing out a failing business with your life savings or home equity has caused some to file personal bankruptcy and even lose their homes.

If you're purchasing an existing business or a franchise, banks and savings and loan institutions often are willing to provide funding. These institutions offer start-up loans and lines of credit (sources of credit that can be drawn on at the borrower's discretion) that help businesses make payroll during slower periods as well as capital loans to buy equipment or machinery. In fact, roughly half of all small businesses use bank loans and lines of credit as part of their financing strategy.

Can I apply for grants to help start my business? Grants are financial awards that are usually offered by federal and state governments and some private organizations. Although grants do not need to be repaid, the application process is quite substantial and includes considerable amounts of paperwork. The biggest hurdle in applying for a grant is writing the proposal. Make sure you understand the grant writing procedure, as many a good submission has not been funded because of an oversight in the grant application. Depending on the nature of your business, federal grants are usually not available, but state governments typically offer grants to small businesses that are in an industry that the state is nurturing to expand in their state economy. Make sure, however, you read through the entire grant application and understand any requirements that may be expected of a grant recipient. Failure to comply with grant requirements will generally result in the grant proceeds being converted to a loan, with interest.

Angel and Venture Capital Financing

What if I need additional sources of funds through investors? There are other sources of funding if you choose not to finance your business with loans or if loans are not an option. For example, businesses can be financed by outside investors such as angel investors, venture capital, or small business investment companies (SBICs).

- **Angel investors.** Angel investors are wealthy individuals who are willing to put up their own money in hopes of a profit return later on. Angel investors fund approximately 30,000 small companies each year, with investments that range between 25,000 to $1 million.[54] Palmer "Pam" Reynolds, founder of Phoenix Textile Corp. in St. Louis, Missouri, attributes her success to an angel investor. Out of work with thirteen years of experience in the textile business, Pam decided to start her own company. If not for an angel investor who put up $250,000, Pam would not be running a $43 million textile company today. Angel investors often provide funding in the earlier stages of a business, when more money is needed than friends and family can or are willing to contribute, but before bringing in the venture capitalists. Angel investors typically have industry experience in the area in which they are investing and can provide guidance and advice. Unlike venture capitalists, angel investors usually do not seek a management position or control of the business. If you don't personally have any rich friends or connections to rich friends, then finding an Angel investor can begin with a simple search on the Internet. There are regional groups, such as New York Angels (New York), The Old Hand (Chicago), and The Professionals (Palo Alto, CA). Social networking sites such as Angel List and Investors' Circle match entrepreneurs to investors.

- **Venture capitalists.** Venture capitalists are the next step in funding a start-up. Venture capital funding is generally sought when the business is more mature, and needs large sources of capital to take the business to the next step. Venture capitalists are corporate entities that use funds from other investors and manage that money by investing it in businesses with a prospect of high growth. Venture capitalists invest in a business in return for some form of equity—a piece of ownership—in the business. Venture capitalists are very picky about the projects in which they invest as they want to minimize the risk of failure. They often look for the potential of a public stock offering; therefore, such financing is generally available only to those businesses that have been operating for several years and have the potential to become larger, publicly owned, regional or national companies. To protect their investments, venture capitalists sometimes require that they play an active role in the management of the company, so business owners must be open to the idea of relinquishing control when they seek venture capital funding.

  Shark Tank, the ABC reality show, offers a peek into the venture capital arena. The show features high-profile investors who listen to a line-up of several new business pitches every week. Although many business ideas are turned down, several receive offers. For example, Mr. Tod's Pie Factory (a pitch in the premier episode in 2009) tripled its sales within the first year after receiving a Shark Tank investment. Mod Mom Furniture owner, Kiersten Hathcock, received $90,000 for a 33% stake in the business and a royalty percentage after sales reach $500,000. The investment took the furniture company out of the owner's garage where she could barely keep up with the rising demand for her modernly designed eco-friendly toyboxes and into a local manufacturing company. Mod Mom Furniture now offers a full line of children's furniture and storage accessories.

- **The SBIC program.** If venture capital is not available or suitable, an alternative is a **small business investment company (SBIC) program**. SBICs are private venture capital firms licensed by the SBA to make equity capital or long-term loans available to small companies. The size of the financing provided by SBICs is generally in the $250,000 to $5 million range.

As mentioned above, a downside of using outside investors is that, to protect their investments, these investors often are looking for some controlling or managerial role in the business. However, it's the investor's level of business acumen that is often necessary to take a business to the next stage of growth, so generally it's a win/win for both owner and investor.

Funding a business is a task fraught with challenges and difficult decisions, as Fred DeLuca would attest. Beginning with just the money offered by a family friend and his own savings, Fred turned a simple sandwich shop into a global franchise operation. But whether the money comes from your own pocket, a friend, or an outside investor, the stakes—personal, professional, and financial—are quite high. Thorough research and careful planning are essential to navigating these tricky issues. By understanding the available options and being prepared to deal with financial predicaments, business owners give themselves the best chance at success. ■

Biz CHAT

Conducting a SWOT Analysis

Recently, you and a fellow engineer friend have been working to boost the performance of hybrid car batteries. As you've learned more about the hybrid car industry, you've discovered a potential unmet need for the service and replacement of these batteries. Some dealerships offer these services, but there may be an opportunity for you to open a specialty shop in your area that focuses solely on these batteries. Can you become the Donald Trump of hybrid car batteries?

CHAPTER 5
SUMMARY

MyBizLab

Go to **mybizlab.com** to complete the problems marked with this icon ⭐.

1 **What is the role and structure of the small business within the U.S. economy?** (pp. 131–134)

- A **small business** (p. 131) is a business that is independently owned and operated, is not dominant in its field, and has fewer than 500 employees and less than $6.5 million in annual revenue.

- Small businesses are important to the economy for several reasons. They account for more than one-half of America's economic output, help foster innovation, supply larger companies with products and services that larger companies do not or cannot supply themselves, supply products and services to consumers that large companies cannot or will not provide, and employ approximately 50 percent of the private workforce.

2 **What are the traits of an effective entrepreneur, and what are the different types of entrepreneurs?** (pp. 138–142)

- An **entrepreneur** (p.137) is someone who assumes the risk of creating, organizing, and operating a business.

- Entrepreneurs are innovative, risk-taking individuals who are motivated to succeed and who are flexible and self-directed. They work well with people, possess good leadership skills, and are "system thinkers."

- Not all entrepreneurs are the same: **lifestyle entrepreneurs** (p. 140) look for a business that matches their desired lifestyle, **micropreneurs** (p. 140) are satisfied with keeping the business small to achieve a balanced lifestyle, **home-based entrepreneurs** (p. 140) run their businesses out of their homes, and **Internet entrepreneurs** (p. 141) run their businesses strictly online. **Growth entrepreneurs** (p. 141) strive to create fast-growing businesses and look forward to expansion, and **social entrepreneurs** (p. 142) start businesses with a social mission in mind. Lastly, **intrapreneurs** (p. 141) are entrepreneurs who work in an entrepreneurial way within an organizational environment.

3 **What are the advantages and disadvantages of franchising?** (pp. 145–146)

- A **franchise** (p. 144) is a method of doing business whereby the business sells a company's products or services under the company's name to independent third-party operators.

- The advantages of franchising include that the business is a proven system of operation, franchises benefit from economies of scale, and the franchisor often offers training and marketing support as well as market research.

- The disadvantages of franchising include a lack of control over the look of the store and the product or service being offered, start-up costs and monthly fees that must be paid to the franchisor, and a heavy workload. Too, franchises will be affected by negative news involving the franchisor or another franchisee of the same company.

4 **Why is a business plan crucial to small business success, and what factors lead to small business failure?** (pp. 149–151)

- A **business plan** (p. 151) outlines the goals and strategies of a company, including company information, marketing plans, financial forecasts, a risk analysis, and an operational plan. Neglecting to consider any of these options can doom a business from the start.

- The reasons new businesses fail include accumulating too much debt, inadequate management, poor planning, and unanticipated personal sacrifices.

5 **What resources are available to provide assistance and guidance to small business owners?** (pp. 151–153)

- The **Small Business Administration** (p. 131) offers assistance in the legalities associated with starting and operating a business as well as education and training, financial assistance, disaster assistance, and counseling.

- **SCORE** (p. 152) volunteers provide free assistance by reviewing business plans, helping with tax planning, and offering new ideas and fresh insights. Other mentoring sources include industry-related conferences and other organizations, such as the EO.

- Business owners can receive formal classroom training at two- and four-year colleges and participate in internships with companies in similar industries for hands-on training.

- **Business incubators** (p. 153) support start-up businesses by offering resources such as administrative services, technical support, business networking, and sources of financing that a group of start-up companies share.

- **Advisory boards** (p. 153) offer guidance to new business owners, but they generally do not have authority to make decisions.
- **Enterprise zones** (p. 153) are geographic areas targeted for economic revitalizing by state and federal governments. Businesses receive generous tax benefits for locating and hiring in these enterprise zones.

6 **What are the potential benefits and drawbacks of each major source of small business financing?** (pp. 154–157)

- The benefit of using cash borrowed from friends and family members is that, unlike banks or other lending institutions, these contacts often do not require a high rate of return or demand to see the business turn a quick profit. However, the potential drawback is that these types of personal loans can sometimes be handled unprofessionally.
- The benefit of credit cards is that they are a convenient means of acquiring short-term cash. However, the risk associated with using credit cards for initial business financing is the high rate of interest charged on unpaid balances.
- When more money is needed than credit cards, friends, or family can provide, another source of financing are small business loans from banks and savings and loan institutions. Lines of credit or start-up loans are also available and can be used to bridge short-term capital needs. Federal and state **grants** (p. 155) may also be available, depending on the nature of the business.
- **Angel investors** (p. 156) are wealthy individuals who are looking to invest in interesting businesses that have a prospect of growth and return. Generally, angel investors do not want a managerial role in their investment and often have a longer timeframe to receive a return on their investment.
- **Venture capitalists** (p. 156) invest in a business in return for some form of equity or ownership in the business. Venture capitalists usually require playing an active role in the management of the company, so this funding option may not be attractive to business owners who aren't open to the idea of relinquishing control.

Key Terms

advisory board   (p. 153)

angel investors   (p. 156)

bootstrap financing   (p. 154)

business incubator   (p. 153)

business plan   (p. 151)

due diligence   (p. 148)

enterprise zones   (p. 153)

entrepreneur   (p. 137)

entrepreneurial team   (p. 142)

franchise   (p.144)

franchisee   (p. 144)

franchisor   (p. 144)

goodwill   (p. 147)

grants   (p. 155)

growth entrepreneur   (p. 141)

home-based entrepreneur   (p. 140)

Internet entrepreneur   (p. 141)

intrapreneur   (p. 141)

lifestyle entrepreneur   (p. 140)

micropreneur   (p. 140)

opportunity niche   (p. 137)

Service Corps of Retired Executives (SCORE)   (p. 152)

small business   (p. 131)

Small Business Administration (SBA)   (p. 131)

small business investment company (SBIC) program (p. 157)

social entrepreneur   (p. 142)

social intrapreneur   (p. 142)

venture capitalists   (p. 156)

Self-Test

Multiple Choice   You can find the answers on the last page of this book.

1. Which is a key trait of an entrepreneur?
   a. Flexibility
   b. Risk taking
   c. Creative thinking
   d. All of the above

2. Sally started her new business venture five years ago. The business now operates in three locations and her sales have increased by 20 percent every year, which is exactly what Sally had in mind. Which type of entrepreneur best describes Sally?
   a. Social entrepreneur
   b. Lifestyle entrepreneur
   c. Growth entrepreneur
   d. Gazelle

3. One of the first things someone needs to do before starting a business is to write which of the following?
   a. A business plan
   b. A loan application
   c. A partnership statement
   d. A franchise agreement

4. Which of the following is not a characteristic of a small business?
   a. They generally have between 500 and 1,000 employees.
   b. On average, the annual revenue is $6.5 million.
   c. It is independently owned and operated.
   d. It is not considered a dominant player in its industry.

5. Steven Ye wants to start a company. He has a rough draft of his business plan and some tentative funding but needs some additional advice and guidance to help him through the start-up process. The best source for Steve is
   a. an angel investor.
   b. a SCORE volunteer.
   c. his parents.
   d. a bank loan officer.

6. Kazuto is interested in starting a new business. Which is a reason Kazuto should consider a franchise over starting a business from scratch?
   a. He will operate a tried and tested business strategy.
   b. He will be able to make all the decisions.
   c. He will need less capital up front.
   d. He will need to work fewer hours.

7. Wayland wants to open up a deli, but doesn't want the risk of opening one up from scratch. There is a deli in the area that the owner is selling, but the owner has put too high a value on the business's goodwill. Goodwill is:
   a. the value of the left-over products the deli gives to the local food pantry.
   b. the value of the donations the deli gives to charity.
   c. the value of the business's reputation with the current owner.
   d. All of the above

8. Rebecca has been operating a pet grooming business for several years and has already maxed out her personal credit and savings. She has designed a device that will make the pet grooming process more efficient but needs about $500,000 to take the idea further and perhaps sell it to other pet groomers. Which is the most likely source of financing that Rebecca could use?
   a. Credit cards
   b. Line of credit
   c. Funds from an angel investor
   d. Venture capital financing

9. Which of the following factors commonly leads to small business failure?
   a. Not enough planning
   b. Too much accumulated debt
   c. Unanticipated personal sacrifices
   d. All of the above

10. Rashid is starting a consulting business. He doesn't want to rent an office right now, but he needs a receptionist, a place to meet clients, and other aspects of an office. A good solution for Rashid to consider would be a(n)
    a. mentoring group.
    b. advisory board.
    c. business incubator.
    d. entrepreneurial team.

True/False You can find the answers on the last page of this book.

1. Being part of a franchise allows you to have access to tried and true marketing strategies.

   ☒ **True** or ☐ **False**

2. A social intrapreneur is someone who provides funding for those in third-world countries who want to begin their own businesses but have no capital with which to do so.

   ☐ **True** or ☒ **False**

3. According to the SBA, to be considered a small business, a company can have only one location.

   ☐ **True** or ☒ **False**

4. A growth entrepreneur is best described as one who starts a business in the agricultural industry.

   ☐ **True** or ☒ **False**

5. Credit cards can be a convenient way to help finance business expenses as long as the balances are paid in full every month.

   ☒ **True** or ☐ **False**

Critical Thinking Questions

⭐ 1. Companies that encouraged its employees to pursue entrepreneurial activities within an existing business created products such as Post-it Notes and Sony Play-Station. What aspects of the corporate environment would benefit intrapreneurial activities?

⭐ 2. Discuss how social media has affected small businesses at all stages of their development such as financing, marketing, and communications.

⭐ 3. Compare the different sources of funding available to small business owners. What types of funding are better at the beginning stages of a business? What types of funding may be better once the business is better established and is looking to expand?

Team Time

STARTING A BUSINESS: BRAINSTORMING

Assemble into groups of four or five.

1. Before meeting as a group, think about what you are passionate about and whether there is a potential market involving your interests. Develop one or two ideas for potential businesses based on your passions. Do not consider any idea impossible at this stage.

   a. Consider if there is something missing in the current market. For example, are you passionate about locally grown organic vegetables but are frustrated that there isn't a place nearby to purchase these items? If so, you've developed an idea for a local farmers' market.

   b. Consider combining two ideas together. When school has a half-day or full-day off, consider having high school students form a daytime child care service for elementary students.

   c. Consider business ideas that have potential but aren't doing very well now. Are there ways to make them better?

2. Gather your group and go over each other's ideas. Refine the list to two or three ideas.

Team Time (continued)

3. Have each group member refine an idea even further, identifying the target market and outlining the business goals and objectives.

4. Meet as a team one more time to pick one business idea.

5. If time permits, the group can develop this idea further by using the Business Plan project template. See Mini Chapter 2 for more information.

Ethics and Corporate Social Responsibility

SOCIAL ENTREPRENEURSHIP: PEPSI REFRESH PROJECT

The soft drink company PepsiCo now runs the Pepsi Refresh Project, a program in which the company awards millions of dollars to fund consumer-generated ideas that will have a positive impact on their communities. Grants range from $5,000 to $250,000.

Step 1. Visit refresheverything.com to see the types of projects that are being proposed and the recipients of awards. Download the toolkit to learn more about how to submit an idea to the Pepsi Refresh Project.

Step 2. In groups, discuss the needs your school or community has and create a list of ideas that your group feels would be good candidates for the Pepsi Refresh Project.

Step 3. Each group should present their idea to the class; as a class, vote on the best idea to send to the Pepsi Refresh Project.

Web Exercises

1. **Angel Investor for a Day**
   Congratulations! You just won the lottery! You are looking for some start-up businesses in which to invest some of your winnings. Go to Angel List (angel.co) and research the types of businesses that have received funding or are looking for funding. Pick three different businesses and discuss why you would or would not invest in them.

2. **Micro-Financing: A Little Money Can Go a Long Way**
   Visit www.kiva.org and click on the "Lend" tab to view the list of entrepreneurs. Use the drop-down menus in the "Find Loans" search bar to locate an entrepreneur or entrepreneurial team to whom you would consider lending. In a brief report, discuss the entrepreneur or group you chose, including information on the loan amount requested, the percentage of funds raised, the entrepreneur's country of origin, and a summary of the entrepreneur's business venture. In your report, explain your reasons for choosing to loan to this particular entrepreneur.

3. **Do You Have What It Takes to Be an Entrepreneur?**
   In this chapter, you learned that there are several personality traits common to successful entrepreneurs. Do you possess any of these traits? Using a search engine, find an entrepreneurial quiz that will help you determine if you have what it takes to be an entrepreneur. What aspects of your personality make you a good candidate to be an entrepreneur? What is holding you back?

4. **Build a Business with a Conscience**
   What does it take to create a socially conscious business? Play the game on the New Heroes from PBS to see if you have what it takes: www.pbs.org/opb/thenewheroes/engage/business.html.

5. **Small Business Owners: Where to Go for Help**
   If you were a new small business owner, where would you go for help? Many colleges have a small business development center (SBDC). These centers, which are affiliated with the SBA, provide information and guidance to current and prospective small business owners. Use the SBDC Locator (www.sba.gov/aboutsba/sbaprograms/sbdc/sbdclocator/SBDC_LOCATOR.html) to identify the nearest SBDC in your area; then research the services it can provide.

MyBizLab

Go to **mybizlab.com** for Auto-graded writing questions as well as the following Assisted-graded writing questions:

5-1. Why would someone want to buy an existing business rather than start a business from scratch? What are the drawbacks of buying an existing business?

5-2. Discuss the benefits of using an incubator when beginning a small business. Are there drawbacks to using an incubator?

5-3. MyBizLab Only – comprehensive writing assignment for this chapter.

Sole Proprietorships

When an entrepreneur starts a business, choosing the proper business structure is vital to the company's success. When Patty Jacobs decided to start her own cleaning business, she became a sole proprietor. Her business began growing so fast, and she now doesn't know if being a sole proprietor is the right business structure for her new venture. Do you know when it's best to operate as a sole proprietorship?

Partnerships

Trying to do a job alone can sometimes be overwhelming. Because of this, entrepreneurs may partner together to share resources and talents for the benefit of everyone involved. Partners Hang Win and Stefan Brown brought their skills and finances together to begin a new venture. Why might a partnership be a good business structure for a business? What difficulties should new partners prepare for?

Corporations

Brandon Jacobson and his sister, Sonya, found themselves unexpected landlords when they inherited properties that were owned and operated by their mother. Their mom reported the rental income on her personal income taxes as a sole proprietor. Brandon and Sonya were looking into creating a partnership, but they were advised that a partnership may not be the best corporate structure for them to operate under. Why isn't a partnership a good choice for Sonya and Brandon? What are their other options?

Not-for-Profits and Cooperatives

Darrell Hammond knew he could make a difference in the life of inner-city children by giving them safe places to play. He quickly outgrew his modest volunteer activities and knew he wanted to expand to help more children. He needed a corporate structure that would allow him to take his profits and put them back into communities nationwide. What type of alternative business structure would work best for him?

Mergers and Acquisitions

Companies constantly search for opportunities to expand by adding to their product lines, to enter into different geographic areas, or to gain a competitive advantage. The rationale behind mergers and acquisitions is that the resulting combined firm will be more valuable than the individual companies on their own. What is the difference between a merger and an acquisition? When do they occur?

MyBizLab®

⭐ Improve Your Grade!

Over 10 million students improved their results using the Pearson MyLabs. Visit **mybizlab.com** for simulations, tutorials, and end-of-chapter problems.

Sole Proprietorships pp. 165–169

Kurhan/Fotolia

Patty Jacobs runs a small cleaning business from her home. She has no employees, and she reports the business's income and expenses on her personal income taxes. However, the business has begun to grow quickly and she is considering hiring a few employees. She is concerned about the added liability she faces with an expanded business and new employees. As a sole proprietor, she knows that she is held responsible for any and all damages her company commits. In addition, now that Patty's small business is becoming successful, it may make more sense to report its earnings on a separate tax return, rather than running them through her personal tax return. She realizes that being the owner of a growing company requires more decisions than she had anticipated. ■

Patty Jacobs chose to begin her company as a sole proprietorship because it was quick and easy to establish. No legal paperwork is required to begin a sole proprietorship, and all the financial information can be reported on the owner's personal tax returns. Because of these advantages, a sole proprietorship is a common form of business ownership for start-up businesses. Many businesses also start out as a sole proprietorship because the owner is unfamiliar with other forms of business ownership.

Choosing the right legal structure for Patty's business may have initially seemed simple, but has her fast business growth outgrown a sole proprietorship? How do you know which form is best for your company? Choosing a form of ownership depends on many factors:

- **Legal liability**
- **Tax implications**
- **Future capital needs**
- **Cost of formation and ongoing administration**

Your decision on business ownership can affect the personal liability you face, the amount you pay in taxes, your ability to borrow money, and the amount of paperwork your business is required to file.

The U.S. economy—as well as the global economy—is based on a variety of enterprises, including sole proprietorships (businesses owned by one person), partnerships (where two or more people legally share ownership of a business), and corporations (businesses that are formed as separate legal entities). In addition, there are different classifications of corporations to consider, such as Limited Liability Corporations and S Corporations. ■ **FIGURE 6.1** shows these common forms of business ownership that are represented in the United States, as well as

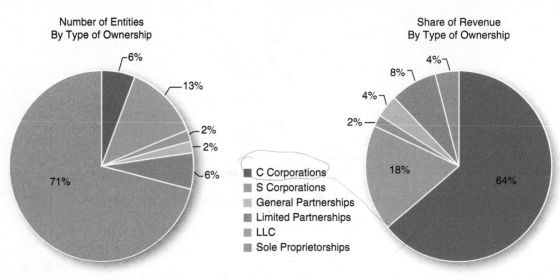

Number of Entities
By Type of Ownership

Share of Revenue
By Type of Ownership

■ C Corporations
■ S Corporations
■ General Partnerships
■ Limited Partnerships
■ LLC
■ Sole Proprietorships

■ **FIGURE 6.1**
U.S. Businesses by Type of Ownership and by Revenue
Sole proprietorship is the most common type of business ownership, but corporations generate the most revenue.
(*Source:* Data from "Table 1. Number of Returns, Total Receipts, Business Receipts, Net Income (less deficit), Net Income, and Deficit, Tax Years 1980-2008." U.S. Internal Revenue Service. http://www.irs.gov/pub/irs-soi/80ot1all.xls)

the share of revenue generated by each form of ownership. In this chapter, we'll explore each of these forms of business ownership in greater detail.

Why is sole proprietorship a popular form of business ownership? A **sole proprietorship** is a business owned, and usually controlled, by a single individual. Because no legal paperwork is necessary to establish a business as a sole proprietorship, many small business owners are sole proprietors without even knowing it. Although a sole proprietorship has only one owner, it can have any number of employees. For example, you can be the owner of a plumbing business with several other plumbers working for you and still operate as a sole proprietorship. Other characteristics of a sole proprietorship are listed in ■ **FIGURE 6.2**.

> ① What are the advantages and disadvantages of a sole proprietorship?

Starting a Sole Proprietorship

How do I start a sole proprietorship? The minute you begin doing business by yourself—that is, collecting income as a result of performing a service or selling a good—you are operating as a sole proprietor. There are no special forms to fill out, and there are no special filing requirements with state and federal governments. At a minimum, you might need to obtain local licensing or permits, or you might have to ensure that you're operating in an area zoned for such business activity. You might also need to register your company name and obtain an employer identification number (EIN) from the Internal Revenue Service if you're hiring employees.

Advantages and Disadvantages

Are there advantages to being a sole proprietor? There are several advantages in forming your business as a sole proprietorship—one of which we have already discussed: ease of formation. With only one person making all

■ **FIGURE 6.2**
Characteristics of a Sole Proprietorship

Preliminary Paperwork	• No special forms required
Period of Existence	• Ends when proprietor dies or leaves business
Liability	• Unlimited liability
Operational Requirements	• Minimal legal requirements
Management	• Full control of management and operations
Taxation	• Not a separate taxable entity; taxes paid through owner's personal tax return
Raising Capital	• Funding mostly derived from owner; outside funding difficult to obtain

the decisions and no need to consult other owners or interested parties, sole proprietors also have great control and considerable flexibility to act quickly. Another advantage is that there are no specific corporate records to keep or reports to file, including tax reporting. Because there is no legal distinction between the owner and the business, no separate tax return is required. As a result, the income and expenses of a sole proprietorship flow through the owner's personal tax return. This can be an advantage, especially in the start-up phase of the business when it's likely that the operating costs of the business are greater than the incoming revenues. In this case, the excess expenses (or net loss) can help to reduce any other sources of income, thus lowering your personal income tax obligations.

For example, imagine you run a landscaping business during the summer in addition to your regular job. If the lawn mower breaks down and needs to be replaced, that expense could be more than all the earnings you collected, generating a loss for your lawn-mowing business. You can subtract that loss from the income earned from your regular job, reducing your income tax obligation. ■ **TABLE 6.1** and ■ **FIGURE 6.3** show how a business loss can reduce your tax payment. In this example, a business loss of $3,000 reduces the overall federal tax due by $450.

■ TABLE 6.1

Personal Income With and Without a Business Loss from a Sole Proprietorship

	With Business Loss	Without Business Loss
Wage income	$14,500	$14,500
Business loss	−$3,000	
Net income	$11,500	$14,500
Tax due	$2,437	$2,887
	Difference: $450	

■ **FIGURE 6.3**
The Effect of a Business Loss on Personal Income
Sole proprietors can deduct business losses from their personal taxes, which reduces their overall tax burden.
Image Sources: top to bottom: .shock/Fotolia; Carlos Caetano/Fotolia; Kirsty Pargeter/Fotolia

Working for someone else throughout the year

Working as a waiter

↓

Wages earned from working as a waiter

Running a lawn-mowing business yourself during the summer

Lawn-mowing revenue

Cash collected from customers

New mower, gasoline, oil, and other expenses

Income	$3,500
Expenses	$6,500
Profit	($3,000)

Simplified 1040 Tax Form · Payment to IRS

Wages	$14,500	$2,887
Profit/loss from summer business	($3,000)	
Total taxable income	$11,500	$2,437

Summer job (loss) results in $450 tax savings

Why wouldn't I want to run my business as a sole proprietorship?
One of the biggest disadvantages of a sole proprietorship is exposure to personal liability. A **liability** is the obligation to pay a debt, such as an account payable or a loan. **Unlimited liability** means that if business assets aren't enough to pay business debts, then personal assets, such as the sole proprietor's house, personal investments, or retirement funds, can be used to pay the balance. In other words, the proprietor can lose an unlimited amount of personal assets. As a sole proprietor, the business is not a separate legal entity and all business debts and liabilities are your personal obligations. You are personally responsible for the business's contracts, taxes, and the misconduct of employees or co-owners who create legal liabilities while acting within their employment. Therefore, if the type of business you're running has the potential for someone to sue you because of damages caused by your business, you may not want to operate as a sole proprietorship.

Imagine that you own a catering business. While you're preparing food in someone's house, the oven catches fire because you forgot to take the egg rolls off the paper tray. You are personally responsible, or liable, for paying for any damages if your business assets (or insurance) are not sufficient to cover the damages. If the damages are severe enough—perhaps your client's entire house burns down—you could lose all your assets, including your own home and savings. If you decide that a sole proprietorship is the right business form for you for other reasons, buying insurance—such as errors or omissions insurance, disability insurance, and insurance to protect your assets—will help protect you against unforeseen situations.

Are there other things to consider with running a sole proprietorship?
Although running your own business certainly has its advantages such as flexibility, independence, and financial control, there are some things that you need to consider. While liability is perhaps the most critical reason for not operating as a sole proprietorship, there are some other considerations that may affect your business structuring decisions:

- **Financing/Investment:** A drawback of a sole proprietorship is the potential difficulty in borrowing money to help your business grow. Banks will be lending to you personally, not to your business, so they will be more reluctant to lend large amounts, and the loan will be limited to the amount of your personal assets. Structuring the business as a separate entity may mean more financing options are available. In addition, the business structure would need to change should you decide to bring in investors, who would want some form of ownership in the company.

- **Taxes:** As a sole proprietorship, business income and expenses are included on your personal tax return. Health care, retirement, and other benefits are not tax deductible for sole proprietorships. If your business were to be so successful that taxes became an issue, the legal structure of the business would need to change.

- **Selling:** If you ever wanted to sell the business, it's much more difficult to sell a sole proprietorship.

- **Financial sacrifices:** Financial control is great, but it can come with a price. Generally, after paying employees, suppliers, and other creditors, the owner is often the last person to get paid. If the budget is tight, payments for the owner's health care and retirement are sometimes postponed, which can be problematic. It's often helpful to run a sole proprietorship as a part-time business and still work for someone else until the business is running well so that you have the security of another salary as well as health-care benefits.

- **Spreading yourself thin:** Most importantly, running a sole proprietorship means that all the management duties fall on one person—you! Many owners of sole proprietorships neglect to consider that there are other responsibilities to running a business besides performing the service or making the good. There is a lot of paperwork and time involved to ensure that invoices are created, payments are collected, and salaries and benefits are paid (if there are other employees). This, as well as generating new business, following up on prior jobs, and performing the tasks of the business, makes for a commitment of time that many sole proprietors do not anticipate and that can undo many new businesses quickly.

Other business structures, which we will discuss later in the chapter, are more helpful should any of these considerations apply to your business.

Remember Patty Jacobs? Soon after starting her business, Patty realized that a sole proprietorship wasn't the best form of ownership for her because she didn't want to risk losing her personal assets in the event of an employee error. Patty, like many other small business owners, learned that making decisions about choosing the correct corporate structure is complex. After getting advice from other business owners, Patty decided that her business needed to undergo some corporate restructuring so that the company's business form would be more conducive to her needs. ■

Partnerships pp. 169–173

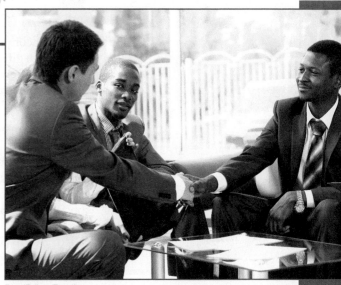

FotolEdhar/Fotolia

Daniel Ramirez had his eye on a piece of property for a storefront in an up-and-coming neighborhood. Because of the recent economic and real estate market downturns, it was more affordable but still slightly out of his reach. It also needed some renovations and modest reconstruction—skills that Daniel did not have. Stephan Brown, a friend of Daniel's college roommate, had some construction and carpentry experience and was also looking for a business opportunity but didn't have as much capital. After much thought and conversation, Daniel and Stephan agreed to form a partnership, buy the property, and embark on the renovations together. What contributions did Daniel and Stephan each bring to the partnership? What might be some difficulties the two new partners should prepare for? ■

Starting a new venture can be a difficult task, so sometimes a partner or two is needed to share the burden. Even large companies such as Target find partnerships useful in keeping their business up to date and running at its best. In this section, we'll look at partnerships in more detail.

Advantages and Disadvantages

When is it good to bring in a partner? Sometimes running a business by oneself can be a daunting task, so adding one or more owners can help share the responsibilities. A **partnership** is a type of business structure in which two or more

> **2** What are the advantages and disadvantages of a partnership and a partnership agreement?

entities (or partners) share the ownership and the profits and losses of the business. The reasons why joining with someone else makes sense include sharing the initial and ongoing finances as well as the management responsibilities and workload. More owners help contribute to the starting and ongoing capital of the business. Multiple people are involved in partnerships, so there is more time available to increase sales, market the business, and generate income. Sharing the financial responsibility brings on more people who are interested in the company's overall profitability and are as highly motivated as you are to make the business succeed. Therefore, additional owners, unlike employees, are more likely to be willing to work long hours and go the extra mile.

Adding partners to help share the workload also allows for coverage for vacations or when a partner is out due to illness or personal issues. Moreover, if partners have complementary skills, they create a collaboration that can be quite advantageous. Partners can help discuss ideas and projects as well as make the big decisions. For example, if you're great at numbers but hate making sales calls, bringing in a partner who loves to knock on doors would be beneficial for your business.

Are there disadvantages to adding partners? For every advantage a partner can bring, adding the wrong partner can be equally problematic. Obviously, adding partners means sharing profits and control, so if you don't want to give these up, a partnership may not be the right structure. A potential partner may have different work habits and styles from you, and if the partner's style isn't complementary, the differences can be challenging. In addition, as the business begins to grow and change, your partner might want to take the business in a different direction than you would want. Like entering into marriage, you want to consider carefully the person(s) with whom you will be sharing your business.

As a business form, how does a partnership compare to a sole proprietorship? Partnerships and sole proprietorships are very similar; in fact, the biggest difference between the two is the number of people contributing resources and sharing the profits and the liabilities. It's just as easy to form a partnership as to form a sole proprietorship. The government does not require any special forms or reports, although some local restrictions may apply for licenses and permits. For example, you and your brother-in-law form a small partnership called "All in the Family Electricians." Before you are able to do business, you might have to apply for a license, but you do not need any special papers to create the partnership itself. Also, like a sole proprietorship, partnerships do not file a separate tax return. All profits and losses of the partnership flow directly through each partner's individual tax return. ■ **FIGURE 6.4** outlines other characteristics of a partnership.

Biz CHAT

How Do You Find the Right Business Partner?

Business partners are like spouses: finding each other is often through circumstance and happenstance. Because of the high financial stakes, many look to partner with those whom they trust most: spouses, friends, or relatives. Hiring friends or relatives can have its benefits, but what do you do if your best friend doesn't do the job well?[1] You might instead want to turn to your casual acquaintance network—your gym buddy, a parent of your child's friend, a classmate—to find a business partner. If your network isn't turning up any promising leads, turn to others' networks. Similar to finding a job, write a description of the "perfect partner" and send it to as many people as you can. Make sure you interview the candidates and look for those who have similar goals but complementary skills. By all means, "date" the prospective partner before jumping into a business marriage; there is too much at risk to proceed too quickly.

Elements of a Partnership Agreement

What goes into a partnership agreement?

Although no formal documentation is required to create a partnership, it's a good idea to draw up an agreement between partners. A partnership can begin with a handshake, and many of them do, but it is best for all involved parties that a written document, called a **partnership agreement**, formalizes the relationship between the business partners. Think of a partnership agreement as a business prenuptial agreement. It helps settle conflicts when they arise and may discourage small misunderstandings from erupting into larger disagreements. Many points can be included in a partnership agreement; however, the following items should always be included:

Preliminary Paperwork	• No special forms required; partnership agreement recommended
Period of Existence	• Ends upon death or withdrawal of a partner unless otherwise provided for in partnership agreement
Liability	• Unlimited liability
Operational Requirements	• Minimal legal requirements
Management	• Roles specified in partnership agreement; partners generally have equal voice
Taxation	• Not a separate taxable entity; taxes paid through owner's personal tax return
Raising Capital	• Funding raised through partner contributions

■ **FIGURE 6.4**
Characteristics of a Partnership

1. **Capital Contributions.** The amount of **capital,** or investments in the form of money, equipment, supplies, computers, and other tangible things of value, that each partner contributes to begin the business should be noted in the partnership agreement. In addition, the agreement should also address how additional capital can be added to the business—who will contribute it and whether there will be a limit to a partner's overall capital contribution.

2. **Responsibilities of Each Partner.** To avoid the possibility of one partner doing more or less work than others, or a conflict arising over one partner assuming a more controlling role than desired by other partners, it is best to outline the responsibilities of each partner from the beginning. Unless otherwise specified, any partner can bind the partnership to any debt or contract without the consent of the other partners. Therefore, it is especially important to spell out the policy regarding who assumes responsibility for entering into key financial or contractual arrangements.

3. **Decision-Making Process.** It is important to consider how decisions will be made. Knowing whether decisions will be the result of mutual consent of all or several partners or whether just one or two partners will make the key decisions is essential to help partners avoid disagreements. What constitutes a key decision should also be defined in the agreement. In a partnership of two, where the possibility of a deadlock is likely, some partnerships provide for a trusted associate to act as an acting third "partner" whose sole responsibility is to be the tiebreaker.

4. **Shares of Profits or Losses.** Not only should the agreement specify how to divide profits and losses between the partners, but it should also specify how frequently this will be done. One partnership agreement might stipulate that the profits and losses will be proportional to each partner's initial contribution to the partnership, as reflected in ■ **FIGURE 6.5**, whereas another partnership agreement might split the profits evenly. It is also important to detail how adjustments to the distributions will be made—if any at all—as the partnership matures and changes.

5. **Departure of Partners.** Eventually, the composition of partners may change as original partners leave and new partners come onboard. The partnership agreement should have rules for a partner's exit, whether voluntary, involuntary, or due to death or divorce. Provisions to remove a partner's ownership interest are necessary so the business does not need to end (i.e., liquidate). The agreement should include how to determine the amount of ownership interest and to whom the departing partner is permitted to transfer his or her interest. It is important to consider whether a partner can transfer his or her ownership

solely to the remaining partners or whether individuals outside the existing partnership can buy the departing partner's share.

6. **Addition of Partners.** The partnership agreement also helps spell out the requirements for new partners entering the partnership. How the profits will be allocated and whether there will be a "junior partner" period during which the new partner can prove himself or herself before obtaining full partner status should also be included.

Types of Partnerships

Are there different types of partnerships? There are two common types of partnerships: *general partnerships* and *limited partnerships*. The distinction between the two types involves who accepts most or all of the business liability.

What is a general partnership? A **general partnership** is the default arrangement for a partnership and is, therefore, the simplest of all partnerships to form. For instance, if two friends, Juan and Franklin, set up an ice cream stand at the local park, sell ice cream cones, and split the profits at the end of the day, they have created a general partnership. For Juan and Franklin, this is a logical arrangement because they share the profits equally, and there is little worry about liability. In a general partnership, each partner has unlimited liability for the debts and obligations of the partnership, meaning every partner is liable for his or her own actions, as well as the actions of the other partners and the actions of any employees.

FIGURE 6.5
Share of Profit and Loss in a Partnership
Partners' shares of profits and losses can be dependent on the capital contribution and the assumed responsibilities of each partner.
Image Sources: top to bottom, left to right: Anatoly Maslennikov/Fotolia; nattstudio/Fotolia; Antonio Gravante/Fotolia; Wong Sze Fei/Fotolia; Wrangler/Fotolia; picture5479/Fotolia; hacohob/Fotolia

What is a limited partnership? Sometimes, a business can bring on additional "limited" partners who mostly provide capital and earn a share in the profits but who are not involved in operating the business. To encourage investors to contribute capital to a business without risking more capital than they have contributed, a **limited partnership** is created. In a limited partnership, there are two distinctions of partners. **General partners** are full owners of the business, are responsible for all the day-to-day business decisions, and remain liable for all the debts and obligations of the business. **Limited partners** are involved as investors and, as such, are personally liable only up to the amount of their investment in the business and must not actively participate in any decisions of the business. To continue the example above, assume that Juan and Franklin needed to buy a freezer. Because they didn't have enough money, they asked Juan's brother Carlos to invest in their business with the necessary cash to buy the freezer. Carlos becomes a limited partner in the business since he will not participate in any of the business operations. Should something go wrong, Carlos would contribute to the payment of damages only up to the value he contributed (the price of the freezer). Limited partnerships can be much more complex to form than our simple example, so it may be worth exploring other business structures before deciding on this strategy.

Another kind of limited partnership is a *master limited partnership (MLP)*. This business structure combines the tax benefits of a limited partnership, but it is similar to a corporation (which we discuss next) in that it is publicly traded on a securities exchange. MLPs are mostly restricted to certain businesses pertaining to the use of natural resources (such as petroleum or natural gas) and real estate.

Will partnerships work well when liability is a concern? Although forming a general partnership for Juan and Franklin's ice cream business makes sense for them, it's not right for every business. In some situations, especially if liability is a concern, neither a sole proprietorship nor a partnership will protect the owner(s) from unlimited risk. For instance, if Sarah and Hannah decide to form Personal Training Partners, a personal training and fitness motivation company, they know that each partner is liable—not only for her own business debts and actions but also for each other's business debts and actions. If a client claims that Sarah mistreated him or her and the client sues the business, not only are the business assets at risk, but Sarah's and Hannah's personal assets are also at risk. Therefore, they need a type of structure that would protect their homes and savings and other personal assets from being lost in case of a business disaster. Both partners want to be protected so that only the business assets, like the building they bought for their gym, the exercise machines, and the computers they use, are at risk, not any of their personal assets. In this case, a partnership is not the best business structure because a partnership has unlimited liability and does not protect against losses of personal property. There are some options available for Personal Training Partners that are like partnerships in many ways but also help insulate an owner's personal liability from the business. We'll discuss these next.

Daniel and Stefan's partnership benefitted from complementary skills and resources that each partner brought to the table. Because Daniel had more financial exposure, it was important to him that he and Stefan sign a partnership agreement. After the renovations were complete and the space was ready for commercial use, Daniel and Stefan brought in one more partner, Lily Ye, who had considerable retail and marketing experience—just what they needed to move forward in their venture. But Lily was concerned about the personal exposure she would have. She suggested the partnership look into a different kind of corporate structure. What other options do the partners have? ■

Corporations pp. 173–180

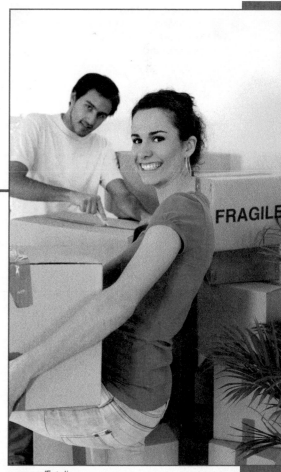

Brandon Jacobson and his sister, Sonya, found themselves unexpected landlords when they inherited properties that were owned and operated by their mother. Their mom was a simple person, and these few properties provided her with some extra income. She reported the rental income she received from the properties on her personal income taxes as a sole proprietor. Brandon and Sonya were looking into creating a partnership, but they have been advised that a partnership may not be their best option. They would still like to report the income through their taxes if possible. Why won't a partnership work? What are their choices? ■

auremar/Fotolia

Preliminary Paperwork	• Incorporation paperwork must be filed with state and federal agencies
Period of Existence	• Separate entity; existence not dependent on owners, founders; ownership transferred easily
Liability	• Owners (shareholders) are not personally liable for debts of corporation
Operational Requirements	• Must have board of directors, corporate officers, annual meetings, and annual reporting
Management	• Shareholders elect board of directors, which provides strategic management of corporation; board appoints senior management
Taxation	• Not a separate taxable entity; taxes filed through owner's personal tax return
Raising Capital	• Capital is raised through sale of stock and debt issue

■ **FIGURE 6.6**
Characteristics of a C Corporation

The U.S. writer Ambrose Bierce once defined a corporation as "an ingenious device for obtaining profit without individual responsibility."[2] Unlike partnerships and sole proprietorships, corporations provide business owners with better protection of their personal assets. What is a corporation? Why might a business owner choose to form a corporation? What are the different types of corporations? In this section you'll find the answers to these questions and more.

What is a corporation? A corporation is a specific form of business organization that is legally formed under state laws. A corporation is considered a separate entity apart from its owners; therefore, a corporation has legal rights like an individual, so a corporation can own property, assume liability, pay taxes, enter into contracts, and can sue and be sued—just like any other individual. Most corporations are run as a **C corporation**, which refers to Subchapter C of the Internal Revenue Code by which it is governed, though sometimes a corporation can be run as an S corporation (which we discuss next). Other characteristics of a C corporation are listed in ■ **FIGURE 6.6**.

Advantages of Incorporation

When does it make sense to form a business as a corporation? Some business owners incorporate just to be able to end a company's name with "Company," "Co.," "Incorporated," or "Inc." Having corporate nomenclature such as "Co." or "Inc." at the end of the business name can give a start-up business an air of legitimacy, which can be a perceived benefit to prospective clients and lenders and potentially a greater threat to the competition. More importantly, forming under a corporate structure provides many advantages not found with other business structures.

> **How is a corporation formed, and how does it compare with sole proprietorships and partnerships?**
>
> ③

How can a business owner protect his or her personal assets? Contrary to much "conventional wisdom," a C corporation can be the right choice for many small entities because a corporation is a separate legal entity and is responsible for its own debts and obligations; it has separated liability from an owner's personal assets. This is one of the main reasons owners incorporate their business. When a corporation runs into problems, only the corporate assets can be used to remedy the situation; the owners are not personally liable for business debts.

What happens to a corporation when an owner leaves? Sole proprietorships and partnerships, by their nature, are dependent on their founding owners. When an owner dies or otherwise leaves the business, the partnership or sole proprietorship is usually terminated. On the other hand, corporations enjoy extended life and ownership transfer because shareholders own the corporation, so its existence doesn't depend on its founding members. Shares of ownership are easily exchanged, so the corporation will continue to exist should an owner die or wish to sell his or her interest in the business. As long as it is financially viable, a corporation is capable of continuing forever.

Is it easier for corporations to get funding and to raise capital? Becoming incorporated offers a business greater flexibility when raising capital. Banks and venture capitalists are more likely to lend money to an incorporated business because lenders and investors are not limited to the credit profile of the sole proprietor or general partners. When a corporation has reached a significant size, it can extend its ownership by "going public"—selling shares of ownership in the corporation to the general public. A stock certificate is the tangible evidence of investment and ownership.

Are corporations taxed the same as other types of businesses?
Because sole proprietors and partners run their business income through their personal income tax statements, these two types of business structures pay taxes at the owner's or partners' tax rates. Corporations have a separate scale of tax rates. At the lowest income levels for a corporation, the corporation has a tax advantage over individual tax payers. The corporate tax rate is 15 percent for the first $50,000 in annual profits, whereas the same amount of profits from a sole proprietorship or partnership would be taxed at a rate of 25 percent through individual taxes.[3] However, most corporations will generate more than $50,000 in net income. Businesses generating more than $50,000 in taxable income will pay taxes at an equal or higher tax rate than individuals.

Structure of a Corporation

How is a corporation structured? A corporation's organizational structure is comprised of three basic groups: shareholders, a board of directors, and corporate officers, as shown in ■ **FIGURE 6.7**. Each group has different responsibilities.

Shareholders

Whether or not a corporation is privately owned or publicly owned, it has shareholders. **Shareholders** (or **stockholders**) have an ownership interest in the company. For their investment, they receive stock certificates from the corporation, identifying the number of shares (called *apportioned ownership interest*) they own. A **publicly owned corporation** is a corporation that is regulated by the Securities and Exchange Commission because the shares of ownership can be traded on public stock exchanges. Although shareholders of a publicly owned corporation serve as the owners of the corporation, they have no involvement in the direct management of the corporation. Instead, they influence corporate decisions by electing directors, overseeing the laws and rules that govern the organization, and voting on major corporate issues.

In **privately held** (or **closed**) corporations, corporations are owned, in most cases, by the company's founders, a management team, or a group of private investors. The owners are generally involved in the management and daily operations of the business, assuming more decision-making responsibilities than do shareholders of publicly owned corporations. The owners of privately held corporations are generally the sole shareholders. Any shares of privately held corporations are not traded on public stock exchanges.

Directors

The shareholders elect the board of directors, and the board of directors select and hire the management team of corporate officers. By doing so, shareholders can influence the very nature of a business. In an effort to

■ **FIGURE 6.7**
Organizational Structure of a C Corporation
In a C corporation, the shareholders have the power to elect a board of directors. The board, in turn, has the ability to hire (or fire) the company's corporate officers.

separate ownership and management, the directors—or the **board of directors**—usually set policy for the corporation and make the major business and financing decisions. Directors authorize the issuance of stock, approve loans to or from the corporation, and decide on major real estate transactions.

The board is also responsible for ensuring that the corporate managers are doing their jobs. Not all boards are effective in doing so, however, as has been demonstrated by many corporate scandals, including those that most recently occurred in the financial sector. In a reaction to incidences of board negligence at the beginning of the century, the Sarbanes-Oxley Act of 2002, a U.S. federal law, was enacted to provide a new set of standards of accountability for the board of directors. If the members of a board of directors ignore their responsibilities of managing the internal controls of a company, they incur the risk of long prison sentences and huge fines.

Officers

Officers, often referred to as senior management, are elected by the board of directors and are responsible for the daily operation and management of the company. The typical lineup of officers includes the CEO, the CFO, and the COO. The **chief executive officer (CEO)** is typically responsible for the entire operations of the corporation and reports directly to the board of directors. Sometimes the CEO is a member of the board of directors, as well. The **chief financial officer (CFO)** reports directly to the CEO and is responsible for analyzing and reviewing the financial data, reporting financial performance, preparing budgets, and monitoring expenditures and costs. The **chief operating officer (COO)** is responsible for the day-to-day operations of the organization and reports directly to the CEO. Often there is a chief legal officer or general council, and, depending on the needs of the company, there might also be a chief information officer (CIO). In actuality, any "officer" position can be formed if it makes sense for the company.

In large companies, the responsibilities of each officer are demanding enough that separate positions are necessary. In smaller companies, only one or two persons might perform the role of several different officers. After having worked as a yoga instructor for local gyms, Maureen Priest opened Moyo, her own yoga studio, in a Philadelphia suburb. "I wanted to be an instructor, but found in my first year that I needed to be the marketing manager, finance director, and chief operating officer, as well. I had to learn quickly how to get my name and my new studio to many people; and I had to learn how to price my services and figure out my expenses so I could come close to breaking even, if not making a profit. Lastly, I had to locate a studio, negotiate a rental contract, and renovate the space to accommodate my specific business needs. I wore many hats that first year."[4]

Disadvantages of Incorporation

Are there any disadvantages of structuring a business as a corporation? Forming a corporation is a much more cumbersome process than forming a sole proprietorship or a partnership. ■ **FIGURE 6.8** shows the steps involved in forming a corporation.

Because a corporation is a separate legal entity, there are many more filing and process requirements that must be fulfilled to maintain corporate status. For example, all public companies must file an annual report, and all corporations,

■ **FIGURE 6.8**
Steps in Forming a Corporation
Corporations provide owners with more protection than other business structures, although forming a corporation is a more complex process.

Choose a Name → Appoint Directors → File Articles of Incorporation → Draft Bylaws → Hold a Meeting of the Board → Issue Stock → Obtain Licenses and Permits

both private and public, must maintain written minutes of annual and other periodic board of director and shareholder meetings. Resolutions or consents of major decisions must be recorded, including decisions involving the issuance of stock; the purchase of real property; the approval of leases, loans, or lines of credit; the adoption of or changes to stock options; and retirement plans. A corporation must also record financial transactions in a double-entry bookkeeping system and file taxes on a regular basis (quarterly or annually).

Another disadvantage of the corporate structure is the idea of double taxation. **Double taxation** occurs when taxes are paid on the same asset twice. The classic business example of double taxation is the distribution of dividends. Double taxation happens because a corporation is first taxed on its net income, or profit, and then distributes that net income to its shareholders in the form of dividends. The individual shareholder must then pay taxes on the dividends (which have already been taxed at the corporate level). Therefore, the same pool of money—corporate profits—has been taxed twice: once in the form of corporate profits and again as dividends received by the shareholders. Although this is a commonly mentioned disadvantage of corporations, it affects only those corporations that pay dividends to their shareholders.

Can a business have the protection of a corporation but not pay corporate taxes? When choosing a legal structure for their businesses, most entrepreneurs will cite two goals: protecting personal liability and flowing taxes through their individual tax returns. As has already been discussed, operating as a sole proprietorship or a partnership allows business profits and losses to flow through an owner's individual tax return, but an owner of a sole proprietorship or members in a partnership assume the risk of personal liability exposure. A corporate structure offers the reverse; it protects an owner's personal assets from being touched if the corporation is in financial difficulty, but the corporation is taxed as a separate entity without flow-through to the owner's returns. Fortunately, there are two forms of business structures in which both goals can be met: the *S corporation* and the *LLC*.

S Corporations

What is an S corporation? An **S corporation** is a regular corporation (a C corporation) that has elected to be taxed under a special section of the Internal Revenue Code called Subchapter S. Like C corporations, S corporations have shareholders, and they must comply with all the other regulations involving traditional C corporations.

How is an S corporation different from a C corporation? Unlike C corporations, S corporations do not pay corporate income taxes. Instead, as with a partnership or a sole proprietorship, the shareholders in an S corporation owe income taxes based on their proportionate share of the business profits they receive and pay taxes through their own individual tax returns. Passing taxes through personal tax returns is one of the primary advantages of forming a business as an S corporation. However, even though S corporations do not pay corporate taxes like C corporations, they still must file a corporate tax return every year. In addition, S corporations must comply with the meeting and reporting requirements established for C corporations. Other characteristics of an S corporation are shown in **■ FIGURE 6.9**.

4 What are the major differences between a C corporation, an S corporation, and a limited liability company?

■ FIGURE 6.9
Characteristics of an S Corporation
(*Source:* Section 1361, Internal Revenue Code)

Preliminary Paperwork	• Incorporation paperwork must be filed with state and federal agencies
Period of Existence	• Separate entity; existence not dependent on owners, founders; ownership transferred easily
Liability	• Owners (shareholders) are not personally liable for debts of corporation
Operational Requirements	• Must have board of directors, corporate officers, annual meetings, and annual reporting
Management	• Shareholders elect board of directors, which provides strategic management of corporation; board appoints senior management
Taxation	• Taxed at entity level; if dividends are distributed, they are also taxed at individual level (double taxation)
Raising Capital	• Capital is raised through sale of stock and debt issue

How does an S corporation handle personal liability? The beauty of an S corporation is that it offers the best of both worlds: profits and losses pass through to the shareholders, *and* the corporate structure provides some limitations on personal liability of the owners. Although an owner's personal assets will be protected in case of a large claim against the corporation, the S corporation does not assume liability for an owner's personal wrongdoings. This is true for any corporate structure—whether it is a C corporation, an S corporation, or an LLC (discussed later). So, if an owner directly injures someone or intentionally does something fraudulent, illegal, or reckless that causes harm to the company or someone else, he or she will be held personally responsible and is not protected under the corporate umbrella.

For example, suppose William is the owner of a boating business that offers day cruises in the San Francisco Bay. Unfortunately, one foggy day, William's boat collides with another boat, causing his boat to capsize. Before leaving the dock that morning, William failed to provide sufficient life jackets for all his passengers and overloaded the boat. As a result, William most likely would be held personally liable for his negligent actions if any of his passengers were harmed because there were not enough life preservers, even though he had structured his company as an S corporation. William would not only be in danger of losing the business but also may be forced into personal bankruptcy if his personal assets were needed to help satisfy the claims on the company.

Can any business elect to be an S corporation? There are certain qualification requirements a business must meet to elect an S corporation status. According to the Internal Revenue Code,[5] an S corporation must have the following characteristics:

- The company must not have more than 100 shareholders.
- Shareholders must be U.S. citizens or residents.
- The company must issue only one class of stock.
- The company must distribute proportionately all profits and losses to each shareholder based on each one's interest in the business.

S corporations are the most appropriate business structure for small business owners who want the legal protection of a corporation but also want to be taxed as if they are the sole proprietor or a partner of a business. However, if a business does not meet these standards but personal liability protection with pass-through tax benefits is still desired, an LLC might be a suitable alternative corporate structure.

Limited Liability Companies

What is an LLC? A limited liability company (LLC) is a distinct type of business that, like an S corporation, combines the corporate advantages of limited liability with the tax advantages inherent in sole proprietorships and partnerships. LLCs are the relatively new kid on the block, and they have received quite a bit of interest in the business community because of their many benefits and flexibility that suit a start-up business. Similar to creating an S corporation or a C corporation, an LLC requires articles of organization, so it is a separate legal entity (thus providing limited liability). But an LLC is free of many of the annual meetings and reporting requirements imposed on C and S corporations, so it is simpler to maintain. LLCs do not issue stock; rather each member's ownership is determined by the value of their capital account. A capital account tracks the member's capital contributions to the LLC. Distributions of profits and losses also flow through capital accounts in proportion to ownership percentage. Because of fewer corporate formalities, inherent limited liability provisions, and the reporting of taxes at the individual level, it is a popular business structure choice for many new businesses.

It is important to note that some states may have restrictions on the types of businesses that can form as an LLC. Other characteristics of an LLC are outlined in ■ **FIGURE 6.10**.

What's the difference between an LLC and an S corporation? Although LLCs and S corporations share certain similarities, there are several distinctions between LLCs and S corporations that should be considered before choosing either form:

■ **FIGURE 6.10**
Characteristics of an LLC

- **Ownership.** S corporations are restricted as to the number of owners the company can have, but LLCs can have an unlimited number of owners (called *members*). In addition, LLC members are not limited to just U.S. residents and are not subject to other ownership restrictions imposed on S corporations.

- **Perpetual life.** When a member leaves an LLC, the LLC must dissolve. In addition, some states also require that a dissolution date be listed in the articles of organization, so an LLC has a limited life span.

- **Stock transfer.** Stock in an S corporation, like a C corporation, is freely transferable, whereas the ownership interest in an LLC is not and the transfer generally requires the approval of other members.

- **Profit and loss distributions.** LLCs may allocate profits in whatever manner best suits the owners, but the profits of an S corporation are allocated in proportion to a shareholder's interest. So, if two members own a business, and one contributes 75 percent of the capital but only does 25 percent of the work while the other member contributes 25 percent of the capital but does 75 percent of the work, the two members can decide that a fair allocation of profits is 50/50. This arrangement would be possible with an LLC, but with an S corporation, the profits would need to be distributed based on the 75/25 ownership interest.

- **Owner and employee benefits.** An S corporation may offer fringe benefits to its owners, such as qualified retirement plans, employee-provided vehicles, and educational expenses related to the job. Because S corporations have stock, they can also offer their employees stock options and other stock bonus incentives. LLCs are limited in the benefits their members can be offered, and because LLCs do not issue stock, they cannot offer stock benefits to their employees.

What kinds of businesses are best suited as an LLC? There are many types of businesses in which an LLC structure is appropriate, but in particular, LLCs are often used by professional corporations formed by accountants, attorneys, doctors, and other similar professionals who want to separate themselves from partner liability but still reap the other benefits of a partnership. LLCs may be a good choice for start-up businesses, not only for the tax benefits but also because it is easier to obtain financing because the number of investors (owners) is not restricted.

Comparing Forms of Ownership

Which form of ownership is best? There is no one entity that works for everyone. A CPA or a specialized tax attorney may be a good source to assist you in choosing the right structure for your business. The important considerations are the operational, legal and tax aspects of each structure as they apply to your unique situation. See ■ **FIGURE 6.11** to see how the most common forms of ownership stack up to one another.

■ **FIGURE 6.11**
Comparing the Forms of Business Ownership
(Based on Forms of Business Ownership, Nevada Small Business Development Center, University of Nevada, Las Vegas, College of Business, 7/31/05)

Comparing the Forms of Business Ownership

Type of Business	Sole Proprietorship	General Partnership	C Corporation	S Corporation	LLC
Ownership	Business owned and operated by one person.	Two or more partners jointly own and operate the business.	Formed under state and federal law; separate entity from owners.	Structured like a C corporation but taxed like a partnership.	Created by statute; owned by members.
Start-up requirements	Easiest form to set up; no required state or federal filings.	Easy to form and operate; no required paperwork; written partnership agreement is recommended.	File articles of incorporation with the state in which it is incorporated; specific paperwork required.	Meet S corporation requirements; articles of incorporation are required.	Articles of organization are required; specific paperwork required by the state.
Taxes	Profits taxed once; profits and losses reported on individual's tax return.	Profits taxed once; each partner's share of profits and losses reported on individual return.	Subject to double taxation; profits and losses reported on corporate tax return.	Each shareholder reports share of profits and losses on individual return. S corporation does not pay taxes.	Taxed like a general partnership or an S corporation.
Liability	The owners' personal assets are at risk.	Each partner's personal assets are at risk.	Owners' personal assets are not at risk, unless personal negligence or fault is involved.	Same as a C corporation.	Same as a C corporation.
Termination	Termination Terminates by desire or death of owner.	Terminates by agreement of partners, or death or withdrawal of partner, depending on the partnership agreement.	Formal dissolution required; not affected by death or departure of owner.	Same as a C corporation.	Same as a general partnership.

A corporation is different from a sole proprietorship and a partnership because it is considered its own legal entity. It has its own tax return, and it can sue and be sued. Some businesses choose to use the corporate structure to appear more stable and legitimate to clients and lenders, but a more significant advantage is that the owners' personal assets are protected should claims be made against the corporation. Brandon and Sonya were looking to form a partnership structure around their inherited real estate properties, but they have been advised that a partnership will not protect their personal assets if something terrible goes wrong and they are sued by a tenant. Because they still would prefer to report the income through their taxes, the siblings decided that an LLC would be the best choice as it would give them the protection of a corporation, but the ability to report the business income through personal tax returns. ■

Not-for-Profit and Cooperatives pp. 181–183

goodgold99/Fotolia

Darrell Hammond had volunteered to make playgrounds while he was in college. Then, several years later, he read about two inner-city children who had suffocated while playing in an abandoned car and realized that if the children had a safe place to play, the tragedy could have been avoided. Shortly afterward, Darrell and his friend, Dawn Hutchinson, built a community playground for a day of service they led, and a year later they founded KaBOOM!, a not-for-profit organization that helps communities to build playgrounds.[6] How could he structure KaBOOM! to protect himself financially, gain credibility, and continue to serve the community? ■

In some business ventures, the goal is not to generate a profit but rather to make a difference in the lives of community members. These businesses can be educational, scientific, religious, or charitable. What are some of these alternative business arrangements? What are the benefits and drawbacks of using these forms of ownership? We'll answer these questions next.

Not-for-Profit Organizations

What is a not-for-profit organization? Legally, a **not-for-profit organization** (or nonprofit organization) is a business that does not seek a profit. Instead, after paying normal operating expenses—such as salaries, rent, and purchases of inventory, supplies, materials, and equipment—a not-for-profit organization uses the remaining revenue for the business's declared cause and mission rather than paying stockholders. Not-for-profit organizations must apply for tax-exempt status with the federal government and sometimes with the state in which they are operating. Not-for-profit organizations generate their revenues primarily through fund-raising and donations. To maintain their tax-exempt status, not-for-profit organizations must demonstrate that a substantial portion of their income or revenue is spent on services to achieve their goals.

Can not-for-profit organizations act like corporations? Not-for-profit organizations are incorporated and, as such, are subject to most of the laws that govern for-profit corporations. Not-for-profit organizations receive limited liability protection when they become incorporated and are established as a separate legal entity. Similar to a for-profit corporation, a not-for-profit is required to hold board meetings and keep complete books and records. The greatest distinction between a for-profit organizations and a not-for-profit organization is—profit! A not-for-profit corporation cannot be organized for any person's private gain—that is, no profits are retained, and any excess revenue is distributed back to the organization for the purposes of supporting its mission. Not-for-profit organization do not issue shares of stock, and their members (or owners) may not receive personal financial benefit from the organization's profits (other than salary as an employee). However, some not-for-profit organizations do provide employee

> **5** What are the characteristics of not-for-profit organizations and cooperatives?

THE List

Successful Not-for-Profit Organizations[7]

1. United Way
2. Salvation Army
3. Feed the Children
4. Good 360
5. Americares
6. YMCA
7. The Red Cross
8. Catholic Charities USA
9. Feeding America
10. Mayo Foundation

benefits, such as health insurance. In addition, should the not-for-profit organization dissolve, the organization's assets must go to a similar not-for-profit organization.

Are there benefits to being tax-exempt? Being tax-exempt means that the organization has met the qualifications provided in section 501(c)(3) of the IRS code. As an organization that has received 501(c)(3) status, the donations that are the organization's primary source of revenue are tax deductible to the donor, which encourages funding. Another benefit of tax-exempt status is that the not-for-profit organization is exempt from paying most federal and/or state corporate income taxes and may also be exempt from state sales and property taxes. Such not-for-profit organizations are able to apply for grants and other public or private distributions, as well as discounts on postal rates and other services.

Cooperatives

What structure would be best for groups of businesses with common goals? Cooperatives are businesses that are owned and governed by members who use its products or services, not by outside investors. Cooperative members can be individuals, such as individual farmers in an agricultural cooperative, or businesses, such as individual hardware stores, florists, or hotels that have come together to create cooperatives. You might be surprised to learn that Ace Hardware, Land O'Lakes, and Florida's Natural Growers are all cooperative ventures.[8] Cooperatives are motivated to provide services to people with common interests and/or needs and are not motivated by profits. Any profits made by a cooperative are returned to members in proportion to their use, not their investment or their ownership share.

How are cooperatives structured? Members are the most important part of a cooperative. They buy shares to help finance the cooperative, elect directors to manage the cooperative, and create and amend the bylaws that govern the cooperative. Cooperatives depend on their members to volunteer for projects supported by the cooperative and serve on boards and committees. The board of directors in a cooperative appoints committees for specific purposes, such as member relations and special audits. The board of directors also hires the cooperative manager who handles the daily affairs.

Are cooperatives not-for-profit? Cooperatives are incorporated under state co-op statutes as a business that is organized to serve its members. Like not-for-profits, cooperatives don't exist to maximize profit. Instead, any profits generated are reinvested into the cooperative to continue to maintain and improve the business. Profit that is truly surplus—that is anything not needed for reinvestment into the business—is available for distribution to the member-owners. The cooperative status is also recognized by state and federal tax codes so that any distributed profits to member-owners are exempted from income tax.

What is the benefit of cooperatives? Cooperatives form because a group of individuals or businesses become dissatisfied with how the marketplace is providing the needed goods or services at affordable prices or acceptable quality. Cooperatives use the benefit of group power, individuals (people or companies) coming together for a single cause, to negotiate within their marketplace. Therefore, members enjoy reduced costs due to greater bargaining power and marketplace strength associated with a large member group.[9]

For example, Florida's Natural Growers is a cooperative of citrus growers who own their own groves in Florida. A group of growers formed the cooperative in 1933 to market their crops. Today, the Florida's Natural Growers Cooperative processes 129,000 boxes of fruit per day—an improvement from the original 3,000 boxes of fruit the cooperative originally handled.[10]

Some businesses don't fit the mold of sole proprietorship, partnership, or corporation due to the underlying cause or purpose of the business. When this occurs, business owners might form not-for-profit organizations or cooperatives. Darrell Hammond did not care about personal profit; he just wanted to create an organization that would help improve communities, so he found that forming a not-for-profit organization was best for him. ■

Mergers and Acquisitions pp. 183–187

Google began in 1998 as a search engine, but nearly 15 years later, the company has made its mark as a Web browser (Google Chrome), mapping and directional service (Google Maps, Google Earth), online productivity and communications center (Google Docs, Gmail) and social media facilitator (Google+). In addition, Google runs the Android mobile platform, Picasa image manager, Blogger, and YouTube. How did Google expand into all these products and services? ■

From top left: Eric Carr/Alamy; Anatolii Babii/Alamy; PhotoEdit/Alamy; Netpics/Alamy; Ingvar Björk/Alamy; Eric Carr/Alamy; PhotoEdit/Alamy

Sometimes, in the evolution of a business or in response to market forces, companies seek opportunities to expand by adding new product lines, spreading out into different geographic areas, or growing the company to increase their competitive advantage. Often product or market expansion is done gradually by slowly adding new product lines or penetrating new areas. However, it takes time and investment to research and develop new products or to locate and build in new areas. Sometimes, especially to remain competitive, expansion needs to happen more quickly. In that case, it may be easier to integrate another established business through the process of mergers or acquisitions. Acquiring or merging with another company are strategies that companies can use to increase their competitive advantage and gain synergy.

Mergers Versus Acquisitions

What is the difference between a merger and an acquisition? The terms *merger* and *acquisition* are often used interchangeably, but there is a difference. When two companies come together cooperatively to form one company, a **merger** takes place. Generally, a merger implies that the two companies involved are about the same size and have mutually agreed to form a new combined company. An **acquisition,** on the other hand, occurs when one company completely buys out another company. In some instances, companies claim a merger has occurred, but in reality, one company has acquired the other. Merger has a better connotation than acquisition, and therefore is used to allow the acquired company to "save face." Often, the combined organization reflects the names of the individual companies, for example, when Sprint Corporation, a global Internet carrier, merged with Nextel Communications, a U.S. telecommunications company, to form Sprint Nextel. In other situations, just one company name is kept; for example, Delta merged with Northwest and the combined airline operates under the Delta name.

Sometimes, a completely new name is derived, such as when Bell Atlantic acquired GTE to form Verizon Communications.

Are all mergers and acquisitions mutually desired by both companies? Often, acquisitions are friendly, as was the case when Google purchased Android in 2005. At the time, Android was just a start-up, but had demonstrated its ability to produce a working operating system for mobile devices. Post-merger, Android continues to be run by its co-founder Andy Rubin, but benefits from the significant resources that Google offers. In turn, Google benefits by having a viable mobile operating system that it uses to challenge industry giants Apple and Microsoft.

Although many mergers and acquisitions are "friendly" and mutually agreed on between companies, some acquisitions are "unfriendly." An unfriendly acquisition occurs when one company tries to take control over another company against its wishes. Unfriendly acquisitions are referred to as *hostile takeovers*. An unfriendly or hostile acquisition attempt occurs through a *tender offer*, where the acquiring firm offers to buy the target company's stock at a price higher than its current value, which is meant to induce shareholders into selling.

Another method of acquiring a company against its wishes is through a *proxy fight* in which the acquiring company tries to persuade the shareholders of the target company to vote out existing management and introduce management that is sympathetic to the goals of the acquiring company. This is the strategy Microsoft pursued when it unsuccessfully tried to take over Yahoo! in 2008.[11]

Some takeovers that are initiated by an outside group of investors, employees, or management are financed with debt. The acquiring group borrows the funds necessary for the acquisition, using the assets of the acquired company as collateral. This type of transaction is called a *leveraged buyout (LBO)*. LBOs can be either friendly or hostile, and companies of all sizes have been the targets of LBO transactions. Some of the more recent and largest LBOs involved the Hertz Corporation, Metro-Goldwyn-Mayer, and Toys"R"Us.

Advantages of Mergers and Acquisitions

Why do mergers and acquisitions occur? *Synergy* is the business buzzword often used to justify a merger or an acquisition. **Synergy** is the effect achieved when two companies combine, in which the result is better than each company could achieve individually. Synergistic value is created when the new company can realize operating or financial economies of scale. Combined firms often lower costs by trimming redundancies in staff, sharing resources, and obtaining discounts accessible only to a larger firm. In other instances, synergy is achieved by combining resources that could not have been created independently by either party. Such was the case with the merger of satellite radio providers Sirius and XM. Each satellite radio provider had exclusive contracts with different sports programmers. Customers were having a hard time choosing between one and the other. The merger gives customers the benefit of both.

Is competition a driving force for mergers and acquisitions? Achieving a greater competitive advantage is another reason mergers and acquisitions take place. Often, companies join to become a more dominant force in their market. For example, in 2009, Pfizer, the world's largest drug maker, acquired rival Wyeth and claimed that the newly combined company would be "one of the most diversified in the industry."[12] One of the compelling reasons Pfizer pursued the acquisition was to become more competitive by gaining access to Wyeth's portfolio of new vaccines and biotechnology medicines.

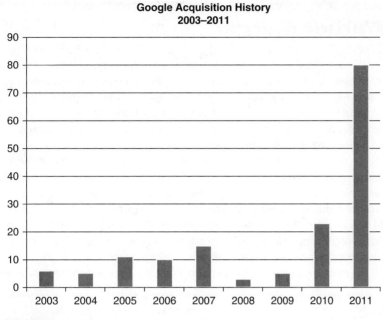

FIGURE 6.12
Google Acquisition Activity
(*Source:* Based on Figure: "Google Acquisition Activity" from Jason Hesse, "Google's 2010 Acquisition
Activity—Analysis." Real Business. Sept. 29, 2010. http://realbusiness.co.uk)

Do companies add value to their product line by mergers? Many times,
larger companies acquire smaller companies for their innovativeness, and a smaller
company will agree to merge or be acquired if it feels it wouldn't have the opportunity to go public and couldn't survive alone otherwise. Much of Google's
growth can be attributed to their innovative creativity within the company, but
some has also come from their acquisitions of small, innovative companies such as
Feedburner, Like.com, Applied Semantics, Postini, YouTube, and DoubleClick.[16] As
shown in ■ **FIGURE 6.12**, Google has had a very aggressive acquisition strategy,
especially compared to other companies in the same industry (see ■ **FIGURE 6.13**).

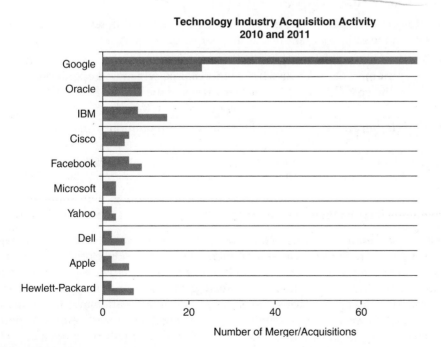

FIGURE 6.13
Technology Merger and Acquisition Activity—2010 and 2011

AOL-Time Warner Merger

Although it took place more than a decade ago, the merger between America Online (AOL), an Internet services company, and Time Warner, a media and communications company is still viewed as one of the worst mergers in U.S. history. Valued at $111 billion, the merger also was (and still is) the largest merger in the United States. At the time, it was believed that the combination of an Internet giant and a media behemoth would, in the words of Gerald Levin, CEO of Time Warner, "create unprecedented and instantaneous access to every form of media and to unleash immense possibilities for economic growth, human understanding and creative expression."[13] According to AOL cofounder Stephen Case, the merger was "a historic moment in which new media has truly come of age."[14] However, the deal began to sour almost immediately, as it was soon quite apparent that the two companies had very different cultures. In addition, AOL, "the crown jewel of the transaction,"[15] ran into great financial difficulties as the dot-com bubble began to burst only months after the merger. Moreover, investigations by the SEC and the Department of Justice revealed that AOL had been improperly inflating its advertising revenue. In 2009, Time Warner spun off AOL as an independent company.

6 What are the different types of mergers and acquisitions, and why do they occur?

Types of Mergers

Are there different types of mergers? The rationale and strategy behind every merger is different, but, as illustrated in ■ **FIGURE 6.14**, there are some consistencies, distinguished by the relationship between the two companies that are merging:

- **Horizontal merger.** Two companies that share the same product lines and markets and are in direct competition with each other, such as Exxon and Mobil and Daimler-Benz and Chrysler.

- **Vertical merger.** Two companies that have a company/customer relationship or a company/supplier relationship, such as Walt Disney and Pixar or eBay and PayPal.

- **Product extension merger.** Two companies selling different but related products in the same market, such as the merger between Adobe and Macromedia.

- **Market extension merger.** Two companies that sell the same products in different markets, such as when NationsBank, which had operations primarily on the East Coast and in southern areas of the United States, merged with Bank of America, whose prime business was on the West Coast.

- **Conglomeration.** Two companies that have no common business areas merge to obtain diversification. For example, Citicorp, a banking services firm, and Travelers Group Inc., an insurance underwriting company, combined to form one of the world's largest financial services group, Citigroup Inc.

Disadvantages of Mergers

Are there disadvantages with mergers? Despite the perceived advantages of mergers, more than one-half of all mergers fail completely or don't live up to financial expectations.[16] The primary culprit of a failed merger is poor integration following the transaction. After an exhausting process, which may cause top executives to take their eyes off business, little energy or motivation may be left to plan and manage how the two companies will come together to work as one. Although cost cutting may be the initial primary focus of some mergers, revenues and profits may ultimately suffer if day-to-day activities are neglected. Additionally, corporate cultures may clash, and communications may break down if the new division of responsibilities is vague. Conflicts may also arise due to divided loyalties, hidden

FIGURE 6.14 Different Types of Mergers Companies merge for different strategic reasons. Sometimes, companies merge to enter new markets, whereas others want to expand into new fields and save costs.

Image Sources: m.u.ozmen/ Fotolia; Sean Gladwell/ Fotolia; stootsy/Fotolia; Maksim Shebeko/Fotolia; Natika/Fotolia; thewhitelight /Fotolia; Fotolia365/Fotolia; Scanrail/Fotolia

Horizontal Merger
Companies that share same product lines and markets

Vertical Merger
Companies that have company/supplier or company/customer relationship

Product Extension Merger
Companies selling different but related products in the same market

Market Extension Merger
Companies selling same products to different markets

Conglomeration
Companies that have no direct common business areas merge to obtain diversification

agendas, or power struggles within the newly combined management team. Employees may be nervous because most mergers result in the elimination of jobs, and more turnover may be created as those employees whose jobs may not be threatened by the merger seek employment in a more stable environment.

Google, like many technology companies, acquired other companies that helped to extend and complement Google's existing product line. In many industries, it's often easier and quicker to buy a start-up with an innovative product or service rather than trying to build one from scratch. Some acquisitions didn't work out, but others did. Google, once just a company with a great search engine, is striving to maintain its market dominance, and maybe then some by acquiring into different markets. ■

CHAPTER 6
SUMMARY

MyBizLab

Go to **mybizlab.com** to complete the problems marked with this icon ⭐.

1 **What are the advantages and disadvantages of a sole proprietorship? (pp. 166–169)**

- A **sole proprietorship** (p. 166) is a business owned and usually operated by a single individual.

- The sole proprietorship is a common form of business ownership because it is the easiest to establish, but there are both strengths and weaknesses inherent in this business form.

- The advantage of establishing a business as a sole proprietorship is that there are no formal, legal requirements for starting the business, and the revenues and expenses are reported directly on the business owner's personal income tax return.

- The primary disadvantage of a sole proprietorship is that personal and business assets are at risk in the event of a business catastrophe.

2 **What are the advantages and disadvantages of a partnership and a partnership agreement? (pp. 169–172)**

- A **partnership** (p. 169) is a business structure that is easy to establish and has no formal, legal requirements.

- Partnerships offer the benefit of two or more individuals sharing aspects of the business, including financial management and sales and marketing responsibilities. Income and expenses flow directly through each partner's individual tax return.

- Partnerships are recommended to have a **partnership agreement** (p. 171), which is a formal document that outlines the responsibilities for each partner and includes provisions when there are disputes among partners.

- Problems can occur when partners do not agree on the nature of the business or have different work ethics.

- Partners' personal and business assets are at risk, with each partner being solely liable for any part of the business. Responsibility is not limited to each partner's financial contribution to the business.

3 **How is a corporation formed, and how does it compare with sole proprietorships and partnerships? (pp. 174–175)**

- **Corporations** (p. 174) are businesses structured as separate legal entities. Corporations are structured with different levels of management, including shareholders, board of directors, and corporate officers, such as the **chief executive officer (CEO)** (p. 176), the **chief**

financial officer (CFO) (p. 176), and the **chief operating officer (COO)** (p. 176).

- Corporations differ from sole proprietorships and partnerships for the following reasons:

  - Corporations are difficult to set up.

  - Corporations require much ongoing paperwork, including annual reports, corporate minutes, and formal financial records.

  - Corporations must file separate tax returns.

  - Corporations can sue and be sued.

  - Corporations protect an owner's personal assets.

4 **What are the major differences between a C corporation, an S corporation, and a limited liability company? (pp. 177–180)**

- **S corporations** (p. 177) are like **C corporations** (p. 174) that offer the protection of limited liability, but S corporations allow the shareholders to flow the corporate revenues and expenses through their personal tax returns.

- S corporations have certain restrictions, which include having no more than 100 shareholders, requiring shareholders to be residents of the United States, allowing for the issuance of only one class of stock, and basing profits and losses on the proportional interest of each shareholder.

- The corporate structure of a **limited liability company (LLC)** (p. 178) is similar to an S corporation that offers the protection of limited liability of a corporation. LLCs differ from S corporations because they can have unlimited members, must dissolve when any member leaves, and do not base distribution of profits on the direct proportion of a member's financial contribution.

5 **What are the characteristics of not-for-profit organizations and cooperatives? (pp. 181–182)**

- **Not-for-profit organizations** (p. 181) are corporations whose purpose is to serve the public interest rather than to seek to make a profit. Not-for-profit organizations are tax exempt, and donations to the organization are deemed tax deductible.

- **Cooperatives** (p. 182) are businesses that are owned and governed by members who use its products and services, not by outside investors.

- Cooperatives are motivated to provide services or goods to people with common interests or needs.

- All profits generated by the cooperative are returned to the members in direct proportion to their share of ownership.
- Cooperatives use the benefit of group power to negotiate within their marketplace.

6 **What are the different types of mergers and acquisitions, and why do they occur?** (pp. 186–187)

- Mergers and acquisitions are business practices that bring companies together (in two distinct manners) for the purpose of achieving better **synergy** (p. 184).
  - An **acquisition** (p. 183) occurs when one company buys another company outright. The purchased company ceases to exist and starts to operate under the buying company's name and management. Acquisitions can be friendly (mutually agreed on) or unfriendly (one company buys the other against the wishes of the management and/or owner).

- A **merger** (p. 183) occurs when two companies of similar size mutually agree to combine to form a new company. Some types of mergers are as follows:
  - **Horizontal mergers** (p. 186): Two companies that share the same product lines and are in direct competition with each other merge.
  - **Vertical merger** (p. 186): Two companies that have a company/customer relationship or a company/supplier relationship merge.
  - **Product extension merger** (p. 186): Two companies selling different but related products in the same market merge.
  - **Market extension merger** (p. 186): Two companies that sell the same products in different markets merge.
  - **Conglomeration** (p. 186): Two companies that have no common business areas merge to obtain diversification.

Key Terms

acquisition (p. 183)
board of directors (p. 176)
C corporation (p. 174)
capital (p. 171)
chief executive officer (CEO) (p. 176)
chief financial officer (CFO) (p. 176)
chief operating officer (COO) (p. 176)
closed corporation (p. 175)
cooperatives (p. 182)
conglomeration (p. 186)

corporation (p. 174)
double taxation (p. 177)
general partners (p. 172)
general partnership (p. 172)
horizontal merger (p. 186)
liability (p. 168)
limited liability company (LLC) (p. 178)
limited partner (p. 172)
limited partnership (p. 172)
market extension merger (p. 186)
merger (p. 183)
not-for-profit organization (p. 181)

partnership (p. 169)
partnership agreement (p. 171)
privately held corporation (p. 175)
product extension merger (p. 186)
publicly owned corporation (p. 175)
S corporation (p. 177)
shareholder (p. 175)
sole proprietorship (p. 166)
stockholder (p. 175)
synergy (p. 184)
unlimited liability (p. 168)
vertical merger (p. 186)

Self-Test

Multiple Choice You can find the answers on the last page of this book.

1. Omar and Sam are physical therapists who work together. Their office is on the first floor of an apartment building Omar owns. They need protection of their personal assets. Which business structure would best suit their company?

    a. A general partnership

    b. A sole proprietorship

    c. A not-for-profit organization

    d. An LLC

2. Why might a potential business owner want to establish a business as a sole proprietorship?

    a. The owner can use personal assets to satisfy any business liabilities.

    b. The owner can take into consideration the opinions of other business owners.

    c. The owner can generate a separate tax return for business expenses.

    d. The owner is not required to file legal paperwork to start up the business.

3. Trudy and Yvonne have come together to run Salford Children's Center, a place where parents on welfare can drop their children off to be cared for while the parents are looking for work. The center receives income from state and federal grants, and whatever is left over is put back into the Center for additional resources. Salford Children's Center would best be described as a(n)

    a. partnership.

    b. LLC.

    c. not-for-profit organization.

    d. sole proprietorship.

4. Jackson Eats is a partnership owned by Jesse and Robert Jackson. They need additional capital to expand to a new location, so they have decided to bring in Sean, who will not only contribute some capital but will also manage the new restaurant. Sean would best be considered as a(n)

    a. general partner.

    b. limited partner.

    c. owner.

    d. None of the above

5. Which of the following is a reason for creating a new business as a C corporation?

    a. The owner's personal assets would be protected.

    b. The owner could raise greater sources of funds by selling shares of ownership.

    c. The corporation would continue to exist even if the owner left the business.

    d. All of the above

6. Suzanne wanted to invest in her friends' new business, but cannot be involved in the daily management and activities of the business. If the business is structured as a partnership, Suzanne would be what kind of partner?

    a. A general partner

    b. A limited partner

    c. A managing partner

    d. An unlimited partner

7. If you were concerned about protecting personal liability but still wanted to flow income and losses through to your personal taxes, which form of corporate structure would be best?

    a. A C corporation

    b. A sole proprietorship

    c. A general partnership

    d. An LLC

8. Which is a benefit of cooperatives?

    a. The group power enables them to negotiate for goods and services at a favorable price.

    b. They are exempt from paying federal and state taxes.

    c. They are established to serve the public interest rather than make a profit.

    d. They provide services to people with a variety of interests and needs.

9. If Mom's outdoor clothing store combined with Dad's camping equipment store to form Mom & Dad's Outdoor Store, which of the following best describes the type of transaction that occurred between the two companies?

    a. A vertical merger

    b. A product extension merger

    c. A horizontal merger

    d. A conglomeration

10. The management team of Company A decides to offer to buy the stock from all the shareholders of Company B at a higher price than current market value. Company A is launching a

    a. proxy fight.

    b. tender offer.

    c. friendly acquisition.

    d. friendly takeover.

True/False You can find the answers on the last page of this book.

1. Any business can elect to be an S corporation.
   ☑ **True** or ☐ **False**

2. A company's officers are responsible for electing the board of directors.
   ☐ **True** or ☐ **False**

3. A small, privately owned company can be structured as a corporation.
   ☑ **True** or ☐ **False**

4. A significant disadvantage of forming a corporation is the amount of paperwork and reporting that is required.
   ☐ **True** or ☐ **False**

5. A partnership agreement should include procedures that handle a partner's departure from the business as well as how any new partners are to be brought in.
   ☑ **True** or ☐ **False**

Critical Thinking Questions

1. Why might it be important to structure your business as a C corporation, even if you are the only person running the business?

2. Investigate a nonprofit organization in your area. What cause is it serving? What is the primary source of its income? What are its main expenses?

3. Approximately 70 percent of all businesses are sole proprietorships. Why is sole proprietorship a popular form of business ownership? What are the circumstances when it might be important to consider a different form of ownership?

Team Time

WHAT'S THE PLAN?

Imagine that you work for the SBA and have the opportunity to advise new business owners on the form of ownership their businesses should take. Form groups of three to five people and choose one of the business ideas below. Work as a group to create an outline of a business plan for each business idea. What kind of business forms would you suggest for each idea and why? Be sure to consider the potential risks and liabilities, the potential income tax situations, and the current and future investment needs of each business. Assume in five years, the business needed additional capital to expand by adding a new building in a different location. Would your business structure support raising the necessary capital? Why or why not?

Business Ideas

- Roofing and siding company
- Ice cream parlor
- Yoga instruction
- Lawn mowing company
- Clothing donation company

Team Time (continued)

Process

Meet as a group to discuss your business idea. Remember that you must prepare an outline of a business plan. Use what you know about the forms of business ownership to create the business plan.

Step 1. Prepare an individual report that explains the form of ownership your business should take and outline why it should take this form.

Step 2. Determine who will be the group's primary spokesperson for your business plan.

Step 3. Your group will have five minutes to present your recommendations.

Step 4. After each group has presented, discuss any differences of opinion about the proposed business structures.

Ethics and Corporate Social Responsibility

SARBANES-OXLEY

Sarbanes-Oxley has been called the "most sweeping corporate regulation measure in decades," and yet, as has been evidenced by the ethical and legal violations incurred by some large banks and investment banks since the passing of Sarbanes-Oxley, it seems as though the measure was not enough. The surge of scandals continues to be fueled, in part, by trying to improve stock value to meet shareholder expectations. Often this results in companies avoiding actions that might result in short-term losses but that would be overall beneficial in the long run. Instead, companies favor transactions that improve share value for a short period of time but which may not be in the long-term best interest of the company. Moreover, because top-level executives are compensated by stock performance, they, too, are driven by such transactions.

Questions for Discussion

1. How do you think executive pay is tied into corporate integrity? Do you think executives' compensation should be tied to corporate performance? Why or why not?

2. How do you think managing a company for stock market performance might lead to risky behavior from the corporate officers and board of directors?

Web Exercises

1. **Business Combinations**
   Look on the Internet for a current example of a business merger, takeover, or acquisition. Explain the circumstances of the event. What companies are involved? Was the event friendly or unfriendly? What are the reasons given for the combination? What is your opinion of this business combination? Do you think it is a good business decision? Why or why not?

2. **Student-Friendly Businesses**
   You have decided to start your own business. You want it to be something you can do while you're still a student. Research on the Web ideas for small businesses for students. Describe at least three different ideas and include what form of business ownership you would use to structure each business.

3. **The Perfect Partner**
   Go to www.inc.com/guides/leadership_strat/23041.html and read the advice for how to pick the perfect business partner. Using information you learned from this chapter and the website, write a list of rules for picking the perfect business partner. What factors should be taken into account? What can you do to avoid trouble in the future?

4. **Plan with the End in Mind**
   Beginning a business requires a lot of planning, but even still, the business often fails. However, most business owners do not have an "exit plan" in mind when they start the venture. Research the main causes of business failures and what kind of exit strategies can be set in place at the beginning to ease the pain if the business needs to close.

5. **Preparing for Business**
   Think of a business idea you might like to pursue some day. Imagine that "some day" is today. Visit the Score.org website, search for the business quizzes, and then take the quizzes there to see if you're prepared to start your business. Are you really ready to begin your business venture?

MyBizLab

Go to **mybizlab.com** for Auto-graded writing questions as well as the following Assisted-graded writing questions:

6-1. Discuss the various types of mergers and give examples of each.

6-2. Describe a corporation's organizational structure. What are the three basic groups, and what are their roles?

6-3. MyBizLab Only – comprehensive writing assignment for this chapter.

Constructing an Effective Business Plan

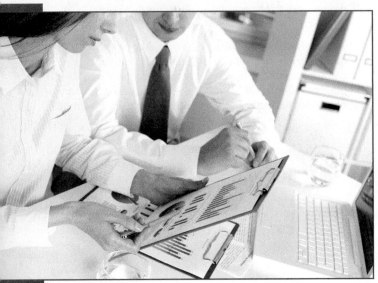

pressmaster/Fotolia

From the moment you received money for mowing your neighbor's lawn or babysitting your neighbor's child, you've been interested in starting your own business. But where do you begin? Do you purchase business cards? Do you create and distribute flyers? Although these might be good ways to get your business moving, they are not the first things you should do when starting a business. The Small Business Association (SBA) suggests that the very first step in starting a business is *planning*. Writing a business plan is usually the first step in that planning process. A business plan is a written document that details a proposed or existing venture, describing the vision, current status, the markets in which it operates, and the current and projected results of a business.

Traditionally, a potential business owner writes a business plan *before* a business is launched, but it can be written after a business has been established. In some instances, and especially in industries in which change occurs rapidly, a business opportunity might be lost if you do not start operations immediately; you may not have time to take the weeks or months often required to write a business plan. In this situation, you should still begin by answering a few discrete and pointed questions, such as those shown in ■ FIGURE 1. This will help you determine whether the business you're pursuing will be worth the effort. Eventually, a formal business plan should be written to more thoroughly define the goals and objectives of the business and the means to achieve them.

Planning—It's Never Too Late

In 1958, college-aged brothers Dan and Frank Carney borrowed $600 from their mother to open a pizza parlor in Wichita, Kansas. This venture marked the inception of the Pizza Hut empire. The brothers had neither a formal business plan nor a clear vision of the path their business would take. In fact, the Carneys simply gave away pizza on their opening night to garner the public's interest. Although their gimmick was impulsive, it worked. Less than a year later, the boys incorporated and opened their first franchise unit in Topeka, Kansas. Within the next 10 years, more than 150 franchises opened nationwide, and one international franchise opened in Canada. However, in 1970, the company's growth became explosive. Pizza Hut went public, and the brothers quickly became overwhelmed. "We about lost control of the operations," Frank Carney said in 1972. "Then we figured out that we had to learn how to plan."[1] Ultimately, Frank and

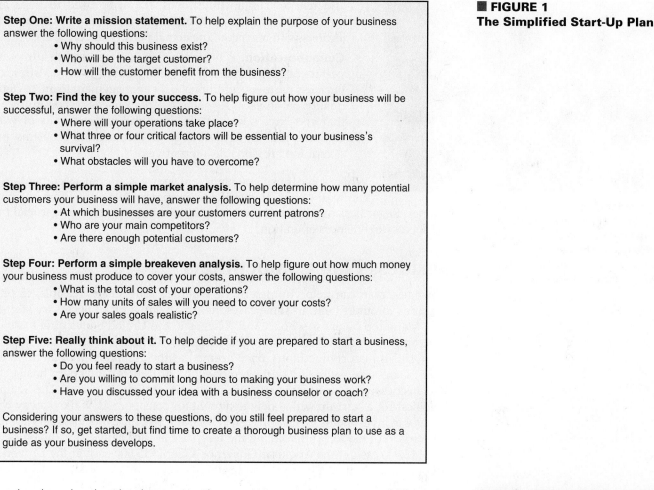

Step One: Write a mission statement. To help explain the purpose of your business answer the following questions:
- Why should this business exist?
- Who will be the target customer?
- How will the customer benefit from the business?

Step Two: Find the key to your success. To help figure out how your business will be successful, answer the following questions:
- Where will your operations take place?
- What three or four critical factors will be essential to your business's survival?
- What obstacles will you have to overcome?

Step Three: Perform a simple market analysis. To help determine how many potential customers your business will have, answer the following questions:
- At which businesses are your customers current patrons?
- Who are your main competitors?
- Are there enough potential customers?

Step Four: Perform a simple breakeven analysis. To help figure out how much money your business must produce to cover your costs, answer the following questions:
- What is the total cost of your operations?
- How many units of sales will you need to cover your costs?
- Are your sales goals realistic?

Step Five: Really think about it. To help decide if you are prepared to start a business, answer the following questions:
- Do you feel ready to start a business?
- Are you willing to commit long hours to making your business work?
- Have you discussed your idea with a business counselor or coach?

Considering your answers to these questions, do you still feel prepared to start a business? If so, get started, but find time to create a thorough business plan to use as a guide as your business develops.

■ **FIGURE 1**
The Simplified Start-Up Plan

Dan developed a plan that kept operations constant and under control. They also created a corporate strategy that enticed PepsiCo to purchase Pizza Hut in 1977. At that time, Pizza Hut sales had reached $436 million a year.[2] The Carneys' story is a success; however, if they had developed a clear business plan from the beginning, they may have been better prepared to handle their company's incredible growth.

Although Pizza Hut owners Dan and Frank Carney launched a successful business without a formal business plan, they soon found that planning was necessary for continued success.

The Purpose of a Plan

A business plan is your "business story"—a story that you will tell to a wide variety of people, from personal friends and casual acquaintances to potential partners, suppliers, customers, and investors. There are three purposes to writing a business plan: development, management, and communication.

- **Development.** Writing down your business plan solidifies and defines your intentions. It forces you to think through many aspects of a business that might otherwise be overlooked, identify roadblocks and obstacles, and determine ways to resolve or avoid them. Business plans can be used to get the entire management team, and perhaps the employees of the company, to understand where the company is and where it is heading.

- **Management.** Of course, the goal of most businesses is to make money, so a business plan should summarize how a business opportunity will translate into profits. A business plan also helps in the management of a company. Because it is a living document, it should be modified as the business changes

One notable winner of the MIT 100K Entrepreneurship's Business Plan Competition was Harmonix, the video game development company responsible for creating Guitar Hero and Rock Band.

and reaches certain milestones. It can be used to track and monitor the progress of the company, as well as evaluate projections with respect to the actual performance.

- **Communication.** A business plan is often used to attract investors or obtain loans. It can also be used to attract strategic business partners, additions to the management team, or high-quality employees. As such, the plan needs to communicate that you have taken an objective and realistic view of your company and thought through all the potential problems and determined reasonable alternatives.

While some business plans are lengthy, formal documents that can take weeks or months to prepare, others are short, informal outlines. Regardless of when or how it is written, a business plan is a crucial part of a successful business operation.

Business Plan Competitions

A business plan can help you determine whether your idea is feasible, to pitch your idea to others, and, in some cases, help you win a bit of necessary start-up cash. Many top business schools and colleges in the United States offer business plan competitions, with cash prizes that range from $10,000 to $100,000.

Business plan competitions, once deemed as the culmination of an academic exercise, are now sources of serious money. In 2010, Rice University hosted the first business plan competition to offer over $1 million in prizes. The winner, BiologicsMD, a start-up with a new treatment for osteoporosis, walked away with $300,000 in investments, $39,250 in cash grants, and $80,100 in business services and gift cards. Not too long after taking the top prize at Rice University, BiologicsMD won $12,000 cash at the Arkansas Governor's Cup, $15,500 cash at the University of Louisville Cardinal Challenge, and $10,250 cash at the University of Cincinnati Business Plan Competition.[3]

Business plan competitions have given life to hundreds of business ideas. The venerable MIT (Massachusetts Institute of Technology) 100K Entrepreneurship's Business Plan Competition is the final step of a trio of contests, including the Elevator Pitch and the Executive Summary Contest. The MIT competition has been giving away prizes since 1990 and has sparked the formation of approximately 130 companies. One of the more notable winners is Harmonix, the company that created Guitar Hero and Rock Band. Harmonix was acquired by MTV Networks in 2006 for $175 million. In 2008, the founders, Alex Rigopulos and Eran Egozy, were named as two of the 100 most influential people in the world in *Time Magazine*.[4]

Before the Business Plan: Finding the Right Fit

Before you begin to think about writing a business plan, you should do some soul searching to determine your own goals and objectives and whether they match those of the business that you've imagined. You might want to visit the SBA's website to find questionnaires and quizzes that can help you focus your ideas.

Not everyone wants to be (or can be) the next Bill Gates. Some individuals are quite content running a successful business that consists of a few employees and that never sees revenues in the millions. However, some ambitious entrepreneurs would like to have their ideas realized on a much larger scale. Regardless of the size of business you would like to own, it is important to articulate your own personal business plan by answering questions like the following:

- Do you want to have a balance between your business life and your personal life? Or is it okay for your business to be your life?
- How do you define "success"? Is it a monetary goal, a production goal, or a lifestyle goal?

■ **FIGURE 2**
Basic Components of a Business Plan

- What is your timeline for "success"? Do you want to achieve it quickly, or is it acceptable to work slowly toward graduated markers of success?

Determining the answers to these questions will help to crystallize your focus, realize what your priorities are, and clarify your business goals and objectives. Once this preparation is complete, you're poised to begin writing your business plan.

Components of a Business Plan

There is no one right way to write a business plan. Each business is unique, so business plans can be drawn up in a variety of ways. Still, most business plans share a few basic components. A typical business plan for a start-up company is about 35–60 pages in length and contains eight key elements, as illustrated in ■ **FIGURE 2**. The order in which the key elements are included is not random; they should be in the order of importance to the person reading the document. Therefore, although a complete description of your product may be of utmost importance to you, your investors and key contributors first need to know about the market before the specifics of your product. Let's look at each of the basic components of a business plan in more detail.

The Cover Sheet and Table of Contents

The *cover sheet* of a business plan is like the cover of a book; it provides the first impression of your plan and your business. This component is crucial, but many business planners don't include the right information on the cover sheet, which may turn off potential investors. As shown in ■ **FIGURE 3**, the cover sheet should include the following:

- Basic company information (name, address, phone number, and Web address)
- The company logo (if applicable)
- Contact information of the owner(s) and any officers (name, titles, addresses, phone numbers, and e-mail addresses)
- The month and year the business plan was created
- The name(s) of those who prepared the plan
- A unique record number so that you can track who received which copy so you can easily follow up with him or her

■ **FIGURE 3**
Sample Business Plan Cover Sheet

AB Environmental Consulting
21 N. LaSalle Street
Chicago, IL 60611
(312) 555-6439
www.abenvironmentalconsulting.com

Business Plan

Prepared by:

Adam Bernard
President & Owner
(312) 555-6438
abernard@abenvironmentalconsulting.com

January 2013

#AB5336

The *table of contents* follows the cover sheet. It should be well organized so that the reader can quickly find information on any aspect of the business. It should also include the page number of the first page of each section, and all pages in the document should be numbered.

The Executive Summary

An **executive summary** is a clear and concise (abbreviated) form of the entire business plan, generally no more than two or three pages long. After reading the executive summary, a person should understand the business's purpose, value, operating methods, and profitability outlook. An executive summary should contain information about the company's unique competitive advantage and projections for future sales, growth, and profits. If the business plan is to be presented to potential investors, the executive summary should also include a statement regarding the amount of and uses for capital, as well as plans and a timetable for repaying investors.

Ultimately, the executive summary should convey excitement and entice the reader to want to read more. Because this is often the only part of a business plan that is read completely, it is the most critical and, as a result, requires more of your time, thought, and attention than the rest of the business plan. Executive summaries are especially important when presenting your business plan to potential investors. If investors don't get excited about your business and the prospects of success after reading the executive summary, they'll stop reading and most likely file your plan in the trash. Because the executive summary is meant to condense the entire plan into a few pages, many people often write the summary as the last step in the business plan process. Writing your summary after completing the rest of your plan ensures that you've worked out all the kinks and made sure the other sections of the plan are sound.

The Company and Management Team

The next section of the business plan presents the "big picture" and defines the company and its purpose. The company section should include the following elements:

- **The mission and vision statements.** As discussed in Chapter 7, the *mission* and *vision statement*s should spell out what the founder ultimately envisions the business to be with respect to growth, values, and contributions to society. They may also offer the company's business strategy that defines the business, identifies the intended customer, and explains how the business will benefit them.

- **Industry profile.** The *industry profile* describes the context in which the business will operate. This section discusses economic trends that affect the business and provides background on the industry, the current outlook for the industry, and future growth potential.

- **Company profile and strategy.** The *company profile* provides details regarding how the business works and why it has a unique chance to impact the industry. The *company strategy* summarizes the company's plans for growth and profits. It is important to be optimistic while also being realistic in discussing goals and strategy. It is even more important to back up the strategy with details of the company's past and present conditions so that the strategy is convincing.

- **Anticipated challenges and planned responses.** This section discusses potential vulnerabilities from competition, suppliers, resources, industry, or economic situations. It also discusses legal factors that might affect the business—either positively or negatively—including changes to legal restrictions, pending lawsuits, expiring patents, copyrights, and the like. This section should also state possible resources the company could make available should the need arise. Finally, the section should mention any protection from copyrights, trademarks, or patents.

- **The management team.** This section should list the members of the management team—finance, marketing, and production specialists—and the pertinent experience, knowledge, or creative ability that each member brings to the team. If your company is large enough to have a board of directors, those members should be listed in this section as well. Because résumés of key personnel will be attached to the back of the business plan, keep this section brief, and dedicate only a paragraph or two to each individual.

A successful business plan weighs both the positive and negative aspects of a business.

Market Analysis

The **market analysis** section identifies who your customers are and explains how you will reach them. The main purpose of this section is to explain the *benefits* of your product. It should answer the question, "What is it about your product that creates a competitive advantage?" For example, your product might be homemade pasta. Your customers might benefit from an authentic Italian taste at a price that is lower than the competition's price. Or, your product could be made with all organic ingredients, which benefits health-conscious consumers. Consumer benefits are those things that do something better for the customer. They affect a person's feelings, pocketbook, or both. The market analysis section should include an assessment of the general market and, more specifically, the competition, as follows:

- **Market research.** This section should contain an analysis of the market to determine whether enough customers exist and will continue to exist to make your business profitable now and in the future. First, you need to describe exactly what you see as the target market for your product—that is, identify your customer. For example, is your ideal customer teenagers heading off to college, owners of pets with little time to walk them, or those needing a great meal in a relaxing location? Once you've identified and described your customer, you need to determine whether the market is growing or shrinking. Your analysis should reach the conclusion that the market is big enough for your business to enter with adequate growth potential to make your time and investment worthwhile.
- **Assess the competition.** It is important to show that you have a clear understanding of your competition. Therefore, you should list your main competitors and their perceived strengths and weaknesses. You should then clearly articulate your plan to take advantage of their weaknesses and respond to their strengths.

The Product

In the next section of the business plan, you describe your product and list its important details. Your product's description should include any testing you've conducted and approvals you've received, as well as trademarks, copyrights, or patents to protect your product. It is also important to discuss ongoing service aspects that are provided with the product, such as warranties and repairs. Your business plan should articulate how the product will be produced. If part of your product is dependent on outside suppliers, you should list those suppliers and verify their reliability. If your business is a service, you should discuss how you intend to find and train personnel who will deliver your service.

Most importantly, whether for a good or a service, this section should cover your pricing strategy. In your pricing discussion, detail any aspects of the product that require a higher price, such as using premium materials. Additionally, you

How will you promote your business? A business plan will help you decide whether to post a flyer on a busy street corner or place an ad in a popular magazine.

must conduct a thorough analysis of what the competition is charging for a similar product, noting the differences in their product or your product that justify a price differential. Lastly, the section should list what you expect customers will be willing to pay for your product.

Sales and Promotion

The sales and promotion section of the business plan explains how you intend to implement the marketing plan. It should describe the approaches you'll take to promote the product. This should include promotional avenues beyond basic advertising. Include your social media strategy, such as using blogs, Facebook, Twitter, Foursquare, or YouTube, and also how you are monitoring the feedback derived from your social media strategy.

This section should also describe your selling approach. For example, are you selling the product with a sales force, over the Internet, through direct mail, via retail outlets, or simply by word of mouth? Include evidence of promotional success, such as current newspaper articles, customer referrals, or letters of satisfaction.

Financials

This section includes several pages of financial statements: the income statement, the balance sheet, and the cash flow statement. In addition, you should cover the financial history of the company to date and have several different forecasts and scenarios projecting the anticipated performance of the business in the next several years. You should put your financials through a stress test by showing how you expect the business to perform under worst-case, expected-case, and best-case scenarios. If one of the primary purposes of this business plan is to seek outside financing assistance, then another component of this section is a statement of funding requirements indicating information such as the amount of capital needed, the type of funding, the term of loan, and how funds will be used. Investors will also want to see how you intend to pay them back—the timing, the return on investment, and an exit strategy that you might want to suggest to investors.

Don't underestimate the importance of preparing the financial information or be misled into thinking that developing the financial information will or should be easy. This exercise forces you, as a new business owner, to face up to the reality of your business's finances beyond daily cash flow. The numbers need to show that you can be successful in the short term as well as over the long term.

Oddly, more is not better in presenting the financials of a company. More importantly, if you use a software program to generate financials, make sure you understand and can defend and explain every number in every line. It's not uncommon for someone who is reviewing the financials of a business plan to ask very specific questions, such as "What does the figure on line 24 in the income statement mean?" If your answer is, "I'm not sure, the software program generated that number," you are not creating investor confidence in your ability to understand and manage the financial aspects of the business. If necessary, consult an accountant to help you prepare and/or interpret the financial statements and projections included in the business plan.

Including the actual financial statements, forecasts, and scenarios in the business plan is not enough. You need to explain and summarize the key information from those statements and specifically state how they relate to the marketing, sales, and production plans already discussed.

Appendices

The final pages of a business plan should be devoted to appendices. Any additional information that adds to the credibility of your business, the management team, or the industry that is not included in the body of the business plan is included in the appendices. Appendices will include information such as the following:

- Résumés of key managers
- Pictures of the product, facilities, production, and so on
- Letters of recommendations, professional references
- Published information
- Contracts and agreements; copies of patents, copyrights, trademarks
- Media, articles

Writing a business plan can seem like a formidable task. But if you have a clear idea and vision of your business venture, your task will become a little easier. It is also important to know that you're not alone. The SBA and SCORE provide a wealth of information and resources for the potential small-business owner.

Remember, your business plan should be exciting, dynamic, and compelling. The plan's purpose is to make others as excited about your business idea as you are. If you carefully follow the steps for writing a business plan and strongly believe in your idea, you may soon have investors beating down your door to be a part of your project.

Business Management and Organization

1 What are the levels of management, and what skills do managers need to be successful? (pp. 204–207)

2 How are the strategic plan, the corporate vision, and the mission statement defined for a business? (pp. 208–210)

3 Why do managers need tactical plans, operational plans, and contingency plans? (pp. 211–213)

4 What is the significance of organizing, and how are most companies organized? (pp. 215–216)

5 How do managers ensure that the business is on track and moving forward? (pp. 218–221)

The Foundations of Management
Xerox Corporation CEO Ursula Burns started her career at Xerox in 1980 as a mechanical engineering intern. What kind of management skills did she display over the years to rise to the top of a multibillion-dollar corporation?

The Functions of Management: Planning
Planning is critical as a business gets off the ground, and every day after that. How does a tattoo artist take his skills forward into a real business? What sequence of planning stages and what tools can he use to accomplish his ultimate goals?

The Functions of Management: Organizing
Carrie Witt and Mark Healy have the same position at competing firms, but their day-to-day experiences differ greatly. Why is this?

The Functions of Management: Controlling
It all sounded so good. The planned reorganization was going to push the company to the next level of competition. So why was everything such a mess now?

MyBizLab®

⭐ **Improve Your Grade!**

Over 10 million students improved their results using the Pearson MyLabs.
Visit **mybizlab.com** for simulations, tutorials, and end-of-chapter problems.

CHAPTER 7

The Foundations of Management pp. 203–207

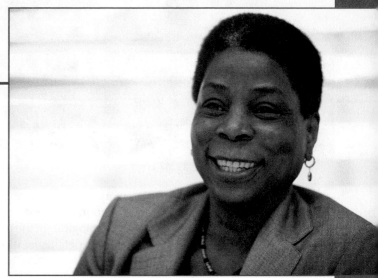
Bloomberg/Getty Images

U rsula Burns, the current CEO of Xerox Corporation, didn't start at the top. Instead, she rose from a position as a mechanical engineering summer intern at Xerox in 1980 to assume the role of chairperson and CEO in 2010. This was a historic event: It was the first time that a female CEO of a major U.S. company, Anne Mulcahy, handed the reins of a company over to another woman. Burns' personal story is dramatically American. She was raised by a single mother in a New York City housing project and now heads a $23 billion company.[1] It hasn't been all smooth sailing for Burns, however. Xerox Corporation faces serious challenges as business moves increasingly into electronic communication, therefore printing and copying less. But Burns has a track record for pushing forward new products with vision. In 1997, she helped direct Xerox into the field of color copying. Her vision moved Xerox out of manufacturing and diversified the set of products it offers. She is also willing to take the company in entirely new directions. An early move in her reign was the $6.4 billion acquisition of Affiliated Computer Services, leading Xerox into the arena of providing full solutions to business data processing and document management problems. In addition, many note her talent at being able to communicate her understanding of technology to the board of directors and other key members of the management team, an important trait. ■

What makes Ursula Burns such a talented and effective manager? What skills does she possess, and how does she apply them? In this chapter, we'll study what management is and discuss the skills integral to successful management.

Business Management

What exactly is management? Have you ever been in a team situation in which one person has been instrumental in making the group work more effectively? That person could have been a peer or a superior, but somehow he or she knew exactly what had to be accomplished, assessed the resources that were available to achieve the goal, and organized and led other group members to accomplish that goal. If so, you've seen management in action.

PLANNING
• Setting Goals
• Developing Strategies
• Determining Resources

ORGANIZING
• Allocating Resources
• Creating an Organizational Structure
• Recruiting and Placing Employees

CONTROLLING/ MONITORING
• Measuring Results Against Goals
• Monitoring Performance
• Correcting, When Necessary
• Rewarding

LEADING
• Guiding and Motivating
• Achieving Results and Milestones
• Maintaining Unit or Organization's Focus on the Goal or Vision

■ **FIGURE 7.1**
The Four Functions of Management
Image sources, clockwise from top left: Jasper James/Getty Images; Henrik Sorensen/Getty Images; Harry Briggs/ Getty Images; Vladimir Rys Photography/ Getty Images

1 What are the levels of management, and what skills do managers need to be successful?

Management is the process of working with people and resources to accomplish the goals of an organization. An organization can be a simple working group, a corporate department, or a multibillion-dollar company. The size of the group doesn't matter, but the skills of a manager and the process a manager goes through are similar across all management levels.

What are the four functions of management? As illustrated in ■ **FIGURE 7.1**, management involves four primary functions: planning, organizing, leading, and controlling/monitoring. These functions integrate all of a company's resources, including human, financial, and technological. In the remainder of this chapter, we'll examine three of these functions in more detail: planning, organizing, and controlling/monitoring. In Chapter 8, we'll examine leadership as a function of management.

Levels of Management

What are the different levels of management? The term *manager* is used in common English to describe any position that has employees reporting back to a supervisor. In the study of management, the company's management team has different levels of managers, with increasing levels of responsibility. ■ FIGURE 7.2 shows a traditional managerial pyramid with examples of jobs held by managers at each level and the tasks they perform.

What do top managers do? At the peak of the pyramid, **top managers** are the corporate officers who are responsible for an organization as a whole. Most established corporations determine the corporate offices, especially the chief executive officer (CEO), or president. Depending on the size and organizational complexity of a company, top management can also include the chief financial officer (CFO), the chief operations officer (COO), and the chief information officer (CIO).

Top managers generate the "big picture" for a company, defining its long-term goals and its strategic vision. Then they create plans that will take a company in that direction. They establish the culture of an organization and inspire employees to adopt senior management's vision of the organization. In smaller corporations,

■ **FIGURE 7.2**
The Managerial Pyramid

POSITIONS   TASKS

| President CEO Executive Vice President | **Top Managers** | Generating strategic plans, long-term goals, mission statement, and vision for the organization |

| Controller Sales Manager Marketing Manager Operations Manager | **Middle Managers** | Tactical planning and coordinating specific plans with the established strategic vision |

| Supervisor Department Head | **First-Line Managers** | Carrying out operational planning and supervising employees involved in the daily operations of the company |

How Are Managers Responsible for Employee Behavior?

Ani Chopourian was a physician assistant at Mercy General Hospital in Sacramento, California, for two years. In that time she had filed numerous complaints about sexually inappropriate workplace conduct by male physicians on the cardiovascular team she was part of—all of her complaints were ignored. After filing her eighteenth complaint, she was fired. In the legal action that followed, a jury awarded her $168 million in damages.[2]

The hospital administrators were not accused of any global practices that discriminated, but the jury heard from a parade of employees who depicted a culture that allowed female employees to be humiliated and bullied, even to the extent that it put patients at risk. What responsibility do the managers of the hospital have to provide a safe workplace culture? Are they able to control cardiac surgeons, who know that they bring in the most money to the hospital? What kind of tools do managers need to be able to navigate these challenges?

especially small start-up companies, top managers may also be responsible for planning and carrying out the day-to-day tasks of a company. But as the business grows, such companies will need to add more employees and divide the work into smaller tasks and areas of specialty, requiring a new layer of management.

What do middle managers do? **Middle managers** can be thought of as top managers for a division or segment of an organization. As such, they are responsible for creating specific plans that coordinate with the strategic vision set by the top managers. Included in this management layer are functional positions such as division managers (finance, marketing, sales, operations, and IT) or team leaders who are not arranged by function but are responsible for a cross-functional group of employees who must carry out specific tasks for an organization.

Are the people who supervise the day-to-day operations also managers? The bottom of the managerial pyramid includes **first-line managers**. These managers fill a supervisory role over those employees who carry out the day-to-day operations of a company.

Does every company have all these different managers? Not all companies have all three layers of management; some have more, and some have fewer. Typically you'll find the extra layers are middle managers.

The Skills of Successful Managers

What skills should a manager have? Because managerial tasks are so varied, a successful manager needs to possess the following types of skills:

- *conceptual*—the ability to think abstractly
- *technical*—specific knowledge for the discipline
- *time management*—the ability to be effective and productive with time
- *interpersonal*—the ability to motivate and communicate easily with others
- *decision-making*—the ability to analyze and implement the best plan of action

It is a rare person who is a master of all these skills. Moreover, because they are responsible for a variety of jobs and because these jobs can change quite rapidly, managers must assess the skills that are required in any given situation. Managers must also be willing to acquire these skills if they are lacking in a specific area, by studying, taking training, or finding a mentor to help.

What do we mean by conceptual skills? To make good decisions, a manager must have **conceptual skills**—the ability to think abstractly and to picture an organization as a whole and understand its relationship to the remainder of the business community. Such skills also include understanding the relationships between the parts of an organization itself. Whenever new market opportunities or potential threats arise, managers rely on their conceptual skills to help analyze the impending outcomes of their decisions. Conceptual skills are extremely important for top managers and are often developed with time and experience.

What technical skills do managers need? Every job has a specific set of technical skills that is important for business managers to possess. **Technical skills** include the abilities and knowledge that enable employees to carry out the specific tasks required of a discipline or a department, such as drafting skills for an architect, programming skills for a software developer, or market analysis skills for a marketing manager. Technical skills may also include how to operate certain machinery. Managers must be comfortable with technology and possess good analytical skills to interpret a variety of data. In addition to having the skills pertinent to their own jobs, managers must also know how to perform or at least have a good understanding of the skills required of the employees they supervise.

What time management skills does it take to succeed as a manager? Managers who possess **time management skills** are able to be effective and productive with their time. As a manager, how do you do this? Eliminating time wasters, such as constant interruptions, setting aside time each day to return phone calls and e-mail, ensuring that meetings have a clear agenda, and successfully delegating work to others, can increase the productive use of your available time. Analyzing your day to track carefully how your time is spent can also be an important key to improving time management.

Why are interpersonal skills important for managers? Managers achieve their goals by working with people both inside and outside an organization, so it is critical that they have strong interpersonal skills. **Interpersonal skills** enable managers to interact with other people to motivate them. It is important that managers develop trust and loyalty with the people they interact with, so they can motivate and encourage employees to work together.

Interpersonal skills are important skills at any management level. Top managers must be able to communicate with the board of directors, investors, and other leaders in the business community. They must also communicate with middle managers to clearly outline the goals and strategies of an organization. Middle managers must communicate with all levels of management and act as liaisons among groups. Lower-level managers must be able to motivate employees, build morale, and train and support those who perform the daily tasks of an organization. As workforce and business relationships continue to become more diverse, it is becoming increasingly important for managers to take into consideration the needs, backgrounds, and experiences of many different people when communicating with individuals and groups in an organization.

Why do some people consistently make better decisions than other people? It is critical that managers have good **decision-making skills**—the ability to identify and analyze a challenge, identify and examine the alternatives, choose and implement the best plan of action, and evaluate the results. When making important decisions, managers often go through a formal decision-making process similar to that shown in ■ **FIGURE 7.3**. Analyzing data and

■ **FIGURE 7.3**
Stages of Decision Making

Biz CHAT

Social Media: How Do Web-Based Tools Make Time Management Easier?

Calendars have traditionally been a tool used by individuals to manage their personal schedules. But with modern social media tools, Web-based calendars can provide for an easy exchange of information and synchronization of schedules. Various Web-based planning tools are available that allow multiple viewers to add new content to the calendar, thus making the scheduling of meetings more effective. For

example, Meeting Wizard is a product that sends out e-mail invitations with a poll of suggested meeting times. It then creates a report for you with the group responses and will send a confirmation e-mail of the final time chosen to all participants. NeedtoMeet is another application that allows you to have the entire group enter their available times on a Web-based calendar. Doodle (also available for iPhone or Android) is scheduling software that lets you check out the yes/no votes for suggested meeting times, even on your phone.

Such tools have proven useful to many managers, but some people argue that Web-based tools can make simple tasks more complicated and can make us actually less productive. What do you think? Do we rely too much on fancy tools to manage our lives and our time?

looking for trends allow a manager to *identify unseen problems or opportunities*. Examples may include poor growth in sales, an increase in customer dissatisfaction, or an opportunity to expand into a new market. Next, managers work with their teams to *generate possible solutions*. They can then *evaluate each potential solution* based on various criteria, such as cost, feasibility, and time and resources needed. Once they have evaluated the potential solutions, managers *select the best plan of action*. At this point, managers may seek customer or market opinion on the chosen plan of action before completely committing to this choice. If market or customer feedback is not positive, management may look to pursue another alternative. When the final choice has been made, plans are established to *implement the plan of action*. Finally, managers *evaluate the results of their decisions*. If changes need to be made, the entire process begins again.

Think back to Ursula Burns, the CEO of Xerox Corporation. How did her education equip her with the technical skills she uses to achieve success? Do you think her success reflects strong interpersonal skills? What does the direction in which she is taking Xerox say about her decision-making and conceptual skills? How might time management skills come into play in her ability to manage a giant corporation? Clearly, Burns' prominence and success in business demonstrate that a combination of management skills is vital. ∎

The Functions of Management: Planning pp. 207–213

William Lee knew his skills as a tattoo artist could lead into his own business if he did the right things. But where does he start? First, he sat down and wrote a vision of why he wanted to start the business and what he hoped to see it add to the world: "To inspire self-expression and creativity through fine arts tattoos." Seeing it written on a page

Jasper James/Getty Images

helped solidify some ideas in his mind, even though it seemed like a grandiose statement. Next was the *how*—how could he create a business from this idea? What were his goals for the future? How would he find a space to rent, the money to set up shop, and the expertise to help him run it? What was his competitive advantage over other tattoo artists, and how would he communicate it? There was a lot of work ahead. ■

In today's busy world, it is easy to become distracted, just as William Lee felt when beginning to plan for his business. Goals and plans focus our intentions in a way that leads to results. **Planning** is the process of establishing goals and objectives and determining the best ways to accomplish them. **Goals** are broad, long-term accomplishments an organization wants to achieve within a certain time frame—in most companies, usually about five years. **Objectives** are short-term targets that are designed to help achieve goals. Planning happens at all levels of an organization. In this section, we'll discuss the different levels of planning that occur in an organization.

Strategic Planning

What is the highest level of planning in an organization? A strategic plan is the main course of action created by top-level managers that sets the approach for achieving the long-term goals and objectives of an organization. Simply put, a strategic plan points an organization to where it wants to be in the future and identifies how it will get there. A strategic plan helps to answer three questions:

1. Where is the company going?
2. What should the company focus on?
3. How will the company achieve its goals?

To be effective, a strategic plan should be realistic and obtainable and should look at the big picture. Although individual goals sometimes contribute to the plan, the overall strategic plan is focused on an entire organization or an entire department.

> **2** How are the strategic plan, the corporate vision, and the mission statement defined for a business?

How is a strategic plan developed? A good strategic plan reflects what is happening inside and outside an organization and shows how those conditions and changes will affect the organization in the future. Those making strategic plans must pay attention to the capabilities and resources of an organization, as well as changes in the environment. There are several steps to the process of developing a strategic plan, as shown in ■ **FIGURE 7.4.**

Consider the strategic plan development for the Wikimedia Foundation (WMF). WMF supports the online collaborative encyclopedia Wikipedia, as well as nine other projects with a common goal (Wikibooks, Wikiquotes, Wikiversity, etc.). The long-term goal of the organization is as follows: "Imagine a world in

■ **FIGURE 7.4**
Strategic Planning Process

which every single human being can freely share in the sum of all knowledge. That's our commitment."[3]

In 2009 and 2010 WMF began to modify its strategic plan, a vision for the company out to 2015.[4] It began by assessing where WMF stood in achieving its vision. The organization found that only about 15 percent of the world was using Wikimedia products. For example, even in the United States, only about one-third of online users had ever accessed a Wikimedia product. The organization set their goal clearly, to increase the total number of people served to a billion. Next the organization examined the challenges in achieving its vision. One problem was that participation and contributions to WMF projects had begun to decline—in fact, over 50 percent of the content was coming from about 1 percent of the contributors. In addition, the organization wanted to enhance the ability of the WMF community to think strategically, with long-term focus on achieving WMF's vision.

To develop a plan that could address these problems and challenges, WMF relied on engagement from their community of contributors and asked for proposals. Every submission was available for the entire WMF community to view and comment on. Together the community created goals and decided how to achieve these through specific actions. The process is ongoing but has the unique feature of being conducted primarily online, appropriate for the tech-savvy WMF community.

Vision and Mission Statement

What helps define the direction of a business? The first step in creating a strategic plan is to establish a corporate purpose through a clearly defined *vision*. A **vision** identifies what the business wants to be in the future, what you would like to see as the end result of all your work. The vision should be made clear to all employees and stakeholders. The vision statement for General Electric (GE) under the former CEO Jack Welch read as follows: "To become the most competitive enterprise in the world by being number one or number two in every business in which we compete."[5] A single clear vision worked for GE—during the 20 years Welch was CEO, the company's market value went from $14 billion to more than $410 billion.[6]

What helps define the purpose of a business? People often confuse the vision of a company with its mission statement. The vision statement sets the long-term objective of a company and tells where the company is headed. A **mission statement** is a more current description of an organization's purpose, basic goals, and philosophies. A mission statement not only helps management remain focused but also lets employees understand the core values of the company for which they work.

Mission statements reflect the personality of a company, so even companies in the same industry can have mission statements that vary greatly in design and content. Some use scientific jargon in a no-nonsense manner directed specifically to a certain target audience. Others may try to reach a larger audience by using a simple, direct statement that inspires the average consumer. You may find that a company uses its mission statement to highlight its environmental awareness or to set an abstract goal for the firm's employees, like working to make the world better able to communicate. Other companies may discuss only their own business goals. The mission statement is a chance for consumers and employees to get a peek into the central values of a company.

What makes an effective mission statement? If employees feel an owner's passion for the business through the mission statement, it has a positive impact. Employees then incorporate the goals and objectives of the mission into their daily work and pass these on to customers and suppliers through their words and actions. A clear message of mission throughout a company tends to strengthen a company's position.

An effective mission statement does not to be flowery—even simple mission statements can be very effective if they are written clearly and convincingly. Read over several mission statements at www.missionstatements.com. The Culver's restaurant chain has a concise statement of mission: "Every guest who chooses Culver's leaves happy,"[7] while the cosmetics firm Avon has a 240-word mission statement. Both are effective and reflect a passion for excellence.

What are some benefits of well-defined vision and mission statements? The vision and mission statements lead to important benefits like:

- keeping management on track by ensuring strategies are consistent with the organization's goals,
- inspiring employees, and
- giving investors insight into the values of the organization.

Are mission statements only for businesses with a profit? No, mission statements are useful for not-for-profit companies as well. The mission statements of not-for-profit organizations are focused on outreach to the community or a specific public service rather than on investor return. For example, the American Cancer Society's mission statement reads: "The American Cancer Society is the nationwide, community-based, voluntary health organization dedicated to eliminating cancer as a major health problem by preventing cancer, saving lives, and diminishing suffering from cancer, through research, education, advocacy, and service."[8] This statement reflects the organization's commitment to serving the community, the range of goals they have, and the set of avenues they use to accomplish their goals.

Where can I find a company's vision and mission statements? Both the vision and mission statements are usually found on an organization's website. However, because the mission statement is directed toward customers—unlike the vision, which is directed toward employees—the mission statement is often used alone on advertising materials or on the actual product.

SWOT Analysis

How does the management team begin to move a company toward achieving its vision? Once a company's vision and mission statements have been articulated, management must assess the company's own strengths and weaknesses as well as its position among its competitors. In addition, management must assess what changes are anticipated to occur both inside and outside the organization and determine whether the company is poised appropriately to respond to such changes.

What is a SWOT analysis? This analysis of strengths, weaknesses, and anticipated changes is called a **SWOT analysis** and helps determine the strategic fit between an organization's internal, distinctive capabilities and external possibilities relative to the business and economic environments. SWOT stands for

Strengths,

Weaknesses,

Opportunities, and

Threats.

■ FIGURE 7.5 gives a brief explanation of each component of the SWOT analysis.

In evaluating a company's internal *strengths* and *weaknesses*, management must analyze a company's internal resources, including such elements as its financial health; the strengths of its employees; and its marketing, operations, and technological resources. For example, a company's strength might be its strong marketing department, but its weakness could be an unfavorable location.

SWOT Analysis

Internal Strengths
Potential internal assets that give a company a competitive advantage
Examples for Walmart:
- Powerful brand
- Reputation for value, convenience
- Wide range of products in one store

Internal Weaknesses
Lack of internal capability or expertise compared to the competition
Examples for Walmart:
- Not as flexible as competitors who sell just one type of product (clothing)
- Global but still in only a few countries

External Opportunities
Foreseeable external changes that could favorably affect a company's competitive capability
Examples for Walmart:
- Expand to new locations and new types of stores
- Take over or form alliances with other global retailers in Europe or China

External Threats
External conditions that could negatively affect a company's competitive capability
Examples for Walmart:
- Intense price competition increasing
- Global retail exposes Walmart to political problems in the countries where it operates
- Being Number 1 makes Walmart the target of competition

■ **FIGURE 7.5**
SWOT Analysis
(Based on Marketing Teacher.com. www.marketingteacher.com/SWOT/walmart_swot.htm.)

To evaluate a company's external *threats* and *opportunities,* management should assess various external elements, such as economic, political, and regulatory environments as well as social, demographic, macroeconomic, and technological factors that could affect the company and industry. It also must perform analyses on the state of the industry and market as well as the company's competitors. For example, a recession could threaten an alternative energy company, whereas increasing awareness of global warming may provide greater opportunity for market growth.

What happens after a SWOT analysis is completed? After conducting a SWOT analysis, managers establish a set of goals and objectives. In defining exactly what a specific goal is, it is best to make sure clear deadlines are specified and measureable outcomes are included. The acronym SMARTER is helpful when designing and wording goals and objectives. Goals should be Specific, Measurable, Acceptable (to those working to achieve the goals), Realistic, Timely, Extending (the capabilities of those working to achieve the goals), and Rewarding to the employees as well (see ■ **FIGURE 7.6**).[9]

Tactical and Operational Planning

How does management decide how to execute a strategic plan? The next part of the process of creating a strategic plan is to have middle management generate *tactical plans* to carry out the goals of a company. **Tactical plans** specifically determine the resources and the actions required to implement particular aspects of a strategic plan. Whereas strategic plans have a long-term focus, tactical

3 Why do managers need tactical plans, operational plans, and contingency plans?

S	M	A	R	T	E	R
Specific	Measureable	Acceptable	Realistic	Timely	Extending	Rewarding
Clear and concise statement	Success can be defined and monitored	To those working toward the goals	Reasonable given resources available	Time frame is reasonable	Extends the capabilities of those working to achieve goals	To the employees

■ **FIGURE 7.6**
SMARTER Design of Goals
(Based on Carter McNamara, "Strategic Planning (in Nonprofit or For-Profit Organizations)," Free Management Library. www .managementhelp.org)

plans are made with a one- to three-year horizon in mind. Determining a company's annual budget, for example, is one function of a tactical plan. Let's say one goal of the strategic plan of a paper supply company is to sell more products to large offices on the East Coast. One part of this company's tactical plan might be to determine how much money should be allocated to advertising in that area.

How is a tactical plan translated into instructions for employees?
The specifics of carrying out tactical plans are *operational plans*. In an **operational plan**, first-line managers precisely determine the process by which tactical plans can be achieved. Operational plans depend on daily or weekly schedules and focus on specific departments or employees. For example, once the paper supply company determines how much of its budget can be allocated to advertising, specific department managers might have to determine which employees will travel to advertise the product.

Contingency Planning

What if unforeseen events occur? **Contingency planning** is a set of plans that ensures that an organization will run as smoothly as possible during an unexpected disruption (see ■ **FIGURE 7.7**).

Sometimes extreme circumstances occur that force a company to move outside of their plans and find alternative means to survive. We have seen all too frequently the effects that natural disasters can have on businesses. The massive earthquake and tsunami that devastated Japan in 2011 led to power shortages, disrupted supply chains, and drastically impacted factory output. The resulting shortage of semiconductors led to worldwide disruption of manufacturing facilities that relied on Japanese parts.[10]

We have also seen companies quickly fall into disfavor due to unexpected failures in product quality, such as the lead paint found on Mattel toys that resulted in millions of toys being recalled. All the best corporate strategies can be negated quickly if an unexpected crisis occurs and a plan is not in place to deal with it adequately. What happens if a company suddenly has more sales than production can handle, or if the best-selling product is recalled due to a defect? Who would run the company if the CEO or the company owner unexpectedly died? How should a company fight off an unpredictable takeover threat from a competitor or a rapidly spreading computer virus that threatens to shut down all internal and external lines of communication?

How can planning help companies weather unexpected events? Contingency planning encompasses how management will communicate, both internally and externally. Internally, management must inform its employees how they should continue to do their jobs. Externally, an organization must have a plan in place to deal with requests for information either from employees, the families of employees, or even the media. Contingency planning involves determining what departments within a company are vital to the immediate needs of the organization when an unexpected crisis occurs. The particulars of each plan differ depending on the size and function of a

■ **FIGURE 7.7**
**Contingency Planning—
Are You Ready?**

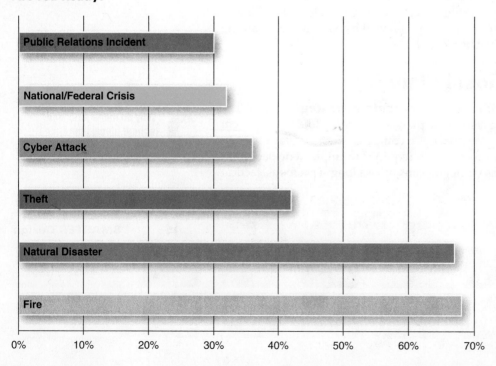

company and the magnitude of crisis for which the plan is needed.

For example, the Vanguard Group, an investment management company, has in place specific, formal business contingency plans to respond to a range of incidents—from worst-case scenarios, such as the loss of a data center, buildings, or staff, to more common occurrences, such as power outages.[11] As important as it is to have plans in place, it is just as important to ensure that the plans are tested and that key individuals know exactly what is expected of them. Similar to fire drills in school, companies should periodically review and rehearse their plans. Vanguard officials put their contingency plans through rigorous testing, including full-scale practice drills in which the company closes a building and works from a remote location. The company also conducts mock disaster drills together with local, state, and federal authorities. Because Vanguard's business would be impacted significantly should a disruption in any of its technical systems occur, it also conducts tests to determine how quickly its IT systems can become operational in the event of a disruption. ■ **FIGURE 7.8** summarizes the types of plans that companies such as Vanguard use to carry out their goals.

Strategic Plan   **Top Management**

- Sets the approach for achieving an organization's long-term goals and objectives
- Acts as a framework for decisions
- Assists in setting corporate benchmarks

Tactical Plan   **Middle Management**

- Determines resources and actions necessary to implement strategic plan
- Made with a one- to three-year horizon in mind

Contingency Plan   **Middle Management**

- Keeps an organization running in the event of a disruption
- Details internal and external communication procedures for such an event
- Determines which departments are most vital to an organization during a crisis

Operational Plan   **First-Line Management**

- Involves planning the execution of the tactical plan
- Depends on daily or weekly schedules
- Focuses on specific department or employees

■ **FIGURE 7.8**
The Four Types of Management Plans

Now that a few years have passed, William Lee smiles when he thinks of the early planning of his business. There have been hundreds of decisions along the way to opening the tattoo shop he now owns. At many points, he needed to think tactically and conduct a full SWOT analysis to determine where his strengths and weaknesses were so he could set the long-term and short-term goals. He also has contingency plans in place if he runs into problems in the future. "You never know what the future will bring," he says, "but you know if you don't plan, you won't win." ■

The Functions of Management: Organizing pp. 213–218

Carrie Witt and Mark Healy have a lot in common: They both graduated with degrees in business, and they both acquired jobs as marketing associates at medium-sized firms that design solar energy panels for commercial use. Nevertheless, their professional experiences have been markedly different. At her firm, Carrie is part of the marketing department. She is training to become an expert in getting new clients within a specific region of the state. She reports directly to the department head, but her work is also overseen by several middle managers, including the marketing

Henrik Sorensen/Getty Images

department supervisor and the marketing manager. They, in turn, take their orders from top managers: the executive vice president, the CEO, and the president. At his firm, Mark works on a team with individuals from a variety of areas, including marketing, R&D, finance, and operations. They work on a variety of projects as a comprehensive unit. One manager supervises his team and coordinates the team's efforts directly with the goals and instructions from the firm's CEO and president. ∎

Carrie's and Mark's jobs seem similar, yet their everyday experiences contrast significantly. Why is this? It's all about organization structure. Which organization structure does Carrie's firm implement? Which one does Mark's firm use? Why are these structures necessary, and what are the benefits of each? Every company, regardless of its size or specialty, needs a solid organization structure. Without one, employees may have trouble making decisions and assigning responsibility. But this doesn't mean there's just one way to organize a company. In this section, we'll explore different aspects of organization.

Organization Structures

How do managers put their plans into action? Once goals have been finalized and plans have been made, the next step in the management process is to put those plans into action. **Organizing** is the process of structuring the capital, personnel, raw materials, and other resources to carry out a company's plans in a way that best matches the nature of the work. Part of organizing is to establish an organization structure. Organization structure depends on a variety of factors, such as the number of employees in the organization, the speed at which decisions need to be made, the subjectivity of the business to rapid change, and the collaborative nature of the work.

How do companies document the structure of an organization? Smaller companies tend to be organized differently than large corporations, using much simpler organization structures compared with large companies. Regardless, to accomplish many tasks at the same time, organizations have some division of labor and allocate work into smaller units. An **organization chart**, like that shown in ∎ **FIGURE 7.9**, shows how groups of employees fit into the larger organization structure.

∎ **FIGURE 7.9**
Organization Chart

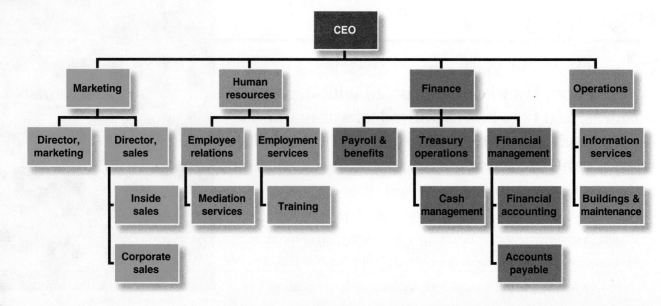

How is power distributed in an organization? There are two common approaches:

4 What is the significance of organizing, and how are most companies organized?

1. **vertical organization** (or a *tall organization*)—the power belongs to a few, and most people are in positions where they obey a supervisor, or
2. **horizontal organization** (or a *flat organization*)—power is distributed, with many people organized in teams or groups.

In a vertical organization, power is centralized with a small controlling group. The organization chart tends to have long vertical columns showing which positions report to which managers.

In a horizontal organization, the traditional managerial pyramid is flattened, and the management layers are collapsed. Decision control is decentralized and spread out across many more people than in a traditional hierarchical structure. A horizontally structured organization still has some of the pyramidal aspects, including a CEO and perhaps another layer of middle management, but then the organization concentrates the majority of the remaining employees into working teams or groups. Here the organization chart would be flat and wide because there are many people with authority and fewer people in positions of direct control. ■ **FIGURE 7.10** illustrates the basic differences in organization charts of a vertically structured organization and a horizontally structured organization.

What are the pros and cons of vertical organization? In a vertical organization, a company is organized by specific functions, such as marketing, finance, purchasing, IT, and human resources. Levels of expertise within functions are developed, and managers have direct authority and reporting responsibility for their area.

Potential problems may arise because integration between functions and divisions is not always easy. Vertical organization usually calls for long lines of communication and "reporting up." This makes it difficult for a company to respond

■ **FIGURE 7.10**
Vertically and Horizontally Structured Organizations

Vertical organization (5 levels)

recent hires, temps, interns, etc., each working for and within a specific division

Horizontal organization (3 levels)

teams and groups of employees

3

quickly to changes in a market or provide new innovation because keeping each division updated means spending time doing so.

The primary structure of business since the Industrial Revolution has been vertical organization. This traditional pyramidal management has its benefits because there is ultimately one person in charge and a clear point of authority for decisions. However, in the early 1990s, vertical organization structures were criticized as being overspecialized, fragmented, and inflexible. Some businesses, such as Ford Motor Company and Barclay's Bank, found that they were more successful when they organized differently and formed management groups around areas of specific production.[12]

What are the pros and cons of horizontal organization? The benefit of a horizontal organization is that each team has more responsibility for the outcome of its work. There is less of a sense of competition for power and more of a push toward collaborative work. Each employee is empowered to have more responsibility and contribute more directly to the company. There are fewer layers of management, so fewer reporting issues arise, and, if needed, the bosses' approval can be sought and received much faster. The company can be more responsive because individuals in a horizontal organization are more empowered to make decisions.

Horizontal structures have been deemed the model for the knowledge age. Now everyone has equal access to information, which many argue makes the horizontal structure more effective. They are suitable for industries that require rapid responses to quick changes.

Changing Structures

Does a company's organization structure ever change? Yes, sometimes when companies have grown so large that there are a variety of product lines, geographic regions, or manufacturing processes that can be difficult to manage, they restructure from a vertical organization to a horizontal one. In these situations, managers often try to reorganize by function. For example, they might structure the organization into divisions of employees who work on just one product line. Or they might divide a company into teams to specialize in one geographic region or work through one manufacturing process.

In essence, these divisions work like separate mini-companies. Each division has its own set of functional expertise, so separate managers are in charge of finance for that division, marketing for that division, and so on. In today's business environment, there are fewer and fewer organizations structured vertically by function.

One company that made the shift from being a vertical organization to a horizontal one is the Xerox Corporation. It was once arranged in a traditional vertical structure, organized by function, such as R&D, manufacturing, and sales. To allow the business to become closer to the customer, the company realigned itself in the early 1990s around individual business markets, such as small businesses, office document systems, and engineering systems. Each individual group had its own set of financial reports, and factories were focused on individual product lines. "We've given everyone in the company a direct line of sight to the customer," said Paul Allaire, the CEO at the time of the restructuring.[13] Today, the company continues to maintain a flat organizational structure organized by product category, as well as by region, to take into account the company's global presence.

Alternative Organizational Structures

What is a matrix organization? In vertical organizations, employees are grouped together based on their function—all accountants are in one department, all engineers in another, and so on. A **matrix organization** is a type of management

THE List

Bits of Advice for Managers

1. Keep your cool.
2. Accept opportunities outside your comfort zone.
3. Put your employees first.
4. Earn loyalty from others. Give respect to others.
5. Be able to admit when you are wrong.
6. Never stop learning.
7. Your success comes when those around you are successful.
8. Encourage creative thinking.
9. Be the change you want to see in your workplace.
10. Listen first.

system in which people are pooled into groups by skills and then assigned to projects as needed. So an employee might answer to the engineering supervisor but suddenly be assigned to a critical project and become accountable to a project manager as well. The matrix organization is useful when the business is project based because it promotes resource sharing. The shared authority and responsibility can mean better coordination between management and lead to better project results. However, having two bosses can create conflicts, so the matrix style is useful only in specific settings.

What is an inverted organization? The traditional vertical hierarchy can be mated with another structure that is quite different, the **inverted organization**. In this structure, management is answerable to employees. The role of management in an inverted organization is to enable, encourage, and empower employees to do what they do best. Empowered employees can make decisions on the ground without the delay of forwarding requests upward through layers of management. Most firms end up implementing inverted structure along with the traditional vertical structure. So although employees still have supervisors, and supervisors answer to managers, managers are equally accountable to their employees. The rationale for this approach is that the core business of the company is to create value. The value creators in the company are the front-line employees. So management contributes to the company's success by empowering the employees, putting employees first.[14]

One company that has grown with this philosophy is HCL Technologies, a provider of IT services. Founded by Vineet Nayar, HCL introduced an inverted organization in 2005 and saw growth of over 20 percent per year between 2005 and 2012, during a worldwide recession.[15] HCL tripled annual revenues and is ranked as India's best employer. "How did I do this?" asks Nayar. "I didn't. The people of our company accomplished the transformation. How did I persuade them to do it? I spoke the truth as I saw it, offered ideas, told stories, asked questions, and even danced." Nayar wrote a book documenting the experience, titled *Employees First, Customers Second*.[16] The result of taking care of employees was that customers were more satisfied and received better services and products.[17] Many other companies, such as Southwest Airlines, have employed elements of the inverted organization.

What organizational structure works across multiple companies? Although the majority of companies are structured with the more traditional vertical structure or the group-oriented horizontal structure, another new business structure is emerging. Instead of the customary means of producing a product or a service in which one company is responsible for all functions, **network organizations** are collections of **independent**, mostly single-function firms that collaborate on a product or a service. For example, Boeing completed production of its latest airplane, the Boeing 787 using a network organization structure. In the past, airplanes were assembled in one hangar. This time, however, Boeing relied on the expertise of hundreds of manufacturers worldwide to independently manufacture the components of the plane and ship the individual pieces for assembly in its main plant. Subassemblies come from India, Japan, Korea, Italy, France, Sweden and the United States. Components are then shipped to Everett, Washington, where they are finally assembled into a single 787 plane.

In addition to Boeing, other companies are using a network arrangement, including Nike, which owns only one manufacturing plant, and Reebok, which designs and markets but does not produce any of its products. Operating with a network structure requires that companies have the following characteristics:

- Are highly flexible and innovative
- Are able to respond quickly to threats and opportunities

Companies that successfully operate in a network structure find that they can save time and can reduce costs and risks.

Reflect back on Carrie and Mark. Carrie works under the supervision of the marketing department head and several middle managers in the same department, who in turn report to top management. Mark works on a team with people from various departments at his company. Is it clearer now why their experiences were so different despite the seeming similarity between their jobs? Carrie's company is a vertical, or tall, organization. The company is organized around specific business functions, and there are several levels of first-line and middle managers. Mark, however, works at a horizontal, or flat, organization. There are fewer middle managers, and employees work in groups. How would their work lives change if their companies reorganized to a matrix organization style? To an inverted organization? ■

Harry Briggs/Getty Images

The Functions of Management: Controlling pp. 218–221

It wasn't supposed to end like this. Over many months, company executives had worked together to make plans for the reorganization of the company. Matt Finley remembered the excitement of it; everyone knew moving toward a horizontal organizational structure would benefit managers, employees, and customers alike. It felt like great times were ahead. But six months later, sales are down, morale is low, and no one knows quite why. Matt believed in the goals the management team had established. What went wrong? ■

The best-laid plans are meaningless if they aren't put into place effectively. As managers form plans and carry out strategies to meet the goals of an organization, they must also determine whether their plans and strategies are generating the desired results. In this section, we'll look at how managers *control* (or *monitor*) their organizations, and why doing so is so important.

Controlling to Stay on Course

Why does a company need to adapt to stay on course? Controlling (also called **monitoring**) is the process by which managers measure performance and make sure the company's plans and strategies are being or have been properly carried out. Through the control process, managers ensure that the direction a company is moving toward aligns with its short- and long-term plans. The controlling process also can detect errors in systems, so if a plan is not meeting its goals, it can be modified.

Control Strategies

5 How do managers ensure that the business is on track and moving forward?

How is moving toward the corporate vision measured? Most companies have control systems that help measure the plans they set in place to carry out the goals of the organization. In general, the control system forms a cycle, as shown in ■ **FIGURE 7.11**: Performance standards are set, and actual performance is measured and compared against the standard. To measure performance, reporting tools such as financial statements and sales reports are used. These reports help determine whether the products are competitive, are using capital wisely, and are being produced efficiently. Based on the results, adjustments are made, and the cycle begins again.

Are financial, production, and sales measures the only tools for assessing performance? No, in addition to meeting financial, production, and sales measures, another measure of performance is quality—the goods or services a company provides must meet and exceed customer expectations. Many managers use **total quality management (TQM)**, an integrated approach that focuses on quality from the beginning of the production process up through the final monitoring to detect and correct problems.

What are the basic tools managers use for monitoring quality? There are seven basic tools managers use to monitor quality-related goals:

1. **Check sheet.** A simple sheet recording the number of times certain product defects occur (■ **FIGURE 7.12A**).
2. **Control chart.** A graph that shows the average and fluctuations of a process being monitored to determine whether it is behaving within the limits of

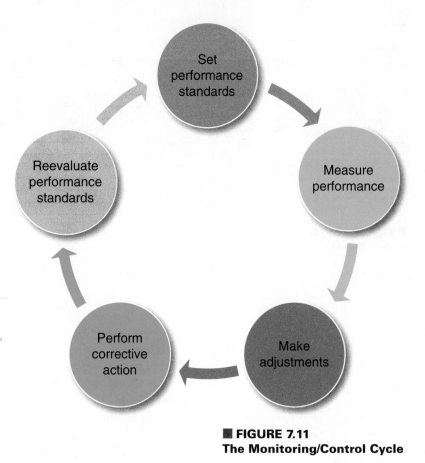

■ FIGURE 7.11
The Monitoring/Control Cycle

Pest Control Company Controls Its Fleet

Anchor Pest Control is a small pest control service with a fleet of 15 vans and trucks. When a van is down for repairs, the company experiences a serious loss of income. So keeping the entire fleet in top operating condition with a minimum of cost and downtime is an important business goal.[18] Another key goal is customer satisfaction. This includes drivers arriving on time, driving to and from sites carefully, and completing their work in a timely manner. Initially, Anchor owner Don Wolf tried using GPS devices in each van to monitor whether these business goals were being met. But he soon realized these systems would track the vehicles but were not helping him answer the business questions he had: When did each van need to go in for maintenance? How hard was the engine working? Which driver was making the most stops in a day?

Wolf found a monitoring device called CarChip that he could afford to install in each vehicle. By downloading the information from CarChip to a software program, each vehicle can be sent in for maintenance at just the right moment, before it breaks down but not before it is required. CarChip can set a top speed for each vehicle so he knows drivers are being careful on the road. Wolf is able to rank top performers by safety rating or total miles driven and give rewards accordingly.

As a good manager, Wolf had to know what his goals were for Anchor and then investigate the right products and tools to monitor performance. Using data to check the business's progress toward meeting those goals has helped the company be the most efficient and profitable it can be.

Name of Data Recorder: Jigme Patel

Location: Bowie, AZ

Data Collection Dates: 10/1–10/15

Defect Types/ Event Occurrence	Sunday	Monday	Tuesday	Wednesday	Thursday	Friday	Saturday	TOTAL
Overheated		IIIIIIII	IIIIIIII	IIII	II			20
Cooled too long			II	I		II		5
Weak welds								0
Misaligned			I	II				3
Broken								0
Discolored		II		IIII				6
Spotting					II			2
Paint defect								0
Irregular shape				I				1
Inaccurate measurements						IIIII		5
TOTAL		10	10	12	4	7		

■ FIGURE 7.12A
Check Sheet

Xbar Quality Assessment of Weld Strength

Lot Number

■ FIGURE 7.12B
Control Chart

proper functioning. **■ FIGURE 7.12B** shows the average weld strength (35.5) and the fluctuations around the average according to the lot number.

3. **Histogram.** A graph that displays the count of the number of times a specific event occurs (e.g., the number of times the smoothness of a tube produced was in the range 5 to 10) (**■ FIGURE 7.12C**).

4. **Pareto chart.** A combination bar and line graph that shows different categories of problems and the total (cumulative) number of problems. The Pareto chart in **■ FIGURE 7.12D** shows the breakdown of types of complaints leading to returned merchandise.

5. **Scatterplot.** A graph that displays the values of two variables to see if there is a relationship between the variables. For example, the scatterplot in **■ FIGURE 7.12E** would help in deciding if more time in the kiln creates tiles that have a higher smoothness value.

6. **Run chart.** A graph that displays the value of some data across a specific set of dates. Managers can then identify problems that occur in a certain cycle, for example, once a month. Does the run chart in **■ FIGURE 7.12F** show there is a pattern to the production of higher brilliance bulbs?

7. **Cause-and-effect diagram.** Also called a fishbone diagram, this illustrates all of the contributing factors in the product design that might lead to faulty production (**■ FIGURE 7.12G**). For example, if the defect being analyzed is

■ FIGURE 7.12C
Histogram

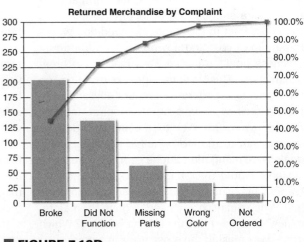

■ FIGURE 7.12D
Pareto Chart

■ **FIGURE 7.12E**
Scatterplot

■ **FIGURE 7.12F**
Run Chart

a soldering defect, the cause-and-effect diagram would show that contributing factors could be from the machinery operator, materials, or methods.

There are many more advanced statistical tools available, but managers often begin their drive toward TQM with these seven basic tools.

What is the Six Sigma strategy for quality? Another well-known quality initiative is **Six Sigma**, a statistically based, proactive, long-term process designed to examine the overall business process and prevent problems. To achieve the "Six Sigma standard," a business must not allow more than 3.4 defects per million opportunities. To achieve such levels, it can take years to train and implement a staff that understands the approach. The techniques of Six Sigma produce results that are consistent and repeatable, which translates into very few defects and very consistent high levels of customer satisfaction.

Jack Welch, CEO of GE from 1981 to 2001, was a huge proponent of the Six Sigma method and pushed it into every corner of the company with great success. However, there is controversy around the proper use of Six Sigma monitoring in the business community.[19] For example, Robert Nardelli worked under Jack Welch and left GE to become CEO of Home Depot, where he applied Six Sigma practices with great fervor. Home Depot initially saw great growth in profits, but the huge amount of paperwork and data collection began to take a toll on store workers. It left them less time for customer interaction, causing customer satisfaction to plummet, falling from first to last place in the American Customer Satisfaction Index. The current CEO of Home Depot, Frank Blake, has modified Six Sigma's approach to allow store managers to make more decisions independently.

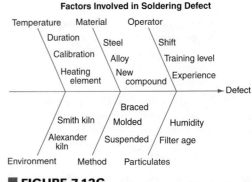

■ **FIGURE 7.12G**
Cause and Effect Diagram

The missing piece for Matt Finley's company, which was struggling despite a promising reorganization plan, turned out to be a lack of adequate control. The company began its reorganization with well-designed goals but never chose which tools it would use to monitor the results. Matt recognized this and established a set of procedures so managers could measure both financial progress as well as product quality. He had to bring himself up to speed on some new tools for quality reporting—Pareto charts and cause-and-effect diagrams—but once the processes for collecting and reporting data were in place, the picture became clear. The new organization structure began working once these important adjustments were made. ■

MyBizLab

Go to **mybizlab.com** to complete the problems marked with this icon ⭐.

1 **What are the levels of management, and what skills do managers need to be successful?** (pp. 204–207)

- **Management** (p. 204) is the process of working with people and resources to accomplish the goals of an organization. Management involves four primary functions: **planning** (p. 208), **organizing** (p. 214), leading, and **controlling/monitoring** (p. 218).

- **Top managers** (p. 204) are the corporate officers who are responsible for the organization as a whole. **Middle managers** (p. 205) can be thought of as top managers for one division or a segment of an organization. **First-line managers** (p. 205) fill a supervisory role over those employees who carry out the day-to-day operations of the company.

- Because managerial tasks are so varied, a successful manager needs to possess a variety of skills, including **conceptual** (p. 205), **technical** (p. 206), **time management** (p. 206), **interpersonal** (p. 206), and **decision-making skills** (p. 206).

2 **How are the strategic plan, the corporate vision, and the mission statement defined for a business?** (pp. 208–210)

- Managers use planning, goals, and objectives to help achieve the corporate vision and stay on task. **Planning** (p. 208) is the process of establishing goals and objectives and determining the best ways to accomplish them. **Goals** (p. 208) are broad, long-term accomplishments an organization wants to achieve in about a five-year time frame. **Objectives** (p. 208) are the short-term targets that are designed to help achieve goals.

- Top managers put together a **strategic plan** (p. 208), or a main course of action, that maps out the means by which the corporation will achieve its goals.

  - Before the strategic plan is in place, management must define the organization's purpose, basic goals, and philosophies through **vision** (p. 209) and **mission statements** (p. 209). The corporate vision is what the business wants to be in the future. A mission statement is a more current description of the organization's purpose, basic goals, and philosophies.

  - Part of the strategic planning process is conducting a **SWOT analysis** (p. 210) to help management determine the strategic fit between an organization's internal capabilities and external possibilities. The SWOT analysis stands for strengths, weaknesses, opportunities, and threats.

3 **Why do managers need tactical plans, operational plans, and contingency plans?** (pp. 211–213)

- **Tactical plans** (p. 211) specifically determine the resources and the actions required to implement particular aspects of a strategic plan. Tactical plans are made with a one- to three-year horizon in mind and are determined by middle management.

- **Operational plans** (p. 212) determine the process by which tactical plans can be achieved. Operational plans depend on daily or weekly schedules and focus more on specific departments or employees. Operational plans are determined by first-line managers.

- **Contingency planning** (p. 212) is a set of plans that ensures that an organization will run as smoothly as possible during a disruption and determines how management will communicate, both internally and externally.

4 **What is the significance of organizing, and how are most companies organized?** (pp. 215–216)

- **Organizing** (p. 214) is the process of structuring the capital, personnel, raw materials, and other resources to carry out a company's plans in a way that best matches the nature of the work. An **organization chart** (p. 214) shows how groups of employees fit into the larger organization structure.

- A **vertical organization** (p. 215) is organized by specific functions, such as marketing, finance, purchasing, IT, and human resources. Managers can better keep track of economic and environmental conditions that affect their functional area. However, potential problems may arise because integration between functions and divisions is not always easy. Vertical organization usually calls for long lines of communication and "reporting up."

- A **horizontal organization** (p. 215) is flattened, and the management layer is collapsed. This type of organization concentrates the majority of employees into working teams or groups. Teams have more responsibility for the outcome of their work. Bosses' approval can be sought and received much faster.

- **Matrix organization** (p. 216) is type of management system in which people are pooled into groups by skills and then assigned to projects as needed.

- **Network organizations** (p. 217) are collections of independent, mostly single-function firms that collaborate on a product or a service.

- In an **inverted organization** (p. 217), management is answerable to employees, and management's role is to empower and encourage employees to do what they do best.

5 **How do managers ensure that the business is on track and moving forward?** (pp. 218–221)

- **Controlling** (also called **monitoring**) (p. 218) is the process by which managers measure performance and make sure a company's plans and strategies are being or have been properly carried out.

- Performance standards are measured with reporting tools, such as financial statements and sales reports. Quality measures are also in place to ensure that products or services meet customer requirements. **Total Quality Management (TQM)** (p. 219) focuses on quality control throughout the entire production process. Basic mathematical and graphical tools, such as scatterplots and Pareto charts, are used to monitor quality goals.

Key Terms

conceptual skills   (p. 205)

contingency planning   (p. 212)

controlling (or monitoring)   (p. 218)

decision-making skills   (p. 206)

first-line manager   (p. 205)

goal   (p. 208)

horizontal organization   (p. 215)

independent   (p. 217)

interpersonal skills   (p. 206)

inverted organization   (p. 217)

management   (p. 204)

matrix organization   (p. 216)

middle managers   (p. 205)

mission statement   (p. 209)

network organization   (p. 217)

objective   (p. 208)

operational plan   (p. 212)

organization chart   (p. 214)

organizing   (p. 214)

planning   (p. 208)

Six Sigma   (p. 221)

strategic plan   (p. 208)

SWOT analysis   (p. 210)

tactical plans   (p. 211)

technical skills   (p. 206)

time management skills   (p. 206)

top managers   (p. 204)

total quality management (TQM)   (p. 219)

vertical organization   (p. 215)

vision   (p. 209)

Self-Test

Multiple Choice You can find the answers on the last page of this book.

1. The four primary processes of management are
   a. planning, optimizing, leading, and controlling.
   b. organizing, controlling, planning, and leading.
   c. prioritizing, leading, controlling, and organizing.
   d. planning, leading, organizing, and deciding.

2. SWOT analysis
   a. is an important part of developing a strategic plan.
   b. is one type of contingency planning.
   c. helps translate the tactical plan in instructions for employees.
   d. leads to an effective mission statement.

3. Julius knows how to identify the key problems on a project, examine alternatives, and implement a plan of action. His last performance review mentioned this when it read as follows:
   a. "Julius shows very polished interpersonal skills."
   b. "Julius has demonstrated excellent decision-making skills."
   c. "Julius exhibits advanced conceptual skills."
   d. "Julius has marketable skills that contribute to a project's success."

4. The organization you work for just hired a new CEO. Within the first week in her new position, the CEO drafted a memo for the board and members of senior management that defined the purpose of the business, as well as the basic goals and philosophies of the business. This document serves as a draft of a new
   a. vision.
   b. mission statement.
   c. goals and objectives statement.
   d. tactical plan.

5. A good strategic plan
   a. determines the best ways to accomplish goals of an organization.
   b. is specific and tactical.
   c. concentrates only on what is going on inside an organization, not outside an organization.
   d. is wide ranging.

6. The controlling function of management is best described as
   a. keeping employees in line.
   b. watching employees carefully by monitoring e-mail and phone usage.
   c. measuring performance to make sure company plans are on track.
   d. All of the above

7. A horizontal organization requires
   a. more use of collaborative teams.
   b. a strict chain of command.
   c. a tall organization chart.
   d. None of the above

8. The seven basic tools for monitoring a business include all of the following except
   a. Pareto analysis.
   b. Monte Carlo statistical simulations.
   c. scatterplots.
   d. cause-and-effect diagrams.

9. Shauna is the sales manager for a regional chain of bookstores. Shauna reports to the executive vice president of sales and marketing, and each sales manager reports to Shauna. Shauna would be considered a
   a. top manager.
   b. middle manager.
   c. first-line manager.
   d. Both b and c.

10. Which would *not* be something that might describe a company's organization structure?
    a. Vertical
    b. Inverted
    c. Network
    d. Spiral

True/False You can find the answers on the last page of this book.

1. A company with a vertical organization cannot use an inverted organization.
   ☐ **True** or ☐ **False**

2. A SWOT analysis is used to determine the strategic fit between an organization and its internal and external environments.
   ☐ **True** or ☐ **False**

3. Conceptual skills mean a person has the ability to think abstractly.

    ☒ **True** or   ☐ **False**

4. Every manager has responsibility for planning, organizing, leading, and controlling.

    ☐ **True** or   ☒ **False**

5. The Six Sigma initiative is focused on improving communication.

    ☐ **True** or   ☐ **False**

Critical Thinking Questions

1. Recall your own personal working experiences and the managers with whom you have had interaction. Discuss the skills that define the best manager with whom you have worked and discuss the skills that define the worst manager with whom you have worked.

2. Would you prefer to work in an organization with a vertical structure or a flat, horizontal structure? Would your answer change if you were the CEO instead of a new hire? How would you feel about working in an inverted organization as a manager?

3. Analyze your own ability to be a manager. What skills do you have now that are already polished? What skills would you need to improve? What skills would you still need to acquire? How could you go about acquiring or improving those skills you do not have?

Team Time

ON A MISSION

Research and print out several mission statements. Be sure to choose statements from both not-for-profit organizations and for-profit organizations. Bring these mission statements to class.

Process

Step 1. Assemble into groups of four or five.

Step 2. As a group, evaluate the mission statements you've chosen for similar components, such as:

- a statement of the product or service
- the primary market
- an indication of commitment to quality
- an indication of a commitment to social responsibility, and
- a declaration of corporate philosophy.

Step 3. Make notes of the components that are included in the majority of mission statements and those that are included in only a few mission statements.

Step 4. As a group, decide which mission statement is the most inspiring. Why? Which is the least inspiring? Why?

Step 5. As a class, compare the statements deemed most inspiring from each group and determine which is the most effective. Finally, openly discuss with your classmates how the winning statement would affect their inclination to work for this organization.

Ethics and Corporate Social Responsibility

ASSESSING SOCIAL RESPONSIBILITY

One of the functions of management is control, which includes measuring financial performance. But how often and with what tools does a manager assess an organization's social responsibility?

Process

Step 1. As a class, in small discussion groups, discuss the following:

- the planning and organizational changes that might need to be implemented
- the controls that a manager might use to measure and monitor the results of his or her social responsibility initiatives

Step 2. After this discussion, research companies that are known for their social responsibility efforts. Then discuss what impact their efforts have had on management.

Web Exercises

1. **Employees First**

   Research on the Internet for a company that has implemented an inverted organization by emphasizing "Employees First." Is this reflected in the company's mission statement? Does it seem to be improving the company's performance? How has this message changed customer relationships?

2. **Tools for TQM**

   Using online resources like YouTube and Office.Microsoft.com, see if you can teach yourself to create a Pareto chart in Excel. Can you create a histogram? A scatterplot? Can you find a PowerPoint template for a cause-and-effect diagram?

3. **How Well Do You Manage Your Time?**

   Time management skills are important for a manager to have to work efficiently and accomplish all the tasks a manager is expected to handle on any given day. How are your time management skills? Even as a student, you are your own manager and can benefit from being more in control of your time. Find a quiz online that assesses your ability to manage your time. Write a brief report answering the following questions:

   - What online assessment did you find?
   - What were the results?
   - How can you improve your time management skills?

4. **Predictably Irrational**

   Visit the Ted.com website and search for the 20-minute video "Are We in Control of Our Own Decisions?" by Dan Ariely, a behavioral economist. Watch the video and concentrate on the example of the doctor and the patient. Are there business decisions that managers make where factors outside their decision-making process influence the outcome?

5. **Get SMARTER**

   The acronym SMARTER reminds us that goals should be specific, measurable, acceptable, realistic, timely, extending, and rewarding. Using the resources at http://www.hr.ecu.edu.au/mps/html/mps-smart.cfm, create two goals for yourself for next semester. Document how they are SMARTER goals.

MyBizLab

Go to **mybizlab.com** for Auto-graded writing questions as well as the following Assisted-graded writing questions:

7-1. Contingency plans are important in any business. Discuss what kinds of plans your school might have in place to recover from a disaster. How would these plans differ, if at all, from those of a local business in your area? What are a few possible scenarios that would require contingency plans in your school or at a local business?

7-2. How does the complexity of a project impact quality control? As software projects grow to have many millions of lines of code, can that industry still achieve Six Sigma quality? What kind of tools and processes would it require?

7-3. MyBizLab Only – comprehensive writing assignment for this chapter.

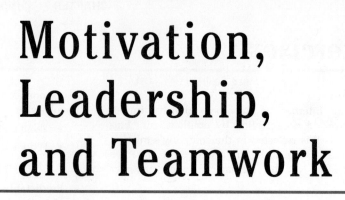

Motivation, Leadership, and Teamwork

Motivation

At Ana Gutierrez's public relations firm, employees were suffering from a severe case of demotivation. Translating motivational theories into practical applications is a challenge many business managers face. How can Ana use abstract concepts about human behavior to inspire her workforce and turn around her struggling company?

Leadership

Every young person dreams big—but dreaming of changing the world's transportation systems and economic systems and creating the tools for space travel seems like too much for any one person. But Elon Musk is accomplishing it all through his leadership skills.

Teamwork

Teamwork can bring about great success. For all teams, team work is important, but for some teams, it is essential. If a surgical operating team does not work together effectively, patients can suffer complications or even die. How could one surgeon make a difference worldwide by studying the dynamics of his operating room team?

MyBizLab®

⭐ **Improve Your Grade!**

Over 10 million students improved their results using the Pearson MyLabs.
Visit **mybizlab.com** for simulations, tutorials, and end-of-chapter problems.

Motivation pp. 229–236

Brian Jackson/Fotolia

"**A**ll of my employees were so . . . *uninspired*," Ana Gutierrez laments. "People seemed to be just 'showing up'; the sense of apathy in the office was almost palpable. The quality of our work was suffering. I wasn't sure what to do."

Ana, the founder and CEO of a small public relations firm, was facing a crisis of motivation within her workforce. The sales team hadn't scored a new account in months, and existing clients were complaining about their representation. "You're not delivering on your promises," one client, the leader of a local not-for-profit organization, blurted during a particularly tense conference call. "A recent event was poorly advertised and poorly attended. There were errors in the latest press release. And your associates take two days to respond to my e-mails."

Ana had already tried a variety of tactics to motivate her employees. She dangled the possibility of additional bonuses and free dinners to the sales teams—to no avail. She instituted a new policy requiring all employees to work nine hours a day, plus two weekends a month. It didn't work. She told her associates she was prepared to promote at least three of the highest-performing employees among them to more lucrative positions within six months. No one was interested.

How could Ana apply what she knows about motivational theories to light a fire under her employees and save her business? ■

We hear the word *motivation* often. When students seek out extra learning opportunities to go beyond a course's general requirements, they are described as motivated learners. But what does motivation have to do with working in a business? Are all of a business owner's actions motivated solely by profit? Does an employer who pays well always have strongly motivated employees? In this section, we'll examine motivation in detail and look at techniques used in the past and the present to motivate employees.

Personal Motivation

What drives you to do your personal best? Even when pursuing personal goals, everyone retains and loses motivation for very singular reasons. Think of times you have pushed to be your best, whether at school, in sports, or in other activities. Is it easier for you to build enthusiasm for tasks you're sure you can accomplish? Or do you set difficult goals and draw energy from the challenge of attaining them? Some people need immediate gratification to stay motivated. Others are able to postpone short-term success in pursuit of long-term gains. Which setting motivates you more?

Now think about how hard you work when you receive positive feedback (either financial or emotional). Are you driven more by the values of the place where you work, your beliefs, or by the rewards from doing a job well? For some people, being part of the accomplishments of a team is what motivates them. Are you one of those people?

What does it feel like to be optimally motivated? Have you ever been working on a project in which you were so immersed in what you were doing that, when you looked at your watch, four hours had gone by? Psychologist Mihaly Csikszentmihalyi refers to this state of rapt attention as **flow**.[1] A flow state happens when you are completely involved and focused on what you are doing. Often people produce their best work, make the best use of their skills, and feel the most pleasure when they are in flow. They feel a strong match between their own abilities and the challenge of a task—it is neither too difficult, which can lead to frustration, nor too simple, which can lead to boredom. They report a sense of control over what is happening and a feeling of effortlessness in their work. How do you create this sense of flow? This is the subject of **organizational psychology**—the study of how to create a workplace that fosters motivation and productivity among employees.

Motivating Employees

How motivated is the U.S. workforce? The Q12 is a 12-question survey of employee engagement administered by the Gallup Organization. According to Q12 survey results, 73 percent of U.S. employees are not engaged or are actively disengaged in their work.[2] Based on respondents' answers to a series of questions, it classifies employees as "engaged," "not engaged," or "actively disengaged" (see ■ **TABLE 8.1**). Imagine a workplace in which three out of four employees are complaining or even disrupting activities during the day. This statistic makes it clear that encouraging flow in the workplace is an important challenge.

How does a work environment encourage "flow"? There is no fixed recipe, but there are companies who have succeeded in building motivated, engaged environments that support workers and support the creative experience of flow.

One such company is SAS, a business software firm in North Carolina. With an incredibly low employee turnover rate of just 2–5 percent[3] and annual revenues of over $2.7 billion,[4] the company has created such an atmosphere in part thanks to the policies of CEO Jim Goodnight. Goodnight lists the following as ways in which SAS works to foster a creative environment:

- It keeps employees intellectually engaged.
- It removes distractions so employees can do their best work.
- It makes managers responsible for sparking creativity.
- It has managers eliminate the arbitrary distinctions between administrative "suits" and more abstract "creatives."
- It engages customers as creative partners.

| 1 | How do motivation and work environment encourage "flow"? |

■ TABLE 8.1

Motivation Levels of Employees

Engaged	Not Engaged	Actively Disengaged
• Work with passion	• Work with minimal effort	• Work in a disruptive manner
• Feel connected and obligated to the company	• Are indifferent to the company	• Are unhappy with the company
• Add to the success of the company	• Make little or no contribution to the company	• Combat the efforts of engaged workers

Source: Based on "Employee Engagement." Employee Engagement. Gallup, 25 June 2012. http://www.gallup.com

In addition to fostering strong professional lives, SAS supports its employees in their private lives as well. On the SAS campus, you'll find medical facilities for employees and their families, a Montessori day care center, and a cafeteria where families can eat lunch together. "The corporate philosophy is, if your fifth grader is in his first school play, you should be there to see it," says Goodnight. Such a philosophy has led to SAS earning a spot on *Fortune* magazine's Best Companies to Work For list[5] and a spot on *Working Mother* magazine's list of best companies.[6]

What are the benefits of keeping employees motivated? Both employer and employee benefit from a motivated workforce. Employers find that workers are more productive, more creative, and have much better retention levels when care is taken to provide a motivating environment and motivating tasks. According to Gallup's calculations, the cost to the U.S. economy from disengaged employees is up to $300 billion a year in reduced productivity.[7] Gallup results have shown that companies with high engagement have a four times greater growth rate of earnings compared to companies in the same industry struggling with disengaged workers.

The Atlanta-based chain Chick-fil-A is an example of a company that has benefited from strong employee motivation. The founder and current CEO Truett Cathy builds employee motivation with strong monetary motivators like scholarships and free cars to the operators of strong-performing stores. The chain has never allowed any store to be open on Sunday as both a practical and spiritual decision that all employees should have an opportunity each week to rest and spend time with family so they can return motivated on Monday morning.[8] Employees are not micro-managed but trusted to perform. Chick-fil-A employees respond with highly engaged behavior, delivering extra special services like refilling customers' drinks or watching to see if someone needs extra napkins delivered to the table. The results of that are seen in the chain's explosive growth with total sales now exceeding $4 billion.[9]

Traditional Theories of Motivation

What are the traditional theories describing what motivates people?
Several theories have been proposed to explain how and why people are motivated:

- Maslow's hierarchy of needs
- McClelland's "three needs" theory
- Herzberg's motivator-hygiene theory

What is Maslow's hierarchy of needs? One early researcher in the area of human motivation was Abraham Maslow (1908–1970), who published the book *Motivation and Personality* in 1954. In his theory of motivation, Maslow suggests that humans have a **hierarchy of needs**, and that primary needs are met first, before higher-level needs are addressed (see ■ **FIGURE 8.1**). The first needs to be met are inborn, basic needs—termed **physiological needs**—such as the need for water, food, sleep, and reproduction. This means that before we as humans can think about anything else in our lives, we must ensure that these basic physiological needs are met.

Once our physiological needs have been met, Maslow's theory holds that people strive to satisfy **safety needs**. This includes establishing safe and stable places to live and work. Once both physiological and safety needs have been met, we can consider social or **belonging needs**. This includes the need to belong to a group and feel accepted by others. The next level in Maslow's hierarchy includes **esteem needs**. These are satisfied by the mastery of a skill and the attention and recognition of others. Finally, **self-actualization needs** are at the top of the hierarchy. These needs include the desire to maximize your own potential through

2 What are the main theories of motivation, and how are they applied to the workforce?

■ **FIGURE 8.1**
Maslow's Hierarchy of Needs
Source: Vitezslav Valka/Alamy

Self-fulfillment, creativity, beauty

Recognition, respect

Feeling accepted by others

Safe and stable place to live and work

Food, water, sex, sleep

Self-actualize
Self-esteem
Love & belonging
Safety & security
Physiological needs

education and self-fulfillment as well as experiences of beauty and spirituality. These higher-level self-actualization needs cannot be addressed unless and until the lower level needs have been met adequately.

Maslow suggested that different people find themselves at different places in the hierarchy, and so their motivations may be different. Although an offer of overtime pay may be a successful motivator for a person concerned with safety needs, it might be the opposite of what someone working to satisfy their need for self-actualization finds motivating.

What is McClelland's "three needs" theory? Other researchers have proposed different models to map human needs to motivation. Psychologist David McClelland's (1917–1998) **three needs theory** suggests there are three main motivators:

1. *The need for achievement*—to accomplish something difficult on your own
2. *The need for affiliation*—to form close personal relationships
3. *The need for power*—to be able to control the behavior of others

Although an individual may have multiple needs, McClelland suggests that one tends to be dominant over the others. Which need we try to satisfy depends on a variety of complex factors, including our cultural background. In a workplace, this theory could account for differences in motivation among coworkers. For example, a person whose main need is for affiliation may have little motivation to perform a solitary task, whereas a person with a high need for achievement may be highly motivated to perform a difficult task alone.

How does Herzberg's motivator-hygiene theory explain motivation? In 1959, psychologist Frederick Herzberg (1923–2000) proposed a theory for job satisfaction called the **motivator-hygiene theory** (or the **two-factor theory**). According to the theory, two factors influence a person's motivation.

Hygiene factors are factors such as a safe working environment, proper pay and benefits, and positive relationships with coworkers. People rarely notice hygiene factors if those factors are present. However, if hygiene factors are absent or inadequate, people tend to be dissatisfied. If there suddenly is no heat in the place where you work or if your pay is cut, you may be motivated to find a way to meet these needs. But if these are already in place, they are taken for granted and may not serve to motivate you.

Motivator factors represent the second set of factors in Herzberg's theory. These factors include a sense of responsibility, recognition, promotion, and job growth. If there is no path for growth in your job or little recognition of your achievements, you probably would not immediately quit, but their absence would create a set of conditions that would fail to motivate you.

Motivational Theories in the Modern Workplace

Do managers actually use theories of motivation? Theories of motivation can be very abstract. How can a team leader at a software development company take what researchers know about human behavior and use it to increase productivity and the satisfaction of employees? The theories of human motivation you have just read about have given rise to several different approaches for organizing and motivating people in the workplace.

What can a manager do to enhance employee motivation? In the workplace, there are some external motivating factors that managers can control. These motivators, called **extrinsic motivators**, include pay, promotion, and verbal praise.

Other factors, called **intrinsic motivators**, are beyond a manager's control because they are internal to each individual employee. These motivating influences are based on a person's actual interest in his or her work and stem from the sense of purpose or value a person derives from the work being done. A manager will have difficulty motivating an intrinsically motivated employee to take on unsatisfying work by using offers of just bonuses or promotions.

Research is investigating if there are some intrinsic motivators common to all of us. At Cornell University, Evan Polman and Kyle Emich studied a large number of undergraduates to see if the motivation and the quality of their work would change depending on whom the work benefited.[10] Two separate groups of students were given puzzles and creative projects. One group was told they were solving the puzzle to save themselves and that they were illustrating a story that they would later publish themselves. The second group was told they were doing the work to benefit someone else—solving the puzzle would save the life of another person who was imprisoned, and that they were illustrating a story that someone else would publish. In each case the group who were working for someone else produced better results—66 percent of the altruistic group solved the puzzle versus less than 50 percent of the self-focused group, and the creative level of the work for an unknown author was of much higher quality. If decisions for others are more effective and creative than decisions we make for ourselves, can mangers structure their organizations in ways that promote that?

What other motivational models exist? In addition to the theories proposed by Maslow, McClelland, and Herzberg, several models have been developed that provide theoretical explanations of what motivates employees specifically in a business or workplace context:

- Theories X, Y, and Z
- The Vroom model
- Strength-based management

What are the Theory X and Theory Y models? In 1960, social psychologist Douglas McGregor proposed the Theory X and Theory Y models of behavior (see ■ **FIGURE 8.2**). The **Theory X** model suggests a view of people as inherently disliking work and wanting to avoid it. Theory X management

> **3** How have motivational theories and industrial psychology changed the work environment since the early twentieth century?

■ FIGURE 8.2 Comparison of Theory X and Theory Y
Based on D. McGregor, The Human Side of Enterprise (New York: McGraw-Hill 1960)

Theory X		Theory Y
Not motivated	**Motivation**	Naturally motivated
Must use heavy control of workers	**Management**	Will create their own motivation
Follow rather than solve	**Leadership**	Creative problem solvers
Avoid responsibility	**Responsibility**	Seek added responsibility
Security seeking	**Needs**	Need intellectual stimulation

suggests that employees must be coerced and controlled by management to be productive. This leads to an authoritarian, hard-line management style. In contrast, the **Theory Y** model suggests that people view work as being as natural as playing and resting. People are naturally motivated and will direct themselves to work for the aims of the organization if they are satisfied with their jobs. Theory Y managers believe that, on average, people will accept and seek out responsibility. Such managers have a softer style of management that involves the participation of many.

Clearly, Theories X and Y would not work equally well in all situations. Theory X style management—which is authoritarian and hard line—is often seen in large-scale operations such as mass manufacturing. In the knowledge industry, in which there is a mix of professionals working together to solve complex problems, Theory Y is more likely to be seen with a participative, gentler management style.

How is the Theory Z model different? In 1981, William Ouchi, a professor at UCLA, put forward a **Theory Z** model based on a Japanese management style that relied heavily on collaborative decision-making. In many corporations in Japan in the 1980s, one person might be responsible for many different aspects of a single project. Employees tended to become generalists rather than specialists who were trained in a very narrow set of tasks. Theory Z style management offers long-term employment with an emphasis on individual responsibility. Workers tend to show a desire to cooperate and be loyal to an organization. As a result, companies that apply Theory Z management often reap the benefits of low turnover, high productivity, and strong morale among the workforce. Morale, a sense of purpose and enthusiasm toward one's work, is an important factor in an employee's level of motivation.

Do any motivational models describe an individual person's motivation? Although Maslow's hierarchy and other theories describe human motivation, they do so in terms of an overall model for all employees. In 1964, Victor Vroom proposed a theory named **expectancy theory**, which has since been developed by other researchers. Expectancy theory suggests an individual's motivation can be described by the relationship between three psychological forces. He put forward the following formula to describe the motivation a person feels in any given situation:

Motivation = Expectancy * Instrumentality * Valence

Expectancy is the idea that a person's effort has an appreciable effect on a situation's result—whether it is a success or failure. Does working harder lead to a more positive outcome for an employee and/or a company? Or does it not make a difference?

Instrumentality refers to the idea that the outcome of a situation is related to rewards or punishment. For those who are extrinsically motivated, instrumentality answers the question, "What are the chances I'm going to be rewarded if I do a good job?" For those who are intrinsically motivated, instrumentality answers the question "How good will I feel if I can accomplish this task?"

Valence is the importance that the individual places on the expected outcome of a situation. It answers questions such as "How great a reward will there be if my performance is exemplary?" and "How serious a punishment do I expect if I under-perform?"

In common terms, Vroom's formulas for high and low motivations read as follows:

High Motivation = (My work actually affects the outcome.) * (There's a good chance I'll get a reward if this works out.) * (It'll be a really big reward!)

Low Motivation = (Nothing I do is going to impact this situation.) * (Even if it does go well, I probably won't see any benefit.) * (The only reward from this will be incredibly small.)

The Vroom formula can be used to analyze factors such as how satisfied employees are at their jobs, how likely it is they will remain at their jobs, and how hard they will work at their jobs. In addition, unlike Maslow's and McClelland's models, which address typical needs across large groups of people, Vroom's model, with its three independent variables can generate a much more specialized result, attuned to the mental state of a specific individual.

What is unique in strength-based management? Management often works to help employees improve skills in areas in which they are weak. But **strength-based management** is a system based on the belief that, rather than improve weak skills, the best way to help employees develop is to determine their strengths and build on them.[11] This system is supported by research that shows that people can learn the most about areas in which they already have a strong foundation. Strength-based programs identify employees' current talents and skills and then provide additional training and support to develop them into areas of excellence.[12] By designing a match between an employee's strengths and his or her daily activities, and working around his or her weaknesses, each employee becomes more motivated and engaged.

Evolution of Motivational Theories

How have motivational theories changed? In the early twentieth century, as the Industrial Age saw the creation of large corporations, issues of efficiency and labor costs became critical. Researchers like Frederick Taylor (1856–1950) began to study how to manage people optimally. In 1911, Taylor published his findings in *The Principles of Scientific Management*. Based on his research and experimentation, he proposed ways that managers could increase productivity. He encouraged managers to use scientific study to determine the best methods to complete tasks and then train employees in these methods. Many of his ideas were implemented in factories. By the 1920s and 1930s, a field of academic study called **industrial psychology** was created to further address these issues. The objective of industrial psychology is to understand scientifically how to manage employees and work optimally.

Other researchers, such as Frank and Lillian Gilbreath, used photography to study employee work patterns and then analyzed these patterns to increase productivity. For example, they used time-motion studies to analyze factory jobs and then train workers in the precise sequence of steps that would make them most productive.

Another famous study of the period was work of Elton Mayo, a professor at Harvard University, at the Hawthorne plant of the Western Electric Company in Illinois. The study ran from 1927 to 1932 and examined physical influences on the workplace (such as lighting and humidity) as well as psychological aspects (such as group pressure and working hours). The major finding, known as the **Hawthorne effect**, was that *regardless of the experimental changes made*, the production of the workers improved. Researchers concluded that the increase in productivity was based on the attention the workers were receiving. Because they knew they were being studied, the employees felt special and produced more, regardless of the conditions Hawthorne studied. The Hawthorne effect is used now as a term to describe the increase in productivity caused by workers being given special attention. After World War II, the direction of research in management theory shifted from management of an individual worker toward management of the entire organization, its structure, and policies.

Marek/Fotolia

For knowledge workers, autonomy, mastery of skills, and a sense of purpose in their work are key motivators.

What motivational theories fit the modern workplace? The fields of organizational psychology and industrial psychology are still very active, and new theories of management practices continue to appear. A motivational theory that is important for the modern workplace comes from examining the open-source movement (software projects that are developed, tested, and maintained for free by a worldwide network of volunteers). Sample open source projects include Wikipedia and the Linux operating system. These have been hugely successful and were created by professional people working many hours for free—outside their regular jobs. What is causing people to behave this way?

Four academic economists explored this by running an experiment where people were recruited to perform a range of tasks—some that required motor skills, some creative, and some needing concentration. Monetary rewards were promised for three levels of performance, with the top performers receiving the equivalent of five months' pay! The result was that the higher the incentives, the *worse* the performance. Similar results were seen when the London School of Economics reviewed corporate pay-for-performance plans.[13] Using economic rewards to motivate employees can actually lead to poorer performance when the work is a creative, cognitive task.

Additional study has shown that modern knowledge workers value three commodities much more highly than money:[14]

- Autonomy—having some control over the key decision in their work lives
- Mastery—having a sense of skill and having time to develop and improve skills
- Purpose—wanting their lives and work to have a higher meaning

Top-performing companies in our modern knowledge-based environment will need to find ways to offer opportunities for autonomy, mastery, and purpose to their employees. Companies that can adjust their incentive structure to recognize this will see great benefits.

Remember Ana Gutierrez and her team of uninspired public relations professionals? "I realized that extrinsic motivators didn't have much of an effect on my employees, nor did a hard-line management style based on the Theory X model," she says. "So I changed my approach, and I soon saw positive results." In an attempt to increase the level of intrinsic motivation among her employees, Ana met with her associates and asked them which accounts they found most meaningful and satisfying to work on. She modified her staff appropriately and found that levels of motivation increased when employees worked with clients with whom they felt a personal connection. Ana also eliminated the nine-hour day mandate, but soon found that many of her newly motivated employees voluntarily worked at least that many hours—if not more! The company, once struggling, now flourishes: Sales are up, and clients are thrilled. With experimentation and careful thought, Ana achieved the goal of all business managers: translating motivational theory into business success. ∎

Leadership pp. 237–243

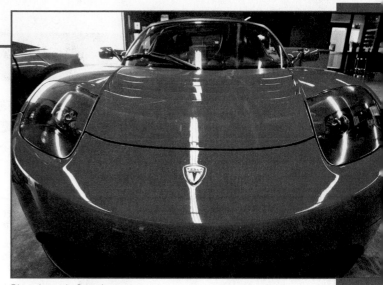
Bloomberg via Getty Images

Elon Musk showed his technical talents early, selling a computer game he designed at age 12 for $500. After he finished his undergraduate education with degrees in economics and physics at the University of Pennsylvania, he made plans to attend Stanford and study physics. But his interests spanned more than one field—he wanted to impact the future of the planet through the revolution of the Internet, by generating solutions to the energy crisis, and by exploring the possibility of mass space travel. How could one person hope to accomplish significant goals in so many different industries? ■

An organization is often successful when employees have a strong leader to demonstrate what it takes for a company to achieve its goals. **Leading** is the process of influencing, motivating, and enabling others to contribute to the success and effectiveness of an organization by achieving its goals. As we discussed in Chapter 7, leading is one of the four functions of management (other functions include planning, organizing, and controlling/monitoring).

Are all managers leaders? Famed management researcher and author Peter Drucker once noted that "management is doing things right; leadership is doing the right things."[15] Both leaders and managers strive to motivate people, but they have different scopes. Typically, managers spend their time making sure that specific tasks are done well and completed on time. The leadership of a company, on the other hand, is focused on setting the long-term vision and strategies a company will need to survive and flourish. Truly great leaders are able to be both managers and leaders: They define a vision, foster agreement across the company, and then implement the strategy.

What styles of leadership exist? Many different leadership styles exist, and leaders often employ different styles in a given situation depending on a complex mix of their own personality, the corporate culture, the type of company, and the employees they manage. ■ **TABLE 8.2** lists four of the most common leadership styles:

- Democratic
- Autocratic
- Affiliative (laissez-faire)
- Visionary

What are democratic and autocratic leaders like? A **democratic leader** delegates authority and involves employees in the decision-making process. An **autocratic leader** makes decisions without consulting others.

Consider Henry Chang, who runs the kitchen of a large restaurant. Henry allows his staff to offer opinions as he develops the menu. He also lets them experiment with different recipes and food presentations and features their work on the main menu when possible. The kitchen staff members love working with Henry because he allows them to be creative and innovative. He also encourages them to cultivate the skills they need to run their own restaurant someday. However, Henry's restaurant

4 What are the various identifiable leadership styles and traits, and how do they affect business leadership?

■ TABLE 8.2

Styles of Leadership

	Democratic	Autocratic	Affiliative (Laissez-Faire)	Visionary
	VOTE tribalium81/Fotolia	kikkerdirk/Fotolia	NLshop/Fotolia	freshidea/Fotolia
Leader characteristics	• Listens well • Is a team worker • Collaborates • Influences	• Commands—"Do it because I say so" • Threatens • Has tight control • Monitors studiously • Creates dissonance • Contaminates everyone's mood • Drives away talent	• Promotes harmony • Empathizes with others • Boosts morale • Solves conflicts	• Inspires • Believes in own vision • Is empathetic • Explains how and why people's efforts contribute to the "dream"
Benefits to style	Values people's input and gets commitment through participation	Soothes fear by giving clear direction in an emergency	Creates harmony by connecting people to one another	Moves people toward shared dreams
When style is appropriate	To build buy-in or consensus or get valuable input from employees	In a crisis, to kick-start an urgent turn-around; with problem employees; traditional military	To heal rifts in a team, motivate during stressful times or strengthen connections	When changes require a new vision or when a clear direction is needed; radical change

often attracts important political dignitaries and famous entertainers. Sometimes, the restaurant becomes unexpectedly busy. In these circumstances, Henry doesn't leave anything to chance, and dictates exactly what needs to be done and who should do it. Henry knows he might hurt someone's feelings, but ultimately, his staff trusts him to make the right decisions to obtain the best results for the restaurant.

For the most part, Henry is a democratic leader because he knows that by involving his employees they become more invested in the process. The trade-off, Henry recognizes, is that his democratic style of leadership requires more time and advanced planning. When such time is not available, Henry must take complete charge. In those instances, he becomes an autocratic leader. A good leader knows that such commanding leadership can be an effective style in certain circumstances when quick decisions need to be made or when it seems as if the group cannot come to a consensus.

What are affiliative leaders? Some leaders take a more hands-off approach to management and act more as consultants than participants. **Affiliative (or laissez-faire) leaders** are more advisory in style, encouraging employees to contribute ideas rather than specifically directing their tasks. This style of leadership is often best used with groups and teams. Affiliative leadership implemented properly can give employees a sense of challenge, commitment, and

Gordon Ramsey is an accomplished chef, famous for an autocratic style of leadership in his restaurant kitchens.

jeremy sutton-hibbert/Alamy

renewed energy as they are left to handle tasks on their own. As businesses continue to reduce the layers of management, affiliative and democratic styles are becoming the leadership styles of choice. However, it is possible for affiliative leaders to lose too much involvement in the group's processes. If the group or team members feel that management is virtually absent, team members may choose actions and strategies that are easy and not in line with the goals of a company.

What makes a leader a visionary? Visionary leaders are able to inspire others, believe in their own vision, and move people toward a shared dream. John Lasseter was an animator in Disney's computer animation department when George Lucas' company Lucasfilm opened a computer animation division. Lasseter was drawn to the vision of what might be possible with the advances in technology he saw in use at Lucasfilm, so he left Disney in 1984 to spend a month at Industrial Light and Magic (ILM), a division of Lucasfilm. He has been there ever since. In 1986 that division was purchased by Steve Jobs and became its own company, Pixar. Lasseter is currently Pixar's chief creative officer. He has assembled a uniquely creative collection of employees and led them to producing a series of new classics in animated film—including *Toy Story*, *A Bug's Life*, and *Cars*.

As a visionary leader, Lasseter had to create the special environment that would allow creative people the freedom to be inventive but also the structure to meet the deadlines required on a multimillion-dollar film schedule. One example of his leadership is in the production of *Toy Story*. At that time, Pixar had never produced anything longer than a short, five-minute film; it was not clear whether the company could actually produce a full-length film. *Toy Story* was being produced and distributed by Disney (in a partnership with Pixar), and Disney executives called a meeting to see a segment. Disney wanted to make sure the film had the quality it wanted from its new partner. Lasseter remembers the meeting: "I was pretty much embarrassed by what was on the screen. I had made it. I directed everybody to do this . . . but it was a story filled with the most unhappy, mean people." Disney wanted to shut down production and fire staff. But Lasseter negotiated a two-week reprieve and returned to lead his team of cowriters and animators. "Let's make the movie we wanted to make," he told them, and the story took on a gentler, sweeter tone. The team had to work nonstop for the two-week reprieve, with the threat of massive lay-offs over their heads. The ending of the story is well known: *Toy Story* went on to achieve $190 million in domestic box office receipts, and Lasseter earned an Honorary Oscar for the achievement. Lasseter has since used visionary leadership to guide the studio to successes with many movies.[16]

Traits of Leadership

What are the traits of great leaders? As illustrated in ■ **FIGURE 8.3** the best leaders share some common traits.

- Great leaders *challenge the process* by not always accepting conventional beliefs and practices as the only way to accomplish tasks. They set goals and have a vision of the future that may be different from the norm. Leaders are not afraid to alter their methods or plans, if the situation calls for change. They continually brainstorm for solutions to problems and more effective ways of reaching goals.

- Great leaders *inspire a shared vision* and motivate people to care about the corporate

■ **FIGURE 8.3**
Traits of Effective Leadership

goals or an important mission. Leaders influence in a positive and moral way (rather than in a selfish and destructive way) and garner trust, respect, and commitment to their vision. They can communicate a vision throughout the organization and inspire others to adopt the same vision and work toward common goals.

- Great leaders *model the way* by serving as a living example of the ideals in which they are asking their employees to share. Leaders have a good handle on their business and industry. They are willing to admit mistakes and constantly seek more information to make informed and reasoned decisions. Good leaders base their decisions on facts. They are well organized and detail oriented. Strong leaders often model the ethical tone they want to set for their businesses through their choices in speech and action.

- Great leaders *exhibit emotional intelligence*. Most successful leaders possess a high degree of **emotional intelligence**—the ability to understand both one's own and others' emotions. It is a term for the set of skills including self-awareness, self-management, social awareness, and relationship management. Leaders can use their awareness of others' emotional states to inspire people to feel more positive and connect with others by being honest and open about their own ideals, concerns, and goals. In working with these types of leaders, people tend to feel secure and free to explore and share their creative ideas.

- Great leaders *enable others to act* by giving people the access to information and empowering them to perform to their fullest potential.[17] Leaders need to

OFF THE MARK

Masataka Shimizu

Masataka Shimizu, head of the Tokyo Electric Power Company (Tepco) faced a horrible natural disaster in the earthquake that rocked the Fukushima nuclear reactor complex in Japan in March 2011. The earthquake led to a tsunami and the meltdown of three reactors, resulting in the worst radiation release since Chernobyl. At hearings later it was found that the amount of radiation released was over twice what had initially been reported. Damages exceeded $100 billion. The country's economy was disrupted for over a year, and national plans to increase the role of nuclear power in Japan were derailed.

It is hard to rise to such a challenging set of events but in the investigations that followed, much troubling information came to light. Reports were found that senior Tepco engineers had known for years that half of the reactors in Fukushima had a dangerous design flaw, but the company failed to make upgrades.[18] When the disaster hit, Shimizu disappeared for days. His communication with government ministers caused confusion. At stake was a complete evacuation of Tokyo if all six reactors at Fukushima were to melt down. Masataka Shimizu resigned amid scandal in 2012.

A protester holds a picture of Masataka Shimizu, president of Tokyo Electric Power Co. when the disaster at Fukushima nuclear station occurred.

Bloomberg via Getty Images

achieve and have a high energy level. True leadership drive, however, does not come at the expense of others, and successful leaders delegate authority and responsibility to others to promote their success also. They are the catalysts for positive action.

These traits are essential to effective leadership and are common to most good leaders.

Are there systems for measuring leadership potential? There are many personality tests that can provide information to assess leadership potential and improve leadership skills. Popular personality assessments include the *Big Five*, the *Cattell 16 PF*, and the *Thematic Apperception Test*. Although no one personality test is recognized as the perfect tool, all of them strive to provide us with a better understanding of the traits that are the foundation of successful leadership.

Leadership and Corporate Culture

How does the management's leadership style influence the work environment? The **corporate culture** is a collection of values, norms, and behavior shared by management and workers that defines the character of an organization. Corporate culture will dictate what style of dress is appropriate at work, the work environment itself, rules for getting ahead and being promoted, what is valued, who is valued, and even what kind of work/life balance is expected. Typically this is done without written rules and open guidance; it is an attitude of "this is how we do things here" and a consistent pressure to make employees fall in line with that model. This is why it is important that your personal goals and style match the corporate culture of the organization you choose to work for.

In a corporation in which the culture is not well-defined—or even worse, one that supports questionable behavior—problems result. This was the case for the natural gas giant Enron, which eventually went bankrupt because of a significant lack of control and the poor ethical behavior of top management. On the other hand, when the corporate culture is strong and all employees accept the culture as their own, they are motivated to maintain it and monitor their own behavior.

How does a leader establish corporate culture? Tony Hsieh of Zappos .com, the online shoe giant, is a powerful example of how a leader can establish corporate culture. Hsieh started Zappos at a time when selling a product like shoes online was thought to be impossible. He was sure that top-notch customer service would be the difference. In his book *Delivering Happiness*: *A Path to Profits, Passion and Purpose*,[20] he explains how first establishing a corporate culture naturally led to the customer service levels he wanted, the profits he wanted, and the purpose he wanted in his life and for his employees. Hsieh and the two other founders

---

Biz CHAT

Do You Have to Be Tall to Be a Leader?

What does height have to do with successful leadership in business? A lot, according to many industry experts and observers. Lara Tiedens, an organizational behavior professor at the Stanford University Graduate School of Business,

cites height is a tool business leaders use to appear powerful. In addition, her research shows that looking directly at others, vigorous hand gesturing, speaking loudly, and interrupting others all promote dominance in a negotiation or in the board room.[19]

What do you think? Does appearance affect success in business? If you interrupt and shout down other voices, will your opinions rise to the top? Or is the idea that height and rudeness, rather than skills and talents, lead to promotion, a myth?

Deliver Wow through Service	Embrace and Drive Change	Create Fun and a Little Weirdness	Pursue Growth and Learning	Be Adventurous, Creative and Open-Minded

■ **FIGURE 8.4**
Zappos Core Values Frog
The corporate culture at Zappos shines through its web page describing the company's core values using the Zappos Core Values Frog!
Image Sources: From "Our Unique Culture," Zappos.com. (c) 2013 Zappos.com, Inc.

developed a list of ten core values and the slogan, "What would Core Values Frog do . . . ?" ■ **FIGURE 8.4** shows the company's 10 core frog values.[21]

The corporate culture shines through, even in the hiring process. For example, value 10 is "Be Humble." Candidates are picked up from the airport with a Zappos shuttle bus. Later, the bus driver is interviewed to see how the candidates treated the driver; in this way, the interview started before the candidates realized it. Another key interview question relates to value 3, "Create Fun and a Little Weirdness." Candidates are asked "How weird are you on a scale of 1 to 10?" Zappos is looking for employees who are willing to bring their personality to the office, not hide behind what they think is expected. (You can see evidence on blogs.zappos.com, where the video from the Zappos Prom is posted.) And one week after they have been hired, every employee is offered $2,000 to leave Zappos if they don't think it is for them.[22]

Hsieh is willing to take his corporate culture out of the office. His Downtown Project is an investment of over $350 million to develop downtown Las Vegas, where he plans to relocate Zappos. The money will support education

ON TARGET

Southwest Airlines

One company that has shown to be on target in using strong leadership and strong employee motivation is Southwest Airlines. They have an amazingly low turnover rate for their industry (7.5%) and credit it to allowing people to express their individuality. Singing flight attendants and comedic reports from pilots are common on Southwest flights. The management encourages input from all levels—position does not prevent anyone from contributing a new idea. Southwest has never furloughed employees, a common industry practice where more people are hired to cover busy travel seasons, but then "placed on hold" when traffic drops. Because of the job security, Southwest employees are confident that they can grow into new positions. The largely union environment has a similar pay structure to other airlines but the company implements a profit-sharing plan, with employees owning 5 percent of the company.[24] A number of employees have become millionaires after 20 years of service.

The company now has had 39 consecutive years of profitability and has operating revenue of over $15 billion. They have won numerous awards for customer service, as one of the best places to work, and as one of the most admired companies in the world. CEO Gary Kelly describes what it takes to live the Southwest way by listing three key criteria: "a Warrior Spirit, a Servant's Heart, and a Fun-LUVing Attitude."[25]

initiatives, new small businesses, and technology start-ups. Instead of following the model of building a corporate campus that meets all the employees' needs, Hsieh envisions building the perfect community—complete with artists, musicians, yoga shops, and cheese stores so his employees will want to live and work in the area.

What did all this focus on building a corporate culture do for the company? Zappos has become a company with a "higher purpose of vision that is more than just about money or profits or being No. 1 in the market," describes Hsieh.[23] Along the way, the staff has become renowned for outstanding customer service, being friendly, even spending hours on the phone with a single caller if needed. That has translated into over $1 billion in annual sales; the company was acquired by Amazon.com for $1.2 billion in 2009.

Elon Musk at 40 has proven himself as a visionary leader. He has founded PayPal, the Internet company that changed online commerce. He is CEO and chief designer of the first company that sent a spacecraft to the International Space Station (SpaceX). He is also CEO of Tesla Motors, whose all-electric line of cars includes the Tesla Roadster, a sports car that goes 0–60 mph in 3.7 seconds. How can one person create disruptive change in three industries? By being a powerful, transformative leader.

Musk has consistently been willing to challenge the status quo—he had to fund Tesla Motors for two years with millions of his own investment because no one else was willing to imagine a business success with all-electric vehicles.[26] He inspires others with his vision and lures talented engineers from other great companies. The engineers know that at SpaceX and Tesla they will push the envelope and create products never seen before at the two companies. Musk's clarity of vision and dedication to creating important and beautiful products serves as a model of what is expected and what is possible at his companies. ■

Teamwork pp. 243–249

There is probably no team you want to be more efficient, communicative, and effective than the operating team that is doing your surgery. The OR team may be comprised of seven or more members, and most often they have never met each other before the day of the surgery. As medicine has become more sophisticated, even the most routine tasks have become so complicated that mistakes are all too common. Dr. Atul Gawande saw this happening and wanted to develop a way to make his team function better. But where to begin? ■

Andres Rodriguez/Fotolia

It's challenging to develop effective teams, but the benefits can be extraordinary. Although different personalities have the potential to create conflict within a team, they can also create unique ideas. In this section, we'll discuss teamwork and how it affects organizations.

The Advantages of Teams in the Workplace

What is the value of using teams in the workplace? In good, working teams, there's agreement on the objectives at hand and the best approach to solve a problem.[27] Teammates depend on one another's ideas and efforts to successfully complete tasks. There is a sense of accountability, and members are committed to one another's success.

One product that benefited from team development is the Microsoft Kinect. A breakthrough product for the video gaming industry, the Kinect is an accessory for the game console Xbox 360. It allows the player to control the system with voice commands and with gestures, without holding any controller at all. The Kinect was not designed by a single team but was made up of seven teams from seven different disciplines. A very small team began exploring ways to track player's body movements. Another small team of computer vision experts from Microsoft Research worked on the key algorithms. Once demos of the team's work began spreading through the company, engineers began to volunteer to come in and work through the night. Kinect sold 8 million units in its first 60 days and holds the Guinness World Record for the fastest selling consumer electronics device.[28]

The Challenges of Teams in the Workplace

Do teams always improve the development process? Although teams have been shown to be effective in many situations, some people suggest that teamwork does not always bring more creative output. Research conducted by Barry Staw at the University of California at Berkeley found that when college students were asked to think of business ideas—either individually or in teams—the individuals came up with more ideas than did the teams. In addition, the individuals' ideas were voted as more creative than were the teams' concepts. Staw concluded that collective thinking does not lead to increased creativity and can, in fact, hamper it. One possible reason, Staw proposes, is that team members often want to "fit in" rather than "stand out," and true creativity and original thinking is largely dependent on one's willingness to stand out and take risks.[29]

If a team is not carefully selected, this behavior of "wanting to fit in" can lead to narrow-mindedness. This is a phenomenon referred to as **groupthink**. People who are from similar backgrounds and sectors of a company tend to have a set of familiar ideas and work with the same set of unspoken assumptions. These may lead to rejecting different ideas without fair examination. The impact of groupthink can be chilling to the creative output of a team, although this challenge can be minimized with thoughtful design in team membership.

In the twenty-first century, another challenge to successful workplace teams is the fact that there is now a wide mix of generations in the workforce (see ■ **TABLE 8.3**). In fact, it is possible for there to be three or even four generations assigned to a single team. People from separate generations have grown up with social and educational experiences that are so different that they take on distinct styles in the workplace.

Are generational differences really that significant? In their book *Millennials Rising: The Next Great Generation*,[30] researchers Neil Howe and

Not every team performs at its best.

© NBC/Courtesy: Everett Collection

William Strauss discuss the three dominant generations in the workplace today:

- *Baby boomers*—those born between 1943 and 1960. The baby boomers are the veterans in the workforce, and many have been with the same company for more than 30 years.
- *Gen-Xers*—born between 1961 and 1981. Gen-Xers, who are known for their independent thinking and hankering for change, are the first generation of workers to value family life over work life.
- *Millennials*—born between 1982 and 2002. Like Gen-Xers, Millennials want their jobs to accommodate their personal lives, but they also have very high expectations for achievement in their careers.

■ TABLE 8.3

Three Generations in the Workplace

Generation	Birth Years	Famous Man	Famous Woman
Boomer	1943–1960	Steven Spielberg	Oprah Winfrey
Gen-X	1961–1981	Matt Damon	Jennifer Lopez
Millennial	1982–2002	LeBron James	Miley Cyrus

Source: Neil Howe and William Strauss, *Millennials Rising: The Next Great Generation* (Vintage, 2000).

Millennials, who are now entering college campuses and the workforce, believe in their self-worth and value—whether deserved or not.[31] They feel they have the capability to change the companies they work for and the world. According to Howe and Strauss, members of this generation expect to make their greatest marks in society by using technology to empower the community. Also important to note is that this generation is the focus of marketing efforts because they are the biggest youth spenders in history, most often in "copurchases" with their parents. Teamwork, good behavior, and citizenship are much more important to Millennials than to earlier generations, and they see equality between different races and genders.

How will this affect business? Strauss predicts, "Young workers will demand that employers adjust to the needs of workers who wish to build careers and families at the same time and lead lower-stress lives than their parents did. Older employees will admire their skills, confidence, and team spirit, but will question their creativity and toughness."[32]

Best Practices for Teams

5 What are the best ways to create, manage, and participate in teams?

What kinds of practices set the stage for the best team performance? Psychologist Mihaly Csikszentmihalyi has extended his idea of flow, discussed earlier, into the team setting. **Group flow** occurs when a group knows how to work together so that each individual member can achieve flow. The characteristics of such a setting are as follows:

1. **Creative spatial arrangements.** Pinning ideas on the walls and using large charts to combine ideas from the entire group tend to lead to the open consideration of ideas. Tables are used less because working while standing and moving promotes more discussion and interaction.

2. **Playground design.** This begins with creating a "safe space," agreeing it is safe to bring out ideas that normally one might just keep to himself or herself. Often a large number of charts display information inputs, graphs, and the project summary. Wall space can be used to collect results and lists of open topics.

3. **Constant focus on the target group for the product.** At Amazon.com, CEO Jeff Bezos has the nickname "the empty chair" because he often keeps a

Red Teamers in the Military

ON TARGET

Teamwork is a critical part of business, but one place you might not think of team decision making is in the military. Military organization is based on unquestioning obedience to orders. But the military is sensitive to how this conditioning could contribute to groupthink in team decision making. So a program of study was developed to produce "Red Teamers," officers trained in analyzing problems from a wide range of points of view—how the decision will impact military allies, how the decision will impact allied countries' military forces, and how the different cultural perspectives of the occupied country will respond. Red Team students study military theory but also Eastern philosophy, for example. "We want them to understand that their view of the world is very narrow," says Bob Topping, who develops the curriculum for the program. "We look at the world through a straw. We're shielded."[33] In Iraq, Red Team officers were used, for example, on teams making decisions regarding the use of military dogs because Iraqi citizens generally consider dogs unclean and even evil. A Red Teamer is responsible for raising issues that the group might not have considered, but then stepping out of the way and not obstructing the decision making. The same idea of injecting a skeptic into a group to promote a variety of points of view is used in other government agencies. For example, the Federal Aviation Administration (FAA) uses Red Teams to conduct airport testing to find and resolve security weaknesses. Is there a Red Teamer in your group . . . or do you need one?

seat open at team meetings. The empty seat is the most important one in the room as it represents the customer.[34]

4. **Visualization.** Heavy use of visualization and prototyping are used to construct early models. These are then refined to make the models more efficient.

How do managers create the best teams? Some important aspects a manager should consider in forming a team include the following:

- **Size.** A team that is too large may struggle with cohesiveness. At the same time, a large group can offer the benefit of diverse perspectives.
- **Time Frame.** Some teams may be formulated to work on a specific problem or project within a short time frame, while others may work together for longer time periods on everyday tasks.
- **Status.** A team that is formally created by a company may be required to provide progress reports and updates, and it often has access to company resources. Less formal teams may need to take initiative in maintaining lines of communication.

According to business writer and theorist R. M. Belbin, effective teams are comprised of people with diverse skills, talents, and points of view. Team members' respective skills and talents should complement one another so the team can perform at an optimum level. For example, what might happen if everyone on a team is extremely creative yet inexperienced in effective time management? What if five of six team members are all aggressive leaders? Clearly, a balance of people who embody different team roles is key in the success of a team.

Belbin's model of nine team roles is outlined in ■ **TABLE 8.4**. Considering both these roles and the personality traits of potential members can be helpful when designing teams.

What are cross-functional teams? Traditionally team members were often chosen from the same department, all reporting to a common supervisor. But today's markets demand such quick response and adapting to conditions that a new model is emerging: cross-functional teams. In a **cross-functional team**, members

■ TABLE 8.4

Belbin's Nine Team Roles

Role	Personality Traits
Plant	Creative and imaginative
Resource investigator	Extroverted and communicative
Coordinator	Mature and confident
Shaper	Challenging and dynamic
Monitor evaluator	Serious and strategic
Teamworker	Cooperative and diplomatic
Implementer	Disciplined and reliable
Completer/finisher	Painstaking and conscientious
Specialist	Dedicated and self-starting

Adapted from R. M. Belbin, "Team Role Descriptions," Belbin Associates. www.belbin.com/content/page/731/Belbin_Team_Role_Descriptions.pdf. Adapted with permission from Belbin Associates, www.belbin.com

are selected across a range of critical functional divisions of a business. For example, in 2004 the LEGO Group was near bankruptcy.[35] Investments in the LEGO theme parks had failed, and some products like Clikits had struggled in the marketplace. The management created a cross-functional team named the Executive Innovation Governance Group. It consisted of employees who could contribute in product innovation, pricing, business processes, marketing, and community building. The group ushered through modifications to existing product lines as well as new products, such as the series of LEGO board games, a new product category for LEGO. In 2010, during a declining toy market overall, LEGO saw a 30 percent increase in revenues.

What effect does technology have on team design? Modern telecommunications allows team members to live far from each other. In a **virtual team**, members are located in different physical locations but work together to achieve a goal. The need for virtual teams has grown out of the increased globalization of business. Familiar tools like conference calls and e-mail have evolved to include video conferencing and live broadcasting of key meetings and events over the Web. Webcasts can now support interactive participation of the viewing audience. In real time, audience members can ask questions, exchange electronic files with the group, and record the presentation for repeated viewing. Web conferencing software like WebEx and Microsoft Office Live allow participants in any geographic location to brainstorm together in real time on a common "virtual whiteboard," watch demos and presentations live, and record and annotate these discussions for later playback.

How can social media tools like wikis help modern teams? Modern tools for collaboration are now often replacing endless streams of e-mails with file attachments. Wikis are one example. *Wikis* are websites that support editing by multiple authors. Team members can work on one common document all at the same time, watching each other make editing changes, having a live chat window open at the same time. Changes are archived and can be recalled; if a member of the team later reads the document and wants to revert back to an earlier version, he or she can do so with just one click. The problem of having multiple versions of a document is eliminated, so there are no concerns about synchronizing the different versions between all team members; the most current version is always available on the wiki.

One of the best known public wikis is the encyclopedia project Wikipedia. Wikipedia is not the only use of wikis, however. Wikis can be run and maintained by individuals or within a specific corporation. Sites like wikimatrix.org can help identify the type of wiki software best suited to a specific virtual team. Products like Blackboard and Microsoft Windows SharePoint contain wiki tools as part of the main product.

Is designing a strong virtual team the same as creating a strong face-to-face team? The best practices for creating strong virtual teams are emerging as virtual teams become a more accepted and useful teaming solution.[36] Most successful virtual teams include some periodic face-to-face meetings. Very few virtual teams are 100 percent virtual. Although technology allows teams to communicate without ever meeting face-to-face, it is still important to have the group occasionally meet with each other in the same space to build social connections. Keeping the team connected is a key priority for a virtual team, and it can be difficult to keep contacts strong from a distance. There can be communication delays from working across time zones or using e-mail as a primary mode of communication. Establishing team rules, such as agreeing to respond to e-mail messages within a certain window of time or initiating global office hours, can minimize these problems. (For more on communicating with teams, see Mini Chapter 3, "Business Communications.")

Your Role on a Team

How can I be a valued team player? It is important to begin now to build the skills that will make you successful in team settings. As we have seen, the best teams are carefully planned and selected and can be the place where some of the most exciting and innovative work in the company is happening. Preparing yourself to contribute in a team setting may be the most important thing you can do to increase your value to an organization, no matter what position you hold.

What habits will give me the best chance to contribute to a team? There are many skills that you can build to enhance your success as a member of a team. One model that organizes these skills is the **Seven Habits model** developed by famed management author Stephen Covey.[37] He has found that there are seven habits of behavior exhibited by successful people:

1. **Be proactive.** This is the ability to control your environment rather than have it control you. Proactive team members are constantly looking "down the road" in terms of their time management, work, and obstacles coming that may impede the success of a project.

2. **Begin with the end in mind.** This means that you are able to see the desired outcome and concentrate on activities that help in achieving it. Staying focused on the ultimate goal allows you to avoid taking the team in directions that will cause divisiveness and waste resources and energy.

3. **Put first things first.** This skill works together with the second habit in pushing you toward success in your team role. Manage your time and energy so that the required tasks are prioritized.

4. **Think win-win.** This is the most important aspect of interpersonal leadership because most achievements are based on cooperative effort; therefore, the aim needs to be win-win solutions for all.

5. **Seek first to understand and then to be understood.** In communicating with other members of the team, it is critical to develop and maintain positive relationships. This style of communication recommends listening and working to give your teammates the feeling they have been heard as key to your own success in being understood and contributing.

6. **Synergize.** This is the habit of creative cooperation—the principle that collaboration often achieves more than could be achieved by individuals working independently toward attaining a purpose.

7. **Sharpen the saw.** This catch phrase comes from the metaphor of chopping down a tree. If you are constantly sawing and never take time to stop and sharpen the saw, you'll feel as if you're investing tremendous energy, but the results will not be what they could be if you just stopped to sharpen the saw first. Strong team contributors avoid the work mode of continually reacting to crises. Instead, they take time to step back and develop skills and analyze the task at hand so that they can work more efficiently.

If you work to develop and use these habits in your role on teams, you will find that your teams become more successful—and that you are in demand for the next team.

The key to promoting better team function for Dr. Gawande was to develop a checklist. His book, *The Checklist Manifesto*, describes how he worked with his staff to create a checklist they would use during surgeries. Issues were identified, like the need for a mandatory introduction of each person on the team before the opening cut, and giving a clear authorization to nurses to stop the surgery if an item on the checklist was missed. By having every member of the team involved in developing the checklist, critical items were included that could easily be overlooked. The result? At a multihospital study, there was a drop in the number of surgical deaths by 47 percent. ■

CHAPTER 8
SUMMARY

MyBizLab

Go to **mybizlab.com** to complete the problems marked with this icon ⭐.

1 **How do motivation and work environment encourage "flow"?** (p. 230)

- **Flow** (p. 230) is a state of feeling completely involved and focused on a task. Managers can increase motivation and foster flow by keeping employees intellectually engaged, removing distractions, encouraging creativity and flexibility, and supporting employees in all aspects of their lives.

2 **What are the main theories of motivation, and how are they applied to the workforce?** (pp. 231–233)

- Maslow's hierarchy describes motivation as a response to a progressive set of needs for **physiology** (p. 231), **safety** (p. 231), **belonging** (p. 231), **esteem** (p. 231), and **self-actualization** (p. 231).
- McClelland's **three needs theory** (p. 232) states the main motivators are the need for achievement, affiliation, and power.
- Herzberg broke the idea of motivation into two categories: **hygiene factors** (p. 232) and **motivators** (p. 232).
- **Extrinsic motivators** (p. 232) are external factors that generate engagement with the work, such as pay or promotion.
- **Intrinsic motivators** (p. 232) are internal drives that come from the actual interest of the work or from a sense of purpose and value in the work being done.
- **Theory X** (p. 233) posits that humans inherently dislike work and will try to avoid it if they can. As a result, managers should adopt a hard-line, authoritarian style.
- **Theory Y** (p. 234) proposes that people view work as natural and will be motivated to work as long as they are satisfied with their jobs. Thus, managers should implement a softer style that involves ample employee participation.
- **Theory Z** (p. 234) suggests that workers want to cooperate and be loyal to an organization. It emphasizes collaborative decision making.
- The **Vroom model (expectancy theory)** (p. 234) states that an individual's motivation can be described by the relationship between expectancy, instrumentality, and valence.

3 **How have motivational theories and industrial psychology changed the work environment since the early twentieth century?** (pp. 233–236)

- **Industrial psychology** (p. 235) is a field of academic study developed to scientifically understand how to optimally manage people and work.

- A 1932 study by Elton May concluded that when workers feel important, productivity increases. This is called the **Hawthorne effect** (p. 235). After World War II, research began to focus on the management of entire organizations rather than individual workers.
- Modern workplaces are influenced by studies that have shown that today's workers value autonomy, mastery, and purpose more than they do economic rewards. Studies of people engaged in creative work are showing they are demotivated by traditional financial incentives and highly motivated by offers of autonomy, mastery, and purpose.

4 **What are the various identifiable leadership styles and traits, and how do they affect business leadership?** (pp. 237–241)

- Leaders may exhibit a **democratic** (p. 237), **autocratic** (p. 237), **affiliative (laissez-faire)** (p. 238), and/or **visionary** (p. 239) style. Many top executives demonstrate one or more of these styles in their business dealings.
- Certain traits are common among effective leaders. They challenge conventional beliefs, inspire a shared vision, model by example, use emotional intelligence, and enable others to perform to their fullest potential.

5 **What are the best ways to create, manage, and participate in teams?** (pp. 245–249)

- Teams can benefit the workplace, allowing creative exchanges, organization, and positive competition.
- Effective teams must be designed and managed thoughtfully. The modern workplace includes workers spanning many generations, and it takes care and insight to make them mesh well on a single team.
- **Group flow** (p. 245) is achieved when a group knows how to work together so that each individual member can achieve flow. Best practices for creating strong teams include considering the size, the life span, and the status of the team.
- R. M. Belbin outlined a model of nine team roles. An effective team requires a variety of roles, and the members must be matched carefully to the team needs.
- Technology allows for virtual teams in which members are in different locations around the country or the world. Webcasts, electronic file exchange, and Web conferencing software make this more effective each year.
- Stephen Covey's **Seven Habits model** (p. 248) can help employees enhance their success as members of a team.

Key Terms

affiliative (or laissez-faire) leader (p. 238)

autocratic leader (p. 237)

belonging needs (p. 231)

corporate culture (p. 241)

cross-functional team (p. 246)

democratic leader (p. 237)

emotional intelligence (p. 240)

esteem needs (p. 231)

expectancy (p. 234)

expectancy theory (p. 234)

extrinsic motivators (p. 232)

flow (p. 230)

group flow (p. 245)

groupthink (p. 244)

Hawthorne effect (p. 235)

hierarchy of needs (p. 231)

hygiene factors (p. 232)

industrial psychology (p. 235)

instrumentality (p. 234)

intrinsic motivators (p. 232)

leading (p. 237)

motivator factors (p. 232)

motivator-hygiene theory (or two-factor theory) (p. 232)

organizational psychology (p. 230)

physiological needs (p. 231)

safety needs (p. 231)

self-actualization needs (p. 231)

Seven Habits model (p. 248)

strength-based management (p. 235)

Theory X (p. 233)

Theory Y (p. 234)

Theory Z (p. 234)

three needs theory (p. 232)

valence (p. 234)

virtual team (p. 247)

visionary leader (p. 239)

Self-Test

Multiple Choice You can find the answers on the last page of this book.

1. **The Q12 survey shows**
   a. whether you have the personality to be a successful motivator.
   b. almost three-quarters of U.S. employees are not engaged at work.
   c. whether the work environment is set up to support the state of flow.
   d. whether extrinsic or intrinsic motivators are influential.

2. **When employees are motivated,**
   a. they often take more time to be with their families.
   b. they often move on to other companies.
   c. net profits tend to decline.
   d. they are more productive and creative.

3. **Maslow's hierarchy of needs**
   a. is a theory of why people are motivated.
   b. uses three factors to compute the motivation of a person in a situation.
   c. was developed to address the Hawthorne effect.
   d. was displaced when Theory Z was introduced.

4. **With creative and abstract work, studies find that the principle motivators are**
   a. financial incentives.
   b. autonomy, mastery, and purpose.
   c. competitive push for advancement.
   d. reduction in hours involved at work.

5. **Teams improve creativity**
   a. when the phenomenon of groupthink sets in.
   b. no matter what the makeup of the team.
   c. when best practices for selecting the team members and roles are followed.
   d. when individuals work with others who are just like them.

6. **An example of Herzberg's hygiene factors is**
   a. feeling of belonging.
   b. creativity.
   c. safe working environment.
   d. respect.

7. **Theory Z is different than Theory X or Theory Y because**
   a. it relies heavily on collaborative decision making.
   b. it is authoritarian and hard line.
   c. it is often seen in mass-manufacturing settings.
   d. managers believe people will seek out responsibility.

8. **Virtual teams are teams that**
   a. are incomplete and need to be dissolved.
   b. communicate only through face-to-face meetings.
   c. primarily focus on technology-based projects.
   d. work in different physical locations.

Self-Test (continued)

9. **The Vroom model of motivational theory uses**
   a. expectancy, instrumentality, and valence.
   b. Rorschach inkblot testing.
   c. openness, conscientiousness, extraversion, and neuroticism.
   d. visualization that leads to daydreaming and lost time.

⭐ 10. **Extrinsic motivators include such things as**
   a. knowing your supervisor cares about you.
   b. believing your opinion matters.
   c. knowing there is a large financial bonus for good work.
   d. working for a company whose mission is meaningful to you.

True/False   You can find the answers on the last page of this book.

1. **Organizational psychology studies why people organize labor movements.**
   ☐ **True** or ☒ **False**

2. **Autocratic leaders cannot manage large companies effectively.**
   ☐ **True** or ☒ **False**

3. **Intrinsic motivators come from a sense of purpose and value in the work employees are doing.**
   ☒ **True** or ☐ **False**

4. **Strength-based management believes the best way to develop talent is to help employees add skills and knowledge that build on their existing strengths.**
   ☒ **True** or ☐ **False**

5. **Groupthink is the convergence of the group on the best idea.**
   ☐ **True** or ☒ **False**

Critical Thinking Questions

1. When in your life have you been motivated by external factors like rewards, money, or promotion? In what kind of setting would the combination of autonomy, mastery, and purpose be more successful in focusing you to go above and beyond?

⭐ 2. Consider the traits of effective leaders presented on pages 239–241 in the chapter. Then consider your own personality traits. How could you strengthen the leadership traits you do not currently see in yourself?

3. Stephen Covey's Seven Habits model is focused on making you a more successful, efficient person. What impact would these seven habits have on your relationships with your friends and family?

Team Time

FORMING A SUCCESSFUL TEAM

A shoe manufacturer wants to diversify its successful product line of hiking boots. The company wants to appeal to young people, a rapidly growing consumer base with increasing amounts of disposable income. The company has decided to give one team almost unlimited resources and freedom to develop a flip-flop sandal for modern, gadget-loving youth.

You need to apply the best-practices principles in team formation to determine the personalities and strengths of each member and assign roles in which the members will be motivated to contribute.

Process

Step 1. Break up into teams of three or four individuals.

Step 2. Begin by deciding what tool you will use to evaluate each member for personality traits, strengths, and weaknesses.

Step 3. Develop a strategy for assessing what work needs to be done and then how your team will assign appropriate responsibilities to each member.

Step 4. How will you evaluate the level of motivation and creativity for the team? What changes can be made if the team's performance is not adequate?

Step 5. Present your findings to the class for discussion.

Ethics and Corporate Social Responsibility

ETHICS IN TEAMWORK

Being a member of a team means you are accountable for your actions and the actions of your fellow teammates. Review the following scenario.

Scenario

Imagine you work at an advertising firm. You're on a team that is developing an advertising campaign proposal for a chain of fitness centers. The firm has been struggling and needs your team to land this account. At a meeting, one of your teammates reveals that he has hacked into a competing firm's network and has a draft of its proposal for the same account. Your teammate wants to steal the idea and use it in your team's proposal. Most of your teammates agree with this idea, but you think it is unethical.

Questions for Discussion

1. How would you handle this situation? Would you voice your objection or go along with the team?

2. If you decide to voice your objection, do you address the entire team or speak to members individually? Why?

3. How would you reconcile your role as a loyal employee and team player with your need to uphold ethical standards?

Web Exercises

1. **Testing 1, 2, 3 . . .**
   Find three online leadership, team roles, and/or personality assessment tools. See testyourself.psychtests.com for examples. How consistent are the results in describing your personality or tendencies? How accurate would you rate the results?

2. **Great American Leaders**
   Visit www.hbs.edu/leadership/database/index.html, the twentieth-century great American leaders database maintained by the Harvard University Business School. Select one leader from your state, one of your gender, one leader of the same ethnicity, and two additional people profiled from different industries. What similarities and differences do you see in this group of five great leaders?

3. **Drive**
   View the animated version of a talk given by Dan Pink on intrinsic motivation titled "Drive" at www.youtube.com/watch?v=u6XAPnuFjJc. Describe his presentation in terms of what motivates you in school and in your free time.

4. **More Motivation**
   Review the set of motivational theories described on changingminds.org/explanations/theories/a_motivation.htm. Select three theories that were not discussed in this chapter and compare them to the motivational theories presented. How are they similar, and how are they different? How would using these theories change how employees were treated in a workplace?

5. **Measuring Your Team's Health**
   Consider a team that you are part of and complete the Team Effectiveness Assessment form at www.mindtools.com/pages/article/newTMM_84.htm#Explanation. Submit the form and examine the summary for your score. Do you agree with the analysis of team dynamics? Use the material following the score interpretation to spark useful discussion in your team. What action steps can you take personally and as a group to become more effective?

MyBizLab

Go to **mybizlab.com** for Auto-graded writing questions as well as the following Assisted-graded writing questions:

8-1. Is it better for a business to respond to a changing climate by hiring a different style of leader or expect the current leadership to adapt its style to new conditions?

8-2. What factors are the most important for creating a team that works efficiently together? What problems have you seen in your own academic career when working in group settings, and how could they be prevented?

8-3. MyBizLab Only – comprehensive writing assignment for this chapter.

Human Resource Management

Human Resource Management

H and R—two simple letters that together represent a vital component of any successful business. Indeed, a well-managed human resource (HR) department is essential to the smooth operation of all organizations. HR managers like Leslie Booth are responsible for many tasks, from hiring to firing and everything in between. Why is human resource management so important?

Training and Evaluating Employees

Training allows a business to leverage the talents of its employees across a whole company. George Hensel knows how to run the perfect meeting. How can his company use him most efficiently to train others?

Compensating, Scheduling, Promoting, and Terminating Employees

To attract high-caliber applicants, companies need compensation packages that are comparable with their competitors or better. Kathy Sanchez is a full-time graphic designer but is struggling to afford health insurance. What other types of benefits are important in a good compensation package?

Managing Workplace Diversity

Diversity is encouraged because it benefits a company, but it has been a challenge for Chandraki Patel to manage the widely diverse group she is responsible for. What issues do companies and managers face when establishing more diversity in the workplace?

Labor and Union Issues

Workers form unions in an effort to protect their interests. If management makes a decision to reduce health care or salaries, union leaders are there to fight for the rights of workers. What happens when the governor decides the power of unions needs to be limited for the sake of a balanced budget?

MyBizLab®

⭐ **Improve Your Grade!**

Over 10 million students improved their results using the Pearson MyLabs.
Visit **mybizlab.com** for simulations, tutorials, and end-of-chapter problems.

Human Resource Management pp. 257–263

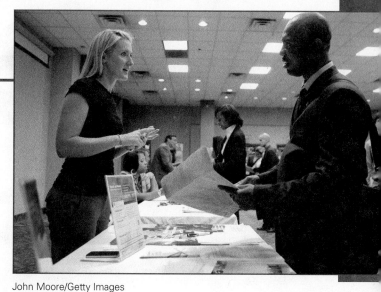

John Moore/Getty Images

When HR manager Leslie Booth was assigned to find a new senior account executive, she weighed her options carefully. To fill such a senior position required patience. She hired a recruiter to find outside candidates to interview for the position, and, to keep her options open, she also placed job postings in local newspapers and in the top accounting journals. When no one with the right qualifications had shown up in four weeks, she began to feel serious pressure from her boss to get the position filled. What should she do? ■

When you think about the resources required to run a business, you probably think about things like money, space, equipment, and supplies. Although those resources are key components, the "human" resource—people—is often taken for granted, but is arguably the most important. People provide ideas, creativity, knowledge, and ingenuity that make a business run.

Human resources—the people in an organization—need to be managed just as carefully as the material and financial resources of a business. **Human resource management (HRM)** is the organizational function that deals with the people in the business. HRM encompasses every aspect of the "human" in a business, including hiring, training, motivating, evaluating, and compensating personnel, as shown in ■ **FIGURE 9.1**. In addition to the traditional functions, HRM also works through many challenges in today's workplace, such as diversity issues, work/life preferences, and global business considerations. In this section, you'll learn the ins and outs of human resource management.

Managing Staffing Needs

How does planning for staffing needs change as a company evolves? A small business start-up may initially have one person serving in every function—as the company's CEO and financial manager, as the sales executive and the marketing director. Once the business begins to grow, new people are brought into the organization. Although keeping track of HR needs at small businesses can be fairly simple, companies that add employees and continue to grow require more specific HR planning.

Poor staff planning can be costly. Being overstaffed burdens a company with the unnecessary expense of maintaining salaries, benefits, and training for surplus employees. An understaffed organization can lead to a loss of sales and competitiveness if customer needs are not met. Planning staffing requires:

- Determining the optimal number of employees the business needs
- Clearly identifying the exact job positions and the requirements of those positions

> **1** What processes are involved in human resource management (HRM)?

■ **FIGURE 9.1**
The Functions of HRM

How does a company determine whether it has the correct number of employees? The process begins with gathering information on the current workforce and on the future demand for workers within the company. The current supply of employees is determined by developing a workforce profile. A **workforce profile** is a personnel inventory that includes information about each employee, such as age, education, training, experience, specialized skills, and current and previous positions held within the company.

The future demand for employees is determined in a process called **forecasting**. Forecasting is based on several factors, such as the predicted sales of a company's goods or services, the current workforce skill level, the effect of technology changes on staff needs, and changes in employment practices (such as using more or less temporary staff). In addition, staffing changes that are expected to occur through normal turnover, retirement, and any planned reassignments are also taken into consideration. If forecasting indicates an imbalance between the supply of and the demand for employees, adjustments can be made. Such actions may include recruitment, training, retraining, labor reductions, or changes in workforce utilization.

How do companies identify the exact jobs they need to staff? The HR department also completes a study of the tasks to be performed within the organization. A **job analysis** defines in detail the duties and requirements of the tasks an employee is required to perform. A job analysis includes:

- A **job description**—a formal statement that summarizes what the employee will do in that role. It includes the responsibilities of that position, the

Job Analysis

Company: Nelson Wireless

Position title: Marketing manager

(a) Job description	(b) Job specifications
Join a team of marketing professionals focused on mobile technologies in the consumer market segment. The marketing manager is responsible for coordinating and/or implementing marketing projects designed for the consumer market segment. Working in cooperation with the sales team, product offers, and other headquarters marketing teams, the marketing manager will coordinate public relations projects and other promotional activities to drive Nelson Wireless brand awareness and product demand and generate consumer purchases. The marketing manager will provide strategic oversight for regional-level industry events, and be responsible for planning and executing customer events. The marketing manager will be responsible for coordinating budgets and timelines, maintaining accurate records of expenditures, and compiling reports of activity results. Additionally, he/she will be responsible for managing a team of 8–10 marketing associates. The marketing manager role will also include administrative elements such as invoice processing, event scheduling, and maintenance of a promotional calendar.	• College degree required with emphasis in marketing, business administration, or communications preferred • 3+ years marketing/communications experience required • Excellent demonstrated verbal and written communication skills • Demonstrated experience in event execution • Demonstrated ability to coordinate cooperative working relationships across multiple parties • Ability to work well under pressure • Extremely well organized, strong project management and time management skills and strong ability to multi-task • Proven ability to operate in a fast-paced, high-growth professional environment

conditions under which the job will be performed, and its relationship to other functions in the organization. Job descriptions are important because they define job objectives that are used later in performance appraisals. They also can become a part of the legal contract between the employee and the employer.

- **Job specifications**—the skills, education, experience, and personal attributes that candidates need to possess to successfully fulfill the role.

■ **FIGURE 9.2** shows a job analysis with a sample job description and the job specifications.

Once a job is well defined, how does HR find the best candidates to interview? Matching the right person for each job depends on a well-devised recruiting plan. **Recruitment** is the process of finding, screening, and selecting people for a specific job. The recruitment process uses a variety of methods and resources.

Internal recruiting, or filling job vacancies with existing employees from within a business, is the first choice of many companies. Often, companies post job openings on the company intranet, in in-house newsletters, and in staff meetings. Internal recruitment has several advantages. It tends to be a morale booster for employees because they know that the company has an interest in promoting its own employees. In addition, because employer and employee have established a working relationship, there is a reduced risk of selecting an inappropriate candidate for a desired position. Additionally, choosing from within is potentially quicker and less costly because it reduces the costs associated with outside recruiting and often shortens the length of training time.

However, there are disadvantages to solely looking internally and not considering outside sources. This includes the possibility of not getting the best candidate due to a limited search process. In addition, another internal vacancy is created that must be subsequently filled. Moreover, relying on internal employees may discourage new perspectives and ideas and eventually make a business resistant to change. As a result, businesses also rely on external recruiting to meet staffing needs.

External recruiting looks outside a business to fill job vacancies. Posting ads in local newspapers, on Internet job sites, or in specialized trade magazines are methods used to reach a wide audience. ■ **FIGURE 9.3** lists various resources HR staff use when recruiting externally. Depending on the type of position, employment agencies may be used. Employment agencies often specialize in specific sectors, such as accounting, sales, or clerical services. They provide a pool of screened candidates, which reduces the hiring company's administrative burden of recruitment. Recruitment consultants, often referred to as "headhunters," conduct more specialized searches, usually for senior management or key employees. Using external firms to help with the search is often expensive, but the costs of finding the wrong candidate can be even higher.

How do social networking sites impact recruiting? You're familiar with social networking sites like Facebook and Twitter. The same concept is applied to the professional community through sites such as LinkedIn (linkedin.com), Jigsaw (jigsaw.com), and Spoke (spoke.com). LinkedIn is an online network of more than 161 million[1] experienced professionals from around the world whose connections

■ **FIGURE 9.3**
External Recruitment Resources

are made through college, graduate school, or professional affiliations. Most people would like to hire or work with someone they know, and LinkedIn can provide helpful colleague and customer recommendations. Using applications such as SlideShare and Google Presentations, LinkedIn members can post presentations they have given as well as showcase their portfolios of work. This helps recruiters quickly evaluate and sort prospective candidates. With versions supporting most mobile devices, such as Android and the iPhone, LinkedIn is always available when an HR recruiter wants to follow a lead. Additionally, LinkedIn may assist job seekers by providing them with "insider" information on companies and employees. For example, before an interview, LinkedIn might be able to provide background information on the person with whom you are meeting. Knowing more about the interviewer and the company can provide good conversation during the interview.

Does technology help or complicate recruiting? One of the challenges facing recruiting specialists is the use of technology. People looking for a job and companies looking to hire use online job and résumé posting sites, Web and video blogs, virtual job fairs, and podcasts to find job prospects and job candidates. When the use of technology was new, these methods were often highly successful and cost-effective. The dramatic growth of job and résumé postings has made the efficient and effective use of technology in recruitment more challenging. Online job postings yield many responses and thus a large pool of candidates, so sifting through these responses to find the right person for the job can be a time-consuming process for HR professionals. In fact, one of the greatest recruiting challenges cited is the difficulty of finding qualified candidates for critical positions.[2] Therefore, HR managers must know how to skillfully use technology. At a basic recruiting level, this means learning how to make a posted job description appeal to the most qualified candidates as well as stand out from competitors in the online environment so the right person can find the open position more readily. It also means becoming familiar with social networking technologies and techniques to post jobs and find recruits.

Hiring

What happens in the hiring process? As shown in ■ **FIGURE 9.4,** hiring is a multistep process. The first step is to form a select pool of candidates from the original group of applicants. To do this, HR managers compare the candidates'

HR and Social Media Risks

Social media force us to consider new questions about the boundaries between work and personal life.

What are the risks of posting information on social media sites? Consider corporate hiring practices. As a job applicant, should you expect that the HR department will review any public information posted—such as reading your Facebook Wall and checking out the Facebook pages of your friends? What if during an interview an employer asks that you "friend" them into other areas of your Facebook site as part of the interview process? The proper workplace use of public information is not yet clearly defined so some employers watch public postings to see what kind of comments employees are making about the company. What if

confidential information that is sensitive to the company appears on your Twitter feed—can the company take action against you? If you are using geolocation apps like FourSquare, your location becomes public information that might give away important clues to a savvy competitor. Companies are finding it important to establish policies for employees on how to use social networking. The site Social Media Governance provides the current policies from many major corporations. For example, Cisco requires employees to disclose employment relationships when commenting on Cisco's products/services on social media.[3]

On a positive side, social media can be used as your own personal marketing agency, creating a "brand" for you as a prospective employee. More and more HR directors are using LinkedIn and Facebook as places to find talent for the positions they need to fill. Does your Facebook page attract a second look from a professional recruiter? Consider including presentations and videos that show your abilities and potential.

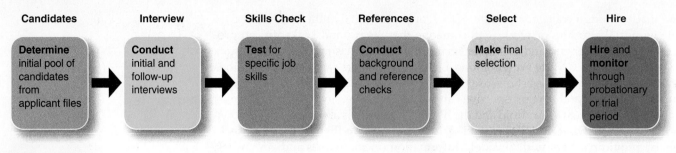

Candidates	Interview	Skills Check	References	Select	Hire
Determine initial pool of candidates from applicant files	**Conduct** initial and follow-up interviews	**Test** for specific job skills	**Conduct** background and reference checks	**Make** final selection	**Hire** and **monitor** through probationary or trial period

■ FIGURE 9.4
The Hiring Process

qualifications to the job specifications. In addition, many companies use special applicant-tracking system software to quickly sort through résumés and job applications. The automation process has made it easier to apply for jobs but has also led to an overwhelming number of applications for HR departments to handle. This has pressured human resource departments to automate even more of the hiring process.[4]

HR managers also use software systems to help prescreen for certain personality traits. The software program Unicru is used by many retail stores to screen candidates for dependability, honesty, and other qualities. Some firms have seen a successful reduction in turnover rates of employees once introducing the screening. Others argue it makes hiring more difficult as it eliminates potentially strong employees who may be "different" in any way, for example, people who are more socially withdrawn. Another controversy around automated screening with Unicru is that the "solutions" to the questions have been posted at various online sites so job seekers may feel pressured into cheating, ironically, to pass the exam that detects if they are ethical.[5]

After identifying a small pool of appropriate candidates, department and HR managers interview each candidate to gauge his or her personality, clarify information in the candidate's résumé, and determine whether he or she is the best match for the position. The candidate might also need to complete some skills-related tests. If necessary, an applicant will be brought back for follow-up interviews.

Before offering a candidate a position, it is important that the company completes thorough background and reference checks. It's not uncommon to hear stories about companies that failed to conduct background checks and hired someone who falsified his or her educational or professional experiences or who had been in trouble with the law. Even if the employee has a significant work history, details in their background can be worth verifying. The former CEO of Bausch and Lomb Ronald Zarrella stated he had an MBA degree from New York University. His claim was never checked by former employers but the background check at Bausch and Lomb revealed he had started the program but never graduated. He was forced into giving up a $1 million bonus.[6]

What legalities must be considered when hiring? Several federal laws must be observed during the hiring process:

- **Federal Equal Employment Opportunity.** Established in 1965, the Federal Equal Employment Opportunity Commission (EEOC) works to "ensure equality of opportunity by vigorously enforcing federal legislation prohibiting discrimination in employment." This legislation consists of a number of different acts and laws, known as equal employment opportunity (EEO) laws. As part of this mission, the EEOC investigates claims of discrimination and files lawsuits against companies when necessary.[7]

- **The Civil Rights Act of 1964.** The Civil Rights Act of 1964 prohibits discrimination based on race, color, gender, religion, and national origin. Title VII of the act also established the EEOC to enforce antidiscrimination laws.

- **Americans with Disabilities Act.** The Americans with Disabilities Act of 1990 (ADA) prohibits discrimination based on disabilities (or perceived disabilities). It also requires employers to make reasonable accommodations to the known disability of a qualified applicant or employee as long as it does not impose an "undue hardship" on the operation of an employer's business. Reasonable accommodations might include providing wheelchair accessibility, modified equipment, or interpreters.[8]

- **Age Discrimination in Employment Act.** The Age Discrimination in Employment Act (ADEA) of 1967 makes it unlawful to discriminate against a person because of his or her age with respect to employment. It also prohibits the inclusion of age preferences in job notices or advertisements, except in specific circumstances where age is considered necessary to the job's function.[9]

HR departments take care of a company's biggest resource—its employees. HR managers like Leslie Booth must possess a variety of skills to capably oversee a wide array of complex tasks. Although these tasks—planning, recruiting, and hiring—may not seem directly related to the overall success of a company, they are, in fact, closely entwined. After not finding a strong candidate for four weeks, Leslie decided to rewrite the job description to more carefully match the job specifications. She expanded the search into virtual job markets and LinkedIn and offered a bonus to employees for word-of-mouth referrals. Applications began to arrive that were from higher-caliber candidates, and she is confident that she'll hire soon. ■

Training and Evaluating Employees pp. 263–268

WavebreakmediaMicro/Fotolia

George Hensel is an expert at running meetings—and everybody knows it. A meeting with George in charge will be just the right length, everybody will have their voice heard, and creative results often emerge. Employees throughout the national company would love to run a meeting like George does, but there is no time or budget to send him around the country to train them on how to do so. How can George's skills be leveraged to help the entire company? ■

Employee training is important for many reasons because it leads to:[10]

- Increased job satisfaction, motivation, and morale among employees
- Greater efficiency in work
- More effective use of new technologies and methods
- The development of new strategies and products
- Lower employee turnover
- Fewer interpersonal conflicts and better communication

Companies that emphasize training and development experience greater employee productivity, loyalty, and retention—all of which are good for the

The Center for Advanced Medical Learning of the University of South Florida draws 30,000 health professionals to practice skills on simulators.

2 How are employees trained and evaluated?

■ **TABLE 9.1**

New Employee Orientation

Action

Your First Day

✓ You will be introduced to the current staff and your appointed mentor.
✓ You will see your new workspace and have a tour of the facilities.
✓ You will review the job description, including the job's responsibilities and expectations.
✓ You will receive a copy of the company handbook.
✓ You will review any health or financial benefits that are available.
✓ You will be introduced to general administrative practices used by the department.
✓ You will have an opportunity to ask questions.

Your First Week

✓ You can expect to have brief, daily meetings with your direct manager so that you understand your responsibilities for the day.
✓ You will meet with your appointed mentor to discuss issues or problems.
✓ At the end of the week, you will have a meeting with your employer to discuss any professional questions or personal concerns you may have.

bottom line. In this section, you'll learn about how training and evaluating employees can enhance the success of a business and ensure that employees stay in top form.

Training Methods and Requirements

What kind of training do new employees receive? Initially, when an employee is hired, an organization uses an **orientation program** to integrate a new employee into the company. Orientation can be as simple as an overview of an organization and the distribution of basic information, such as company procedures and expectations. Today, however, many companies are going beyond the traditional orientation program of explaining rules and regulations, as reflected in the orientation checklist in ■ **TABLE 9.1**. Orientation is more effective if it becomes a means of familiarizing the employee with a company's mission, discussing how a new employee's contribution can add to a company's success. In addition, employees should be introduced to associates in their department so they feel at ease and can quickly become as productive as possible. A failure to adequately integrate new hires into a company leads to low retention rates.

What other training is required of new and current employees? Training begins where orientation ends. Training should teach employees skills or ways to improve on existing skills. For example, a salesperson might know how to sell a product but may not know all the intricacies of selling a new product. Often, other employees in the department or the recent hire's mentor can conduct **on-the-job training**. With on-the-job training, employees learn skills by performing them. For example, there are many training and certification programs to become a pharmacy technician. But the specialty of nuclear pharmacy technician, a position that requires dispensing radiopharmaceuticals for use as therapies or for diagnostic testing in hospital settings, requires 500 additional hours of on-the-job training.[11]

Some trades require an apprentice training program. An **apprentice training program** trains individuals through classroom or formal instruction and on-the-job training. For example, there is a growing need for underwater welders to repair the infrastructure of bridges and other structures where the key components are underwater. The training to be an underwater welder requires completing a surface welder program and a commercial diving program. Next you would apply to a commercial diving company that offers underwater welding as a service. You would begin your career as a diver tender (apprentice diver) to build experience in the trade. Once you have proven sufficient skills, you can advance to welder-diver status.

Some jobs are more readily learned through a **programmed learning approach** in which an employee is asked to perform step-by-step instructions or respond to questions. These often come in the form of computerized multiple-choice tests that provide immediate feedback. The benefit of programmed learning is that an employee can progress at his or her own pace, picking up information piece by piece. For some settings, though, this kind of training may not match the type of complex decision making needed to teach employees. It also requires a commitment in providing computer access to employees and in acquiring and maintaining the automated training software.

What kind of impact does technology have on training? Improvements in technology provide companies with other training options, such as simulated training and interactive multimedia training. *Gamification*, the application of game design concepts to nongame settings, has led to some training tools that are very engaging. Cold Stone Creamery, the U.S. Army, and Hilton are all turning once-dull training into an interactive video experience by taking advantage of "serious games" to train their employees. One study by the Entertainment Software Association showed that 70 percent of major U.S. employers have used interactive software and games for training.[12]

Videoconferencing and teletraining allow employees at various remote locations to train and work together easily.

Other companies are offering simulation training that allows their employees to really get a taste for their jobs. **Simulation training** provides realistic job-task training in a manner that is challenging but does not create the threat of failure. It is suitable for airline pilots, astronauts, and medical professionals for whom making mistakes during training is not an option or is too costly. However, other organizations take advantage of simulation training as well. For example, at the Institute for Simulation & Training at the University of Central Florida, students interact with virtual students in a classroom simulation program.

Online training allows employees to take college classes on the Internet at their convenience, enabling them to obtain specific job-related education or pursue a degree. Other forms of Internet-based distance learning training involve instructors in a centralized location teaching groups of employees at remote locations via television hookups (*teletraining*) or through a combination of audiovisual equipment (*videoconferencing*). Modern webconferencing allows users to share documents, share application software, and swap control of an attendee's desktop. Attendees can ask questions in real time, comment to the group as videos are being shown, and archive the session for later viewing.

Electronic Performance Support Systems (EPSSs) are another form of training technology. These systems provide employees with information and training when they need it, automatically, instead of sending employees to long, formal trainings, disconnected from their daily work. EPSSs can act as an in-house automated training alternative. With the quality of training interaction that users have with modern technologies, this is an increasingly attractive option. One case study reported that a client implemented EPSS and saw the system answer over 300,000 requests for support the first year, generating savings of $2.6 million.[13]

Do managers need training? Yes, but because of their roles in the organization, managers require different training than their frontline workers. Managerial training often focuses on leadership, communication, teamwork, and relationship-building skills. In addition, managers need to keep abreast of changes in employment laws, such as discrimination and harassment, as well as updates in using new tools for electronic communication.

In addition to managerial training, many companies offer **management development programs** that prepare management trainees to become managers within an organization. These programs may have trainees participate in an on-the-job training program, which might include *job rotation*, in which an employee rotates through different departments to learn firsthand the various aspects of the business, or a *coaching/understudy program*, in which an employee works directly with senior management in planning and other managerial functions. *Action learning*, another management development training approach, focuses on solving real problems on actual work projects. Action learning allows trainees to work together on teams to analyze real-time corporate problems that extend beyond their areas of expertise. Companies such as Microsoft, DuPont, and Boeing have successfully implemented action-learning teams as part of their management development programs.[14]

Some companies use **off-the-job training and development** techniques that require employees to participate in outside seminars, university-conducted programs, and corporate universities. Hamburger University, McDonald's system of 22 corporate training facilities, trains employees for management roles. Nineteen full-time professors offer training for restaurant managers, department heads, and executive development. Through interpreters, they can even deliver courses in over 28 languages.[15]

How are experienced managers developed? Senior managers often use *executive coaches* to further develop their effectiveness. Executive coaches identify a manager's strengths and weaknesses by interviewing those who work closely with the manager. They then meet with the manager to work on eliminating weaknesses and further developing strengths.

Mentoring is another option that companies use to enable their experienced employees to work closely with inexperienced employees. **Mentors** are individuals established in the company who help a newer person by explaining how to perform specific tasks, creating opportunities to learn new skills, and counseling about the consequences of particular actions and decisions. Like other forms of training and management development, mentoring increases employee performance, satisfaction, and loyalty.

Performance Appraisals and Alternatives

Why are performance appraisals necessary? A performance appraisal is an evaluation of an employee's performance that gives feedback about how well an employee is doing, as well as where changes and improvements are needed. A sample appraisal form is shown in ■ **FIGURE 9.5**. Managers use the results of performance appraisals in decisions about promotion, raises, additional training, or reassignments. The performance appraisal process is

■ **FIGURE 9.5**
A Sample Performance Appraisal

Annual Employee Performance Evaluation

Employee's Name:		Supervisor:	
Job Title:		Date Hired:	
Department:		Date of Review:	

Evaluation

This form is designed to assess your current performance and to help in setting goals for the future. This form is considered confidential and will only be reviewed by you and your supervisor(s).

Overall Job Knowledge/Experience Level

Consistently meets requirements	
Generally meets requirements	
Does not meet requirements	

Comments:

Quality of Work

Exceeds expectations
Meets expectations
Does not meet expectations

Comments:

Attendance

Rarely tardy or absent
Sometimes tardy or absent
Frequently tardy or absent

Comments:

Cooperation

Consistently participates and contributes to the team
Generally participates and contributes to the team
Does not participate or contribute to the team

Comments:

Future Goals:

important for both employees and the organization as a whole and includes three aspects:

- *Determining standards* that employees should aim for in their work
- *Evaluating performance* of an employee in comparison with these standards
- *Providing feedback* to reduce and eliminate poor performance and improve or enhance positive performance

When employees are hired, they should have a good understanding of what is expected of them. These expectations become the performance standards on which they'll be measured. Appraisals act as a confirmation of these standards and help employees establish quantifiable and measurable goals for improvement in the upcoming year.

Are there problems with performance appraisals? Performance appraisals, when conducted properly, are very helpful to an employee and ultimately an organization; however, they are often not effective. Because appraisals often lead to criticism, many managers shy away from them because they are uncomfortable delivering negative comments. Additionally, some managers have a difficult time quantifying performance and fear not being able to defend their ratings if questioned. Although performance appraisals often suggest means to improve weak performance or enhance solid performance, the process does not always offer the opportunity to follow up and ensure that such means have been acted on. Typically, it is not until the next performance appraisal that it is recognized that such training and development did not occur. And when the next appraisal can be a year away, more immediate crises can take time away from the focus on an appraisal's recommendations.

What alternatives exist for performance appraisals? An alternative to a performance appraisal is performance management. **Performance management** is an approach that combines goal setting, performance appraisals, and

---

■ TABLE 9.2

Aspects of Performance Management

Direction sharing	Communicating an organization's higher-level goals, such as vision, mission, values, and strategy
Role clarifying	Defining roles in terms of daily work tasks
Goal setting and planning	Redefining organizational or departmental goals into specific employee goals, which includes an employee's development of the steps necessary to achieve goals
Ongoing performance monitoring and feedback	Periodic performance reports regarding progress on meeting goals as well as feedback regarding progress toward goals
Coaching and support	Ongoing as a part of the feedback process
Performance assessment (appraisal)	An element in the performance management process that offers specific, defined knowledge on how an employee's performance is improving company results
Rewards, recognition, and compensation	Given as appropriate to motivate an employee toward achieving current and future goals
Workflow, process control, and return on investment management	Making sure an employee's measurable performance is linked to measurable goals of company

Source: Dessler, Gary, Human Resource Management, 13th, © 2012. Printed and electronically reproduced by permission of Pearson Education, Inc., Upper Saddle River, New Jersey.

training and development into a unified and ongoing process. As such, it is more of a cyclical and fluid process than the single occurrence of a performance appraisal. Employees are constantly receiving feedback and given opportunities for training and development to ensure that they have the right tools with which to perform their jobs. ■ **TABLE 9.2** summarizes several aspects of the performance management process. The concept, while often applied to employees, is also applicable to other components of an organization, including an entire department, a product or a service, or an organization as a whole.

Performance management, appraisals, and training can play a significant role in keeping a business productive and efficient. At George Hensel's company, management decided that knowing how to run and participate in a productive meeting was a skill that all employees should have. They therefore created online learning modules that featured videos in which George explained how people often allow meetings to go off track. The company then created a "serious" game that allowed players to simulate conducting a virtual meeting and to be "scored" for how efficient they were. Employees who logged a certain number of attempts at the online training and simulation received special credit in their performance appraisal. The commitment to training created more productive meetings throughout the company. ■

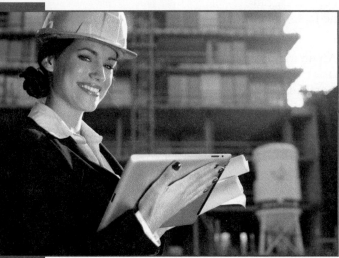
berc/Fotolia

Compensating, Scheduling, Promoting, and Terminating Employees pp. 268–274

Kathy Sanchez loves what she does. Since graduating from college two years ago, she has worked for a small start-up company as a graphic designer, creating brochures and other materials for a wide variety of clients. Because the company is so small, she gets to work on projects she would never have a chance to work on in a bigger company. She also loves the relaxed atmosphere of the office and feels like her coworkers are actually her friends. So what's the problem? Because the company is just getting on its feet, it isn't able to offer her much in the way of pay or benefits. Although she loves her work, she is tired of reaching the end of each pay period with no money left. And don't even ask her about her retirement plan or health insurance! What should she do? ■

Having the right pay system in place is very important for a company to become and remain competitive. A good compensation package attracts high-quality employees and keeps them from leaving. But compensation is not just about monetary rewards. In today's workplace, employees frequently receive compensation in a variety of forms, including work/life benefits, health insurance, and retirement plans. Because there are many ways to structure compensation, the decision is not an easy one. It's often a delicate balance between paying to attract and keep the best and not jeopardizing the financial security of a company.

Compensation Strategies

3 What are the main components of compensating and scheduling employees?

Are all employees paid in the same way? There are many ways to pay workers for their time and effort.

Compensation, payment for work performed, is generally offered through direct financial payments in the form of fixed **salaries** (annual pay for a specific job) or **wages** (payments for hourly work). Usually, on an annual basis, an employee's compensation level has the potential to increase based on the results of employee evaluations.

Incentive-based payment structures are better compensation strategies for some positions, such as those in sales. These typically have a lower base salary and then are enhanced with **commissions**, compensation based directly on an employee's performance. Incentive-based compensation rewards employees that achieve strong measurable results.

Bonuses, compensation based on total corporate profits, help tie employees' efforts to the company's bottom line. Higher corporate profits mean higher bonuses.

What types of retirement plans do companies offer employees? The most popular retirement plan offered today is the 401(k) plan.

A **401(k) plan** is a defined contribution plan in which pretax dollars are invested in a bundle of investments that are generally managed by an outside investment company, such as the Vanguard Group or Fidelity Investments. The amount of the annual contribution is determined by the employee as a percentage of salary up to a specified legal limit. In some cases, a company will match a portion of the employee's contribution to the account.

Pension plans are another kind of retirement benefit that some companies offer their full-time employees. There are two types of pension plans:

- With *defined benefit plans*, employees know ahead of time how much pension they will receive when they retire. Defined benefit plans are not popular with employers, as a company takes on the financial risk if the fund's investments do not perform as expected.

- *Defined contribution plans* specify the annual amount employees will contribute to their pension plan through payroll deductions. With defined contribution plans, the actual amount received at retirement depends on the amount contributed and the fund's investment earnings. The burden of risk falls on employees with defined contribution plans, and there is no way they can determine how much will ultimately be available until they actually retire.

Profit-sharing plan is a term used for a range of different types of compensation options. At many businesses, profit sharing means that if the company hits certain profit targets, then there is a bonus structure for employees. Sometimes the term *profit sharing* is used for company contributions to an employee retirement plan. Profit sharing plans are often offered as a part of executive compensation in larger companies, but in many small companies, they are a way to motivate employees, especially during the start-up phase when cash is tight and salaries may be low.

What other financial incentives do companies offer as compensation? Stock option agreements allow an employee to purchase a specific number of shares of stock at a specific price but only at a specific point in time. If the stock value increases beyond that point, the employee can reap a huge financial reward. If not, however, the employee gains little. Facebook used stock options as a common part of the compensation package to lure top engineers. Recruiters for Facebook say experienced engineers received stock options that would yield a profit of over $12 million, after the company went public. Estimates are that the 2012 IPO for Facebook created thousands of millionaires within the company.[16]

Employee stock purchase plans allow employees to buy company stock at a discount (usually at 85 percent of market value). Companies typically limit the amount of stock an employee can purchase this way to 10 percent of their total salary. **Employee stock ownership plans (ESOPs)** use a company's pension plan for employees to invest in company stock, effectively giving employees significant ownership in a company. For example, in 1994, United Airlines was failing and needed to negotiate dramatic wage reductions with its unions (pilots, flight attendants, etc.). The employees formed the United Airlines ESOP and then agreed to 8–15 percent wage cuts for the next five years. In return, the ESOP acquired 55 percent ownership of United Airlines. An advantage of providing employees with ownership in a company via stock transactions is that employees feel more connected to the business and are motivated to ensure that the business succeeds. For United Airlines, the next several years saw the value of the company rise by $4 billion.[17]

Benefits

What are noncash forms of compensation? An important part of the business planning and management process is determining the type and amount of **employee benefits**, or indirect financial and nonfinancial payments an employer offers that supplement cash compensation. Benefit compensation often enables a company to attract, motivate, and retain the best employees. Benefits come in many forms, including health and disability insurance, vacation and sick pay, and retirement plans. Vacation time, holidays, and pensions, once referred to as "fringe benefits," constitute a significant percentage of total compensation.

Some companies offer **flexible benefit plans** (or **cafeteria plans**) that permit an employee to pick from a menu of several choices of taxable and nontaxable forms of compensation. Flexible benefit plans allow employees to choose the benefits that are most important to them, while reducing the cost of offering all benefits to all employees.

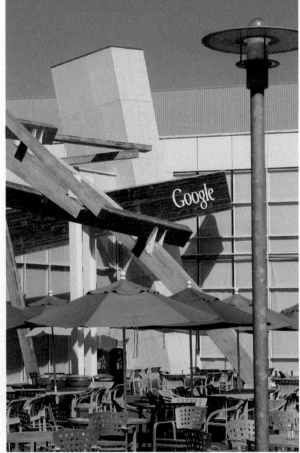

The Googleplex, Google's Mountain View, California, campus, has several pools, 11 free gourmet cafeterias, volleyball courts, and massage services.

ZUMA Press/Newscom

What are work/life benefits? **Work/life benefits** are benefits that help an employee achieve a balance between the demands of life both inside and outside the workplace. Work/life benefits include flexible schedules, relaxed atmospheres, and child care and fitness/gym programs. For example, the SAS Institute, the largest privately held software developer in the United States, offers employees unlimited sick leave, an on-site fitness club with indoor pool, on-site car detailing, massages, and a hair salon. There are four subsidized childcare centers on-site and pantries stocked with free food. Although seemingly expensive, this strategy of keeping its employees happy saves the company approximately $70 million per year because it experiences low turnover. In fact, compared with an industry average of 20 percent turnover, SAS has kept its turnover rate below 5 percent.[18]

What are some other trends in employee benefits? In the early '80s, the *Village Voice,* a free alternative weekly newspaper in New York City, began offering *domestic partner benefits.* These benefits provide for an employee's unmarried partner of the same or opposite sex. Since then, domestic partner benefits have become increasingly common components of compensation packages. In fact, almost 60 percent of Fortune 500 companies offer domestic benefits to their employees.[19] Benefits such as health care and family leave policies are extended to domestic partners. Recently, companies have also begun to address taxation inequities for domestic partner benefits. Same-sex couples pay a tax on the health benefits for their partners that married couples do not. Kimpton Hotels, Google, and other companies will reimburse same-sex couples the $1,069 they pay in federal taxes for their domestic partner benefits.[20]

The Family and Medical Leave Act states that companies with more than 50 employees must allow all eligible employees to take up to 12 weeks of unpaid time off to be with family because of medical issues, births, or adoptions. Upon the employee's return, the act guarantees that the employee can return to his or her job or a comparable job. This benefit compares weakly to those of other countries. At least 178 countries have laws that guarantee paid leave for new mothers; more than 50 countries offer paid leave for new fathers as well.[21]

Alternative Scheduling and Work Arrangements

What work schedules are possible outside of the traditional workday? An increasing number of employees are finding that managing the demands of work and personal life results in doing neither well. The added stresses that employees today face from child care, elder care, commuting, and other work/life conflicts have led to a decrease in productivity and an increase in employee absenteeism and tardiness. As a result, more and more employers are offering alternatives to the traditional 9 A.M. to 5 P.M., Monday to Friday workweek. In fact, a study looking at the behavior of over 24,000 IBM employees found that employees with flexible schedules and the ability to work from home worked an additional 19 hours per week.[22]

The most popular flexible work arrangements include the following:

- **Alternative scheduling plans (flextime).** In *alternative scheduling plans* or **flextime**, management defines a total number of required hours as a core workday and is flexible with the starting and ending times. Managers must rise to the challenge of ensuring that required hours are met and monitoring employee performance. However, overall, flexible arrangements allow for increased productivity due to reductions in absenteeism and tardiness.

- **Permanent part-time.** Permanent part-time employees are hired on a permanent basis to work a part-time week. Unlike temporary part-time workers who are employed to fill short-term needs, permanent part-time employees enjoy the same benefits that full-time employees receive.

- **Job sharing.** **Job sharing** is an arrangement in which two employees work part-time to share one full-time job. Those who share a job have been found to be very motivated to make this flexible situation work, so productivity and employee satisfaction increase. On the other hand, conflicts may arise if the job sharers don't have a clear understanding of who is in charge of what, or if there is confusion from other employees about whom to contact and when. Therefore, job sharers must carefully coordinate and communicate both with one another and their employer to ensure that all responsibilities are met.

- **Compressed workweek.** A compressed workweek allows employees to work four 10-hour days instead of five 8-hour days each week, or 9 days instead of 10 in a two-week schedule for 80 hours. Such arrangements can reduce worker overtime, make more efficient use of facilities, and provide employees with longer blocks of personal time and less commuting time. The disadvantages are a potential increase in employee fatigue and conflicts with state labor laws that cite overtime requirements for hours worked in excess of 8 per day.

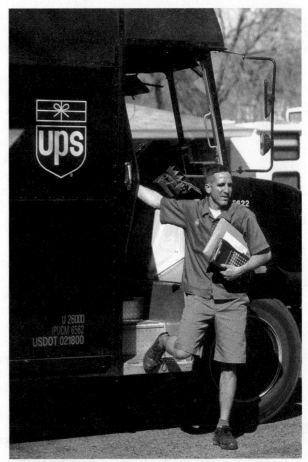

UPS offers a permanent part-time package handler position in which employees work about four hours per day, Monday through Friday, with no weekend or evening work required. In addition to traditional health insurance, vacations, and a stock purchase plan, UPS offers tuition assistance as an additional benefit.

David R. Frazier Photolibrary, Inc./Alamy

- **Telecommuting.** Telecommuting allows employees to work in the office part-time and work from home part-time or work completely from home, making only occasional visits to the office. Telecommuting reduces commuting costs and allows employees to take care of home needs while also fulfilling work responsibilities. For example, Cisco now has a workforce that telecommutes an average of two days per week.[23] Cisco estimates it has saved the company $277 million.[24]

The disadvantages of telecommuting include monitoring employees' performance at a distance, servicing equipment for off-site employees, and communication issues. Additionally, employees who telecommute may become isolated from other employees.

What benefits do employers see from supporting alternative work schedules? Despite the costs associated with designing and implementing flexible working arrangements, employers can expect positive bottom-line results due to increases in employee satisfaction, decreases in absenteeism, and increases in worker productivity. Similarly, reductions in employee turnover lead to a decrease in time and costs associated with employee recruiting and replacement training.

Contingent Workers

Why does a company hire contingent workers? Contingent workers are people who are hired on an as-needed basis and lack status as regular, full-time employees. These workers often fulfill important and specific functions. Contingent workers are most likely hired by companies in business and professional services, education and health-care services, and construction industries. Companies hire such temporary workers to fill in for absent employees or augment the staff during busy periods. Long-term temporary staff is often hired for indefinite periods of time to work on specific projects. In many cases, temporary staffing is part of a company's HR "temp to perm" strategy in which temporary employees are evaluated and then moved to a permanent position if they are found to be reliable and skilled.

Independent contractors and **consultants** are another form of contingent workers who are generally self-employed. Companies hire them on a temporary basis to perform specific tasks. Often, contractors are hired for those jobs that involve state-of-the-art skills in construction, financial activities, and professional and business services. For example, it might be most cost-efficient to hire a Web-page developer as an independent contractor rather than keeping one on staff permanently. Consultants are hired to assist with long-term projects, often at a strategic level, but also with a specific end in sight. For example, a company that is reviewing its executive management compensation arrangements might hire a compensation consultant.

Is temporary work a common situation for people? The U.S. Bureau of Labor Statistics estimates that the temporary workforce accounts for more than 2 percent of the U.S. workforce.[25] Temporary staffing is a $70 billion industry, represented by companies such as Kelly Services and Manpower.

Working for a temporary agency means assignments are short-term and temporary workers are able to experience working in many different companies, doing different jobs, and meeting numerous people. Recent college graduates and college students may find that temporary work is a means to gain real-world experience in an industry they are interested in pursuing on a full-time basis. But temporary workers are often paid less than full-time workers and are less likely to receive benefits.

Promotions

How can employees increase their level of responsibility in a company? After performing successfully in a position, many employees look to

4 How does employee status change through promotions, termination, and retirement?

increase their level of responsibility and stature in a company or a department through a promotion. Employers like to promote from within because they can reward exceptional behavior and fill positions with tested employees. However, promotion may not always result in a positive situation if it is seen as being draped in secrecy, unfairness, or arbitrariness. Therefore, management must ensure that promotions are based on a distinct set of criteria, such as seniority or competency.

Do promotions always move you into management positions? Consider an engineer who succeeds on the job but has no desire to manage. Some companies provide two career paths: one toward management and the other for "individual contributors" with no management aspirations. Therefore, engineers, for example, with a desire to manage can pursue one track, and other engineers without managerial aspirations or capabilities can be promoted to a position such as "senior engineer." Alternatively, it's always possible to keep employees in their same job but give them more responsibility, thus enriching their experience while continuing to prepare them for further advancement.

Terminating Employees

Why do companies lay off workers? At times, it becomes necessary to re-evaluate an employee's contribution or tenure at a company or reevaluate the composition and size of the workforce altogether. Downsizing and restructuring, the growth of outsourcing and offshoring, the pressures of global competition, and the increased uses of technology are also reasons companies look to reduce the number of employees. **Termination** refers to the act of permanently laying off workers due to poor performance or a discontinued need for their services. Companies often offer a set of benefits for terminated employees, including the continuation of health-care coverage, severance pay, and outplacement services like résumé writing and career counseling.

Terminating employees due to poor performance or illegal activities is a complex process. Most states support **employment at will**, a legal doctrine that states that an employer can fire an employee for any reason at any time. Likewise, an employee is equally free to resign at any time for any reason. Exceptions to the employment-at-will doctrine include the inability for employers to discriminate and fire someone because of legally protected characteristics or activities, such as race, religion, age, gender, national origin, or disability. In addition, companies cannot terminate employees because of whistle-blowing (revealing company wrongdoing to authorities), filing a worker's compensation claim, jury service, or testifying against a company in a legal proceeding.

How does a manager prepare to terminate an employee? Before firing an employee for wrongful acts or incompetence, managers must take steps to avoid a wrongful discharge lawsuit. These steps include maintaining solid records so that they can build a case for dismissal with sufficient documentation and evidence. Courts have sided with the terminated employee, especially when not enough evidence of poor behavior is brought forth. Written evidence is the only material evidence accepted, which makes building an employee's personnel file with documented proof of poor performance critical. Hearsay and rumors do not stand up in legal proceedings. Consider Monique Drake, a medical secretary in the same physician's practice for 12 years. The doctor married, and his new wife began running the office. This new office manager told Drake her salary was being cut from $54,000 to $40,000, sick days would be eliminated and her vacation time cut, listing a number of issues with her performance. A month later Drake found she was being terminated. Drake sued and won her case for wrongful dismissal based on the lack of any documentation of weak performance and no ongoing discussion with Drake about her work habits.[26]

THE List

Top Ten Ways to Get Promoted

1. Get a mentor.
2. Learn outside of work.
3. Self-promote your successes.
4. Volunteer.
5. Ask questions.
6. Be consistent.
7. Help your colleagues.
8. Tell your boss you want to be promoted.
9. Be a team player.
10. Create your own opportunities.

Retirement

Is there a set age when employees retire? It used to be that employees retired when they became 65 years old. **Retirement** is the point in one's life where one stops participating full-time in a career. Current economic conditions in the United States have forced many to rethink their retirement plans. Over a third of those surveyed responded that they now intended to work five years or more than the age they had once targeted for retirement.[27] The major factors contributing to this shift is the higher cost of living and concerns over the cost of health care.

One impact of this shift in workforce demographics is more competition for younger employees to be promoted into certain jobs. For employers, an aging workforce may present other challenges, such as age-discrimination lawsuits if they aggressively lay off older workers. Therefore, to encourage older workers to retire, companies have offered financial incentives, known as **worker buyouts** (or *golden parachutes*). The U.S. Postal Service is using buyouts to try to consolidate operations and reduce costs. In the first three months of 2012, the Postal Service lost $3.2 billion. That resulted in a buyout offer to nearly all 45,000 mail handlers. The plan included a $15,000 payment to workers who take early retirement or leave the position.[28] Additional changes will be needed in services and workforce reduction, but the worker buyout was an opening step.

Remember Kathy Sanchez, who loved her job but was struggling with deciding what to do because of her low pay and benefits? After some serious soul-searching, Kathy decided to stay on at the small company, but she has set a limit of two more years before she starts looking for a job elsewhere. She is hoping that within that timeframe, the start-up company will get a solid footing and be able to offer its employees not only a positive work environment but also an attractive and competitive compensation package as well. ■

Yuri Arcurs/Fotolia

Managing Workplace Diversity pp. 274–277

Chandraki Patel always thought of herself as someone who was familiar with a range of types of people and cultures. Though she was born in Detroit, her parents came from India, and she has often traveled abroad for vacations. But now that she is a manager at an international marketing firm, she is faced with issues she never anticipated. She has a staff that includes men and women from six different nationalities with five different religions (each with different holiday calendars). In addition, she is responsible for remotely managing a site in Dublin, Ireland, and one in Beijing, China. The language and cultural differences there have caused misunderstandings more than once. How could anyone manage so many different types of people and locations? ■

Most likely, you interact with people who are of different than you—in gender, age, religion, and race. In this section, you'll learn about what makes the modern workplace so diverse and how diversity introduces both challenges and benefits to organizations.

Benefits and Challenges of Diversity

5 | How does incorporating diversity affect the workforce?

Why has the modern workplace become so diverse? Several changes have led to increased diversity in the workforce.

Advancements in technology have made it possible for businesses to operate with relative ease on a global basis. It's not unusual for companies to outsource or offshore work to other countries to decrease labor costs or establish operations in other countries to broaden their market reach.

Hiring patterns are adding to the diversity of the workforce as U.S.-based companies hire workers who have emigrated from other countries. European and Middle Eastern companies are experiencing similar increases in immigration.

More women are entering the workforce than ever before. Many more employees than ever are indicating that they plan to work beyond the traditional retirement age, meaning increased age diversity in the workforce. For all these reasons, the modern workplace is now very diverse in age, gender, and ethnicity.

How is a diverse workforce beneficial? Diversity is an important component of the modern workplace. For many companies, hiring to diversify the workforce initially meant fulfilling an **affirmative action** requirement by filling positions with a certain number of women, Hispanics, or African Americans. Some criticized this strategy as unfair and bad for a company if the best candidate was not hired in favor of meeting such a requirement. Over time, however, many companies have come to embrace the idea of diversity beyond just satisfying a requirement. It's now becoming clear that companies should embrace diversity as a strategy and resource to become more competitive in the global market.

Promoting diversity in the workplace is more than affirmative action that prescribes that a company employ a certain number of minorities and women. Instead, diversity should be aggressively pursued as a means to improve a company's competitiveness and its bottom line. A diverse workforce helps companies offer a broad range of viewpoints that are necessary to compete in a world that is more globalized. Such variety in viewpoints promotes creativity in problem solving with improved results.

In addition, products and services need to cater to customers and clients with diverse backgrounds, so it's vital to have a workforce that understands the nuances of different cultural needs. Additionally, a diverse staff helps strategize ways to handle markets that have become segmented, both culturally and demographically.[29] For example, PepsiCo's Frito-Lay division launched a Doritos guacamole-flavored tortilla chip to appeal especially to Latino consumers. The Latino Employee Network provided valuable feedback on taste and packaging to ensure that the Latino community would consider these chips as authentic. The product generated more than $100 million in sales in its first year, making it the most successful product launch in the company's history.

What issues do companies face while managing diversity? Despite its many benefits, a diverse workforce can pose challenges. For example, a more culturally diverse population naturally brings about a wider variety of religious beliefs and practices, with more employees trying to integrate their religious practices into their workday. As employers struggle to accommodate workers'

David Gee 2/Alamy

Harley-Davidson realized that to remain competitive it needed to understand the needs and wants of customers beyond the traditional stereotype of the white male. The motorcycle manufacturer has made a significant effort to hire and retain women and minority managers.

religious needs, they must also try to avoid the potential friction that open demonstrations of religious practices might provoke. Many employers strike a balance by allowing employees to take prayer breaks, enabling employees to take time off to observe religious holidays, catering to dietary requirements, and permitting differences in dress. Surveys show that 64 percent of companies now use floating religious holidays to accommodate employee needs, and 70 percent have introduced on-site religious accommodations, such as prayer rooms.[30]

Although the number of women in the workforce is growing, women are still battling some of the same issues that their mothers and grandmothers faced: sexism, salary inequities, and sexual harassment. Historically, women in similar positions as their male counterparts were paid less and experienced fewer promotions, despite documented higher performance ratings. Many gender-discrimination and sexual harassment lawsuits continue to receive national press and indicate that gender-related challenges have not gone away.

The aging workforce also creates several challenges. Compared with younger workers in the same position, older workers often expect higher salaries and better benefits. Health-care costs, for example, are higher with an older workforce. However, many employers find that hiring and retaining older employees has several benefits, including less turnover and absenteeism, lower training costs, and a willingness to learn new skills and help and train younger coworkers. These benefits offer enough savings to a company to negate the higher costs in retaining more senior workers.

How can employees improve their understanding of each other's differences? Differences can create misunderstandings and conflict, even over the most well-intentioned behaviors. Therefore, it is important that employers provide effective **diversity training** for their employees. It is also important for coworkers to learn to look at situations from a perspective that is different from their own. Ultimately, managing diversity is developing a workforce that has a capacity to accept, incorporate, and empower the diversity of human talents and perspectives.

OFF THE MARK

One Diversity Training Does Not Fit All

Because promoting diversity is a priority for most companies in today's global marketplace, so too is the implementation of diversity training programs. These often-costly programs typically involve workshops and seminars that teach managers about the benefits of a diverse workforce. And yet, according to a recent study, most of them simply don't work.[31] After analyzing years of national employment statistics, the study concluded that standard diversity training rarely had an effect on the number of women or minority managers employed at companies where it was used. Why not? Some theorize that mandatory training inevitably leads to backlash; others say altering people's inner biases is a nearly impossible task.

Hope for promoting diversity in the workplace is not lost, however; the study also found that two techniques had significant, beneficial effects on workplace diversity: (1) the appointment of a specific person or committee who is specifically accountable for addressing diversity issues within the company led to 10 percent increases in the number of women and minorities in management positions; (2) mentorships increased the number of African American women in leadership positions by 23.5 percent.

Recall Chandraki Patel who was responsible for a staff with different cultural backgrounds, languages, and beliefs in her position at an international marketing firm? She decided to take on diversity management as an area where her performance could improve. She began by researching all the ways that the diversity of the group she managed had led to innovative solutions to problems. As she counted the many benefits of working with such a varied range of people in the group, she felt more motivated to manage some of the challenges. She began a training program to help employees become more adept at examining issues from a variety of perspectives. Not only did that help within the group she headed up, but it also led to better cooperation with the Chinese and Irish divisions. ■

Labor and Union Issues pp. 277–279

In 2008, the United States experienced a dramatic economic downturn and unemployment figures hit double digits. State revenue fell for many areas as businesses shrank and restructured to weather the hard times. By 2011 many state legislatures and public officials were faced with huge budget shortfalls and argued the fiscal problems were due to government worker unions.

At least 12 states passed laws to restrict the power of unions. Governor Scott Walker of Wisconsin was quoted as saying, "We can no longer live in a society where the public employees are the haves and taxpayers who foot the bills are the have-nots."[32] Tensions continued to grow and before the final vote on legislation to limit negotiation rights of unions, protestors flooded into the State Assembly chanting "We're not leaving."[33] ■

Have you ever passed a picket line and wondered why the workers were on strike? A **strike** occurs when workers agree to stop work until certain demands are met. In this section, you'll learn about the role of organized labor in the workplace and how this role is changing in today's global economy.

AFP/Getty Images

Organized Labor

What is a labor union? A labor union is a legally recognized group dedicated to protecting the interests of workers. Unions represent many types of workers in public-sector industries, such as teachers, nurses, and firefighters; in manufacturing industries such as the automotive industry; and in construction specialty "craft" groups such as engineers, plumbers, and roofers. Entertainers and supporting industries, such as actors and writers, also have unions. Labor unions negotiate various employment issues, such as salary, benefits, and working hours.

6 What are the objectives, structures, and future of labor unions in the global business environment?

What are the objectives of organized labor? Labor unions began as a means to protect workers from the terrible injustices employers inflicted on their workers in the nineteenth century during the U.S. Industrial Revolution. During that time, employers took advantage of workers, subjecting them to long hours, low pay, and health risks. Women and children were often treated even worse and paid less. Labor unions formed to fight for better working conditions and employee rights. These individual labor unions, by joining together, proved to be more effective in bettering working conditions. Two of the more influential unions are the **American Federation of Labor (AFL)**, founded in 1886 to protect skilled workers, and the Industrial Workers of the World, founded in 1905 to represent mainly unskilled workers.

The **Congress of Industrial Organizations (CIO)** was formed in 1935 to represent entire industries rather than specific workers' groups. The CIO was initially a separate organization within the AFL but soon split to form its own organization. In 1955, the two were reunited to form the AFL-CIO, which is still in effect today as a federation comprised of 56 member unions. The Change to Win Federation, formed in 2005 as an alternative to the AFL-CIO, is the newest member to organized labor. Other prominent unions include the United Auto Workers (UAW), the International Brotherhood of Teamsters, and the Service Employees International Union.

How are labor unions structured? To form a union, a group of workers must either have their employer voluntarily recognize them as a group or have a majority of workers form a **bargaining unit** for union representation. A bargaining unit is a group of employees that negotiates with an employer for better working conditions or pay. When a union forms, workers join and pay membership dues. Most unions have paid, full-time staff that is often supplemented with substantial volunteer workers. In addition to dues, some unions create strike funds that help support workers should they strike. Union members elect officers and shop stewards who make decisions for the entire body and represent the members in dealings with management. So that unions can better represent specific interests, union **locals** are created by workers of the same industry, company, region, or business sector.

Collective Bargaining

What is the collective bargaining process? One of the primary roles of a union is to negotiate with an employer for better work conditions and terms of employment. This generally is done through a **collective bargaining** process. Negotiation is between union representatives and employers usually over concerns related to wages, benefits, working hours, insurance benefits, and grievance procedures. A collective bargaining agreement is the result of such negotiations, and it forces an employer to abide by the conditions specified in the agreement. Change can be made only through subsequent negotiations.

What happens if an agreement cannot be reached through collective bargaining? If negotiating does not produce a collective bargaining agreement, and both parties seem to be at an impasse, then other means to settle the dispute are used before workers go on strike. **Mediation** is a process that involves a neutral third party that assists the two parties both privately and collectively to identify issues and develop proposals for resolution. The mediator works with both sides to understand their genuine interests and helps each side generate proposals that address those interests. In **arbitration**, a dispute is sent to an arbitrator for a decision. Arbitrators hear both sides of a dispute, and the parties involved agree in advance that the arbitrator's decision is final. Sometimes, arbitration is nonbinding, meaning that neither party is required to accept the arbitrator's decision.

What happens when negotiations break down? When negotiation reaches an impasse, union workers can take several actions to prompt management to accept union demands. Union members and those who are sympathetic to their cause can stage a **boycott**, in which supporters refuse to buy or handle a company's products or services. However, companies can use a **lockout**, in which management refuses to allow union members to enter the premises. Lockouts are legal only if negotiations have come to an impasse and the company is defending a legitimate position.

As a last resort, union workers may vote to go on strike and agree to stop working. Strikes jeopardize the productivity of an organization, so they are used to force management into making concessions that they might not have made otherwise. Strikes also gain considerable media publicity, especially when workers **picket** a workplace by walking outside a company's entrances with signs that reflect the employees' grievances. Workers do not easily make the decision to strike, as they risk losing income throughout the strike period. For example, a six-week strike would cost a worker earning $700 per week a total of $4,200 in lost wages. If the new contract negotiated a weekly wage increase of $1, it would take about two years to recover the lost wages. Additionally, strikers might be fired or replaced as management has the authority to hire replacement personnel, known as **strikebreakers**, or scabs. Some states prohibit public safety workers, such as police officers and hospital workers, from going on strike. In these cases, workers often have "sick-outs," during which union members are not officially on strike but instead call in sick, refusing to come to work.

AFP/Getty Images

Hostess, makers of Twinkies, has more than 75% of its employees unionized. The company has gone to court to throw out its union contracts arguing they need more concessions to keep operating. Unions are willing to strike, knowing the baker's union pension fund is owed $994 million by Hostess.

The State of Labor Unions

Are labor unions still effective today? In the United States, the role of labor unions is declining. As of 2011, union membership sits at 11.8 percent.[34] Many private-sector unions, such as the automobile workers and construction trade unions, have experienced dramatic reductions in membership. This decline is the result of several factors, but arguably, the most prominent reason is a reaction to their own success by fighting for better working conditions, higher wages, and more benefits. Additionally, the introduction of technology has resulted in a shift from blue-collar–based industries to professional white-collar, service-based industries, for which unions are less common. Despite declining numbers, labor unions continue to be influential in many industries, as well as in other countries.

What is the future of unions and labor-management relations? In response to a more globalized working community, unions have begun to build alliances with unions in other countries. They recognize that when multinational corporations decide to move production abroad, for example, there might be a negative impact on local and international workers. Consequently, in an effort to protect their interests, unions must broaden their reach and make a commitment to international labor solidarity. Immigration is another issue affecting unions. Immigrant workers are crossing borders and threaten to take jobs traditionally supported by labor unions. Unions, especially in California and Florida, continue to grapple with integrating and embracing these potential new members into the organization. Lastly, and perhaps most importantly, unions will need to transform themselves to survive the effects of globalization.

Remember Scott Walker, the Wisconsin governor who limited collective bargaining rights for public workers in the Dairy State? Less than two years into his term he was forced into a recall election by the backlash from his position on labor unions. He easily defeated the pro-union nominee put up against him, raising questions about the strength of the labor movement across the country. The recall election also raised questions about campaign financing as Walker's anti-union position was strongly supported by conservative donors outside the state, allowing the Walker campaign to outspend its opponent seven to one.[35] ■

MyBizLab

Go to **mybizlab.com** to complete the problems marked with this icon ⭐.

1 What processes are involved in Human Resource Management (HRM)? (pp. 257–263)

- **Human resource management (HRM)** (p. 257) is the organizational function that encompasses every aspect of the "human" in a business, including hiring, training, motivating, evaluating, and compensating personnel.

- Staff planning involves determining how many employees a company needs. A **workforce profile** (p. 258) is compiled as a form of "personnel inventory" and includes information about each employee. The future demand for employees is determined in a process called **forecasting** (p. 258).

- **Recruitment** (p. 259) is the process of finding, screening, and selecting people for a job.

- Hiring begins by narrowing down candidates who have been identified in the recruiting process to a select group of applicants.

2 How are employees trained and evaluated? (pp. 263–268)

- An **orientation program** (p. 264) integrates new employees into an organization. Other forms of training include **on-the-job training** (p. 264), **apprentice training programs** (p. 264), and **simulation training** (p. 265).

- **Management development programs** (p. 265) prepare management-trainees to become managers within an organization by having them participate in on-the-job training programs.

- **Off-the-job training and development** (p. 266) require the employee to participate in outside seminars, university-conducted programs, and corporate universities.

- A **performance appraisal** (p. 266) is an evaluation of an employee's performance that gives feedback and suggestions for improvement. They are useful when done properly, but many managers avoid performance appraisals because they do not feel comfortable critiquing employees harshly.

- **Performance management** (p. 267) is an alternative to performance appraisals. It approaches employee evaluations as ongoing and systematic.

3 What are the main components of compensating and scheduling employees? (pp. 269–271)

- **Compensation** (p. 269), or payment for work performed, consists of financial and nonfinancial payments.

- **Salaries** (p. 269) and hourly **wages** (p. 269), **bonuses** (p. 269), **commissions** (p. 269), and retirement **pension plans** (p. 269) constitute financial compensation.

- Defined benefit plans describe the amount of retirement benefit the employee will receive, and defined contribution plans identify the contribution the employee must make to the plan. **401(k) plans** (p. 269) allow employees to contribute pretax dollars to their retirement plans.

- Noncash **employee benefits** (p. 270) come in many forms, including health and disability insurance, vacation and sick pay, and retirement plans.

- **Work/life benefits** (p. 270), such as gym memberships, are important for those employees who are trying to balance busy lives both in and out of work.

- Alternative scheduling arrangements enable employees to have more flexibility in their workday times. **Flextime** (p. 271), **job sharing** (p. 271), **permanent part-time** (p. 271), **telecommuting** (p. 272), and **compressed workweeks** (p. 271) are alternative scheduling methods.

4 How does employee status change through promotions, termination, and retirement? (pp. 272–274)

- Employees increase their level of responsibility through promotion—taking on a job that has more responsibility and stature in a company or a department.

- **Termination** (p. 273) is when companies permanently lay off workers due to poor performance or a discontinued use for their services. Downsizing and restructuring, outsourcing and offshoring, pressures of global competition, and increased uses of technology are reasons companies look to reduce the number of employees through termination.

- **Retirement** (p. 274) occurs when employees decide to stop working on a full-time basis or stop working altogether. Financial security, staying active and engaged, and learning something new are reasons seniors cite for deferring retirement.

5 **How does incorporating diversity affect the workforce?** (pp. 275–276)

- The workforce today consists of employees from many different cultures and religions, which can lead to challenges in helping employees understand one another.
- More women are entering the workforce, but few are reaching executive management levels. Sexism, salary inequity, and sexual harassment remain prominent issues.
- The workforce is getting older as more baby boomers work beyond typical retirement age. An aging workforce increases health-care costs but also increases productivity and decreases training costs.
- A diverse workforce has proven to be more creative and innovative than a nondiverse workforce. Diversity keeps companies competitive in a global business community.

6 **What are the objectives, structures, and future of labor unions in the global business environment?** (pp. 277–279)

- A **labor union** (p. 277) is a legally recognized group dedicated to protecting the interests of workers. Labor unions typically negotiate various employment issues, such as salary, health benefits, and work hours.

- Representatives of the labor union form a **bargaining unit** (p. 278) that negotiates with employers in a **collective bargaining** process (p. 278) in hopes of reaching an agreement that is satisfactory to both sides.
- If satisfactory terms cannot be agreed on by both sides, the process is often turned over for **mediation** (p. 278), in which a neutral third party assists both sides and generates a proposal that addresses each party's interests.
- In the **arbitration** (p. 278) process, a third party settles the dispute after hearing all the issues.
- If negotiations break down, unions may choose to **boycott** (p. 278) a company.
- As a last resort, union members may vote to go on **strike** (p. 277) and agree to stop working altogether.
- As the business community continues to expand globally, unions will need to change their definition of membership to handle the increase in immigration workers.

Key Terms

401(k) plan (p. 269)
affirmative action (p. 275)
American Federation of Labor (AFL) (p. 278)
apprentice training program (p. 264)
arbitration (p. 278)
bargaining unit (p. 278)
bonus (p. 269)
boycott (p. 278)
collective bargaining (p. 278)
commissions (p. 269)
compensation (p. 269)
compressed workweek (p. 271)
Congress of Industrial Organizations (CIO) (p. 278)
consultants (p. 272)
contingent workers (p. 272)
diversity training (p. 276)
employee benefits (p. 270)
employee stock ownership plan (ESOP) (p. 270)
employee stock purchase plan (p. 270)
employment at will (p. 273)

external recruiting (p. 260)
flexible benefit plan (or cafeteria plan) (p. 270)
flextime (p. 271)
forecasting (p. 258)
human resource management (HRM) (p. 257)
incentive-based payment (p. 269)
independent contractors (p. 272)
internal recruiting (p. 259)
job analysis (p. 258)
job description (p. 258)
job sharing (p. 271)
job specifications (p. 259)
labor union (p. 277)
locals (p. 278)
lockout (p. 278)
management development programs (p. 265)
mediation (p. 278)
mentor (p. 266)
off-the-job training and development (p. 266)
online training (p. 265)

on-the-job training (p. 264)
orientation program (p. 264)
pension plan (p. 269)
performance appraisal (p. 266)
performance management (p. 267)
permanent part-time employee (p. 271)
picketing (p. 279)
profit-sharing plan (p. 269)
programmed learning approach (p. 264)
recruitment (p. 259)
retirement (p. 274)
salary (p. 269)
simulation training (p. 265)
stock options (p. 269)
strike (p. 277)
strikebreakers (p. 279)
telecommuting (p. 272)
termination (p. 273)
wages (p. 269)
worker buyout (p. 274)
workforce profile (p. 258)
work/life benefits (p. 270)

Self-Test

Multiple Choice   You can find the answers on the last page of this book.

1. Human resource planning consists of two main focuses:
   a. hiring and firing.
   b. creating job descriptions and creating job specifications.
   c. managing diversity and the relationship with unions.
   d. profiling the current workforce and forecasting future demand.

2. When interviewing candidates for an administrative assistant's job, which of the following interview questions is legally inadvisable?
   a. What church do you attend?
   b. What are your strengths and weaknesses?
   c. What are your hobbies?
   d. Who do you think will win the Super Bowl?

3. Types of training required in some careers include
   a. an on-the-job mentor.
   b. time spent as an apprentice to a master.
   c. programmed learning.
   d. All of the above

4. The performance review process often includes all of the following except a(n)
   a. evaluation of the employee's social standing in the work environment.
   b. assessment of performance as compared to defined standards.
   c. specific feedback on how to enhance positive performance.
   d. clear definition of expectations from the employee.

5. Amit Patel, as part of his compensation package, was offered an opportunity to purchase company stock at a later date but valued at the current, lower price. Which of the following is Amit given?
   a. Stock option
   b. Stock ownership plan
   c. Stock purchase plan
   d. None of the above

6. James Rodriguez wants to spend more time at home with his two-year-old granddaughter and is considering leaving the company. He could receive three months' pay and the same retirement package he will be eligible for in three years' time if he leaves now. This type of offer is called a(n)
   a. independent consultant status.
   b. worker buyout.
   c. retirement.
   d. compressed workweek.

7. Which one of the following is NOT a reason to hire a contingent worker?
   a. To fill in for absent employees
   b. Not enough office space for a full-time employee
   c. To supplement staff during particularly busy times
   d. To evaluate how a person performs on the job before hiring permanently

8. Which of the following are benefits companies have experienced from employing a diverse workforce?
   a. Cultural differences add more perspectives and promote better problem solving.
   b. They fulfill expected affirmative action standards.
   c. Companies become more competitive in the global marketplace.
   d. All of the above

9. The AFL-CIO, the UAW, and the Teamsters are examples of
   a. illegal organizations.
   b. labor unions.
   c. labor relations.
   d. union locals.

10. Which of the following are actions that management can take when threatened with disgruntled employees walking out on their jobs?
   a. Hiring strikebreakers
   b. Boycotting employees
   c. Imposing a lockout
   d. Both a and c

True/False You can find the answers on the last page of this book.

1. Federal laws like the ADA and the ADEA must be followed by every business when hiring.
   ☐ **True** or ☐ **False**

2. Profit sharing could mean that a good year means employees get bonuses or it could refer to the company's contributions to an employee retirement plan.
   ☐ **True** or ☒ **False**

3. Some managers use an alternative to performance appraisals called performance management.
   ☒ **True** or ☐ **False**

4. Free gourmet lunches, on-site child care, and on-site health facilities are benefits provided by some U.S. companies.
   ☒ **True** or ☐ **False**

5. A diversified workforce adds creativity and a variety of viewpoints to the workforce, which often helps improve a company's competitiveness and its bottom line.
   ☒ **True** or ☐ **False**

Critical Thinking Questions

1. Performance management is one alternative to a traditional performance appraisal. Which style of evaluation would you prefer as an employee? Which would be more useful to you as a manager?

2. An inefficient hiring process can cripple a company as the cost of turnover and retraining is so high. Does the automation of collecting and evaluating résumés by computer help companies? Job seekers? How do you feel about taking a personality test as part of an application process? What if it is automated?

3. Describe the "perfect" benefits package that would be most important to you when applying for a job. What kinds of questions could you ask to determine how and when those benefits will be offered to you? How does salary/pay level affect your decision? Would you accept a lower salary/pay level for better benefits?

Team Time

Seeing Both Sides

Walmart has been both praised and criticized for many of its HR policies. Assemble into teams of four students. Divide each team into two subgroups.

a. Subgroup 1—Good HR Practices: Research articles about the positive HR policies and practices Walmart has implemented. Prepare a summary paper outlining your findings.

b. Subgroup 2—Bad HR Practices: Research articles about the negative HR policies and practices Walmart has implemented. Prepare a summary paper outlining your findings.

Process

Step 1. As a group, compile your findings, comparing the positive and negative policies. Were there instances where a policy started out as a positive and ended up as a negative or vice versa? How did their policies work with Walmart's strategic goals? How have their policies affected Walmart's stock price and bottom line?

Step 2. If you were employed as an HR consultant for Walmart, what kind of advice would you give the company based on your findings?

Ethics and Corporate Social Responsibility

THE ETHICS OF INTERVIEWING

The interview and hiring process is fraught with ethical concerns. Form a small group and discuss the ethical implications of the following scenario.

Scenario

Where does a candidate's right to privacy end and a company's right to know begin? As you learned in this chapter, federal laws protect potential employees from discrimination. Hiring managers must observe these laws by refraining from asking certain questions during the interview process, such as direct questions about age and physical disabilities. However, to find out about these topics while still staying within the bounds of legality, managers have devised alternative questions.[36] For example:

Instead of asking . . .	They ask this legal alternative . . .
Which religious holidays do you observe?	Can you work our required schedule?
Do you have children?	What is your experience with "X" age group?
Do you have any disabilities?	Are you able to perform this position's specific duties?

Process

With your group, discuss your opinions on the use of these "legal alternatives" as an HR strategy. They are legal, but are they ethical? Do managers undermine the laws by finding ways around them? Or does a company have a right to know about these topics to make the best hiring decision?

Web Exercises

1. **Analyzing Annual Reports**
   Using the Internet, access the annual reports of three companies in different industries. How are human resources handled in the annual report? What kind of issues do these companies discuss that relate to human resources? What is similar and different among the companies?

2. **Social Media and HR**
   Forbes reports that almost one in five executives says that a candidate's social media profile has caused him or her not to hire a person.[37] Review all of the online materials available about you—Facebook, LinkedIn, blog postings you have made, photographs uploaded—from the perspective of a potential employer. Do you have any materials that might keep you from being hired? What do you think about this issue?

3. **Organized Labor**
   Explore the AFL-CIO website (www.aflcio.org). What are its current concerns and causes? How does one become involved in this organization? What is its history? Which historical, political, and social forces propelled the organized labor movement?

4. **Benefits Packages**
   Many companies have determined that their biggest asset is their employees, so taking care of employees is a mission-critical objective. Research companies that use benefits packages as a way to make their employees feel cared for and that retain a high percentage of employees. Consider both small and large businesses.

5. **Legal Matters**
   Visit the ACLU Action Center website (http://action.aclu.org) to find information about current issues concerning employee rights, antidiscrimination laws, or other HR concerns. What are the circumstances of these cases? What is your opinion on them?

MyBizLab

Go to **mybizlab.com** for Auto-graded writing questions as well as the following Assisted-graded writing questions:

9-1. Job analysis is an important part of human resource management. How does the job analysis work with the development of a workforce profile? How would HR help a company move to innovate in a quickly changing industry?

9-2. Labor unions were born at a time when working conditions were quite exploitive and even dangerous in many parts of the United States. Do labor unions serve a purpose in today's workplace environment? Discuss what functions unions provide that benefit a company as a whole.

9-3. MyBizLab Only – comprehensive writing assignment for this chapter.

Online Business and Technology

Online Business

Sonja Pettingill has a new start-up venture. She can sell her product through local boutique stores, but she knows she needs a strong online business component to succeed. How does being online change her marketing strategy? How does she take advantage of the latest online technologies?

Technology in Business

When Melissa McGregor started working for a hardware store, she was amazed that the technology it used was so outdated. There was no website or customer database, and the cash registers weren't even connected to an information system. How could advancements in technology benefit the store? Who is responsible for keeping the store current in technology?

Security

Kevin Fossbenner knows his business—BMX bikes. Flatland Frames is doing well but one suspicious e-mail to an employee could open the company to dangerous hacking. How do modern business people protect themselves?

Impact of Social Media and Mobile Technology

You make the effort to stay up on current technologies. You add a social media component to your business. It begins to take off but then one upset customer seems to begin to drive customers away. There are positive and negative ways to incorporate new technologies into your business, and they can make or break you.

MyBizLab®

⭐ **Improve Your Grade!**

Over 10 million students improved their results using the Pearson MyLabs.
Visit **mybizlab.com** for simulations, tutorials, and end-of-chapter problems.

Online Business pp. 285–291

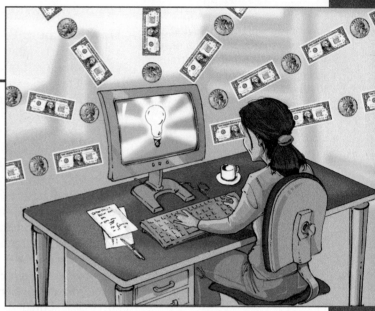

When Sonja Pettingill decided to start a business, she knew she had a great idea. Her Mom Utility Vests (MUVs) would mean moms had all the things they needed for a day out with Baby, but still had their hands free while carrying all that gear. So the idea is solid—but how to kick off a business for such a specialty product? She could travel from one small boutique to another in the area, but she'd never recoup the cost of developing and producing the products. She realizes she needs to take her marketing message to a national audience and take her storefront online . . . but how? ∎

ImageZoo/Alamy

The online business model has become part of every business whether there is a brick-and-mortar store as part of the business or not. It allows access to national and international consumers, around the clock. But it demands a wide set of skills—marketing techniques that work in the cyber environment, technical skills to maintain and support the online business, and security knowledge to recognize and respond to the special threats online businesses face. New technologies like social networking and advances in mobile technologies promise to continue fueling new ways for online business to grow. In this chapter you'll explore the challenges and opportunities technology has brought to business.

Growth of Online Business

Has online shopping hit its peak? You have likely shopped online. More than 80 percent of online users have purchased something at least once. The advantages of online shopping most cited, such as saving time, making it easy to compare prices, and offering more variety with lower prices, have propelled online business to record highs. These advantages are sending e-commerce sales climbing worldwide. Sales are predicted to top $1.4 trillion by 2015. In the United States alone, electronic sales are growing at 10 percent a year. The increase in mobile devices is another trend promoting additional sales, with $23.8 billion of sales from mobile devices alone forecast[1] for 2015. All this means we should think a bit about the special advantages and needs of e-commerce.

Marketing Online

How does the online environment support marketing efforts? Marketing is an aspect of business that has responded to changes in business technology by redefining itself. In today's world, a marketing department must consider the Internet as a tool both for collecting information about its customers as well as

 What does the online environment offer to help market a business?

THE List

Brought to You by PayPal[2]

Each of the following people spent time working at PayPal, the company that pioneered a new style of online purchasing transactions. After leaving PayPal, the 10 here have founded or invested in all these wildly successful businesses. What did PayPal teach them?

1. Reid Hoffman—LinkedIn
2. Chad Hurley—YouTube
3. Steve Chen—YouTube
4. Jawed Karim—YouTube
5. David Sacks—Yammer
6. Keith Rabois—Square
7. Elon Musk—SpaceX and Tesla
8. Premal Shah—Kiva
9. Max Levchin—Slide
10. Peter Thiel—funded Facebook, Palantir, Zynga

distributing information about its products and services. Companies such as Lyris, Topica, and Constant Contact can organize and control mass e-mail campaigns by providing templates for e-mail newsletters or advice on how to create e-mail surveys. They also provide services that generate reports to track the number of people who read the e-mail message, how many followed the links inside, and how many forwarded the e-mail to another contact.

How has an online presence changed marketing strategies? For marketing experts, taking advantage of new advertising outlets offers many new opportunities. **Online advertising** refers to any form of advertising that uses the Internet to market its message to customers. This includes everything from banner ads to Facebook campaigns to spam e-mails. More often than not, the online ad is hyperlinked to another website and tracks how many "clicks" are registered. The ability to track how many eyes have viewed an ad is, in fact, one of the great allures of Internet advertising.

As the number of households with high-speed broadband Internet access has increased, online advertising has become much more sophisticated.[3] QR codes redirect purchasers from magazine ads and from counter displays directly to a company's Web content. Flash and Java technologies allow advertisers to embed animated ads and full-motion video. In addition to the abundance of such rich media ads, programs such as Google's AdWords service and AdSense network employ the process of **pay-per-click (PPC) advertising**. With PPC advertising, advertisers pay only for the number of times a Web surfer clicks on their ad. Google's AdWords and AdSense have been able to translate this simple technique into a successful source of revenue for the company. Mobile platforms are seeing an increase in direct advertising as well. With the release of the iPhone operating system iOS 4.0, Apple introduced the design of iAds. Instead of redirecting a user out of the application he or she is in and into a Web browser, iAds are integrated into the iPhone app so they fade up, interact with the user, and then fade away—all while the user is still in the original app.[4]

PPC ads are effective because they are associated with keywords and are highly relevant to what potential consumers are searching for. The idea was initially conceived by the GoTo search engine before Google began to develop its own AdSense network. Google's popular AdSense network takes PPC ads to the next level. By placing PPC ads on third-party sites, such as blogs and Web forums, they reach readers depending on the content of a particular page instead of search results. Also known as **contextual advertising**, these ads are automatically generated by the content on a specific site. This way, readers of a popular snowboarding blog might see ads with Shaun White promoting Red Bull. Moreover, the AdSense network also allows individual bloggers to generate revenue by hosting these ads on their site. Blogs with a significant readership can earn a great deal of money by giving such ads visibility.

Google AdWords allows you to reach potential customers already searching for products like yours.

digitallife/Alamy

Are there any drawbacks to online advertising? "Click fraud" can occur, in which a competing company clicks on ads to run up the cost of its competitor's advertising. Spam annoys people and fills up their in-boxes. Web surfers also complain about pop-up ads, which open their ads in new browser windows, and interstitials, which are displayed before a viewer can get to the desired content. Also, because the integration of ads on the Internet is so prevalent, many people have grown so used to seeing Web ads that they may not even notice them. ■ **TABLE 10.1** summarizes the pros and cons of online advertising.

How does technology change marketing in a global marketplace? Internet technology allows every company with a website to advertise to anyone in the world with Internet access. The site must

support multiple languages, as seen in ■ **FIGURE 10.1**, but more importantly, it must also make sure the content for different countries is culturally customized. Every marketing campaign is now global.

Budweiser launched a campaign during the 2010 World Cup that demonstrated how these pieces can be woven into a single campaign.[5] The "Bud United" campaign followed 32 soccer fans living in a single house, one representing each nation in the World Cup. As each country was eliminated, that person left the house. Daily video content from the house was published on YouTube, and daily updates were posted to Facebook and Twitter. A worldwide television and online advertising campaign accompanied the "reality ad" video content. Coordinated television ads were run in 20 countries, and online ads in a range of sports-related sites in local markets all worked to drive users to the Bud United site. Each house member had his or her own Facebook and Twitter page in his or her native language, reaching out to fans around the world. Offline, the campaign extended to include display ads in stadiums in South Africa and video content aired in New York's Times Square. For the first time ever, Bud worked with FIFA (the Fédération Internationale de Football Association) so that fans could vote for the most valuable player (MVP) of each match online and through mobile text messaging. Social media technologies, Web, and video technologies were combined with traditional marketing tools and expanded across a global scale for one unified campaign.

What is viral marketing? To get people to notice their advertisements, many marketers are turning to a technique known as **viral marketing**. This practice

TABLE 10.1
Pros and Cons of Online Advertising

Pros	Cons
Reasonable cost: With PPC advertising, the cost of advertising depends on frequency of use.	**Fear of spam:** Web users may avoid clicking ads to avoid receiving spam.
Hitting target markets: Contextual advertising allows for high probability of reaching intended viewers.	**Annoyance factor:** Rather than be drawn in, Web users can become annoyed with flashing ads or pop-ups.
Tracking: Companies are able to keep records of who is clicking ads and where they are located—essential information for designing future campaigns.	**Click fraud:** Companies who invest in PPC advertising may receive unexpectedly large invoices if a competitor purposefully clicks ads in excess.

■ **FIGURE 10.1**
The Global Web
Thanks to Internet technology, every company with a website is now capable of advertising globally. This page markets Pearson publishing products to a Japanese audience.
Reprinted by permission of Pearson Education, Japan. http://www.pearsonkirihara.jp/

DAY 5

CB2/ZOB/Newscom

The 2011 movie *Contagion*, about a rampant virus, put a twist on viral marketing. Custom Petri dishes and specially colored bacteria were created that grew into a living billboard.

involves using social networks, e-mail, and websites to spread the awareness of a particular brand. Rather than being an overt advertising campaign that relies on airwaves with commercials, a viral campaign is more subtle and dependent on the user to be an active participant in spreading a message. It's designed to appeal to consumers who may be resistant to traditional advertising. Essentially, viral marketing is a Web 2.0 version—that is, a more consumer-engaged, interactive, and collaborative type—of old-fashioned word of mouth.[6]

Viral marketing gives a company more than the opportunity to promote a product or brand; it allows potential consumers to feel a personal connection to the brand by becoming a part of a communal experience. Hollywood movie studios have been on the forefront of this kind of viral advertising. Consider the marketing campaign for the science fiction film *District 9*. Before the film's release, public service announcements began to appear in the 15 largest U.S. markets. Bus benches were plastered with signs reading "Bus bench for humans only" followed by a note, "Report nonhumans," and a phone number as well as a website address that took visitors to information about the movie.[7] In two weeks there were over 33,000 phone calls as people on the street agreed to play along with the premise that alien beings were residing in their community. The site had language support for both human and nonhuman visitors, as well as games and training simulations. By generating interest about the extensive campaign, the $30 million film took in over $37 million its first weekend.[8]

This dedication to using advertising as a means to develop content and create an entertainment experience is one way the Internet and viral marketing are shifting the paradigm of advertising's capabilities.

Types of Online Business Transactions

What are the kinds of business transactions that happen online? Interaction between business and the consumer has also changed radically since the introduction of the Internet. The most common modes of transactions are business to business (B2B), business to consumer (B2C), and consumer to consumer (C2C).

What is the focus of B2B transactions? Business-to-business transactions involve the exchange of products, services, and information between businesses on the Internet. B2B websites can be classified as follows:

- *Company websites* target other companies and their employees, similar to an exhibit at a trade show. They are designed to sell goods or services to business clients, rather than to household consumers. For example, UPS has a website that is separate and distinct from the website that consumers use for their personal shipping needs. It is an interactive and user-friendly B2B site for business owners looking for shipping solutions.

- *Procurement exchange* is a group of companies that act together to purchase goods or services at lower prices. Electronic procurement, known as *e-procurement*, is the online purchase and sale of products and services between businesses. Procurement exchanges benefit both purchasers and suppliers. For example, the state of Kentucky has an e-procurement website. Vendors can register, examine current bidding opportunities, and even enter online bidding for contracts through the site.[9]

- *Specialized industry portals* are online gateways to major sources of information, discussion forums, and product listings. To see an example, view the portal page for CEOs at ceoExpress.com. These are also known as *niche portals*

2

What are the types of business transactions that are supported by online commerce?

or *vertical portals* because they provide expanded information on a specific product or market.

- *Brokering sites* are third-party sites that act as liaisons between providers and potential buyers of goods or services. Brokering sites can be found for a variety of rental goods that businesses may need, from projectors and video equipment to backhoes and excavators.

- *Information sites* provide information about a particular industry. Also called an *infomediary*, an information site gives businesses information about current standards and developments. For example, TheMedica.com is an infomediary that posts news about the health-care and medical industries. It also includes information about trade shows, links to medical publications, and a directory of health-care businesses and products.[10] Infomediaries help facilitate and originate B2B traffic.

But often businesses work directly with customers online? Yes, **business-to-consumer (B2C) transactions** refer to e-commerce that takes place directly between businesses and consumers. In fact, it's becoming essential for almost all businesses to sell or at least promote their products to customers online. "Click and mortar" refers to B2C businesses that have both an online presence and a bricks-and-mortar presence. This combination is ideal for customers who like the convenience of online shopping but who also want the convenience of returning products without shipping costs or being able to see a product in person before buying.

To stay in business, B2C companies have gotten savvy with regard to online distribution, advertising, networking, and accessing customers. Some models that have accelerated B2C e-commerce include the following:[11]

- *Online intermediaries* are businesses such as Travelocity and Amazon.com that are not direct producers of products but instead buy goods and/or services and sell them to customers.

- *Advertising-based models* rely on banner ads on other websites to attract customers. The two main approaches that advertisers use are *high-traffic* and *niche*. The high-traffic approach is designed to reach a wide audience, with ads placed on popular sites, such as Yahoo!. The niche approach best serves companies that target a small, specific audience.

- *Community-based models* allow users with similar interests to interact with each other worldwide. Steam from the Valve Corporation is an example of a community-based gaming website where users can purchase and play online games. Steam distributes games from the full range of small, independent video game houses as well as major publishers. With over 30 million active accounts,[12] Steam members always have someone to play with—and someone to encourage them to buy a new game!

- *Fee-based models* require users to pay a subscription fee to view their content. In these systems, website content is restricted until a user registers and pays either a flat monthly rate or a pay-as-you-go fee. Internet dating sites, such as Match and eHarmony, and online journals, such as *Consumer Reports*, are examples of fee-based B2C sites.

Although B2C sites face challenges in keeping regular customers and maintaining a competitive edge, there are advantages to online companies that serve customers directly via the Internet. Many B2C sites have call centers or request forms so customers can ask questions or submit comments to improve the site. Online ads also allow B2C companies to reach a wider audience.

What kind of business happens between customers? Transactions that take place between consumers are called **consumer-to-consumer (C2C) transactions**. In this e-commerce model, consumers sell goods and services to other consumers, sometimes with the involvement of a third party. The artsy storefront

TABLE 10.2

Types of Online Business Transactions

Business-to-Business (B2B) Examples	Business-to-Customer (B2C) Examples	Customer-to-Customer (C2C) Examples
Company websites UPS	**Online intermediaries** Amazon.com	**Exchange through intermediary** eBay
Procurement exchange Kentucky e-procurement	**Advertising-based models** Ads on Yahoo!	**Peer-to-peer exchange** Music files
Specialized industry portals CEOExpress.com	**Community-based models** Steam	
Brokering sites Excavating broker	**Fee-based models** Consumer Reports	
Information sites TheMedica.com		

Etsy is an example of a business based on C2C transactions. A popular C2C marketplace with an intermediary is eBay. File and music sharing are types of C2C exchanges, sometimes referred to as *P2P*, or peer-to-peer. Social networking sites, including Facebook and MySpace, can fill this role as well. The wide variety of business transactions happening online is summarized in ■ TABLE 10.2.

Challenges of E-commerce

How are taxes applied to e-commerce sales? Most Internet sales are tax free, which causes major problems for states that rely on sales taxes to fund their public institutions. The laws regarding e-commerce taxation have been debated since Congress passed the Internet Tax Freedom Act (ITFA) in 1998. This law established a three-year suspension of online sales taxes and was extended for two more years in 2001. It expired in 2003 and was never renewed.[13]

Online sales tax requirements also vary depending on the business. If an e-business also has a physical presence, such as a store or an office, then it must charge sales tax on transactions occurring in the states in which it has a physical presence.[14] Target, for example, has some stores in Maryland, so a customer living in Maryland must pay sales tax on a purchase from Target's website. However, if a customer in Georgia orders a bouquet from the 1800Flowers website, he or she does not have to pay sales tax because 1-800-Flowers doesn't have a brick-and-mortar store in Georgia.

Because tax-free shopping is a major appeal to consumers, some large companies have created online stores that are separate legal entities from their brick-and-mortar stores. This allows customers to purchase from their online stores without paying sales tax, although this practice has outraged many retailers that must collect tax from their customers. Businesses that can avoid charging sales tax have a competitive advantage. State governments, however, are losing considerable revenue, and many have now instituted a "use tax." For example, in Pennsylvania you have one month to pay the 6 percent use tax on anything you purchase over the Internet if the seller did not collect state taxes.

Who has legal jurisdiction over an online business? Jurisdiction is the authority of a government to legislate and enforce its many laws. It is usually territorial, but because the Internet has a geographic territory that is too broad to define, it is difficult to address legal jurisdiction issues for online-only businesses.[15] Disputes over the legal jurisdiction of e-commerce have been occurring since the dawn of the Internet. A large corporation might have offices or stores in several different countries, and it becomes very difficult to comply with the laws of all those countries. In addition, to protect the rights of buyers and sellers and protect

Peer-to-peer is a file sharing system that is an example of consumer-to-consumer (C2C) exchange.

Matthias Pahl/Shutterstock

copyright material, the Digital Millennium Copyright Act, passed in 1998, must be followed.[16] In 2000, the World Intellectual Property Organization (WIPO) assured e-businesses that they would have to comply with laws only where the companies are based.

Sonja decided to start with a significant investment in an online presence. She hired Web developers from India to construct a viral advertising campaign, placing videos and images in a number of popular forums and websites for new moms and those throwing baby showers. While those were building interest in the new product, she began researching how to use Google Analytics to gather useful information about the visitors to her newly opened Web storefront. It requires a lot of time to put all these aspects of the business in place, but she knows she is building a business that can compete in the twenty-first century. ■

It looks like a great deal . . . but do you know if your state enforces a use tax for online purchases?

Elenathewise/Shutterstock

Technology in Business pp. 291–295

When Ian McGregor began working for a hardware store, he thought all he'd be doing was updating their website and maintaining the computer system. But when he saw the outdated technology they were using, he was amazed that the place was still in business. There was no online ordering from the website, no central storage of the sales information, and no way to send out a mailing targeted to certain customers. The store owner told him that he wanted to give the store a makeover and update the technology so he could increase his profits. Ian didn't know where to begin. What role does IT play in business? ■

Sergej Khackimullin/Fotolia

Try to imagine a type of business that doesn't use computer systems for at least some primary functions—it's hard to do! Any modern business must be able to reach consumers via electronic communication media such as texting, Facebook, and websites. Accounting information can be managed electronically so that taxes are filed easily and budgets prepared and monitored, and word processors and databases are vital to any business. In retail, point-of-sale terminals collect information that is fed into inventory and sales computer systems so that stock can be reordered, fast-moving products can be identified, and accounting information can be kept current and accurate. At Apple's retail stores, employees roam the store with mobile "cash registers" in hand.

They complete credit card transactions, e-mail sales receipts, and have customers in and out of the store in no time. The latest version of the Apple Store app takes this even further by allowing customers to check themselves out of the store using their own phones. Many grocery stores, as well as Home Depot warehouses, provide self-service automated checkout systems, reducing the need for cashiers. It's clear that technology is changing fundamental aspects of how business is conducted.

In this chapter we'll examine how technology is helping businesses grow. Whether it's a small family-owned business getting its first electronic accounting system or a huge corporate conglomerate launching a new interactive website, the business world is getting more technologically advanced every day.

The IT Organization

Who is in charge of business technology? Information technology (IT) is the design and implementation of computer-based information systems. In many organizational structures, the person responsible for such technology is the **chief information officer (CIO)**. This is typically a position at the same level as the CFO of a firm, for example. As ■ **FIGURE 10.2** shows, the CIO is in charge of information processing, including systems design and development and data center operations. He or she is responsible for updating or replacing the computer systems and the software the company uses. The CIO must also manage a budget that balances the benefits of technology against the ever-rising costs of upgrading to the latest systems. In addition, CIOs are involved in creating business and e-business opportunities as well as defining governing policies for the company in areas such as privacy and security.

What is a typical decision a CIO has to make? IT demands can pose a financial burden placed on companies trying to stay up-to-date. The full cost of any new piece of technology includes not only the purchase of the software and hardware itself but also potential hardware upgrades required to make the new product useful. For example, suppose management decides it wants to upgrade the operating system that runs on the company's computers. This requires that the firm buy not only licenses for the operating system software but also memory upgrades for computer systems. In addition, the IT department will need to take time to test the software prior to deployment, establish a support staff, install the software, and train users on how to interact with the programs. Before adopting

3

What are the functions of a company's chief information officer (CIO) and information technology (IT) department?

■ **FIGURE 10.2**
The Many Functions of a CIO
Because technology is spread across all divisions and major functions of a modern business, a CIO requires excellent leadership and organizational skills.

- Create and monitor IT budget
- Strive for highest possible return on investment (ROI)

Budget

- Update hardware and software to current business needs
- Introduce appropriate new technologies

Currency of Systems

Policies
- Create policies regarding security, privacy, and intellectual property

Systems Design and Development
- Create specifications for required programs
- Create, test, and maintain custom software programs

e-Commerce
- Create and maintain an Internet storefront
- Drive traffic to corporate Web site
- Maintain secure interactions

new technology, business managers must evaluate whether the benefits of new technology will exceed the costs.

Sometimes, management may feel pressure to upgrade software or hardware because the entire market has switched to a new product or because customers or vendors have already moved to a new version of a program or device. In such circumstances, the CIO must evaluate the available workforce and determine whether there are sufficient people trained with the new software or hardware to make the return on investment significant and worthwhile. Occasionally, software products are released and working, but they are not yet supported by other companies' software products. For example, when Microsoft released the Windows Vista operating system, many mid-size companies found they would be required to upgrade their hardware, adding hard disk drives, more memory, or possibly even buying entirely new computers because their existing processors were too slow for Vista.[17] However, Microsoft predicted a savings of $340 a year per machine in IT labor and support costs. In these cases, the CIO must evaluate whether adopting a new piece of technology is in the best interests of a company.

What happens in an IT department? The IT department is comprised of many professionals responsible for everything from hardware components and software programs to networking strategies. Members of this department are also responsible for security, both in response to computer virus attacks and emergency recovery from power outages and system failures. In addition, the department keeps all the computers, printers, and other equipment operational and current. The IT department manages the design of a company's networks and databases where information is stored. The department is also responsible for selecting the appropriate software programs and providing training to employees. Sometimes, IT professionals must create custom software to bridge the gaps between the products available and the needs of a firm. The IT department also maintains and manages the use of mobile computing throughout the company. Equipment includes notebook computers, Internet tablets like the iPad, smartphones, and other devices. Finally, the IT department is responsible for implementing remote access to computing resources, such as employees' access to work files or e-mail when they are working outside the office.

Information Systems

What's an information system? The main difference between an IT system and an **information system (IS)**, also called a **management information system (MIS)**, is that an MIS is focused on applying IT to solve business and economic problems. For example, the payroll department may need to upgrade to a new accounting system or software package. It is the role of the MIS department to investigate the impact of that change on the other technology systems in the company and rate the amount of gain against the cost required for the new software. So, MIS professionals bridge the gap between purely technical knowledge and how it will impact a business.

What is the difference between data and information? In common usage, the terms *data* and *information* are often used interchangeably, but they have different meanings. **Data** are the representations of a fact or idea. Data may be a number, a word, an image, or a sound. **Information**, however, is data that have been organized or arranged in a way that makes the data useful (see ■ **FIGURE 10.3**).

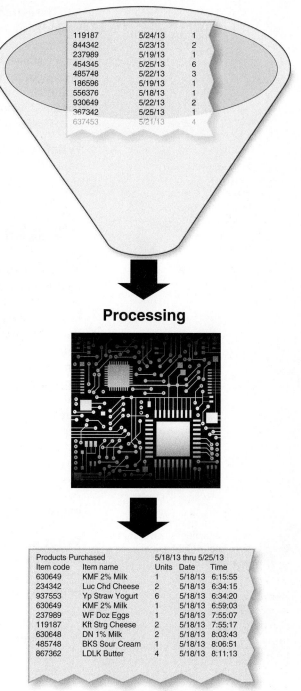

119187	5/24/13	1
844342	5/23/13	2
237989	5/19/13	1
454345	5/25/13	6
485748	5/22/13	3
186596	5/19/13	1
556376	5/18/13	1
930649	5/22/13	2
367342	5/25/13	1
637453	5/21/13	4

Processing

Products Purchased   5/18/13 thru 5/25/13

Item code	Item name	Units	Date	Time
630649	KMF 2% Milk	1	5/18/13	6:15:55
234342	Luc Chd Cheese	2	5/18/13	6:34:15
937553	Yp Straw Yogurt	6	5/18/13	6:34:20
630649	KMF 2% Milk	1	5/18/13	6:59:03
237989	WF Doz Eggs	1	5/18/13	7:55:07
119187	Kft Strg Cheese	2	5/18/13	7:55:17
630648	DN 1% Milk	2	5/18/13	8:03:43
485748	BKS Sour Cream	1	5/18/13	8:06:51
867362	LDLK Butter	4	5/18/13	8:11:13

Information

■ **FIGURE 10.3**
The Processing of Data into Useful Information
The raw data from a grocery store's sales log can be processed into information that will help the storeowner know when to schedule the store's milk shipments.

The extraction of information from raw data is critical to the success of many business enterprises. Businesses try to use all the resources at their disposal to gather raw data. For example, media, credit bureaus, and information brokers often purchase data made public in court proceedings. These data are processed into useful information for that business or later resold to other companies. So, a health club in Massachusetts may request a list of recently divorced women from the family court. The health club's plan is to process that raw data into a mailing list of a specific target audience for its membership services.[18]

What are databases? Database programs allow businesses to quickly enter data, filter and sort information, and generate reports. Forms can be easily designed so that data can be entered and validated for accuracy. These forms, such as weekly time cards or customer surveys, can be delivered through e-mail, and the responses automatically added into tables in the database. The collected data can be queried to create reports that describe specific conditions, such as the addresses of all employees who worked overtime in the past week.

As the amount of data grows, how is it managed? Data are stored in **database management systems (DBMSs)**. DBMSs are collections of tables of data that organize the data and allow simple analysis and reporting. As companies begin to store vast amounts of data in database systems separate from their production databases, **data warehouses** are created. These can hold petabytes of transaction data. (A single petabyte can hold over 13 years' worth of HD television video.[19]) Sometimes, subsets are created to isolate one product or one department. These smaller data sets are called **data marts**. The process of exploring and analyzing the data mart to uncover data relationships and data patterns that will help a business is referred to as **data mining**. Data mining can be used in many ways. For example, suppose a supermarket uses data mining to help decide whether to restock a product that isn't selling well. If data mining reveals that the few people who typically buy the product are among the supermarket's most profitable customers, it will most likely be worth keeping the product on the shelves to retain their business. Although data mining has not yet lived up to its full potential, new advances in hardware and software are making it a larger part of business decision making.

What kinds of tools analyze data to help an organization? Businesses can easily collect and store large amounts of data, but turning them into useful information, "business intelligence," is a challenging task. Several software systems help in this regard.

4 How do businesses transform data into useful business intelligence?

Many businesses use software programs to organize and analyze the data they collect.

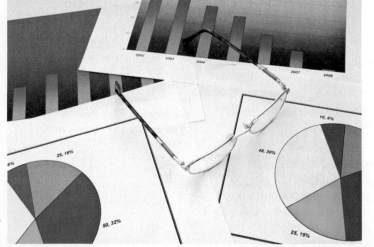

Elnur/Fotolia

- A **decision support system (DSS)** is a software system that enables companies to analyze collected data so they can predict the impact of business decisions. A DSS can also retrieve data from external sources and display results tied to business decision making.

- An **executive information system (EIS)** is a software system that is specially designed for the needs of management. This system can consolidate and summarize the transactions within an organization by using both internal and external sources. The terms *DSS* and *EIS* are sometimes used interchangeably, but usually an EIS has a more graphical interface compared to a DSS, which often uses spreadsheets and can show only one department or product at a time.

- An **online analysis package (OLAP)** is a software application that enables very quick analysis of combinations of different business factors. OLAPs are designed to help analysts combine multiple pieces of information into a clear picture of the state of the business. These software applications are used for tasks such as reporting sales figures and budgeting and forecasting. OLAP products in the marketplace include MS Analysis Studio, the open-source product Openi (pronounced "open eye"), and Jedox Palo software.

What kinds of questions can business intelligence software answer? Business intelligence software can assist managers in reporting, planning, and forecasting workforce performance. Business intelligence software allows managers to analyze the financial states of the company, customer satisfaction, sales analysis, and supply chain status. Managers can quickly display the answers to several questions:[20]

- Who are my top ten revenue-generating customers?
- What factors (e.g., regions, products, or customers) are the greatest contributors to bad debt?
- Which vendors have unpaid invoices, and how much money do these vendors owe?
- How many days' worth of inventory is in each warehouse?
- Which plants have completed the highest number of work orders on time?

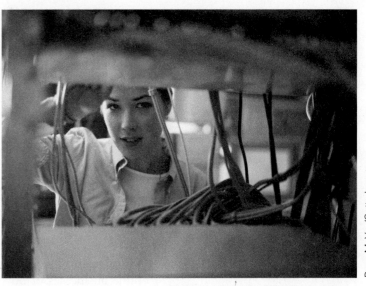

Ryan McVay/Getty Images

The IT department is responsible for everything including hardware, software, and networking.

Even small businesses, like the hardware store where Ian McGregor works, need someone with IT experience to bring their businesses into the modern age. Ian's boss recognized that the success of his business was dependent on upgrading the technology used at his store, but he wasn't sure where to begin. Ian acted in the role of an information officer and began by collecting data on the demographics and purchasing habits of their customer base. By analyzing those data with a suite of business intelligence software, he had information to develop a new marketing campaign. He developed a social media strategy, giving the company a Facebook and a Twitter presence, tying that to the online store at the company website and marketing materials sent out via e-mail. Ian showed his boss that he would better be able to stay in touch with his customers by using this technology. As the store's business improves, and they begin to realize benefits and profits from these initial changes, Ian hopes to have the opportunity to make additional IT changes. ■

Security pp. 295–299

Kevin Fossbenner had grown up biking in BMX races and always was focused on having a bicycle manufacturing company. His dream came true—Flatland Frames produces both custom frames and full custom design race bicycles. In any normal day, the company receives thousands of e-mails, many of them spam. One day an employee received a "phishing" e-mail that looked like it came from

alexskopje/Shutterstock

the IT department. New passwords were being assigned, it explained, and asked the employee to confirm the "administrator password." She hesitated—something just didn't seem right. But she had so much other work to get done. . . . ■

Security issues are important for our personal lives but are even more vital for businesses. It is critical for businesses to be aware of the potential damage from hackers, from data breaches, and even from bad publicity if adware or spyware is unintentionally delivered to a customer over a website. Employers need to protect their business but balance that with their own employees' need for privacy. In this section we'll examine these issues in more detail.

Threats to Online Business

What special security threats do online businesses face? Although online businesses or other businesses with an online component have the most potential for growth and expansion, they are also the most vulnerable to threats, such as security breaches and viruses. If you've ever clicked on a banner ad or downloaded a program, you've run the risk of allowing adware or spyware onto your computer. **Adware** is any software application that displays banner ads or pop-up ads while a program is running. At best, this is annoying. At worst, it installs **spyware**, which tracks your personal information and passes it on to a third party without your knowledge.[21]

Spyware operates in the backchannel of an Internet connection, collecting data and relaying that data to interested parties for fraud or identity theft.[22] This can cripple businesses, as hackers can use spyware to steal money, erase valuable information, or even crash an entire company's system. The most insidious spyware can capture keystrokes, thereby stealing passwords and other confidential information, which can grant hackers unlimited access to company networks.[23]

Can a business protect its online identity? Any business that processes transactions online is at risk of having its customers' credit card information stolen by hackers. Spyware is not the only method that hackers use to obtain private information. **Phishing** is a common way to trick online users into sending their personal information, like credit card numbers, straight to hackers.[24]

Suppose you have an account with Bank of America and you receive an e-mail from them informing you that your online banking account is about to expire. This e-mail requests that you fill out a secure form with your personal information so Bank of America can reactivate your account. The e-mail has the Bank of America logo and background, and it includes a link to the secure form to be filled out. You click on the link, which takes you to an online form on the Bank of America website. After completing the form, which asks for your name, address, password, credit card number, and credit card expiration date, you click the Submit button and send all of that information to Bank of America.

Surprise! You've just been phished. That e-mail was not from Bank of America but from hackers who had broken into the Bank of America network and copied its logo and e-mail design. The link you clicked took you to a fake website that was designed to look like an authentic registration form. You just sent your banking information to phishers, who can now use your credit card to make fraudulent purchases in your name. This identity theft can destroy your credit rating. It also hurts Bank of America because the bank will have to track and cancel any illegal transactions

5 What security challenges arise with the increase of technology?

Phishing uses e-mail impersonating an online business you normally use to try to trick you into entering personal and financial information.

Brian Jackson/Fotolia

and issue you a new credit card account. If you find yourself in this situation, be sure to report it to the company's fraud or abuse center.

Banks are not the only businesses that suffer from phishing. Online retailers, such as eBay, or payment services, such as PayPal, have been the victims of spyware and phishing.[25] This can cost them dearly because customers may no longer trust these websites after they have been scammed. Businesses that have been hacked often spend thousands of dollars on reclaiming lost information and updating their antivirus programs and security systems to prevent future break-ins. Although these security breaches remind us of the risks of online transactions, they also force online businesses to remain current in their network protection and take extra precautions to protect consumers.

What risks does a breach of security pose for management? With so much of the value of a modern business stored in electronic material—whether as documents, software programs, or e-mail files—a company can be vulnerable to hackers. **Hackers** are individuals who gain unauthorized entry into a computer system. Their goal may be to disrupt the operation of the system or gain access to protected data. For example, agents raided a set of homes in Miami-Dade County and retrieved a dozen computers and $422,000 cash. On those computer hard drives they found evidence of a hacking ring that had stolen more than 170 million credit card numbers worth hundreds of millions of dollars. The hackers had committed online thefts from a wide range of stores, such as 7-Eleven, Dave & Buster's, and T.J. Maxx.[26]

One of the largest security breaches ever occurred in 2011 when the Sony PlayStation Network was illegally hacked. The online gaming service had over 77 million members, all of whom had personal information and credit card numbers exposed to an unknown hacker. The network was down for 44 days while company technologists worked to revamp the system to provide better protection, at a cost of about $170 million.[27] Customers were angry at Sony's handling of the break-in—it took over a week for the company to acknowledge that the system had been compromised. Sony ultimately responded with a "Welcome Back" campaign, giving customers a range of free games, free rentals, and free upgrades. It was not enough to stop a series of class action lawsuits over its failure to protect customer information. The PlayStation Network is a free service with no monthly fee required, but this incident showed that companies still must be vigilant in maintaining state-of-the-art security or risk a backlash in the marketplace.

Sometimes it is not an attack from the outside that jeopardizes business stability. The business can also be vulnerable if technology is not implemented reliably. Even a short blackout of vital services, such as internal e-mail or customer access to the corporate website, can damage a company's reputation and value. For example, recently, the Hawaiian airline Go! attempted to sell 1,000 tickets for $1. The promotion caused so many people to access the company's website that it crashed, and customers could not get tickets. The company was forced to double the number of $1 tickets it was offering to assuage upset customers.[28] One survey of managers in the United Kingdom found that 70 percent said IT failure was the top threat to their organizations, whereas only 2 percent cited a concern over terrorism disrupting their business.[29]

Can technology also be used to support ethical conduct? Part of the Sarbanes-Oxley Act of 2002 mandates that all public companies have procedures for handling the concerns of whistle-blowers—persons who report on illicit activities. Several corporations now use their intranet to allow whistle-blowers to make anonymous reports. Organizations such as the Occupational Safety and Health Administration (OSHA) and the American Civil Liberties Union (ACLU)

Actor Ashton Kutcher had his Twitter account hacked in early 2012. His page has nearly 12 million followers.

Glenn Weiner/ZUMA Press/Newscom

Biz CHAT

How a Simple Mistake Can Lead to a Major Data Breach

The U.S. government experienced one of the largest data breaches to date. This occurrence wasn't attributed to savvy hackers though. Rather, an employee for the Department of Veterans Affairs (VA) went against policy and took a laptop home, and it was stolen during a burglary. The laptop contained the names and Social Security numbers of over 26 million veterans. The VA laptop was eventually recovered. Fortunately for the VA and the vets involved, sensitive information on the computer had not been accessed.

Another kind of data breach happened to Apple as they were developing the next generation of iPhone, the iPhone 4. One of their engineers was at a local brew house for his birthday and left the prototype device on his bar stool. The person who found the phone realized what it was and the phone eventually ended up being featured on the Gizmodo website, months before its official release. Threats of legal action came from a number of directions, but any excitement Apple wanted to build before announcing the phone's new features was already compromised.

also have designed their websites to allow people to file reports easily and safely, shielding them from possible retaliation.

This type of reporting system is common in hospitals and medical centers. Staff members can report "near misses"—mistakes that could have occurred but were caught and corrected—through the organization's intranet. This allows an organization to learn from possible mistakes but safeguards the employee from embarrassment or disciplinary action. Without the benefit of anonymity, many mistakes and unethical actions might go undetected.

Other websites are more controversial in how they support similar activities. The site WikiLeaks describes itself as "a multi-jurisdictional public service designed to protect whistleblowers, journalists and activists who have sensitive materials to communicate to the public."[30] But it has sparked several controversies because it has made public confidential documents from the U.S. military, the Central Intelligence Agency (CIA), the U.S. Embassy, and a variety of private corporate reports and e-mails. For example, WikiLeaks made public a video of a 2007 U.S. Army helicopter strike in Iraq against a group that included children and two Reuter's journalists.[31]

Privacy

How has technology impacted employees? Some uses of technology in the workplace have brought about difficult changes. The increasing volume of

OFF THE MARK

Spying Scandal at HP

A serious case of spying occurred at Hewlett-Packard when HP crossed the ethical lines of employee privacy in an attempt to discover the source of an anonymous article that leaked private company information. Chairwoman Patricia Dunn hired private investigators and allegedly authorized them to use illegal tactics to uncover the source of the leak. The private investigators used pretexting, or lying about one's identity, to gain access to phone records, tracer e-mails containing spyware, and the surveillance of journalists. Placing physical spies in a newsroom was even discussed.

Dunn resigned from HP over the scandal, as did board member George Keyworth, who was discovered to be behind the information leak. The scandal ended up costing the company several board members, millions of dollars, and bad press.

Employee privacy concerns are a big issue today, as technology makes it easier to spy on employees. Although HP engaged in illegal methods of observation, companies can legally screen the e-mail and Internet histories of employees, raising ethical concerns about the right of companies to do so.

e-mail can contribute to a breakdown in communication as fewer personal exchanges take place. Communication experts agree that in face-to-face discussions, up to 93 percent of the meaning of the messages exchanged is communicated in nonverbal ways—through gestures, glances, body position, and facial expression.[32] As more office discussions take place via e-mail, the chance of misunderstandings and errors continues to rise.

The boundary between work and home has also blurred because of the increase of technology. Once a worker has access to office files from home, and the office has access to employees via smartphones or live videoconferencing, the workday can extend dramatically.

pn_photo/Shutterstock

Employee monitoring can feel like an invasion of privacy in the workplace.

How does technology affect employee privacy? At home, U.S. citizens are guaranteed specific levels of privacy and freedoms. In the workplace, however, the expectation of privacy is quite different. **Electronic monitoring** is commonly used to track employees' keystrokes and e-mails, examine their Internet browsing histories, and even monitor their cell phone and instant messaging usage.[33] Camera surveillance can be conducted with recording devices so small that employees do not realize they are being recorded. Used appropriately, these technical tools can help a company eliminate a drain of business resources for personal use. But to some employees, the work environment then begins to feel so monitored that they no longer produce their best work. In a study conducted at Bell Canada, a telecommunications company, researchers found that 50 percent of employees in the customer service department reported an increase in stress and anxiety when their calls were being monitored. Employee stress can lead to job dissatisfaction and can prompt health problems.[34] Finding the balance between an appropriate level of monitoring and an optimal work environment is a continuous challenge.

Flatland Frames escaped disaster this time. The employee realized this was an unusual request for sensitive protected data and called the IT manager on the phone before responding to the e-mail request. But phishing schemes and other threats to Flatland's data will continue, and the company will need to stay vigilant in being aware of the latest types of attacks and how to defend against them. ■

Impact of Social Media and Mobile Technology pp. 299–303

The rule of thumb Philippe Durand started out with when he opened his restaurant was that no advertising was bad advertising. Even bad word of mouth would only make people curious, and you'd win them over once they tried the restaurant. But in the new age of blogging and Facebook, what is said about you in

maigi/Shutterstock

Anatolii Babii/Alamy

Social media sites are important to our personal lives but also increasingly to the functioning of good business organizations.

cyberspace can have a real negative impact. For a long time, Philippe's restaurant was the only place to get French American cuisine, but a new competitor just opened across town. Philippe decided to go on the offensive and began posting little quips about his competitor on his restaurant's Facebook page. The reaction was quick—people hated the fact that Philippe was being negative and started complaining about his postings, and then about his restaurant's service and food. How did this all go wrong so fast? And how was Philippe going to make things right? ∎

New technologies emerge every day, and they are changing the face of business in unexpected ways. The advent of social networking has created new employment opportunities, new marketing opportunities, and new dangers in marketing a brand. The rise of mobile devices and the fast increase of their computing power have created new forces in the marketplace. Understanding how mobile technology can be used to enhance the operations of business and anticipating how it will be used by consumers will make or break someone's future as a businessperson.

Social Networking

(6) How have new advances in social networking and mobile technologies impacted business?

How is social networking changing businesses? Social media is a technology that is changing the face of business. Social media decisions are spread throughout an organization. In finance, social networks are being used to generate funding. In addition, organizations now have to decide how they will pay for their social media campaigns. Human resources use social media in recruiting, and the management team often uses social networks to communicate throughout the organization. Let's take a closer look at the specific impact this technology has had on twenty-first-century business.

Are social media apps used within businesses? Enterprise social networking refers to the application of products like Facebook in a corporate setting. In fact, enterprise versions of products like Facebook, Twitter, and workplace wikis are already beginning to appear in the office. Imagine using the collaborative power of Facebook and blogs within a company to increase collaboration and unify the entire business. It is hoped that such tools will speed up decision making and ensure a smoother customer experience.

The Dell Social Media Listening Command Center monitors over 22,000 posts every day, looking to catch the mood of the day on Dell products and services.

How are companies using social media to monitor their business? Keeping watch on the messages and information being spread about their products in cyberspace is critical. **Social media monitoring** has become an important corporate function. There are many products now being sold, like Brandwatch and UberView, which collect social media mentions of a specific product or company and then analyze and report on patterns and trends.

Companies are meeting this need with large-scale responses. The computer manufacturer Dell is a good example. In 2005 the blogosphere was full of furor over poor performance and service from Dell. "Dell

Business Wire/Handout/Getty Images

Hell" continued as it took Dell over a year to understand the significance of having such bad publicity.[35] Today the company has more than 40 Facebook profiles worldwide, and has thousands of staff representing the company on Twitter, where it boasts over 1.6 million followers.[36] @DellOutlet generates over $15 million of sales itself. Dell has entered the Chinese market by becoming a popular brand in the country's top social networking site Ren Ren. Its IdeaStorm website allows customers to take part in product development, posting ideas, promoting others' ideas, and then seeing how the company puts the idea into action. In 2010 Dell opened the Social Media Listening Command Center, where employees monitor over 22,000 posts daily. The average daily number of mentions of Dell on just Twitter is more than the combined circulation of the top 12 daily newspapers[37] in the United States.

What new jobs have been created with the rise of social media?

Matching this new need, many businesses have created a position identified as social media manager or social media marketing specialist. This position is responsible for monitoring and engaging in social media networks to generate positive buzz, to promote products, and to identify potential problem areas. The number of social media-related jobs on Monster.com surged 75 percent in 2011.[38]

The social media manager would watch over Facebook groups who have "liked" a product and make sure they get special updates, offers, and the latest news on promotions and events. With over 800 million users on Facebook and another 200 million on Twitter, it is an important job.

Can social media provide information that is directly useful to a business?

It is important to use social media for marketing, but using it as an avenue for more specific business decision making is happening as well. Using crowdsourcing to control inventory and make purchasing decisions is happening more and more. The clothing franchise ModCloth introduced a "Be the Buyer" program to encourage customers to vote online on clothing samples. ModCloth owner Susan Gregg Koger is faced with tough buying decisions since many manufacturers require a large minimum order. Now the company uses the Web to go to its customers to help with these decisions. By evaluating their feedback and response to a particular item, Koger knows she can risk committing to the larger scale purchase.

Crowdsourcing is directly helping businesses manage inventory.

How can social media help with technical support services?

Companies that are well situated with a strong social media presence can use that to head off potential technical problems that might turn into public disaster. The company iRobot, manufacturer of home robots like

http://www.inc.com/magazine/20100201/using-crowdsourcing-to-control-inventory.html and company is mod cloth.

Tasteless Tweet

Responsible use of social media and sensitivity to your customer base is key in avoiding an off-the-mark backlash. Singer Amy Winehouse was a recording artist in the style of jazz and R&B and had recently released a duet song with Tony Bennett when she died from alcohol poisoning in 2011. After her death, Microsoft sent out a tweet encouraging fans to remember the singer by buying her last album from Zune, the company's digital marketplace. Thousands of Twitter users responded with tweets of their own that included, "utterly tasteless," "vile-leaches—seriously?" and "Microsoft—failing at social media."[39]

OFF THE MARK

the Roomba vacuum cleaner, realized the importance of this when one customer posted to YouTube a video account of the trouble he was having and very quickly racked up 60,000 views. Now iRobot uses software to match social media comments with specific customer records and respond quickly to problems.

How is social media helping people start and fund new businesses?

For several years the microlending movement, begun by Muhammad Yunus, has been used to connect many people in need of funding for very small businesses with those who can loan small amounts. The Grameen Bank became a microcredit lending institution, establishing many very small, very-low-interest-rate loans to the poor of underdeveloped countries. The website Kiva combined this idea with the interconnectivity of the Internet to allow investors to make a loan as small as $25 to borrowers worldwide.

Now social networking is becoming a mechanism for funding start-ups in a variety of business arenas in a similar manner. **Crowdsourced funding** (crowd funding) allows a great number of people who believe in a company or a product to contribute a small amount to help the company get started. In most cases the company gives them something back in return—a free copy of the product or a signed card from the founder. Some of the projects crowd-funded through Kickstarter include five films that premiered at the Sundance Film Festival, an experiment with the idea of a successful restaurant (WhatHappensWhen), and the smart watch named Pebble, which raised over $10,000,000 of funding. ProFounder gives the start-up business owner not just the chance to crowdfund, but also provides tools and resources for handling legal issues, creating pitch documents, marketing, and financial tools. Other sites like RocketHub, IndieGoGo, and Funding4Learning are continuing the crowdfunding trend.

Nobel Prize award winner Mohammad Yunus used micro-lending to improve the lives of the rural poor. Web 2.0 technologies now allow even more people to start and grow their businesses through crowdsourced funding.

LLUIS GENE/AFP/Getty Images/Newscom

Mobile Devices

Why do businesses need mobile devices? Most business organizations today find it critical to have a mobile component both to support their employees and to attract and serve customers. The sales staff requires constant access to e-mail, calendar and contacts, and Internet resources. Being able to make video phone calls, see data mapped to their current location, and create and send photos and videos all can serve the larger mission of the company if implemented well. Customers demand a way to find the closest outlet and to place orders from their smartphone.

Jackson Kayak is a small business that designs, manufactures, and sells kayaks in Tennessee. It works to build the kayaking community through its own social network on its website, a Facebook page, and its own mobile app. The company uses mobile analytics products that allow representatives to quickly display and analyze site traffic when working with dealers. The analysis can point to specific customer behaviors that support stocking certain items, for example. The company developed its own mobile app for customers, which allows users to browse the latest kayak industry news, upload photos and status info and, of course, shop Jackson Kayaks.

How does a business select which mobile devices it needs to understand? There are two kinds of business considerations around mobile devices—what kind employees should use within the company and what kind of devices customers are using. Internally, the CIO must take into account a number of considerations when deciding which mobile devices belong in the organization. How easily will the devices scale out to the full company, if a smaller trial is successful? How do they integrate with existing mail systems? IT also needs to think about what kind of encryption and data protection is available and whether the right applications exist or can be developed in-house.

Externally, a company would ideally provide mobile solutions for the various platforms customers may have, whether an iPhone, an Android device, or a non-smartphone. The expense of developing and maintaining multiple applications, though, means that a business must thoroughly understand its own client base before deciding which mobile products to deploy.

What kinds of mobile apps are useful for business? There are over 500,000 apps available for the iPhone, and other smartphone devices have impressive stores of content as well. For business, many useful apps focus on communications, task management, and managing data. For example, phone applications can allow users to conduct a WebEx conference, integrating a slideshow, file transfer, and multiple voice and audio feeds. Products like Omnifocus organize a schedule beyond a simple calendar format, displaying tasks that require resources that are nearby geographically, or listing which tasks can be run concurrently and which are on hold for input from someone else. Mobile apps for the sales force organize new leads and customer requests, help manage expense reports, or handle invoicing right from the phone.

The number of apps available for mobile devices continues to skyrocket.

How has cloud computing helped grow the mobile device market? Cloud computing refers to the sharing of information, resources, and software over the Internet and is another new trend in business technology. Using cloud computing, online backup systems can work through a "cloud" so that files are automatically backed up and made available instantly to a whole set of users. For those accessing and changing data through mobile devices, this instant synchronization between the data manipulated when on the road and the data seen from their work or home computer makes users very productive. With Apple's iCloud service, for example, a photograph taken on someone's iPhone is instantly available on his or her iPad as well as on his or her home PC. As more services beyond just storage begin to take advantage of cloud computing, businesses will become more agile and efficient.

As you read at the beginning of this section, Philippe Durand tried to become part of the social media revolution. His first foray into this new age of marketing didn't work out the way he'd hoped, but he learned from that. Specifically, he learned that discrediting the competition not only didn't hurt the competition, but also it hurt his own business. Instead, he began to study more closely who was using his Facebook page and who was responding to the QR codes he used in his new ad campaign. He found that his restaurant was attracting a specific demographic of affluent, well-traveled people. He decided to try to appeal to their sense of interest in new cuisines and new experiences. His Facebook page began to highlight the ingredients he used and the stories behind his suppliers. He offered a new way for customers to pay at the end of their meal, using a custom mobile app that kept track of reward points for them. Incorporating new technology needs to be done at the right time and in the right way to bring benefits. ■

iQoncept/Fotolia

C H A P T E R   10
SUMMARY

Go to **mybizlab.com** to complete the problems marked with this icon ⭐.

1. What does the online environment offer to help marketing businesses? (pp. 287–290)

- Online shopping is still growing significantly. **Online advertising** (p. 288) and mass marketing through e-mail campaigns are critical.
- **Pay-per-click advertising** (p. 288) can actually be a source of revenue as well as advertising. Mobile devices now feature in-app direct advertising options. Possible negative impacts of online advertising include click fraud and increasing the annoyance factor of visitors at your website.
- **Viral marketing** (p. 289) can be unpredictable, but very effective if social network traffic and environmental marketing messages work well.

2. What are the types of business transactions supported by online commerce? (pp. 290–292)

- There are three common types of transactions—business to business (B2B), business to consumer (B2C), and consumer to consumer (C2C):
  - **B2B** (p. 290) sites support communication between businesses through encouraging purchases, the exchange of information, and brokering services.
  - **B2C** (p. 291) sites work with customers directly and need to be able to handle online distribution, advertising and networking needs.
  - **C2C** (p. 291) sites use a model of connecting customers to each other directly for sales, as seen in eBay, and in file sharing, as seen in peer-to-peer networking sites.

3. What are the functions of a company's chief information officer (CIO) and information technology (IT) department? (pp. 294–295)

- A company's **chief information officer (CIO)** (p. 294) is the executive in charge of information processing, including systems design and development and data center operations. He or she is also responsible for the following:
  - Updating or replacing computer systems and software a company uses
  - Managing a budget that balances the benefits of technology against the ever-rising costs of having the latest systems
  - Setting policy for privacy and security concerns
  - Creating business and e-business opportunities
  - Designing systems and developing required software programs
- The IT department consists of a number of professionals responsible for everything from hardware components to software programs to networking strategies. The IT department also has the following tasks:
  - Maintaining security both in response to computer virus attacks and emergency recovery from power outages and system failures
  - Keeping all of an organization's computers, printers, scanners, and other equipment operational and current
  - Designing networks used within a company and databases where information is stored
  - Selecting or creating software programs used by the business and providing software training to employees
  - Maintaining and managing the use of mobile computing throughout a company
  - Implementing remote access to computing resources, such as employees' access to work files or e-mail when they are working from home

4. How do businesses transform data into useful business intelligence? (pp. 296–297)

- **Information technology (IT)** (p. 294) is the design and implementation of computer-based information systems.
- **Information systems (ISs)** (p. 295) focus on applying IT to the solution of business and economic problems. IS professionals bridge the gap between purely technical knowledge and how it will impact business.
- Raw **data** (p. 295) must be organized and arranged into useful **information** (p. 295). IS professionals and other decision makers can then use this information to determine which IT solutions to implement.

5. What security challenges arise with the increase of technology (pp. 298–299)

- **Adware** (p. 298) and **spyware** (p. 298) can cause annoyance for online customers or even contribute to theft of their identity information and credit card data.
- **Phishing** (p. 298) is an illicit means of obtaining secure private information by imitating a communication from a legitimate site.
- Businesses of all sizes must protect against data breaches from **hackers** (p. 299). These disrupt business operations and can open the door to expensive legal action against the company if customer data are compromised.
- One of the benefits of technology is that it can support ethical conduct within the workplace. Several federal organizations have websites that allow people

with complaints or allegations of misconduct to file reports easily and safely, shielding them from possible retaliation.

6 How have new advances in social networking and mobile technologies impacted business? (pp. 302–305)

- Businesses need to know what is being said about them in cyberspace, so many use **social media monitoring** (p. 302). Software products keep an eye on social media mentions and watch for trends.

- New positions like social media manager exist now to help companies in creating effective marketing campaigns.

- Crowdsourcing is used to involve customers more closely in business decisions like purchasing.

- **Crowdsourced funding** (p. 304) is used to help start and grow small business ventures by appealing directly to a mass audience for the product or service.

- The increase in the number of mobile devices and the advent of **cloud computing** (p. 305) are supporting a large increase in the growth of mobile technology. Consumers can use mobile devices to make online purchases, to compare item, and even to check themselves out of a physical store.

Key Terms

adware (p. 298)
business intelligence software (p. 297)
business to business (B2B) (p. 290)
business to consumer (B2C) (p. 291)
chief information officer (CIO) (p. 294)
cloud computing (p. 305)
consumer to consumer (C2C) (p. 291)
contextual advertising (p. 288)
crowdsourced funding (p. 304)
data (p. 295)

database management system (DBMS) (p. 296)
data mart (p. 296)
data mining (p. 296)
data warehouse (p. 296)
decision support system (DSS) (p. 296)
electronic monitoring (p. 301)
enterprise social networking (p. 302)
executive information system (EIS) (p. 296)
hacker (p. 299)
information (p. 295)

information system (IS) (p. 295)
information technology (IT) (p. 294)
management information system (MIS) (p. 295)
online advertising (p. 288)
online analysis package (OLAP) (p. 296)
pay-per-click (PPC) advertising (p. 288)
phishing (p. 298)
social media monitoring (p. 302)
spyware (p. 298)
viral marketing (p. 289)

Self-Test

Multiple Choice You can find the answers on the last page of this book.

1. **IT is**
   a. internship technology opportunities.
   b. companywide investigations of office conduct.
   c. building a networking plan for the flow and use of information.
   d. the design and implementation of computer-based systems.

2. **MIS is different from IT because**
   a. MIS focuses on applying IT to solve business problems.
   b. MIS is the branch of IT focused on Internet usage.
   c. IT focuses on hardware, and MIS focuses on software.
   d. MIS is applied, and IT is theoretical.

3. **DSSs are used most often by**
   a. managers who make decisions based on current data.

   b. employees who decide how to solve technical problems.
   c. clerical staff that organize and format documents and reports.
   d. trainers who teach staff and employees new software products.

4. **Data warehousing is**
   a. the storing of terabytes of transaction data.
   b. not used when DBMSs are in place.
   c. is not used now because data marts have replaced it.
   d. is the management of large quantities of paper records.

5. **OLAP**
   a. is illegal in the United States.
   b. allows a company to monitor employees' usage of its technology resources.

Self-Test (continued)

c. is a spreadsheet that supports a number of financial functions.

d. helps analysts compile multiple pieces of information into one clear picture.

6. **Hackers can infiltrate systems**

a. only if they use cookie files to store information.

b. if the systems are isolated as a single corporate extranet.

c. All of the above

d. None of the above

7. **Social media monitoring is best described as**

a. planning events where the sales force mingles with potential clients.

b. regulating the use of e-mail and messaging in the workplace.

c. staying aware of the messages posted about your products in cyberspace.

d. eavesdropping on personal communications.

8. **Phishing can be used to**

a. minimize the taxes owed to the federal government.

b. steal identity information from unsuspecting clients.

c. record the keystrokes typed in when someone is logging into a password-protected site.

d. help save storage space on mobile devices.

9. **Business-to-business transactions include**

a. brokering sites.

b. social networking sites.

c. specialized industry portals.

d. Both a and c

10. **Social media technologies have impacted**

a. marketing campaigns.

b. the time between updates to new hardware systems.

c. the number of required reports filed with tax authorities.

d. All of the above

True/False   You can find the answers on the last page of this book.

1. **The CIO is the director of IT and reports to the CFO.**
   ☐ True or ☑ False

2. **Business intelligence software supports decision making by presenting visual, interactive views of the state of a business.**
   ☐ True or ☑ False

3. **Viral marketing can be prevented by using the proper spyware.**
   ☐ True or ☐ False

4. **Information is data that have been arranged in a way to make the data more useful.**
   ☑ True or ☐ False

5. **Crowdsourced funding is a use of social networking to build capital for a new venture.**
   ☐ True or ☐ False

Critical Thinking Questions

1. There have been several major data breaches in the last few years. How do you see these lapses in corporate security affecting consumers? Does it make you less likely to purchase from certain companies or to purchase certain products? Has it changed how you protect your identity information?

2. What responsibilities accompany the new volume of information we can collect through modern information technologies? If airlines can cross-reference travel data with bank records and identify suspicious patterns, do they have a responsibility to alert authorities? Or should they be forbidden from looking for

patterns as "profiling" (the extrapolation of certain psychological and physical characteristics)? What if a college IT department finds a threatening message that has been sent from a student e-mail account? What if it is not "threatening" but in very bad taste? Where is the boundary of the college's responsibility?

3. Think about how a CIO can determine whether a business will benefit enough from a specific hardware/software upgrade to justify its purchase. What information would he or she need? How might past experience benefit the decision that needs to be made today?

Team Time

THE WINDS OF CHANGE

Assemble into groups of three. Each member of the group should select one of the following areas:

a. Social impact of business technology

b. Ethical impact of business technology

c. Global impact of business technology

Process

Step 1. As a group, determine what innovation in business technology will have the most impact over the next year, five years, and ten years. After the group has selected a specific innovation, each group member should prepare a short presentation on why that particular technology change will be significant in his or her area.

Step 2. Evaluate the innovation by asking the following:

- How many businesses will be impacted?
- How many aspects of business activity will be impacted?
- How many consumers and/or vendors will be impacted?
- Will the innovation lead to additional changes in the business in the future?

Step 3. Optional: As a class, compare the group results. Determine which innovation has the most likelihood of coming to fruition. How will it change your career and the world you will be part of in the future?

Ethics and Corporate Social Responsibility

COMPUTER HACKING: A HIGH PRICE TO PAY

Read the following case study. Then, as a class, discuss the questions that follow.

One night, 21-year-olds Brian Salcedo and Adam Botbyl were driving around in Adam's car with a couple of antennas hanging out the window and a laptop powered up looking for open wireless networks they could access. As they drove past the Lowe's home improvement store, they found one. Lowe's had set up its wireless network so that scanners and other devices could connect to its network without cabling. Six months later the pair decided to place a modified program onto Lowe's computer system. Now, when credit card transactions were processed, a copy of the number would be sent to a special file they could use later. The FBI investigated and arrested them before they ever saw a single credit card number. They pleaded guilty and worked with Lowe's to boost its security. Even so, Brian Salcedo was sentenced to nine years in prison, one of the longest sentences in U.S. history for computer hacking, and Adam Botbyl was sentenced to 26 months.

Questions for Discussion

1. Who holds responsibility for Lowe's customers?
2. How can consumers know that their purchases are safe?
3. Were the sentences given to the pair appropriate? Why or why not?

Web Exercises

1. **WikiLeaks**
Visit the WikiLeaks website and select two of the most current leaks posted. Evaluate the value of these pieces of information being made public. Does it violate the privacy rights of the individuals involved? Does it make available the means to expose a criminal act? Would you argue that the benefits outweigh the violation of confidentiality, or not?

2. **To Censor or Not to Censor**
In 2010, Google reversed its previous position and stopped enforcing censorship of its search engine results to Chinese users. Instead Google began to redirect users to an uncensored search engine based in Hong Kong. What led to the change in Google's corporate position? What response did Google receive from the Chinese government? Contrast this to the deal Microsoft signed with Baidu, the biggest search engine in China.

3. **Online Business Is Global Business**
Visit the BMW website. This international portal redirects customers to one of many hundreds of country-specific sites. Select three countries and investigate the website presented. What elements are kept the same? How does BMW maintain a unified international marketing message? Which components are different? How does your Web browser handle the differences in character sets for different languages?

4. **Data Breach!**
Visit the homepage of Breachalerts (breachalerts.trustedid .com/) and review the recent data breach reports posted there. Select one of these reports and note relevant information about the breaches, such as the source(s) of data loss, the date(s) of the occurrence, the sizes of losses, and the individuals or geographic area(s) affected. How did the losses occur? How might they have been prevented?

5. **Marketing Online**
Find a successful viral marketing campaign and analyze how it was developed. One sample is the video series named "The Entrance" from Heineken. It was the centerpiece for the first national ad campaign Heineken had run in five years. The core television ad was preceded by a series of 11 Facebook videos that gave background on each character. How does viral marketing support traditional marketing efforts?

MyBizLab

Go to **mybizlab.com** for Auto-graded writing questions as well as the following Assisted-graded writing questions:

10-1. There is much concern over the "Digital Divide," the gap in IT resources among industrialized countries and developing countries. The explosive growth of smartphones may be a path that allows developing countries to move quickly into the digital age. What advantages would there be to supporting the growth of smartphone usage over computer usage in a developing country? What infrastructure would be required to take the most advantage? What other devices might be useful to minimize the Digital Divide?

10-2. What kinds of business functions could benefit from input from consumers? How would you collect the best quality data for that purpose?

10-3. MyBizLab Only – comprehensive writing assignment for this chapter.

Production, Operations, and the Supply Chain

The Production of Goods and Services

Steve Schmidt loves his job making custom bicycles. His business partner, Ralph Brinsdorfer, takes pride in providing the best customer service by ensuring that the bikes are delivered on time, offering financing, and providing friendly and efficient repair service. Their goal, like the goal of all businesses, is to deliver a quality good or service to their customers. What is involved in the production of goods and services? How important is production to the U.S. economy and also to world economies?

Operations Management

Arthur Riddle's furniture manufacturing company has had great success in northern California, and he's considering expanding operations to a new location. What factors does Arthur need to consider before choosing a new location? How should the facility be arranged, and how does he determine the best suppliers to use?

Supply Chain Management

Sylvia Ackerman loves the simple lines and clean design of IKEA products and can't wait to furnish her new apartment with IKEA merchandise. Moreover, she knows she'll be able to afford what she needs and can assemble the furniture on her own with minimal help from others. How does IKEA manage the process of producing inexpensive, high-quality goods for its stores around the world?

Production Management

Ted Hoyt and Austen DuPont run a fitness and nutritional consulting firm. For all their clients, especially those with specific food allergies or dietary requirements, they recommend the YouBar, a nutrition bar with customizable ingredients that cater to the tastes and nutritional needs of each of their clients. How does the YouBar provide for such product customization without making each bar by hand?

Operations Control

Jeanette Pae's daughter hurt herself when the tray of her high chair unexpectedly separated from the rest of the chair. The chair was later recalled, but Jeanette's confidence in the quality of the product was shaken. Similar situations happened to her friends and family members, who had experienced the recall of toys, medicine, computer batteries, and cars. What can companies do to ensure the production of a high-quality product?

MyBizLab®

⭐ **Improve Your Grade!**

Over 10 million students improved their results using the Pearson MyLabs.
Visit **mybizlab.com** for simulations, tutorials, and end-of-chapter problems.

The Production of Goods and Services pp. 313–315

Ljupco Smokovski/Fotolia

S teve Schmidt covers his face with the protective shield and begins to weld together the seat tube. This is the third and last bicycle he is putting together today. Steve loves building custom bicycles. Although many bicycles are mass produced, Steve builds bicycles by hand only. Steve has a growing list of customers, mostly professional cyclists and triathletes who appreciate the attention to quality each bike receives during the production process. Steve's reputation is growing outside the country; many of his new clients are based in Europe, Asia, and South America. Ralph Brinsdorfer, Steve's co-owner, provides impeccable service. Ralph ensures that each bike is delivered damage free and on time, and he runs a quick and reliable repair service. Both Steve and Ralph agree that it just couldn't be done any other way. ■

The goal of business is to deliver a good or a service to customers and to make a profit doing so. Every business uses a specific process to produce the good or service it delivers.

Production is the process of getting a good or a service to the customer; it is a series of related activities, with value being added as each activity or stage is completed. All businesses, whether they are strictly manufacturing, strictly service, or a combination of both, require some form of production process. How efficiently a company handles the production process can either help or hinder the overall success of the business and the competitiveness of the good or the service in the marketplace. In this chapter, you'll learn about the various decisions businesses make with regard to the production of goods and services.

The Importance of Production

Why is production a critical component of any business? Companies strive to make a profit by providing goods or services to consumers. To increase their profits and decrease production costs, businesses must find the most efficient production process possible. Increasing competition, global manufacturing pressures, changing customer needs, increasing prices on resources and labor, and a sagging economy are just some of the issues that require companies to scrutinize the efficiencies of their production process. To remain competitive, companies must be cost-effective, efficient, innovative, and flexible. Managing each component of the production process from beginning to end is critical if a company wants to remain profitable and competitive.

1 **How is manufacturing and production important to the U.S. economy and to global economies?**

■ FIGURE 11.1

Manufacturing plays a significant role in the U.S. economy.[2]

Source: "National Data." U.S. Bureau of Economic Analysis (BEA). Web. 09 June 2012. http://bea.gov

How important is manufacturing in the United States? Manufacturing, although it has been hit hard in the past decade by significant increases in imported goods and related job losses, remains a fundamental component of the U.S. economy (see **■ FIGURE 11.1**).[1] Manufacturing generates other service-based economic activities, such as transporting goods, generating software that is needed to assist with processes, and marketing and selling the goods. Moreover, because manufacturing uses a substantial amount of commodities and services as inputs, the manufacturing sector is actually responsible for a large share of total economic output. The manufacturing sector has played a dominant role in stimulating the economy.

Moving to a Service-Based Economy

How important are services to the U.S. economy? Despite the ongoing importance of the manufacturing sector, the United States, like most developed nations, has transitioned itself from an industrial-based, manufacturing economy to a service-based economy. Services make up nearly three-fourths of the U.S. GDP, and over 75 percent of jobs are in the service sector.[3] Service businesses, such as bookkeeping, child care, and even retail operations, are easier to start because they require less capital for real estate, factories, and equipment, which are usually required of businesses in the manufacturing sector.

We may think of service businesses as being the small mom and pop stores in our neighborhood, but not all service businesses are small. Ten of the 30 firms that currently comprise the Dow Jones Industrial Average (DJIA) are in the service sector. These include American Express (which in 1982 became the first services firm to be added), AT&T, Bank of America, Cisco, McDonald's, JP Morgan Chase, Travelers, Verizon Communications, Walmart, and Walt Disney.

Some companies are considered to be both manufacturing and service based. GE and IBM, also on the DJIA, are considered manufacturing companies, and both are also considered as the largest and most competitive service operations in the world. Additionally, transportation and utility companies are service-based industries and are very important to the U.S. economy.[4]

The Global Production Landscape

How does U.S. manufacturing compete globally? When seemingly all product labels indicate that the goods we use are made somewhere other than in the United States, it is hard to imagine that the United States is still a globally important manufacturing country. According to the authoritative *CIA World Factbook*, the United States has "the largest and most technologically advanced economy in the world."[5] Even in the midst of a global recession, the United States is the third largest exporter, having exported a $1.5 trillion worth of goods in 2011.[6] As illustrated in **■ FIGURE 11.2**, the United States has the highest GDP but is less reliant on industrial production, compared to its global counterparts. Nearly one-half of U.S. exports are goods, such as transistors, aircraft, motor vehicle parts, computers, and telecommunications equipment; industrial supplies such as organic chemicals account for another one-fourth of U.S. total exports; and consumer goods, such as automobiles and medicines, make up another 15 percent.[7]

How does manufacturing affect the global economy? As U.S. companies search to reduce their costs of manufacturing, they offshore production to third-world or developing countries, such as those in Asia and Africa to take advantage of lower wage rates. This has been the practice of many companies, including athletic footwear manufactures such as Nike, Reebok, and Adidas.[9] Outsourcing the production of these and other products to third-world countries helps to improve their standard

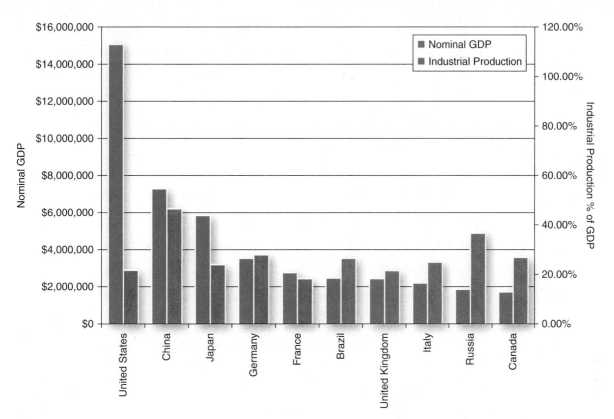

■ FIGURE 11.2
Industrial production as a percent of nominal (not adjusted for inflation) GDP 2012.[8]
Data from World Economic Outlook Database April 2012. Web. (07 June 2012.) http://www.imf.org/external/pubs/ft/weo/2012/01/weodata/index.aspx.

of living, which contributes to overall world economic growth. The opposite effect on the world economy can happen as well when economic downturns occur in some of the leading world economies. The Great Recession of the late 2000s was due to failures in several of the world's leading economies. Thanks to better communication and transportation technologies, the world economy continues to evolve into a single global market with increased trade and better utilization of capital and labor.

In many respects, small bike shops, like the one run by Steve Schmidt and Ralph Brinsdorfer, are significantly different from their larger competitors, such as Trek, Cannondale, and Schwinn. But all local, regional, and global companies share similar concerns with regard to producing a quality product. Where to locate the business or plant, determining which suppliers to work with, ensuring the right inventory is on hand, and achieving and maintaining high quality are all concerns of every business—whether it is big or small or produces a good or a service. ■

Operations Management pp. 315–320

Arthur Ridder owns a furniture company in northern California.

His company has enjoyed a great deal of success; its close proximity to natural resources and

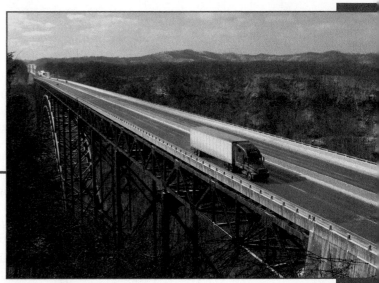
Adam Bies/Fotolia

dependable suppliers, as well as a large employee base, has allowed it to produce large quantities of high-quality furniture. Shipping has been efficient, as the factory is located 3 miles from a major highway and 20 miles from a port for international delivery. Due to the success of his business, Arthur is considering opening a new location in Europe to expand his international presence. The site of the proposed European factory is near the Alps in Switzerland. Natural resources are amazingly abundant—they are what drew Arthur to the area—but finding an adequate number of skilled employees may be difficult. Shipping is also a concern, as the area is not centrally located. Weighing the pros and cons, what should Arthur do? ■

Picking the right location for your business can be a complex issue, but it is only one component of **operations management**. Operations management is the administration and planning of business operations to produce and distribute goods and services as efficiently as possible to maximize the profits of an organization. Operations managers are focused on the big picture: the design, implementation, and monitoring of the process by which a good or a service is created and delivered successfully to the customer.

In this section, we'll look at some of the more important operational issues that a company must consider, such as finding the ideal location and determining how the facility will be organized. In later sections, we'll look at supply chain, production management, and operations control, which are also important components to the entire process.

Determining Facility Location

What factors must businesses consider when determining where to locate their facilities? Where an organization locates its offices, factories, or retail outlets can have a significant effect on its overall efficiency, profitability, and success. Several factors play an important role in determining the best location of a business beyond cost and availability:

- **Proximity to market:** Service businesses, such as restaurants, supermarkets, and retail operations, must choose their locations based on how near they are to their potential customer base. A restaurant that is easily visible to passing cars and pedestrians has more of an advantage in attracting customers than a restaurant tucked away in a remote part of town where few people visit.

- **Proximity to raw materials:** Manufacturing businesses, however, need to be close to raw materials and transportation sources. Being near raw materials may reduce costs associated with spoilage, and transportation costs are one of the major expenses that many manufacturing companies must consider. In fact, transportation costs can be as much as five times the cost of operating a production facility.[10] For example, Tata Steel is one of the world's leaders in steelmaking. One of Tata's success factors is its proximity to raw material sources.[11] Although the company is headquartered in India, Tata Steel operates in 24 countries. Tata secured the iron ore mines in India, and its overseas operations in Southeast Asia, Australia, and parts of Africa are focused on securing raw material sources at these locations.

- **Proximity to utilities: Utility supply** refers to the availability of public infrastructure services, such as electricity, natural gas, water, and communications.

2   What is operations management, and what is important in determining a facility's location and layout?

A company that is establishing a large facility, such as a bottling plant or a warehouse, wouldn't want to situate it in a remote location with little public infrastructure, even if the land is cheap. Because such a large facility requires ample amounts of electricity and running water to operate properly, the cost to establish this infrastructure if it didn't exist could be enormous.

Tata Steel factories, located throughout the world, are situated near transportation and the source of raw materials.

- **Proximity to hazardous waste disposal:** Many businesses, as part of their day-to-day operations, generate large amounts of hazardous waste that must be dealt with within the state, county, and municipal hazardous waste disposal guidelines. Even every-day materials, such as paint and cleaning fluids, are considered hazardous waste and must be disposed of properly.[12] The proper disposal of this waste has ramifications on a business's location. Responsible organizations must be aware of the disposal options that are available in their areas.

How does labor affect location decisions? Another consideration when choosing a production location is the human factor, which refers to how the location decision affects the people in a surrounding community and vice versa. Companies need to hire employees to maintain their operations, but they also need to be aware of how their presence affects the community overall. The human factor has four separate, though interrelated, components:

- **Skilled labor:** One component of the human factor is the availability of labor. After all, labor is a necessary factor of production for a company to operate successfully. Choosing a location for virtually any business requires finding an area with an abundance of workers who possess the necessary skills. California's famed Silicon Valley became a top hub for the tech industry's software and hardware manufacturing businesses because of its proximity to Stanford University, its abundance of local engineers, and the area's history in developing technology.[13]

- **Affordable labor:** However, seeking skilled workers is only part of the decision-making process. Many businesses need to find a workforce that they can afford financially as well. One of the reasons some corporations send their manufacturing operations outside the United States is because those countries contain highly skilled workers who require lower wages than their U.S. counterparts. India is the primary destination for outsourced high-tech labor because it offers an experienced, skilled, and affordable labor pool.[14]

Solar panel manufacturer SunPower provides green collar jobs. Here a 150-acre solar installation uses panels to generate more electricity than conventional systems. This solar system delivers electric power to approximately 8,000 homes.

- **Living conditions:** Businesses can alter an area's living conditions either positively or negatively. A business brings opportunities to a community by creating jobs and a higher standard of living. Many businesses seek areas where the quality of life is already high (good schools, pleasant weather, low crime rates, etc.) to attract a better caliber of employees. Some social entrepreneurs might take it upon themselves to locate their business in an impoverished area

to revitalize the local economy. Environmentally aware politicians advocate green collar businesses precisely for their ability to rejuvenate economically depressed communities. Conversely, a business can have negative effects on a community by exploiting workers or increasing local traffic.

- **Laws and regulations:** To maintain a balance between business and community interests, governments have created many laws and regulations to protect individuals and the environment. Laws and regulations may vary by state or country; therefore companies, as part of their location assessment process, must consider how any government intervention will affect the organization.

Facility Layout and Capacity Planning

Why is facility layout important? **Facility layout** refers to the physical arrangement of resources and people in the production process and how they interact. The design of a facility's layout is important to maximize efficiency and satisfy employees' needs. It involves everything from the arrangement of cubicles in an office space to the position of robotic arms in an automobile manufacturing plant.

When planning facility layout for maximum effectiveness, operations managers must anticipate and plan for future changes in layout, renovation needs, and expansion possibilities. Additionally, the facility layout should be in accordance with Occupational Safety and Health Administration (OSHA) guidelines to ensure worker safety.

How big should the facility be? **Capacity planning** is the process of determining how much product an organization can produce. It requires a balance between the maximum amounts of product or work an organization is capable of producing and the quantity of the product or service demanded by its customers. The overall size of a facility as well as efficient utilization of resources dictates production capacity. Capacity can be increased by introducing new technologies or equipment, increasing the number of workers or machines or improving the efficiency of existing workers or machines, or expanding production facilities.

How does facility layout affect production? A facility layout should be able to handle materials efficiently and in an orderly manner to ensure a smooth flow of production. To do so, designers need to use available space effectively. The distance that a work-in-progress must travel within a facility must also be taken into account. This is true not only for the production of goods but also in the production of services. For example, the layout of a fast-food restaurant can help the employees involved in the different parts of the process—preparing food and serving customers—to work in a more integrated fashion.

The layout of a fast-food restaurant helps employees prepare food and serve customers in an integrated fashion.

David Levenson/Alamy

What are the different types of facility layouts? Different manufacturing processes require different types of facility layouts. There are four common types: process layout, product layout, cellular layout, and fixed position layout.

- **Process layout** groups together similar tasks, and the partially assembled product moves from one station to the next as workers perform a particular step in the production process. Process layout is used mostly to produce low-volume, customized products. For example, Vermont Teddy Bears are produced in a process layout: Each bear is assembled and dressed according to specific customer orders.

- **Product layout** is used mostly for high-volume, standardized products that can be produced in a sequential fashion, such as Crayola Crayons. Batches of crayons go through parallel processes of melting and coloring wax, shaping into molds, wrapping, and then finally coming together and being assembled into boxes.

Both of these layouts are organized by function. However, these arrangements are not always efficient, as production can stall if a problem occurs at one station, and workers can get bored with repetitive tasks. To overcome the shortcomings of process and product layouts, some manufacturers have adopted cellular and fixed position layouts.

- **Cellular layout** places small teams of workers who handle all aspects of assembly, so each station is equipped with the parts and tools necessary to produce a product from start to finish, and the worker moves through the workstation as he or she conducts the assembly process.
- **Fixed position layout** is used for manufacturing large items, such as ships, airplanes, and modular homes. With a fixed position layout, the product stays in one place, and the workers move around the product to complete its assembly.

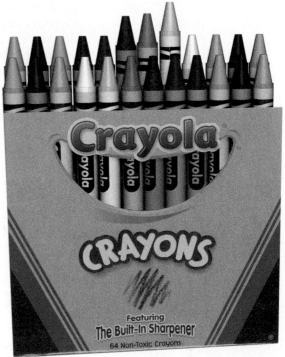

Crayola Crayons are produced using a product layout, which is suitable for high-volume, standardized products.

Working with Suppliers

What is a make-or-buy decision? It is not always necessary for a company to make everything in-house. When starting the production process, one of the first decisions that operations managers make is determining if the company will make the entire product or if the product will be assembled from a combination of parts manufactured in-house and parts manufactured or purchased outside the organization. This is commonly called a **make-or-buy decision**. If it is less expensive to outsource the production of certain parts elsewhere, that may be the best decision. However, it is important that a company can trust the quality of any parts that are outsourced since the product ultimately will carry the company's name and reputation.

How does a company decide which suppliers to use? Selecting suppliers is an important part of the make-or-buy decision. After all, establishing a business relationship with a supplier is like entering into a partnership. A company's first step in finding suppliers involves clearly defining and understanding its needs so that it can find suppliers that truly fit its requirements. Cost is always a factor, but it should never be the sole factor. For example, one supplier may offer to manufacture a part for significantly less but of such poor quality that later repairs or recalls would end up costing a company more than the cost of producing quality parts; its reputation would also be affected.

Customers perceive a product as a single entity—not as component piece-parts provided by different suppliers. Customers will hold the company responsible even if an individual supplier is to blame for making a faulty part or missing a deadline and causing a delay. For example, Mattel had to recall close to one million toys because its supplier in China had coated the toys in paint that contained lead. Mattel was later fined $2.3 million by the Consumer Product Safety Commission because ultimately, the company was responsible for the quality of the finished

Shelves are nearly empty after Mattel issued a recall for Chinese-made toys that could have lead paint.

product.[15] So having a good supplier that meets a company's needs and cares about a company's customers as if they were its own is an invaluable asset. Understanding these needs before choosing a supplier will make the process easier and more beneficial in the end.

A vast collection of resources is available to help businesses connect with suppliers. These resources include the Better Business Bureau, the local chamber of commerce, exhibitions, trade magazines, the Internet, and old-fashioned recommendations from friends and business acquaintances. The challenge for operations managers is in finding the best people for the job and determining which of those suppliers offer optimal solutions for production needs.

Operations Management for Service Providers

Does operations management differ in the service sector? Operations management has been traditionally associated with manufacturing goods, but many of the concepts apply to the service industry, too. There are some inherent differences between the industrial sector and the service sector. Service providers have more contact with their customers than do manufacturers. Also, services are usually customized to satisfy the specific needs of a customer. For example, a house painter applies the colors chosen by the customer, and a doctor treats his or her patients' specific symptoms. However, despite these differences, the ultimate goal of providing a quality product in a cost-efficient manner is similar for manufacturers and service providers. Service providers have implemented much efficiency in their processes. For example, banks and fast-food restaurants have installed drive-up windows. As noted earlier, the location for a manufacturer is dependent on the proximity of resources and suppliers, whereas the location for a service provider needs to be near the customer. The size of a manufacturing facility is dictated by the extent of the production process, whereas the size of a service business must take into consideration fluctuating demands and capacity.

Taking transportation, human, and physical factors into consideration, businesses ultimately choose a location that will allow them to be competitive. In addition, determining the correct facility layout and choosing the right suppliers can further enhance a company's operations management. Creating a proper facility for operations is only the first step for a successful business owner. The next step involves determining and developing a proper production management plan. Think back to the furniture company example that started this section. Given what you know now about choosing a manufacturing location and operations management, is Switzerland the best location for Arthur Ridder's furniture company? ■

Iain Masterton/Alamy

Supply Chain Management pp. 320–322

The ink was barely dry on the lease as Sylvia Ackerman drove to IKEA to pick out furniture for her new apartment. Sylvia loves the Swedish furniture manufacturer because of the simple lines and clean designs of its products. In addition, because she has only herself to rely on, she can move her purchases into her apartment without much help from others because the products are packaged in flat packs.

Sylvia also loves the challenge of assembling the products herself. More importantly, Sylvia knows that it is hard to beat IKEA pricing; she will always get quality products at a low cost. ■

What sets IKEA, the Swedish home products retailer, apart from other furniture companies is the packaging and storage of its products. Most of the furniture it produces is shipped in flat packs to be assembled at the consumer's home. The condensed packaging minimizes shipping and storage costs, which, in turn, lowers the retail cost of IKEA products. The company has many factories worldwide and is constantly opening new locations to supply its growing number of franchised stores.

The Importance of Supply Chain Management

What is a supply chain? A supply chain consists of suppliers, business partners, and service providers, as well as sourced manufacturers, distributors, retailers, and transporters. Internally, the supply chain also includes all the major departments within an organization. And of course, at the end of the supply chain is the customer. A supply chain is fluid and constantly changing, and demands great communication and coordination between all involved parties to achieve the greatest efficiencies. Supply chains are a part of every business—service, manufacturing, profit, and not-for-profit.

Why is supply chain management important? Supply chain management is the management of activities from all organizations involved in the production process. The goal of supply chain management is to maximize value and achieve a sustainable competitive advantage. Moreover, supply chain management helps companies reduce their carbon footprint by critically looking at each component of the supply chain (see ■ **FIGURE 11.3**). Until recently, companies didn't consider the chain of activities that ultimately delivered their product to the final customer. The chain is as strong as its weakest link. A poor relationship within any link of

> **3** What is supply chain management, and how does it help companies create and deliver their goods and services more effectively?

■ **FIGURE 11.3**
As companies try to reduce their carbon footprints, they need to take a closer look at each component of the supply chain.

THE List

Ten Supply Chain Leaders[16]

Amazon.com

Apple Inc.

Cisco Systems, Inc.

Dell Inc.

McDonald's Corp.

PepsiCo

Procter & Gamble

Samsung

The Coca-Cola Company

Walmart Stores, Inc.

the supply chain can have disastrous consequences for all other supply chain members. Supply chain management is important to improving efficiencies, not only within the organization, but also among all the components of the production and distribution process. In addition, companies are seeking ways to strengthen their global presence by positioning inventories so products are available when customers want them, regardless of location, in the right quantity for the right price. This can happen only if all components along the supply chain are working together. The partnering in manufacturing and design with other companies involved along the supply chain has increased the need for better sharing of product information and collaborative product development. Companies like IKEA have been forced to become global enterprises as they seek the lowest cost suppliers, making the supply chain a more complicated process and ripe for inefficiencies if not managed well.

Is supply chain management only for manufacturing companies? Supply chains also exist in service organizations. The goal is the same for service organizations: to maximize value in the delivery process to achieve a competitive advantage; however, instead of managing "things," supply chain management for service organizations (sometimes referred to as service chain management) manages the time and actions of the labor force required to perform the service. Service chain management also measures and forecasts the responses and needs of the customer. In addition, it involves planning, scheduling, workforce management, and enterprise resource planning. Finally, service chain management focuses on establishing strong relationships with customers through enhanced communication technologies.

What's a supply chain system? Virtually every product that reaches an end user, whether or not it's completely manufactured in-house, is derived from an accumulation of efforts from multiple organizations around the globe. Companies acquire raw materials from global vendors to be used in their factories located in different continents. The finished goods then pass through different distribution networks involving exports to different countries or local markets, warehouses, distributors, and retailers, before finally reaching the end customer. The information and communication systems needed to coordinate these activities are also a significant part of the supply chain system. The proliferation of new telecommunications and computer technology has made instantaneous communications a reality. Such information systems can link together suppliers, manufacturers, distributors, retail outlets, and ultimately customers, regardless of location.

In an effort to remain competitive, and to keep their retail prices low without sacrificing quality or customer service, IKEA looked for opportunities to improve operational efficiencies. To achieve cost reduction, quality, and customer satisfaction, IKEA focused on its supply chain management, from product design phase through distribution.[17] With stores and franchise operations, warehouses, and suppliers in all major regions of the world, IKEA's supply chain has a global spread. ■

Production Management pp. 322–328

Ted Hoyt and Austen DuPont have known each other since high school. They became great friends mainly because of their shared interests in sports. While they went their

Mat Hayward/Fotolia

different ways in college, they met years later and started a fitness and nutritional consulting firm. One of the main products they recommend, especially to their clients with food allergies or dietary requirements, is the YouBar, a nutrition bar with customizable ingredients that cater to the tastes and nutritional needs of each customer. YouBar allows customers to choose the ingredients (including vitamin infusion) and even name their bar. The bars are available only via online orders and are sold around the world. How does the YouBar provide for such product customization without making each bar by hand? ■

Goods and services don't just appear; they are created. As you learned earlier in this chapter, production is the process through which resources are converted into finished products and given value. **Production management** refers to the planning, implementation, and control measures used in the process to convert resources into finished products. The act of production gives these finished products value, or **utility**, by satisfying consumers' wants or needs.

To ensure that a product provides utility, production managers must successfully develop and carry out a production plan. A **production plan** is a description of how resources are to be used to develop a product in a specific way. A well-thought-out plan will ensure a smoothly run production process. The scope of production management includes determining what to produce, what processes and machinery to use to increase efficiencies and minimize costs, the number of products that need to be produced, and how to meet the needs of all employees while maintaining quality standards. Production managers are in charge of setting schedules, choosing what parts and supplies to buy for the assembly process, overseeing quality control, and managing other important issues. Production managers who plan effectively are able to increase productivity, reduce costs, and improve customer satisfaction.

The Production Process

What production processes are used by businesses? There are several types of production processes that businesses can use. The type that is chosen depends on the company and what types of goods or services it produces. Some common production processes and techniques are shown in ■ **FIGURE 11.4**.

How are large quantities of goods produced? The method of producing large quantities of goods at a low cost is called **mass production**. This method relies on machines and automated assembly lines to produce goods that are identical to each other and adhere to certain standards of quality. Mass-produced goods are usually manufactured along an **assembly line** (or production line), in which partially complete products are moved from one worker to the next on a conveyor belt.

The cost to run an assembly line is kept low because machines do the majority of the work, and the laborers don't need to be especially skilled to perform their repetitive tasks. This method also cuts down on production time, allowing a large quantity of goods to be produced very quickly. Because machinery is the main component, the risk of human error is virtually eliminated. A major disadvantage, however, is that mass production is inflexible. After a production line is established, it is very difficult

> **4** What is production management, and what production processes are used by businesses?

■ **FIGURE 11.4**
Common production processes and techniques.

Mass Production
- Machines and automated assembly lines

Mass Customization
- Customized mass production through flexible manufacturing systems

Lean Production
- Aimed to increase efficiency by eliminating waste along the production process

Reprinted with the permission of Blank Label, www.blanklabel.com

Blank Label uses mass customization to produce customer-designed men's shirts.

to change or alter the process if an unexpected problem occurs.

Can product customization be done with mass production?
When mass production was initially implemented, if any customization or individualization of product design was desired, production was stopped or slowed down to customize small batches. Now, due to advances in digital and production technologies, the once-difficult, time-consuming, and more costly customization process has become accessible to a wide variety of markets. **Mass customization** is the production of goods or services tailored to meet customers' individual needs cost-effectively. It ranges from the bulk customization of industrial supplies, such as valves, switches, and instruments, to individual customization that is most often seen with clothing, shoes, glasses, and bicycles. For example, Blank Label allows customers to design their own shirts online for nearly the same price as a store-bought shirt. The benefit of this process is that Blank Label does not need to produce shirts of every size and style, thus incurring additional warehousing and shipping expenses. This is the same model that Dell Computers employed in the 1990s. Rather than warehouse potentially unused parts that soon would be obsolete, Dell allowed customers to design their computers to the specifications that best met their needs. Now, most PC manufacturers offer online customization for their products.

How is mass customization achieved?
A solution to the rigid system of mass production is a method of production called *flexible manufacturing*, or a **flexible manufacturing system (FMS)**. In this system, several machines are linked together by one central computer. All the machines in the system can process different part types simultaneously. Unlike a mass-production system, an FMS can adapt to changes in schedules and product specifications. There are four components to an FMS: processing machines, a material handling system, a central computer, and human labor.[18] For example, Victory Motorcycles, a division of the off-road vehicle manufacturer Polaris, uses an FMS to create motorcycles that customers design online to their specific needs and tastes.

Can mass customization be used in service industries?
The technologies of mass customization have also enabled many service-based organizations to meet the individual needs of their customers. Burger King, for example, introduced its "Have It Your Way" campaign*, which took the mass production of standardized fast food to a more personalized delivery and allowed customers to "tweak" what went on their hamburgers to meet their specific tastes. The Ritz Carlton Hotel takes overnight visits to a new level. Most hotel chains offer a preference of bed size and perhaps room location, but the rest is pretty standard no matter which city or country you are in. But the Ritz trains its staff to record unique habits, preferences, and dislikes of each guest, which it enters into a database that is used to further customize a guest's current stay and also make the next stay filled with personal touches. Each guest is greeted by name, the hotel knows whether there is a preference for feather or nonallergenic pillows, and the hotel has the guest's favorite newspaper placed at the

Victory Motorcycles uses an FMS to produce customer-designed, made-to-order motorcycles.

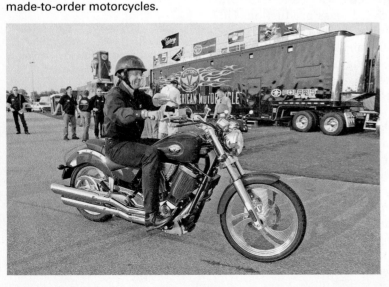

VICTORY MOTORCYCLES/PRN/Newscom

*Source: "Our History." Burger King, www.bk.com

Biz CHAT

3-D Printing: An Industrial Revolution?

Who would have thought that the simple process of printing could innovate and potentially change the manufacturing industry? Indeed, this may be the case with the innovation of the 3D printer. Thanks to a convergence of ingenious technologies, a new twist on printing has emerged. The 3D printer makes objects from a digital file with a process that is similar to inkjet printing. The objects are made from layers of resilient, durable plastic and can be complex in design such as a toy car with movable wheels and different colored parts. The potential of these 3D printers is the mass customization of items specific to individual wants and needs in virtually any environment: at home, at work, or on a remote island. Moreover, since the cost to acquire and run one of these machines is low, it may change outsourcing decisions and bring the manufacturing of small parts and objects back home. What do you think? Could 3D printing change the world?

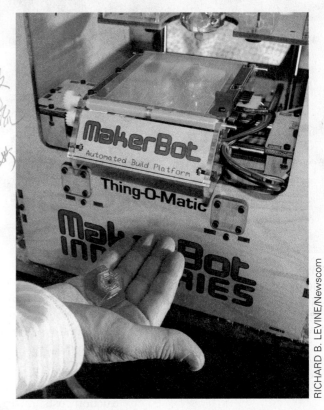

RICHARD B. LEVINE/Newscom

The Thing-O-Matic is a 3D printer from MakerBot Industries that enables users to produce small plastic objects at home as simply as printing from an inkjet printer.

door every morning. They anticipate a customer's every need, without having to ask. The results of this customized program have been a 23 percent increase in guest retention.[19]

What type of production focuses on efficiency? One of the most important aspects of the production process is making sure that work gets done as efficiently as possible. Increased efficiency helps work get done faster, cheaper, and sometimes with better quality. Although efficiency has always been a concern, the success of lean production has made efficiency a primary focus for many companies. **Lean production** is a set of principles concerned with reducing waste and improving flow. The basic tenet of lean production is to do more with less through the elimination of wasteful overproduction, unnecessary wait time, needless transportation, excess inventory, superfluous motion, redundant over-processing, and careless defective units. This system was first defined and employed by Toyota in the 1980s with great success. Although lean production originally was used for manufacturing, the principles behind it are highly flexible and can be used in every step of the production process.

Technology in the Production Process

What is the role of technology in the production process? With thousands of goods to produce at a given time, technology plays an integral role in facilitating the flow of any production process. When managed efficiently, the technological aspect of a production process leads to increases in productivity

How does technology influence the production process?

Rainer Plendi/Shutterstock

Robots play a big part in automobile manufacturing, but they are also used to weld, paint, assemble, package, inspect, and test many other types of products.

and reductions in costs. Technology can improve the quality and increase the variety of products, which influences a customer's buying decisions. Customers are more likely to buy a product that is not only low-priced compared to other similar products but also of high quality and readily available in many varieties. It is essential for businesses in today's globally competitive environment to be up-to-date on new technologies that can improve any or all aspects of the production process.

What has helped automate the production process? Humans are sometimes at a disadvantage when it comes to performing a task repetitively for many hours and with great precision and accuracy. This is where robots come in; an *industrial robot* is any device that performs automatically, typically completing repetitive tasks.[20] Not only can robots work around the clock tirelessly, and with accuracy, but they can also work in potentially hazardous conditions, thereby protecting human workers from dangerous environments. The two biggest industries employing robot applications are the automotive industry—which uses robots for welding, painting, assembly, and handling various materials—and the household appliances industry—which requires sealing, painting, and installing appliances such as microwave ovens.

What is the advantage of robots? Robots offer consistency in reducing production costs, raising productivity, and producing high-quality products. Industrial robots may take away some production-related jobs, but the technology has also created many new jobs for technicians and engineers. Companies that can effectively apply robotic technology in their production processes are more likely to gain an economic advantage in the global marketplace.

How does technology improve the design process? Computer-aided design (CAD) refers to using a computer and software to create two-dimensional or three-dimensional models of physical parts. A product designer first translates the design into a geometric model for the CAD system to display. Once the model data are received, the CAD system provides the designer with tools and a flexible environment so the product can be modified in size or shape, viewed internally,

OFF THE MARK

Technology: Too Much of a Good Thing?

In 1995, the new Denver International Airport boasted a fully automated baggage-handling system. The technology, however, turned out to be too much of a good thing. The system was designed to move luggage along an automated track between airport terminals and baggage claim areas, some of which were as far as a mile apart in the large airport. A centralized computer system would control the entire operation, eliminating the need for human baggage handlers to physically move baggage from one point to another. But after 10 years of misplaced luggage, glitches in the system, and soaring maintenance costs, the error-prone system was finally shut down. In 2005, the only airline to ever use the system, United Airlines, went back to using baggage handlers to complete the tasks previously handled by the automated system. In a test run before the switch was made, human baggage handlers beat the automated system's error rate hands down. With the help of mobile devices, such as handheld scanners, United Airlines is now able to track luggage better than the automated system ever could. In this case, better too little technology than too much.

and rotated on any axis. CAD also facilitates the testing of parts in simulated real-world environments before they are manufactured. By programming a simple design change into the CAD system, a manufacturer can produce custom-designed products, such as clothing and cars, without incurring extra costs. CAD systems are used to design tools and other small products as well as houses, machinery, and commercial structures.

How is CAD used on bigger projects? Some manufacturing processes that are more complicated, such as those for motor vehicles and airplanes, need more than one CAD program to design and incorporate all the different components. For instance, the design of a ship may require one CAD application for the steel structure and another CAD program for the propeller. A disadvantage of this method is that it requires knowledge of all the different software applications used as well as how to integrate them in the end. The model for Boeing Company's 757 aircraft is a good example of how integration can be achieved. The 757 aircraft is comprised of parts from 50 different firms. Boeing's CAD system effectively integrates all the parts, ensuring a precise fit. This system effectively reduces the number of prototypes needed as well as the working hours required for assembly.[21]

CAD uses computer technology for the design of objects in two or three dimensions.

How does CAD information get incorporated into the manufacturing process? Once a design is approved, **computer-aided manufacturing (CAM)** uses the design data to control the machinery used in the manufacturing process. The integration of CAD and CAM systems with the various aspects of a firm's production process is referred to as *simultaneous engineering*. Ford Motor Company's engine division, for example, successfully integrated all its production and design systems into one database that is accessed by employees and suppliers involved with design and production.[22] This type of facilitated communication is a huge benefit for firms with complex systems. One of the main disadvantages of using CAD/CAM systems is that they require considerable time and investment to set up and learn the necessary software, hardware, communications, and integration processes.

Can an entire facility be automated? **Computer-integrated manufacturing (CIM)** systems combine design and manufacturing functions with other automated functions, such as order taking, shipment, and billing for the complete automation of a manufacturing plant. The printing company VistaPrint uses CIM not only to manufacture its products but also to help customers create and place orders for custom-designed business cards, brochures, and even T-shirts. Through the use of CIM, the company has expanded its business and is able to serve more customers while continuing to offer affordable prices.[23]

What effect has automation had on overall productivity? CAD, CAM, and CIM have dramatically improved the process of producing goods by reducing the time between design and manufacturing, thus making a significant impact on productivity. These systems have also increased the scope of automated machinery in the production process. Through the rapid pace of technological advancement, CAD, CAM, and CIM systems are not limited to large mass-production facilities; they are entering smaller companies as well.

Production and Social Networking

How has social networking impacted production? The social networking structure of the Internet, along with hardware and software tools, has created a ready-made distribution system for more creative consumers who want to "have it their way." Using social media tools, such as blogs, Web videos, and podcasts, as well as social networking sites like Facebook and Twitter, consumers cannot only design their own products but also have direct influence on what companies develop and produce.

The Trendwatching website coined the phrase *customer-made*, defining it as the "phenomenon of corporations creating goods, services, and experiences in close cooperation with experienced and creative consumers, tapping into their intellectual capital, and in exchange giving them a direct say in (and rewarding them for) what actually gets produced, manufactured, developed, designed, serviced, or processed."[24] The previously mentioned Blank Label is a relative newcomer to this growing genre, and Adidas with their "mi Adidas" campaign and Converse's "Make One Yours" are proven examples that this design-your-own trend is part of our society.

Beyond design, social media capabilities enable consumers to directly influence what companies develop and produce, as well as give instant feedback on whether their initiatives are worthwhile. Nokia was one of the earliest manufacturers, with its Nokia Experience Lounge site, to invite consumers to "join in" and collaborate, converse, and connect. Starbucks and Dell have similar sites with MyStarbucksIdeas and Dell's IdeaStorm, respectively, that invite their customers to share product development ideas. And third-party sites, such as Engadget, have been running "How Would You Change or Improve" topics that give users a place to voice their insights and suggestions about products such as the Xbox 360, Skype, TiVo, and the Electrolux Roomba. The Internet and social media have created a virtually new world of opportunities for anyone to innovate, produce, and process an idea.

Companies rely on production management to plan, implement, and control the process of converting resources into finished goods. The YouBar uses mass customization techniques to take online orders from around the globe to produce individually designed nutrition bars. Having such customizable products at hand allows Ted and Austen to meet their individual customer's needs, as well. ∎

Operations Control pp. 328–335

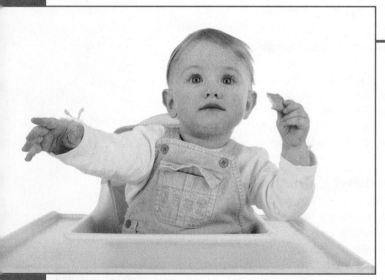

© tompet80/Fotolia

Jeanette Pae could hardly stop her daughter, Rihanna, from crying or stop her own self from shaking after her daughter fell out of her high chair. The activity tray of the high chair unexpectedly separated from the rest of the chair, and Rihanna tumbled out onto the tile kitchen floor, hitting her head and cutting her lip. Shortly after the incident, Jeanette received a product recall notice from the manufacturer offering to replace the faulty chair with a different one from the company. Jeanette had already determined she would be buying a different brand of high chair. Jeanette and her family were no strangers to recalls. Jeanette had owned one of those Dell laptop batteries that were overheating and causing fires, her mother had to return some Mattel toys that she had purchased for Jeanette's older son because of lead paint fears, and her father had been taking Vioxx to control his arthritis when Merck recalled the product due to elevated chance of heart attack or stroke. Even the cherished family Toyota was recalled. What was going on? Why were even the most reliable products having quality issues? ■

In this section, we'll look at some important areas of control in the production process, beginning with key project management and scheduling techniques. Inventory management is a factor in profitability, but also in customer satisfaction to ensure that the product or service is delivered on time. Lastly, the quality of a product is best determined and controlled at every step of the production process.

Controlling the Production Process

How does scheduling shape the production process? When it comes to production, **scheduling** refers to the efficient organization of equipment, facilities, labor, and materials. There are two different types of scheduling: *forward* and *backward*. With *forward scheduling*, you start with the date that materials are available, create the most efficient schedule, and then determine a shipping date based on that schedule. *Backward scheduling* is the exact opposite: you are given a shipping or due date, and you need to determine the start date and the most efficient schedule based on when everything must be finished.

What tools are available to help with scheduling? Two major components go into making an effective schedule: loading and sequencing. *Loading* is assigning a job to a specific machine or an entire work center. *Sequencing* is assigning the order in which jobs are processed. Software systems are used to put together a cohesive schedule of loading and sequencing to ensure that all the right tools are working on the right jobs at the right times. But no matter how complex the system, all configurations are just estimates based on the data input into the system and the rules it uses. Having a person oversee scheduling is still invaluable because that individual can bring experience and judgment that cannot be programmed into a computer.

How are the individual tasks of a process tracked? One method for keeping tabs on the progress of a given project is a **Gantt chart**, a tool developed by Henry Gantt in the 1920s. A Gantt chart is formatted similarly to a horizontal bar graph. It is used to lay out each task in a project, the order in which these tasks must be completed, and how long each task should take. ■ FIGURE 11.5 shows an example of a Gantt chart for a remodeling project. Originally used for large-scale construction projects, such as building the Hoover Dam in the 1930s, Gantt charts are used to manage a variety of both large-scale and small-scale projects. At any point in the process, project managers and manufacturers can see at a glance which tasks have been completed, which tasks are in the process of being completed, and which tasks have yet to begin. In addition, a Gantt chart helps to identify whether tasks were completed on schedule.

What is a PERT chart? The **program evaluation and review technique (PERT)** maps out the steps involved in a project, differentiating tasks that must be completed in a certain order from tasks that may be completed simultaneously. A PERT chart is like a flowchart (see ■ FIGURE 11.6) and emphasizes more the relationships between tasks than it does the timeline.

6 How is the production process developed and controlled?

Remodeling Project

Remodeling Project Job No.: 980015.05	Jul '12			Aug '12				Sep '12				Oct '12	
	15	22	29	5	12	19	26	2	9	16	23	30	7	14
Project Summary														
Soft Demo														
Soft Demo-Structural														
Structural Steel-Fab														
Framing-Rough														
Skylights														
Roof Curbs & Patch														
Electrical-Rough/Finish														
Overhead Doors														
Inspection-Structural Rebar														
Structural Concrete-Pour														
Service/Repair Elevator														
Plumbing Rough														
Data/Phone Cabling														
Structural Steel-Install														
T-bar Grid Repair														
Inspection-Walls														
Inspection-Drywall Screw														
Mud & Tape														
Mezzanine Demo														

■ **FIGURE 11.5**
Sample Gantt chart.
Created with KIDASA Software, Inc's Milestones Software. Reprinted by permission.

A PERT chart identifies the *critical path*, or the path of sequential tasks that will take the most time to complete. This helps managers determine an overall timeline for completing a project or, from a manufacturing standpoint, producing a particular good or service. However, because delays can cause the critical path in a project to change, PERT charts are limited in their ability to predict project completion times.

■ **FIGURE 11.6**
Sample PERT chart.

Purchasing and Inventory Control

How are materials used in the production process acquired? Purchasing is the task of acquiring the materials and services needed in the production process. Production managers need to find reliable suppliers who can provide high-quality resources at the best price. The Internet has made purchasing a much more competitive process. Just like you might use the Internet to search for the best price before buying a particular product, purchasing managers can compare prices and services between suppliers online before embarking in a service agreement.

How does a company maintain inventory control? Inventory control includes the receiving, storing, handling, and tracking of everything in a company's stock, from raw materials to finished products. Inventory often makes up a large portion of a business's expenses. Therefore, proper inventory management is a way to keep costs low while ensuring that all necessary materials are in stock and stored in the proper places. There are four main types of stock: raw materials, unfinished products, finished products, and consumables (such as pens and paper). Maintaining each of these kinds of stock helps determine where money should be spent and where waste occurs. Inventory maintenance helps to manage products with specific shelf lives that could deteriorate as well as products that have become obsolete and need to be removed. In addition, inventory maintenance monitors supplies to determine when too much or too little stock is being purchased. Ensuring an adequate supply of finished products or other types of stock is further complicated when customer demand is variable.

What methods are used to manage inventory? Managing stock or inventory can be achieved in a number of different ways. No single method works best for every business, and sometimes multiple methods are used to manage the different types of stock. Factors such as the size of a business, the necessary amount of inventory, the amount of storage space available for inventory, the perishability of inventory, and the proximity to suppliers all contribute to which inventory control method will work best.

- The least involved way to manage inventory is to simply *eyeball it*. This method works really well for smaller companies or companies that don't maintain large amounts of stock.

- When accuracy is a necessity, a *stock book solution*, where stock on hand is tallied in a book along with stock on order and stock that has been sold, would probably work best.

- Another less complicated management system is called the *reserve stock system*. This is where stock is set aside in reserve so that it cannot be used. The company goes through its inventory as it regularly would, and when it has to dip into the reserve stock, it knows it is time to reorder that item. It is important for managers to keep in mind when using this system that however much stock is in reserve should be enough to last the length of time it takes to resupply.[25]

What inventory system is most efficient for large companies? The systems described above can work well with smaller businesses; larger businesses often require an inventory management system that is more efficient. A **just-in-time (JIT) inventory control** system keeps the smallest amount possible of inventory on hand, and everything else that is needed is ordered so that it arrives when it is needed. Storing fewer items for shorter periods of time can reduce storage costs. Dell Computers made its mark in the PC manufacturing industry by embracing JIT inventory control. Because the company adopted a build-to-order system, the huge expense of carrying components that may not be used and subsequently become obsolete and useless was reduced. Over a four-year period after adopting this system, Dell's revenues grew from $2 billion to $16 billion.[26]

Mr Zach/Shutterstock

With barcodes and RFID tags, inventory is monitored electronically.

This system, however, is not without its drawbacks. To work properly, a company must have a very good relationship with its suppliers to ensure that appropriate quantities arrive on time and are delivered to where they are needed.

How is technology used to streamline inventory control? Many organizations rely on a computerized inventory system that uses a barcode or **radio frequency identification (RFID)** tag on each item, allowing a computer to keep track of the status, and quantity of each item. Each item is logged and classified when it is stocked and an identifying barcode or RFID tag is attached to the item. Both barcodes and RFID tags store all the specific information for each item, such as cost, stock number, and storage location. Using these systems, items in inventory can be scanned when they are used or sold, and the computer can continuously update the information for each item. Computerized inventory makes it easier to analyze the quantitative factors of managing stock, such as how quickly each item is sold, how much really needs to be held in inventory at once, and how often inventory is restocked.

What is materials requirement planning? More appropriate to the production side of inventory management is **materials requirement planning (MRP)**, a computer-based program used for inventory control and production planning. When an order is made, the specifics of that order are input into the MRP system. It uses previous manufacturing data to break the job into components; then the MRP system determines which parts will be needed to complete the job and compares these findings to current inventory. Based on this information; the MRP highlights what parts need to be obtained, either through production or a supplier, as well as when the parts will be needed. The end result is the best project needs estimate based on previous data. Knowing these estimates helps determine both part and labor shortages before a project even starts.

There are many limitations to MRP, the biggest being that it is only as effective as its data. So if the data are not well maintained, the estimates that it provides will become increasingly useless. Another limitation to MRP is its scope: It focuses only on the management of needed component parts in the manufacturing processes of a company and not in any other business areas.

What is enterprise resource planning? One way around the limitations of MRP is to use **enterprise resource planning (ERP)**.[27] ERP systems manage the same inventory control and process scheduling that MRP systems manage, but they can integrate these functions with other aspects of the business, such as finance, marketing, and human resources. Through various types of computer software and hardware, a typical ERP system consolidates information into a central database that is accessible to various system modules. Companies that specialize in ERP systems include Oracle, SAP, and Microsoft.

ERP systems enable companies to streamline workflows and share information across departments, improving employee productivity. With an ERP system in place, various departments of an organization can work together without worrying about compatible software. Unfortunately, there are disadvantages for a business that fails to fully invest in an ERP system. These problems can range from inadequate tech support to limited customization of the system.

Quality Management

Has quality control always been part of the production process? The techniques, activities, and processes used to guarantee that a certain good or service meets a specified level of quality is referred to as **quality control**. Formerly, quality control was a separate department that would inspect and test products for flaws at the *end* of the process after the product had been manufactured. Unfortunately, this method creates several problems. For one, it is expensive in terms of time and labor. Because inspection is performed by outside people instead of by the workers making the product, each inspector can pass or fail a product using his or her own standards and procedures. Moreover, inspecting finished products and discovering defects means some of these defects have to be scrapped or reworked, which can be costly.

What methods are used to improve quality? Merely controlling for quality through inspection and monitoring employees is like visiting a doctor to treat the symptoms as opposed to remedying the source of an illness. So, since the 1980s, firms have been focusing on building quality into every step of the production process instead of scrapping or fixing defects. This concept of "total quality" at every stage of a production process was fully embraced by U.S. companies only after Japanese manufacturers implemented companywide quality-improvement methods and strengthened their presence in the global market.[28] The Japanese produced exports not only at lower prices but also at higher levels of quality. In response, and to remain competitive, companies in the United States began to implement the **total quality management (TQM)** approach in their production processes. TQM involves everyone involved in the production process, including management, customers, employees, and suppliers.

How is TQM carried out? TQM involves ongoing improvement of products, services, and processes. This can be accomplished by undertaking a plan-do-check-act (PDCA) cycle, created by American statistician W. Edwards Deming (see ■ **FIGURE 11.7**).[29] Using the PDCA cycle, organizations first formulate a plan to reduce potential errors, carry out the plan on a small scale, check the outcome and effectiveness of the change, and then implement the plan on a larger scale while monitoring results continually.

What other tools are used to implement TQM? **Statistical quality control (SQC)** describes the set of statistical tools used to analyze each stage of the production process to ensure that quality standards are being met. **Statistical process control (SPC)** is one of the tools used with SQC. SPC inspects a random sampling of products at every phase of production to show any variations that need to be corrected throughout the process. Another common SPC tool is **Six Sigma**, a method that seeks to virtually eliminate defects by implementing a quality focus in every aspect of the organization. Employees are trained in the Six Sigma methodologies and are responsible for implementing any necessary changes in the production process to ensure that total quality is met. A company with

> **7** What is quality control, and how do ISO (International Organization for Standardization) standards help companies produce high-quality goods and services?

■ **FIGURE 11.7**
Total quality management uses the Plan, Do, Check, Act methodology.
Source: Based on "Continuous Improvement," American Society for Quality. www.asq.org

• Define and analyze the problem
• Identify the root cause

• Devise a solution
• Develop action plan
• Implement systematically

PLAN   **DO**

ACT   **CHECK**

• Standardize solution
• Review and define next issue

• Measure results
• Identify deviations and issues

Six Sigma Takes Organizations to the Top

Bill Smith, an engineer at Motorola, developed Six Sigma in the 1980s. It involves using SPC and also builds in TQM ideas of finding assignable causes for variations. Six Sigma strives for *continuous improvement.* Motorola managed to achieve Six Sigma quality in 1992 after adopting continuous quality-improvement methods in the 1980s.[30] Other large corporations, such as GE and Honeywell, have followed suit. Over the past several years, Motorola has taken the concept of Six Sigma even further by adapting it to the innovation involved in creating new products. At Motorola, designers are free to develop new products, and "project hoppers" are on hand to ensure that new projects meet quality standards.[31] As a result, innovation is encouraged, and, at the same time, projects are monitored at every step to uphold quality and increase profitability. But, Six Sigma is not best in all situations, and corporate specifics should be considered before employing this highest standard of quality control.

Six Sigma quality produces at a low defect rate of just 3.4 defects per 1,000,000 opportunities.

How does TQM cater to the customer? It's not enough to simply implement quality-management tools. A significant aspect of TQM is catering to customers' needs and desires. SGL Carbon, a manufacturer of graphite specialties, emphasizes adherence to a TQM approach by giving its customers the final say in determining whether a product meets their requirements of high-quality standards. Although firms may define in the beginning what makes products high quality or low quality, those companies that learn how to simultaneously emphasize quality throughout the production process and incorporate the desires of customers will have a greater presence in the global marketplace.

What is the ISO? The International Organization for Standardization (ISO) is an organization dedicated to creating worldwide standards of quality for goods and services. ISO was created in 1947 and is headquartered in Geneva, Switzerland. The organization has published more than 18,000 standards, and over 1,000 new standards are published every year.[32] ISO's objective is to develop production processes that are equal in quality and capability in all participating countries.[33] More than 161 countries have adopted these standards, and thousands of companies require their products to be ISO certified. Some industries have even developed their own industry-specific set of ISO standards.

The ISO standards apply not to the products themselves but to the production methods and systems used to manufacture them, as well as other areas, such as communication within the company and leadership. Such a standardized system is necessary to avoid trying to comply with various conflicting systems. Most of the standards generated by the ISO are product specific, but there are two "generic" standards that can be applied to any organization regardless of size, product/service, sector, or type of business enterprise. These standards are ISO 9001 and ISO 14001. **ISO 9001** implements a quality management system, and **ISO 14001** implements an environmental management system.

What is the ISO certification process? Certification is usually done by a third-party registrar. This registrar conducts an assessment of a company's quality-assurance manuals and practices. First, a preliminary assessment is conducted, during which the registrar reviews the documents that outline a company's standards and processes. If the manual and other printed documents pass the review, a company can proceed with the rest of the assessment. If the registrar finds errors in these documents, further review is delayed until the mistakes are corrected. During the formal assessment, the registrar reviews the corrected documents and interviews employees and administrators in the company. The goal of this part of the assessment is to ensure that written policies and procedures are being implemented in the company's production methods. Finally, the registrar issues an audit report that summarizes the results of the assessment and lists any areas that need improvement. If corrections are required at this stage, the company can make them and document them in a report to the registrar. After satisfactory corrections have been made, the registrar can then award certification to the company. Once it has earned certification, the company can put the ISO seal on its promotional materials and its letterhead.

After certification, the registrar returns to the company twice a year to make sure the company is still in compliance with ISO standards. These spot-checks are conducted without advance warning, and the registrar focuses on areas that were notably weak during the initial assessment. Every three years, the registrar will complete another assessment and issue a new audit report. The company must also establish an internal auditing program that is responsible for keeping ISO standards in practice.

What are the benefits of ISO certification? Companies that have successfully gone through the ISO certification process have indicated significant benefits, including improved customer satisfaction and international recognition. More tangible benefits include increased efficiency, procedural consistency, and a factual approach to decision making that are all due to the guidelines and training that need to be established to obtain certification. Companies with ISO certification also enjoy marketing advantages because they can now easily publicize that their company has reached this quality standard to attract new and maintain existing customers. As a result, companies have reported increased revenue, due to improved financial performance and increased productivity and a boost in customer satisfaction. For example, after implementing ISO 14001 environmental standards, Ford Motor Company reduced its water consumption by nearly 1 million gallons per day and saved over $65,000 in electricity costs by no longer using fluorescent light bulbs. The company also began to recycle paint waste, thus reducing disposed paint sludge, and began to use reusable plastic or metal containers instead of cardboard and plywood boxes.[34]

I t's no surprise that Jeanette Pae's confidence in the quality of her daughter's high chair was shaken. The loss of consumer confidence in a company to produce quality products is costly. Lost sales result in reduced revenues, but the process needed to repair a company's reputation and earn back the customer's respect can be even more expensive. Mattel, Merck, and Dell each experienced the repercussions of poor quality management, even though some of the problems were due to supplier error. Putting the focus on quality management at the beginning of the production process and adopting a quality-orientation throughout the company can ensure that a consistent product is produced. ∎

CHAPTER 11
SUMMARY

MyBizLab

Go to **mybizlab.com** to complete the problems marked with this icon ⭐.

1 **How is manufacturing and production important to the U.S. economy and to global economies?** (pp. 313–314)

- **Production** (p. 313) is the process of getting a good or a service to the customer; it is a series of related activities, with value being added at each stage. Companies are in business to provide a service or a good to consumers. The more efficiently a company can produce and deliver the product or the service, the greater the profit it will generate.

- Although the manufacturing industry has been declining over the years, it still accounts for more than one-fourth of the U.S. GDP and nearly one-tenth of all U.S. jobs. Moreover, manufacturing uses services and commodities as inputs, so manufacturing is actually responsible for a bigger share of total output.

- The service industry is very important to the U.S. economy, and accounts for nearly 75 percent of the U.S. GDP and about 80 percent of jobs. Service businesses range from small start-ups and home-based businesses to large corporations that are represented on the DJIA.

- Despite the push to outsource and offshore jobs and manufacturing to low-cost locations, the U.S. manufacturing industry is still globally important. The United States is still the leading industrial power in the world.

2 **What is operations management, and what is important in determining a facility's location and layout?** (pp. 316–319)

- **Operations management** (p. 316) consists of managing the activities and processes to produce and distribute products and services. Operations management includes how the facility should be organized, what supplies to purchase, what materials and inventory to keep on hand, and how quality is measured and controlled.

- When determining a location for a facility, companies consider their proximity to market, the cost of transporting raw materials, the presence of highways and other transportation systems, **utility supply** (p. 316), hazardous waste disposal, labor availability, living conditions, and laws and regulations.

- **Facility layout** (p. 318) refers to the physical arrangement of resources and people in the production process and how they interact. The design of a facility's layout is important to maximize efficiency and satisfy employees' needs.

- When starting the production process, one of the first decisions that operations managers make is what needs to be manufactured and what needs to be purchased from outside suppliers. This is commonly called a **make-or-buy decision** (p. 319).

- Although operations management has been traditionally associated with manufacturing goods, many of the concepts also apply to the service industry.

3 **What is supply chain management, and how does it help companies create and deliver their goods and services more effectively?** (pp. 321–320)

- **Supply chain management** (p. 321) is the management of activities from all organizations involved in the production process. The goal of supply chain management is to maximize value and achieve a sustainable competitive advantage. Supply chain management is important to improve efficiencies, not only within the organization, but also among all the components of the production and distribution process.

- A supply chain is made up of information and communication systems that work together to coordinate the path of the product and its components from raw material to finished product delivered to the consumer.

4 **What is production management, and what production processes are used by businesses?** (pp. 323–325)

- **Production management** (p. 323) refers to the planning, implementation, and control measures used to convert resources into finished products. These activities are similar to those in operations management but are more focused on the product.

- **Mass production** (p. 323) is the method of producing large quantities of goods at a low cost. The benefits of mass production include low cost, decreased production time, and virtually no human error, due to the reliance on machinery. A major disadvantage is that mass production is inflexible, making it difficult to alter the process if an unexpected problem occurs.

- **Mass customization** (p. 324) is the production of goods or services tailored to cost-effectively meet customers' individual needs. Mass customization is achieved with a **flexible manufacturing system (FMS)** (p. 324)—a system in which machines are programmed to process different part types simultaneously—allowing a manufacturer to mass-produce customized products. The primary benefit of an FMS is that it provides the flexibility to make products with many slight variations. A challenge of an FMS is that it is not well suited for goods that are in high demand.

- **Lean production** (p. 325) is a set of principles concerned with reducing waste and improving flow. The basic tenet of lean production is to do more with less through the elimination of wasteful overproduction, unnecessary wait time, needless transportation, excess inventory, superfluous motion, redundant over-processing, and careless defective units.

5 How does technology influence the production process? (pp. 325–327)

- Robots offer consistency in reducing production costs, raising productivity, and producing high-quality products.
- **Computer-aided design (CAD)** (p. 326), **computer-aided manufacturing (CAM)** (p. 327), and **computer-integrated manufacturing (CIM)** (p. 327) have dramatically improved the process of producing goods by reducing the time between design and manufacturing, thus making a significant impact on productivity. These systems have also increased the scope of automated machinery in the production process.
- The social networking structure of the Internet, along with hardware and software tools, has created a ready-made distribution system for more creative consumers who want to "have it their way." Beyond design, social media capabilities enable consumers to directly influence what companies develop and produce, as well as to give instant feedback on whether their initiatives are worthwhile.

6 How is the production process developed and controlled? (pp. 329–330)

- Effective **scheduling** (p. 329) can help managers control the production process. Gantt and PERT charts are scheduling tools to ensure that all the right tools are working on the right jobs at the right times.

- **Purchasing** (p. 331) is the task of acquiring the materials and services needed in the production process. In doing so, production managers must find reliable suppliers who can provide high-quality resources at the best price.
- **Inventory control** (p. 331) includes the receiving, storing, handling, and tracking of everything in a company's stock, from raw materials to finished products. A **just-in-time (JIT) inventory control** (p. 331) system keeps the smallest amount of inventory on hand as possible, and everything else that is needed is ordered so that it arrives when it is needed.

7 What is quality control, and how do ISO standards help companies produce high-quality goods and services? (pp. 333–335)

- **Quality control** (p. 332) is the use of techniques, activities, and processes to guarantee that a certain good or service meets a specified level of quality.
- **Total quality management (TQM)** (p. 333) involves every factor in producing high-quality goods-management, customers, employees, and suppliers. At any point, employees and leaders are aiming to produce high quality.
- The ISO has created worldwide standards of quality for goods and services. ISO standards apply not to the products themselves but to the production methods and systems used to manufacture them, as well as to other areas, such as communication within a company and leadership.

Key Terms

assembly line (p. 323)
capacity planning (p. 318)
cellular layout (p. 319)
computer-aided design (CAD) (p. 326)
computer-aided manufacturing (CAM) (p. 327)
computer-integrated manufacturing (CIM) (p. 327)
enterprise resource planning (ERP) (p. 332)
facility layout (p. 318)
fixed position layout (p. 319)
flexible manufacturing system (FMS) (p. 324)
Gantt chart (p. 329)
inventory control (p. 331)
ISO 9001 (p. 334)

ISO 14001 (p. 334)
just-in-time (JIT) inventory control (p. 331)
lean production (p. 325)
make-or-buy decision (p. 319)
mass customization (p. 324)
mass production (p. 323)
materials requirement planning (MRP) (p. 332)
operations management (p. 316)
process layout (p. 318)
product layout (p. 319)
production (p. 313)
production management (p. 323)
production plan (p. 323)
program evaluation and review technique (PERT) (p. 329)

purchasing (p. 331)
quality control (p. 332)
radio frequency identification (RFID) (p. 332)
scheduling (p. 329)
Six Sigma (p. 333)
statistical process control (SPC) (p. 333)
statistical quality control (SQC) (p. 333)
supply chain (p. 321)
supply chain management (p. 321)
total quality management (TQM) (p. 333)
utility (p. 323)
utility supply (p. 316)

Self-Test

Multiple Choice   You can find the answers on the last page of this book.

1. Which is *not* a concern when a company is trying to determine a location of their facilities?
   a. The proximity to the potential customer base
   b. The weather conditions of the area
   c. The skills and education of the residents in the region
   d. The proximity to raw materials and transportation

2. Mass customization is achieved by using which type of system?
   a. Flexible manufacturing system
   b. Lean production
   c. Forward processing
   d. Backward processing

3. Which production process strives to reduce waste and improve production flow?
   a. Mass customization
   b. Mass production
   c. Lean production
   d. Assembly line production

4. If the Ford Motor Company wants to understand the aerodynamics of a new auto body, which of the following would be used to create a virtual three-dimensional model of the auto body?
   a. CAD
   b. Simultaneous engineering
   c. CIM
   d. Robotics

5. Which of the following is a set of environmental quality standards that can be applied to any organization?
   a. Six Sigma
   b. ISO 14001
   c. ISO 9001
   d. TQM

6. An effective plan by a production manager should lead to
   a. increased productivity.
   b. reduced costs.
   c. improved customer service.
   d. All of the above

7. Which feature distinguishes a PERT chart from a Gantt chart?
   a. Creates a timeline of production tasks
   b. Creates a workflow for production equipment
   c. Identifies the critical path of tasks in a project
   d. Predicts the completion time of a project

8. Radio frequency identification is used to
   a. keep track of the status and quantity of each item.
   b. keep track of the customer base for an item.
   c. stay in touch with other workers in a factory.
   d. manufacture stereo systems.

★ 9. Which type of facility layout would be best used for the production of potato chips?
   a. Product layout
   b. Process layout
   c. Cellular layout
   d. Fixed position layout

10. TQM is geared toward
   a. producing the largest quantity of goods in the time allotted.
   b. reducing errors throughout the production process.
   c. eliminating humans from the workplace.
   d. meeting government standards for emissions.

True/False   You can find the answers on the last page of this book.

1. Robots can work around the clock with good accuracy and in potentially hazardous conditions.
   ☐ True or ☐ False

2. CAD and CAM have dramatically reduced the time between the design and manufacturing stages of production.
   ☐ True or ☐ False

3. Supply chain management refers to the process of delivering the supplies necessary for manufacturing.
   ☐ True or ☐ False

4. The make-or-buy decision comes at the end of the production process if a product has not turned out as planned.
   ☐ True or ☐ False

5. The JIT method of inventory control consists of keeping a large amount of inventory in the warehouse to be sure that all deliveries will be made on time.
   ☐ True or ☐ False

Critical Thinking Questions

✪ 1. Supply chain management is the management of activities from all organizations involved in producing and delivering a good or service. If you were in charge of improving the supply chain at your college, what components would it involve? Consider internal and external sources. Where might improvements be made?

✪ 2. You have decided to open a company that produces wooden furniture, and you must select a suitable location for production. The first option is in a remote region of Montana with easy access to abundant raw materials but far away from a skilled worker base. The second option is in Southern California in close proximity to many skilled workers as well as several major highways for distribution, but not close to raw materials. Which location would you choose for your business and why?

✪ 3. A sports equipment company is known for a special grip on its tennis rackets that is imported from South America. The cost of shipping these grips has grown steadily more expensive, and the business would like to produce the grips in-house. What factors does the business need to consider before adding another step to the production process?

Team Time

TO OUTSOURCE OR NOT TO OUTSOURCE . . . THAT IS THE QUESTION

Divide into two teams to represent both sides of the issue:

a. One group thinks the company should make the component.

b. One group thinks the company should outsource the component.

Scenario

The Grindstone Supply Company of New Jersey is attempting to expand its manufacturing of large wall clocks. In years past, the company has outsourced the manufacturing of clock springs to a company in Nebraska. This has been cost-effective in the past, but now that demand for the springs has increased, Grindstone is considering manufacturing the springs in-house. Although the cost of producing the springs in-house is lower, it is unclear whether it will be profitable in the long run, as the manufacturing process will change greatly. New machines for the production of springs will be needed, as the factory works exclusively in wood and plastic. With the new machines comes the need for new technicians to monitor and service them. Should the Grindstone Supply Company alter its manufacturing process to include the production of clock springs or should it continue outsourcing to Nebraska as it has in the past? What factors contribute to this decision? Will this be more profitable in the long run? How will the decision affect employee morale and relations?

Process

Step 1. Record your ideas and opinions about the issue presented in the scenario. Be sure to consider the issue from your assigned perspective.

Step 2. Meet as a team and review the issue from both perspectives. Discuss why the position of your group is the best decision.

Ethics and Corporate Social Responsibility

ENVIRONMENTAL SHIPPING CONCERNS

You have just been promoted as the head of the shipping department for your office supply company, and it is now your responsibility to determine routing. The company is located on the eastern seaboard, near major highways as well as the ocean. In the past, trucking has been the preferred method of shipping, as it was deemed the most cost-effective. Shipping by boat, however, would greatly reduce the negative effects on the environment caused by truck emissions. After calculating the cost on paper, you realize that shipping by sea would have a negative effect on the overall profit margin, but the company would still generate solid profits.

Questions to Discuss

1. What decision would you make in this situation—land or sea?

2. If you were told that you would take a personal pay cut from switching to the more environmentally friendly route, how would that affect your decision?

3. What kind of impact do you think one company switching to less environmentally damaging practices could have on the general atmosphere of the shipping world?

Web Exercises

1. **Have It Your Way**
   Burger King introduced mass customization to its fast-food offerings in the mid-1970s, thus revolutionizing how fast food could be delivered. Today, mass customization is aided by the Internet and other technologies. Search the Internet and find five companies that use mass customization. Is customizing a product to your specific needs important to you? Why or why not?

2. **Greening America**
   Although the United States has become more of a service-based economy, many feel that the focus on creating new, environmentally friendly technologies may bring manufacturing back to the country and help power an economic recovery. Research what kinds of environmental technologies are being manufactured in the United States today. Do you think a greater investment in these technologies could help fuel an economic recovery? Why or why not?

3. **Radio Frequency Identification**
   The use of chips to track goods during the shipping process is becoming more widespread. Use the Internet to research options for RFID. What are some of the options for tracking goods? What kind of range can these products cover?

4. **How Everyday Things Are Made**
   The Alliance for Innovative Manufacturing at Stanford University has put together short videos on how certain products such as jelly beans, airplanes, and bottles are made. These products use various manufacturing processes including forging, casting, and injection molding. Type manufacturing.stanford.edu into your Web browser and click on the "How Everyday Things Are Made" link. Watch a few videos and click on the "Test your Knowledge," "Think About It," and "Apply It" links. Write a brief summary of your experience and outcomes.

5. **Quality Control**
   Quality control is a major issue in the mass production of goods. Many systems have been used to assure quality control in manufacturing. Find two different systems of quality control on the Internet. What are the merits and downfalls of each? If you were in charge of the production of a product, which system of quality control would you choose? Write a paragraph comparing and contrasting these two quality control systems.

MyBizLab

Go to **mybizlab.com** for Auto-graded writing questions as well as the following Assisted-graded writing questions:

11-1. What technological changes have enabled mass customization to take place? What are the advantages and disadvantages of this type of production process compared to mass production?

11-2. Give an example of what the TQM process would involve in a restaurant. What steps can restaurants take to ensure that a high level of quality is maintained consistently in their food delivery process?

11-3. MyBizLab Only – comprehensive writing assignment for this chapter.

Business Communications

endostock/Fotolia

We communicate and interact with others all day, every day. In fact, people in organizations spend at least 75 percent of their time in interpersonal situations—one-on-one; in groups; intra-organizational; or with customers, suppliers, investors, and advisors.[1] Communicating effectively is critical in the business world, yet it can present significant challenges. When you consider the impact poor communication can have on business—such as a loss of customers from poor customer service, a lack of focus on business objectives, and stifled innovation—it becomes clear why effective communication is an important business goal. In this mini chapter, we'll discuss how you can improve your communication skills in the workplace.

Improving Your Presentation Skills

In business, you often need to persuade, educate, or inform a group about your ideas. If you don't have strong presentation skills, your audience won't be receptive. Good presentation skills begin with good oral communication skills, so you need to make sure you speak loudly and clearly. Change your vocal intonation to add emphasis or interest when appropriate. It is important to engage audience members by looking directly at them, often changing your focus to different individuals around the room. Relax and smile, just as you would if you were talking to your friends.

Presentation software, such as Microsoft's PowerPoint, can be a great addition to a presentation if it is used correctly. We have all sat through boring presentations where the speaker read directly from the slides or used too many distracting graphics, animations, and blinding color schemes. When used to its best capabilities, PowerPoint can be a very effective tool. In this mini chapter, you'll find some tips to make your next PowerPoint presentation successful.

Delivering effective presentations requires planning and practice.

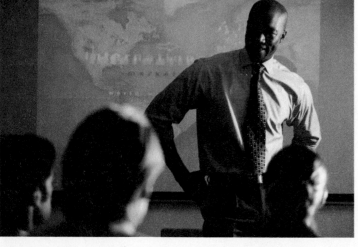

AISPIX by Image Source/Shutterstock

The complement to good oral communication skills is active listening skills. To ensure that you're being attentive when listening, repeat back or summarize the points that you believe were made. Good listening also means asking good questions, but avoid becoming distracted by trying to think of what you're going to say next. If you need clarification, try to respond with statements such as "Tell me more." Finally, keep an open mind to others' ideas and suggestions. You do not necessarily want to have a solution or outcome defined in your mind before you hear what everyone else has to say.

PowerPoint Tips

1. **Keep it simple.** Just because the software is capable of doing amazing things, don't feel as if you have to use all the bells and whistles. Keep the design clean and charts simple and easy to understand. Limit the number of animations and special effects. In addition, use graphics to illustrate or highlight what you're saying—not to serve as the focus.

2. **Follow the 6 × 6 × 24 rule.** Remember, PowerPoint slides should represent only an outline of key points you are making. Don't include everything you plan to say on the slides. Place only those key words or thoughts you want your audience to remember. As you speak, fill in the other details. To help keep the content of your slides to a minimum, presentation experts suggest you use no more than six words in a bullet point, six bullet points on a slide, and a font size that is at least 24-point. Also try to keep the total number of slides to a minimum.

3. **Use graphics and media to convey ideas.** Combining a strong oral presentation with visual cues on slides can make PowerPoint a very effective part of your delivery. We can better remember what someone is saying if we see key words at the same time that we hear them. We remember even better when the right graphic or image is used to convey an entire idea. Consider incorporating short video pieces into your presentation to add a bit of humor, bring in a different "speaker," or convey a message in a different way. YouTube and Google Video are useful storehouses of video, as are Vimeo, Ustream, and Ted.com.

4. **Use color sparingly but effectively.** A light background with dark text is the best color combination for most lighting conditions. Adding color sparingly will help add visual interest and bring special attention to key areas of the presentation. Too much color can be distracting.

5. **Edit and proofread.** Typographical and spelling errors as well as grammatical mistakes make it appear as if you didn't review your presentation slides and leave a bad impression with your audience. If you know that grammar is a weak area for you, ask a friend who is a good editor to review the slides for you.

6. **Practice.** Practice giving your presentation several times aloud before giving it live in front of an audience. If you find yourself stumbling through a part, think more about the exact idea you need to communicate—additional examples you could use, analogies that might explain it better to your audience, and so on. When you practice your presentation, use the Rehearse Timings mode to record how many seconds you are staying on each slide. Review these numbers and make sure you are spending the most time on the sections that are most critical to your message.

Improving Your Writing Skills

In business, written communication is often in the form of a business letter or memo. Let's look at each of these forms of writing.

Business Letters

There is still a place in the business world for nonelectronic communication. For example, when a company offers you a position, it will often mail a business letter documenting the responsibilities and benefits of the offer. Communications sent via U.S. Postal Service are also often used when a formal, documented series

■ FIGURE 1
A Traditional Business Letter
Adapted by Permission from Lynn E. Elfner,
"In search of a lost art: How to Write a
Business Letter." Adventures of Cyberbee.
©2009 Linda C. Joseph.

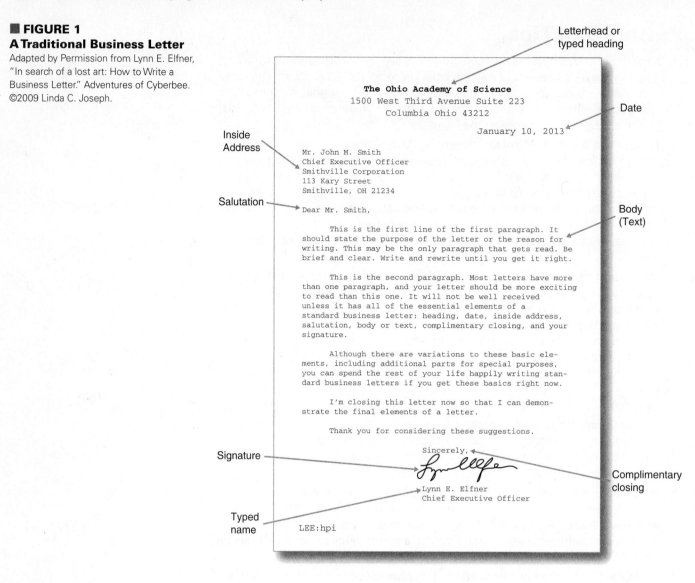

Letterhead or
typed heading

The Ohio Academy of Science
1500 West Third Avenue Suite 223
Columbia Ohio 43212

Date

January 10, 2013

Inside
Address

Mr. John M. Smith
Chief Executive Officer
Smithville Corporation
113 Kary Street
Smithville, OH 21234

Salutation

Dear Mr. Smith,

Body
(Text)

This is the first line of the first paragraph. It
should state the purpose of the letter or the reason for
writing. This may be the only paragraph that gets read. Be
brief and clear. Write and rewrite until you get it right.

This is the second paragraph. Most letters have more
than one paragraph, and your letter should be more exciting
to read than this one. It will not be well received
unless it has all of the essential elements of a
standard business letter: heading, date, inside address,
salutation, body or text, complimentary closing, and your
signature.

Although there are variations to these basic elements, including additional parts for special purposes,
you can spend the rest of your life happily writing standard business letters if you get these basics right now.

I'm closing this letter now so that I can demonstrate the final elements of a letter.

Thank you for considering these suggestions.

Signature

Sincerely,

Complimentary
closing

Lynn E. Elfner
Chief Executive Officer

Typed
name

LEE:hpi

of actions is being conducted between two people. As shown in **■ FIGURE 1**, a traditional business letter has a specific format that includes the date at the top, the address of the person receiving the letter, and a formal salutation. Businesses typically have a stock supply of letterhead paper, imprinted with their logo and design, on hand for mailings.

If you are on a first-name basis with the intended recipient, then your salutation can use the first name, such as "Dear Rebecca." In other cases, use a title and last name such as "Dear Mr. Consuelas." Letters can be more descriptive and include more detail than other summary types of communications, but they still need to be clear and to the point. Assume that the recipient doesn't have time to read through flowery prose. As with any other piece of writing, a business letter should have a beginning, a middle, and an ending. State the purpose of the letter in the first paragraph: "As you requested, I am providing more information . . . ," "I regret to inform you that . . . ," "I am enclosing. . . ." The paragraphs that follow should add supportive details. The final paragraph should offer information about what action will follow or what is expected from the

■ **FIGURE 2**
A Standard Memo

To: All Employees

From: Evan Galvez. CEO

Re: Welcome to our new Vice President of Social Media Communications

---

I would like to announce that Jerry Spangler will be joining the Digital Strategies family as our new Vice President of Social Media Communications.

We are very excited to have Jerry leading our social media communications. He brings with him a wealth of experience having been a social media consultant to many well-known firms in the Silicon Valley area.

Please join me in welcoming Jerry to Digital Strategies!

recipient. Business letters should end with a formal closing, such as "Sincerely," with your full name and title. You may include your contact information after your title if it's not included in the letterhead information. It is important that information in a business letter be written precisely. Make sure the language is clear and simple.

Memos

Memos are used to make announcements, summarize facts from a conversation or a meeting, or request or exchange information. They are either formal or informal, depending on the content. Typically, they're used for communications within an office or a company, not between companies and external contacts or clients. As shown in ■ **FIGURE 2**, memos have a standard heading format that contains the date, the person(s) to whom the memo is addressed (the To: line), the name of anyone else receiving a copy (the Cc: line), the name of the sender (the From: line), and a concise statement of the memo's topic (Subject: or Re:). You can find a large number of pre-designed memo templates for Microsoft Word on the Microsoft Office website. The following tips provide some points to remember when writing memos.

Memo Writing Tips

- Be concise.
- Use headings, bullets, and/or numbered lists to highlight key points.
- Keep each paragraph short and focused on one main idea.
- Always proofread carefully. Check all facts for accuracy.
- Identify any attachments so they don't go unnoticed.
- Closings are unnecessary. The "From" line eliminates the need.
- Remember that memos should be professional in tone and appearance.

What Form of Communication Should You Use?

There are many options when it comes to getting your message across. Should you send an e-mail? Write a letter? Visit your client face-to-face? Let's investigate the specific strengths and weaknesses of each type of communication so you can better match your delivery choice to the situation.

Oral communication allows participants to assess the meanings of the speaker's words and voice intonations. When speaking in person, participants also use "unspoken" messages sent by body language and facial expressions when interpreting the message. The speaker can adapt his or her message by assessing a listener's attentiveness. However, oral communication is not perfect. To deliver your message accurately, especially to those with whom you're not very familiar, it is important to offer clear, unbiased language and avoid clichés, negative metaphors, and culturally specific references. For example, using the expression "down to the last out" is meaningful to an American baseball fan but perhaps not to someone from another country.

Written communication has more permanency than oral communication. You can revise it before sending or review it at a later date. In addition, the receiver has more time to analyze the content before responding. On the other hand, the sender has no control over when the recipient chooses to read the message and does not benefit from immediate feedback; the sender is not always given the opportunity for further clarification. Finally, written communication can lead to misunderstandings due to the lack of face-to-face interaction. Albert Mehrabian from UCLA found that 55 percent of meaning in an interaction comes from facial and body language and 38 percent comes from vocal inflection. The words convey only 7 percent of meaning.[2] Therefore, if the nature of a written communication contains anything sensitive or complicated, it might be wise to follow up with a quick phone call or an in-person meeting.

E-mail

E-mail is perhaps the most used form of digital written communication, although social networks, wikis, podcasts, and blogs are becoming increasingly popular in the business world. E-mail is quick and convenient, and the sender and receiver don't need to be available at the same time to communicate. Popular mobile devices, such as smartphones, and Internet tablets, such as the iPad, enable people to read and reply to e-mail any time they have a phone signal or wi-fi connection.

In the business world, your e-mail is all that many people see of you. It is important to take time to understand the audience to whom you're sending the e-mail, and structure it accordingly. Obviously, an e-mail to a friend will be different from one to your boss or a client. A friend may expect a loosely formatted e-mail—full of slang and spelling errors. However, in a business context, such an e-mail will give people a negative impression of you. Your e-mails represent you and your organization; therefore, sending clear, organized, and thoughtful messages is critical. The following list has some pertinent tips for e-mail writing.

Tips on Writing Effective Business E-Mail

1. **Use a meaningful subject line.** Subject lines help the reader prioritize and organize e-mail messages. Instead of "Here's what you're asking for," try to be more specific, such as "3/3/13 Client X Update." Create agreed-on acronyms for use in subject lines that help to better identify messages and/or actions required, such as AR (Action Required) or MSR (Monthly Status Report). Using consistent identifications can help with filtering/sorting functions as well as help prioritize actions that are required. If possible, condense the entire message into several words that fit in the subject line, such as "2 P.M. meeting on 2/15/13 confirmed."

2. **Watch slang and offensive or potentially damaging content.** E-mails are business documents. Err on the side of being utterly conservative in your language and content. You don't want to offend anyone by using the wrong words or including something deemed inappropriate. Do not use texting abbreviations.

3. **Proofread and edit.** Quickly firing off an e-mail without proofreading can lead to big mistakes or misunderstandings. Make sure the message is free of grammatical and spelling errors.

4. **Keep it brief and focused.** Your e-mail may be one of 200 (or more!) read by the recipient that day, so keep the content brief and focused. Organize with bullets or short sentences so the reader can clearly understand key points. Be specific. If you send a 20-page attachment, for example, tell the recipient that the important information is on pages 2 and 17.

5. **Be considerate of file format.** When you don't know if the recipient has the right software to view an attachment, use a universal format, such as a PDF.

6. **Include previous messages in a reply.** Even if you copy only a phrase from a previous e-mail, including messages in a reply helps when responses are not immediate. You wouldn't pick up a phone and say "I agree," and expect the person on the other end to understand what you're agreeing with if you hadn't spoken in a day or two. However, be careful when including an entire message if you're adding someone new to the e-mail. Long threads of e-mail exchanges may contain information that is not appropriate for a new person to see.

7. **Use a signature line.** The line should include your title and full contact information.

E-mail has other limitations, so users need to be aware of them to avoid problems. Be considerate of the size for attachments. Most e-mail servers have a limit and will not allow an e-mail through if it has exceptionally large attachments. If large files need to be exchanged, consider placing the information on an intraoffice website. There are also free Web services like YouSendIt that allow you to easily send files up to 2 gigabytes in size.

Also, apply caution when using e-mail because it is not as private as a regular letter. E-mail is more like a postcard that can be read, copied, saved, shared, and exchanged by anyone. Work e-mails can be legally monitored by your boss and may be subject to review if a lawsuit is filed against your company.[3] In addition, serious mistakes have occurred when users have mistakenly "replied to all" with comments about one of the people on the distribution list or have forwarded the message to the wrong person. Because of its ease of use and access, many users have gotten into troubling circumstances after shooting off an e-mail in frustration or anger rather than waiting to cool off and responding in a calmer and more professional state of mind. The bottom line is, e-mail should be used with care and should not be used to communicate secure, private, or potentially damaging information.

Companies are beginning to recognize the problems erupting from the high volume of e-mail. The tool that offers us an easier way to communicate is, in some instances, actually making it harder for us to communicate. Companies in all

Texting has become part of business in many settings.

industries are adopting "no e-mail" days in an effort to reduce the e-mail overload and encourage employees to get out from behind their digital devices and actually talk to their colleagues and customers, whether in person or on the telephone. The results have been astonishing. For example, when U.S. Cellular enforced a no-e-mail Friday, two coworkers who had been communicating with each other exclusively by e-mail found out that instead of being across the country from each other, they were only across the hall. Now, their working relationship is much stronger due to their in-person interactions. When people were forced to call public affairs manager Tyler Caroll on no-e-mail Fridays, many were surprised to find out that the person they assumed was "Mr. Caroll" was a woman.[4]

Workdays without e-mail have been highly successful in increasing teamwork, providing better customer service, and helping companies solve problems quickly. As a result, many companies are looking for other ways to reduce the stresses caused by electronic overload and an "always-on" environment, such as "no-meeting Fridays" or "quiet time" to allow employees time to work uninterrupted in an offline mode.

Instant Messaging

Instant messaging (IM) is quickly catching on in the business community as a means for conducting personal chats. Because of its immediacy and streamlined efficiency, many business users prefer IM to phone calls and e-mail. However, like e-mail, IM should not be used to communicate confrontational, sensitive, or confidential information. IM messages can be copied and saved to a Word document or archived in their entirety, so discretion is important. Instant messaging is great when used to convey simple messages, clarify a point, confirm a meeting, and the like.

Texting

Texting is another popular form of digital communication. As a means of exchanging quick messages via a cell phone, texting can be as useful as IM. When texting is done with devices that do not have a full keyboard, the sender has to communicate solely with the 9-digit text/number pad found on phones. Texting users have responded by developing a shorthand-type language that uses abbreviations for traditional words or phrases. Texting is finding more and more uses in business meetings and during business travel; however, avoid using texting abbreviations, which are very informal, in more formal business texting. Many businesses also use text messaging as a means to "push" information to users via their cell phone. For example, airlines use texting to confirm flight information, and real estate agents use it to inform buyers when new listings that fit their specifications come on the market. Advertisers are also finding text messaging a convenient way to alert users to new product information.

Videoconferencing unites attendees in different locations with a real-time audio and video connection.

Using Collaborative Communication Tools

In addition to presentations, memos, e-mail, and so on, there are a variety of tools to aid collaborative business communications.

Videoconferencing

Videoconferencing uses two-way audio and video technology to allow people in two or more locations to interact simultaneously. This means that people in different parts of the country or the world can have virtual meetings in which they can see each other and interact face-to-face. In addition to reducing travel costs, companies that use videoconferencing have found that increasing face-to-face time between employees is beneficial. Videoconferencing has also been implemented as a means of following up with clients and as a mode of effectively training workers in multiple locations.

Popular devices, such as the iPhone, now support videoconferencing. Each iPhone has two cameras, one pointing to the speaker's face and one pointing out the back of the camera. An iPhone user can videoconference with another iPhone user, sending the video of them speaking or switching to a video of something else in the room.

There are other technologies that offer efficient and effective collaborations in a virtual workplace. Online meeting software, such as WebEx, allows users to run and archive meetings with users from any location. Each person can stream in video from a webcam or just join in through voice. Users can participate whether they are at a computer workstation, on a laptop, or using a smartphone. Meeting participants can present slideshows, take live questions, run software applications, and share documents. Remote desktop control allows anyone in the meeting to take control of each user's desktop to make a point or illustrate a feature. Tools like WebEx are used for conferencing but also for interactive customer training, sales presentations, and customer support.

Wikis

A wiki is a collaborative website that allows users to create, add, edit, or remove Web content using any Web browser (see ■ **FIGURE 3**). It's like a shared workspace where everyone has full and equal access to the same project, only better. Because all versions of the Web content are saved, users can revert back to a previous version of a document, as well as track all edits and who made the edits. Wikis provide an excellent means of collaborative writing and allow multiple authors to edit and produce a single document.

Joe provides initial text (represented by black text)

Sheila provides extra detail (represented by red text)

Before hiring additional employees, an analytical study of the tasks to be performed within the organization should be completed. With small businesses, this might be a simple process conducted by the business owner, as small business owners usually have a good idea of the tasks that need to be done and even who is the most qualified person to perform those tasks. As an organization grows, and more employees are required to ensure that the goals of the organization are met, this analysis becomes a function of human resources. A job analysis identifies and defines in detail the particular duties and responsibilities an employee is required to conduct. In a job analysis, each task is defined by a job description, a formal statement that summarizes the job objectives, responsibilities, and conditions under which the job will be performed. Job descriptions are important as they define the job's relation to the rest of the organizational structure. They also define job objectives, which are later used in performance appraisals and can become a part of the legal contract between the employee and the employer.

Steve adds more text (represented by green text)

■ **FIGURE 3**
Professional Collaboration
Wikis are great collaboration tools.
(left: top, vgstudio/Fotolia; bottom, Sergej Khackimullin/ Fotolia; right: ARENA Creative/ Shutterstock)

Unlike exchanging e-mails and attachments, there are no timing and version issues. Moreover, all users can see and comment on the document at any time, thus making the process more collaborative and accessible to all. The cost of using wikis is virtually negligible because the software for wikis is free, and little—if any—additional hardware or IT support is required. Beyond team collaboration, businesses are using wikis to ask questions, offer help, correct and add information to documents and presentations, brainstorm, and keep everyone informed about projects. Although some wikis, such as Wikipedia, the wiki-based online encyclopedia, are available and accessible to the general public, it is possible to make wikis private and available to only a select group of individuals, thus reducing privacy and confidentiality issues. Wikis can contain a variety of formats, such as documents, spreadsheets, and presentations, and they can be arranged into different pages for better content organization.

Blogs

A blog is a Web log that is usually authored by an individual and cannot be changed or edited by visitors. Visitors can, however, add comments to the original content. In some instances, blogging and business have not mixed well, such as when bloggers have written unflattering tales about their employers or when their blogosphere persona is radically different from their corporate persona. For example, Google fired Mark Jen after postings on his blog criticized Google and allegedly revealed sensitive financial information.[5] The PittGirl, a popular blogger in Pittsburgh who used comedy and commentary to jibe the mayor, ran into conflict between the anonymity of cyberspace and the demands of the business world. The PittGirl blog became a popular site, and eventually author Virginia Montanez revealed her identity. The next day she was fired from her job for the Negro Educational Emergency Drive.[6] It is still unclear how anonymous you are as a blogger and when legal action can be taken to force your identity to be revealed.

Many companies recognize that blogs afford them an opportunity to reach a wide audience and elicit feedback via commenting sections. Blogs offer companies the opportunity to interact with their customers in ways that other forms of communication do not. Because companies can sift through blogs to determine the "pulse" of the public—what they are talking about, what is important to them, and what they like and dislike about current trends or products—blogs are a valuable marketing research tool. In fact, more than 22 percent of *Fortune* 500 companies have active business blogs with content about the company and/or its products.[7] For example, Dr. Laundry is a blog created by the Clorox Company about bleaching tips. Marriott on the Move is a blog written by Bill Marriott, chairman and CEO of Marriott International, one of the world's largest hotel chains. When Bob Lutz, vice chairman of GM, began his FastLane blog, readers bombarded it with their critiques and suggestions.

Podcasts

A podcast is another form of digital communication that the business community is embracing—in fact, 19 percent of *Fortune* 500 companies provide podcasts.[8] A podcast is an audio (or video) file stored on the Internet that customers can download to their computers or MP3 players and listen to whenever they want. Podcasts are unique in that customers can subscribe to programs they are interested in and have them automatically downloaded to their computers every time new content is available. Because the

Podcasts are audio or video broadcasts pushed automatically to your computer and mobile device.

Jessmine/Shutterstock

downloading process is quick and automatic, podcasts are simple and convenient for businesses and customers alike. Best of all, most podcasts, as well as the necessary software, are free.

Effective, efficient communication is key in today's dynamic global economy. Fortunately, there are many options from which to choose when it comes to business communications, from traditional phone conversations and letters to high-tech videoconferencing and wikis. Remember to choose the best form for a given situation, and, most importantly, use it wisely.

CHAPTER 12

Marketing and Consumer Behavior

OBJECTIVES

Marketing Fundamentals

Ford Motor Company started production of the first Model T in 1913. Nearly 100 years later, the automobile manufacturer is still producing vehicles. Part of the company's success is that it has changed its marketing concepts to meet the times. How has marketing evolved? How does marketing benefit the customer, the seller, and even society?

Marketing Tactics

Aaron Hoffman has a business idea to start a mobile pet-grooming service. An advisor told him that he needs to create a "marketing strategy." What is a marketing strategy? Why is it necessary?

The Marketing Environment

Amelia Russo runs a store selling inexpensive dress shoes that she imports from overseas. The value of the U.S. dollar has gotten so low that she needs to raise her prices. Her marketing environment is forcing her to change the way she does business. What is a marketing environment? How can it pose constraints on a business?

Marketing Research and Planning

Tiara Watson has decided to start a salon supply business. She knows that there is a demand for her products, but she wants to draw up a carefully organized marketing plan to ensure the success of her business. There are over thirty salons in her city, and Tiara has the connections to offer them products at a lower cost. What steps must she take to get her name known in the salon supply world? What can she do to ensure success in her new business?

Consumer Behavior

Will Giusto needs to buy a computer and is overwhelmed at the selection in front of him at the store. His girlfriend has a Mac, and his best friend has a top-notch gaming machine. Will isn't looking for a name brand or a computer with lots of features. What factors will help him choose one computer over another?

MyBizLab®

⭐ **Improve Your Grade!**

Over 10 million students improved their results using the Pearson MyLabs.
Visit **mybizlab.com** for simulations, tutorials, and end-of-chapter problems.

Marketing Fundamentals pp. 353–359

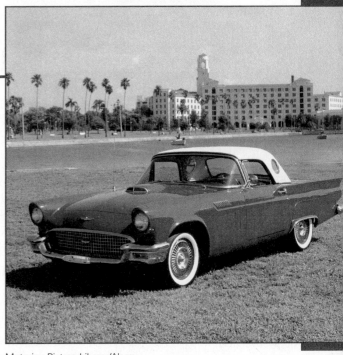

Motoring Picture Library/Alamy

The innovation of the assembly line enabled Ford Motor Company to mass produce millions of Model Ts when production began in 1913. Years later, when customers' needs and tastes changed, and the Model T did not, production of the Model T stopped in 1927. Ford learned its lesson that it needed to respond to the customer. When the new Model A rolled off the line, it responded to a more affluent consumer market, offering both style and comfort. Nearly two decades later, an improved economy and more sophisticated customers' tastes sparked an interest in the '49 Ford. It was offered in a wide range of body styles, with elegance meeting performance, and there was "something for everyone." In 1955, the Ford Thunderbird captured the free spirit of that era. Ford continued along the "road to postwar prosperity"[1] over the next several decades despite stiff competition and financial pressures from economic and gas crises. Now, after some difficult economic times, Ford Motor Company is back—some say better than they were before. As this brief history of the company indicates, the company's marketing strategies have evolved over time. Will it be able to continue its marketing success into the future? ■

In its broadest sense, *marketing* can be thought of as identifying and meeting human needs and wants. However, the degree to which marketers have identified and met people's needs and wants has changed over time, as has the American Marketing Association's (AMA's) official definition of marketing. In 2004, the American Marketing Association (AMA) revised the definition to reflect a new focus on value for customers as well as to recognize the importance of managing customer relationships. The AMA now defines **marketing** as "an organizational function and a set of processes for creating, communicating, and delivering value to customers and for managing customer relationships in ways that benefit the organization and its stakeholders."[2]

What does a marketing department do? Marketing departments serve a variety of functions (see ■ **FIGURE 12.1**). First and foremost, marketers are

■ FIGURE 12.1
Functions of a Marketing Department
Image sources, top to bottom: valdis torms/ Fotolia; zentilia/ Fotolia; Sashkin/Fotolia; CenturionStudio.it/Fotolia; Inllusion/ Fotolia

1 | How has marketing evolved over time?

■ FIGURE 12.2
The Evolution of Marketing
Adapted from Figure "The Alternative Business Philosophies" in "Overview of the Alternative Business Philosophies" by Dr. Kenneth M. Thompson. Introduction to Marketing course site. http://courses.unt .edu/kt3650_1/

responsible for keeping an eye on what people need and want and then communicating these desires to the rest of the organization. Marketing departments help establish desirable pricing strategies and promote an organization by persuading customers that their products are the best. As you've learned, a **product** is any tangible good, service, or idea available for purchase in a market, as well as any intangible benefits derived from its consumption. Marketing departments are also responsible for distributing products to customers at a place and time most suitable to the customer. But perhaps the most important aspect of marketing is to successfully establish meaningful relationships with customers, to instill loyalty, and to ensure repeat business. Marketing is one of the most visible functions of any organization; however, the public sees only the tip of the iceberg. In this chapter, we'll present some basic aspects of this important corporate function, including marketing strategies, the marketing mix, and consumer behavior. We'll start by looking at how marketing has changed over time.

The Evolution of Marketing

How has marketing evolved over time? The nature of marketing has evolved over five general eras (see **■ FIGURE 12.2**):

1. The production concept era
2. The sales concept era
3. The marketing concept era
4. The societal marketing era
5. The customer relationship era

Although each concept experienced a peak in popularity during a specific time period, some companies still employ marketing concepts from an earlier era. Today's most successful marketing campaigns are a sophisticated combination of the best of each of these concepts.

What was the marketing philosophy of the early 1900s? From the Industrial Revolution until the 1920s, most companies focused solely on production—thus the *production concept era* evolved. The prevailing mind-set was that a good quality product would simply sell itself. This approach worked for many organizations during this era because of strong demand and a limited supply of products. Whenever demand exceeds supply, it creates a seller's market. This type of economic climate may have motivated Henry Ford to remark that his Model T cars could be painted "any color, so long as it's black."[3]

What was the sales concept era? From the mid-1920s through the early 1950s, technological advances accelerated production. In the first part of the era, however, the United States was in the middle of the Great Depression, during which unemployment was nearing 30 percent, and people bought only what they absolutely needed. Supply far exceeded demand for most products; therefore, competition for customers became more intense. Businesses began to undertake aggressive sales tactics to sell or "push" their products, and the use of heavy public advertising in all available forms of media became prevalent. Thus began the *sales concept era*. During this era, marketing generally took place after a product was developed and produced. Heavy emphasis was placed on selling existing products, and is characterized by the door-to-door salesman pushing hair brushes, vacuum cleaners, and encyclopedias. Even today, many people associate marketing with selling or advertising; however, it has become much more than that.

What was the marketing concept era? By the 1950s, production continued to expand more quickly than did growth in demand for goods and services. In addition, there were more companies producing similar products competing for a buyer's attention. This created a buyer's market and the start of the *marketing concept era*. Soldiers returning from World War II were getting married, starting families, and willing to spend their money on goods and services. Consumers were beginning to tire of the "hard sell" tactics that companies were using to force them to buy products they didn't necessarily want or need. Eventually, businesses began to realize that simply producing quality products and pushing them onto customers through clever advertising and promotional campaigns didn't guarantee sales.

Companies needed to determine what customers wanted and then produce products that met those wants and needs, as opposed to producing products and then trying to convince customers to buy them. The **marketing concept** changed the focus from finding the right customer for a product to producing the right product for a customer and doing it better than the competition. As you can see in ■ **FIGURE 12.3**, the marketing concept also focuses on aligning all functions of the organization to meet or exceed the customer's needs through superior products and customer service. In addition, the marketing concept focused on satisfying customers over the long term.

General Electric (GE) was one of the first companies to implement this new marketing strategy. GE's 1952 annual report outlined its new marketing philosophy, which stated that GE would provide a product that the customer wants at the price they are willing to pay, and have it delivered to the customer at the right time and location. To do this, the GE marketing team had control of the product through all phases, from planning, through production scheduling and inventory control, as well as sales, distribution, and servicing.[4]

■ **FIGURE 12.3**
The Marketing Concept

The marketing concept requires a company to constantly take the pulse of changing customer needs and wants and then quickly adapt to meet them. Moreover, it may mean anticipating customers' changing preferences—before they are expressed or even known by the customer—and satisfying these preferences before competitors do. Even today, companies such as Apple have had great success following this philosophy. Apple has become a master of anticipating customers' desires and fulfilling them with its range of iPods, iPod accessories, iPhones, iPhone apps, and the iPad.

Does marketing also take into consideration what's best for society?
Companies began to realize that they must also take into consideration the long-term interests of society. *Societal marketing,* an offshoot of the marketing concept and corporate social responsibility, began in the late 1960s and early 1970s. It challenges companies to work for the benefit of both consumers and society while still attaining a profit. The Body Shop, a skin and cosmetics company, sells products that are made with only 100 percent natural ingredients. The company also actively supports and pursues community trade by using highly skilled but small-scale farmers, craftsmen, and rural cooperatives because it is the way to do business that is best for society.[5] Other examples of the societal marketing approach in action include companies that are going green, such as the automotive industry manufacturing more fuel-efficient vehicles, or industries that are influencing healthy behavior and discouraging unhealthy practices, such as the new diet-conscious menu additions at fast-food restaurants.

What marketing philosophy encourages customer loyalty?
The late 1990s saw the beginning of the *customer relationship era,* in which organizations try to intensify their focus on customer satisfaction over time. The result has been the creation of **customer relationship management (CRM)**, the process of establishing long-term relationships with individual customers to foster loyalty and repeat business (see ■ **FIGURE 12.4**). The marketing concept is good for *acquiring* customers by offering customized products, among other things, but customer relationship management goes one step further by trying to please customers after the sale. It combines customer service and marketing communications to *retain* customers so in order to to stimulate future sales of similar or supplementary products. For example, most stores send e-mails with coupons and information about their sales and promotions to customers who join their mailing lists or who "like" them on Facebook. Amazon.com uses its massive database to automatically offer suggestions for future purchases to customers based on their prior purchases or browsing interests.

The idea of customer loyalty programs is to learn as much as possible about customers and their shopping behaviors and create a meaningful one-on-one interaction with each of them. In practice, CRM often involves the sales force gathering information about specific customers to create a customer database. Other companies use CRM software to personalize e-mail or other communications. It enables a company to offer products tailored to specific customers' needs and desires. CRM databases also mean that customers visiting an organization's website or phoning the customer service call center can be quickly and easily recognized so that offerings can be adapted to their preferences. CRM is part of why airlines offer frequent flyer programs and why credit card companies offer customized services and low-interest balance transfer to certain targeted customers.

Marketing for Not-for-Profits and Others

How do not-for-profit organizations market their products?
Many not-for-profit organizations also have an interest in marketing. Rather than a product or a service, these organizations look to market an event, a cause, a place, or a person. For example, organizations such as the Sierra Club and the Red Cross rely on marketing to raise awareness of and

■ **FIGURE 12.4**
Customer Relationship Management
CRM involves marketing, sales, customer feedback, and support to ensure customer satisfaction over time.

Drunk Driving

Buzzed Driving

Buzzed driving is drunk driving.

Ad campaigns from the Ad Council have been effective tools in marketing public service interests.

increase donations to their causes. Countries, states, and cities run marketing campaigns to attract tourists and businesses to their locations. You may be familiar with the public service advertising campaigns run by the Ad Council, such as the current Buzzed Driving Is Drunk Driving campaign.[6]

Is it possible to market a person? Political parties market candidates for elected office. Consider, for example, the revolutionary social marketing campaign for Obama in his run for presidency in 2008. Agents market their clients on TV shows, cereal boxes, and magazine covers. We market ourselves when we interview for a job. You may have marketed yourself for acceptance to your college or university. Regardless of what is being marketed, the essence of marketing remains the same: delivering value to customers and managing customer relationships. The only differences between marketing practices are the stakeholders involved and their objectives.

Benefits of Marketing

How does society benefit from marketing? Society at large benefits from successful marketing because scarce resources are more efficiently allocated or channeled into the production of those goods and services most desired by society. The market mechanism ensures that resources, such as raw materials and labor, flow into the production of those goods and services in greatest demand and away from low-value products with falling demand. For example, if the public demands more Apple iPads, then Apple's profits rise and Apple has a huge incentive to produce more iPads. Because more resources are required to increase production, the demand for resources and labor used in iPad production rises, raising prices and wages. When resources are used more efficiently, society is able to consume more products, increasing the average standard of living.

How do investors and employees benefit from marketing? Investors receive financial rewards for investing in successful organizations. Indeed, more and more investment capital flows to those businesses that are most successful in satisfying customers because investors earn higher returns. Employees benefit from successful marketing because their jobs and livelihoods are more secure. In addition, new job opportunities are created as production expands to satisfy the growing demand for high-value products.

How do sellers benefit from marketing? Of course, if marketing is successful, a company also benefits because it sells more product. As long as the costs of the marketing campaign and the production of a product are less than the revenue generated by the sales of a product, a company generates a profit. Hence, sellers benefit because successful marketing stimulates sales and generates revenue and profits. Profits enable the organization to not only sustain itself but also to prosper and continue to provide value to customers—ideally, it's a win-win arrangement.

2 What are the benefits and criticisms of marketing?

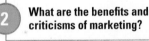

THE List

10 Great Marketing Strategies

1. Stand out from the crowd.
2. Communicate with e-mail.
3. Create a relationship with the customer.
4. Use giveaways, coupons, and contests.
5. Establish a social network presence.
6. Create a great website.
7. Generate PR through community involvement.
8. Use pay-per-click advertising.
9. Establish great customer service.
10. Market consistently.

PR NEWSWIRE/Newscom

FIGURE 12.5
Marketing Generates Five Types of Utility for Customers
Image sources, top to bottom: Africa Studio/Fotolia; wolfelarry/Fotolia; marinini/Fotolia; auremar/Fotolia; Lorelyn Medina/Fotolia

How does marketing benefit consumers? As consumers, we have many needs—food, clothing, housing, medical care, and transportation to name a few. Marketers don't really *create* needs; instead, they *respond* to needs in an effort to *satisfy* them. Subway and Quiznos go to great lengths to convince you to buy their sandwiches to satisfy your need for food, just as Toyota and Ford try to convince you to purchase their vehicles to fulfill your transportation needs. When needs are satisfied, *utility* is created.

Are there different types of utility? There are five kinds of utility that marketing provides to customers (see ■ **FIGURE 12.5**):

- **Form utility:** when a company produces a product from raw materials, such as a swimsuit is made from fabric and supplies. The product takes on a form that pleases the customer.
- **Task utility:** when someone performs a service for someone else, such as when a seamstress alters a swimsuit.
- **Time utility:** when a business makes a product available at a time when it is most needed, such as having the swimsuit available in time for summer.
- **Place utility:** when the product is made available for purchase at a place that's convenient for buyers, such as when the swimsuit is stocked and placed on display at your local department store.
- **Ownership utility:** when a store transfers ownership to the customer by selling the swimsuit.

How is product value measured? Whenever a business satisfies a need or a want, it creates value for a customer. But how do customers measure value? The **value** of a product equals the ratio of a product's benefits to its costs. With a high-value product, its benefits far exceed its costs. A low-value product has few benefits in relation to its costs. Successful marketing finds ways to increase value to customers—to increase the real or perceived benefits of a product or minimize customers' costs by reducing the price or maximizing convenience. Organizations that offer the highest-valued products win the most customers and thrive. Those organizations that offer low-value goods and services lose market share or go out of business entirely.

Criticisms of Marketing

What are the criticisms of marketing? Over time, certain social shortcomings have emerged from marketing techniques. Some of the questionable tactics include price gouging (setting a price that is widely considered unfair), high-pressure selling, the production of shoddy or unsafe products, planned obsolescence (the product becomes outdated after a period of time planned by the manufacturer), poor customer service, the misuse of customer information, confusing and deceptive labeling, and other deceptive practices such as hidden fees and charges.

Let's consider some examples of the costs to society of questionable marketing:

- **Misuse of personal information:** Marketing often involves the collection of customers' personal information. Companies conduct marketing surveys to determine the marital status, annual income, age, sex, race, and other characteristics of current and prospective customers. Many of us feel violated when this personal information is not adequately protected or is resold without our permission.
- **Hidden fees:** Many of us feel taken advantage of when we must pay hidden fees and charges not included in the advertised price. Products that require additional parts or shipping and service fees often make customers upset.

- **Consequences of purchase:** Unscrupulous marketing may take advantage of less sophisticated members of society. To what extent is it reasonable to hold buyers responsible for being aware of the consequences of their purchases? This is especially important when purchasing expensive or sophisticated goods and services, such as a car or a mortgage on a home. Similar concerns emerge when marketing is directed at children.

The many criticisms of marketing should not be taken lightly. These concerns may help explain the strong support for consumer protection laws and other regulations governing business behavior. Too often the social costs of marketing stem from unethical business behavior. As we discussed in Chapter 3, all companies should have a code of ethics and policies in place to curb unethical behavior within their organizations. However, not all companies do, which allows for questionable products to be marketed. The AMA has a statement of ethics that contains guidelines on ethical norms and values for marketers. (Visit www.marketingpower.com/AboutAMA, then select Statement of Ethics.)

A s you can see, the marketing landscape has changed drastically over the past 100 years or so. Companies that have managed to stay in business—such as Ford Motor Company—have changed their products and marketing strategies to match changes in consumers' wants and needs. For Ford, those transitions ranged from mass producing one model of a car to producing dozens of models and styles today that each strive to meet individual customer preferences, tastes, and budgets. ■

Smoke a LUCKY to feel your LEVEL best!

Luckies' fine tobacco picks you up when you're low . . . calms you down when you're tense!

Luckies' **fine tobacco puts you on the right level**—the Lucky level—to feel your level best, do your level best.

That's why it's important for you to remember that LUCKY STRIKE MEANS FINE TOBACCO —mild, ripe, light tobacco that makes a thoroughly enjoyable smoke. No wonder more independent tobacco experts—auctioneers, buyers and warehousemen—smoke Lucky Strike regularly than smoke the next two leading brands combined.

Light up a Lucky! Luckies' fine tobacco picks you up when you're low, calms you down when you're tense. So get on the Lucky level where it's fun to be alive. Get a carton of Luckies and get started today!

L.S./M.F.T. — Lucky Strike Means Fine Tobacco

LUCKY STRIKE CIGARETTES L.S./M.F.T.

Apic/Getty Images

Was it ignorance of the harm their product could have on society or a conscious effort to deceive the public for selfish gain that motivated tobacco companies to undertake promotions like this one in the 1950s? Many believe that ad campaigns such as this one fall under the heading of unscrupulous marketing.

Marketing Tactics pp. 359–363

A aron Hoffman is determined to work for himself, and he knows he can do that with his own mobile pet-grooming service. Because Aaron worked as a pet groomer for seven years, he has enough experience to branch out on his own. Aaron has already found a van to hold all his equipment, and he knows a few of his previous customers are interested in his services, but he isn't sure what the next step should be. Someone suggested he come up with a marketing strategy. What does a marketing strategy do? And how should Aaron apply it to his new business? ■

Willee Cole/Fotolia

All organizations can benefit from a well-developed marketing strategy. In this section, we'll discuss the factors that are involved in the marketing process.

Marketing Strategy: The 4 Ps of Marketing

3 — What are the elements of a marketing strategy and the components of the marketing mix?

What is a marketing strategy? A marketing strategy consists of two major elements:

- The **target market**: a specific group of potential customers on which a firm focuses its marketing efforts.
- The **marketing mix**: the combination of controllable elements of a product's marketing plan designed to serve the target market.

What elements are included in the marketing mix? Traditionally, there have been four elements in the marketing mix, known as the 4 Ps: product, price, promotion, and place. The idea is to provide the *product* that customers need and want at an appropriate *price,* and *promote* its sale, and *place,* or distribute, the good or the service in a convenient location for the customer to purchase. Some feel there is a fifth P that should be added to the marketing mix: people. Particularly when a service is being offered, the people involved can add significant value.

The elements of the marketing mix need to be blended in the most appropriate manner to best meet the needs of the target market. As you can see in ■ **FIGURE 12.6**, finding the best blend of the 4 Ps is constrained by environmental factors beyond a firm's control. We'll discuss these constraints found within the broader market environment later in this chapter. Let's first look at each of the 4 Ps in a bit more detail.

Product

The perfect product is one that provides value for the customer. Companies must determine what a customer wants from a product, or how a product satisfies a particular need. Additionally, distinguishing a product from that of the competitors

■ **FIGURE 12.6**
The Marketing Mix
Effective marketing requires the appropriate blend of the 4Ps directed at targeted customers. This blend is constrained by forces beyond a firm's control and found within the broader market environment.
Image Sources: center: iQoncept/ Fotolia; clockwise from top left: swisshippo/Fotolia; 3ddock/ Fotolia; venimo/Fotolia adisa/ Fotolia

Social Daily Deal Offers— Are They Working?

Who doesn't love a bargain? Sales, coupons, BOGOs, and other discount promotions have been a common way for companies to get you to try something you may not purchase otherwise. Daily deal sites like Groupon, LivingSocial, and Google Offers have merged the concept of discount promotions with social networking and have caught on like wildfire. The question is whether or not they are working— either for the consumer or for the business promoting its product. Perhaps the only party winning is the discounting site, but even that is undecided.

The enticement for a company to offer its product on a daily deal site is that its promotion reaches a large group of people quickly. And, unlike other promotions, the "deal" doesn't take place unless there is a significant mass of interest. The downside that many companies experience is an initial surge of interest surrounding the deal, but with little to no repeat business they had hoped would result. One would also think consumers benefit by being able to try something for nearly half the cost. But many have been caught in the fine print that restricts the time, place, or type of offering. In fact, both Groupon and LivingSocial have been hit with class action lawsuits that claim the expiration dates on the deals are in violation of consumer protection laws. The daily deal sites themselves have grown to become a multibillion dollar industry and may be the only ones receiving long-term benefits, but will they begin to experience growing pains, or can they continue their rapid success? What do you think? Are daily deals here to stay?

is critical. If your product isn't different from or superior to the competition, then why should customers buy from you? *Product differentiation* is the creation of a real or perceived difference in a product designed to attract customers. Product differentiation is one of the most critical ingredients for most businesses and will be discussed in greater detail in Chapter 13.

Price

There's a lot to consider when deciding on the price for a product. The product must be competitively priced to appeal to customers, though competitive pricing doesn't always mean the cheapest. Coupons, discounts, or other services can help reduce cost to the customer, and therefore are appealing, but must be evaluated as to their overall effectiveness. Of course, the price will have to be sufficient to make a profit. Lastly, product pricing must take into account the cost of warranties and returns. We'll investigate the price component of the marketing mix in more detail in Chapter 13.

Promotion

The **promotion** part of the marketing mix consists of all the methods to inform and persuade targeted customers to buy a product and build positive customer relationships. Communicating the benefits of your good or service to customers is done through advertising, sales promotions, personal selling, public relations, direct marketing, and publicity. We'll explore promotion more fully in Chapter 14.

Place

The **place** (or **distribution**) component of the marketing mix refers to all the methods involved in getting a product into the hands of customers. A product isn't beneficial to a customer if it can't be purchased when and where it is needed. When a business is providing a good instead of a service, the delivery component is often more complicated. Many goods, such as grocery store items, go through a *distribution channel*, which is a series of firms or individuals that participate in the flow of a product from the manufacturer to the consumer. The middle players in a distribution channel are sometimes called *distributors* or *wholesalers*. Some goods, such as food products, go through many wholesalers before reaching a retail outlet (e.g., a grocery store) and, finally, the consumer. Other goods, such as automobiles,

■ FIGURE 12.7
The 4 Ps of marketing are being replaced by the 4 Cs to better fit the movement to a more consumer-oriented marketing approach.

typically move from the manufacturer to just one wholesaler, the car dealership, and then the consumer. Still other goods bypass wholesalers altogether and move from the manufacturer directly to the consumer, such as L.L. Bean clothing products, when they are ordered from a catalog and shipped directly to consumers.[7] In Chapter 14, we'll examine finding the appropriate distribution channel and managing it efficiently to get the product to the right place at the right time, in the proper quantity, and at the lowest cost.

The 4 Cs of Marketing

Can the marketing mix be represented a different way? While the 4 Ps of marketing are the backbone of many marketing strategies, they present marketing from the producer's perspective. A more recent revision to this classic classification is a model that looks at marketing from the consumer's perspective, as shown in **■ FIGURE 12.7**.

- **Customer** replaces product: Represents the trend toward niche marketing and a focus on creating individual solutions for the customer rather than forcing the customer into a standard product solution.

- **Cost** replaces pricing: Represents the recognition that price is only a portion of the total cost of ownership. Other factors that affect cost may include the cost to change or implement a new product or service, or the cost of driving to the location or of shipping a product.

- **Convenience** replaces place: The advent of the Internet, online shopping, and other hybrid models of purchasing have reduced the importance of place. Convenience, instead, factors in the ease at which information about a product or the product itself is located and how the actual purchase transaction takes place.

- **Communication** replaces promotion: The proliferation of mobile devices and social networking platforms allows companies and consumers to be in constant communication with each other. Companies need to "listen" to their customers as much as they want their customers to listen to the marketing message.

The Marketing Process

4 How do firms implement a marketing strategy by applying the marketing process?

What are the steps in the marketing process? There are five steps in the marketing process, as outlined in **■ FIGURE 12.8**.

1. **Identify a market need.** Think back to Aaron Hoffman's mobile pet-grooming service. Aaron has his own pets, and before he became a groomer himself, he took his dogs to the pet-grooming service at which he was later employed. Transporting his dogs was a huge hassle, and he felt horrible about leaving them in a cage for part of the day. He didn't know it at the time, but Aaron had identified an unfilled market need: a *mobile* pet-grooming service that eliminates the hassle and guilt that trouble pet owners when they take their pets to a grooming service. This is the first step in the marketing process.

2. **Conduct market research and develop a marketing plan.** The next step is to conduct research on the profitability of a potential business. By analyzing the marketing environment, Aaron can determine if any political, economic, societal, and/or technological factors could affect his business. In addition, he conducts an internal analysis that includes evaluating his potential customers, competitors, and collaborators. These analyses form the foundation for his marketing plan. As Aaron researches, he discovers that many other people share his desire for a more convenient pet-grooming service. It appears

that sufficient demand already exists for the services of his potential business. We'll discuss how to analyze the marketing environment, as well as how to conduct market research and develop a marketing plan in more detail later in the chapter.

3. **Identify target customers.** The third step is to determine a target market. Without this focus, Aaron will waste effort and money promoting a service to individuals who are not interested in his service. When selecting a target market, he must visualize his ideal customer. Aaron considers what his ideal customer does, thinks, and wants, and then uses that image to form his marketing decisions. We'll discuss target marketing in more detail later in the chapter.

4. **Implement the marketing mix.** Once Aaron selects a target market, the fourth step is to implement the marketing mix. He has already identified a *customer need* and has developed a *product* that not only meets that need but also fulfills it better than the competition.

   Then he will want to contemplate his *pricing* strategy to ensure that a profit is made *and* that he remains competitive. In developing his pricing strategy, Aaron needs to be sensitive to any other direct or indirect *costs* that the customer may incur from using his service.

   The *place* component of the marketing mix often involves deciding how his product will be distributed to his customers. The initial size and mobility of Aaron's business affords him great flexibility; he will be delivering his product to his customers, within a reasonable distance, with little or no inventory management required. This service offers his customers much *convenience*. Are there other conveniences he might also consider offering? Can he make scheduling appointments any easier?

   Lastly, *promotion* is the most visible part of the marketing mix. It can be very expensive yet very fruitful. For Aaron's product (i.e., service), he should start by creating a memorable brand name to *promote* his business and to distinguish it from all others. What forms of *communication* should he create to engage with his current customers and to attract other customers? Should he create a Facebook account, generate a mobile app, or set up a website? Should he blog or tweet about pet grooming and other care tips?

5. **Nurture good customer relationships.** The final step in the marketing process is to manage customer relationships. Because the goal of CRM is to establish long-term, trusting relationships with individual customers to foster loyalty and repeat business, Aaron must develop a rapport with his customers and their pets. He should know which customers are returning clients and note any particular grooming preferences. He might even offer discounts for select customers. Aaron should not only solicit but also respond to suggestions by customers on how to improve his services. To build customer trust, he might also offer customers their money back if they are unsatisfied. To maintain and foster interest in his services, he may want to create a Facebook page or offer pet care tips through a Twitter account. Aaron may also want to establish relationships with veterinary clinics and dog breeders. Above all, it's critical to personalize and maintain good customer relationships.

■ **FIGURE 12.8**
The Five Steps in the Marketing Process

Marketing is an ongoing process of tweaking a business to satisfy customers to ensure quality, value, and repeat business. The marketing process may seem simple when it is written on paper, but it's as much an art as it is a science. Aaron Hoffman's mobile pet-grooming service would have a completely different marketing strategy than would a nonmobile stand-alone business producing a good. Each product needs to be looked at individually to tailor an appropriate marketing mix. ■

The Marketing Environment

pp. 364–368

Kadmy/Fotolia

Amelia Russo runs a successful shop selling inexpensive dress shoes for women. She gets most of her stock from France, so the value of the U.S. dollar makes a big difference in her total costs. However, the value of the dollar has fallen so low that Amelia is considering limiting her overseas orders and using domestic distributors. This would save money on purchasing shoes as well as delivery; however, the quality and style would be different than what her customers expect. If she keeps the same stock, she'll be forced to raise her prices, and her sales may fall significantly. What other types of environmental influences might affect Amelia's business? ∎

The components in the marketing mix are variables under the direct control of an organization. However, the **marketing environment** includes environmental influences beyond a firm's control that constrain an organization's ability to manipulate its marketing mix. These environmental influences include the competitive, economic, technological, and sociocultural environments as well as the global, and political, and regulatory environments, as shown in ∎ **FIGURE 12.9**.

Marketers must be keenly aware of the marketing environment when determining the marketing mix. In fact, one of the key responsibilities of managers in any organization is to undertake **environmental scanning**, the process of surveying the marketing environment to assess external threats and opportunities. A successful business detects changes in the marketing environment and adjusts its marketing mix quickly and appropriately, inasmuch as the overall marketing environment will allow it to do so. Let's study each element of the marketing environment in a bit more detail.

> **5** How does the marketing environment influence a firm's ability to manipulate its marketing mix?

The Competitive Environment

Why is analyzing the competition important? The degree of competition facing a firm is critical to creating an effective marketing mix. You may recall from Chapter 2 that the basic market environments with respect to the varying degrees of competition facing firms are perfect competition, monopolistic competition, oligopoly, duopoly, and monopoly. The degree of competition impacts a firm's marketing strategies in many ways. A successful business must be aware of competition and should try to stay one step ahead. Amelia Russo's shoe store had an edge on the competition due to her low prices. As a result of the dollar's weakness, however, Amelia is going to lose her competitive pricing advantage and be forced to create new marketing ideas.

The Economic Environment

Why is the economy important for marketing? The economic environment can affect customers' willingness and ability to spend their money on a product.

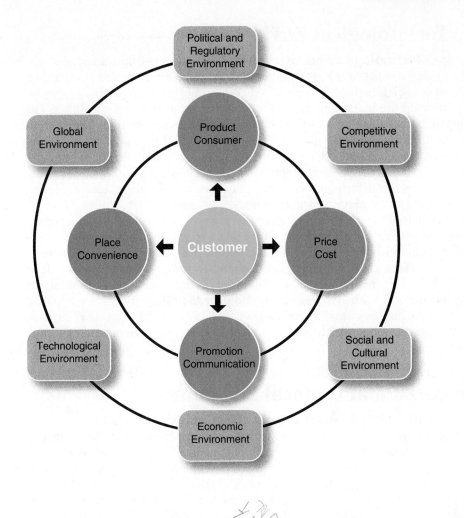

■ **FIGURE 12.9**
The Marketing Mix and the Marketing Environment
The marketing mix can be controlled by marketing managers, but the marketing environment represents external forces that cannot be controlled.

Therefore, marketers must keep abreast of changes in inflation, interest rates, unemployment, and economic growth rates over the course of the business cycle so they can keep their internal costs down, which ultimately affects the product's price. Similarly, the economic conditions have a great effect on the overall cost associated with a product. High gasoline prices may limit how often a customer can get to the store or may increase distribution costs. Awareness of these factors requires keeping up with changes in consumer confidence levels and government fiscal and monetary policies. Moreover, because of globalization, prudent firms follow global economic trends as well. This is especially important if a company has expanded internationally.

How does the economic environment affect a marketing strategy?

The economic environment impacts a firm's marketing strategy in many ways. For example, a rising inflation rate reduces the purchasing power of money, and sales may fall. A recession will reduce the demand for most products. Even the best-laid marketing plans will fail when customers can no longer afford to buy a company's product. If interest rates are low, then the cost of borrowing drops, and consumers who buy on credit, especially the big-ticket items such as houses and automobiles, may purchase more. As a final example, suppose the value of the dollar falls (gets weaker) in foreign exchange markets. This will cause imported goods to become more expensive, like Amelia Russo's French dress shoes. The price of imported goods may need to increase, which could reduce sales. Savvy marketers try to keep their fingers on the changing pulse of the economy to forecast looming problems or potential opportunities and make the necessary adjustments.

The Technological Environment

How does technology affect marketing? Advances in communication technologies may be some of the most influential factors to affect modern marketing. The onset of social media and Web-based communications has been a key influence in moving the marketing mix focus from the product to the consumer. The Internet alone has enabled many small businesses to compete with large corporations around the world by marketing and selling their products online. Moreover, the Internet has opened a new manner of marketing, which better enables a company to deliver its message more quickly to a broader audience. Marketing messages, often in the form of a video, can be passed on to others, easily creating exponential exposure almost instantaneously.

Through technological improvements, modern, sophisticated manufacturing innovations have enabled many firms to more easily customize their products to meet individual needs and to offer them at dramatically reduced prices to satisfy the varying tastes of targeted customers. Technology has enhanced CRM by facilitating the creation and use of computer databases. The availability of mass-produced, inexpensive dress shoes and expedient shipping allowed Amelia Russo to make her shoe store a profitable venture. Successful marketing requires using the latest technologies to reach and satisfy target customers wherever they may be.

The Social and Cultural Environment

How do cultural and social trends affect marketing? In Chapter 4, we examined the critical role that the sociocultural environment has on international business. We noted that many international business blunders have resulted from a lack of sensitivity or understanding of cultural differences. Domestic businesses must realize that culture is dynamic, and effective marketers should adapt to different preferences and keep up with changing social trends. Demographic shifts—such as age, gender, ethnicity, and marital status—and changing values can signal opportunities for businesses. For example, we can expect the demand for medical care, pharmaceuticals, and nursing homes to increase as the average age of the population increases. Amelia Russo recognized the demand for inexpensive, high-quality dress shoes from a younger crowd and took advantage of the opportunity.

ON TARGET

Viral Marketing

Viral marketing has become an efficient marketing tool. It is the digital version of word-of-mouth because individuals pass on the marketing messages they like to others. Like a virus, this form of Internet marketing spreads to vast audiences quickly. A successful viral marketing campaign can have a much larger impact than a nonviral campaign, which explains why many companies are including viral marketing as a part of their overall marketing strategy. Some of the most successful viral marketing campaigns have been created by Dos Equis beer (Most Interesting Man in the World *), Old Spice men's grooming products (the Old Spice guy), and the innovative and popular Blendtec (Will it Blend? **)

campaigns. The key to great viral marketing is to create a marketing message that is novel, entertaining, and intriguing enough to get people to notice and to want to "talk about it" by passing it on to others. What makes a message good enough to go viral? It's harder than you think, but most include an unexpected theme, an incentive to continue to watch, and a follow-up. Most importantly, good viral messages rarely sell the product directly. What are your favorite viral ads? What is it about them that makes you want to pass them on?

*Source: "Meet the Man." Dos Equis. www.dosequis.com
**Source: "Will It Blend? Home." Blendtec. www.willitblend.com

Netflix Angers Everyone

OFF THE MARK

Netflix, the streaming video and DVD-by-mail company, was a major factor that pushed industry icon Blockbuster into bankruptcy. Netflix took advantage of a trend of streaming video and by-mail rentals that Blockbuster didn't recognize quickly enough. But seemingly as quickly as Netflix gained market share, it lost it. In one year, Netflix share price grew from $100 to nearly $300, and in half that time the share price plummeted to lows near $60. Beyond the pure financial impact of this downward spiral is the pure tragedy that this debacle was entirely Netflix's own doing. What caused this self-inflicted nightmare? Netflix lost sight of its customer and the importance of the customer relationship. In an effort to deemphasize the more expensive DVD-by-mail component and focus on the more profitable streaming video component of the business,

Netflix decided to create two separate service lines. The DVD-by-mail would be rebranded as Qwikster, while the streaming video component would continue as Netflix. Customers would have two separate logins to access two separate websites. Netflix completely violated the 4 Cs in the new marketing mix by misunderstanding the customer's needs and wants, the overall cost and lack of convenience the split businesses would have on the consumer, and also did a very poor job of communicating the change to its customer base. Beginning with a quick apology within days of the blunder, CEO Reed Hastings has since been trying to make amends. In the months that followed Netflix attention to customer service and quality recouped many who had left in protest and pushed Netflix back to the top in market share.

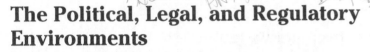

The Political, Legal, and Regulatory Environments

How do politics and legislation affect marketing? It has been said that in a democracy, the squeaky wheel gets the grease. Special interest groups try to influence the political process in various ways. Businesses are no exception. They try to wield political influence through contributions to political parties, individual candidates, and political action committees (PACs) because government laws and regulations significantly impact business interests. In addition, a variety of regulatory agencies enforce laws and regulations constraining marketing efforts. These include the Environmental Protection Agency (EPA), the Consumer Product Safety Commission (CPSC), the Food and Drug Administration (FDA), and the Federal Trade Commission (FTC). Businesses are forced to consider the political and legal environment in making marketing decisions, as these factors can play a major role in overall success.

The Global Environment

How does the global environment affect marketing? Thanks in part to the Internet, world trade has increased significantly. Customers can search globally for attractively priced products, and businesses can search globally for suppliers. In addition, in efforts to tap new markets, companies have expanded internationally. Therefore, marketers have needed a global perspective in many of their campaigns. However, global trade and the marketing efforts that accompany such increases in global trade and consumerism are not without difficulties. Marketers need to be aware of cultural and social differences before launching their products and their marketing campaigns. Political landscapes with differing policies and regulations can also affect how a company does business in another country. Lastly, businesses must also be aware of the complications involved in shipping products to foreign countries.

So what did store owner Amelia Russo decide to do when her stock from France became more expensive due to a weakened dollar? She judged her options and decided to buy domestically until the dollar gets stronger. Her customers were generally satisfied with the domestically produced substitute dress shoes, so Amelia was able to stay in business. Successful businesses like Amelia's are constantly on the lookout for changes in the market environment and are prepared to adjust accordingly. ■

Comstock Images/ Getty Images

Define the marketing need or opportunity

↓

Develop the research design

↓

Collect the relevant data

↓

Analyze and interpret the data

↓

Act on conclusions

■ **FIGURE 12.10**
The Market Research Process

Marketing Research and Planning pp. 368–373

Tiara Watson noticed that the owner of the hair salon she frequented constantly complained about the salon's supply company. The owner's complaints often revolved around increasing delivery costs and lengthening delivery times. The supplier was in a city 70 miles away. Tiara recognized an opportunity to begin a supply company more local to the region. A local supply business could offer convenience as well as reduced delivery costs. Tiara's initial research revealed over 30 salons in the immediate area. Casual conversations with some of the owners indicated that many would be willing to switch suppliers. Tiara knows she can't start out selling supplies to every salon in the area. How can she determine which salons to target initially for a successful start of her new business? ■

Look back at the five-step marketing process shown in Figure 12.8. You'll notice that after a market need is identified, a firm needs to conduct *market research* to determine the profitability of a venture, develop a marketing plan, and determine its target market. In this section, we'll explore each of these processes in more detail.

The Market Research Process

What is market research and what are the steps involved in the process? Market research is the process of gathering and analyzing market information for making marketing decisions. Market research can be as simple as including a brief survey with an invoice or via e-mail, or it can be as complex as conducting a full-blown analysis that is necessary before launching a new product. Although there are dozens of intermediate steps in conducting marketing research, they all fit into this basic process (see ■ **FIGURE 12.10**).

Why is it important to define the marketing needs or opportunity? Although a new need or opportunity seems apparent, perhaps other hidden issues or needs should be addressed. For example, Tiara has identified the need for a salon supply company that is in closer proximity to salons in her area. But, is distance the real problem, or could other factors such as poor service or insufficient product offerings really be the problem? The first step in conducting marketing research is to define the problem, which may involve more research to further identify or enhance the perceived need or opportunity. In this phase of the process, marketing managers and researchers work together to clearly define the need or opportunity. This helps to determine what kind of data needs to be gathered, and the mechanisms by which the information will be gathered. This step will help the researcher determine the approach, establish a budget, and collect relevant and appropriate data for analysis.

<table>
<tr><td>6</td><td>What is the marketing research process, and what are the elements of a good marketing plan?</td></tr>
</table>

What kind of data should be collected? Determining which types of data will be collected and how the information will be collected is critical. Two general types of data exist: primary and secondary.

- **Primary data** are raw data collected by a researcher. The data are frequently collected through observation, questionnaires, surveys (via mail, e-mail, or telephone), focus groups, interviews, customer feedback, samples, and controlled experiments. A **focus group** is typically a group of 8–10 potential customers who are asked for feedback on a good or a service, an advertisement, an idea, or packaging style. They are often used in test marketing an idea or a new product.

- **Secondary data** are data that have already been collected and processed, such as census data. This information is usually much cheaper than primary data to obtain.

By contacting current salon owners, Tiara Watson has begun to collect primary data about the interest of salon owners in changing to a closer, cheaper supplier. She also has collected secondary data about the location of the closest salon supply companies and data regarding the demographics of potential salon customers in her region. Examples of primary and secondary data sources are summarized in ■ **TABLE 12.1**.

How is social media used in market research? Social media sites, such as Facebook and Twitter, are becoming invaluable tools for businesses to get in touch with the public at large (see ■ **FIGURE 12.11**). Not only can companies find out what is being said about their products, but they can also find out what is being said about the competition. Both types of information are invaluable—regardless of whether the opinions are good or bad. The value social media has over traditional focus groups is twofold: size and immediacy. Focus groups are limited in size, and a researcher can never be sure whether he or she has picked the right people. Because of the formality of a focus group, the event often requires much planning and can be quite expensive to implement. Alternatively, social media networks gather quick results from substantial numbers of consumers. Social media gives honest and candid feedback from audiences who are eager to voice their opinions. Not every company or marketing research project will lend itself to social media tools. But, if a fit is determined, social media gives marketers another valuable tool for obtaining consumer insights.

How are the data analyzed and interpreted? Once the data have been collected, they must be assembled into a format that can be easily analyzed and interpreted. The analysis of data requires knowledge of appropriate statistical techniques that are beyond the scope of this text; however, the ultimate goal is to conduct careful analyses that will lead to conclusions about

■ TABLE 12.1

Primary and Secondary Data Sources

Primary	Observations
	Questionnaires and Surveys
	Experiments
	Interviews and Focus Groups
	Customer Feedback
Secondary	Internal Corporate Information
	Trade Associations
	Commercial Sources
	Government Data
	Magazines and Newspapers
	Social Media, Internet Databases, and Search Engines

**■ FIGURE 12.11
Benefits of Using Social
Market Research**

what marketing strategies to implement. Honest analysis is necessary, and researchers should never adjust data to get the results they want. Tiara's research showed over 30 salons in the area in which she was planning on locating her business, indicating she had a strong potential target market. Moreover, through surveys and personal interviews Tiara determined concerns about product offerings, pricing, and relationships with the buyers' current supplier that Tiara could also address.

What happens when the research is completed? The whole purpose of marketing research is to point managers toward better marketing decisions. Once the information is collected and analyzed, it is usually presented in an organized manner to decision makers. A formal presentation may be given to the sales and marketing teams, or a plan outlining a new advertising strategy may require hiring an advertising agency.

Marketing research should be ongoing. Changing market conditions require businesses to continually adapt and constantly search for better ways to provide value to customers. Part of acting on the conclusions of marketing research is creating a marketing plan.

The Marketing Plan

What is a marketing plan? A marketing plan is a written document that specifies the marketing activities that will take place to achieve organizational objectives. It is the roadmap that will help carry out the strategies as determined by marketing research.

What are the elements of a good marketing plan? Four elements emerge from all good marketing plans:

- A clearly written marketing objective
- Performance of a situational analysis
- Selection of a target market
- Implementation, evaluation, and control of the marketing mix

Why is a marketing objective necessary? A marketing objective is a clearly stated goal to be achieved through marketing activities. It should be realistic, quantifiable, and time specific.[8] A marketing objective of having every home in the United States purchase a specific product is unrealistic. Selling 100,000 units in a year is a more realistic, quantifiable, and time-specific marketing objective. When objectives are realistic, they are attainable and can motivate employees toward the goal. When they are measurable, a firm can determine whether they are being achieved. If deadlines are also imposed, then firms know whether they are reaching their goals in a timely manner.

What is situational analysis? Creating clearly stated objectives is the first step in any good marketing plan. The next step is conducting a *situational analysis*. There are several methods that can be used to conduct a situational analysis, which is similar to the SWOT analysis discussed in Chapter 7 in that it includes an evaluation of internal *strengths* and *weaknesses*, as well as the *opportunities* and *threats* found in the external environment; however, it focuses on marketing only, rather than on the entire organization.

What do we mean by internal strengths? In terms of marketing, a company's internal strengths refer to the competitive advantages or core competencies that a company has at its disposal to meet a specified marketing objective. Core competencies provide customer benefits and are not easily imitated by other companies, setting a company apart from its competition. For example, Deere and Company has been very successful in expanding its business by transferring the strength of its John Deere brand-name reputation of superior-quality agricultural equipment into lawn tractors and mowers for urban dwellers, and earth-moving equipment for the construction industry. Indeed, a significant portion of Deere and Company's revenues now come from its nonagricultural sales.[9]

How does a company assess its weaknesses? Assessing internal weaknesses means that a company must perform an audit of current managerial expertise, manufacturing and financing capabilities, and an organization's execution of the marketing mix. By honestly assessing its weaknesses, a company can determine a realistic marketing objective. For example, a company that makes handmade watches and has only three employees cannot expect to produce 75,000 watches a week.

Why look to the external environment? The dynamic and ever-changing external environment offers many opportunities and creates many threats. Changes in the degree of competition facing firms, the economy, technology, and sociocultural forces, as well as changes in the global, and political and regulatory environments have caused some firms to thrive while damaging others. This is especially true for international businesses because the number of market environments compounds the analysis. Rapid changes in technology create new opportunities, such as expanding sales over the Internet, but also pose new threats and challenges. Eastman Kodak, once the leader in cameras and photographic film products, was forced into bankruptcy because of its failure to transition to digital photography more quickly. Successful companies continually evaluate environmental factors as part of their situational analysis to match their strengths with opportunities and address their weaknesses to avoid threats.

Are there other ways to perform a situational analysis? Another useful tool for conducting a situational analysis is by analyzing the factors shown in ■ FIGURE 12.12. This type of situational analysis gathers information about a company and its collaborators and climate, and then extends the information by including an analysis of its customers and its competitors.

Target Markets

How are target markets determined? Determining a target market begins with **market segmentation**, the process of separating the broader market into smaller markets segments. A **market segment** is a subgroup of potential customers who share similar characteristics and therefore have similar product needs and preferences. So, for example, rather than selling to all the salons in the state, Tiara, from the opening story, decided to focus on a smaller market segment of just those salons in the region. Some markets, called **niche markets**, are even more narrowly defined. For example, a company that sells specialized gear shifters for racing bicycles is operating in a niche market.

■ **FIGURE 12.12**
Factors to Consider in a Situational Analysis

Company	Collaborators	Customers	Competitors	Climate
• What does my company do? • What are we selling? • What are our strengths and weaknesses?	• Who am I working with to make my business operate? • How can I grow and foster these relationships?	• Who is my target audience? • Who are my current customers? • Am I selling what they want?	• Who are my primary competitors? • Are there substitutes for my product? • Are there emerging businesses or technologies that might impact me? • What is my uniqueness, and am I leveraging it?	• What's going on in the industry? • Are there laws or regulations that impact me? • How is the current economic situation affecting buying behaviors?

Marketers choose the market segments that offer the greatest profit potential for their products, and these become the target markets. The market segments should be identifiable, accessible, substantial, stable, and have unique needs. For each target market, a company tries to blend the marketing mix to best satisfy its targeted customers. The process of developing a unique marketing mix that best satisfies a target market is known as **positioning**.

How are consumer markets segmented? Consumer markets can be segmented based on many variables or characteristics of customers. Four of the most common market segmentation classifications are geographic, demographic, psychographic, and behavioral. These types of market segmentations are summarized in ■ **TABLE 12.2**.

How are markets defined by location or region? Segmenting markets according to geographic characteristics is called **geographic segmentation**. For example, clothing apparel, skis, snowblowers, four-wheel drive vehicles, air conditioning, and heating needs differ according to regional climate differences. Taste in food products also varies by region. For example, McDonald's offers special menu items to cater to the tastes and preferences of a particular region or country. McLobster Rolls are served in Canada and the northeastern region of the United States, and because people in India do not eat beef, the Maharaja Mac, made of lamb or chicken meat, is the big seller. For Tiara Watson's salon supply company, the prominent hairstyles in some parts of the city may require specialized products that are not as popular in other locations.

How are markets defined by different population characteristics? Often, products are best received by men, or athletes, or seniors. **Demographic segmentation** is market segmentation according to age, race, religion, gender, ethnic background, and other demographics. For example, by the year 2020, one in five Americans is estimated to be of Hispanic origin.[10] Few businesses want to miss out on this growing market segment. It's now common to find labels or instructions written in both English and Spanish. Spanish language television stations and newspapers proliferate, as well as companies marketing their products to this growing segment in the United States.

The market segment that Tiara's salon supply company will focus on primarily is African American women's hair product needs.

Can a market be segmented based on opinions or interests? Harley-Davidson offers a wide variety of motorcycles, and each model attempts to cater to a particular lifestyle.[11] Cat food ads cleverly focus on "cat lover" personalities, whereas many beer commercials target men and sports enthusiasts. Market segmentation based on lifestyles, personality traits, motives, and values is called **psychographic segmentation**. When motives are used to determine the appropriate market, marketers focus on why consumers make a purchase. For example, Whole Foods Market and Trader Joe's focus on consumers interested in healthier, organic foods, and Planet Fitness sells memberships to customers concerned with their health but who are also price conscious. Salons that will purchase Tiara's products are motivated by the need to supply customers with high-quality beauty products.

Sophisticated marketers closely examine their customers'

■ **TABLE 12.2**

Consumer Market Segmentation

Geographic	Demographic	Psychographic	Behavioral
• Region	• Age	• Lifestyle	• Benefit sought
• Suburban	• Race	• Personality traits	• Volume usage
• Rural	• Religion	• Motives	• Brand loyalty
• City	• Family size	• Values	• Price sensitivity
• County	• Ethnicity		• Product end use
• Population density	• Gender		
• Climate	• Income		
• Terrain	• Education		

lifestyles, personality traits, motives, and values because, unlike geographic and demographic variables, these psychographic variables can be manipulated by marketing efforts. Whatever consumers may value, whether it be quality, social status or affiliation, safety, health, privacy, technology, or appearance, you can bet that businesses will offer a good or service to satisfy that real or perceived need. They will be rewarded with profits for doing so.

How can consumer behaviors define a market segment? Do you buy only one particular brand of toothpaste regardless of price? Do you buy cranberry sauce only at Thanksgiving? These types of behaviors define **behavioral segmentation**, the market segmentation based on certain consumer behavior characteristics, such as brand loyalty, price sensitivity, the benefits sought by a product, occasions that stimulate purchases, and the ways in which a product is used.

Brand loyalty is another kind of behavioral segmentation. It can impact price sensitivity: the more loyal the customer, the less sensitive he or she is to a price increase. If a customer has been using the same brand of toothpaste for 12 years and has had no cavities, a small price increase will most likely not be an issue to that customer.

Finally, knowing how a product is actually used can help companies develop packages that appeal to customers. For example, having vitamins for adults packaged with lids that are easily turned by arthritic hands can be useful for some consumers.

The marketing process may involve only a few steps, but each of these takes some time and plenty of focused effort. Tiara Watson has given much thought to whom she wants to target as customers. However, without performing a market analysis, she wasn't sure where to start. Once she stepped back and took time to go through the research process, she knew where to begin. Tiara is off to a good start, but she still has some work ahead of her in implementing her marketing mix and nurturing good customer relationships. The next two chapters explore the implementation of the marketing mix in more detail to nurture good customer relationships. ■

Consumer Behavior pp. 373–377

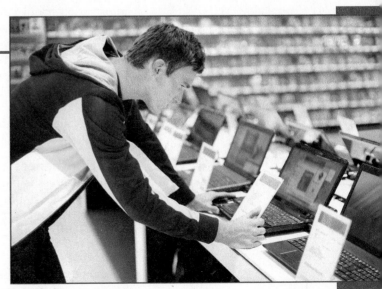

Yuri Arcurs/Fotolia

Will Giusto is standing in front of a display of laptop computers. He has to buy one for school but has left the task to the last minute, and he really can't leave the store without one. Not knowing much about computers, they all look pretty much the same to him, so how is he to decide? His girlfriend has a MacBook Pro and loves it, but she loves everything Apple makes. His best friend has a top-of-the-line Dell and raves about how awesome it is, but he's a gamer. Will isn't looking for a fancy label or a "tricked out" machine; he just needs something to type his papers on and access Facebook from. But staring at the row of similar looking laptops is just plain intimidating. How can Will make the best purchasing decision? What factors will influence his decision? ■

The term **consumer behavior** refers to the ways individuals or organizations search for, evaluate, purchase, use, and dispose of goods and services. Notice that consumer behavior involves the study of individual consumers or business organizations as buyers in the market. Most of us intuitively think of a market as being a consumer market. In a **consumer market**, individuals purchase goods and services for personal consumption. But there are also business-to-business markets. In **business-to-business (B2B) markets**, businesses purchase goods and services from other businesses. In this section, we'll explore both markets and examine the buying behavior differences between consumer markets and B2B markets.

Consumer Markets

7 How do the buying decisions and marketing processes in the business-to-business market compare to those in the consumer market?

Why study consumer behavior? Knowledge of consumer behavior helps marketers select the most profitable target markets and guides the implementation, evaluation, and control of the marketing mix for selected targeted markets. For example, consumers are becoming increasingly concerned about gas mileage. Automobile manufacturers that realize this concern may offer more gas-efficient vehicles or drop the prices on less-efficient models to compensate for poor gas mileage.

How does a consumer make a buying decision? The consumer buying process involves five steps:

1. Need recognition
2. Information search
3. Evaluation of alternatives
4. Purchase or no purchase decision
5. Postpurchase evaluation

Not all consumers go through each step in the process, and the steps do not need to be completed in the same order. The process can be interrupted at any time with a "no purchase" decision.

Consider your decision to purchase the educational services of your college or university. You first recognized the need for higher education. You likely obtained information about colleges from many sources, including your friends, family, counselors, and perhaps even the annual college rankings of the *U.S. News & World Report*. You may have also visited a few college campuses to gather firsthand information. You then evaluated your choices based on a variety of factors, including tuition (price), geographic location, or perhaps where your friends were going to college. Your final choice may have been based on rational analysis or the result of an emotional decision (based on some gut feelings). After making a purchase, we also evaluate our decision in terms of how well our expectations are being met. You'll likely continue to evaluate your college choice long after you graduate.

What influences consumer decision making? The consumer decision-making process is part of a broader environmental context that influences each step. Marketers should be aware of these factors when developing an appropriate marketing mix for the target market. These environmental forces are shown in ■ FIGURE 12.13.[12]

How does culture affect a person's buying behavior? *Culture* is the set of learned attitudes, beliefs, and ways of life that are unique to a society and are handed down from generation to generation. Subcultures are specific groups within a culture that share attitudes and life experiences. Some examples of subcultures include churches, community organizations, and online communities like Facebook and Pinterest. Together, a buyer's culture, subculture, social class, family, and peers comprise the *sociocultural influences* that affect buying decisions. Cultural values change over time. For example, as the obesity epidemic becomes more pronounced, many people today value healthier lifestyles and have begun to change their buying patterns. *Social class* refers to a combination of factors, such as education, income, wealth, and occupation common to a group of people. Social class can have an impact on purchasing decisions, as some possessions are considered status symbols, like the MacBook Pro that Will's girlfriend owns. Apple computers are often viewed as just being "cooler" than other types of computers.

What unique personal influences shape buying behaviors? *Personal influences* on a buyer's consumption choice are often shaped by age, gender, economic situation, lifestyle, and personality. For example, knowing that there is a difference between how men shop and how women shop can help influence a sales strategy. Women often like to browse, linger, and socialize, whereas men often prefer to get in and get out of a store. The owner of a Canadian women's clothing boutique recognized these patterns. To cater to her female customers, she hosts "trunk shows," during which her customers get together with their friends to have a glass of wine while reviewing a designer's new line. Similarly, she caters to her male customers' more efficient buying preferences by keeping a database of their personal information and preferences. Prior to special occasions, she'll contact her male customers and let them know she has the perfect gift for their spouse or partner.[13]

How do attitudes affect buying decisions? One goal of marketing is to shape the perception of a product in the minds of consumers. Attitudes toward a product put customers in a frame of mind that either predisposes them to favorably view a product or not. *Psychological influences* include differences in a buyer's motivation, perception, attitudes, and learning. Equally important is an effort to create positive product experiences. Good experiences with brands result in repeat business; bad experiences stunt future sales. It is more expensive to find new customers than to keep existing customers, so investing in methods to ensure that existing customers' needs are met and that they remain loyal to the brand is very important.

Can temporary conditions affect how buyers behave? *Situational influences* include the physical surroundings, the social surroundings, and the type of product purchased, and these all can influence how a buyer behaves. Some factors, such as where products are placed or how a store is organized, can be easily controlled. However, other factors, such as adverse weather conditions or a consumer's negative mood, are not as easily managed, such as the hurried purchase Will Giusto was about to make because he had left his shopping to the last minute. He may not feel able to make a calm and informed decision due to the immediate pressure of the moment.

How does the marketing mix influence purchases? *Marketing mix influences* include putting forth a product that buyers want at an affordable price, promoting awareness of the attributes of that product, and placing the good or the service in a timely and convenient location for consumers to buy.

■ **FIGURE 12.13**
Major Influences Impacting a Consumer's Buying Decision
Many factors influence consumer buying decisions. Effective marketing attempts to help consumers with their information search and the evaluation of alternatives.

Knowledge of consumer buying behavior and the influences on the buying decision is critical to effective marketing. Some of these influences, like personal influences, are beyond the control of marketers, while other influences, like psychological influences, can be impacted by businesses. All of these influences should be kept in mind when selecting a target market; implementing, evaluating, and controlling the marketing mix; and building customer relationships.

B2B Markets

What is the difference between consumer markets and B2B markets? The difference between consumer and B2B markets hinges on who's doing the buying. If a good or a service is purchased in a B2B market, it is purchased by a business for further processing, for resale, or to facilitate general business activity. The B2B market is larger than consumer markets because virtually all consumer products go through a number of distributors or wholesalers before reaching the final consumer at a retail outlet. In fact, a separate B2B market exists at each stage of the supply chain. Think of all the transactions involved in manufacturing and delivering a car. Most of the components are manufactured by separate firms, each of which needs to purchase the raw materials required to make the part.

What are the characteristics of a B2B market? The first step in selling to a business market is the same as the consumer market: identify the customer and determine why the customer needs the product. However, the rest of the process is distinct for each end market because of the inherent differences among the markets. B2B markets are generally more relationship driven than product driven. The quality of the product remains important, but the emphasis is on the relationship. Some other important characteristics of B2B markets are as follows:

1. **A few buyers that purchase in large quantities.** B2B markets typically involve a few buyers that purchase very large quantities. For example, only a few airline companies buy most of Boeing's jets.

2. **Highly trained buyers.** Most business purchasing agents are highly skilled at their jobs. They often weigh the benefits and the costs in a more systematic fashion and are less influenced by emotional factors than are buyers in consumer markets. This requires sellers to pitch their products at a much more sophisticated level.

3. **Group purchasing decision.** A team of individuals within purchasing departments usually collaborates in making a purchasing decision in B2B markets. This means marketers must be prepared to be patient and mindful of the concerns of all decision makers to seal a deal.

4. **Strong customer relationship.** Because there are only a few sophisticated buyers that purchase large quantities, marketers find it necessary to establish a much closer relationship with customers compared to the relationship with buyers in consumer markets. As a result, B2B marketing is more focused on personal selling compared to the mass advertising campaigns that typify consumer markets.

5. **Geographically concentrated buyers.** Most buyers in B2B markets are concentrated in a few of the most industrialized states, where most large businesses are located. This reduces the costs of reaching buyers.

6. **Direct purchasing.** Buyers in B2B markets often purchase directly from sellers, as opposed to consumer markets where products typically go through many wholesalers before a product arrives at the end user.

These key differences between consumer and B2B markets are summarized in ■ **TABLE 12.3**. These differences can be organized by market structure, the nature of the buying unit, and the purchasing process.

How does a business make a buying decision, and what influences that decision? Similar to consumers, businesses begin by recognizing a need; they seek out information to aid them in the purchase decision; evaluate alternatives; decide to either purchase or not to purchase; and undertake a postpurchase evaluation. However, business purchases are generally more rational, reasoned, objective decisions based on various influences, such as the state of the economy; technological factors; the degree of and regulatory concerns; and organizational objectives, policies, and procedures.

Is the marketing process different for B2B markets? The marketing process remains the same for all markets: identify a need, undertake research to come up with a marketing plan, select a target market, implement and control the marketing mix, and nurture customer relationships.

TABLE 12.3

Differences Between B2B and Consumer Markets

	B2B Market	Consumer Market
Market Structure	• Few customers • Large-volume purchases • Geographically concentrated	• Many customers • Small-volume purchases • Geographically dispersed
Nature of the Buying Unit	• More professional and rational purchase decision	• Less sophisticated and more emotional purchase decision
Purchasing Process	• Highly trained buyers • Group purchasing decision • Complex buying decisions • Formalized buying procedures • Close and personal selling relationship between marketer and buyer • Personal selling	• Untrained buyers • Individual purchasing decision • Relatively simple buying decisions • Informal buying decision • Impersonal relationship between marketer and buyer • Mass advertising

Will Giusto finally made his purchase. After consulting with a sales clerk about each of the brands, he chose a Dell. Was it the quality and reputation of Dell products that swayed his decision? The influence of his friend? Or something else? ∎

C H A P T E R 1 2
SUMMARY

MyBizLab

Go to **mybizlab.com** to complete the problems marked with this icon .

1 How has marketing evolved over time?
(pp. 354–356)

- During the production concept era (from the Industrial Revolution until the 1920s), most companies focused solely on production. Demand was often greater than supply, and the prevailing mind-set was that a good-quality product would simply sell itself.

- During the sales concept era (from the mid-1920s through the early 1950s), technological advances meant that production increased more sharply than demand for goods and services. The use of heavy public advertising in all available forms of media became prevalent.

- During the marketing concept era (from the 1950s through the 1990s), production continued to expand more quickly than the growth in demand for goods and services. The **marketing concept** (p. 355) changed the focus from finding the right customer for a product to producing the right product for a customer and doing it better than the competition.

- During the societal marketing era (1960s to the present), companies began to realize that they must also take into consideration the long-term interests of society. Companies began to work for the benefit of both consumers and society.

- During the customer relationship era (from the late 1990s to the present), organizations have worked to establish long-term relationships with individual customers to foster loyalty and repeat business.

2 What are the benefits and criticisms of marketing? (pp. 357–359)

- **Marketing** (p. 353) identifies and satisfies human needs and wants. It provides value to customers by providing benefits that exceed their costs. In turn, sellers benefit because marketing enables firms to survive.

- Businesses that are most successful in satisfying customers generate higher profits, and investors benefit from the profits earned. Employees benefit from successful marketing as well because their jobs and livelihoods are more secure.

- Society at large benefits from marketing because scarce resources are more efficiently allocated to those goods and services most desired by society.

- Criticisms of marketing include price gouging, the production of shoddy or unsafe products, and confusing and deceptive practices. The criticisms of marketing should not be taken lightly. All companies should

have a code of ethics and policies in place to curb unethical behavior within their organizations.

3 What are the elements of a marketing strategy and the components of the marketing mix? (pp. 360–362)

- The two basic elements of a marketing strategy are the **target market** (p. 360) and the **marketing mix** (p. 360).

- The four Ps of the marketing mix are **product** (p. 354), price, **promotion** (p. 361), and **place** (p. 358).

4 How do firms implement a marketing strategy by applying the marketing process? (pp. 362–363)

- The marketing process involves (1) identifying a need, (2) conducting market research and developing a marketing plan, (3) determining a target market, (4) implementing the four Ps of the marketing mix, and (5) nurturing good customer relationships.

- The application of the marketing process is as much an art as a science. Producing a high-quality product with a unique brand properly promoted that consistently delivers value to customers at a fair price when and where customers want a product are common ingredients for marketing success.

5 How does the marketing environment influence a firm's ability to manipulate its marketing mix? (pp. 364–367)

- The **marketing environment** (p. 364) includes environmental influences, such as the competitive, economic, technological, and sociocultural environments, as well as the political, legal, and regulatory environments. Because these factors are beyond a firm's control, they constrain an organization's ability to manipulate its marketing mix.

6 What is the marketing research process, and what are the elements of a good marketing plan? (pp. 368–371)

- **Market research** (p. 368) is an ongoing process of gathering and analyzing market information to gauge changing market conditions that may suggest better ways and opportunities to provide services to customers.

- The marketing research process involves (1) defining the marketing need or opportunity, (2) collecting relevant data, (3) analyzing and interpreting the data, and (4) acting on research conclusions.

- A **marketing plan** (p. 370) is a written document that specifies marketing activities designed to achieve organizational objectives.

- Four elements emerge from all good marketing plans: (1) a clearly written marketing objective; (2) performance of a situational analysis; (3) selection of a target market; and (4) implementation, evaluation, and control of the marketing mix (the 4 Ps).

- Another type of situational analysis is looking at other factors of marketing: company, collaborators, customers, competitors, and climate.

7 **How do the buying decisions and marketing processes in the business-to-business market compare to those in the consumer market?** (pp. 374–377)

- In a **consumer market** (p. 374), buyers are households that purchase final consumer goods. In a **business-to-business (B2B) market** (p. 374), businesses buy from other businesses. There are many more B2B markets than consumer markets. In B2B markets, purchases are often undertaken by a small group of highly trained individuals who buy in large volumes and have a much closer relationship with marketers. B2B buyers are also more geographically concentrated and often avoid distributors.

- Consumers and businesses undertake the same five-step decision-making process when making a purchase. However, some of the influences that impact the business purchase are different.

- The marketing process remains the same for all markets: identify a need, undertake research to come up with a marketing plan, select a target market, implement and control the marketing mix, and always remember to nurture good customer relationships.

Key Terms

behavioral segmentation (p. 373)
business-to-business (B2B) market (p. 374)
consumer behavior (p. 374)
consumer market (p. 374)
customer relationship management (CRM) (p. 356)
demographic segmentation (p. 372)
environmental scanning (p. 364)
focus group (p. 369)
form utility (p. 358)
geographic segmentation (p. 372)
market research (p. 368)

market segment (p. 371)
market segmentation (p. 371)
marketing (p. 353)
marketing concept (p. 355)
marketing environment (p. 364)
marketing mix (p. 360)
marketing objective (p. 370)
marketing plan (p. 370)
niche market (p. 371)
ownership utility (p. 358)
place (or distribution) (p. 361)
place utility (p. 358)

positioning (p. 372)
primary data (p. 369)
product (p. 354)
promotion (p. 361)
psychographic segmentation (p. 372)
secondary data (p. 369)
target market (p. 360)
task utility (p. 358)
time utility (p. 358)
value (p. 358)

Self-Test

Multiple Choice You can find the answers on the last page of this book.

1. Which marketing era occurred during the Great Depression when manufacturers almost had to force consumers to purchase their products?

   a. Production concept era

   b. Sales concept era

   c. Marketing concept era

   d. Customer relationship era

2. When a car is purchased, *form utility* refers to the value customers receive from

   a. owning the car.

   b. the styling and function of the automobile.

   c. ready availability and speed with which the dealer made the car available for purchase.

   d. close proximity to the car dealership.

3. LinYee created a document that included a situational analysis and a discussion of the target market. LinYee's document is called

   a. marketing research.

   b. a marketing mix.

   c. a marketing plan.

   d. marketing segmentation.

4. Tenitia Reynolds opened a small community bookstore several years ago. When a new book comes out, Tenitia e-mails those clients she thinks will enjoy the book based on their past purchases. Which part of the marketing process do Tenitia's actions reflect?

   a. Conducting market research

   b. Identifying a market need

   c. Implementing the marketing mix

   d. Nurturing customer relationships

5. Bill Wertz runs a transportation service that caters exclusively to the residents of retirement communities. Bill's business is taking advantage of which of the following marketing environments?

   a. The competitive environment

   b. The sociocultural environment

   c. The technological environment

   d. The economic environment

6. Which of the following does *not* define a B2B Market?

   a. The market consists of small-volume purchases in a geographically dispersed area.

   b. Buyers make complex purchasing decisions, often with formal buying procedures.

   c. The purchasing process involves much personal selling and requires a close relationship between buyer and seller.

   d. Buyers are more professional and make more rational purchasing decisions.

7. Market segmentation based on lifestyles, personality traits, motives, and values is called

   a. geographic segmentation.

   b. demographic segmentation.

   c. psychographic segmentation.

   d. behavioral segmentation.

8. Which of the following represents a shift from the 4 Ps to the 4 Cs of marketing?

   a. Taking into consideration the complete cost to the consumer

   b. Making the product convenient to buy

   c. Focusing on consumer wants and needs

   d. All of the above

9. Environmental scanning is

   a. market segmentation according to geographic characteristics.

   b. market segmentation based on certain consumer behavior characteristics.

   c. the process of developing a unique marketing mix that best satisfies a target market.

   d. the process of surveying the marketing environment to assess external threats and opportunities.

10. Which is *not* an example of primary data?

    a. Census data

    b. Customer feedback

    c. Surveys and questionnaires

    d. Data collected through controlled experiments

True/False You can find the answers on the last page of this book.

1. The main difference between the B2B and consumer markets is that B2B markets have many more buyers that purchase smaller individual quantities.
   ☐ **True** or ☒ **False**

2. A product is defined as any tangible good, service, or idea available for purchase.
   ☐ **True** or ☒ **False**

3. A market niche is a narrowly defined market segment.
   ☒ **True** or ☐ **False**

4. Employees benefit from successful marketing because new job opportunities are created as production expands to satisfy the growing demand for high-value products.
   ☐ **True** or ☒ **False**

5. The information gathered from a meeting with a group of potential customers to gain feedback on a product is considered secondary data.
   ☐ **True** or ☒ **False**

Critical Thinking Questions

1. Think of an example of how a specific organization (for-profit or not-for-profit) tried to establish a better customer relationship with you. What did the organization do? Was it effective? Why or why not? What recommendations would you make to the organization?

2. In an effort to help recover some financial losses due to the economic crisis of the Great Recession, Bank of America announced a $5 monthly debit card fee it was planning to impose on consumers. This plan spurred great opposition from Bank of America's customers, causing the bank to abandon the plan. At the time, other banks already had been charging such fees, so why was the revolt against Bank of America's announcement so strong? What part of the message delivery process could have been improved?

3. Suppose you were hired by Apple to develop a marketing campaign for their latest iPad. What would be the target market? List at least four characteristics and the corresponding market segment category that define the ideal customer. Repeat the exercise for a Toyota Prius and a vacation package to a luxury spa in Arizona.

Team Time

TOBACCO WARS

Divide into two teams, one to represent each group:

a. Tobacco company employees; pro-cigarette advertising in magazines

b. Anti-tobacco advertising activists

Scenario

Does a company have a fundamental right to market its products wherever it wishes? Cigarette advertising in magazines has been a topic of great controversy. The large tobacco companies provide publications with a great deal of revenue by purchasing expensive advertising space, but many antismoking groups and some magazine publishers are questioning the ethical nature of this. Antismoking groups argue that these ads appeal to children and glamorize smoking. Tobacco companies claim that they are merely making attractive advertisements with no intention of encouraging children to use their products. The European Union has banned tobacco advertisements from magazines entirely, and many U.S. publications have stopped selling ad space to tobacco companies. Do tobacco companies

Team Time (continued)

have the right to advertise their products as they see fit? Is it morally wrong to advertise a product that is known to cause health problems?

Process

Step 1. Collaborate with team members to discuss both sides of the issue, analyzing the arguments from each perspective.

Step 2. Prepare the most effective argument for your team's perspective, and think about counterpoints to arguments that the other team may raise.

Ethics and Corporate Social Responsibility

SUBPRIME MORTGAGE CRISIS

Subprime loans are home loans made available at temporarily reduced or zero interest rates that adjust or increase to much higher interest rates over time. These loans allowed many people to qualify for loans to buy expensive homes that they otherwise would not have been qualified to buy. Because of the long-standing expectation that home prices would continue to rise over time, as they have historically, and that recipients of subprime loans would be able to refinance their loans into traditional fixed-interest loans, many people thought these subprime loans would turn out to be great deals. However, when the price of homes began to fall in 2006 and 2007, it became difficult to refinance these subprime loans. At the same time, the temporary low interest rates on subprime loans were rapidly adjusting upward as specified in the loan contracts. Some people found themselves unable to make their monthly mortgage payments, and they couldn't sell their homes because they owed more than the homes were worth. Many people were forced into foreclosure and lost their homes. Foreclosures also hurt many banks, and this downturn negatively affected the U.S. economy as a whole.

Questions for Discussion

1. Do you feel that it is unethical to offer loans at low "teaser" rates that adjust upward rapidly over time to people who may not fully understand the consequences of increased house payments or allow people to purchase homes that they otherwise would not be able to afford?

2. As a bank owner, do you feel that the benefits of giving subprime loans outweigh their potential risks?

3. Do you think the banks that gave the loans should take responsibility for their payment?

4. Should the government provide assistance at taxpayers' expense to those people who received these subprime loans and now have trouble keeping their homes?

Web Exercises

1. **Apple's Marketing Mix**
   Go to Apple's website and click on the iPad link. Describe Apple's marketing mix strategy: product/customer, price/cost, promotion/communication, and place/convenience. How does Apple attempt to foster good customer relations? What marketing recommendations would you make to Apple?

2. **Mobile Marketing**
   Marketers recognize that nearly everyone owns a mobile phone or other mobile device, and so are instituting mobile marketing campaigns such as offering mobile coupons, sending alerts for special sales or discounts, using QR codes, and creating special mobile applications. Starbucks is a leader in mobile marketing. Research and comment on Starbuck's mobile marketing efforts. In your opinion, what are they doing right? What might they be doing better?

3. **Organic Differences**
   Visit the websites of Trader Joe's and Whole Foods Market. Both companies are in the organic and health-conscious food industries. Compare the two websites. What marketing techniques does each site use? Do you think the companies are targeting the same type of customer? Why or why not?

4. **Freebies: Long-Term Gain or Loss?**
   Visit Sephora's website, and click on Weekly Specials. This company gives bonus offers, including free samples with every purchase from its website. Do you think that this strategy will be profitable for the company in the long run? How might this strategy help with customer relationships?

5. **The Jeep Experience**
   The Jeep brand uses a nontraditional marketing approach by offering Jeep owners invitations to special events. Go to the Jeep website and research the events that this company offers to its customers. How effective do you think engaging customers in ongoing events is in getting them to be repeat buyers?

MyBizLab

Go to **mybizlab.com** for Auto-graded writing questions as well as the following Assisted-graded writing questions:

12-1. Briefly compare the marketing environments for a pizza parlor and a flower shop. What do they have in common? What is different?

12-2. Think of the last major purchase you made. Discuss how sociocultural, personal, psychological, situational, and marketing mix influences impacted this purchase.

12-3. MyBizLab Only – comprehensive writing assignment for this chapter.

Product Development and Pricing Strategies

Developing Goods and Services

Evelyn Robinson and Juan Delgado each drink zero-calorie soft drinks made by Coca-Cola. Evelyn drinks Diet Coke, and Juan drinks Coke Zero. Each thinks his or her soda is the best! Are the products really different or are they basically the same with different labeling and names?

Branding

Robin Green loves homemade bread. When her bread-making machine needed a new part, she contacted the manufacturer, and, surprisingly, was told that the company didn't actually make the machine and would not service it. The company had licensed its name to a different manufacturer! Robin felt let down by the brand she thought was so good. When you go shopping, how important is the brand of a product?

New Product Development

Jessica Smith wants to open a yoga studio in her neighborhood. She also wants to sell yoga supplies. The closest studio is 15 miles away and in poor condition, so she thinks her location would be great. What else does Jessica need to do to develop her studio? What steps are involved in the product development process?

Pricing Goods and Services

When Eugene Whitaker wanted to increase profits at the store he managed, he revisited the pricing strategies that the previous manager had set in place. How could Eugene get customers to think differently about the unique items in his store? Could he compete with the big chain store with the items they had in common? What approach should Eugene pursue with pricing?

MyBizLab®

⭐ **Improve Your Grade!**

Over 10 million students improved their results using the Pearson MyLabs.
Visit **mybizlab.com** for simulations, tutorials, and end-of-chapter problems.

Developing Goods and Services pp. 385–391

Art Directors & TRIP/ Alamy

Evelyn Robinson and her boyfriend, Juan Delgado, were ordering lunch. "I'll have a Diet Coke," Evelyn added after placing their sandwich orders, "and he'll have a Coke Zero," pointing to Juan. Evelyn laughed at Juan. "You know, they're both the same. I don't understand why you won't drink Diet Coke." "I've never liked Diet Coke. For some reason, Coke Zero tastes better. If you think they're the same, why don't you just drink Coke Zero?" he quipped back. "I couldn't imagine drinking anything besides Diet Coke. You can keep your Coke Zero; I have to have my Diet Coke."

Are Juan and Evelyn right? Are the two zero-calorie cola products produced by Coca-Cola the same, with just different labels and names, or are the products really different? Why would Coca-Cola make two very similar products? What are they trying to accomplish? ■

In Chapter 12, we saw that successful marketing requires identifying a need, using market research to determine a target market, and implementing a marketing plan that satisfies customers over time. This may sound easy, but it's not. Applying the marketing process is as much an art as it is a science. Making a high-quality product with a unique brand that is properly promoted and that consistently delivers value to customers at a fair price and is available when and where they want it presents significant challenges to marketers all over the world.

This chapter focuses on two of the 4 Ps of the marketing mix: *product* and *price*. Chapter 14 will focus on the other two components—*promotion* and *distribution* (place).

We begin by looking at the product because all marketing begins with a product. Most businesses must regularly modify their product offerings or offer entirely new products to meet rapidly changing market conditions with the goal of distinguishing or differentiating the product from the competitors' products. To do this, a product should be seen not only in regard to its physical components but also in regard to other attributes that make up the total product offer.

The Total Product Offer

What is the total product offer? A **product** is any good or service that might satisfy a want or a need. An Apple iPhone, a college education, a doctor's advice,

1 How is a product distinguished from a total product offer?

■ FIGURE 13.1
The Three Levels of a Product
The three levels of a product define the benefits to be derived from a total product offering.
Based on "Three Levels of a Product." from Marketing Teacher.
www.marketingteacher.com

and even a Caribbean vacation package are all products. Consumers buy products for a number of tangible and intangible benefits. The **total product offer** consists of all the benefits associated with a product that impact a consumer's purchasing decision. For example, when you buy a car, you're not just buying a mode of transportation; you're also buying some intangible benefits, such as style or image. Marketers know this; when planning a total product offering, they think about products on three levels: the *core product*, the *actual product*, and the *augmented product*. Each level adds more value to a product. **■ FIGURE 13.1** summarizes the three levels of a product.

What is the core product? The **core product** is the primary benefit or service that satisfies the basic need or want that motivates a consumer's purchase. For a car, the core product is convenient transportation. For a soft drink, it's the thirst-quenching capability. For a camera, it's the ability to capture and share memories. Notice that the core product is intangible. You can't touch it. Companies use the benefits of their products to lure customers. That is why BMW uses "Sheer Driving Pleasure" as an advertising slogan*.

What is the actual product? The **actual product** is the tangible aspect of the purchase that you can touch, see, hear, smell, or taste. It provides core benefits when it is used. Consumers often assess the tangible benefits of actual products by comparing brands, quality (often associated with a brand's reputation), features, styling, or packaging. For a car, the actual product is the automobile itself. The core benefits of an automobile could be numerous safety features, leather seats, or an in-car entertainment system. For a soft drink, the actual product is a refreshing taste or the caffeine buzz that consumers are looking for when they purchase some sodas.

What is the augmented product? The **augmented product** consists of the core product and the actual product *plus* other real or perceived benefits that provide additional value to a customer's purchase. These benefits might include customer service and support, delivery, installation, a warranty, or favorable credit terms. The value-enhancing elements of an actual product are an important part of the total product offering because they help provide a more satisfying customer experience. For a car, augmented benefits might include a reasonable price, an easy payment plan, a 10-year warranty, or just the security of owning a brand-new car.

When developing products, marketers must begin with a basic customer need or want that represents the core product. Then marketers develop the actual product to satisfy that need for targeted customers. Successful product developers then augment the product to create a total product offering that provides a benefit package superior to that of the competition. This is the essence of successful *product differentiation*, which we'll discuss next.

Product Differentiation

2 What is product differentiation, and what role does it play in product development?

How important is product differentiation? It is critical for a product's success. **Product differentiation** is the process of distinguishing a product from its competition in real or perceived terms to attract customers. Products are differentiated by establishing concrete or intangible differences among similar products. For example, Southwest Airlines began to set itself apart from other airlines with low-cost fares and minimum hassle. It has continued to distinguish itself with a "bags fly free" campaign**. If a product doesn't stand out, there is no motivation for customers to buy that product over a competing product.

How does consumer input affect product development? Companies rely on customer input to help shape their products. Listening to customers and

*BMW Corporation. www.bmw.com
**Southwest Airlines. www.southwest.com

incorporating their suggestions are effective ways to foster good customer relationships, which is a critical component in establishing repeat business and long-term success. In fact, using customer feedback is one of the most important elements of sound customer relationship management. You have to know what your customers want in order to tailor a product offering to their needs. Many companies have found that social media sites, such as Facebook, Twitter, and Pinterest, are great ways for companies to know what is on their customers' minds. This provides insight into not only their own products but also their competitors' products, which can be equally informative. Consumer input often provides information that prompts companies to divide a large market and focus on narrowly defined, targeted customers. For example, a breakfast cereal company might find that most consumers buy its cereal because it is high in fiber. That company can differentiate its product from competing products by labeling the cereal "a good source of fiber" and target the product to health-conscious adults.

Hair care products are differentiated by packaging, scents, and perceived beauty benefits.

Companies might also use consumer input to differentiate their products by improving an existing product or creating an entirely new product. SC Johnson, the makers of cleaning products found consumers were using a competing product, Lysol Disinfectant Spray, because they thought the spray killed bacteria in the air, when in fact the spray kills bacteria only on surfaces. SC Johnson used this information to create a new product, Oust Air Sanitizer, and differentiated it from Lysol and other similar products by stating that Oust Air Sanitizer is different because it kills airborne bacteria.[1]

Product Lines and the Product Mix

What are a product line and a product mix? Customer feedback also gives rise to the creation of a **product line**, a group of similar products marketed to one general market. A **product mix** is the combination of all product lines offered for sale by a company. For example, Honda offers a full line of automotive products, which can be broken down into various product lines, including its cars, minivans, and sport utility vehicles (SUVs), as well as plane and boat motors, power equipment, and all related accessories. Honda also offers a financial services product line to dealers and their customers for the purchase or lease of Honda vehicles. Honda is involved in several other nonautomotive business activities as well. One of these product lines is the manufacture and sale of environmentally friendly home energy devices.[2] All of Honda's combined activities constitute its product mix.

Does it matter how many products are in a product line? An important marketing decision involves product line length. **Product line length** is the number of items in any given product line. The addition or removal of items from a product line affects a company's profits. For example, the Coca-Cola Company has found it very profitable to pursue a long product line length given the huge variety of drinks it offers for sale. Coke is the biggest-selling soft drink in history. The company offers 450 different types of beverages to satisfy the specific tastes of the 1.8 billion customers worldwide it serves each day.[3] The company offers a wide variety of regular, diet, caffeine-free, and flavored varieties of Coca-Cola. Those who do not want a soft drink can choose from over 3,500 Coca-Cola beverage offerings, including fruit juice drinks, waters, sports and energy drinks, teas and coffees, and milk and soy-based beverages that appeal to the various wants and needs of the company's global consumer base.[4]

Product mix width refers to the number of different product lines a company offers. This, too, is determined by profitability. General Electric (GE) has hundreds of product lines, ranging from light bulbs and home appliances to jet engines and medical machinery.[5] GE aims to achieve maximum profitability by stretching its

Product Mix Width

	Soft Drinks	Energy Drinks	Juices/Juice Drinks	Water
Product Line Length	Coca-Cola	Full Throttle	Fuze	Dasani
	Diet Coke	Rehab	Five Alive	Aquarius Spring
	Coke Zero	TaB Energy	Minute Maid Juices	Glaceau Smartwater
	Fanta			Glaceau Vitaminwater
	Sprite			

■ **FIGURE 13.2**
Coca-Cola's Product Mix Width and Product Line Length
Image Source, Eric Carr/Alamy

■ **FIGURE 13.3**
Consumer Products Versus Industrial Products
Consumer products are classified by shopping patterns, while industrial products are classified by production uses. Each type of product is distinguished further by pricing, promotion, and distribution strategies.

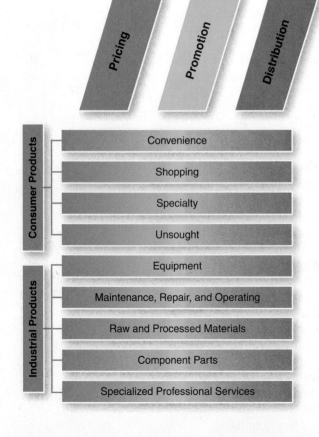

capabilities across multiple markets. Product line length and product mix width are the result of companies striving to offer differentiated products to satisfy targeted customers. ■ **FIGURE 13.2** displays a small sampling of Coca-Cola's product line length and product mix width.

Consumer and B2B Products

What's the difference between consumer products and B2B products? In Chapter 12 we explored the differences between consumer markets and B2B markets. Similarly, there are differences between **consumer products**, goods and services purchased by households for personal consumption, and **business-to-business (B2B) products** (sometimes called *industrial products*), goods and services that are purchased by businesses for further processing or resale or for use in facilitating business operations. The distinction depends on whether it's used for personal use or for business use to generate a profit. For example, if a homeowner purchases a lawn mower for personal use, then it would be a consumer product. If a landscaper purchases the same lawn mower but uses it in his business, then it would be a B2B product.

It's convenient for marketers to classify consumer and B2B products differently because the buying behavior in these two categories is different. Differences in buying behavior impact how the marketer prices, promotes, and distributes the product.

As shown in ■ **FIGURE 13.3**, the shopping patterns of consumers help to establish classifications of consumer products. Industrial products are classified by how they are used in the production of other goods. Each of these types of products has unique pricing, promotion, and distribution strategies.

Consumer Product Classifications

What are the different consumer product classifications? Consumer products can be divided into four categories, as shown in ■ **FIGURE 13.4**:

- Convenience goods and services
- Shopping goods and services
- Specialty goods and services
- Unsought goods and services

What constitutes a convenience product? Those products that customers purchase frequently, immediately, and effortlessly are considered **convenience goods and services**. Because they are normally consumed quickly, they are also referred to as *nondurable goods*. Milk, soap, and newspapers are all considered convenience goods. A car wash is an example of a convenience service. These purchases are usually based on habitual behavior, meaning consumers routinely purchase a particular brand with which they're familiar and comfortable. Convenience goods and services are relatively low-priced items. They're usually promoted through brand awareness and image (which we'll discuss shortly) and are widely distributed through convenience stores or local grocery stores.

What is the classification for those products that are purchased less frequently? Some products require more effort and time for comparison and are typically purchased less frequently than consumer goods. These products are referred to as **shopping goods and services**. Consumers usually base their comparison on attributes such as suitability, quality, price, and style. Shopping goods are typically *durable goods*—goods that can be used repeatedly over a long period of time. Examples of shopping goods include automobiles, clothes, furniture, and major appliances. The features and price of these products are often compared between stores such as

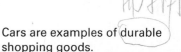

Best Buy, Sears, and Lowe's. Examples of shopping services include hotels, airlines, and other travel services. Because consumers carefully compare brands and models, companies that sell shopping services compete on the basis of price, quality, and brand-name image.

What if a consumer is very particular about the type of product he or she wants? Sometimes buyers are willing to spend a considerable amount of time and effort searching for particular brands or styles. Customers know exactly what they want, and they will not accept substitutes. These types of unique or specialized products are **specialty goods and services**. Examples of specialty goods and services include Ferrari sports cars, Rolex watches, high-fashion designer clothing, and the services of prestigious medical and legal experts. Because there are no suitable substitutes, buyers of specialty products do not comparison shop. They already know the specific good or service they want, and they are willing to seek it out regardless of its price and location. Businesses that successfully differentiate their products to the point that they are considered specialty goods or services can set a much higher price than similar products that are considered shopping goods or services.

What about products that are purchased only when a special need arises? **Unsought goods and services** are products buyers don't usually think about buying, don't know exist, or buy only when a specific problem arises. We don't usually think about or want to think about buying some products, such as life insurance or cemetery plots. These goods and services require a lot of persuasive advertising and personal selling to encourage consumers to buy products that will help them prepare for life's uncertainties. Other unsought goods and services are products that are completely new to consumers. New and innovative products, such as pharmaceutical drugs, must be introduced to consumers through promotional advertising before consumers can actively seek out these products. Emergency medical services and automobile repairs are also unsought purchases where prepurchase planning is rarely considered. In these cases, resolving the immediate problem is more important than comparison shopping that is based on price or other features. Sales of unsought products require personal selling or promotional advertising, and price may not be an important consideration if the good or the service is urgently needed.

■ FIGURE 13.4 Consumer Product Classifications
Image sources, left to right: Patrikeevna/Fotolia; Vanessa/Fotolia; Elena Baryshkina/Fotolia; Balint Radu/Fotolia

3 What are the different classifications of consumer products and business-to-business products?

Cars are examples of durable shopping goods.

HappyAlex/Fotolia

■ **FIGURE 13.5**
B2B Product Classifications
Image sources, left to right: Marc Dietrich/Fotolia; Africa Studio/Fotolia; Željko Radojko/Fotolia; karlstury/Fotolia; Scanrail/Fotolia

Equipment	Maintenance, Repair, Operating	Raw and Processed	Component Parts	Specialized Professional Services
Capital items for production or support	Frequently used items that support operations	Raw materials in original form / Processed materials for use in other products	Assembled portions of the finished product	Services that support operations

B2B Classifications

What are the different B2B product classifications? B2B products can be divided into five categories, as shown in ■ **FIGURE 13.5**:

- Equipment
- Maintenance, repair, operating (MRO) products
- Raw and processed materials
- Component parts
- Specialized professional services

Each of these types of products has unique pricing, promotion, and distribution strategies.

What is considered equipment? *Equipment*, also known as *capital items*, includes all the physical facilities of a business. These physical items are further defined as *production goods* (factories, warehouses, and office buildings; heavy equipment) or *support goods* (computers, printers, and copiers). Many of these capital items are expensive, unique, and intended to last for a long time; therefore, the acquisition process may require special negotiations involving top management and stretch out over many months or even years. Marketers frequently offer a variety of services to help sell this type of equipment, including financial packages to ease the large price associated with the purchase, maintenance, and repairs after the sale.

How do you classify operating supplies? Products that facilitate production and operations but do not become a part of the finished product are classified as *MRO (maintenance, repair, operations) products*. These products include paper, pens, and cleaning materials. They are often marketed based on convenience, just like consumer convenience goods and services.

How are unprocessed products that are used to make other products classified? Unprocessed materials that are sold in their original form before being processed for use in other products, such as crops, crude oil, iron ore, and logs, are examples of *raw and processed materials*. These products are the basic inputs that become part of a finished good. Many raw products and some processed farm products go into the production of numerous grocery items. Raw materials like wood and processed materials like steel are used to make a variety of products. Raw and processed materials are usually purchased in large quantities at prices that are based on the quality of the materials.

How are parts used in an assembly process classified? *Component parts* are assembled portions of the finished product. Examples include brakes and engines for a car or drywall and electrical wire for a house. Businesses purchasing component parts make their decisions based on quality and brand-name recognition because, ultimately, the quality of a business's product will be based on the quality of its component parts.

Do specialized services have a separate classification? Businesses often require the use of services, just as individuals do. *Specialized professional services* help support a firm's operations. They include advertising; management consulting; and legal, accounting, and IT services. Managers compare the costs and the quality of these specialized services with their in-house operations before deciding whether to *outsource* these activities. For example, a local grocery store owner might assess his or her ability to handle the business's financial records before hiring an outside accounting firm.

Considering the variety of types and classifications of products, it's clear that product development is an exciting yet challenging area of business. Remember Evelyn and Juan? Evelyn loved Diet Coke, and Juan preferred Coke Zero. Both products are zero-calorie cola-flavored soft drinks manufactured by the same company, but the two sodas have different flavors, marketing strategies, and targeted demographics. Coca-Cola came up with an idea to differentiate a diet cola product to appeal more to men and produced Coke Zero.[6] The can is darker to convey a bigger flavor, and ads for the beverage are male dominated. Coke Zero shows it is important to differentiate products not only from their competitors but also to meet the needs of a broader market. The key is considering and understanding the many complex factors involved in creating a differentiated product. ∎

Branding pp. 391–398

Robin Green loves homemade bread and has used her bread-making machine a lot. After baking many loaves of her favorite bread, honey whole wheat, the paddles started to slip and needed to be replaced. To her surprise, when she contacted the manufacturer, she was told that the company didn't make such products nor did it service them. In fact, the company had licensed its brand name to a completely different manufacturer! The trust Robin had in this company and its products was tainted. Robin, like so many of us, bought a product based on the inherent trust she had in a brand name to deliver a quality product, but she didn't get quite what she expected. ∎

What are the benefits of a brand? Why are some brands perceived to be better than others? How is brand loyalty built and kept? These questions are important components of another complex aspect of product development—branding. In this section, we'll discuss branding, its benefits, brand loyalty, and branding strategies.

Robert McLean/Alamy

Branding Benefits

What are the benefits of branding? Branding is one of the most important tools of product differentiation, and it benefits both buyers and sellers. A **brand** is a name, a term, a symbol, or a design that distinguishes a company and its products from all others. For buyers, well-recognized brands reduce the shopping time necessary to find the quality and consistency they desire in a product. Branding also reduces the risks involved in some purchases for which buyers are unable to objectively determine quality. We rely on established brands to consistently deliver an expected level of quality. Comparing product descriptions and ingredients takes a lot longer than simply picking up your favorite brand. Consumers are also able to express themselves by buying brand names with which they wish to be identified. For example, some buyers seek prestige by buying exclusive brands, such as Mercedes-Benz, Rolex, or Dom Pérignon, or "cool" things by buying trendy items, such as UGG boots.

Branding also helps sellers define special qualities of their products, thus promoting repeat purchases as well as new sales at higher prices. Because certain brands, such as those from Kraft, are associated with quality and value, the companies with these brands are able to introduce new products quickly and at a relatively low cost. By expanding their brands, companies add length to their product lines, widen their product mix, and enhance their profitability. Marketing a product using the same brand name but in a different product category is known as **brand extension**. Because Kraft has a wide diversity in its product mix, the company can market its brand to just about any person in the world. Kraft's product line has something for everyone. Well-branded companies are generally recognizable by a trademark. A **trademark**, a legally protected brand, can also benefit sellers by distinguishing their brands from the competitors' *knockoff brands*, which are illegal copies or cheap imitations of another product.

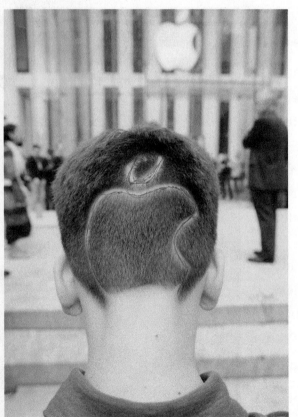

One benefit of branding for sellers is brand loyalty, such as that displayed by many Mac users for Apple products.

James Leynse/CORBIS

Can a company's trademark legally be put on a different company's product? **Brand licensing** is an agreement between the owner of a brand and another company or individual who pays a royalty to use the brand in association with a new product, such as the bread-making machine in our opening story. Brand owners use licensing to extend a trademark or character onto different products. The Walt Disney Company is a good example. Characters such as Mickey Mouse appear on toys, books, and clothing that are not made by Disney. The national sports leagues are also big licensors and leading retail sellers of licensed products.

How does a logo help to build a brand? No doubt you can describe the logo for Nike, Mercedes Benz, and Ralph Lauren. Logos are an important element of a company's identity. They help make a company stand out from the competition, build trust and confidence about the brand, and increase customer loyalty. A good logo makes it easy for customers to associate products with a company's set of standards. When you are miles away from home and see McDonald's "golden arches" rising above the horizon, you know exactly the type and quality of food you'll be served if you go there.

Brand Loyalty and Brand Equity

What is brand loyalty? **Brand loyalty**, the degree to which customers consistently prefer one brand to other brands, is another major benefit of branding. In fact, companies hope that customers not only recognize (*brand recognition*) and then prefer (*brand preference*) but also eventually insist (*brand insistence*) on their brands. Brand insistence is the highest degree of brand loyalty. It can turn a product into a specialty good or service that can command a much higher price. Ultimately, the degree of brand loyalty depends on satisfied customers. Perhaps the most significant contemporary example of brand loyalty is the fervent devotion of many Apple customers.

What is brand equity? Strong brand loyalty contributes to **brand equity**, the overall value of a brand's strength in the market. Perceptions of quality contribute significantly to brand equity. Quality products are not only free from defects but also consistently perform at high levels. For example, many customers will purchase Levi's jeans because of the brand's high quality and durability. This reputation adds significantly to Levi's brand equity.

What contributes to brand equity? Besides quality, two other perceptions of a brand lead to fierce loyalty: *brand awareness* and *brand association*.

- **Brand awareness** refers to the extent to which a particular brand name is familiar within a particular product category. Companies participate in mass advertising as a way to help their product's brand name become synonymous with the actual name of the product. For example, what brand first comes to mind when you think of diapers? If it's Pampers, then P&G has succeeded in its brand awareness campaigns for its disposable diapers.

- **Brand association** involves connecting a brand with other positive attributes. Hiring celebrities to endorse a product can be an effective tool for nurturing brand associations. Nike was so successful with Michael Jordan's endorsement that it launched its Air Jordan line of sport shoes. Disney has been successful in associating its brand with wholesome family values. Images invoked by symbols and slogans can also be very powerful brand association techniques.

Companies understand the passion of NASCAR fans, so they display their logos on cars and drivers' jumpsuits to associate their brand with the sport.

Branding Strategies

What strategies are employed in branding products? Branding strategies are important to building brand equity. There are several different branding strategies. The strategy marketers choose to use is based on how they want to define their products. Is the brand meant to convey thriftiness or luxury? A different branding strategy would be chosen for each of these objectives. Similarly, branding strategies differ depending on the characteristics of the target customer. There are several different types of brands that a product could be categorized into (see ■ **FIGURE 13.6**):

- Manufacturer's brands
- Family brands
- Individual brands
- Private brands
- Co-brands
- Generic brands

What is a manufacturer's brand? A manufacturer's brand is a brand created by producers. A manufacturer's brand is also known as a *national brand*, even though the brand may be distributed globally. Well-known brands, such as Nike, Ben & Jerry's, and Google, are considered manufacturers' brands. Manufacturers spend a lot of money creating, promoting, and building

Christa L Thomas/Cal Sport Media/Newscom

■ **FIGURE 13.6**
Branding Strategies

their brands. There are two types of manufacturers' brands: *family brands* and *individual brands*.

What is a family brand? A **family brand** is a brand that markets several different products under the same brand name. Sony home and portable electronics and Keebler snack food products are examples of companies that have family brands. Consumers are more likely to try new products from an established brand that is familiar and trusted. These established companies are therefore able to penetrate new markets successfully with their brand names. Bic, most known for its disposable ink pens, successfully added Bic disposable razors and Bic lighters to its family brand. Family brands have the advantages of brand awareness and brand association. This affiliation can foster more brand loyalty and still greater brand extension. However, an unsuccessful extension can dilute an established brand name or even create a negative brand image.

What is an individual brand? An **individual brand** is a brand assigned to each product within a company's product mix. For example, Sara Lee uses individual brands among its many food, beverage, household, and personal care products. Some of the brands may be familiar to you: Ball Park Franks, Hillshire Farm meat products, and, of course, Sara Lee's frozen and packaged foods. A major advantage of individual branding is that if a new product fails, it won't damage the image of the other products.

What is a private brand? A **private brand** is a brand created by a distributor, or a middleman. These middlemen can be wholesalers, dealers, or retail stores. As a result, private brands are also called *distributor, wholesaler, dealer, store,* or *retail brands.* The key characteristic of a private brand is that the manufacturer is not identified on the product. Examples include Sears's line of DieHard batteries, Kenmore appliances, and Craftsman tools. These products are made by other well-known and recognized manufacturers but are sold under the private brand label. Often, the manufacturer makes special products just for the private brand. The advantage of private branding is that an individual distributor has more control over a product's price and promotion. The competition is heating up between manufacturers' brands and private brands, as many private brands have gained national recognition.

What is a co-brand? A **co-brand** is using one or more brands affiliated with a single product, such as Gillette M3 Power shaving equipment with Duracell

Retailers and Their Private Brand Labels[7]

Company	Private Brand Labels
Best Buy	Insignia, Dynex, Geek Squad
CVS Caremark	CVS, Fieldbrook Farms, Just the Basics
Home Depot	Hampton Bay, PowerCell
Kroger	Private Selection, Comforts, Kroger
Lowe's	Kobalt, allen + roth,
Safeway	Eating Right, Lucerne, Captain's Choice
Sears Holdings	Craftsman, Kenmore, DieHard
Target	Archer Farms, Market Pantry, Sutton & Dodge
Walgreens	Walgreens, Deerfield Farms
Walmart	Equate, Sam's Choice, Great Value

batteries. The objective is to combine the prestige of two brands to increase the price consumers are willing to pay. Co-branding is also used to foster brand loyalty for one product while extending loyalty to the contributing product.

What is a generic brand? A **generic brand** is a product that has no brand at all. The product's contents are frequently identified by black stenciled lettering on white packages. A generic brand may mimic a branded product, but the generic brand is not associated with the branded product's manufacturer. For example, a generic brand of cream-filled sandwich cookies may look like Oreo cookies, but they are not associated with Nabisco. Generic brands are typically lower in price and not advertised. Yet generic products are often made by the same manufacturer as the name brands; in this way, the manufacturer can capture both cost-conscious and brand-loyal customers. Often consumers will buy generic brands for those products they use routinely and do not have a brand preference or if they understand that the product is exactly the same, such as generic drugs.

Packaging

How does packaging affect a brand? A product's package, the encasement of an external cover on a product, sends a message about a product and its brand. Packaging is the frontline of marketing and through its design and labeling communicates features and differentiates the product. In addition to promotion, packaging serves other functions: it provides protection, facilitates convenience and portion control, and provides information through labeling.

Recently, environmentalists are taking a closer look at packaging to assess and curtail the impact packaging has on the environment. Offering an environmentally-friendly package can also send a message about the brand and the company that is important to many in today's society.

Procter & Gamble's Tide teaming up with the American Breast Cancer Association is an example of how two organizations can come together to form a co-brand.

Myrleen Pearson/Alamy

Brand You: Creating a Personal Brand

What do Lady Gaga and Donald Trump have in common? They both are their own brands. Each celebrity has a unique image that is as much of a brand as are Nike, Apple, and Starbucks. But celebrities are not the only ones who can create a personal brand. Everyone, including you, can create a personal brand. Personal branding is the process by which we market ourselves to others. If we develop our personal brand carefully, it can build brand equity similar to well-known corporate brands.

Business management guru Tom Peters actually coined the phrase *personal branding*. "We are CEOs of our own companies: Me Inc.," he writes. "To be in business today, our most important job is to be head marketer for the brand called You. It's that simple—and that hard. And that inescapable."[8] Enhancing your own personal brand is important to your success; it's what will give you a competitive edge in almost everything you do.

There are a variety of ways you can create your own personal brand, and many of them are similar to the ways companies promote their own brands. For example, you can start by using social media tools, such as Facebook, LinkedIn, and Twitter. Make sure your brand image is consistent and professional with all these tools. Write a blog or have a website with your own name in the title or domain name and establish your brand in your e-mail address by using something like firstname.lastname@email.com. Take charge of your brand. It's the first step you can take toward your own success.

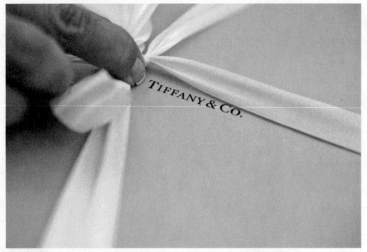

Simon Lord/Alamy.

Tiffany's robin's-egg-blue box often makes the recipient happy without even looking inside!

How does packaging help promote a product? Packaging helps to define the character and quality of a product. Because packaging is the first interaction a consumer has with a product, packaging often is the first criteria consumers use in their purchasing decision. Getting the consumer to notice a product and choose it from among many products on crowded shelves is extremely important. The package design, shape, color, and texture all influence buyers' perceptions and buying behavior. Luxury items, such as jewelry or high-end cosmetics, typically package their products to create an impression of extravagance, sophistication, and exclusiveness.

Coca-Cola has an iconic package that defines the brand, the shape of which is distinctive and immediately recognizable. That contoured shape was initially created in 1915 to differentiate Coke from its competitors. It was such a success that the bottle design was trademarked in 1977. The little blue box from Tiffany & Co. is another example of an iconic package that promotes both a brand and a lifestyle. The robin's-egg-blue jewelry box has been a symbol of elegance and excitement since it was introduced in 1837. The packaging is so desirable that some consumers simply want to buy the box. However, it is an ironclad rule of the company that no Tiffany & Co. blue box can leave the store unless it encloses a purchased item.[9]

How does packaging protect a product? Packaging is intended to preserve and protect a product. This is the most obvious purpose of packaging. Most products are handled several times as they are distributed from the manufacturing site to the final consumer. Many of these products also need to be protected from adverse conditions. Additionally, packaging must protect a product from tampering. Products, such as medicines or infant formula, need to be tamper-proof and must meet the minimum requirements set by the FDA. The Consumer Product Safety Commission (CPSC) has also established guidelines concerning packaging that require that a manufacturer must be able to determine the exact

ON TARGET

OFF THE MARK

Q-tips Brand Cotton Swabs

Branding acts as a tool to help differentiate one product from other similar products. However, what happens when the brand itself becomes the category? When was the last time you purchased a box of cotton swabs? How about Q-tips? Well, if you bought cotton swabs that didn't display the brand name Q-tips, then you didn't buy Q-tips, but you probably still referred to them as Q-tips. The Q-tips brand is a trademark or brand name that has become synonymous with a general class of product or service. Someone shopping for Q-tips may actually buy another brand of cotton swabs. The competitor's price and/or packaging could

convince a consumer to choose that particular brand over the Q-tips brand. All companies want to guard against their brand name becoming a generic description for a product category because then their brand name becomes public property, which means the owner loses all rights to it! This happened to not only Q-tips but also to *Kleenex, Xerox, aspirin, escalator, shredded wheat, kerosene, Jell-O, Band-Aid,* and *Thermos.* If these companies had trademarked their brand names, they could have prevented them from becoming public property and would have preserved their product differentiation.

source of the product and its components. Such labeling helps trace defects and contaminations (such as *E. coli* bacteria) to the source for a more expedient remedy.

Why is convenient packaging so important? Packaging should facilitate use and convenience. Sellers want packages that are easy to ship, store, and stock on shelves. More importantly, consumers want products that handle easily, open, reseal, and store conveniently, and, for perishable items, have a long shelf life.

Packages that are convenient to use and that are also physically attractive sell better. Heinz ketchup experienced a significant increase in sales when it began offering ketchup in a squeezable bottle. It has recently introduced a dual-function individual serving package to give users the choice of dipping or squeezing when they are on the go. Campbell's soup has responded to changing consumer tastes and preferences for greater convenience by offering pull-top lids, and sippable soups, microwave soup lines, and ready-to-serve soups. Many sellers also offer different-sized packages dependent on serving size. For example, salt, sugar, and breakfast cereal packages come in many different sizes for added convenience.

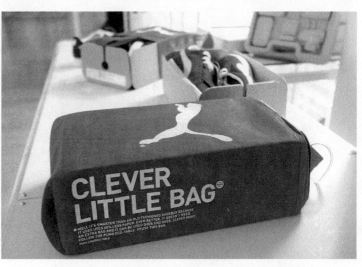

Puma is packaging its shoes in cardboard frames wrapped in reusable shoe bags, which saves nearly 8,500 tons of paper.

Bloomberg/Contributor/Getty Images

How does packaging affect the environment? A growing concern among many consumers is whether a product and its package are environmentally sound. Landfills contain discarded products and packaging materials, which often are not biodegradable. Some packaging, especially the single-serve packages, can be considered wasteful and environmentally unfriendly. Consequently, many companies are going green and placing increased effort on reusing, recycling, and developing new products that are eco-friendly. Puma is a company that has developed a new eco-friendly packaging concept for its shoes. Instead of the traditional cardboard shoebox that has been criticized as wasteful, Puma is packaging its shoes in cardboard frames wrapped in reusable shoe bags. This repackaging saves nearly 8,500 tons of paper and reduces the resources required for production and transportation.[10] Even companies that are selling services are trying to go green. For example, Kimpton Hotels has instituted an EarthCare Program that is run by employees with support of management. In keeping with the green mission of the program, the hotel chain uses environmentally friendly practices such as using green cleaning products, installing recycling bins in every room, switching to water-saving fixtures, and providing local and organic ingredients for their restaurants. They even give parking discounts for guests with hybrid cars.[11] This type of service "packaging" will appeal to those who share a concern for the environment.

The Importance of Labels

What does the government have to say about product labels? Labeling serves two functions: to inform and to persuade. The government has initiated several acts that regulate what must go on a product's label. The Fair Packaging and Labeling Act of 1966 requires that companies communicate specific information about their products to consumers. The act requires that all labels include the name and place of business of the manufacturer, the packer or the distributor, and the net quantity of the contents.

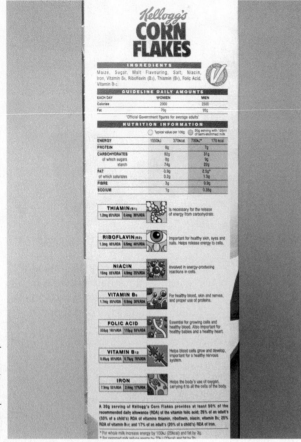

sciencephotos/Alamy

Labels can be used to communicate nutritional value to the consumer.

Other government attempts to make labels more useful for consumers to evaluate products include the Nutrition Labeling and Education Act of 1990. This legislation requires that all nutrient content claims, such as high-fiber or low-fat, and health claims are consistent with agency regulations. Clearly, labels should inform consumers about a product, its uses, and any safety concerns. However, labels can be confusing or misleading. For example, the FDA criticized General Food's claims that Cheerios, the best-selling cereal in the world, lowers cholesterol and treats heart disease.[12] Now, instead of boasting that Cheerios lowers cholesterol by a specific percentage over a specific period of time, the box carries a more general statement that the cereal helps to lower cholesterol. Businesses that wish to foster good customer relationships must be careful to label their products ethically.

Why is labeling important to establishing a brand image? Labels are also used to promote and persuade customers to buy a product. Labels can educate consumers of the features and other benefits of a product. Many companies label their products with their brand logo to distinguish their products. If a label comes to represent consistent quality and dependability, then the label can perpetuate a positive brand-name image.

How are digital media and the Internet affecting branding strategies? With the Internet and its capabilities being so widespread, many companies are incorporating digital media into their branding strategies. Initially, that meant creating a website, but companies are now creating blogs, providing online customer chats, and placing ads in Google searches as a means to build their brands. In addition, the proliferation of social networking sites (such as Facebook and Pinterest) and geolocation applications (such as Foursquare and Gowalla) has started to cause marketing managers to rethink their strategies. Companies such as Zagats and HBO have partnered with Foursquare to incorporate their products into the location-based mobile application that lets users compete for points as they frequent bars, restaurants, and other sites. For example, Zagats, the restaurant rating guide, is using Twitter and placing tips and recommendations into Foursquare. Zagats is also using a new technology, called *augmented reality*, in its mobile app Zagat To Go. The iPhone application merges restaurant ratings and reviews with the camera view and displays the information in the camera lens.

As media has changed over time, so have branding techniques and strategies. This new set of technologies has caused some companies to rethink, redefine, and replace their prior branding practices.

Robin Green was disappointed that the brand that she chose for its quality was not at all what she bought. The next time Robin needs to buy an appliance, it most likely won't be from the same manufacturer. And, she'll be sure to check out the servicing and warranty information before purchasing anything. Branding is important for both the buyer and the seller. Making products memorable and appealing is a priority for all companies, and branding plays an important role in achieving this goal. ∎

New Product Development pp. 399–403

Jessica Smith had a dream—to open a yoga studio in her hometown. There was only one other yoga studio in the area, but people were becoming dissatisfied with the service. Jessica formerly taught classes there but quit because it was so poorly run and maintained. There weren't enough mats for students, the locker rooms were tiny, and the paint on the walls was peeling off. So Jessica decided it was time to open her own studio. Not only did she want to teach classes, but she also wanted to sell yoga equipment. How does Jessica go about creating her new product? And what happens to the product after it's been created? ■

Companies need to introduce new products or they face losing market share and potential extinction. However, developing a new product takes a lot of research and planning, and often the commitment of financial resources. New product development starts with an idea, like Jessica's idea to open a yoga studio, and then must go through testing, analysis, and more testing before it becomes a reality. In this section, we'll look at how products are developed and the path a product takes in the course of its existence.

Pete Saloutos/Fotolia

New Product Development

What is involved in new product development? "Innovate or die" is a phrase often associated with new product development. Introducing new products is important to the future success of many organizations. The process, which begins with generating an idea for a new product and ends with launching it to the public, is outlined in ■ FIGURE 13.7. The process of developing new, high-quality products involves several steps:

> **5** What steps take place during new product development, and what is the product life cycle?

1. **Idea generation.** Ideas for entirely new products or improved versions of existing products are often obtained by listening closely to customers or focus groups. In fact, customer complaints may signal a need for a new product or service. Suppliers, employees, and salespeople also generate ideas by assessing the competition and visiting trade shows. Some companies foster internal innovation and brainstorming sessions to spur new ideas.

2. **Idea screening.** The objective of idea screening is to identify the best ideas and eliminate unsound concepts before devoting costly resources to their development. Screening involves estimating the level of consumer demand for a product, its profitability, and its production feasibility given the company's current technical capabilities or outsourcing costs. Acceptable ideas move on for further analysis.

3. **Product analysis.** The few viable candidates are analyzed further to determine the market need for the product and whether it is financially feasible

Step 1: Idea Generation
- Brainstorm new product ideas
- Think of ways to improve an existing product

Step 2: Idea Screening
- Ask yourself: will my target market benefit from this product?
- Ask yourself: can this product be competitive with similar products?

Step 3: Product Analysis
- Determine a desired sale price
- Assess the cost of production

Step 4: Development and Testing
- Produce a virtual or conceptual prototype
- Get feedback from potential customers

Step 5: Product and Marketing Mix Development
- Produce physical prototype
- Obtain more feedback from potential customers

Step 6: Market Testing
- Place product in select target market
- Virtual reality or simulated tools can help customers

Step 7: Commercialization
- Introduce the product to the market
- Begin the rollout process

■ **FIGURE 13.7**
The New Product Development Process
Kotler, Philip; Keller, Kevin Lane, Marketing Management: Analysis, Planning, Implementation and Control, 12th Ed., © 2006. Reprinted and electronically reproduced by permission of Pearson Education, Inc., Upper Saddle River, New Jersey.

to produce the product. Product analysis estimates the costs of production, the selling price, sales volume, and profitability, which will vary depending on competition. The costs of production depend on the features of the product deemed necessary to meet the targeted customers' needs.

4. **Concept development and testing.** Concept testing involves soliciting customer responses to a new product idea, generally conducted through focus groups. Potential targeted customers are asked to evaluate different features, prices, packages, and a host of other factors surrounding a product. Often storyboards or a virtual mock-up are used to present the product. Sometimes advertising concepts are shown. Ultimately, the goal of the focus group process is to determine what the participants liked and disliked about the concept, and whether or not they would purchase the product and at what price point. The idea is to come up with the best, most profitable total product offering.

5. **Product and marketing mix development.** Once a product has gone through initial development and testing, and business analysis indicates that there is financial merit to the idea, an initial design or prototype is developed. Previously, the design and prototype were in conceptual or virtual format. At this stage, a physical product is developed and introduced for additional consumer feedback to the product as well as to aspects of the marketing mix, such as pricing, promotional techniques, and distribution options (retail stores, online, etc.).

6. **Market testing.** Sometimes this step is skipped if enough information and feedback has been obtained in the previous step. But often a product is placed in trial phases to test its acceptance even further. This is usually done with a product launch in a specific geographic area, aimed at a select target market. Sometimes marketers must convince distributors or store managers to make shelf space available. P&G forgoes real market testing and relies on computer-simulated virtual reality to mimic in-store environments and conduct a more controlled test.[13] Peapod, the online grocer, has taken virtual simulations one step further by lining the walls of a commuting train station tunnel with a virtual store. By scanning the barcodes with the downloaded Peapod mobile app, passersby can place orders and schedule deliveries as they wait for or walk to their train.[14] Although still new, simulation tools and virtual stores are helping to reduce development costs and the time required to bring a new product to market.

7. **Commercialization.** If a product makes it this far in the process, it is ready to be launched. Commercialization is the decision to market a product. Introducing a new product can be costly due to manufacturing investments, advertising, personal selling, and other promotional activities. The returns from such investments can take time. This may explain why many

companies introduce their new products in one region at a time—sometimes called *rolling out the product.*

Despite the scientific nature of new product development, a large proportion of new products still fail. In contrast to the success of Coke Zero, one of the most interesting cases of a new product failure was Coca-Cola's New Coke, launched in 1985. In an attempt to revitalize its brand, the company toyed with the formula of its popular soda and almost destroyed it. People didn't want their favorite soft drink modified, and New Coke was pulled from the shelves only three months after being introduced.[15] Coca-Cola returned to its original formula and renamed it Coca-Cola Classic. More recently, Netflix's more recent attempt to spin its DVD-by-mail service into a separate company named Qwikster was met with immediately negative reaction and a loss of nearly a third of their subscribers. Many compared the Qwikster launch to the similarly disastrous launch of New Coke.

Peapod, the Internet grocer, uses an innovative on-the-go virtual grocery store in Chicago's commuting train tunnel.

The Product Life Cycle

What is a product life cycle? Once a product is developed, it begins the product life cycle. A **product life cycle** is a theoretical model describing a product's sales and profits over the course of its lifetime. During this cycle, a product typically goes through an introductory stage, a growth stage, a maturity stage, and a declining stage. The product life cycle can be applied to a specific product or an entire product category.

You can see how the theory works if you consider the life cycle of vinyl musical recordings. Vinyl records were first introduced in 1930 by RCA Victor but became popular in the 1950s as a replacement for the brittle and easily broken 78-rpm records. This was their introductory stage. Sales grew rapidly in the 1950s and the 1960s, representing the product's growth stage. Vinyl records came in the 33⅓-rpm long playing (or LPs) and the 45-rpm singles. In the early 1970s, vinyl records hit their maturity stage. By the late 1970s and early 1980s, cassette tapes gained wide acceptance and caused the sales of vinyl records to decrease drastically, representing their declining stage. After compact discs, or CDs, were introduced, the decline continued. Vinyl records are now sold mostly as collectors' items.

It is important to note that, like all models, the product life cycle model presents a simplified version of reality and should not be used prescriptively because of the diversity of products, environmental factors, and consumer behavior. For example, the product life of fad items like Beanie Babies can be as short as a few months; for some products, such as automobiles, a product's life can be as long as a century or more. In addition, not all products strictly follow these stages. Some products are introduced but never grow in sales, whereas others never seem to decline.

How do marketing decisions affect a product's life cycle? The product life cycle model may be useful as a general description of a product's sales and profits over time, but it should be used with caution when forecasting or predicting future sales and profits. The time frame involved with each stage can vary dramatically, and some stages may be skipped. In fact, marketing decisions can affect each phase of a product's life cycle. Knowing which stage of the product life cycle a particular product is in helps determine the appropriate marketing mix strategy for that stage. ■ **FIGURE 13.8** summarizes

FIGURE 13.8
The Product Life Cycle Model
Kotler, Philip; Keller, Kevin Lane, Marketing Management: Analysis, Planning, Implementation and Control, 12th Ed., © 2006. Reprinted and electronically reproduced by permission of Pearson Education, Inc., Upper Saddle River, New Jersey.

Characteristics

	Introduction	Growth	Maturity	Decline
Sales	Low sales	Radically rising sales	Peak sales	Declining sales
Costs	High cost per customer	High cost per customer	Low cost per customer	Low cost per customer
Profits	Negative	Rising	High	Declining
Customers	Innovators	Innovators	Middle majority	Laggards
Competitors	Few	Growing number	Stable number beginning to decline	Declining number

Marketing Objectives

	Introduction	Growth	Maturity	Decline
	Create product awareness and trial	Maximize market share	Maximize profit while defending market share	Reduce expenditure and milk the brand

Strategies

	Introduction	Growth	Maturity	Decline
Product	Offer a basic product	Offer product extensions, services, warranty	Diversify brands and models	Phase out weak items
Price	Cost-plus or Price Skimming	Price to penetrate market	Price to match or beat competitors	Cut prices
Distribution	Build selective distribution	Build intensive distribution	Build more intensive distribution	Go selective; phase out unprofitable outlets
Advertising	Build product awareness among early adopters and dealers	Build awareness and interest in the mass market	Stress brand differences and benefits	Reduce to level needed to retain hard-core loyals
Sales Promotion	Use heavy sales promotion to enhance trial	Reduce to take advantage of heavy customer demand	Increase to encourage brand switching	Reduce to minimal level

the characteristics, marketing objectives, and strategies for each stage of the product life cycle.

How can a product's life be extended? Because most products eventually decline and may have to be withdrawn from the market, companies must continuously seek to develop new products to replace older ones. At the same time, marketers work hard to extend the life of existing products to derive as much profit from them as possible. Some tactics used to extend the growth stage of a product include:

- **Lower the price.** Some auto manufacturers have used discounted prices, rebates, and low-interest loans to extend the life of their models.

- **Create a new use.** Arm & Hammer, a company that produces baking soda, extended its product's life by advertising and creating a new use for its product as a refrigerator deodorizer. Jell-O extended its knowledge and applied new technology to raw gelatin to create puddings and other snacks.
- **Find a new market.** Home Depot and Lowe's are creating new markets for their businesses by expanding into do-it-yourself training on home projects within their stores.
- **Use new labels or different container types.** Repackaging is another popular method to extend a product's life. For example, Sally Hansen, the nail care company, put nail polish in a pen-like applicator that is portable and spill-proof.
- **Create a new vision.** A company can also reposition its product as Oldsmobile attempted to do with its "This isn't your father's Oldsmobile" campaign. These strategies are not always effective. The Oldsmobile, despite the revised campaign, has been discontinued.[16]

As you've just learned, developing a high-quality product is not so much an end in itself as it is a beginning. After a product is developed, the product life cycle begins, and appropriate marketing strategies must be conceived and implemented accordingly. Jessica Smith is experiencing this now. Three years after opening her yoga studio and equipment store, she changed her marketing and pricing strategies on products that were experiencing declining sales. At the same time, she expanded offerings of her most popular classes to maximize profits during the critical growth and maturity stages. As Jessica quickly learned, a dynamic market calls for dynamic product development. ■

Pricing Goods and Services

pp. 403–409

Pavel Losevsky/Fotolia

As the new store manager of Bitsy Baby, Eugene Whitaker needed to increase profits. Under the previous manager, Bitsy Baby was barely surviving, and the owner was contemplating closing the doors forever. Eugene was his last hope. The previous manager insisted on carrying many of the same items the big chain store in the nearby mall sold, but tried to undercut the big store's prices. Bitsy Baby also carried a small assortment of unique baby items that were casually displayed in a back corner of the store. Eugene felt those items could be their "niche." The question Eugene struggled with was the pricing. Could he try to compete with the big stores on the items they had in common? What pricing strategy should he use with the unique goods? ■

Pricing is important to consumers and producers alike, and it is an essential component in the marketing mix. We conclude this chapter by discussing the pricing component of the marketing mix. We'll discuss promotion and distribution strategies in the next chapter.

6 What are some pricing objectives, and how do they relate to the marketing mix?

Product Pricing and Pricing Objectives

Why is price an important component in the marketing mix? As consumers, we know a product's price means what we must pay to acquire it. From the seller's perspective, price is the only revenue-generating component of the marketing mix; product, promotion, and distribution strategies are all cost components. Therefore, price is an important factor in determining profit.

Price can also serve as a marketing tool and is often used in promotional campaigns. Trying to set the right price can be a real challenge for marketers. The price of a product has to be low enough to generate enough value to customers to motivate sales yet also high enough to enable a company to cover costs and earn a profit. Setting the right price is a challenge because market conditions are always changing. As a result, companies must constantly tweak prices to remain competitive. Moreover, some companies operating in very competitive markets may have little or no control over their prices. Instead, prices are determined in the market through the interaction of supply and demand. For example, farmers have virtually no control over the prices of their agricultural commodities. These companies may therefore be called *price-takers* (not *price-setters*). However, most companies have at least some control over the prices they charge.

How does value affect price? Price is what customers actually pay for a product, but value is the derived benefit of the entire product offering. Recall that the total product offer consists of all the benefits associated with a product, and each level of benefit (core, actual, and augmented) adds more value to a product. Often price plays into how a customer views a product's value. In addition, there can be other costs associated with purchasing a product, such as the cost of learning how to use a product or the costs associated with removing the old product that may affect the product's overall value.

What are some pricing objectives? Pricing is more than simply calculating the cost of production and then tacking on a markup for profit. The price often impacts how consumers view a product and may determine whether they will purchase it. Price also helps to differentiate a product from the competition. Setting a specific pricing objective is important to do before establishing the price point. There are a variety of pricing objectives; some of the most common ones include the following:

- **Maximize profits.** This occurs when price is set so that total revenue exceeds total cost by the greatest amount.
- **Achieve greater market share.** A company's market share is the percentage of total industry sales or revenues it is able to capture. Unfortunately, achieving greater market share does not always translate into higher profits.
- **Maximize sales.** Maximizing sales often means charging low prices that can result in losses. Firms cannot survive for long with losses. However, maximizing sales may be an appropriate short-run objective to rid the company of excess inventory, such as last year's models.
- **Build traffic.** Many retail stores, such as grocery stores and department stores, may advertise a sale price on a few goods to increase traffic in their stores and build a stronger customer base. They also hope customers will purchase other, more profitable items while they are shopping for the bargains.

- **Match the status quo prices.** The objective of status quo pricing is to match competitors' prices, possibly to avoid a price war that could be damaging to everyone. The airfare wars of the past hurt every airline carrier, so they have chosen to compete on nonprice factors instead.

- **Cover costs to survive.** If a company is struggling to build a customer base, it may choose to set prices to generate just enough revenues to cover costs. However, this is not a suitable long-term objective. Survival prices might generate sales, but they will not generate profits.

- **Create an image.** Some products are priced high because firms hope that consumers will associate high prices with high quality. This is the case for many specialty goods, such as luxury cars, perfume, and designer jewelry.

- **Ensure affordability to all.** Some companies may charge low prices to enable the poor to afford their products. For example, many governments have been involved in ensuring that staple food products, such as grains, are affordable to all.

How do you choose the right pricing objective? The most appropriate pricing objective is determined by considering the business and financial goals of a product or a company. If one of the business goals is to become a market leader and amass the greatest market share, then maximizing quantity of sales may be a more appropriate choice over building traffic; if a business objective is aggressive production growth, then profit maximization will be important. Survival and status quo pricing may be better suited when market conditions are poor or unstable or when entering a market for the first time. Pricing objectives will change over the life cycle of a product. Marketers must develop their pricing strategies in coordination with their product branding, packaging, promotion, and distribution strategies as well. Indeed, price is only one element in the marketing mix.

Pricing Strategies and Price Perceptions

7 What are the major pricing strategies?

What are the major pricing strategies? After determining the pricing *objective*, choosing the best pricing *strategy* to achieve that objective is next. Although there is no one right way to determine the price of a good or service, there are several strategies that sellers can use. Certain strategies work better with certain objectives, and some pricing strategies may be used at different times to fit in with changes in marketing strategies, market conditions, and product life cycles. The most common pricing strategies include *cost-based pricing, demand-based pricing, competition-based pricing*, and *everyday low pricing*.

There are also several alternative pricing strategies and strategies that affect price perceptions. ■ **FIGURE 13.9** outlines these pricing strategies.

What is cost-based pricing? One of the easiest and simplest ways to price a product is **cost-based pricing**. This pricing strategy (also known as *cost-plus pricing*) is based on covering costs and providing for a set profit. Suppose you manufacture 100 units of a product at a total cost of $2,000. The average (or per unit) total cost would be $20. If you want to make a unit profit margin, or *markup*, of 20 percent, which is $4 (0.20 × $20), you would price the product at $24. Total revenue would equal $2,400; profit would equal $400, or 20 percent above costs.

There are many advantages of cost-based pricing. Besides being easy to calculate and easy to administer, it requires a minimum amount of information. However, it has several disadvantages as well. Cost-based pricing ignores whether a price is compatible with consumer demand or expectations and is competitive to the prices for similar products. It also provides little incentive to be efficient and hold costs down. Many pharmaceutical companies undertake cost-based pricing to recover the expensive research and development costs associated with a new

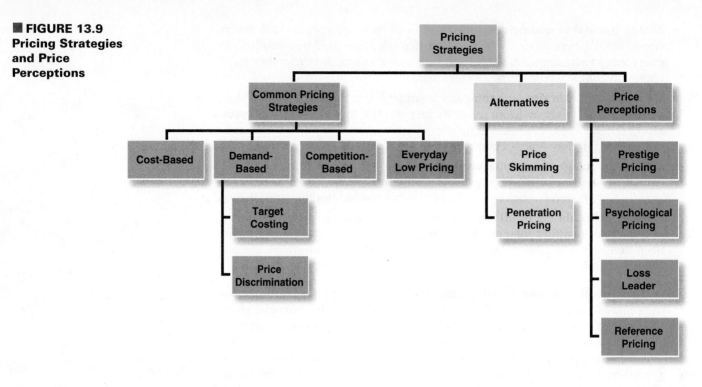

**FIGURE 13.9
Pricing Strategies
and Price
Perceptions**

drug and to earn a targeted profit level. The monopoly power granted by patents on new drugs means there is no competition, and pharmaceutical companies find little need to consider consumer demand when setting prices on drugs.

How does product demand impact pricing? Demand-based pricing (sometimes called *value-based pricing*) is pricing based on the demand for a product or its perceived value. A high price will be charged when demand or the perceived value of a product is high, and a lower price will be charged when demand or perceived value is low. This pricing strategy assumes firms can accurately estimate the perceived value or demand for their goods or services. Sometimes this is the case, but it's usually very difficult to do in practice. Nevertheless, many firms try.

Demand-based pricing can be defined further by other pricing strategies: target costing and price discrimination.

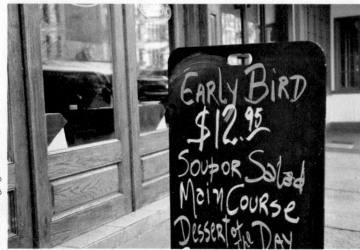

Early bird specials are a form of price discrimination that offer meals at reduced prices when ordered during predinner hours.

- **Target costing** estimates the value customers receive from a product and, therefore, the price they are willing to pay and then subtracts an acceptable profit margin to obtain a desired cost. Firms then work to get costs down to this targeted level. The Boeing Company and Caterpillar have successfully used target costing as a pricing strategy.[17]

- **Price discrimination** occurs when a business charges different prices to different customers for an identical good or service, for reasons not associated with costs. Successful price discrimination charges higher prices to targeted customers who are price insensitive and lower prices to targeted customers who are more price sensitive. Price discrimination requires firms to successfully segment customers based on their differences in demand and price sensitivity, and it requires that a product cannot be easily resold among customers. One example of price discrimination includes hotels and resorts charging different rates based on different

© Judie Long/age fotostock

days of the week or seasonal variations. Movie theaters may also charge different prices for different viewing times. In some cases, even salespeople charge different prices to customers based on their perceived demand for big-ticket items, such as cars and furniture, so don't tell them how much you value or love their good or service! Many organizations price discriminate because it's profitable.

What pricing strategy would work best in a highly competitive market? Competition-based pricing is a pricing strategy based on what the competition is charging. Revenues and costs are secondary. The degree of competition in markets affects a company's price-setting ability.

- *Perfectly competitive markets,* markets with many suppliers and homogenous products such as gasoline, agricultural, and raw material commodities, have little, if any, control over their prices. Firms charge prices equivalent to all others' prices.

- *Monopolistically competitive markets,* markets in which many firms compete on the basis of doing something unique, have some firms that charge higher prices if they are successful in their product differentiation strategies. Other companies may charge lower prices to get an edge on the competition. Most real-world competition rests on product differentiation and the customer's perception of value. For example, Oakley, Inc., which makes sunglasses and goggles for sports and fashion, has successfully differentiated its products and can charge higher prices.

- *Oligopolies,* markets with a few dominant sellers, such as those in the airline and oil industries, often avoid competing on the basis of price to avoid price wars. Instead, they compete aggressively on product differentiation and charge higher prices if their total product offerings are unique. However, periodically, a price leader may charge a different price, and all other firms will follow with similar price changes.

- *Monopolies,* markets that are controlled by one dominating firm, possess the greatest price-setting ability because there is no competition. In some extreme cases monopolies may capture their markets through *predatory pricing*, the practice of charging very low prices with the intent of destroying the competition. Predatory pricing is illegal, but that hasn't prevented it from occurring.

What pricing strategy offers low prices all the time? Some retail stores offer **everyday low pricing (EDLP)**, a strategy of charging low prices with few, if any, special or promotional sales. Walmart has successfully used this strategy because it has been able to give the impression that its brand means everyday low cost. JC Penney is revising its policy with a new "fair and square" pricing strategy that promotes everyday values.

Are there pricing strategies that work better with certain phases of the product life cycle? When launching a new product, companies may need to use a different type of pricing strategy than they would on an existing product (refer back to Figure 13.8).

- **Price skimming** involves charging a high price for a product initially and then lowering the price over time. Price skimming coincides with the introductory stage of a product's life cycle, during which there are few, if any, competitors. The idea is to skim off as high a price as possible to recoup the expensive new product development costs. However, the high price may encourage competitors to enter the market at a lower price.

- **Penetration pricing** involves charging the lowest possible price for a new product. This pricing strategy is designed to quickly build market share for a product. If the increased production to satisfy growing sales results in lower per unit costs, then profits can actually rise even though the price is lower. Penetration pricing is also appropriate during the growth stage of a product's life cycle and when customers are price sensitive. It may also create goodwill among consumers and inhibit competitors from entering the market. Its drawbacks include the establishment of low price expectations or a poor-quality image for a brand and a company, which may make it difficult to raise prices later.

What are some strategies used to impact price perceptions? For many consumers, a high price indicates good quality. Although this is not always the case, many consumers make this association when products are complex, do not have a strong brand identity, or are services with which they are unfamiliar. The less they know about a product, the more consumers rely on price as an indicator of quality. Businesses have to be careful not to lower their prices too much; otherwise, a product may be perceived as low quality. There are several types of pricing strategies that have an impact on price perceptions.

- **Prestige pricing** (also known as *premium pricing*) is the practice of charging a high price to invoke perceptions of high quality and privilege. For those brands for which prestige pricing may apply, the high price itself is a motivator for consumers. The higher perceived value because of the higher price actually increases demand and creates a higher price that becomes self-sustaining. Some people have called this the *snob effect*. Examples of this strategy include the pricing of luxury cars, jewelry, and designer clothes.

- **Psychological pricing** (sometimes called *odd* or *fractional pricing*) is the practice of charging a price just below a whole number to give the appearance of a significantly lower price. For example, charging $9.99 as opposed to $10.00 is an example of psychological pricing. Gas stations often use psychological pricing.

- **Loss leader** is a product that is priced below its costs. Stores use loss leaders to attract customers into the store and then motivate them to buy more expensive items as well. Reference pricing is another strategy used to attract customers.

- **Reference pricing** refers to listing an inflated price (the regular retail price or the manufacturer's suggested retail price) that is then discounted to appear as if it is a good value. A variation of this strategy occurs when stores provide both a more expensive "gold-plated" version of a product and a lower-priced alternative. This makes the alternative appear as a bargain.

How might production be affected by pricing strategies? No matter which pricing strategy is selected, it is important to determine how much product can be produced at that price level before generating a profit. A **breakeven analysis**, which determines the production level for which total revenue is just enough to cover total costs, is useful to conduct with any pricing strategy. At the breakeven point, no profit has been made, and no losses have been incurred. The first step in conducting a breakeven analysis is to determine costs. There are two types of costs that make up the total product cost: fixed costs and variable costs. *Fixed costs* (sometimes called *overhead costs*) are any costs that do not vary with the production level. Fixed costs typically include salaries, rent, insurance expenses, and loan repayments. *Variable costs* are costs that vary with the production level. Examples include wages, raw materials, and energy costs. *Average variable costs* (or *per unit variable costs*) equal total variable costs divided by the production level. A convenient formula for calculating the breakeven production level is as follows:

$$\text{Breakeven volume of production} = \frac{\text{Total Fixed Costs}}{\text{Revenue Per Unit} - \text{Average Variable Costs}}$$

For example, suppose that the total fixed costs equal $600, the selling price is $24, and average variable costs are $14. The breakeven volume of production is therefore $600 ÷ ($24 − $14), or 60 units. Any production level below the breakeven volume will result in losses, and any production level above the breakeven level will result in profits. Any changes in the fixed or variable costs, or changes in the price, will affect the breakeven volume of production.

Adjusting Prices

What are common types of price adjustments? Most businesses adjust their prices to promote their products. Several tactics are used, as shown in ■ FIGURE 13.10. One way is to use **discounts**, a deduction from the regular price charged. Discounts come in many forms:

■ FIGURE 13.10
Price Adjustments (Tactics)

- Cash discounts (a reduced price for paying with a method that does not require processing)
- Quantity discounts (a lower price for buying in large quantities)
- Seasonal discounts (a price reduction if you buy out of season)
- Forms of allowance, such as a trade-in allowance (a reduced price if you trade your old good for a new good)

Another way to adjust prices is to use rebates. **Rebates** are partial refunds on what a customer has already paid for a product. An example is mail-in rebates, where a manufacturer gives a debit card to be used against future purchases or may write a check to the customer after the customer provides proof of purchase.

Bundling is another type of price adjustment. In **bundling**, two or more products that usually complement one another are combined and sold at a single price. To be attractive, the single price is usually lower than the sum of the individual products' prices. Bundling is quite common in the fast-food industry, where products are bundled to make a complete meal. Bundling also occurs with cable, DSL, or satellite television sales; when a package of channels is sold at a single price; or when phone, Internet, and television plans are combined. Many vacation packages are also bundled products consisting of airfare, car rental, hotel accommodations, and other amenities.

Dynamic pricing is another price-adjustment technique. In **dynamic pricing**, prices are determined directly between a buyer and a seller, unlike the more traditional fixed pricing in which a seller sets prices. Auctions are a traditional form of dynamic pricing. More recent examples exist in e-commerce, such as eBay and Priceline.com. Dynamic pricing often results in quick price adjustments.

Eugene moved the unique goods to the front of the store and created a much nicer display. He began to notice that more customers were coming into Bitsy Baby for those unique items to buy them as gifts. He also began to gradually increase the prices as he realized that customers were willing to pay just a bit more to get that unique gift. Eugene began to pursue a different pricing strategy. He competitively priced those items that the chain store also carried and continued to price the unique items just high enough that customers would think they were special but not too high to deter interest. In addition, Eugene had special bags, boxes, tissue paper, and ribbons designed with the company logo and colors, so his items stood out even when they left the store. Eugene's pricing and packaging strategy paid off. Within two years Bitsy Baby's financial woes were in the past, and Bitsy Baby had found its niche. ■

CHAPTER 13
SUMMARY

MyBizLab

Go to **mybizlab.com** to complete the problems marked with this icon ⭐.

① How is a product distinguished from a total product offer? (pp. 385–386)

- A *product* is any good, service, or idea that might satisfy a want or a need. A **total product offer** (p. 386) consists of all the tangible and intangible benefits associated with a good, a service, or an idea that impact a consumer's purchasing decision. Marketers know this. When planning a total product offering, they think about products on three levels:

  - A **core product** (p. 386) satisfies the basic need or want that motivates a purchase. Because it is the basic benefit provided by a product, you can't touch it; it is intangible.

  - An **actual product** (p. 386) is the tangible aspect of a purchase that you can touch, see, hear, smell, or taste. It provides core benefits when it is used.

  - An **augmented product** (p. 386) consists of the core and actual product plus other real or perceived benefits that provide additional value to the customer's purchase.

② What is product differentiation, and what role does it play in product development? (pp. 386–387)

- **Product differentiation** (p. 386) is the process of distinguishing a product from its competition in real or perceived terms to attract customers.

- Customer input and feedback guide product development and product differentiation. It also gives rise to the creation of a **product line** (p. 387), a group of similar products marketed to one general market. A **product mix** (p. 387) is the combination of all product lines offered for sale by a company. Product lines and mix result from trying to tailor total product offerings to unique targeted customers.

③ What are the different classifications of consumer products and business-to-business products? (pp. 388–391)

- The four classifications of **consumer products** (p. 388) are convenience goods and services, shopping goods and services, specialty goods and services, and unsought goods and services:

  - Customers purchase **convenience goods and services** (p. 388), such as gum, soap, and milk, frequently, immediately, and effortlessly.

  - **Shopping goods and services** (p. 389) are products that are less frequently purchased and require that

the customer spend more time and effort in comparing the products. Examples include clothes, electronics, and furniture.

  - **Specialty goods and services** (p. 389) have unique characteristics and no suitable substitutes. Examples include designer clothing or the services of prestigious lawyers.

  - **Unsought goods and services** (p. 389) are products buyers don't usually think about buying, don't know exist, or buy only when a specific problem arises. An example is funeral services.

- There are five categories of **business-to-business (B2B) products** (p. 388): equipment, MRO products, raw and processed materials, component parts, and specialized professional services.

④ Why is branding beneficial to both buyers and sellers, and what are some different branding strategies? (pp. 392–395)

- Branding reduces shopping time for buyers and helps consumers express themselves. Branding helps sellers define the special qualities of their product, encouraging repeat purchases and new sales at higher prices.

- Marketing a product using the same brand name but in a different product category is known as **brand extension** (p. 392). **Brand licensing** (p. 392) is an agreement between the owner of a brand and another company or individual who pays a royalty for using the brand in association with a new product.

- For sellers, branding creates **brand loyalty** (p. 392) among consumers. Brand loyalty contributes to **brand equity** (p. 393), the overall value of a brand's strength in the market. **Brand awareness** (p. 393) refers to the extent to which a particular brand name is familiar within a particular product category. **Brand association** (p. 393) involves connecting a brand with other positive attributes.

- There are six different types of brands: **manufacturer's brands, family brands, individual brands, private brands, co-brands,** and **generic brands** (pp. 393–395).

- How a product is packaged and labeled sends a message about a product and a brand.

⑤ What steps take place during new product development, and what is the product life cycle? (pp. 399–402)

- The steps in new product development are idea generation, idea screening, product analysis, concept development and testing, product and marketing mix development, market testing, and commercialization.

- The **product life cycle** (p. 401) is a theoretical model describing a product's sales and profits over the course of its lifetime. Stages in the product life cycle include introduction, growth, maturity, and decline.

6 **What are some pricing objectives, and how do they relate to the marketing mix?** (pp. 404–405)

- Common pricing objectives include maximizing profits, achieving greater market share, maximizing sales, building traffic in stores, matching status quo prices, covering costs to survive, creating an image, and ensuring affordability to all.

- Price is the only revenue-generating component of the marketing mix. Marketers must carefully consider their pricing objectives to develop the best pricing strategy.

7 **What are the major to pricing strategies?** (pp. 405–409)

- The major approaches to pricing strategy are **cost-based pricing** (p. 405), **demand-based pricing** (p. 406), **competition-based pricing** (p. 407), and **everyday low pricing (EDLP)** (p. 407).

- **Price skimming** (p. 407) and **penetration pricing** (p. 407) are tactics used for launching new products.

- **Prestige pricing** (p. 408), **psychological pricing** (p. 408), the use of **loss leaders** (p. 408), and **reference pricing** (p. 408) are pricing strategies that impact price perceptions by consumers.

- **Discounts** (p. 409), **rebates** (p. 409), **bundling** (p. 409), and **dynamic pricing** (p. 409) are common types of price adjustments.

Key Terms

actual product (p. 386)
augmented product (p. 386)
brand (p. 392)
brand association (p. 393)
brand awareness (p. 393)
brand equity (p. 393)
brand extension (p. 392)
brand licensing (p. 392)
brand loyalty (p. 392)
breakeven analysis (p. 408)
bundling (p. 409)
business-to-business (B2B) products (p. 388)
co-brand (p. 394)
competition-based pricing (p. 407)
consumer products (p. 388)
convenience goods and services (p. 388)

core product (p. 386)
cost-based pricing (p. 405)
demand-based pricing (p. 406)
discounts (p. 409)
dynamic pricing (p. 409)
everyday low pricing (EDLP) (p. 407)
family brand (p. 394)
generic brand (p. 395)
individual brand (p. 394)
loss leader (p. 408)
manufacturer's brand (p. 393)
penetration pricing (p. 407)
prestige pricing (p. 408)
price discrimination (p. 406)
price skimming (p. 407)
private brand (p. 394)
product (p. 385)

product differentiation (p. 386)
product life cycle (p. 401)
product line (p. 387)
product line length (p. 387)
product mix (p. 387)
product mix width (p. 387)
psychological pricing (p. 408)
rebates (p. 409)
reference pricing (p. 408)
shopping goods and services (p. 389)
specialty goods and services (p. 389)
target costing (p. 406)
total product offer (p. 386)
trademark (p. 392)
unsought goods and services (p. 389)

Self-Test

Multiple Choice You can find the answers on the last page of this book.

1. The level of a product that satisfies the basic need or want that motivates a purchase is the
   a. total product offering.
   b. augmented product.
   c. actual product.
   d. core product.

2. Product mix width refers to
   a. a total product offer.
   b. a group of similar products marketed to one general product market category.
   c. the number of product lines a company offers.
   d. the number of items in a product line.

3. When companies compete aggressively on the basis of price, quality, and brand-name image because consumers carefully compare brands, these businesses are most likely selling _____ goods and services.
   a. convenience
   b. shopping
   c. specialty
   d. unsought

4. When businesses hire celebrities to endorse their products and connect their brands with positive attributes, they are focusing on enhancing their brand
   a. loyalty.
   b. awareness.
   c. association.
   d. extension.

5. A brand that markets several different products under the same brand name is a
   a. manufacturer's brand.
   b. family brand.
   c. private brand.
   d. co-brand.

6. Siobhan Clark just bought a Philadelphia Phillies jersey with player Roy Halladay's name and number on the back, as well as a hat and jacket that display the Phillies logo. The type of branding strategy used for these products is
   a. generic branding.
   b. manufacturer's branding.
   c. private branding.
   d. brand licensing.

7. In what stage in the product life cycle would you consider the RIM Blackberry phone to be?
   a. Introduction
   b. Growth
   c. Maturity
   d. Decline

8. Stephanie Ling has been asked to conduct a breakeven analysis. Which of the following would be considered a variable cost?
   a. Price of gasoline
   b. Property insurance
   c. Salaries
   d. Interest on loan

9. Rocco Valentino shops only at Walmart. Because Walmart rarely has sales, Rocco believes he'll receive the lowest price without further hassles. This type of pricing strategy is known as _____ pricing.
   a. dynamic
   b. everyday low
   c. competition-based
   d. penetration

10. Which pricing strategy sets prices just below a whole number to give the appearance of a lower price?
    a. Predatory pricing
    b. Price discrimination
    c. Target costing
    d. Psychological pricing

True/False You can find the answers on the last page of this book.

1. The augmented product provides additional value to a customer's purchase.
   ☑ **True** or ☐ **False**

2. Trademarking benefits sellers by helping to distinguish their products from knockoff brands.
   ☑ **True** or ☐ **False**

3. Loss leader pricing is used to move a product quickly off the shelves.
   ☐ **True** or ☑ **False**

4. MRO B2B products are marketed much like consumer convenience goods and services.
   ☑ **True** or ☐ **False**

5. A product's packaging is used only to provide protection of the good's contents.
   ☐ **True** or ☑ **False**

Critical Thinking Questions

1. How are brand loyalty, specialty goods and services, and prestige pricing related?

2. In 2011, Starbucks came out with a new design of their iconic logo that removed the words "Starbucks Coffee" and emphasized the image of Siren. What is your reaction to the new logo? Why do you think they redesigned it?

3. Describe the conditions when it might be appropriate to use each of the following pricing strategies: discounting, rebates, bundling, dynamic pricing, prestige pricing, psychological pricing, loss leader pricing, and reference pricing.

Team Time

Developing a Product

Divide into teams of three or four. As a team, use what you have learned in this chapter to discuss how you would develop a new product.

Process

Step 1. Begin with the first step in the new product development process: idea generation. Work as a group to decide what your new product will be.

Step 2. Proceed through the idea screening, product analysis, product development and testing, and commercialization steps. What do you estimate the consumer demand and production feasibility for this product to be? How much will it cost to produce, and what should be its selling price? How might you test-market this product? How will it be marketed? Discuss the answers to these questions as you address their corresponding steps.

Step 3. Prepare a summary of your findings and present them to the class.

Ethics and Corporate Social Responsibility

THE ETHICS OF RX

The pharmaceutical drug industry is an ethical minefield. The development of prescription medications is one topic among many that can present significant ethical challenges. Consider the questions raised by the following scenario. If possible, discuss your thoughts with a classmate or participate in a group debate on the topic.

Scenario

You are an executive at one of the top drug companies in the United States. At the most recent product development meeting, two teams of scientists reported that each is within one year of having a new drug ready for clinical trials. Team A is developing a drug to cure a rare but fatal bone disease. Team B is developing a drug to treat a common, non–life-threatening skin condition. To make the deadline, however, both teams need an additional $10 million in funding. You know that the company can afford to fund only one team. According to the product analysis, Team A's drug will be expensive to produce, difficult to market, and yield only modest profits. Team B's drug has the potential to yield massive profits.

Questions for Discussion

1. Which team would you recommend the company fund? Why?

2. How do the potential profits of Team B's drug affect your stance, from both financial/business and medical/ethical perspectives?

3. What about pricing? How might you reconcile the need to keep the drug company profitable with the ethical responsibility to make medications affordable for those in need?

Web Exercises

1. **The iPhone as a Product**
   Go to Apple's iPhone website. Describe Apple's marketing mix strategy for its product and its price. When would an iPhone be a consumer product, and when would it be a B2B product? What does Apple do to augment its product? What type of branding strategy is Apple pursuing? What stage of the product life cycle is the iPhone in? Is Apple undertaking the appropriate strategies, given this stage of the product's life cycle?

2. **Organic Coke?**
   Organic products are increasing in popularity. Suppose Coca-Cola came out with an organic soda product. Use the Internet to research other organic beverages and sodas. Where would this fit in Coke's product mix? How would Coca-Cola's established branding help or hurt the product launch? What kind of pricing strategy do you think it would use to introduce the product?

3. **Research a Brand**
   Choose a favorite brand of clothing or food and use the Internet to gather information about it. What type of brand is it—manufacturer's, private, individual, or other? Is it

part of a brand extension? Is it associated with a co-brand or a licensing arrangement? How do packaging and labeling affect the image the brand projects? Summarize your findings in a brief report.

4. **Toothpaste Differential**
   Look at Walmart's website or a website for an online drugstore. List the various manufacturers of toothpaste. Then, under each one, list the various products they make. How are companies trying to differentiate their products from each other? How do you think consumers react to these various types of toothpaste?

5. **"Innovate or Die"**
   Research in Motion (RIM) released the BlackBerry smartphone in 2003. The device was wildly successful and had few true competitors until Apple introduced the iPhone in 2007. Research the market share of the two phones since the iPhone's release and discuss the possible reasons for Blackberry's decline. What, if anything, is RIM doing now to gain back market share? Do you think they'll be successful? Why or why not?

MyBizLab

Go to **mybizlab.com** for Auto-graded writing questions as well as the following Assisted-graded writing questions:

13-1. Why is it important for marketers to think of a good or a service as a total product offering?

13-2. What part of the product life cycle would a product like the energy drink Red Bull be in? What about Gatorade?

13-3. MyBizLab Only – comprehensive writing assignment for this chapter.

Promotion and Distribution

Promotion and the Promotional Mix

When Danny Perez started his own lunch cart business, he thought that being in a location with other lunch carts and giving away samples would generate business. Unfortunately, things didn't turn out as he anticipated the first day. How could Danny create an effective promotional strategy?

Advertising and Public Relations

Monica Garcia and Steven Alvarez have opened their own new interior design business. They have a website and are using Pinterest and Facebook to connect with their customers and hear what people are saying about their business. But how can they monitor all the comments made in these social networking sites? Do they need other, more traditional means of advertising? What other advertising options are best for them?

Personal Selling and Sales Promotion

Keith Jefferson works for a trucking company and is giving his first sales pitch alone. When his potential client asks a question about shipping rates, Keith freezes. He has no idea how to answer the question. What is personal selling? What traits do good salespeople have?

Distribution: Marketing Intermediaries

Liv Karlsen needs a book that was on the *New York Times* best-sellers list for her modern U.S. literature class. The college bookstore had no more copies, so she used her smartphone to order a copy online. What is the distribution process for online products? Are all distribution processes the same?

MyBizLab®

⭐ **Improve Your Grade!**

Over 10 million students improved their results using the Pearson MyLabs.
Visit **mybizlab.com** for simulations, tutorials, and end-of-chapter problems.

CHAPTER 14

Promotion and the
Promotional Mix pp. 417–419

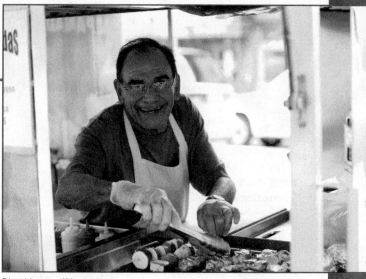

Blend Images/Alamy

Danny Perez dreamed of having his own business. When he decided to take the leap and switch careers, he was nervous but excited. He loved to cook and wanted to get people to taste his food, but he didn't have the money to open a full-fledged restaurant. Instead, he decided to operate a food cart and was able to set up in a busy commercial area that already had several other lunch carts. Danny's son suggested he start a Facebook page and a Twitter account, but Danny didn't trust those techy things. Instead, he decided to begin by giving away samples of some of his menu items. Unfortunately, not many people took the free samples, and even fewer bought anything. In the end, he was out $400 in food the first day with nothing to show for it. Was it his food, his location, or how he promoted his product? Should he have taken his son's advice about the social media sites? ■

Danny's plan to promote his business was well intentioned, but it didn't work out quite the way he had hoped. What should he have done differently? What other options does he have? In this chapter, you'll learn about the promotion and distribution (or place) components of the 4 Ps of the marketing mix.

Promotion

What is promotion? Few products—no matter how well they are developed, priced, and distributed—will sell well if they are not properly promoted. **Promotion** involves all the techniques marketers use to inform targeted customers of the benefits of a product and persuade them to purchase it. Promotion is designed to increase brand awareness, brand loyalty, and sales and is, therefore, one of the most visible components of the marketing mix.

Finding the best way to communicate the benefits of a product and persuade customers to buy it is a critical job of marketers. Should a product be advertised, or is personal selling more appropriate? If advertising is used, is it best to advertise through newspapers, television, the Internet, or another source? Beyond advertising and personal selling, what types of public relations activities might be most appropriate? These are just a few of the questions that marketers must ask themselves when promoting a product.

■ FIGURE 14.1
The Promotional Mix

1 What is a promotional mix, and what is its function in a promotional campaign?

Billboards such as the one shown here may be part of an IMC strategy.

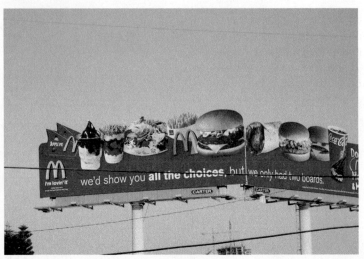

David P.G. Phillips/Alamy

What are the most popular tools marketers use to promote a product? The following four basic promotional tools are used to promote a good or a service:

- Advertising
- Public relations
- Personal selling
- Sales promotions

The **promotional mix** is the strategic combination of these promotional tools used to reach targeted customers to achieve marketing objectives. The elements of the promotional mix are illustrated in ■ **FIGURE 14.1**. Notice that the product is also included as an element in the promotional mix. It can be a promotional tool because its features may be promoted by giving away free samples of the good or service, as Danny Perez did.

Efficient organizations search for the optimal or most cost-effective promotional mix given their marketing objectives and budgetary constraints. The optimal promotional mix for a given product will vary depending on the goals of a business.

What are the steps involved in a promotional campaign? It's best to plan out a promotional campaign to determine the right balance of activities and timing to increase awareness in the marketplace. Although each campaign will differ to suit the specific needs of the product, the basic steps are as follows:

1. **Identify the target market.** Recall from Chapter 12 that a *target market* is a specific group of potential customers on which to focus marketing efforts. The promotional campaign should devote its promotional activities to that market, first.

2. **Determine marketing objectives.** Is a business trying to maximize profits, sales, or market share? Is the goal to build traffic, brand awareness, or brand image? Is a business trying to introduce a new product or respond to an attack by a competitor? Whatever the marketing objective is, the goal should be clearly understood and measurable.

3. **Determine the budget.** The best combination of promotional activities can be determined by finding the mix that has the biggest bang for the buck—but it still needs to stay within a predetermined budget.

4. **Design the message.** The message should inform customers of the benefits of a business's product and be echoed by all elements of the promotional mix for a unified communication.

5. **Implement the promotional mix.** It is important to ensure that the variety of tools and resources required of a typical promotional campaign all work together harmoniously. **Integrated marketing communications (IMC)** is a strategy to deliver a clear, consistent, and unified message about a company and its products to customers at all contact points. This strategy contrasts with allowing members of an organization to develop in isolation their own communications with customers, which could give rise to conflicting messages, consumer confusion, and ultimately a loss of sales.

6. **Evaluate and adjust as needed.** The effectiveness of any promotional mix depends on clear and measurable objectives. Each element of the

mix, as well as the entire combination of the mix, will need to be adjusted as necessary for growth, for changing marketing objectives, or to correct ineffective promotional techniques.

Promoting a product involves choosing the best combination of promotional tools to persuade customers to purchase a good, a service, or an idea. As Danny Perez's initial experience with his food cart business shows, achieving this blend can be a challenge. Having learned his lesson, Danny is now putting careful thought into each of the steps of developing an effective promotional campaign to determine the best promotional mix for his business. ■

Advertising and Public Relations pp. 419–427

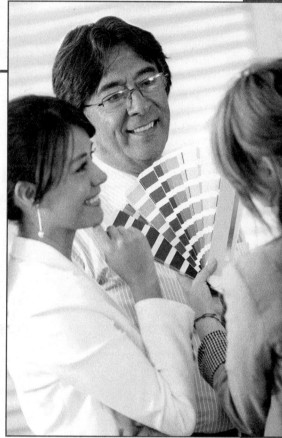

After graduating from design school, Monica Garcia and Steven Alvarez rented a small studio and opened their interior design business. They already had several clients—friends and family connections—but they knew they had to get the word out in a more formal and broader context if they ever wanted their business to grow. Steven was in charge of the website and creating a fan page on Facebook. Monica loved Pinterest, so she began to pin little design images each day, but she wondered how she would monitor all the conversations that were happening in response to their efforts. Monica and Steven were also wondering if these avenues were enough or whether they needed to advertise in magazines and/or newspapers or create and distribute flyers. What kind of advertising would be best for Monica and Steven? ■

Andres Rodriguez/Fotolia

Advertising is paid, impersonal mass communication from an identified sponsor to persuade or influence a targeted audience. When we think of advertising, many of us first think of television commercials. But advertising is much more.

The Role of Advertising

What role does advertising play in business? Advertising plays a huge role in business as one of the promotional tools designed to communicate with targeted customers. Businesses use advertising to:

> 2 What are the different categories of advertising, and what role do these categories play in business and society?

- Help build mass brand awareness and brand association, and so it is especially important in the introduction and growth stages of a product's life cycle.
- Emphasize product differentiation, and is especially helpful for a product in the maturity stage.
- Build brand loyalty and brand equity.

THE List

Successful Advertising Campaigns

1. "Drivers Wanted" (Volkswagen, 1998)
2. "Have It Your Way" (Burger King, 1973)
3. "Just Do It" (Nike, 1988)
4. "Campaign for Real Beauty" (Dove, 2004)
5. "The Duck" (Aflac, 1999)
6. "Priceless" (MasterCard, 1997)
7. "Breakfast of Champions" (Wheaties, 1930s)
8. "A Diamond Is Forever" (De Beers, 1999)
9. "Don't Leave Home Without It" (American Express, 1975)
10. "Good to the Last Drop" (Maxwell House Coffee, 1959)

Sources: Volkswagen, 1998. www .vw.com; Burger King Corporation, 1973. www.bk.com; Nike, 1988. www.nike.com; Dove, 2004. Unilever Corporation, www.unileverusa .com.; Aflac, 1999. www.aflac.com; Mastercard Worldwide, 1997. www.mastercard.com; General Mills, 1930s. www.generalmills .com; DeBeers, 1999. www .debeers.com; American Express, 1975. www.americanexpress.com; Maxwell House. Kraft Foods, 1959. http://www.kraftrecipes.com

- Inform consumers of the value inherent in products and educate the public in their uses. However, critics argue that advertisers often mislead the public into perceptions of value or qualities that may not exist. This debate continues. It echoes the need for ethical business behavior and can explain the existence of government laws and regulations that constrain advertising and other marketing practices.
- Lead to lower prices for consumers. The more people know about a product and like it, the more sales and production increase. Given the economies of scale associated with increased volumes of production, consumers get lower per-unit costs and lower-priced products.

What's the economic impact of advertising? Advertising impacts the economy because of the huge sums of money spent on it. For example, Google's 2012 advertising budget of $213 million nearly quadrupled the previous year's $53 million budget,[1] and a 30-second spot during the Super Bowl has exceeded $3.5 million![2] Those advertising dollars are dispersed throughout the economy in a variety of ways. Immediately, the advertising dollars help fund the platform the advertisement is using: commercials help pay for the television programming, and print ads help pay for the publishing of newspapers and magazines. A positive economic impact occurs if advertising is successful. A well-received campaign results in increased sales profits, which ultimately lead to business growth, more jobs, and more discretionary income available to spend. However, the opposite can also be true, so if a company doesn't spend money on advertising, or has a poor campaign, sales can stagnate quickly, resulting in corporate retrenchment and lost jobs.

Types of Advertising

What are the different types of advertising? There are several different forms of advertising, with firms using just one or a variety of advertising techniques. No matter the form used, advertising is undertaken by virtually all organizations. Some of the more common types of advertising are reflected in ■ **FIGURE 14.2**.

Advertising Media

What are the different types of advertising media? Advertising media are the means of conveying a message about a product, and companies use a variety of media to implement their advertising strategies. Some of the more traditional media used include television, newspapers, the Internet, and outdoor media. Outdoor media include billboards, signs in sports arenas, ads painted on the sides of vehicles, and even skywriting. The Internet and social media have become popular means of advertising, as well.

ON TARGET

Blendtec: Will It Blend?*

How do you advertise a new blender and make it exciting? That was the problem George Wright, the marketing manager of Blendtec, faced. Wright needed to find a unique and creative venue to demonstrate the significant capabilities of the Blendtec Blender. He recognized that traditional television and print ads were becoming less effective, so he opted for online video and introduced a "fun" factor. The videos, posted to Blendtec's own channel on YouTube, feature Blendtec successfully grinding up rather untraditional items, such as marbles, cell phones, action figures, skis, an entire Thanksgiving dinner, and even the iPad. This series of videos has collected more than 117 million views on YouTube, and demand doesn't seem to be dying down. The company is still receiving requests for what items to blend next. More importantly, sales have grown an amazing 500 percent.[3]

Source: "Will It Blend? Home." Blendtec. www .willitblend.com

Product advertising promotes a specific product's uses, features, and benefits. This is the type of advertising we most often think of.

Advocacy advertising promotes an organization's position on a public issue, such as global warming or immigration. We are familiar with advocacy advertising undertaken during political campaigns by organizations that are independent of a political party or candidate.

Corporate (or institutional) advertising focuses on creating a positive image toward a government, an organization, or an entire industry as opposed to a specific product.

Interactive advertising uses interactive media, such as interactive video catalogs on the Internet or kiosks at shopping malls, to connect directly with consumers in a personal and engaging way.

Comparative advertising compares a brand's characteristics with those of other established brands. Examples include television commercials comparing toothpaste, pain relievers, and detergents.

Internet advertising displays messages on websites as banner ads, pop-ups, videos, and the like. The advantages of online advertising are that it is immediately delivered, can be interactive and customized, and is reasonably cost-effective.

Retail (or local) advertising focuses on attracting customers to a fixed location, such as a department store or a grocery store.

Mobile advertising is delivering advertising messages via mobile phones or other mobile devices. Since more people own mobile phones than any other device, this form of advertising will continue to increase in the near future.

B2B advertising is directed to other businesses rather than to consumers. For example, Caterpillar, the earth-moving equipment company, advertises to construction companies.

Non-profit and public service advertising focuses on promoting organizations such as the Red Cross or on behalf of a good cause such as the prevention of wildfires.

■ FIGURE 14.2
Common Types of Advertising
Image sources: left, top to bottom: Rog999/Fotolia; Michael Matthews/Alamy; Richard Levine/Alamy; Alex/Fotolia; viktor88/Fotolia; right, top to bottom: Barry Barnes/Fotolia; imagebroker/Alamy; Yanik Chauvin/Fotolia; Scanrail/Fotolia; © Franck Fotos/Alamy

Direct mail advertising still remains one of the largest forms of advertising. You're probably familiar with direct mail advertising; you just have a different name for it—junk mail. Direct mail advertising ranges from coupon offers to brochures and catalogs. Surprisingly, direct mail spending grew by almost 6 percent to $45.8 billion in 2011 and is expected to reach nearly $47 billion in 2012.[4] Direct mail advertising allows companies to target their advertising dollars to customers who are most likely to buy their products and offer customized product offerings to these customers.

What are the advantages and disadvantages of the different types of advertising media? The marketer's task is to find the most effective and efficient medium for transmitting his or her message to targeted customers—given marketing objectives and budget constraints. Every type of advertising media has certain advantages and disadvantages. For example, television advertising reaches a huge audience, but it's very expensive. Social media also reaches large numbers but can demand a great deal of manpower to follow and interpret the results. **■ TABLE 14.1** lists some of the advantages and disadvantages of each major medium.

■ TABLE 14.1

Advantages and Disadvantages of Advertising Media

Media	Advantages	Disadvantages
Direct Mail	High levels of segmentation; allows personalization; high flexibility; ad can be saved; measurable impact	High cost; can be rejected as junk mail and viewed as a nuisance
Television	Good mass-market coverage; low cost per contact; combines sight, sound, and motion; good attention span	High cost; low recall; channel surfing or digital video recorders (DVRs) skip over ads; short exposure
Newspaper	Timing and geographic flexibility; good local market coverage; high credibility and acceptability	Short life span; lots of competition for attention; poor-quality reproductions
Magazine	High market segmentation; high-quality color; long life; longer attention span; high credibility	Declining readership; lots of competition for attention; high cost; long ad-purchase lead time
Radio	High geographic and demographic selectivity; low cost; creative opportunities with sound	Low attention span; short exposure time; information overload; limited coverage
Internet	Global and interactive possibilities; ease of segmentation; high audience interest; easy to measure responses	Audience controls exposure; clutter on each site; skewed demographically to surfers
Social Media	Relatively inexpensive to set up; results in immediate consumer feedback; provides access to consumer feedback on competition; builds customer relationships	Can be difficult to monitor; not a passive strategy—must be actively maintained
Outdoor	Able to select key geographic areas; low cost per impression; high frequency on major commuter routes	Short exposure time; brief messages; creative limitations; little segmentation possible

(*Image sources,* top to bottom: raven/Fotolia; T/C; Patrikeevna/Fotolia; Studio 101/Alamy; Tengu/Fotolia; AMATHIEU/Fotolia; bloomua/Fotolia; magann/Fotolia)

Recent Advertising Developments

What are some important recent developments in advertising? One of the most important trends emerging from modern advertising has been the development of **Internet advertising**. In fact, it is one of the fastest-growing media because, in part, it allows firms to focus their advertising dollars on targeted customers. Other developments include product placement, infomercials, and global advertising.

How does advertising take place online? Companies use the Internet for basic advertising functions, including spam (junk e-mail), pop-ups, banner ads, and other links found at websites to attract potential customers to a company's web page. A banner ad is a graphic element that displays across the top or along the side of a Web page. Generally, when you click on a banner ad, you are hyperlinked to the sponsor's website. Banner ads are often more favorable to static print ads in that they can present multiple images as well as change appearances in a number of other ways in an effort to catch the viewer's attention. To get a banner ad on a website, the advertiser must either arrange to pay a website directly to post the ad on its site or pay a service like DoubleClick to post the banner on a variety of sites.

An alternative to banner ads is Google's advertising services: Google AdWords and Google AdSense. With Google AdWords, advertisers submit text-only ads to Google along with a list of relevant keywords. When a user types one of the keywords into the Google search engine, the text-only ad appears in a sidebar of the Google search results. The advertiser pays Google only when a user clicks on the ad. For example, if you are searching for a new couch and type *sofa* as a keyword, an advertisement from a local furniture store may appear in the sidebar. If you click on the advertisement, that furniture store will need to pay Google.

The benefits of using Google AdWords over traditional banner ads are that you pay only when someone clicks on the ad, and you receive the benefit of the millions of searches conducted on Google using the keywords that are relevant to your product rather than trying to target the specific websites your potential customers might visit. The potential downside to Google AdWords is that they are text-only, whereas banner ads are designed with more eye-catching graphics. Facebook has similar advertising capabilities to Google AdWords, and the pricing (at least for now) is more affordable.

Lastly, Google AdSense is a free program that enables website owners to earn money by displaying relevant ads on their websites. As an advertiser, you can pay Google to post your ad (similar to hosting a banner ad). Your ad will display only on those websites that are relevant to your product. For example, a blogger writing about landscaping ideas can choose to display an AdSense sidebar on his blog that might display ads from nurseries, garden supply shops, outdoor furniture retailers, and the like.

What is the benefit of online advertising? The tools of the Internet allow a company to work with customers and create a customized product offering that best meets the customers' unique tastes and preferences. Once customers visit a company's website, the company can learn a lot about their preferences and shopping habits based on where and how often they click within the website. Businesses can also interact with their customers by offering a chat service, providing helpful videos, or posting a blog. If a business is able to consistently deliver high-quality value using these modern techniques, then Internet advertising can help businesses maintain positive customer relations.

Google AdWords is one of several effective online marketing tools.

digitallife/Alamy

Social Media

How is social media being used in advertising? The emergence of Web 2.0 technologies—tools that allow users to connect, share information, communicate, and collaborate with each other online—has caused many companies to rethink how they can connect and communicate with their customers. Social media is a part of many IMC plans. Using social networks such as Facebook and Pinterest, companies are building customer support and gaining better insight into their customers and competitors. Companies create blogs and tweets to announce new products or corporate developments, post help tutorials and product demonstrations videos on YouTube, and create fan pages on Facebook that prompt interactions with their customers.

H&R Block posts tax tips via podcasts and Twitter, and has rather amusing YouTube videos. Starbucks and Dell each have sites (MyStarbucksIdea.com and IdeaStorm.com, respectively) that allow customers to post ideas and suggestions as well as vote on which ones should be implemented. All of these are an effort to keep the customer engaged with the product.

Mobile Marketing

How is mobile marketing being used? Mobile phones are the most pervasive technology ever invented. Surprisingly, it's been documented that more people own mobile phones than they do toothbrushes![5] Given that ubiquitous market penetration, mobile phones make the best platform for advertisers. Companies are embracing technologies such as QR codes, text messages, and mobile app platforms to connect with their customer base nearly 24/7. Universal Pictures uses mobile advertising to help promote its movies. The movie production company runs ads on certain apps that the user clicks on to watch a trailer of the movie as well as to purchase tickets.[6]

Product Placement

What is product placement? When a company pays for its product to be prominently displayed in television shows, movies, and video games where they will be seen by potential customers, it's known as **product placement**. This promotional technique has been around as long as the media itself. However, the advent of DVRs, which allow viewers to record shows and then fast-forward through ads, has driven companies to increase their product placement in television shows. Just turn to any reality show and you'll see some featured product or service.

Another variant of product placement is the banners of brand names, symbols, and slogans found on the walls of professional sports stadiums so that camera shots of the televised games will frequently display the banners' messages.

Infomercials

How are infomercials useful as an advertising technique? Infomercials (also known as **paid programming**) run longer than traditional commercials, and many run as long as regular television programs. Unlike normal commercials, infomercials are designed to elicit a specific, direct, and quantifiable response from viewers. Infomercials typically appear as actual television programs, often in the form of a talk show, with little direct reference to the fact that they are actually ads. They have the advantage of showing the features of the advertised products in great detail. Infomercials often use "experts" or celebrities as guests or hosts to endorse and push their products. Some successful infomercials include ads for the Bowflex Home Gym and Proactiv Solution Acne Treatment.[7]

Advertising in a professional sports stadium is a variant of product placement.

Robert Landau/Alamy

Global Advertisements

How has advertising gone global? The globalization of advertising is another important development in advertising. Most products have to be customized to satisfy foreign customers. This means that products are tailored to meet the unique local tastes, preferences, and cultural sensitivities of foreign customers or satisfy the regulatory standards of different governments around the globe. Likewise, some advertising campaigns can be exported intact, while others have to be modified. Advertisers prefer to use the same message because it is cheaper, allows for a more globally integrated message, and allows for the pooling of talent to design the most compelling advertising message. But transferring domestically created, successful advertising messages abroad can be tricky. As we discussed in Chapter 4, marketers have to carefully consider the interpretations of their messages in the underlying cultural context of the foreign market. Increasingly, marketers are realizing that customized advertising campaigns to globally segmented markets work much better, just as domestic market segmentation is more effective.

Public Relations

What is public relations? Another important part of the promotional mix is public relations. **Public relations** is the management function that establishes and maintains mutually beneficial relationships between an organization and its stakeholders, including consumers, stockholders, employees, suppliers, the government, and the public in general. In other words, public relations promotes the image of a company or an individual.[8] All organizations are interested in public relations.

> **3** What is public relations, and how is it used in the promotional mix?

Biz CHAT

Groupon: Is It a Good Promotional Tool?

On the surface, social coupons seem like a fantastic way to promote your business: a website offers heavily discounted goods and services to incentivize buyers to try your business' product. Once the buyer experiences your great offering, he or she will certainly return. You win by increased exposure with limited downside, since you control the price and the terms of the offering. In addition, the website takes a cut of the action, and the consumer saves a bundle. It's a win-win-win . . . or is it?

The rapid growth of daily deals websites such as Groupon and LivingSocial seem to indicate that this business model is a huge success. Certainly for the consumers, and most likely for the website, these daily deals are generally paying off. But what about the businesses offering the deals? Is this really a great promotional tactic?

The logic behind social coupons is that business owners are encouraged to use the deals to attract new customers. And, they do . . . once. Unfortunately, statistics are showing that most customers who take advantage of these deals rarely return with repeat business. In reality, for some businesses, these daily deal offerings may end up being a poor business choice. But not always.

So, when might using Groupon make sense for a business? Why in some instances don't these daily deals generate repeat business?

Net photos/Alamy

What steps are involved in developing public relations plans? There are three steps to a good public relations program:

1. **Assess the public opinion.** The idea behind public relations is to create and maintain a positive image of an organization in the minds of stakeholders. This begins with assessing public attitudes and perceptions of the organization. Sometimes, public opinion may be based on perceptions that have little to do with facts. Nevertheless, an honest audit of public opinion is necessary before specific public relations programs can be implemented to shape the image and reputation of an organization.

2. **Change the policies and procedures.** Sometimes, a corporation requires public relations to correct or build back a corporate reputation after a significant mishap. British Petroleum (BP), Toyota, and Netflix have all had to run public relations campaigns to build back the trust of their customers. Once an organization has listened carefully to public concerns and interests, it needs to respond by changing its behavior or correcting misperceptions.

3. **Inform public of actions planned or taken.** Finally, an organization needs to inform the public of any changes it has made or educate the public about the facts associated with it.

What are some common public relations tools? Several specific types of public relations tools exist to build a positive business image. They can be classified by whether the news transmitted is controlled, semi-controlled, or uncontrolled by the organization.[9] The degree of control hinges on how and when the message is delivered.

- *Controlled messages* include corporate (or institutional) advertising, advocacy advertising, and public service advertising. A company may also disseminate annual reports, brochures, flyers, and newsletters or provide films or speakers to send a controlled message to targeted audiences.

- *Semi-controlled messages* are placed on websites, in chat rooms, and on blogs. In these forums, what people say about a company is not strictly regulated. Other semi-controlled messages include sponsorships of sporting events and other special events because participation by the press and stakeholders is not under the control of the sponsoring company.

- *Uncontrolled messages* generally take the form of *publicity*.

How is publicity helpful? Information about an individual, an organization, or a product transmitted through mass media at no charge is called **publicity**. Publicity has two advantages over advertising. First, it is free. Second, it is more believable because it is often presented as a news story. Publicity, when it is positive, saves companies a great deal of money because they don't pay for it; it just happens. However, publicity is *not* controlled by the seller; it is controlled by the media, which can be its disadvantage, and often generates the need for good public relations. For example, in 2008 Chrysler and other American automobile manufacturers were in the news due to their failing financial situations. Moreover, after receiving bailouts from the U.S. government (which were controversial in themselves), the companies received further press regarding the top management receiving huge salaries and bonuses, which solicited further public outrage. America's disenchantment with Chrysler and the other manufacturers needed to be turned around. Chrysler implemented an advertising/public relations campaign, "Imported from Detroit." The campaign began with an Eminem spot in the Super Bowl that generated lots of positive press.

How does a company generate positive publicity? Naturally, keeping friendly relations with the press increases the probability that a "newsworthy" story will be covered and treated with a favorable spin. Nevertheless, public relations managers need to ensure that publicity releases are timely, interesting, accurate, and in the public interest. For example, when GE launched its "ecomagination" campaign to portray itself as an environmental leader, the company wanted to ensure the public that it was sincere about the environment, and not just jockeying for a favorable marketing impression. GE's publicity releases were timely, interesting, accurate, and in the public interest. This may explain why the campaign won the prestigious Silver Effie Award for effective marketing communications in the category of Corporate Reputation, Image, and Identity.[10]

BP's public relations used the company's website to provide up-to-date reports on the oil spill clean-up efforts.

Another example of positive publicity is the favorable press companies receive when they contribute to some humanitarian purpose. Corporate philanthropy is generally good publicity, especially if it results in getting a company's name on a building or is associated with an annual event that is visible to the public. Some large corporations renowned for their philanthropic and charitable efforts include Microsoft and Target. Many smaller companies give to local organizations.

Whether motivated by publicity needs or a sense of social responsibility, giving back to the community can be financially beneficial. Most of us like buying products from companies if we believe that some of our money will be used to give back to the community or reward companies for doing the right thing. Giant Foods, the grocery store chain, links a customer's loyalty card to a local school that participates in its A+ School Rewards Program. In the 2011/2012 program, Giant gave away $2 million to local schools, with the top winner receiving nearly $20,000.[11] Parents will be more likely to shop at Giant than at another store if they know it will have such a positive impact on their children.

How does a company respond to negative publicity? A final role of public relations personnel is managing a crisis. *Damage control* is a company's effort to minimize the harmful effects of a negative event. Negative publicity can, in a matter of days, tear down a firm's image that took decades to build up. For example, ExxonMobil still suffers from the *Exxon Valdez* oil spill accident that occurred over two decades ago. BP has tried to learn from ExxonMobil's mistakes, so soon after the oil-rig explosion that caused millions of barrels of oil to leak into the Gulf of Mexico, it began to run spots on television explaining all the things the company was doing to help the communities hurt by the disaster recover. BP continues to sponsor ads outlining BP's continued response years later. Sometimes, bad news doesn't come from the media but from word of mouth. In the event of bad news, a company must stand ready to react—and react quickly. No easy remedies exist for crises, but being honest, accepting responsibility, and making other ethical responses are the first steps toward regaining credibility and reestablishing a positive image.

Advertising, public relations, and publicity are important elements in the promotional mix. Monica and Steven consulted with a friend who is a public relations specialist and asked for advice on how best to get the word out about their new venture. For now, it seems they are generating just enough business with their current promotional efforts. They will continue to get the word out via their friends, relatives, and business contacts as well as work the social media sites. They can't afford to do too much more, but they also know they can't afford to do any less. ■

AISPIX by Image Source/Shutterstock

Personal Selling and Sales Promotion pp. 428–434

Keith Jefferson is nervous about giving his first big sales pitch alone. He's trying to convince an electronics wholesaler to switch from its current trucking company to his company. Despite his nerves, the presentation goes well, and the client seems receptive. After the presentation, the client asks him how fluctuating oil prices will affect shipping rates. Keith has no idea what to say, and the client defers closing the deal. This was much more difficult than he imagined. How could he have been more effective with his potential client? ■

Personal selling is more complicated than simply suggesting to a customer that he or she should buy your product. It's a complex process that involves several steps, each of which must be executed with great planning and care.

Personal Selling

What is personal selling? **Personal selling**, another component of the promotional mix, is direct communication between a firm's sales force and potential buyers to make a sale and build good customer relationships. For example, a laboratory supplies company may deploy a representative to a research facility to demonstrate new products. Good salespeople don't just want to sell their products; they want to serve customers. A salesperson should help customers with their buying decisions by understanding their needs and presenting the advantages and disadvantages of a product. Salespeople must effectively represent their companies by establishing good customer relationships that foster repeat business and long-term company success.

Why is personal selling important? The sales staff is often the first contact point for many customers. To build good customer relationships, a salesperson should be customer oriented, competent, dependable, honest, and likable. Good salespeople are also able to listen carefully to customer needs. They possess knowledge of a company's total product offerings and make the buying process as easy as possible for the customer. In many B2B or industrial sales, millions of dollars may be involved in a single purchase, such as buying an airplane or constructing an office building. You can see why businesses want nothing less than truly professional salespeople—people who can deliver carefully prepared presentations, establish rapport with customers, and negotiate details with skill. In fact, the demand for well-educated, well-trained professional salespeople today explains why some salespeople are top earners in their companies. The unflattering stereotype of the backslapping, fast-talking salesman of the past certainly doesn't depict the modern sales consultant.

What are the advantages and disadvantages of having a sales force? Obtaining and keeping good salespeople is expensive. In addition to direct compensation (salaries and commissions) and employment benefits, additional expense goes to training and the tools needed to keep track and maintain customers and territories. Personal selling is the most expensive part of the promotional mix for most companies. Generally, personal selling is preferred over advertising when selling a high-value, custom-made, or technically complex product. Advertising is more cost-effective when selling a low-value, standardized product that is easily understood.

What are the different roles of salespeople?

There are four general roles taken on by salespeople. Of course, some salespeople, especially in smaller businesses, may be required to fulfill some or all four roles.

Personal selling is preferred when selling a complex product such as life insurance or financial planning services.

1. **Order getters.** An **order getter** is a salesperson who increases a company's sales by selling to new customers and increasing sales to existing customers. Salespeople use current customers as sources for leads on new prospects. This task is sometimes called *creative selling*. It requires recognizing customer needs and providing information to potential buyers of a product's uses and features. Many businesses such as real estate, insurance, and automobile dealerships depend on their sales personnel to generate new sales. Telemarketers are also order getters. Although telemarketing has been restricted by U.S. laws, the practice is still widely used. The responsibility of order getters is not always restricted to getting orders. Once the initial sale is through, they then focus on building a customer relationship. To enhance repeat sales, salespeople stay in touch with current customers to ensure satisfaction. Some of the same people who are order getters are also order takers.

2. **Order takers.** An **order taker** is a salesperson who handles repeat sales and builds positive customer relationships. One of the major roles of an order taker is to ensure that buyers have sufficient quantities of products when and where they are needed. This is especially true in B2B sales, such as selling food and paper products to restaurants. Order takers, such as retail clerks, generally handle routine orders for standardized products that do not require a lot of technical sales expertise. The role of order takers also includes customer service representatives who identify and solve problems. The Internet and other technologies have enabled companies to replace some or all tasks associated with order takers with automated services. For example, it is becoming more common for orders to be placed electronically using the Internet, or to have issues/resolved by a controlled automated response system, though some companies offer live chat capabilities using a "real" person to assist with questions and then take your order online.

3. **Order influencers.** **Order influencers** are not engaged in direct selling, but rather they concentrate on selling activities that target those who influence purchases made by the final customer. There are two kinds of order influencers: missionaries and word-of-mouth promotions.

   • *Missionary salespeople* are in industries where customers require advice or requirements of others. For example, pharmaceuticals discuss products with doctors (the order influencers) who then write a prescription for the patient (the final customer). Similarly, your college professors act as the order influencers recommending specific textbooks for you to purchase.

   • *Word-of-mouth* also acts as an order influencer. Social networks have emphasized the influence and power of word-of-mouth promotion.

4. **Support personnel.** **Support personnel** are salespeople who obtain new customers but also focus on assisting current customers with technical matters.

Support personnel also include the office staff that assists the salespeople. They are most common in B2B sales, where manufacturers assist wholesalers and retailers with the best ways to sell and promote their products to ultimate consumers.

All salespeople, whatever their specific role at any given time, are ambassadors for a business. They need to listen carefully, act as sounding boards, and relay customer feedback to an organization. This allows firms to improve existing products or create new products to better meet customer needs and preferences. Serving customers better is a large part of what building good customer relationships and promotion are all about.

4 **What are the steps in the personal selling process?**

What are the steps in the selling process? The steps involved in the selling process are essentially the same for selling a consumer product and for selling a B2B product, though the sale of a B2B product is usually more complex. In all cases, a salesperson has to be knowledgeable about his or her product and competitors' products.

No two salespeople are alike, and no two selling situations are the same. However, six steps emerge from all personal selling: prospecting, approaching the prospect, presenting, overcoming objections, closing the sale, and following up. This six-step personal selling procedure is outlined in ■ **FIGURE 14.3**.

How are customers identified? The first step in the personal selling process is to identify qualified potential customers. This is known as **prospecting**. Notice that businesses need to not only find potential customers but also identify those who are *qualified* to buy. To be qualified to buy means that a potential customer has the ability and the authority to purchase. Prospecting can be a daunting task; it often involves cold calling. Cold calling is approaching a prospect over the phone unexpectedly. Some salespeople find leads at trade shows, from those who have scouted a company's website, or, better yet, from currently satisfied customers who are willing to recommend them to others because of their superior product and service.

What is the best way to approach a prospect? The second step of the personal selling process involves two parts: the *pre-approach* and the *actual approach.* The pre-approach involves salespeople doing their homework. This is especially critical if they are trying to sell a B2B product, such as an inventory

■ **FIGURE 14.3**
The Personal Selling Process

Prospecting	Approaching the Prospect	Presenting	Overcoming Objections	Closing the Sale	Following Up
• Identify qualified potential customers	• Preapproach: gathering information • Approach: Initial contact	• Tell the product's "story" • Conduct demonstrations	• Provide additional information to answer questions or resolve doubts	• Conduct physical purchase	• Answer questions • Provide training or solutions

software system. Salespeople must learn as much as possible about their potential customers to determine their likely needs and think about how they might be able to satisfy those needs. The timing decision of the actual approach should also be carefully planned not to catch the prospect at a busy time or at an off time in the budget cycle.

In the actual approach, the idea is to meet, greet, and put the prospect at ease. First impressions are lasting impressions! This is the salesperson's first chance at building a long-lasting relationship. Good salespeople present themselves as knowledgeable and friendly professionals who are genuinely interested in serving customers. The first impression is followed by asking some questions to learn about a potential customer's needs. Then the salesperson must listen carefully to those responses.

How are the details of the product explained? The next step in the personal selling process is the actual presentation of the product to the prospective customer. Often salespeople demonstrate the product and let the prospect use it as well. The presentation should be carefully planned using the most advanced presentation technologies that allow for the full use of multimedia effects. It is important that probing questions are asked during the presentation and that the prospect's responses are listened to carefully. Listening is more important than talking to fully understand the customer's needs.

What happens if the prospect has an objection? Objections to buying are common. Good salespeople anticipate concerns and are prepared to counter them. Once objections surface, a salesperson will provide more information about the product and turn these objections into reasons to buy. Often bringing in other experts from the company to address any objections is helpful to address areas outside of a salesperson's expertise. This provides an opportunity to establish a rapport based on trust between the salesperson, the company, and the prospect. Overcoming objections can be the beginning of a mutually beneficial and lasting relationship.

How is the sale finalized? After overcoming objections, the next step is to close the sale and ask for a purchase. Great salespeople know the physical cues, comments, or questions that signal the time to ask the buyer for an order. This is also the time to review points of agreement, ask the buyer which model he or she prefers, ask how many units are needed, or sweeten the deal by offering more favorable credit terms or throwing in an extra quantity free of charge. Closing the sale is an art that is learned with practice.

What happens after the sale is made? To ensure a long-term relationship and repeat business, the salesperson must follow up with the customer to ensure that he or she is happy with his or her new product. Any feedback from the new customer is relayed back to the company as input for improving existing products or designing new ones. Good follow-up service and rapport can give rise to referrals or testimonials that can be used to enhance future sales. Following up is all about building and nurturing relationships.

Sales Promotion

What is sales promotion? The final element of the promotional mix is sales promotion. A **sales promotion** is a short-term activity that targets consumers and other businesses for the purpose of generating interest in a product. Sales promotions encompass activities designed to inform, persuade, and remind targeted customers about a product, which have not already been undertaken by advertising, public relations, or personal selling. As consumers, we see sales promotions almost everywhere: from coupons in newspapers to rebate offers on a new car purchase,

■ FIGURE 14.4
Common Sales Promotion Techniques

Coupons	Rebates	Frequent-user incentives
Point-of-Purchase displays	Free samples	Contests and sweepstakes
Give aways	Bonuses	Cents-off deals

from e-mail announcements offering discounted prices on airline tickets to end-of-aisle displays of potato chips at a local grocery store tempting impulse purchases.

What are the two general types of sales promotions? Most companies' products go through a distribution system before they reach the final consumer. These companies encourage **wholesalers** (e.g., middlemen) to push their products through to end users. Any incentives to push a product through the distribution system to final consumers are called **trade** (or **B2B**) **sales promotions**. In addition, **consumer sales promotions** are incentives designed to increase final consumer demand for a product. The whole idea behind all sales promotions is to generate interest and excitement around a product. Businesses need to create a reason why stores should not only carry their products but also encourage their purchase by consumers. Companies want consumers to be so excited about their products that they seek the products out and ask for them by name. In short, companies want all involved to opt for their products instead of competitors' alternatives.

⑤ What are the two types of sales promotions, and what types of tools are commonly used as incentives?

What are some consumer sales promotional tools? Some of the most common consumer promotional tools are listed in **■ FIGURE 14.4**. Consumer sales promotions are aimed at the end users, or final consumers. Consumer promotions are intended to increase demand for a good or a service by providing that extra incentive to tip consumers in favor of a specific brand. They are also aimed at providing customers with another reason to feel good about their purchases. The timing of consumer sales promotions is important to get maximum impact. They need to be strategically coordinated with other elements in the promotional mix. This kind of promotional tool is becoming more common because it helps segment markets and is cost-effective.

What are some trade sales promotional tools? Some of the specific tools used to promote a product to other businesses are listed in **■ FIGURE 14.5**. However, if you want other businesses to become interested and excited about carrying your product, it is important to generate in-house enthusiasm. Fully educate the sales staff about the product and its many uses, features, and benefits. This also may require some formal training on how to best present the product. To generate leads, it is often beneficial to participate in trade shows equipped with sophisticated multimedia presentations, full-color brochures, and giveaways embossed with your product logo. Creating some internal buzz and excitement for your product is necessary to get other businesses interested in carrying and promoting your product. Finally, the same level of energy and excitement should be created with distributors. When it comes to trade sales promotional techniques, firms have many options from which to choose. If one doesn't work, they can easily adopt new strategies until they find the best combination.

IKEA offered "free samples" of its products by leaving displays of their furniture in several busy Paris subway stops.

LAURENT GARRIC/WOSTOK PRESS/MAXPPP/Newscom

Social Media Promotions

What is social media? **Social media** uses technologies that are designed to interactively share information. This type of media includes a wide range of technologies, including blogs and microblogs

(Twitter), podcasts, and wikis. In addition, social media technologies create communities in which users can exchange personal information such as social networks (Facebook, Pinterest), and exchange opinions and recommendations (Yelp, Urban Spoon).

How is social media used to promote products? In essence, social media is today's form of word-of-mouth communication. If you had a wonderful meal at a restaurant, you can Tweet about it, post a picture of the dessert on Pinterest, or check in on Facebook to let all your friends immediately know of your great experience. Similarly, news of a bad experience can travel just as fast.

Companies are well aware of this, and are using social media not only to hear from their customers but also to communicate with them. The term **viral marketing** (viral advertising, marketing buzz) refers to using social media tools and techniques to spread a marketing message quickly. As important as it was two decades ago for a company to have a website, it's equally important now for a company to have a presence on at least one, but generally several social media sites. Accordingly, companies have begun to shift their marketing and promotion budgets from traditional print and broadcast advertising to social media and website initiatives.

What are the advantages and disadvantages of the promotional mix? As you've learned, when developing the best promotional mix for a product, companies must weigh the advantages and disadvantages of each of the four main options—advertising, public relations, personal selling, and sales promotions. ■ **TABLE 14.2** summarizes some of these key advantages and disadvantages.

■ **FIGURE 14.5**
Common Business-to-Business Sales Promotion Techniques

KFC Marketing Campaign Gone Wrong

OFF
THE MARK

Not to be outdone by a free Grand Slam Breakfast promotion by Denny's, KFC offered a free grilled chicken meal on the Oprah show. The coupon was available on both Oprah's and KFC's websites for the following 24 hours. Simple enough; but the company underestimated the power of the Internet (and Oprah) to make the KFC meal coupon one of the top trends on Twitter. Four million people printed the coupon!

KFC had not expected this amount of interest and so their stores were not prepared. In some areas, customers wanting to redeem their coupons were lined up out the door and around the block. Stores ran out of chicken and staff refused to honor the coupons. Pandemonium followed. Police had to break up riots of unhappy customers.

KFC had a huge problem on their hands. The entire situation reflected terribly on KFC. In response, the president of KFC announced on Oprah two days later that the company would offer rain checks, and add a free drink, too! In the end, this episode cost KFC nearly $42 million in free food.

Amazingly, however, the story does not end there. Nearly a year later, KFC offers a similar deal in China. This time, the offer was for half price, but still available for only 24 hours. When coupons were brought in, some were rejected, with the KFC staff offering varying excuses. Once again, KFC posted a compromised response, but the majority of customers left feeling cheated and mishandled.

You would think KFC would have learned the first time around!

Chinese customers mob a KFC restaurant in Beijing, angry that a coupon deal had gone awry.

TABLE 14.2

The Advantages and Disadvantages of Promotional Tools

Promotional Tool	Advantages	Disadvantages
Advertising	• Builds brand awareness and brand loyalty • Reaches a mass audience	• Expensive • Impersonal • Not good at closing a sale
Public Relations	• Often seen as more credible than advertising • Inexpensive way of reaching many customers	• Risk of losing control • Cannot always control what other people write or say about your product
Personal Selling	• Highly interactive communication between the buyer and the seller • Excellent for communicating a complex product, information, and features • Good for building customer relationships and closing a sale	• Expensive • Not suitable if there are thousands of buyers
Sales Promotions	• Can stimulate quick increases in sales by targeting promotional incentives on particular products • Good short-term tactical tool	• If used over the long term, customers may get used to the effect • Too much promotion may damage the brand image

Recall Keith Jefferson? He wasn't prepared to answer questions about the service he was offering when giving his sales pitch to a potential client. As a result of his lack of preparedness, he wasn't able to land the account. In retrospect, he should have done more homework and researched potential concerns his prospect might have. Or, he could have offered to get back to the client with the answer. Next time, he will be more prepared. As Keith's story shows, determining which promotional tool to use is merely half the battle. Effective execution—whether it is an ad campaign, a public relations event, a sales pitch, or a sales promotion—is equally important. ■

Distribution: Marketing Intermediaries pp. 434–444

Liv Karlsen listened as the professor of her modern U.S. Literature class rattled off the book requirements for the new semester. Most were from the *New York Times* best sellers list, and Liv was required to

shotsstudio/Fotolia

have the first book read by the end of the week. After class, she ran over to the campus bookstore, only to find that the bookstore had run out. What other sources does Liv have to find her book? Are all distribution processes the same? ■

Distribution is the process that makes products available to consumers when and where the consumers want them. Distribution is a very complicated but essential process in the world of business today. Most of us don't think about the transfer and storage of the products we buy—unless something goes wrong and we are unable to get the products we want, when and where we want them, like Liv Karlsen. You can imagine the challenges companies face trying to guarantee that customers have access to their products at the right time and in the right quantity and place and are handled correctly if they are returned unused or due to a defect or expiration. The distribution (or place) function of the 4 Ps of marketing is often overshadowed by the more visible product, pricing, and sales promotional strategies.

Distribution Channels and Marketing Intermediaries

What is a channel of distribution? A channel of distribution is the part of the supply chain that focuses on getting the product to the ultimate consumers. More specifically, a **distribution channel** is a set of marketing intermediaries who buy, sell, or transfer title (or ownership) of products as they are passed from producer to consumer or business user. Some distribution channels involve several intermediaries, while others are shorter with fewer intermediaries.

What are marketing intermediaries? A **marketing intermediary**, formerly known as a *middleman* or *wholesaler*, is a business or person that moves goods and services between producers and consumers (in a B2C environment) or between business users (in a B2B environment). Marketing intermediaries, therefore, pass along products from manufacturers to end users. Sometimes no intermediaries are needed, such as when you buy a dozen ears of corn from the farmer down the road. But usually many intermediaries of different types work to ensure that a product reaches consumers.

What are the different types of marketing intermediaries? The main types of marketing intermediaries, as outlined in ■ **FIGURE 14.6** include:

- **Merchant wholesalers** buy and resell products to other wholesalers, retailers, and industrial users. For example, your local grocery store probably purchased Tide laundry detergent from a wholesaler who bought it from P&G, the manufacturer.
- **Agents/brokers** facilitate negotiations between buyers and sellers of goods and services but never take title (ownership) of the products traded. Examples include real estate agents and brokers, stockbrokers, and agricultural brokers. eBay also can be considered an agent/broker because the company facilitates the transfer of ownership from sellers to buyers.

We will look at each type of intermediaries in greater detail later in this section.

Why are marketing intermediaries necessary? You might wonder why we need all of these intermediaries and whether they serve to only drive up prices. It's certainly true

> **6** Why are marketing intermediaries and distribution channels important elements in marketing?

■ **FIGURE 14.6**
Types of Wholesale Intermediaries

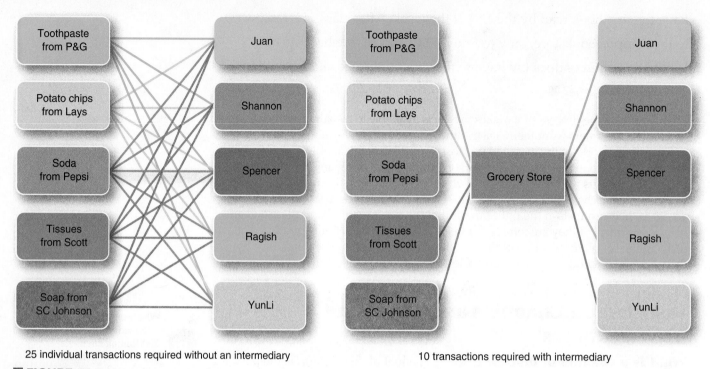

25 individual transactions required without an intermediary   10 transactions required with intermediary

■ FIGURE 14.7
The Efficiencies of Intermediaries
The introduction of an intermediary reduces the number of exchange relationships between manufacturers and retailers.

that each link in the distribution channel incurs costs, and intermediaries must cover these costs and earn a profit to remain in business. Intermediaries' added value is efficiency.

To examine the efficiencies provided by intermediaries, review **■ FIGURE 14.7**, which shows five consumers and five producers. Without an intermediary, each consumer would have to contact each producer to order the desired goods. Without intermediaries, if Juan, Shannon, Spencer, Ragish, and YunLi each wanted toothpaste, potato chips, soda, tissues, and soap, they would each have to go to the individual companies to get the items. That would involve 25 transactions (five transactions for each person). Now suppose a grocery store stocks and resells each of the five manufacturers' products. Now the five manufacturers and five customers have only one intermediary (the grocery store) to deal with. Each of the manufacturers makes one trip to the grocery store to deliver the items, and Juan, Shannon, Spencer, Ragish, and YunLi each make only one trip to the grocery store to get those products. This reduces the number of exchange relationships from 25 to 10. Intermediaries therefore reduce the time and costs of providing products to customers.

In short, intermediaries are a necessary part of the distribution process. If they are not available to do the job, someone else (ultimately the consumer) would need to perform the task of retrieving a product directly from a manufacturer. Intermediaries also help to transport and store goods and are often involved in other parts of marketing, such as advertising and relationship building. Some intermediaries even serve as interim bankers, financing inventories or giving credit. Historically, intermediaries have proven that they can add value, despite some additional costs.

What are the different types of distribution channels? Not all channels of distribution are the same. As illustrated in **■ FIGURE 14.8**, the type of distribution channel needed depends on the type of product being brought to the consumer. The number of intermediaries within a distribution channel

■ **FIGURE 14.8**
Distribution Channels for Consumer Products

depends on whether greater efficiency or additional value is provided by adding another link to the distribution system. For example, in Figure 14.8, Jeanne buys cosmetics directly from Avon without the need for any intermediary, but when Kevin buys a Goodyear tire, the tire is manufactured at a Goodyear plant and then delivered to TiresPlus, a Goodyear dealer that sells it to Kevin. Adding the extra component to this channel of distribution adds value to the product because the retail shop can provide information and service more easily than can the manufacturing plant and also provide convenience because Kevin lives closer to the store than to the plant.

Other products such as food and clothing have more complicated distribution systems, requiring the use of brokers, wholesalers, and finally retail stores to get the products to the consumer, but all are necessary to achieve efficiency. Similar channels of distribution also exist in B2B markets. Competitive markets determine what number of intermediaries will be required to achieve the greatest level of efficiency.

Merchant Wholesalers

What services do merchant wholesalers provide? Merchant wholesalers are intermediaries that buy and resell products to retailers, other wholesalers, and industrial users. They are different from retailers in that retailers sell products only to final consumers. One of the most effective ways to distinguish wholesalers from retailers is to remember that wholesalers *primarily* sell B2B products, while retailers sell *only* consumer products. Nevertheless, merchant wholesalers provide a host of services to their customers, some of which are listed in ■ **TABLE 14.3**.[12]

What are the different types of merchant wholesalers? Merchant wholesalers are independently owned businesses that take ownership (title) of the products they handle. There are several types of merchant wholesalers as illustrated in ■ **FIGURE 14.9**.

Merchant wholesalers include *full-service wholesalers* and *limited-service wholesalers*.

Full-service wholesalers provide a full line of services: carrying stock, maintaining a sales force, offering credit, making deliveries, and providing management assistance. There are two types of full-service wholesalers: *wholesale merchants* sell primarily to retailers, and *specialty distributors* sell to manufacturers and institutions, such as hospitals and the government.

> **7** What types of services do wholesalers and agents/brokers provide?

■ TABLE 14.3

Services Provided by Merchant Wholesalers

Service	Description
Bulk breaking	Wholesalers save retailers money by buying in bulk and breaking bulk packages down into smaller quantities.
Financing	Wholesalers finance retailers by giving credit, and they finance manufacturers by ordering early and paying bills on time.
Management service and advice	Wholesalers often help retailers train their sales clerks, improve store layouts and displays, and set up accounting and inventory control systems.
Market information	Wholesalers give information to manufacturers and retailers about competitors, new products, and price developments.
Risk bearing	Wholesalers absorb risk by taking title to merchandise and bearing the costs of theft, damage, spoilage, and obsolescence.
Selling and promoting	Wholesalers' sales forces help manufacturers reach many smaller retailers at a low cost. The wholesaler has more contacts and is often more trusted by the retailer than the distant manufacturer.
Transportation	Wholesalers can provide quicker delivery to buyers because they are closer than the producers.
Warehousing	Wholesalers hold inventories, thereby reducing the inventory costs and risks of suppliers and retailers.

As intermediaries, limited-service wholesalers offer fewer services than full-service wholesalers. The major types of limited-service wholesalers include:

- **Cash-and-carry wholesalers** carry a limited line of fast-moving goods and sell to small retailers for cash. They normally do not deliver. For example, a small fish store may drive to a cash-and-carry fish wholesaler, buy fish for cash, and bring the merchandise back to the store.

- **Truck wholesalers** (or truck jobbers) sell and deliver directly from their trucks. They generally carry semi-perishable items that regular wholesalers prefer not to carry. For example, trucks that deliver bread or snack food to convenience stores and restaurants are truck wholesalers.

- **Drop shippers** don't carry inventory or handle products. On receiving an order, they select a manufacturer, who ships the merchandise directly to the customer. Drop shippers assume title and risk from the time of the order to delivery. They operate in bulk industries, such as lumber, coal, and heavy equipment.

- **Rack jobbers** serve grocery stores and drug retailers, mostly in nonfood items. They send delivery trucks to stores, where the delivery people set up racks or displays within the stores. Rack

■ **FIGURE 14.9**
Major Types of Merchant Wholesalers

Merchant Wholesalers
Take title, assume risk, buy & resell to others

Full-Service   **Limited-Service**

| Wholesale merchants | Specialty distributors | Cash & carry | Truck wholesalers | Drop shippers | Rack jobbers |

jobbers retain title to the goods and bill the retailer only for the goods sold to consumers.

Because of their limited functions, these limited-service wholesalers usually operate at a lower cost than full-service wholesalers.

■ **FIGURE 14.10**
Types of Agents and Brokers

Agents and Brokers

What distinguishes agents and brokers? Agents and brokers are unique among intermediaries because they do not take title to the products traded. They merely facilitate the buying and selling of products and earn a commission on the selling price. What distinguishes agents from brokers is that agents represent the buyers or the sellers who hired them on a more permanent basis, while brokers are hired on a temporary basis.

What are some common types of agents? The common types of agents are manufacturers' agents, selling agents, and purchasing agents, as shown in ■ **FIGURE 14.10**.

- *Manufacturers' agents* can represent two or more manufacturers of complementary lines. A formal written agreement with each manufacturer covers pricing, territories, order handling, delivery service and warranties, and commission rates. Manufacturers' agents are often used in such lines as apparel, furniture, and electrical goods. Most manufacturers' agents are small businesses with only a few skilled salespeople. Small manufacturers may hire an agent if they cannot afford their own field sales forces, while larger manufacturers rely on agents to open new territories or cover territories that cannot support full-time salespeople. Some manufacturers' agents work directly for the manufacturer and directly distribute the company's products to retailers. In some instances, these agents deal directly with the consumer, skipping the retail middleman altogether.

- *Selling agents* have contractual authority to sell a manufacturer's entire product line. The manufacturer is either not interested in the selling function or feels unqualified. The selling agent serves as the sales department for the manufacturer. Selling agents are common in the industrial machinery and equipment businesses; coal, chemicals, and metals industries; and real estate and stock brokerage industries.

- *Purchasing agents* generally have long-term relationships with buyers and make purchases for them, often receiving, inspecting, warehousing, and shipping the merchandise to buyers. They provide helpful market information to clients and help them obtain the best goods and prices available.

Retailers

What are the different types of retailers? A retailer sells products directly to the consumer. Many retailers sell products they manufacture themselves. In some instances, retailers purchase products from a manufacturer or directly from a wholesaler and then sell them to the consumer.

Retailing constitutes a major sector of our economy. Although approximately a half million wholesalers exist in the United States, there are well over a million retail stores that employ approximately 15 million people.[13] You're likely familiar with retail distributors because most of your personal shopping experiences have occurred at retail stores. There are two main types of retailers: *in-store retailers* and *nonstore retailers*. ■ **TABLE 14.4** describes the major types of retail stores and lists some examples of each.

■ TABLE 14.4

Types of Retail Stores

Type of Store	Description	Examples
Specialty store	A retail store that carries a wide selection of products in one category	Gamestop, Foot Locker
Department store	A retail store that carries a wide variety of products organized by departments	Nordstrom, Saks, Neiman Marcus, JCPenney
Supermarket	Large, low-cost, high-volume grocery stores that also sell household products	Safeway, Albertson's, Kroger
Convenience store	Small stores located near residential homes that are usually open long hours seven days a week and carry the most frequently purchased convenience goods	QuikTrip, 7-Eleven
Discount store	Stores that offer lower prices by accepting lower profit margins and sell at a higher volume than department stores	Target, Walmart
Factory outlet	Stores owned and operated by a manufacturer that normally carries surplus, discontinued, or irregular goods	Nordstrom Rack, Banana Republic Factory Outlet Stores
Warehouse club	Stores that sell a limited selection of brand-name food and nonfood items at deep discounts that usually require an annual membership fee	Sam's Club, Costco, BJs

What kinds of in-store retail organizations are there? In-store retail organizations consist of **corporate chain stores**, individually-owned retail stores, cooperatives, and franchises.

- *Corporate chain stores* are two or more retail outlets owned by a single corporation. They attempt to realize economies of scale by buying large volumes at reduced prices. Corporate chains appear in all types of retailing. But not all retail stores are corporate chains. Individually owned retail stores, sometimes referred to as "mom and pop" stores are also prevalent.

- *Cooperatives* are formed when independent companies voluntarily band together and buy in bulk to experience economies of scale that reduce costs. Examples of wholesalers that have banded together to buy in bulk and have agreed to common merchandising include the Independent Grocers Alliance (IGA) and True Value (hardware stores). Examples of independent retailers that have banded together and have created jointly owned, central wholesale operations include Associated Grocers (groceries) and Ace (hardware stores).

- *Franchises* are a distribution system where a *franchiser* sells a proven method of doing business to a *franchisee* for a fee and a percentage of sales or profits. Subway, Jiffy Lube, and Holiday Inn are familiar franchises. Franchisees are typically required to purchase necessary items from the franchiser and must meet strict rules and regulations to ensure consistency and quality.

What is nonstore retailing? Little has drawn as much attention in modern retailing as the growth of nonstore retailing. **Nonstore retailing** is a form of retailing in which consumer contact occurs outside the confines of a traditional brick-and-mortar retail store. Of course, the Internet is a big component of nonstore retailing, but there are other forms of nonstore retailing that you commonly interact with. For example, vending machines, kiosks, and carts are convenient and inexpensive ways of providing products and services. Some other important nonstore retailers include:

- **Telemarketers** sell products over the phone. Sometimes the sales pitches are recorded messages. To avoid such sales pitches, many have signed up for the National Do Not Call Registry.

- **Direct sellers** sell goods and services door-to-door at people's homes and offices or at temporary or mobile locations. Direct selling is also known as *multilevel marketing* (*MLM*) because of the marketing structure that defines the corporate strategy of many of these organizations. Often MLM companies are referred to as pyramid structures because of the resulting hierarchy of compensation levels. The sales force is compensated not only by the products sold but also they are incentivized to bring other sales members to an organization. When they bring in other sales members, they receive a percentage of the sales generated by the new associates, creating multiple levels of compensation. Avon cosmetics, Pampered Chef kitchen products, and Herbalife health products are sold through MLM.

- **Direct marketers** are those retailing a good or a service and bypassing intermediaries. Such retailers include catalog sales and direct mail, and infomercials.

How has the Internet impacted retailing? Electronic retailing, or the selling of consumer goods and services over the Internet, is a subset of e-commerce. It is now almost mandatory that any business, especially a retail store, have an online as well as a social network presence.

In addition, the Internet has enabled consumers to access data and information about products and competitors quickly. The ability to purchase products online has changed a consumers' expectation of an in-store experience. Often, consumers come into a store to touch and interact with a product before purchasing or to seek more information. If a sales associate is not familiar with a product, or cannot access information more quickly than can the customer with his or her smartphone, the store risks losing a sale.

Stores are also keenly aware of other factors that can potentially turn customers away, such as long lines or insufficient store inventory. If customers have to wait too long or if the product is not on the shelf, they may decide to leave and order the product online when they get home—or they may ultimately not purchase the product or purchase it from somewhere else. Either way, the sale is lost.

Retail Strategies

What are the important retail strategies? All companies that sell products need to decide how intensively they wish to cover any geographic market. Companies can choose to sell either through all available retail outlets or only through a more selective distribution (see ■ **FIGURE 14.11**).

- An **intensive distribution** is most appropriate for companies selling convenience goods, such as newspapers, chewing gum, and milk. Companies want these products to obtain the widest possible exposure in the market, and so strive to make these products convenient for purchase at as many convenience stores and supermarkets as possible.

Christina Kennedy/Alamy

Vending machines are not just for food. Best Buy has placed in airports vending machines that are stocked with frequently forgotten electronics.

■ **FIGURE 14.11**
Distribution Strategies
Image sources: TheStoreGuy/Alamy; Helen Sessions/Alamy; Kristoffer Tripplaar/Alamy

Intensive Distribution
Selling convenience products

Selective Distribution
Selling shopping products

Exclusive Distribution
Selling specialty products

Why are retailing and physical distribution key aspects of distribution?

- A **selective distribution** strategy uses only a portion of the many possible retail outlets for selling products. This approach is appropriate for the sale of shopping products and durable goods, such as stereos, televisions, and furniture. Buyers spend more time comparing competitors' prices and features when buying shopping products. A sale often depends on providing buyers with information on these features to successfully differentiate one brand's product from another. Naturally, producers want to selectively determine where their products will be sold to ensure successful differentiation. Moreover, customers often want other services, such as installation, to be properly distributed. Again, producers are selective in determining outlets and may provide training to outlets to ensure the best service.

- An **exclusive distribution** strategy uses only one outlet in a geographic area. This is most appropriate when selling specialty products, such as high-quality cars or high-end jewelry and clothing. Because these products carry a certain degree of prestige, sellers often require distributors to carry a full line of inventory, offer distinguished high-quality service, and meet other exclusive requirements. Another common form of exclusive distribution exists with franchises. Often, to avoid competition between franchises within the same company, only one outlet is allowed in a given geographic area, and the retail distributors are required to meet strict quality and service standards to protect brand-name integrity.

Distribution Logistics

What do we mean by distribution logistics? Logistics refers to managing the flow of materials, information, and processes that are involved in getting a product from its initial raw stages to the point of consumption. Different kinds of logistics are involved at various stages of the production and distribution processes, as shown in ■ **FIGURE 14.12**. Bringing raw materials, supplies, information, and any other goods and services from suppliers to the producer is *inbound logistics*. Managing the movement of resources throughout the production process is *materials handling* and *operations control*. Lastly, managing the **physical distribution** of produced products to customers in the quantities needed, when and where they want them, is *outbound logistics*. It is also important to properly manage *reverse logistics*, bringing products back to the producer when they are defective, overstocked, outdated, or returned for recycling. If part of the process is outsourced, then managing that process is *third-party logistics*.

The Benefits and Costs of Transportation Modes

What are the benefits and costs of various transportation modes? Transportation is often the most expensive distribution cost. To keep costs as low as possible, a company looks for the most economical mode of transportation. However, companies also have to consider other factors beyond cost—such as speed, dependability, flexibility in product handling, frequency of shipments, and accessibility to markets. ■ **TABLE 14.5** outlines the benefits and costs of the five major modes of transportation according to these criteria. Businesses have to carefully weigh these benefits and costs in making a mode-of-transportation decision. They look at different transportation methods when receiving materials from suppliers as well as when delivering orders to customers.

■ **FIGURE 14.12**
Distribution Logistics Process

■ TABLE 14.5

Benefits and Costs of Various Transportation Modes

Mode	Percentage of Freight (Tons)[14]	Cost	Speed	Dependability	Flexibility in Handling Products	Frequency of Shipments	Accessibility to Markets
Railroads	12.0%	Moderate	Average	Average	High	Low	High
Trucks	58.2%	High	Fast	High	Average	High	Very High
Waterways	14.8%	Very Low	Very Slow	Average	Very High	Very Low	Limited
Airways	0.1%	Very High	Very Fast	High	Low	Average	Average
Pipelines	10.5%	Low	Slow	High	Very Low	Very High	Very Limited

Source: http://www.bts.gov/publications/freight_shipments_in_america/html/table_04.html

A firm might rely on one method of transportation or a combination of methods for each component.

How does a company determine the transportation method? Routing is simply the way in which goods are transported to a client, from suppliers, or anything in between. Proper routing ensures that any transportation of goods, be it with a company's own equipment or through a courier, is done at a minimum of cost, time, and distance without sacrificing quality. The best way to understand all the variables of each transportation option pertinent to a specific company is to develop a comprehensive *routing guide* that provides detailed routing solutions for a company's every possible shipping situation.

Warehousing and Inventory Control

How important is warehousing? Warehousing, or storing products at convenient locations so they are ready for customers when they are needed, is critical for customer service. There are two types of warehouses:

- *Storage warehouses* store goods from moderate-to-long periods of time.
- *Distribution warehouses* (or distribution centers) are designed to gather and move goods quickly to consumers. Walmart operates approximately 100 distribution centers in the United States. Each center is over one million square feet of space (about 29 football fields) under one roof.

Warehousing today uses sophisticated technologies to effectively store and distribute products.

How is inventory tracked? One of the challenges in managing a supply chain is managing inventory levels to ensure that there is neither too much nor too little inventory on hand. Encountering either situation can be costly, as having too much inventory involves extra warehousing fees, and too little inventory means lost sales. As we mentioned in an earlier chapter, companies use bar codes, or Universal Product Codes, on almost all products to help identify and track products.

RFID tags are intelligent bar codes. RFID technology, although more costly than bar codes, is more versatile and provides a richer amount of information about the movement and details of a product. Companies use bar codes and RFID tags to help reduce inventory costs by generating information on a real-time basis, thus providing accurate stocking information and reordering information.

Recall the dilemma faced by Liv Karlsen? She couldn't find the book she needed for class in her college's bookstore. Liv immediately used her smartphone to check for the book online. Fortunately, she was able to find several copies of the book, both used and new, from a variety of retailers—the large chain stores, online distributors, and a local independently owned bookstore. She also had her choice of paying to have the book delivered to her home, or having the book shipped to the local store free of charge. The bookstore is only one part of the channel of distribution for Liv's book. The channel of distribution for the book involves different marketing intermediaries, including a wholesaler and a retailer. Her online search revealed other channels through which she could obtain her book, one of which was a website with no retail stores. The distribution process is not the same for all products—some are longer and some are shorter, but the process is carefully determined to be as efficient and cost-effective as possible. Although it might not always work to ensure that all products are always available when needed, the distribution process ultimately adds value to the consumer. ■

MyBizLab

Go to **mybizlab.com** to complete the problems marked with this icon ⭐.

1 **What is a promotional mix, and what is its function in a promotional campaign?** (pp. 418–419)

- A **promotional mix** (p. 418) is the strategic combination of promotional tools used to reach customers to achieve marketing objectives. It includes advertising, public relations, personal selling, and sales promotions.

- Implementing the promotional mix is part of an effective promotional campaign. Promotional campaigns involve six steps:
  - Identify the target market.
  - Determine marketing objectives.
  - Design the message.
  - Determine the budget.
  - Implement the promotional mix.
  - Evaluate and adjust as needed.

2 **What are the different categories of advertising, and what role do these categories play in business and society?** (pp. 419–421)

- **Advertising** (p. 419) is paid, impersonal mass communication from an identified sponsor to persuade or influence a targeted audience.

- Advertising plays several important roles in business:
  - It helps businesses build brand awareness and product differentiation.
  - It also has economic benefits, by lowering the costs and prices of products providing many jobs.

- Advertising also plays a societal role:
  - Society benefits from advertising because it informs and educates us about new and different products.
  - Advertising can also persuade us in ways that can have positive or negative social ramifications.

- Many categories of advertising emerge from marketing: **product corporate comparative retail B2B nonprofit public service advocacy interactive, Internet advertising** and **mobile advertising**.

3 **What is public relations, and how is it used in the promotional mix?** (pp. 425–427)

- **Public relations** (p. 425) is the management function that establishes and maintains mutually beneficial relationships between an organization and its stakeholders.

- Public relations tools consist of controlled, semi-controlled, and uncontrolled news messages. **Publicity** (p. 426) is uncontrolled and can be a powerful public relations tool.

- Damage control is the effort to minimize the harmful effects of a negative event. It is critical to respond to crises honestly to reestablish a positive image.

4 **What are the six steps in the personal selling process?** (pp. 430–431)

- **Personal selling** (p. 428) is direct communication between a firm's sales force and potential buyers to make a sale and build good customer relationships. Establishing and maintaining good customer relationships through personal selling is critical for a firm's success.

- Six steps are involved with personal selling:
  - **Prospecting** (p. 430) is identifying qualified potential customers.
  - Approaching the prospect has two parts. In the pre-approach, the salesperson learns as much as possible about potential customers to determine their likely needs and think about how those needs might be satisfied. In the actual approach, the idea is to meet, greet, and put the prospect at ease.
  - Presenting involves telling a product's story, demonstrating its use, asking questions, and listening to customers' answers.
  - Overcoming objections involves countering customers' reasons for not buying with reasons to buy.
  - Closing the sale is when a salesperson asks for a purchase.
  - Following up is when a salesperson ensures that a customer is happy with a product and asks for feedback. Following up is critical to establishing and maintaining good customer relationships that are conducive to new and repeat business.

5 **What are the two main types of sales promotions, and what types of tools are commonly used as incentives?** (pp. 431–432)

- **Sales promotions** (p. 431) are short-term activities that target consumers and other businesses for the purpose of generating interest in a product, which have not already been undertaken by advertising, public relations, or personal selling.

- One type of sales promotion is **consumer sales promotion** (p. 432). Tools used for consumer sales promotions include coupons, rebates, frequent-user incentives, POP displays, free samples, contests and sweepstakes, and advertising specialties.

- **B2B** (or **trade**) **sales promotion** (p. 432) is another type of sales promotion. Tools used as incentives for trade sales promotions include trade shows, trade allowances, cooperative advertising, free merchandise, sales contests, dealer listings, store demonstrations, quantity discounts, and training programs.

6 **Why are marketing intermediaries and distribution channels important elements in marketing?** (pp. 435–437)

- **Marketing intermediaries** (p. 435) are middlemen in the distribution process. Wholesalers, agents/brokers, and retailers constitute the different types of intermediaries.

- A **distribution channel** (p. 435) is a whole set of intermediaries. There are many different types of distribution channels, including consumer channels, consumer/business channels, and business channels. The type and length of the distribution channel depends on the type of product that is being brought to the consumer.

- Intermediaries are important because they reduce the costs of products to consumers by increasing the efficiency of the distribution of goods and services.

7 **What types of services do wholesalers and agent/brokers provide?** (pp. 437–439)

- **Wholesalers** (p. 432) provide many services that add efficiency to the distribution of merchandise. These include selling and promoting, warehousing, transporting, financing, and providing market information.

- **Agents/brokers** (p. 435) are intermediaries that facilitate negotiations between the buyers and the sellers of goods and services but never take title (ownership) of the product traded.

- Manufacturers' agents represent two or more manufacturers of complementary lines.

- Selling agents have contractual authority to sell a manufacturer's entire product line and serve as the sales department for the manufacturer.

- Purchasing agents make purchases for buyers and receive, inspect, warehouse, and ship merchandise to buyers.

8 **Why are retailing and physical distribution key aspects of distribution?** (pp. 441–442)

- Several types of retailers exist: specialty stores, department stores, supermarkets, convenience stores, discount stores, factory outlets, and warehouse clubs.

- In **nonstore retailing** (p. 440) consumer contact occurs outside a traditional retail store. Examples include electronic retailing, vending machines, kiosks, carts, telemarketing, direct selling, and direct marketing.

- Retailers can cover their markets using an **intensive** (p. 441), a **selective** (p. 442), or an **exclusive distribution strategy** (p. 442).

- Physical distribution is one of the most expensive parts of marketing a product. In the broadest sense, it entails the management of the entire supply chain.

- Transportation options include railroads, trucks, waterways, airways, and pipelines. Careful measurement of the advantages and disadvantages of these options is important before selecting a mode of transportation.

Key Terms

advertising (p. 419)

advocacy advertising (p. 421)

agents/brokers (p. 435)

B2B advertising (p. 421)

cash-and-carry wholesalers (p. 438)

comparative advertising (p. 421)

consumer sales promotion (p. 432)

corporate (or institutional) advertising (p. 421)

corporate chain stores (p. 440)

direct marketers (p. 441)

direct sellers (p. 441)

distribution (p. 435)

distribution channel (p. 435)

drop shippers (p. 438)

electronic retailing (p. 441)

exclusive distribution (p. 442)

infomercials (or paid programming) (p. 424)

integrated marketing communications (IMC) (p. 418)

intensive distribution (p. 441)

interactive advertising (p. 421)

Internet advertising (p. 423)

logistics (p. 442)

marketing intermediary (p. 435)

merchant wholesalers (p. 435)

mobile advertising (p. 421)

nonprofit advertising (p. 421)

nonstore retailing (p. 440)

order getter (p. 429)

order influencers (p. 429)

order taker (p. 429)

personal selling (p. 428)

physical distribution (p. 442)

product advertising (p. 421)

product placement (p. 424)

promotion (p. 417)

promotional mix (p. 418)

prospecting (p. 430)

publicity (p. 426)

public relations (p. 425)

public service advertising (p. 421)

rack jobbers (p. 438)

retail (or local) advertising (p. 421)

retailers (p. 439)

routing (p. 443)

sales promotion (p. 431)

selective distribution (p. 442)

social media (p. 431)

support personnel (p. 429)

telemarketers (p. 441)

trade (or B2B) sales promotions (p. 432)

truck wholesalers (p. 438)

viral marketing (p. 433)

warehousing (p. 443)

wholesaler (p. 432)

Self-Test

Multiple Choice You can find the answers on the last page of this book.

⭐ 1. Which of the following is *not* part of the promotional mix?
   a. Personal selling
   b. Product placement
   c. Advertising
   d. Public relations

2. Advertising that promotes a specific product's uses, features, and benefits is _____ advertising.
   a. corporate
   b. retail
   c. comparative
   d. product

3. Your college professors take on what kind of sales role when they select books for you to read for their class?
   a. Order taker
   b. Order influencer
   c. Support personnel
   d. None of the above

⭐ 4. When a company sells its product through all available retail outlets, what is its retail distribution strategy?
   a. Exclusive
   b. Intensive
   c. Selective
   d. Franchise

5. Managing the process of getting products out the door and to consumers is _____ management.
   a. wholesale
   b. retail
   c. supply chain
   d. production

6. Which type of logistics is involved in bringing raw materials, supplies, and information from suppliers to the producer?
   a. Inbound
   b. Outbound
   c. Reverse
   d. Third-party

⭐ 7. Which of the following would most likely be an advantage associated with the sales promotional element of the promotional mix?
   a. Highly interactive communication between the buyer and the seller
   b. Excellent for communicating a complex product, information, and features
   c. Good short-term tactical tool to stimulate sales
   d. Reaches a mass audience

8. *American Idol* judges often have tall glasses on their desk featuring the name Coca-Cola. This advertising strategy is known as
   a. product placement.
   b. viral marketing.
   c. an infomercial.
   d. a direct pitch.

9. Which of the following would be considered a consumer sales promotion tool?
   a. A 10 percent off coupon from the newspaper
   b. A $10.00 mail-in rebate
   c. A frequent buyer card
   d. All of the above

10. QR codes, text messages, and apps are part of what kind of promotional strategy?
   a. Viral promotions
   b. E-commerce
   c. Mobile marketing
   d. Social promoting

True/False You can find the answers on the last page of this book.

1. The product itself can be considered part of the promotional mix because samples of the product can be given away to demonstrate its features.
   ☐ **True** or ☒ **False**

2. Advertising can reduce the costs of production and improve quality.
   ☐ **True** or ☒ **False**

3. RFID tags are similar to bar codes except that they do not need a physical scanner to process the information.
   ☐ **True** or ☒ **False**

4. Brokers work with buyers and sellers on a permanent basis, while agents are more temporary.
   ☐ **True** or ☐ **False**

5. The last step in the selling process is closing the sale.
   ☐ **True** or ☒ **False**

Self-Test (continued)

Critical Thinking Questions

⭐ 1. Describe *mobile marketing*. Why is it such a growing promotional trend? Describe a mobile marketing technique that has made you notice a product. Why did it work (or not work)?

⭐ 2. How might DVRs impact media selection for advertising?

⭐ 3. Describe which distribution strategy—intensive, selective, or exclusive—would be most appropriate for each of the following products and explain why: laundry detergent, cigarettes, Mercedes sports cars, and Snickers candy bars.

Team Time

DEVELOPING A PROMOTIONAL MIX

The company you work for, Fit Foods, is launching a new product, Shine Breakfast Bars, which are all-natural, vitamin-fortified granola bars. The company has enlisted you and your teammates to design an optimal promotional mix for this product.

Process

Step 1. Assemble into teams of four. Each team member should be assigned as the "lead" for one of the four components of the promotional mix—advertising, public relations, personal selling, and sales promotions.

Step 2. Use knowledge gained from this chapter to develop a promotional mix for Shine Breakfast Bars that integrates each promotional component. What will be the key aspects of the advertising campaign? What media will be used? What public relations tools will be used? What will a sales pitch for this product consist of? How will sales promotions be implemented?

Step 3. Summarize the key points of the promotional mix plan in a poster or PowerPoint presentation.

Step 4. Present your findings to the class for discussion.

Ethics and Corporate Social Responsibility

JUST WHAT THE DOCTOR ORDERED?

In Chapter 13, you considered the ethics involved with the pricing of prescription drugs. Now turn your attention to the promotion of these products and the ethical issues raised by such advertising. Read the following scenario and then discuss the questions that follow in a small group.

Scenario

Currently, the United States and New Zealand are the only two countries in the world that permit widespread use of direct-to-consumer (DTC) advertising for prescription drugs. Such advertising has become big business in the United States: More than $4.9 billion was spent on direct-to-consumer advertising of prescription drugs in the United States in 2007.[15] Some people argue that DTC advertising is unethical because it encourages the overuse of medications, preys on the elderly and/or the chronically ill, and does not fully inform consumers of the risks and side effects of drugs. Others say that DTC advertising puts the power where it belongs—in the hands of consumers—and allows people to be advocates for their own health.

Questions for Discussion

1. If you were a legislator voting on a bill that proposed a ban on DTC advertising of pharmaceuticals in the United States, would you vote for it or against it? Why?

2. Is DTC advertising more appropriate for certain drugs? For example, do the ethics of advertising cholesterol-lowering drugs differ from the ethics of advertising antidepressants? Why?

3. Consider the tactics used in print and television ads for pharmaceuticals. What type of style is typically employed? Why? When and/or where are the side effects mentioned? Are these ads helpful in raising awareness of certain illnesses and treatments, or are they irresponsible in giving false hope and/or incomplete information about powerful medications? Explain.

Web Exercises

1. **The Perks of Internet Advertising**
Go to the Google website and click on "Advertising Programs" at the bottom of the website. What are the benefits of advertising on Google as opposed to advertising in a nationally circulated magazine, such as *Newsweek*, a nationally circulated newspaper, such as the *New York Times*, or a national television network?

2. **Getting to the Top of the List**
Many companies spend a significant part of their marketing budget on search engine optimization (SEO). Research what SEO is. Why is it so important for companies to do? Discuss why you think companies feel it's worth spending millions of dollars to do.

3. **Viral Marketing**
Find an example of a viral marketing campaign on YouTube. Discuss the features of this campaign that made it go viral. Research to see if the company reported any benefit from this campaign. Discuss whether you think viral marketing is an effective type of marketing.

4. **Personal Selling**
There are many different careers in sales. To determine whether sales is a good career path for you, use the Internet to research careers in sales. You might want to start by looking at the *Occupational Outlook Handbook* on the Bureau of Labor and Statistics website. What are the pros and cons of a career in sales? Describe several of the sales careers. Is this a field you are interested in entering? Why or why not?

5. **Multilevel Marketing**
Suppose you want to earn a few dollars but don't want a full-time job. Research the benefits and requirements of working for an MLM company doing in-home product demonstrations. Some companies to consider are the Pampered Chef, Amway, Discovery Toys, Herbalife, or MonaVie. How does the compensation structure work for these companies? Is this something you can make a career out of?

MyBizLab

Go to **mybizlab.com** for Auto-graded writing questions as well as the following Assisted-graded writing questions:

14-1. How has social media impacted the promotion and advertising processes?

14-2. Discuss the value created by marketing intermediaries. Is their service worth the extra costs? Why or why not?

14-3. MyBizLab Only – comprehensive writing assignment for this chapter.

Finding a Job

According to the U.S. Bureau of Labor Statistics, there were approximately 14.6 million people applying for 3.2 million job openings in the United States in May and June 2010.[1] One might conclude from these statistics that there are approximately five applicants for every job opening. However, in reality, the number of applicants for job openings ranges from 50 to 400 applicants for some positions.[2] Clearly, the job search landscape is a challenging one. As a job seeker, it is essential that you stand out in a crowd. In this mini chapter, you'll learn how to effectively market yourself, search for jobs, and interview and negotiate with a company so that your job searches will be successful.

Marketing Yourself

amasterphotographer/Fotolia

Standing out in a crowd requires that you sell yourself. This starts with developing a powerful résumé and cover letter.

Developing a Résumé

A **résumé** is a fact sheet that outlines your work history, experience, and accomplishments. It lets an employer know what you've done and what you want to do. There are two main types of résumés: chronological and functional. A *chronological résumé* lists jobs in date order, beginning with the present. Use this type of résumé if you're staying in the same field or just getting started in the job market. *Functional résumés* detail your work history by pointing out your skills and achievements, not your titles and the companies you've worked for. This is a good type of résumé to use when you're switching fields. Your skills show employers what you can do for them because your previous job experience may not be related.

Getting Started

Before you start typing, take some time to evaluate yourself. Consider the following:

- What are your strengths and weaknesses?
- What type of skills do you possess?
- What do you want from an employer?

Aside from technical skills, think about your soft skills. Soft skills include personality traits and interpersonal skills, such as honesty, responsibility, leadership, and teamwork. Some employers find these traits more desirable than technical skills because technical skills can be taught, while soft skills are innate.

When you begin your résumé, remember that organization is key. Employers generally spend about 15 seconds reviewing a résumé,[3] so you need to quickly capture the attention of the reviewer. Organize your résumé clearly, with bold headings and bulleted information; no one will take the time to read a lengthy paragraph about your achievements. The following headings can help you organize a basic chronological résumé: Contact Information, Objective, Education, Experience or Work History, Skills/Interests, and References. Depending on how you format your résumé, you may or may not use all of these headings.

Contact Information

Your **contact information** is typically centered at the top of the page, with your name in the largest font. Include your mailing address, phone number, and e-mail address. Remember that prospective employers may hear your outgoing phone message, so be sure it's appropriate.

Objective

An **objective** is a short summary of the job you're seeking and how your skills will apply to that job. Objectives should be specific to the job for which you're applying. Generalized objectives don't tell a prospective employer anything about you and don't get anyone's attention.

Read the following objective and analyze it from an employer's perspective.

> OBJECTIVE: To employ my advertising knowledge by working for a successful company that will help me get experience to kick-start my career.

What position is the applicant applying for? This objective doesn't specify the position. It also describes what the applicant wants the job to do for him or her, not what he or she can contribute to the company. Employers already know that you want to learn and gain experience; reiterating it makes you look selfish.

A good objective is specific and short. Here's an example.

> OBJECTIVE: To obtain a position at Doyle and Associates as an entry-level graphic designer where my creativity and technical ability will add value to operations.

With this objective, an employer knows what position you want and why you think you're the right person to fill the opening. It also shows you're serious about the position because you took the time to tailor your résumé to this specific position.

Education

Begin your education list with your most recent educational experience. Be sure to detail your degree, major, minor, dates of attendance, and the name and location of the school. If you haven't graduated yet, list your expected degree and graduation date. Include your GPA if it is 3.0 or higher. Including a GPA that is lower may inadvertently invite questions about your studying skills that you may not be comfortable answering, or you may be passed over altogether.

If you don't have relevant work experience, list your educational background first. If you have pertinent work experience, reverse the sections so that work history comes before education.

Experience or Work History

List your previous work experiences chronologically, starting with the most recent, and include each company's name, its location, your dates of employment, and your title or position. For each experience listed, include at least three bullet points that highlight your achievements or undertakings. You don't have to put specific dates of employment but do list the month and year. If you include the years only, you may give the impression that you have gaps in your employment history. If possible, include specific, quantifiable data about your accomplishments and how you benefited your employer.

Skills/Interests

This section should include your hidden talents or skills, such as whether you speak a foreign language or are knowledgeable about a certain software package. Also include extracurricular activities or professional organizations you belong to that relate to your career field. You don't want to restate anything you've said in your education and experience sections, so if you don't have anything to add, omit this section.

References

References can attest to your work ethic and skills and are important to have ready to go. You should have three professional references expecting to be called on to help you. If you have no professional references, obtain references from teachers, instructors, professors, clergy, and other people who know about your character. Avoid using family members and friends. Always ask permission to use someone as a reference before listing him or her. Be sure your references know you're engaging in an active job search in case a potential employer calls them so your references can be prepared to answer questions accurately.

Employers generally won't need references until they interview you, so it's customary to include at the bottom of your résumé the line "References are available upon request." However, if you choose to provide information for each reference on your résumé, you should include for each reference the name, title, employer, contact information, the nature of your relationship, and the length of time he or she has known you. Including references shows that you have professional contacts with people willing to recommend you. When you are invited to an interview, bring additional copies of your references with you.

Résumé Showdown!

To get yourself noticed, you need to make your résumé pop. Look at the two examples (on the following pages) from the perspective of an employer who has a pile of résumés to look through. Both résumés are for the same person. Consider the strengths and weaknesses of each and which one you feel makes the best impression.

Which résumé do you think an employer would be more impressed with? Most likely the second one—right? It has a better organizational structure and a cleaner appearance. The résumé also focuses more on the candidate's achievements than on her responsibilities, with specific and detailed actions and outcomes. Overall, the second résumé gives a prospective employer a stronger idea of what the candidate can offer the company.

Writing a Cover Letter

Along with your résumé, you need to include a cover letter. A **cover letter** introduces you to a prospective employer. This is an opportunity for you to market yourself by demonstrating sound communication skills. A cover letter may be more important than a résumé in the eyes of a prospective employer because it gives you a voice. Even if you're the most qualified person for a job, a poorly written cover letter may end your chances before anyone ever looks at your résumé. If you follow these basic tips, your cover letter may get you an interview all on its own.

Tip #1: Tailor Your Cover Letter to Fit the Job You're Applying for.

There are three main types of cover letters: an application letter, a prospecting letter, and a networking letter. An *application letter* is sent as a response to a job opening. A *prospecting letter* is sent to a company where you want to work, asking

Jane Doefield
4117 Blank Street
Cincinnati, OH 45202
(513) 555-4529
Janedoefield@email.com

Education
Ohio State University, Columbus, OH, 2008–2013
BS, Biology with a concentration in Medical Technology
GPA: 2.57

Work History
Johnson and Webb, Columbus, OH, January 2013–May 2013
Intern
My main responsibilities were to organize a computerized file-retrieval system for research and create a tracking spreadsheet to keep track of tested drugs. I also worked hands-on in the lab testing cells for sensitivity to different drug treatments.

BookZilla, Columbus, OH, 2009–2012
Sales Associate
While working at BookZilla, I was responsible for stocking and straightening the magazine and stationery sections. When needed, I also worked on the cash register and sold BookZilla discount cards.

Pepe's Garments, Cincinnati, OH, 2007–2009
Sales Associate
I provided customer service by helping customers pick out garments and ringing up there purchases. I maximized sales by signing people up for Pepe's credit cards. I was also responsible for keeping an accurate sales drawer.

Skills/Interests
I am proficient in Microsoft Office and fluent in French. I enjoy playing the piano, painting, and swimming. While in college, I played on an intramural softball team.

References
Mario Rodríguez
Supervisor, BookZilla
(614) 555-7619

Andrea Zimmerman
Owner, Pepe's Garments
(513) 555-9723

Résumé #1.

Jane Doefield
4117 Blank Street
Cincinnati, OH 45202
(513) 555-4529
Janedoefield@email.com

Objective: To obtain a position as a quality-assurance technician in AIF's lab.

Education
Ohio State University, Columbus, OH, 2008–2013
BS, Biology with a concentration in Medical Technology

Work History
Johnson and Webb, Columbus, OH, January 2013–May 2013
Intern
· Tested cells for sensitivity to a variety of drug treatments at a rate of 4 assays per day, enabling our department to exceed company testing expectations
· Developed a tracking mechanism to organize drugs tested, preventing the inadvertent retesting of drugs, which saved our department over 10 hours of lost time per month
· Streamlined retrieval process for locating researched materials, adding 5 hours of additional analysis time per month

BookZilla, Columbus, OH, October 2009–December 2012
Sales Associate
· Organized and maintained periodical and stationery sections containing more than 200 items
· Marketed and sold five BookZilla discount cards a week to boost sales
· Provided excellent customer service while processing purchases

Pepe's Garments, Cincinnati, OH, June 2008–August 2009
Sales Associate
· Assisted customers with making purchasing decisions
· Used sales strategies to register customers for Pepe's credit cards
· Provided customer service to achieve sales goals

Skills
· Proficient in Microsoft Office
· Fluent in French

References
· Available upon request.

Résumé #2.

454

about potential positions. A *networking letter* is sent to ask for information regarding your job search.[4] Each cover letter you send out needs to be tailored to fit the job opening you're applying for or inquiring about. Look at the requirements in the ad. Find the key words and phrases used to describe the position and then describe your skills and experience using the same terms. Highlight a major relevant accomplishment in terms used by the employer. Include how you have or will address the needs of the employer. Overall, demonstrate in your cover letter that you fulfill the specific requirements the company is looking for.

Tip #2: Indicate What You Can Do for the Employer.

All cover letters should explain to potential employers what you can do for them, not what they can do for you.[5] Don't tell them how the job will give you experience in a particular field. Instead, tell them how you have what it takes to perform the required tasks.

Tip #3: Clearly Explain Why the Company Should Hire You.

After you've explained that you can do the job, discuss why the company should hire you.[6] Think about what sets you apart from the competition; remember to be assertive and descriptive. Instead of saying, "I'm flexible," say, "My years in customer service have taught me how to effectively interact with people of different ages and backgrounds. As a result, I have learned to be flexible, persuasive, and tactful. These abilities have allowed me to maintain long-term customer relationships that have boosted sales for my previous employers." Use concrete examples to show how you can be an asset to the company.

Tip #4: Keep It Short.

Each cover letter you send out should be limited to one page with at least three paragraphs. The first paragraph explains why you are writing, whether it is to respond to a job opening or to ask about available positions. The goal of the first paragraph is to start strong and get the reader's attention. Here is an example:

> I am responding to your advertisement on Monster.com regarding an entry-level sales position. My background in customer service and advertising is a perfect fit for your company. I am interested in being part of a company that has a fast-paced environment, like ATI Corp., and feel I can be an asset to your expanding team.

The body of the letter lets the employer know your experience as it relates to the desired position. For example:

> My background includes three years of experience in sales. I have extensive experience working with customers and implementing sales strategies. I have coordinated and advertised events, including fashion shows and cooking demonstrations that have boosted sales over 20 percent and led to successful product launches. I am skilled at motivating teams and have consistently met or exceeded my sales goals.

The final paragraph thanks the reader and leaves contact information:

> I would appreciate an opportunity to sit down with you and discuss how I can become a valuable member of the ATI Corp. team. Feel free to call me at 443-555-2728. I look forward to hearing from you. Thank you for your time and consideration.

Because your résumé states only facts, your cover letter is a valuable opportunity to highlight your skills, show a bit of your personality, and sell yourself. Consider time invested in writing your cover letter as time invested in your future.

Multimedia Portfolios and Personal Websites

Because résumés and cover letters only *say* what you can do, creating a portfolio to *show* what you've already done may be beneficial. Don't worry if you're not an artist or a writer; anyone can have a multimedia portfolio. A **multimedia portfolio** is a collection of work that is displayed in the form of photographs, pictures, audio clips, and video clips. The goal is to choose some of your best work for inclusion in your portfolio—papers, projects, posters, videos of presentations, or photos of you volunteering for a charitable organization. Whatever you choose, it should be your most exceptional work. You can prepare your portfolio as a display binder or save it on a portable storage device and bring it with you to interviews. You can also create your own website that has a list of all your accomplishments and give your interviewer the Web address to check out your work during or after the interview.

All these things show who you are and will help leave a mark in the mind of the interviewer. However, it takes time to create a good portfolio or an impressive website, so don't throw something together just to have it for an interview. The portfolio is meant to help you stand out in the eyes of the interviewer in a positive light, not hinder you by exemplifying rushed or shoddy work.

Search Strategies

When searching for a job, you need to use a variety of strategies and methods to be successful. Don't expect to e-mail a few résumés on Monday and be invited to an interview on Tuesday. In this section, you'll learn about how tools such as networking, online and newspaper job postings, recruiting companies, cold calling, college-campus career resources, and informational interviews can help you get a job.

Networking

Networking is the process of building relationships that can potentially create business opportunities. Networking is best done face-to-face, but it can take place online as well. There are numerous social networking sites, such as LinkedIn, where you can connect with colleagues and professional acquaintances. Professional organizations also offer opportunities to connect through social networks. Other organizations hold regularly scheduled face-to-face social networking opportunities to generate job leads.

The benefit of networking in person is that it can happen anywhere. You can meet someone while you're grabbing a cup of coffee, or you can attend a formal networking event, a conference, or a job fair. No matter where it happens, you need to know what to say and how to say it to make a good first impression. Don't mistake a networking event for a party. Remember, networking is about making business contacts, not a new best friend. The first thing you need to do is create an elevator pitch. An **elevator pitch** is a brief statement that clearly summarizes your skills and what you can offer. It's called an elevator pitch because it should be a crisp, concise statement you could make on a short elevator ride. You should focus on three or four key points and sound informal.[7] Try practicing your pitch in front of a mirror or on your voicemail.

When you attend networking events, be prepared. First of all, dress to impress. If you're going to a job fair, you may encounter people who may want to hire you, so dress the part. If others are dressed casually, you'll stand out as someone serious about your future. Don't forget to take along copies of your résumé or business cards. Before attending an event, try to find out what companies or types of companies will be there. Research

Networking is best done face-to-face but can take place online as well.

Yuri Arcurs/Fotolia

the companies that interest you so you'll have more to say than "What does your company do?" Representatives will likely be impressed by your initiative and enthusiasm for a particular job. Once you meet someone, don't ask for a job right away. Instead, if it seems appropriate, ask to meet him or her again to discuss possible opportunities.

Building a network takes commitment. You can't meet new contacts sitting around waiting for someone to call you. Get connected on some of the reputable online social networking sites. Attend a free social networking seminar. Check your local newspaper for conferences or jobs fairs. Enroll in classes to further your skills or meet other people with the same interests. Look for professional networking groups for people with your area of expertise. Be open to networking opportunities outside professional settings. You could meet a person who works in your desired field at the gym, at the grocery store, or in line at Starbucks. This is why it is important to always be prepared to present your pitch at a moment's notice. Finally, be patient. You can't expect to create a network overnight. It takes time, but know that after all your work, you'll have a solid group of people who can give you valuable support, advice, and perhaps the opportunity to get ahead.

Spot the Truth

Which of the following is NOT a myth related to job hunting?

a. Posting your résumé on websites will have employers lining up to hire you.

b. If you are in need of a job, take the first offer you get.

c. The majority of job openings are never publicized.

Answer: C. Most jobs, especially higher positions, are never advertised.[8] The key to finding out about these openings is through networking and, to a lesser extent, cold calling, which you'll learn about later in this mini chapter.

Although you don't literally need to deliver your "elevator pitch" during an elevator ride, the pitch should be concise enough that you theoretically could.

Doreen Salcher/Shutterstock

Internet Research

If you're sure of the field you want to work in, create a list of potential employers. Find each company's website and read about each company's history and its mission and vision statements. You want to know as much as you can about a company and the industry so that you can make an informed decision about where you want to work. You can also look online for job openings and contact information. Looking at online job postings, such as those on Monster.com, is also a popular way to look for a job. You can search these sites and then e-mail your cover letter and résumé at any time—day or night. You can also post your résumé so companies can contact you if they think you're the right fit for a job. Many people view online job sites, so openings fill fast; check sites often for new postings and make sure your résumé really stands out.

Newspapers

As with online postings, classified ads can be a starting point for your job search. Generally, the Sunday paper has the most classified job ads, but that shouldn't stop you from looking in the paper every day. Once you find a position that sounds good, research the company. Check to see whether the position is still open and send your cover letter and résumé. Newspapers don't have the same number of postings as does the Internet, but you can look at a newspaper anywhere.

Recruiters

The job of a **recruiter** is to find qualified employees to work for a company. They can work full-time for a large corporation, or they can be contracted for part-time help at multiple companies. Recruiters may get in touch with you to learn more about your capabilities or determine whether you're a good fit for a particular company. If a recruiter contacts you, be sure to ask why he or she is interested and to which companies your résumé is being sent. If the recruiter has multiple positions to fill, be clear about the types of companies and jobs that work best for you. If you don't like a strict nine-to-five schedule or a corporate atmosphere, let the recruiter know. Once you're both on the same page, you can figure out whether the job available is right for you.

You can contact a recruiter yourself if you're seeking help with your job search. His or her large pool of contacts can be useful; however, be aware that you may be one of many job seekers the recruiter is assisting. It is best to continue your job search on your own as well as with the help of a recruiter.

Cold Calling Pros and Cons

Cold calling is a method of job hunting in which you make unexpected and un-invited phone calls to potential employers to express your interest, inquire about openings, and request interviews. It's a practice that is somewhat controversial because an uninvited contact may seem off-putting to some employers but resourceful to others. If you decide to make cold calls, there are some things you should do before you start dialing. First, make a list of companies that interest you. Then make preliminary calls to obtain the name, title, and phone number of the person in charge of the department you're interested in working for. You may also be able to find this information on a company website. Send your cover letter and résumé directly to the person you want to impress before you make a call. Don't forget to tailor your cover letter to the specific company and position. Finally, call the people you sent your résumé to and request an interview.

This process is hard and can end up producing mixed results. An employer may view your call as bothersome or pushing, and an opportunity that could have been an option if you would have waited for the employer to contact you could then be lost. On the other hand, an employer may see your phone call as ambitious. He or she may view you as a self-starter who is motivated to reach your goals. Unfortunately, there's no easy way to tell which way the process will go. It is up to you decide whether cold calling is right for you and the situation.

Cold calling is controversial as to its effectiveness, and can end up producing mixed results.

Monkey Business/Fotolia

College Campus Career Resources

Your college's career center can help you determine your skills and strengths, focus on your goals, explore potential career paths, and find current job openings. Most centers have manuals, informational books, and career-planning guides available. In addition, you can meet with a counselor to talk about your career goals and interests. Your counselor may administer an assessment test that can help you gain a deeper understanding about yourself. These tests don't tell you what you should do, but they can give you an idea about what kinds of preferences you have and provide career suggestions based on those preferences.

Also, check your career center's website for links to other informational sites that can help you. For example, the Bureau of Labor Statistics publishes the *Occupational Outlook Handbook* on its website, a publication that holds a wealth of information about various career fields. This is a great place to start researching a career field. There should also be listings for local job fairs and other career-related events on your college's career center's website. Career centers can also help you find internships that allow you to explore a career field and begin to build networking contacts. Many career centers can provide you with help writing résumés and cover letters; they also might offer seminars on proper etiquette and how to dress for success that many students find useful.

Informational Interviews

The goal of an **informational interview** is to gain firsthand knowledge from someone who currently works in the field. This gives you a chance to hear about the reality of what you think is your dream job. If you don't know anyone personally to interview, you can check your local career center or your school's alumni office for contacts. You can also contact a business directly and ask the HR office to direct you to the best person to interview. Be sure that you're interviewing the right person, though. If you're just getting started, you shouldn't be interviewing the president; you should be speaking with a junior-level employee. The idea is to gain insight into what your job, not the boss's job, would be like in that field.

Informational interviews enable you to gain firsthand knowledge from someone who currently works in the field.

When you meet for the informational interview, you should have a list of organized questions to ask. The following examples are general questions you would have about any job. You may want to include one or two in your interview but try to formulate questions directly related to a specific field.

- What duties do you perform daily?
- What type of degree do you need to be considered for this job?
- What types of skills are employers looking for when filling positions? Technical? Soft?
- What do you enjoy most about your job? Least?
- Do you have any advice for me if I decide to pursue a job in this field?

If your interviewee is not forthcoming and gives vague or off-putting answers, don't jump to conclusions. Set up another interview with someone in the same field. Also, although this isn't a formal job interview, you should dress professionally. An informational interview is another opportunity to network; your interviewee may be impressed with you and give your name to someone higher up or know about an opening elsewhere. Try to give the best impression possible because you never know—one meeting could turn into your dream job.

Interviewing and Negotiating

Congratulations, you've landed an interview! Interviews can be a breeze if you're properly prepared or a nightmare if you're not. The goal of the interview is to convey that you're the best person for the position, so confidence is key.

Interview Red Flags

Not all interview questions are created equal. Some are even illegal. Interviewers cannot ask questions about your race, gender, sexual orientation, religion, age, national origin, marital status, or family matters.[9] If your interviewer asks you any of the following questions or makes any inappropriate comments, it may be a red flag, a warning signal that you should look elsewhere for employment:

- Where were you born?
- How old are you?

Stephen Coburn/Fotolia

Preparation is key when it comes to interviews.

- Are you married?
- Do you attend church?
- Do you plan on having children soon?

Preparing for the Interview

There is so much to do before the big day, so if you have the option, give yourself a few days to prepare. Go over everything on your résumé. Be prepared to talk about anything listed, from previous jobs to your educational background. Research the company as much as you can. Look at its history, mission and vision statements, and current projects. Try to relate previous experiences to the position you're applying for, such as "While I served as vice president of the student body, I learned a lot about persuasion and compromise, which I know are two skills a marketing representative must have."

Next, practice your answers to standard interview questions, such as "What's your biggest weakness?" Think about the questions and jot down your answers. Stage a mock interview with a friend. You might feel silly, but practicing your responses will make you feel more confident.

Interview Questions

No matter which field you're in, certain interview questions show up everywhere:

- What can you tell me about yourself?
- Why do you want to work here?
- What kind of position are you looking for?
- Why did you leave your last job?
- What is your greatest strength? Weakness?
- Describe a problem you faced at your previous job and explain how you handled it.
- How do you handle stress?
- What is your proudest accomplishment?
- Where do you see yourself in five years?
- How would you describe your work style?
- What motivates you?
- How do you evaluate success?

By preparing your responses ahead of time, you'll boost your confidence and give yourself a little room to relax.

Once you know what you want to say, work on looking the part. You want to make a good impression, so be careful what you choose. Because you don't know the person interviewing you, stick with a conservative look. Don't wear baggy clothes, tennis shoes, short skirts, funky jewelry, or other inappropriate attire, and don't overload yourself with cologne or perfume. Also, be sure to consider the job and whether tattoos, body piercings, or extreme makeup will present a negative impression.

During the Interview

Aim to arrive 10–15 minutes early. Being late is a signal to the person interviewing you that you're not serious about the job. If you know you're going to be late, call and apologize as soon as you realize it. Once you arrive, give another quick apology and sit down for the interview.

When you meet your interviewer, give a firm handshake, smile, and make eye contact. Have questions prepared to ask at the end of the interview. If you need to, write them down ahead of time and take them to the interview with you. Some examples of interview questions are as follows:

- Can you describe an ideal employee?
- What kinds of growth opportunities are available?
- Can you describe the company's management style and the type of employee that fits well with it?
- What do you consider to be the most important aspects of this job?

Also, ask about the overall responsibilities of the position, the day-to-day tasks associated with it, associated travel requirements, and any other questions you might have. Avoid asking directly about the salary. If you feel it is important and appropriate, though, ask about salary at the very end of the interview.

Interview Take-Alongs

There are some things you need to take to your interview besides your winning personality. Grab a briefcase or folder and include the following items:[10]

- Copies of your résumé
- A list of your references
- A portfolio if you have made one
- Paper and a pen
- Directions
- A cell phone, in case something happens, but leave it in the car or turn it off during your interview

At the end of the interview, if you still want the job and feel you're a good fit, say so directly. Ask the interviewer what the next step entails—a second interview, a background/reference check, and so forth—and when you can expect to hear from him or her again. Before leaving, remember to thank the interviewer for the opportunity. Following up with a personal thank-you note or e-mail is also highly recommended.

Negotiating Strategies

You aced the interview, and the company has offered you a job. Now you have to think about negotiating a salary. Negotiating may be uncomfortable, but it helps set the tone for your career. The following steps can help guide you through the negotiation process:

1. Before you negotiate, figure out a reasonable salary for the position you're interested in.
2. Using websites such as Salary.com, research the median salary for your profession based on your zip code, educational background, and experience.
3. Ask for a day to consider the salary offer. This will give you time to do further research and come up with a negotiating plan.

THE List

Interview Tips

1. Be confident.
2. Listen carefully to the interviewer's comments and questions.
3. Think before responding to questions.
4. Don't feel rushed. If you are uncertain about what a question is asking and want clarification, ask for it.
5. Never interrupt anyone.
6. Answer questions succinctly yet thoroughly.
7. Avoid nervous habits, such as bouncing your leg, rolling your pen, or biting your nails; these things can be distracting and undesirable.
8. Keep a continuous yet natural level of eye contact.
9. Do not ask any questions that are clearly answered on the company website or in any literature provided to you.
10. Be sincere and genuine.

Stephen Coburn/Fotolia

Negotiating a salary may be uncomfortable, but it sets the tone for your career.

4. Don't forget that you can negotiate factors aside from salary, such as benefits, vacation time, or a more flexible schedule.

5. When you sit down to negotiate, make it clear you want the job, make reasonable requests, and have a positive attitude.

6. Sell yourself and defend your goal if you have a specific salary in mind.

7. If you succeed in getting what you want, be sure to obtain the agreement in writing. If you don't get what you want, consider how much you want the job. It may be beneficial to gain valuable experience even though you aren't getting paid what you want.

8. If you decide to turn down the offer, let the company know you are still interested in a position if something else opens up.

Marketing yourself, searching for employment, interviewing, and negotiating all present their share of challenges. Now you have the knowledge to successfully land a job that fits your skills, talents, and goals. Go for it!

Financing and Tracking Business Operations

Financial Management

In an effort to remain competitive, the company that Cindy Li works for needs to launch a new device to quickly match the competitor's latest gadget. As CFO, Cindy was asked to assess the company's financial ability to pull this off. What kind of financial information does she need to pull together? What are her company's options for financing such a project?

Financing Small Business Activities

Ginny McIntyre runs a small clothing tailoring business out of her home. She is so overwhelmed with business that she doesn't have enough space for her orders and equipment. She wants to expand her business into a small shop, but she doesn't have enough money. Where can Ginny find financing for her business?

Financing Big Business Activities: Debt and Equity

Joseph Cortez was planning large growth for his company. He needed capital and knew he needed outside investors for funds. Should he use stocks or bonds? What factors are involved when making the decision?

Accounting Functions

Arnold Sawyer always thought he was good with figures, and for years he was able to help his niece manage the books for her catering business. Then, after an appearance on a local newscast, catering sales went through the roof. Could the company mobilize quickly enough to fill the requests? Where was the money going to come from?

Financial Statements

Mateo Morales had just received a huge bonus check. After a great deal of excited contemplation on what "big ticket item" he could purchase, Mateo reined in his enthusiasm and decided a more prudent action would be best. He would invest the money, so now he was trying to decide between two companies. Where should he begin? What numbers should he look at, and how should he make sense of them?

MyBizLab®

⚙ **Improve Your Grade!**

Over 10 million students improved their results using the Pearson MyLabs. Visit **mybizlab.com** for simulations, tutorials, and end-of-chapter problems.

Financial Management pp. 465–469

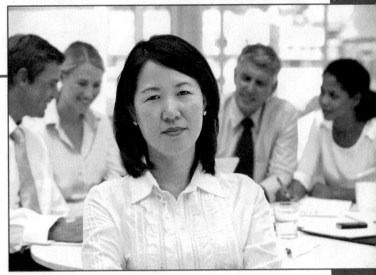
Monkey Business Images/Shutterstock

Cindy Li had no idea how her company was going to pull this off. In the past, board members had come up with some far-reaching projects, but this one was the most aggressive by far. As a part of the strategic plan, the board was suggesting the company launch a new kind of portable handheld computer to keep up with its competitor's latest gadget. Putting this together would require significant cash and capital investments.

As CFO, Cindy was asked if the company currently had the resources to pull off this venture, and, if not, what its options for financing such a project were. Cindy knew that her days would be full for the next few months. ■

Financial managers are vital to the success of any company. In this section, you'll learn about what financial management entails, what responsibilities a financial manager must fulfill, and how financial managers guide their companies to success.

The Financial Manager

What is financial management? You understand that a business is created to sell a good or a service and make a profit. Producing, marketing, and distributing a product are important aspects of generating a profit. Even more important, however, is a company's ability to manage the financial resources required to accomplish these tasks. Without financial management, there is no business! Situations like the one at Cindy Li's company can arise quickly. Without good financial controls and planning, a company, no matter what its size or how long it has existed, will not be able to respond to unexpected challenges or planned expansion. Just as you might save money to ensure that you can pay next month's rent or make plans for a big purchase such as a car or home, businesses must also plan and save. To remain competitive, businesses make large strategic investments, such as buying or building a new factory or investing in more advanced machinery or technology. At the same time, businesses also must ensure that they can pay their monthly bills.

Financial management involves the strategic planning for and budgeting of short- and long-term funds for current and future needs. Financial management establishes and monitors controls to make certain the plans and budgets are managed sufficiently so that the business can reach its financial goals. Tracking past financial transactions, controlling current revenue and expenses, and planning for a company's future financial needs are the foundation of financial management. All successfully run businesses have people designated to manage the financial needs of the company. In many small companies, the owner makes most of the financial decisions, with or without the help of outside consultants. But as a company grows, it is

> **1** What is financial management, and how do financial managers fulfill their responsibilities?

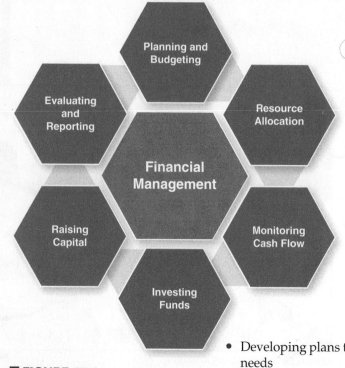

often necessary to establish a finance department. Generally, the finance department has two divisions: accounting and financial management. Accounting, which we'll cover later in this chapter, is concerned primarily with creating historically factually financial reports useful to those who are making financial decisions for the company as well as to investors and lenders. Financial management is more introspective, and is used for management purposes.

What is the role of a financial manager? A financial manager oversees the financial operations of a company. In smaller companies, the financial manager may be the owner, or someone who may have other responsibilities within the business, as well. Eventually, companies may opt to have a *chief financial officer (CFO)*. CFOs are brought on when a business's finances become complicated, or when the business is in a high growth phase and extra financial expertise and planning is critical. As shown in ■ **FIGURE 15.1**, a financial manager is responsible for planning and managing a company's financial resources, including the following:

- Developing plans that outline a company's financial short-term and long-term needs
- Defining the sources and uses of funds that are needed to reach goals
- Monitoring the cash flow of a company to ensure that obligations are paid in a timely and efficient manner and that funds owed to the company are collected efficiently
- Investing any excess funds so those funds can grow and be used for future developments
- Raising capital for future growth and expansion
- Evaluating financial outcomes and expectations, and generating financial reports

Planning for Financial Needs

How does the financial manager plan for financial needs? A company's financial needs are both short term and long term in nature, and a financial manager must plan for both by developing a financial plan. In addition, a financial manager must ensure that funds are used optimally and that the firm is ultimately profitable. To meet these objectives, a financial manager oversees three important processes: forecasting financial needs, developing budgets and plans to meet financial needs, and establishing controls to ensure that the budgets and plans are being followed.

What is involved in managing financial needs? To successfully ensure that the financial needs of a company are met, good financial management begins with a **financial plan**. As shown in ■ **FIGURE 15.2**, a financial plan uses information from the overall corporate strategic plan, the financial statements, and the external financial environment to identify the amounts and types of capital needed to meet short-term and long-term goals. For example, a priority among the goals and objectives that Cindy Li's company's board of directors and management team discussed was to produce a new device to go head-to-head with a competitor's product. As the head financial manager, it is Cindy's responsibility to manage revenue and expenses for this plan. In addition, she has to develop short- and long-term financial forecasts to ensure that the strategic goals and objectives are financially feasible.

In developing financial plans, financial managers take many factors into consideration, including a company's current and future plans, the current and future state of the economy, and the competition's current and anticipated actions.

Financial managers coordinate with other areas of a company to formulate answers to certain questions: How much product do we need to sell? Do we need to expand to meet demand? Do we have the human and capital resources to expand our product line? Financial forecasts are especially important when strategic goals include large capital projects, such as acquiring new facilities, replacing outdated technology, or expanding into a new product line. It's critical that such forecasts are as accurate as possible because erroneous forecasts can have serious consequences.

In addition, financial managers must anticipate the impact external factors will have on a company's financial situation. For example, if economic forecasts predict a slowdown in six months, financial managers know such a forecast will affect a company in many ways. Therefore, additional planning is required during general economic downturns to handle the possibility that payments might be harder to collect or that sales could be lower. Because of the result from either or both of these possibilities, plans for expansion of buildings or equipment might have to be postponed.

How does a company know it has enough resources to meet forecasted needs? The accounting area of the finance department generates financial statements. These statements include the *income statement*, the *balance sheet*, and the *statement of cash flows*. We'll discuss financial statements in more detail later in the chapter, but for now you just need to know that together they create a financial landscape that explains where a company has been over the current year and in past periods. Moreover, they serve as a basis for management to develop expectations of where a company will be in future periods.

Using these expectations, a financial manager develops a **budget**—a management tool that outlines a company's planned cash flows, expected operating expenses, and anticipated revenue. An **operating (master) budget** includes all the operating costs for an entire organization, including inventory, sales, purchases, manufacturing, marketing, and operating expenses. The operating budget maps out the projected number of units to be sold and estimated income for the coming year, in addition to all anticipated costs of operating the business to produce and sell the estimated level of business.

How are funds made available for large projects? Another component of the budgeting process is the capital budget. The **capital budget** considers a company's long-range plans and outlines the expected financial needs for significant capital purchases, such as real estate, manufacturing equipment, plant expansions, or technology. Because capital investments are often financed with borrowed money or money raised through the sale of stocks or bonds, it is important to plan ahead to ensure that necessary funds are available when they are needed. During the capital budgeting process, each department in an organization makes a list of its anticipated capital needs. Then senior management and the board evaluate these needs to determine which will best maximize a company's overall growth and profitability. Some capital needs are the routine replacement of equipment or technology and may not require much evaluation. Other requests

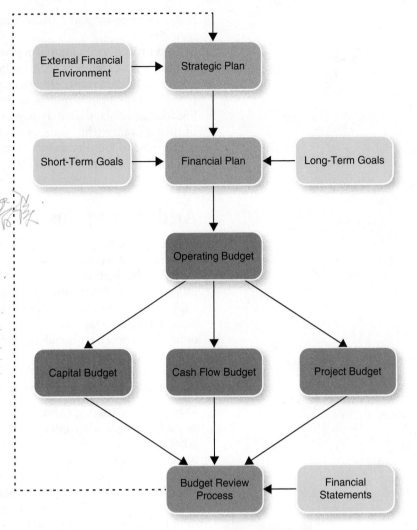

■ **FIGURE 15.2**
The Financial Planning Process

might be necessary to move a company in a new direction and should be evaluated closely.

According to its annual report, Apple's capital expenditures during 2011 included "approximately $614 million for retail store facilities and $4.0 billion for other capital expenditures".[1] Barnes and Noble in their 2011 annual report indicate that although their current sources of cash will be sufficient for short-term operating requirements, they may need to raise additional capital to fund the expansion of their eReader (the Nook) and eBook businesses.[2] Sometimes, a **project budget** is prepared to identify the costs needed to accomplish a project—an endeavor that has a specific start and end date, such as installing and upgrading a computer system, or renovating an existing building.

Addressing Cash Flow and the Budget

What helps to plan for short-term cash needs? Cash flow is the amount of money that a company actually receives and spends over a specific period. The **cash flow budget**, as illustrated in ■ FIGURE 15.3, is a short-term estimate of cash inflows and outflows, and predicts any cash flow gaps for the business. Cash flow gaps occur when cash outflows are greater than cash inflows. Cash flow budgets help financial managers determine whether a business needs to seek outside sources of funds beyond traditional income sources to manage anticipated cash needs. They also indicate whether a business will have enough cash to grow and help to fund future investment opportunities. Moreover, financial managers use the cash flow budget to help plan for debt repayment or to cover unusual operating expenses.

Why is monitoring cash flow important? A company can have the best-selling product on the market, but if the flow of funds coming in and going out of a business is not managed properly, a company can easily fail. Monitoring cash flow is important because it measures a company's short-term financial health and financial efficiency.

Cash flow specifically measures whether there are sufficient funds to pay outstanding bills. For seasonal businesses, such as ski shops and pool installation companies, cash management is critical for carrying a business through the slow months. Seasonal business owners must be disciplined to not spend surplus cash generated during the busy season. Although many investors focus on a company's profitability as an indicator of strength, a company's *liquidity*—how quickly an asset can be turned into cash—is often a better indicator. After all, companies go bankrupt when they cannot pay their bills, not because they are unprofitable. As you'll read later in this chapter, accountants also play a big role in helping financial managers monitor cash flows.

How does a company know if it's staying on budget? After a budget is developed, it must be compared periodically to a company's actual performance. It is very important that management regularly compare actual performance to the

■ FIGURE 15.3
Cash Flow Budget
Image Sources, left to right, top to bottom: Texelart/Shutterstock; slaved/Fotolia; lucadp/Fotolia; Arthur Eugene Preston/Shutterstock; SDuggan/Fotolia; Pawel Burgiel/Fotolia; Paul Fleet/Fotolia; scusi/Fotolia; Stoyan Haytov/Fotolia

budget. Ideally this happens every month. Without such a comparison, it's hard to determine whether a company is actually performing as expected. To understand this concept better, we can apply the same principle to your personal financial situation. Let's say you decide to save some money for one month; at the end of the month, you have $50 in your savings account. Is that good or bad? It all depends on what you originally planned to save. If you intended to save only $35 but end up with $50, that's great. If you intended to save $75, then the outcome is not as good, and you should modify your spending to bring you back into budget.

The same is true with the financial performance of a company. If the actual numbers generated by a company closely match the budget, this shows that the company is fulfilling its plans. However, if the actual numbers differ greatly from those projected by the budget, this indicates that corrective actions must be taken. Businesses strive to stay on budget and to fund needs through monies generated by business operations. However, there are many situations, even with the best planning, when a financial manager needs to consider funding operations with additional internal cash sources or finding outside sources to fund large projects or unexpected expenses.

What must financial managers consider when seeking outside funds? In your personal life, you most likely have different types of financing options to help you manage your financial needs. For example, you may have a credit card to pay for short-term expenses. In addition, you might also have loans to pay for bigger, long-term expenses, such as school tuition, a car, or your home. Likewise, a company may have several different types of borrowing options to finance small operating costs and large projects. There are many sources of outside funds available to a company. How does a financial manager evaluate the best financing option? The financial manager must assess several criteria, including how much and how quickly the money is needed, how long the financing is needed, the cost of the financing, and the riskiness of the project being financed. Short-term financing options for small businesses and start-ups generally include grants, short-term loans, or lines of credit from banks as well as credit from suppliers. Long-term financing needs may be met with bank loans or mortgages, venture capital, or funds from an angel investor. Larger, more established companies that need to finance growth or expansion many need to determine whether it is best to finance by raising **equity**—ownership interest in the form of stocks—or issuing debt. We'll discuss all of these options later in the chapter.

Financial managers like Cindy Li have myriad responsibilities. To determine the feasibility of the company's planned launch of a handheld computer device, Cindy developed short- and long-term financial forecasts. Taking into account the state of the economy and the future plans of the company, Cindy found that while producing the new product would be challenging, it could be done. Next she would need to take a closer look at the capital budget and evaluate funding options. ■

Financing Small Business Activities pp. 469–473

Ginny McIntyre runs a tailoring business from her home. Her customers have been recommending her work to

Diego Cervo/Shutterstock

other people, so in the last six months her customer base has almost doubled. Her house isn't big enough to accommodate all the orders and her equipment, so she wants to buy a small shop that is for sale and hire one or two employees. Ginny has identified the perfect location and is already interviewing candidates. The problem is that her family and friends aren't able to completely finance the expansion, and she's not sure her operating revenue will completely cover her new expenses. What financing options does Ginny have? ∎

You probably have heard the adage "It takes money to make money." When small businesses find it necessary to expand, or the operating revenue is not sufficient to cover operating costs, small-business owners must make some important decisions regarding financing. In this section, you'll learn about what financial resources are available for small businesses and how business owners decide which option is best.

Short-Term Financing Options

How are the operations of a small business financed? Every business has varying financial needs. It's important that all companies have a plan to finance those needs. One of the most important responsibilities of the financial manager is the careful monitoring and management of short-term financial needs. As mentioned earlier, cash flow budgets are prepared to predict a company's cash flow gaps—periods when cash outflows are greater than cash inflows. When these gaps are expected, and depending on the size of the business and the cash flow gap, there are several short-term sources available to help fill the temporary gap.

Short-term financing is any type of financing that is repaid within a year or less. It is used to finance day-to-day operations, such as payroll, inventory purchases, and overhead (utilities, rent, leases).

- **Self-financing/family/friends.** Smaller start-up businesses often fund cash flow gaps by tapping into personal funds or appealing to friends and family. Personal loans are not a recommended long-term or permanent strategy because they can lead to severed relationships if loans are not paid back promptly. However, when used, it is important that both parties understand and agree to formal payment arrangements.

- **Credit cards.** Another approach that many smaller businesses take to fund cash flow gaps is using credit cards. Credit cards are a good way to defer payments, but they can become very expensive if credit balances are not paid off completely every month. Business credit cards should be used instead of personal credit cards, if possible. Doing so protects the owner's personal credit if he or she were to default on payments. However, if the business is a sole proprietorship, owners can be held responsible, regardless of whether a business card or personal card is used. One of the few benefits of using credit is the potential for cash back and other rewards offered by several credit card companies. If the card is used wisely, and balances are paid off regularly, these rewards can be a significant bonus.

- **Trade credit.** Businesses with good credit and an established relationship with their suppliers can take advantage of another credit relationship to help bridge the temporary gap. Companies will often purchase inventory and supplies on trade credit. **Trade credit** is the ability to purchase from the supplier inventory and supplies on credit without interest. Suppliers will typically request payment within 30, 60, or 90 days, or give a discount for early payments. Trade credit terms are often expressed with three numbers, such as 2/10/60. The first number is the discount if you pay within the discount

2 How do companies finance their short-term business needs?

period, which is expressed as the second number. The third number is the number of days by which the balance must be paid in full. So, for the example given, the business owner will receive a 2 percent discount if the balance is paid within 10 days; otherwise the full balance is due in 60 days. Another way these terms are often expressed is 2/10, Net 60.

Taking advantage of the discount is wonderful if cash flow is not problematic. Deferring payment with trade credit is a good strategy to bridge a temporary cash flow gap, and it does not tie up cash unnecessarily. Moreover, using trade credit keeps debt levels down, which is always attractive to outside investors and lenders. However, there may be disadvantages associated with using trade credit. If payments extend beyond the trade credit period, delinquency penalties are charged, and, if allowed to accrue, can be very costly.[3] Financial managers must weigh the costs and benefits of paying early for a discount or paying on time without a discount so that their cash is available longer. ■ **FIGURE 15.4** illustrates this decision.

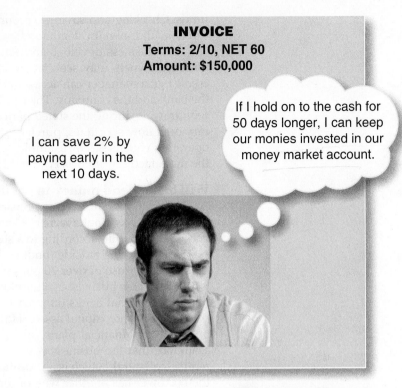

■ **FIGURE 15.4**
Using trade credit can be advantageous, but always must be evaluated and monitored carefully.
Image source: The Supe87/Shutterstock

- **Commercial paper.** Sometimes a large corporation needs funds for a short time, but doesn't want to pay the high interest rates banks charge for short-term loans. In these situations, companies can sell commercial paper. **Commercial paper** is unsecured, short-term debt that matures in 270 days (9 months) or less. The interest rate is stated in the agreement. Because the debt is unsecured, only companies with excellent credit reputations are able to sell commercial paper. Commercial paper does not need to be registered with the Securities and Exchange Commission, and therefore can be used only on current assets and not fixed assets. Buyers of commercial paper are those who want to invest their cash for short periods of time.

Can businesses turn accounts receivables into cash? Another strategy that uses accounts receivable to obtain quick sources of cash is factoring. **Factoring** is the process of selling accounts receivable for cash instead of using them as collateral for a loan. This takes monies that are owed to a company by clients or suppliers and turns them to cash that a company can then use almost immediately. The factoring company pays the value of the past-due invoices to the company selling them, less a fee. Companies often use factoring to help manage their cash flow, such as making payroll or buying materials or inventory, and to keep a business going when revenue or cash is low. Although more costly than collecting the invoices, factoring can be an important strategy for companies to bridge cash flow gaps and is easier to obtain than a business loan.

Often companies will rely on commercial banks, savings and loan institutions, or other commercial lenders for interim credit arrangements and other banking services.

Short-Term Loans and Grants

How do commercial banks help with financial management? Commercial banks are financial institutions that raise funds from businesses and individuals in the form of checking and savings accounts and then use those funds to make loans to businesses and individuals. Small start-up businesses rely on commercial banks for savings and checking services to pay bills and store excess

 What kinds of loans and grants are available to finance short-term business needs?

funds. Checking and savings accounts are a form of **demand deposit**, funds that can be withdrawn (or demanded) at any time without prior notice.

As a business develops and establishes a good relationship with a bank, the business owners may seek to open a line of credit. A business **line of credit** is credit that a manager can access at any time up to an amount agreed on between the bank and the company. The funds can be withdrawn all at once or in multiple withdrawals during the stated period. This is a common way of covering temporary cash flow shortages, purchasing seasonal inventory, or financing unforeseen operating expenses. For example, car dealerships purchase their inventory from the manufacturer, such as Ford or Honda, with a line of credit.

Will banks lend money to small businesses? The credit crunch in 2009 and 2010 made it difficult for many businesses, small and large, to seek financing solutions from banks. Banks were not lending, and if they were, the requirements were very stringent. But, according to a study conducted by Capital One, of those small businesses seeking outside funding, 85 percent were able to obtain bank approval. This is an increase of over 70 percent of the year before.[4] The economy has begun to rebuild, more businesses are seeking loans, and banks are beginning to respond. Many commercial banks offer loans to businesses for the purchase of equipment, property, or other capital assets. However, most banks require owners to provide business and financial plans, and personal and business financial statements as assurance that the business is viable and worth financing. In many cases, banks require **collateral**, which is an additional form of security that assures a lender that the borrower has another way of repaying the loan. Loans that require collateral are **secured loans**. Sometimes the collateral is the asset that is being financed. For example, if a bank were to approve a loan to a company to purchase a building, the building could serve as the collateral. If the company was unable to pay down the loan, the bank would then take possession of the building as a substitute for the remaining loan payments. Other forms of collateral can include a business's inventory, cash savings, or equipment. Some small-business owners put up their personal assets as collateral, risking their homes, or retirement or other savings accounts. If the firm has an excellent credit history and a solid relationship with the lending institution, it may get an **unsecured loan**, which doesn't require collateral.

Are there other short-term loan options? Sometimes, a company is unable to secure a short-term loan from a commercial bank. In these cases, an alternative source of financing is a **commercial finance company**, a financial institution that makes short-term loans to borrowers who offer tangible assets as collateral. Commercial finance companies, such as GE Capital, provide businesses with loans but are not considered banks. Dave Capps, owner of Capps Van and Truck Rental in Dallas, Texas, needed to replace his fleet of vans, which are rented to schools and church organizations, but Capps was unable to secure financing from the lender whom he had used for the past 20 years. Fortunately, GE Capital stepped in to help with a loan.[5] GE Capital and other commercial finance companies also use accounts receivable (payments that are owed to a company by clients or suppliers) and inventory as collateral for their loans.

Microloans are small, short-term loans specific to small businesses. The maximum loan amount for a microloan is $50,000, but the average microloan is about $13,000.[6] According to the Small Business Administration (SBA), which runs the Microloan Program, microloans may be used for ongoing business needs such as working capital, purchase of inventory or supplies, purchase of furniture or fixtures, or machinery or equipment. Businesses seek microloan funding through a local lending organization that is part of the SBA Microloan Program.

Is there a way to obtain loans without involving financial institutions? **Peer-to-peer lending** is a growing source of financing for small businesses. As its name implies, peer-to-peer lending is the process of individuals lending to each other. Similar to eBay, where individuals sell their goods to other individuals, sites such as Prosper.com and Peer-Lend.com facilitate lending between individuals. This trend became popular as it became more difficult to obtain financing through traditional banking sources. Peer-to-peer loans generally have lower interest rates than commercial loans. ■ FIGURE 15.5 illustrates how peer-to-peer lending works. For example, prospective borrowers with Prosper.com create an account that describes the purpose for and amount of the loan and a maximum interest rate they are willing to pay. In addition, borrowers must provide financial information from which the site creates a "credit grade" that helps prospective lenders evaluate the worthiness of a project and borrower. Loans may be funded by one or several lenders. Loans are repaid directly through Prosper.com, which automatically debits the borrower's bank account each month, then in turn credits the accounts of the affiliated lenders.

Are grants available to finance small business operations?
Although most small business grants are targeted for specific research and development of scientific and technical innovation, grants can be found to help small businesses finance their ongoing operations. The federal government does not provide grants for starting or expanding a business, as their grants are specific to not-for-profit organizations. State and local governments are better sources for business grants, though often these grants are targeted toward specialized businesses that the state or local government are trying to develop, such as child care centers, businesses that improve tourism, or businesses developing an energy efficient solution.

- Borrower creates loan listing
  - Specifies reason for loan
  - States loan amount
- Company grades borrower
  - Reviews credit history
  - Provides risk grade for lenders
- Lenders make loans
  - Lenders bid on loans
  - Quote rate they are willing to accept
- Borrower makes monthly payments
  - Payments made to company
  - Company credits lenders' accounts

■ FIGURE 15.5
How Peer-to-Peer Lending Works

Businesses have a variety of options for financing their operations and expansions. Although friends and family weren't able to help Ginny McIntyre expand her tailoring business, she was able to get a loan to help her purchase a small shop. In a few years, she plans to expand her business to include more staff and additional shops. She will likely enlist the help of a commercial finance company to fund this venture. Ginny, like all business owners, hopes that securing financing for these expenditures will lead to beneficial growth and profits. ■

Financing Big Business Activities: Debt and Equity pp. 473–478

Three years ago, Joseph Cortez secured equity investments from a venture capital group to help his company expand its product line for Playthings, Inc., a toy manufacturing company. Since then, his company has continued to expand faster than he expected. This year, they have the good fortune of producing the latest "hot" toy that is flying off the shelves. He is now contemplating opening up retail stores and building a much larger plant to handle the increased manufacturing demand. How should Joseph meet the financing needs of Playthings, Inc.? Should it issue company stock or bonds? What factors does Joseph need to consider? ■

RTImages/Shutterstock

In the financial planning process, a financial manager must take into consideration the company's long-term goals and objectives, how much these long-term goals and objectives will cost, and how they will be financed.

Long-Term Financing Options

Why do companies need long-term financing solutions? Remember that to grow, companies need expansion projects, such as establishing new offices or manufacturing facilities, developing a new product or service, or buying another company. These projects generally cost millions of dollars and may take years to complete. **Long-term financing** is needed because it provides funds for a period greater than one year. For example, BMW, the German automobile, motorcycle, and engine manufacturing company, is investing $900 million into its Spartanburg, South Carolina, plant so it can produce the X4, a new line of utility vehicles beginning in 2014. This will be the fourth expansion of the plant, with all expansions totaling over $6 billion.[7] These types of large capital projects require significant long-term planning to ensure that all the financing and other business components are ready when needed. In most cases, a company will use several sources of long-term financing, even for one project.

4 What is the purpose of each type of long-term financing?

What are the different types of long-term financing? For large capital-intensive projects or general expansion, business owners can use **securities**—investment instruments such as bonds (debt) or stock (equity). **Debt financing** occurs when a company borrows money that it is legally obligated to repay, with interest, by a specified time. Contrary to debt financing, **equity financing** occurs when funds are generated by the owners of a company rather than being borrowed from an outside lender. These funds might come from a company's own savings or from a partial sale of ownership in a company in the form of stock.

5 What are the pros and cons of debt and equity financing?

How do companies choose between debt and equity financing? Most companies use debt (loans or bonds) to finance large projects such as the purchase of real estate, equipment, or building construction. Equity is often used to provide funds for ongoing expansion and growth. Debt and equity financing are very different forms of financing and are complementary financing options. Most large companies will use both types of financing, aiming to achieve an optimal balance between both.

Financing with Bonds

Why finance with bonds? In our personal lives, when we want to buy something that costs more than what we have saved, such as a house, our best option is to borrow money. We take out a loan (such as a home mortgage) specifically to pay for the item, and that item is used as collateral in case we cannot repay the loan. Similarly, when a company has a project or desired asset that it cannot finance with existing company assets, it can take out a business loan. Common lenders include banks, finance companies, credit card companies, and private corporations.

Eventually, a company's financing needs may grow beyond what these common lenders can provide. In these situations, companies may use bonds to acquire the needed funds. **Bonds** are debt instruments issued by companies or governments with the purpose of raising capital to finance a large project. Simply put, bonds are like loans, but the lenders are investors, not banks. A bond consists of the principal (the amount borrowed) and interest (the fee charged by the lender for using the borrowed money). Investors loan money to a company by purchasing bonds. In return, investors generally receive interest on the bonds they purchase. Although some bonds do not pay interest, all bonds require repayment of the principal.

What are the advantages of financing with bonds? Financing with bonds allows a company to use money from investors to create or obtain business assets. Using debt increases a company's leverage. **Leverage** is the amount of debt used to finance a firm's assets with the intent that the rate of return on the assets is greater than the cost of the debt. In simple terms, assume a company borrows by issuing bonds at say 5 percent and the return on the business operation is 12 percent—the company is using debt, or leverage, to grow the business. This is smart borrowing.

Although there is a cost to borrowing, the intention is that the project or company expansion will ultimately have a positive rate of return after paying for the cost of the debt. However, it can be risky to take on too much debt, so lenders consider how much debt a company has relative to the amount of equity (or assets) a company owns before they borrow. A common leverage ratio is for a company to have at least twice the amount of equity as it has debt. If a company is unwilling or cannot take on additional debt, it must consider equity financing to meet its long-term business needs.

In addition, unlike stocks, financing with bonds does not dilute ownership of a company. For many business owners, giving up or diluting ownership or control of a business through the issuance of stock is not a feasible or a desirable option. Unlike shareholders, bondholders have no voice or control in how a business is managed. Their only requirement is that the loan is paid back on time and with interest.

What must financial managers consider before choosing to finance with bonds? Financial managers must consider several factors before choosing to finance with bonds. First and foremost, the cost of the loan—the interest rate the lender will demand—is an important consideration. If the interest rate is too high, it can force the cost of the project into something that is not affordable or that just doesn't make economic sense. A high interest rate may provoke a company to consider a different line of financing or postpone the project until interest rates are more attractive.

The interest rate is determined by a combination of several factors, including *issuer risk* and the *length of the bond term.* Issuer risk is a measure of a company's ability to pay back the loan. Credit rating agencies, such as Standard & Poor's and Moody's, assess the creditworthiness of a company. As the risk increases, so does the interest rate. Often, as you'll learn in Chapter 16, issuers use *bond insurance* to help lower the risk. Although there is a cost to having bond insurance, the amount of money saved by having a lower interest rate is greater than the cost of bond insurance. In addition to issuer risk, the *length of the bond term* (known also as the maturity) affects the rate. Longer-term bonds have a greater chance of the issuer not being able to pay principal or interest when it's due. Therefore, bonds that have a term of 30 years carry additional risk and a higher interest rate than bonds with a term of 5 years.

Before making a final decision to issue bonds, a financial manager must also consider how this additional debt obligation affects the overall financial health of a company. From a balance sheet perspective, too much debt may impair a company's credit rating and increase its risk. The statement of cash flows will help determine whether there will be sufficient cash flow to repay the debt. Too much stress on cash flow can quickly launch a company into a disastrous financial tailspin.

How do companies pay back their bond debt? As noted already, bond investors receive two types of payments: *principal* and *interest*. Most bondholders periodically receive interest payments in amounts and at the times specified in the bond agreement. Most interest payments are semiannual. Interest is calculated on the amount of principal outstanding and the periodic interest rate associated with the debt. So, if you held a $10,000 bond with a 5 percent interest rate, paid semi-annually, you would receive ($10,000 * 0.05)/2, or $250, in interest payments twice a year. At the end of the loan period, the company is responsible for paying you the entire initial amount you invested (the principal), which in this case is $10,000.

To ensure that there is enough money at the end of the loan period to pay back the principal to all the bondholders, companies annually set aside money in a **sinking fund**—a type of savings fund into which companies deposit money regularly to help repay a bond issue. ■ **FIGURE 15.6** explains the payment cycle of a bond issue.

Financing with Equity

What kinds of equity financing are available? If a company is successful, finding long-term funding can be as simple as looking at its balance sheet for *retained earnings,* or *accumulated profits.* Using retained earnings is an ideal way to fund long-term projects because it saves companies from paying interest

Payment Cycle of Bond Issue

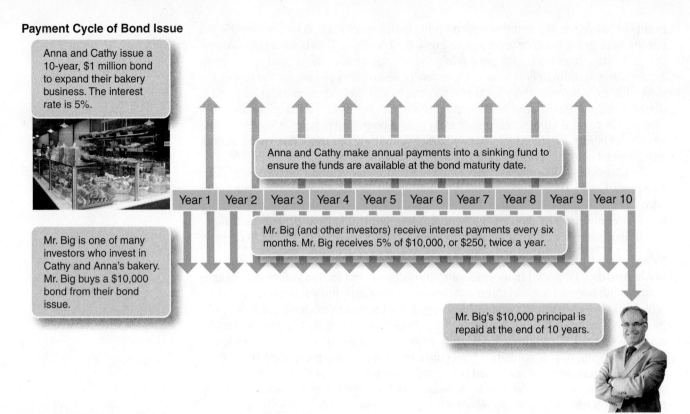

Anna and Cathy issue a 10-year, $1 million bond to expand their bakery business. The interest rate is 5%.

Anna and Cathy make annual payments into a sinking fund to ensure the funds are available at the bond maturity date.

| Year 1 | Year 2 | Year 3 | Year 4 | Year 5 | Year 6 | Year 7 | Year 8 | Year 9 | Year 10 |

Mr. Big is one of many investors who invest in Cathy and Anna's bakery. Mr. Big buys a $10,000 bond from their bond issue.

Mr. Big (and other investors) receive interest payments every six months. Mr. Big receives 5% of $10,000, or $250, twice a year.

Mr. Big's $10,000 principal is repaid at the end of 10 years.

■ **FIGURE 15.6**
Payment Cycle of a Bond Issue
Image Sources, left: Stephan Coburn/ Shutterstock; right: Yuri Arcurs/ Shutterstock

on loans or underwriting fees on bonds. Unfortunately, not all companies have enough retained earnings to fund large projects. In particular, start-up businesses find themselves with few options for long-term financing. Each business owner can contribute money to a company for expansion, purchases, operations, and so forth. However, at some point the individual owners contribute as much as they can or are willing to and still need additional funds to keep their business growing.

What kind of private equity financing is available? A company may look for long-term financing in the form of venture capital. **Venture capital** is an investment in the company by a group of outside investors, called *venture capitalists*, who take an active role in a company's management decisions. Venture capitalists seek their return in the form of equity, or ownership, in a company. They anticipate a large return on their investments when a company is sold or goes public. Venture capitalists are willing to wait longer than other investors, lenders, or shareholders for returns on their investments, but they expect higher than normal results.

Why finance with stock? The most common forms of financing for small businesses are personal savings or contributions from family, friends, or business associates. As a business grows, venture capital or funds from angel investors are also possible sources of new capital. Eventually, however, those options are not sufficient to finance large capital needs. Companies issue stock (often referred to as *equity*) to finance long-term general funding and ongoing expansion rather than a specific project or need, which is usually funded by bonds.

Stock is a unit of ownership in a company that is sold with the intention of raising capital to finance ongoing or future projects and expansions. A **stock certificate** represents stock ownership and includes the details of the stock issue, such as the company name, the number of shares the certificate represents, and the type of stock being issued. Paper stock certificates, however, are rarely being issued these days because companies are opting to keep such investor records electronically. The first sale of stock to the public by a company is called an **initial public offering (IPO)**. Offering shares of ownership in a company to the general public—called "going public"—can be a great option. A company can choose to go public when it feels it has enough public support to attract new shareholders.

Using Social Networks for Venture Capital

ON TARGET

Businesses need money, and venture capitalists need investments. How do the two meet? You might find it surprising that today many connections are made online through social media sites, such as blogs and Twitter, and social networks, such as LinkedIn. For example, Chris Sacca of Lowercase Capital is always looking for new investment opportunities. In an off-chance, he sent a tweet asking if there were any "bootstrapped, profitable start-ups with founders working late on a Friday night"* and, to his surprise, one replied. The connection was made, and the investment is still one of Chris' favorites.

Social media allows investors to get a sense of the personality of the start-up founders of their potential investments before sinking a lot of time and effort into cultivating a relationship. Investors use social media to find deals and create relationships with entrepreneurs so they can close the deals that seem most attractive. Searching through Twitter streams can turn up valuable insight into a company's culture and viability, as well as the individual nature of the employees. Social networks can also help forge connections between investors and founders. If an investor doesn't know the management team of the potential investment, he or she can see if there are any common connections between them. If there are common connections, they can prove to be good sources of information—even if it's only about character and business acumen.

Twitter searches can be valuable to venture capitalists to see if users are having good experiences with a product, or whether they are disgruntled. It helps to uncover the real-world problems that might otherwise be purposely ignored by a company's management team. But it's not just a one-way street. Investors also need to build their online reputations to differentiate themselves from other venture capitalists. Venture capitalists can also use the social web to build up a reputation for their investments.

Source: How Venture Capitalists are Using Social Media for Real Results. Mashable Social Media, May 17, 2010 by Jolie O'Dell. http://mashable.com/2010/05/17/vcs-social-media/
*Tweet from @sacca (Chris Sacca). Twitter.com

Are there disadvantages to financing with stock? The biggest disadvantage that financing with stock brings is a dilution of ownership. Stockholders become owners of the company. Especially in smaller companies, new stock owners may have a dramatic impact on the way a business operates and is managed. Shareholders do not have direct control over the day-to-day management of a company, but they do have a say in the composition of the board of directors. The board of directors is charged with hiring the senior management team. This means that although shareholders do not directly control how a company is managed, they do directly control who manages the company. As a result, shareholders can have a strong influence on management's decisions.

What are the advantages to financing with stock? Unlike bonds and other forms of debt, equity financing does not need to be repaid, even if a company goes bankrupt, so no assets need to be pledged as collateral. In addition, financing with equity enables a company to retain cash and profits rather than use the funds to make interest and principal payments. In many instances, financing with equity can make the balance sheet look stronger, as high levels of debt can be problematic to lenders and investors.

How does a company choose between debt and equity? The choice between financing large projects with debt or equity is a fundamental decision. It depends on many factors, including the maturity, the size and financial worthiness of a company, the number of assets and liabilities a company already owns, and the size and nature of the project being financed.

Managers can reach the best decision by understanding the financing needs of the project itself and the impact the financing decision has on corporate earnings, cash flow, and taxes. In addition, a company must consider how much debt it already has before issuing bonds or whether it wants to dilute ownership by issuing stock. Lastly, a company must also consider external factors at the time of financing, such as the state of the bond or stock market, the economy, and the anticipated interest of the investors. In reality, companies use both debt and equity to finance projects and business expansion. It is important to note that debt and

■ TABLE 15.1

Debt or Equity Financing: What Does Each Mean for the Company?

Debt	Equity
Company profits are used to repay debt.	Company profits retained or paid to shareholders.
Must be repaid or refinanced. Requires regular interest payments.	No required payments to shareholders.
Company must generate cash flow to pay interest and principal.	Company is not required to pay dividends out of cash flow. Dividends, if paid, are paid out of profits.
Collateral assets are usually required.	No collateral required.
Interest payments are tax deductible.	Dividend payments are not tax deductible.
Debt does not impact control of a company.	Equity requires shared control of a company and may impose restrictions.

equity financing are very different and should not be considered as substitutes for one another. Instead, they should be viewed as complementary financing; most large companies will use both types of financing.

■ **TABLE 15.1** summarizes the differences between financing with debt and financing with equity. The overall goal is to strike a balance between debt and equity, take advantage of the positives of each type of financing option, and minimize the negative consequences that too much of each option might bring.

When it comes to deciding how to finance the expansion of a business, there are many factors involved, such as current debt, ownership dilution, the state of the bond and stock markets, and the interests of investors. The decision is not always obvious, as the ever-changing state of the economy determines which choice is more cost-effective. Also, business owners must decide if they are willing to compromise the vision they have for their companies by allowing stockholders to have a say in company decisions.

There is no easy answer to this question, as Joseph Cortez discovered. After weighing the pros and cons of both options, Joseph decided that stock was the best way to finance the ongoing expansion of Playthings, Inc. He also decided to postpone plans for building a new manufacturing facility, but felt that when the time comes, issuing bonds may be the best option to finance that project. Joseph felt confident that his decisions would help his company achieve growth and maintain a good balance between debt and equity financing. ■

Robert Kneschke/Shutterstock

Accounting Functions pp. 478–484

Arnold Sawyer was pretty good at handling figures. When his niece Josephine asked him to oversee the finances for her vegan catering business, he figured he could handle it. Arnold's background was in sales, but he assumed he was smart enough to handle accounting. He used the software program QuickBooks to create a basic bookkeeping system. Because the company had a small but steady stream of clients, the accounting side didn't seem complicated. However, after Josephine appeared on a newscast to talk about the benefits of a vegan diet, sales skyrocketed. With the significant increase in catering contracts, the workload doubled. Josephine needed to increase her staff and supplies, but the company didn't have enough cash to cover the initial costs. Arnold wasn't sure what to do. ■

Accounting is often called "the language of business" because it provides financial information for decision making, planning, and reporting. When companies are small, accounting can seem relatively simple. However, as a company grows and diversifies, accounting becomes increasingly complex. In this section, we'll look at the fundamentals of accounting, the types of accounting, and accounting standards and processes.

Accounting Fundamentals

What is accounting? Remember Cindy Li from earlier in the chapter? She was asked to make a decision about her company's ability to finance a large project. To make an informed decision, Cindy and her staff relied on financial data that her accounting staff prepared. Similarly, Arnold Sawyer must decide how his niece's catering business will acquire the extra funds it needs to keep the business moving. Arnold will need to review the company's financial information and possibly enlist outside consultants before making a decision. Both situations illustrate how accounting helps business managers make well-informed decisions about the financial needs of a company.

Accounting involves tracking a business's income and expenses by recording its financial transactions. The transactions are then summarized into key financial reports that are further used to evaluate a business's current and expected financial status. Accounting is not just for large organizations. In fact, as Arnold Sawyer can attest, it is vital for businesses of all sizes. Accounting defines the heart and soul of even the smallest business as it helps to "account for" what the business has done, what it is currently doing, and what it has the potential to do. Although accounting involves a great deal of precision, there are also some degrees of interpretation in the process of accounting. This makes accounting both an art and a science.

Types of Accounting

Are there different types of accounting? *Accounting* is a general term, to say the least. Because different forms of business have varying needs, a multitude

> **6** What are the functions of the different types of accounting?

How's This for an Accounting Goof?

OFF THE MARK

The assessor's office in Carver County, Minnesota, made an accounting goof that affected 34,000 taxpayers across the county. One of the clerks who was entering property values into the county's database typed the value of a vacant lot as $189 million instead of $18,900. The typing error went unnoticed. Not even the accounting software the county used detected anything out of the ordinary. The county assumed it would be getting $2.5 million in property tax payments and planned accordingly. Jurisdictions in the county created their budgets with the error still in place. Taxpayers received tax estimates from the county and thought they were catching a break because the estimates included the $2.5 million payment. No one was aware of the error until the owner of the vacant lot received a bill for $2.5 million and called officials to complain. Carver County officials had to hustle to adjust budgets properly for the following year. Many taxpayers, who thought they were getting a tax cut, were livid because they actually got a tax hike.[8]

**■ FIGURE 15.7
Primary Accounting
Disciplines**

of specialty areas reside under the accounting umbrella. The main accounting disciplines are *corporate accounting* (including *managerial* and *financial accounting*), *auditing, government and not-for-profit accounting,* and *tax accounting,* as outlined in **■ FIGURE 15.7**.

What is corporate accounting? Financial managers must make many important decisions. Some decisions may involve determining whether a company's financial assets are working most efficiently (that is, earning as much money as possible), evaluating what kind of financing strategy is best, or choosing a way to obtain needed funds. The answers to these decisions and many more are found in the reports and analyses performed by corporate accountants. **Corporate accounting** is the part of an organization's finance department that is responsible for gathering and assembling data required for key financial statements. Corporate accounting has two separate functions: *managerial accounting* and *financial accounting.*

What is managerial accounting? Managerial accounting provides information and analyses to managers within an organization so they can make informed business decisions. Managerial accountants help management in planning by preparing budgets and forecasts, and in controlling through the analysis of sales performance, production efficiencies, and actual performance as compared to budgeted expectations. For example, a managerial accounting budget can help management determine whether it should increase staff or institute layoffs. Managerial accountants also prepare short-term reports that help managers with the day-to-day operations of the business, such as weekly sales reports that managers can use to direct and motivate their sales force. Moreover, they help determine which business activities are most profitable and least profitable. Based on their analyses, management is better equipped to make decisions about whether to continue with, expand, or eliminate certain business activities. In addition, by monitoring the activities involved in planned budgets, managerial accountants help determine and anticipate in what areas a company strays from its budgeted expectations.

What is financial accounting? Financial accounting is an area of accounting that produces financial documents to aid investors and creditors. Managerial accounting is used by managers *inside* a company to make decisions, while interested parties *outside* a company depend on financial accounting. **■ FIGURE 15.8** compares the two corporate accounting disciplines.

Prospective and current investors and creditors rely on financial accounting information to help them evaluate a company's performance and profitability. Such information is generally found in key documents, such as *annual reports*—

**■ FIGURE 15.8
A Comparison of Managerial
and Financial Accounting**

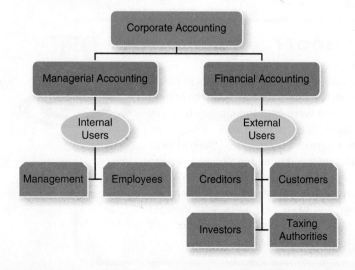

documents produced once a year that present the current financial state of a company and future expectations. These documents help investors determine whether it is wise to put funds into a company. Banks and other creditors analyze financial accounting statements to determine a business's financial health and creditworthiness. Some companies employ a **private accountant** to perform financial accounting tasks, while others hire a **public accountant**, someone who works independently. Those public and private accountants who have passed a rigorous series of examinations given by the American Institute of Certified Public Accountants and who have also met state requirements are given the designation of **Certified Public Accountant (CPA)**.

What is auditing? Auditing is the area of accounting responsible for reviewing and evaluating the accuracy of financial reports. Large corporations may have internal auditors on staff who work independently of the accounting department to determine whether a company's financial information is recorded correctly and has been prepared using proper procedures. Generally, however, most companies hire independent auditors from outside the organization to ensure that their financial reports have been prepared accurately and are not biased or manipulated in any way. Companies can avoid devastating budget problems, such as the one experienced by the assessor's office in Carver County, Minnesota (described in the Off the Mark box), by performing audits.

What accounting is used by governments and not-for-profit corporations?

Accounting is not only for organizations that strive to make money; government institutions and not-for-profit organizations use accounting as well. **Government and not-for-profit accounting** refers to the accounting required for organizations that are not focused on generating a profit, such as legislative bodies and charities. Although their goal is not to make a profit, organizations such as the American Red Cross and the United Way must distribute and manage funds, maintain a budget, and plan for future projects, just like for-profit companies. Government and not-for-profit organizations must also report their financial activities so taxpayers and donors can see how funds are spent and used.

Are there accountants who focus just on taxes?

Paying taxes is an important part of running a business. State and local governments require individuals and organizations to file tax returns annually. **Tax accounting** involves preparing taxes and giving advice on tax strategies. The process for filing taxes can be complicated and is ever changing, so companies often have tax accountants on staff or hire a self-employed tax accountant, or an outside accounting firm, such as H&R Block or Jackson Hewitt, to prepare their taxes.

Accounting is so important to a business that accountants of all kinds are in high demand. ■ **TABLE 15.2** explains some types of accountants.

THE List

Top Accounting Scandals[9]

Rank	Company	Description
1.	Bernie Madoff	Owner operated the biggest Ponzi scheme.
2.	Lehman Brothers	Company hid billions of loans, classifying them as sales.
3.	Enron	Company used "special purpose entities" to keep huge debts off the firm's balance sheet.
4.	HealthSouth	CEO was convicted of directing company employees to report greater than actual company earnings so as to meet shareholders expectations.
5.	WorldCom	CEO convinced board to use loans to cover margin calls on his leveraged stock options when the stock price of WorldCom decreased.
6.	Tyco	CEO and CFO were convicted of misappropriating hundreds of millions of dollars, which they claimed the board of directors had approved as compensation. Both had also tried to inflate the company's income by more than a half billion dollars.
7.	Satyam	Executives increased revenue by 20 percent, or approximately $1 billion, by falsifying loans.
8.	AIG	Nearly $2 billion loans were improperly booked as revenue.
9.	Waste Management	Management manipulated depreciation schedules to artificially increase profits by nearly $2 billion.
10.	Freddie Mac	Committed widespread accounting errors.

Accounting Standards and Processes

Are there specific standards accountants must adhere to? For any financial information to be useful, it is critical that the information is accurate, fair and objective, and consistent over time. Therefore, accountants in the United States follow a set of **generally acceptable accounting principles (GAAP)** that are standard accounting rules defined by the Financial Accounting Standard Board (FASB), an independent organization.

Although GAAP provides accountants with general rules, they are often subject to different interpretations, which can lead to problems. In 2002, Congress passed the **Sarbanes-Oxley Act**, which was created to protect investors from corporate accounting fraud in reaction to companies like WorldCom, Enron, and Tyco that made headlines and fell into financial ruin in the early

■ TABLE 15.2

Accountants in High Demand

Certified Management Accountant (CMA)	Provides financial information to managers and other corporate decision makers "inside" a corporation and helps formulate policy and strategic plans.
Certified Public Accountant (CPA)	Provides financial information to stockholders, creditors, and others who are "outside" an organization. CPAs are licensed and must satisfy rigorous requirements.
Independent auditor	Provides a company with an accountant's opinion that attests to the accuracy and quality of a company's financial report. Independent auditors are not otherwise affiliated with companies for which they offer opinions.
Public accountant	Provides a broad range of accounting, auditing, tax, and consulting activities for individual and corporate clients. Not all public accountants are CPAs. Many have their own businesses or work for public accounting firms.
Private accountant	Employed by an organization for the purpose of maintaining financial control and supervising the accounting system.
Tax accountant	Assists taxpayers in the preparation of tax returns. Taxpayers can be individuals or corporations. Corporate tax accountants assist decision makers in strategic plans to minimize tax obligations.

2000s due to very aggressive and fraudulent accounting practices. The act established the Public Company Accounting Oversight Board, which is responsible for overseeing the financial audits of public companies. Unfortunately, as evidenced by the fraudulent accounting practices conducted by Lehman Brothers in 2009, Sarbanes-Oxley may not be as effective as Congress had expected. Read the BizChat to find out more.

Do all countries have the same accounting standards? Outside the United States, other countries have their own accounting standards, which may differ from U.S. GAAP. For example, U.S. GAAP is different from Canadian GAAP. A movement is in place toward international convergence of accounting standards to remedy these global differences. Most other countries are beginning to accept a common set of country-neutral accounting standards, which are known as *International Financial Reporting Standards (IFRS)*. By doing so, multinational companies with operations in the United States and other countries, such as Toyota and Guinness, may avoid the need to convert the financial reports prepared to meet their own country's accounting standards into U.S. GAAP specifications.

Is the Sarbanes-Oxley Act Working?

The Sarbanes-Oxley Act was passed in 2002 as a reaction to several major corporate and accounting scandals that cost investors billions of dollars. The act was designed to improve corporate responsibility and accounting transparency. The question remains whether this legislation has been effective. Proponents feel that "SarbOx" has helped to restore investor confidence by strengthening corporate accounting controls. Others, however, claim that the overly complex regulations imposed by the act are not only expensive for companies to implement but also have made U.S. companies less competitive internationally. Moreover, the downfall of Lehman Brothers due to fraudulent accounting practices seems to highlight the belief that it may be impossible to regulate an industry that prides itself on taking advantage of loopholes. The debate continues with no decisive and apparent "winner."

漏洞

Assets = Liabilities + Owners' Equity

What is the accounting process? When people think of accounting, most think of the systematic recording of a company's every financial transaction. This precise process is a small but important part of accounting called **bookkeeping**. The process of bookkeeping centers on the fundamental concept that what a company owns (*assets*) must equal what it owes to its creditors (*liabilities*) plus what it owes to its owners (*owners' equity*). This balance is illustrated in ■ **FIGURE 15.9** and is better described as the **fundamental accounting equation**:

Assets = Liabilities + Owners' Equity

Does the accounting equation always stay in balance? To maintain the balance of assets and liabilities plus owners' equity, accountants use a recording system called double entry bookkeeping. **Double entry bookkeeping** recognizes that for every transaction that affects an asset, an equal transaction must also affect either a liability or owners' equity. For example, let's say you started a business mowing lawns. Your initial assets are a lawn mower that is worth $500 and $1,500 in cash that you have saved and are willing to use to start the business. Your assets total $2,000. Because the cash and lawn mower were yours to begin with, you do not owe anyone any money, so you have zero liabilities. If you were to close the business tomorrow, the cash and the lawn mower would belong to you; therefore, they are considered owners' equity. The accounting statement for your lawn mowing business would look like the one in ■ **FIGURE 15.10**.

Now say the business is growing rapidly. You realize you need to buy a bigger lawn mower; you also want to buy a snow blower so you can expand your business to include snow removal. Together these items cost $2,500. You don't have enough cash to buy either outright, so you have to borrow the money. Although you are increasing your assets with a new lawn mower and a new snow blower, you are also adding a liability—the debt you have incurred to buy the new equipment. If the business closed tomorrow, your owners' equity would not change because you could sell the lawn mower and the snow blower to pay off the debt (assuming no loss in value for the equipment). The accounting statement for your lawn mower business would look like the one in ■ **FIGURE 15.11**. What would the accounting statement look like if you were to purchase office equipment to help run the business, such as a computer for $900?

> **7** How is double entry bookkeeping used to maintain the balance of the fundamental accounting equation?

■ **FIGURE 15.10**
Business with No Liability
Without any liabilities, assets equal owners' equity.

Accounting is necessary for businesses of all sizes to help figure out what they have the potential to do. Arnold Sawyer was initially able to handle the finances for his niece's catering business, but when business boomed, he didn't know what to do. He realized he was in over his head and convinced his niece that she needed to hire a full-time accountant to handle these important matters. Having someone on staff knowledgeable about accounting is vital to a company's success. ■

■ **FIGURE 15.11**
Business with Liability
Borrowing to buy assets increases assets and liabilities.

Financial Statements pp. 485–495

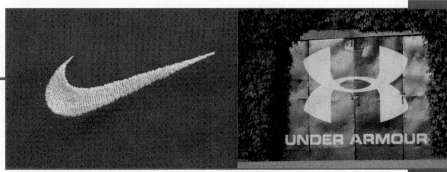

Howard Harrison/Alamy Images   SMI/Newscom

Mateo Morales was beyond excited. He had just received a huge bonus check, and his mind was spinning with all the things he could buy with the money: a bigger flat-screen television, a long weekend trip to Las Vegas—the possibilities were endless. But then he came to his senses. Although he would love to buy those things, he knew the best choice would be to invest his bonus. Hopefully, over time, the investment would reap rewards and *then* he could buy some great things. But what should he invest in? Perhaps Nike, Inc. would make a great choice, but how could he know? What about Under Armour, Inc.? Both companies are in the same industry, the stock prices are about the same, but the sizes of the companies are different. So is one a better investment than the other? What numbers should he look at? Where can he find the information? ■

Financial statements are the formal reports of a business's financial transactions that accountants prepare periodically. They represent what has happened in the past and provide management as well as outsiders, such as creditors and investors, with a perspective of what is going to happen in the future. Publicly owned companies are required to publish annual reports. Annual reports contain a lot of information about the company and its financial condition, and include these financial statements (see ■ **FIGURE 15.12**):

> **8** What is the function of balance sheets, income statements, and statement of cash flows?

- A **balance sheet** shows what a company owns and what it has borrowed (owes) at a fixed point in time and shows the net worth of a business.
- An **income statement** shows how much money is coming into a company and how much money a company is spending over a period. It shows how well a company has done in terms of profit and loss.
- A **statement of cash flows** shows the exchange of money between a company and everyone else it deals with over a period of time. It shows where cash was used.

Let's look more closely at each of these financial statements.

The Balance Sheet

What is the balance sheet used for? A balance sheet is a snapshot of a business's financial condition at a specific moment in time. It reflects what a company owns (assets), what it owes to outside parties (liabilities), and what it owes to the owners (owners' equity). At any point in time, the information in the balance sheet is used to answer questions such as: "Is the business in a good position to expand?" or "Does the business have enough

■ **FIGURE 15.12**
The Financial Statements

Balance Sheet Summarizes Assets and Liabilities

- Shows a company's financial condition as of a particular date
- Summarizes Assets, Liabilities, and Owners' Equity
- Thought of as the company's report card
- A snapshot of a company's financial position

Income Statement Summarizes Costs and Profits of Operations

- Shows total amount of sales, costs incurred to achieve sales, and other operating costs
- Reflects a profit/loss for a period of time

Statement of Cash Flows Summarizes Changes in Cash Position

- Tracks changes in cash position in operations, investments, and financing activities over a particular period of time
- Similar to a checkbook register
- Reflects how efficiently management uses cash

Nike, Inc. Summary of Balance Sheet as of May 31, 2011 (in millions)					
Assets			**Liabilities**		
Current Assets			Current Liabilities		
Cash and Cash Equivalents	$	1,955	Accounts Payable	$	1,469
Short-Term Investments	$	2,583	Other Current Liabilities	$	2,489
Net Receivables	$	3,138	**Total Current Liabilities**	$	**3,958**
Inventory	$	2,715	Long-Term Liabilities		
Other Current Assets	$	906	Long-Term Debt	$	276
Total Current Assets	$	**11,297**	Other Liabilities	$	921
Fixed Assets			**Total Long-Term Liabilities**	$	**1,197**
Property, Plant, Equipment	$	2,115	**Total Liabilities**	$	**5,155**
Other Assets	$	894			
Total Fixed Assets	$	**3,009**	**Owners' Equity**		
Intangible Assets			Common Stock	$	3,947
Goodwill	$	205	Retained Earnings	$	5,801
Intangible Assets	$	487	Other	$	95
Total Intangible Assets	$	**692**	**Total Owners' Equity**	$	**9,843**
Total Assets	$	**14,998**	**Total Liabilities and Owners' Equity**	$	**14,998**

■ **FIGURE 15.13**
Summary Balance Sheet for Nike, Inc.

cash to ride out an anticipated lull in sales?" In addition, by analyzing how a balance sheet changes over time, financial managers can identify trends and then suggest strategies to manage accounts receivable and payable in a way that is most beneficial to a company's bottom line. ■ **FIGURE 15.13** is a summary balance sheet for Nike, Inc. as of May 2011.[10] Summary financial statements present the data in a condensed format without a lot of detailed information.

What does a balance sheet track? Balance sheets are based on the fundamental accounting equation described earlier:

Assets = Liabilities + Owners' Equity

It is important to remember that assets (the items on the left side of the balance sheet) must always equal liabilities plus owners' equity (the items on the right side of the balance sheet). Liabilities and owners' equity can also be thought of as claims on assets. Let's look at each of the components of the balance sheet in more detail and then see how they all fit together to provide meaningful information.

Assets

Assets are the things a company owns, including cash, investments, buildings, furniture, and equipment. On a balance sheet, assets are organized into three categories: current, fixed, and intangible. These categories are listed on the balance sheet in order of **liquidity**—the speed at which assets can be turned into cash.

- **Current assets** are those assets that can be turned into cash within a year. Examples of current assets include cash, accounts receivable, inventory, and short-term investments, such as money market accounts. As you can see in Figure 15.13, as of May 31, 2011, Nike, Inc. had nearly $11.3 billion in current assets.
- **Fixed assets** are assets that have more long-term use, such as real estate, buildings, machinery, and equipment. Often, the value of a fixed asset, such as

machinery or equipment, decreases over time due to usage or obsolescence. To compensate for such reduction in value over time, accountants use **depreciation** to spread out the cost of the equipment over its useful life. Depreciation helps keep the accounting equation in balance by matching the expense of the asset with the revenue that asset is expected to generate. As of May 31, 2011, Nike, Inc. had approximately $3.0 billion in fixed assets.

- **Intangible assets** do not have physical characteristics (you can't touch or see them), but they have value nonetheless. Trademarks, patents, and copyrights are examples of intangible assets, in addition to strong brand recognition and excellent customer or employee relations. Intangible assets are often reflected on financial statements and reports as **goodwill**. Nike's goodwill and intangible assets amount to nearly $700 million.

Liabilities

Liabilities are all debts and obligations owed by a business to outside creditors, suppliers, or other vendors. Liabilities are listed on the balance sheet in the order in which they will come due.

- **Short-term liabilities**, also known as *current liabilities*, are obligations a company is responsible for paying within a year or less, and are listed first on the right-hand side of the balance sheet. They consist of accounts payable, accrued expenses, and short-term financing. *Accounts payable* are obligations a company owes to vendors and creditors. They are similar to those bills you need to pay every month, such as cable fees, credit card payments, and cell phone charges, and other obligations that are paid less frequently, such as taxes and insurance. *Accrued expenses* include payroll, commissions, and benefits that have been earned but not paid to employees. Trade credit and commercial paper make up *short-term financing*. Nike, Inc. has nearly $4 billion in current liabilities.

- **Long-term liabilities** include debts and obligations that are owed by a company that are due in more than one year, such as mortgage loans for the purchase of land or buildings, long-term leases on equipment or buildings, and bonds issued for large projects. Nike's long-term liabilities are approximately $1.2 billion.

Owners' Equity

Owners' equity is what is left over after you have accounted for all your assets and taken away all that you owe. For small businesses, owners' equity is literally the amount the owners of a business can call their own. Owners' equity increases as a business grows, assuming debt has not increased. It is often referred to as the owners' capital account.

For larger, publicly owned companies, owners' equity becomes a bit more complicated. Shareholders are the owners of publicly owned companies. Owners' equity, in this case, is the value of the stock issued as part of the owners' (shareholders') investment in the business plus **retained earnings**, which are the accumulated profits a business has held onto for reinvestment into the company. The owners' equity (or stockholders' equity because it's a public company) for Nike, Inc. is approximately $15 billion.

Analyzing a Balance Sheet

What information is important on a balance sheet? A lot of information about a company can be determined by its balance sheet. For example, just looking at the amount of inventory a company keeps on hand can be an indicator of a company's efficiency. **Inventory** is the merchandise a business owns but has not sold. Inventory on hand is necessary to satisfy customers' needs quickly, which makes for good business. However, there are costs associated with keeping inventory, the most obvious being the money spent to purchase the merchandise. In addition to the initial cost, storing unused inventory incurs warehousing costs and ties up money that could be used elsewhere. An even worse situation can arise if the value of unused inventory decreases over time, causing a company to lose money. This is a big concern for computer hardware companies, such as Apple, Inc., whose inventory consists of computer parts and other technology-related components that can become obsolete very quickly.

For now, understand that it's okay to have a lot of inventory on hand if it's being sold quickly enough to avoid becoming outdated or spoiled. Inventory turnover varies greatly by industry, and companies must always have enough inventory to keep business moving and keep up with competitors. Some service-related companies or online businesses like Google Inc. or Yahoo! Inc. do not carry inventory.

Other important features to watch for on a balance sheet include how efficiently a company handles its current assets and current liabilities, and whether a company is carrying too much long-term debt. These indicators will be discussed next.

How can I compare data from two different companies? Although looking at a balance sheet is a good way to determine the overall financial health of a company, the data presented on the sheet can be overwhelming and useless to investors if they are not organized. This is why ratio analysis is crucial when analyzing financial statements. **Ratio analysis** is a comparison of numbers and therefore is used to compare current data to data from previous years, competitors' data, or industry averages. Ratios eliminate the effect of size, so you can reasonably compare a large company's performance to a smaller company's performance. There are three main ratios one can use with information from a balance sheet to determine a company's financial health and liquidity:

- **Working capital.** Current Assets − Current Liabilities
- **Current ratio.** Current Assets ÷ Current Liabilities
- **Debt-to-equity ratio.** Total Liabilities ÷ Owners' Equity

In addition, different industries have different standards to compare companies in each industry. For example, supermarkets have different ratio standards than drug companies or automobile manufacturers. Comparing an individual company's performance against the industry average provides information about how well the company is doing amongst all its peers, not just one or two.

What measures how financially efficient a company is? One of the most important reasons one looks at a company's balance sheet is to determine the company's working capital. Working capital tells you what is left over if a company pays off its short-term liabilities with its short-term assets. It is a measure of a company's short-term financial fitness, as well as its efficiency. The working capital ratio is calculated as follows:

Working Capital = Current Assets − Current Liabilities

If a company has positive working capital (its current assets are greater than its current liabilities), it is able to pay off its short-term liabilities. If a company has negative working capital (its current assets are less than its current liabilities), it is currently unable to offset its short-term liabilities with its current assets. So, even after adding up all of a company's cash, collecting all funds from accounts receivable, and selling all inventory, the company would still be unable to pay back creditors in the short term. When a company's current liabilities surpass its current assets, many financial difficulties could occur, with bankruptcy being the most severe. It is important to watch for changes in working capital, as a decline in positive working capital over time can be an indication that a company's financial health is in trouble. For example, a company that is experiencing a decrease in sales will have a decrease in accounts receivable (current assets).

On the other hand, situations like the one faced by Arnold Sawyer and his niece's catering company can arise when a company experiences a sudden spike in sales. It's possible to have positive working capital but not have enough immediately available to handle a large, unexpected cash need. A good financial manager and accountant must maintain a balance between having enough cash on hand and keeping the available short-term assets from being idle. Because of this, working capital can also be an indicator of a company's underlying financial efficiency.

What measures whether a company can pay its bills? It's hard to compare a company's efficiency to the rest of the industry or to its competitors, especially if companies vary significantly in size. The current ratio (sometimes called *liquidity ratio*) is a measurement used to determine the extent to which a company can meet its current financial obligations. The current ratio is calculated as follows:

$$\text{Current Ratio} = \frac{\text{Current Assets}}{\text{Current Liabilities}}$$

Look back at Figure 15.13. Nike's current ratio ($11,297 ÷ $3,958) equals 2.85. As an individual measure, the current ratio tells you that Nike, Inc. can pay off its current liabilities with current assets and still have cash left over. A benchmark for a current ratio is 2:1, meaning that a company has twice as many current assets as current liabilities. Having too high of a current ratio indicates a company may not be very efficient with its cash; having too low of a current ratio may indicate a company will face potential problems paying back its creditors. What does Nike's current ratio say to you about the company?

Can a company have too much debt? Another way to analyze the activities of a company is to use the debt-to-equity ratio. Although leverage can be beneficial by freeing up cash for other investments, too much debt can become a problem. Companies with too much long-term debt may end up financially overburdened with interest payments. The debt-to-equity ratio measures how much debt a company has relative to its assets by comparing a company's total liabilities to its total owners' (or shareholders') equity. The debt-to-equity ratio is calculated as follows:

$$\text{Debt-to-Equity Ratio} = \frac{\text{Total Liabilities}}{\text{Owners' Equity}}$$

The debt-to-equity ratio can give a general idea of a company's financial leverage. As you may remember from the beginning of this chapter, *leverage* is the amount of debt used to finance a firm's assets. The debt-to-equity ratio indicates the relative proportion of debt and shareholders' equity used to finance a company's assets. A lower debt-to-equity ratio means that a company is using less leverage and has more equity. A high debt-to-equity ratio usually means that a company has been more aggressive in financing its growth and indicates greater risk because shareholders have less of a claim on the company's assets.

To get a better idea of how ratio analysis is used as a comparison tool, look at the data for Nike, Inc. and Under Armour, as shown in ■ **TABLE 15.3**. Although the two companies are in the same industry, Nike is much bigger than Under Armour ($15 billion total assets vs. $675 million total assets), so comparing absolute numbers is not effective. But looking at ratios makes the comparison more meaningful. How do you think the balance sheet data of the two companies compare?

Income Statements

What information does an income statement show? An income statement reflects the profitability of a company by showing how much money a company takes in and how much money it spends. The difference of money in and money out is the profit or loss, referred to as **net income** (or loss), or simply the bottom line. Besides showing overall profitability, income statements also indicate how effectively management is controlling expenses by pinpointing abnormal or excessive expenditures, highlighting unexpected increases in cost of goods sold, or showing a change in returns.

■ TABLE 15.3

Comparison of Balance Sheet Data*

Company	Working Capital (Current Assets − Current Liabilities)	Current Ratio (Current Assets ÷ Current Liabilities)	Debt-to-Equity Ratio (Total Liabilities ÷ Owners' Equity)
Nike	$7,339 ($11,297 − $3,958)	2.85 ($11,297 ÷ $3,958)	0.52 ($5,155 ÷ $9,843)
Under Armour	$407 ($556 − $149)	3.73 ($556 ÷ $149)	0.36 ($178 ÷ $497)

*Numbers in millions of dollars.

Sources: Data from Nike, Inc. Balance Sheet, May 31, 2011 and Under Armour, Inc. Balance Sheet, December 31, 2010.

What are the components of an income statement? Recall that the balance sheet relates directly to the fundamental accounting equation: Assets = Liabilities + Owners' Equity. Similarly, income statements also work around an equation:

$$\text{Revenue} - \text{Expenses} = \text{Net Income (or Loss)}$$

Expenses are generally broken down into cost of goods sold (how much does it cost to generate the product being sold) and operating expenses (how much does it cost to run the business).

■ **FIGURE 15.14** shows a summary income statement for Nike, Inc. Let's look at each of these components and then see how they all fit together on an income statement.

■ FIGURE 15.14
Summary Income Statement for Nike, Inc.
Data from Nike, Inc. www.nike.com

Nike, Inc. Summary of Income Statement as of May 31, 2011 (in millions)	
Revenues	$ 20,862.00
Cost of Goods Sold	$ 11,354.00
Gross Profit	$ 9,508.00
Operating Expenses	
Research & Development	$ -
Selling and Administrative Expenses	$ 6,693.00
Other Operating Expenses	$ (29.00)
Total Operating Expenses	$ 6,664.00
Net Income before taxes	$ 2,844.00
Income Tax Expense	$ 711.00
Net Income (or Loss)	$ 2,133.00

Revenue

Revenue is the amount of money generated by a business by either selling goods or performing services. If a company has several different product lines or businesses, the income statement shows each product or division in categories to distinguish how much each area generated in revenue. For example, Nike and Under Armour have only one source of revenue, which is their athletic clothing and accessories. Starbucks, on the other hand, breaks down its revenue into two sources: retail and specialty. Revenue generated from retail sources is from sales made at all Starbucks stores. Specialty sales include sales made from its website and licensing fees from arrangements with Barnes & Noble, Target, and other locations, which pay for the right to operate Starbucks in their stores.[11] As shown in Figure 15.14, Nike's revenue for 2011 was nearly $21 billion.

Cost of Goods Sold

An income statement delineates several categories of expenses. The first category of expenses, **cost of goods sold**

(COGS), comprises the expenses a company incurs to manufacture and sell a product, including the price of raw materials used in creating the good along with the labor costs used to produce and sell the items. Nike's cost of goods sold is approximately $11.4 billion.

When you subtract cost of goods sold from revenue, the result is gross profit (gross margin). **Gross profit** tells you how much money a company makes just from the sale of its products and how efficiently management controls costs in the production process. In addition, analysts use gross profit to calculate one of the most fundamental performance ratios used to compare the profitability of companies: *gross profit margin.* In service-related companies, generally there is no cost of goods sold, so gross profit could equal net sales or revenue.

Operating Expenses

Although it is certainly important to identify the costs associated with producing a product or a service, it is also important to identify **operating expenses**, the overhead costs incurred with running the business. Operating expenses include sales, general, and administrative expenses such as rent, salaries, wages, utilities, depreciation, and insurance. Expenses associated with research and development of new products may also be included. In Nike's case, another expense is the cost of managing the risk associated with changes in foreign currency exchange rates and interest rates.

Unlike cost of goods sold, operating expenses usually do not vary with the level of sales or production and are constant, or "fixed." Outside interested parties (lenders and investors) watch operating expenses closely as an indication of managerial efficiency. Management's goal is to keep operating expenses as low as possible without negatively affecting the underlying business. The amount of profit realized from a business's operations (operating income, or net income before taxes) is determined when operating expenses are subtracted from gross profit. Nike's operating expenses are $6.664 million.

Is operating income adjusted further? Management focuses on operating income as budgets are prepared and monitored. Some feel that operating income is a more reliable and meaningful indicator of profitability than gross profit because it reflects management's ability to control operating expenses. But, it is still not the "bottom line." Adding or subtracting any other income or expense, such as interest payments on outstanding debt obligations or earnings from investments, adjusts operating income further. Lastly, taxes paid to local and federal governments are subtracted to determine net income (or net income after taxes).

Net income after taxes is the "bottom line" and is usually stated on the very last line of an income statement. For publicly owned companies, however, net income may be further adjusted by dividend payments to stockholders, resulting in *adjusted net income.*

Analyzing Income Statements

How do I analyze an income statement? One of the main purposes of the income statement is to report a company's earnings to its shareholders. However, as noted already, an income statement reveals much more about a company, such as how effectively management controls expenses or how a company's profits compare to others in its industry. Specifically, the measurements that reveal this information are as follows:

- **Gross profit margin** = (Revenue − COGS) ÷ Revenue
- **Operating profit margin** = (Gross Profit − Operating Expenses) ÷ Revenue
- **Earnings per share (EPS)** = Net Income ÷ Outstanding Shares

Let's look at each measurement in detail to understand the differences among them and how they are used to analyze a company's financial health.

How can I determine a company's overall profitability? A company's profitability and efficiency can be determined at two levels: profitability of production and profitability of operations. The **gross profit margin** determines a company's profitability of production. It indicates how efficient management is in using its labor and raw materials to produce goods. The gross profit margin is calculated as follows:

$$\text{Gross Profit Margin} = \frac{\text{Revenue} - \text{Cost of Goods Sold}}{\text{Revenue}}$$

The gross profit margin should also be compared to that of prior years. It's noted in Nike's 2011 Annual Report that gross margin increased more than five percentage points from the previous year. The **operating profit margin** determines a company's profitability of operations. It indicates how efficiently management uses business operations to generate a profit. The operating profit margin is calculated as follows:

$$\text{Operating Margin} = \frac{\text{Gross Profit} - \text{Operating Expenses}}{\text{Revenue}}$$

Gross profit margin and operating profit margin are equally important to management and investors.

You may notice they are both ratios, and, as you have learned in this chapter, ratios are best used when comparing two or more companies. Look at ■ **TABLE 15.4**. Nike's gross profit margin (revenue less cost of goods sold) divided by revenue is 45.6%. Under Armour's gross profit margin of 49.87% is slightly better than Nike's, indicating that Under Armour is slightly more efficient at producing its apparel than Nike. However, Nike's operating margin of 13.63% is slightly better than Under Armour's 10.62%, indicating that Nike operates the general business more efficiently than does Under Armour.

How much of a company's profit belongs to its shareholders? The portion of a company's profit allocated to stockholders on a per-share basis is determined by calculating **earnings per share (EPS)**. Earnings per share is calculated as follows:

$$\text{Earnings Per Share (EPS)} = \frac{\text{Net Income}}{\text{Outstanding Shares}}$$

■ **TABLE 15.4**

Comparison of Income Statement Data*

Company	Gross Profit Margin	Operating Margin
	Revenue − COGS / Revenue	Gross Profit − Operating Expenses / Revenue
Nike	45.58% = $\dfrac{\$20,862 - \$11,354}{\$20,862}$	13.63% = $\dfrac{\$9,508 - \$6,664}{\$20,862}$
Under Armour	49.87% = $\dfrac{\$1,064 - \$533.4}{\$1,064}$	10.62% = $\dfrac{\$531 - \$418}{\$1,064}$

*Numbers in millions of dollars.

Sources: Data from Nike, Inc. Balance Sheet, May 31, 2011 and Under Armour, Inc. Balance Sheet, December 31, 2010.

As with some of the other ratios, looking at the EPS number in isolation is not completely meaningful. For example, it might seem reasonable to assume that a company with a higher EPS will be the better company to invest in than one with a lower EPS. However, a highly efficient company—and potentially good investment—can have a low EPS ratio simply because it has a large number of outstanding shares. Still, shareholders and prospective investors monitor EPS closely.

In some instances, the pressure of maintaining a continued growth record in net income or EPS has led management to "cook the books" or misrepresent financial information so that the business's bottom line appears better than it actually is. As noted earlier, such fraudulent behavior was the notable downfall of companies such as Enron, WorldCom, and Tyco and is the reason why the Sarbanes-Oxley Act was enacted. It's also how companies like AIG, Lehman Brothers, and Citibank spurred on the economic crisis that began in 2008. Therefore, it is best not to rely on any one financial measure and to look at all the financial statements and other information as a whole.

Statement of Cash Flows

What is the statement of cash flows? You have just looked at two important financial statements: the balance sheet and the income statement. The cash flow statement (or statement of cash flows) is the third important financial statement. The balance sheet is a snapshot of a company's financial position, and the income statement reflects a company's profitability over a specific period. A statement of cash flows reflects changes in a company's cash positions, similar to a checkbook register. It provides aggregate data on incoming and outgoing *cash* transactions, rather than transactions that have been recorded using accrual accounting. The statement of cash flows helps to identify whether a company is managing cash flow efficiently.

As illustrated in ■ **FIGURE 15.15**, the statement of cash flows organizes and reports cash generated in three business components: operating, investing, and financing activities.

- *Operating activities* measures cash used or provided by the company's actual operations. This is the most important section because it shows how well a company generates cash. Unlike the other statements that show assets and revenue as accrued but not necessarily received, the operating activities section of the Cash Flows Statement reflects what has actually been received.
- *Investing activities* shows how the company is building its capital through the purchase of property, plants (factories), equipment, and other investments.
- *Financing activities* shows the cash exchanged between a company and its owners (or shareholders) and creditors, including dividend payments and debt service.

Why is the statement of cash flows important? The statement of cash flows tells a story that the income statement does not. The income statement reports revenue receipts and expense payments. Because revenue and expenses often are accrued (earned but not paid), the income statement does not tell how efficiently management generates and uses cash. The statement of cash flows, because it focuses specifically on cash exchanges, provides this important information. For example, when customers make purchases on credit, the sales have been recorded in the income statement as revenue and reflected as accounts receivable on the balance sheet. However, these purchases are not included in the statement of cash flows because no cash has been received at the time of purchase. Although revenue is being generated in this situation, a company may look profitable, but until accounts receivable have been collected the company may not have sufficient cash to pay bills or to meet payroll. Similarly, if a company purchases

■ **FIGURE 15.15**
Components of a Statement of Cash Flows
Data from Nike, Inc.

Cash Flow from Operations

- Measures cash used or provided by the core business of a company.

Cash Flow from Investing

- Represents cash involved in the purchase or sale of investments or income-producing assets (such as buildings and equipment).

Cash Flow from Financing

- Shows cash exchanged between a company and its owners (shareholders) and creditors, including dividends and debt service.

inventory with trade credit, the inventory may be noted in the balance sheet as an asset. The transaction would be recorded as a liability on the balance sheet as an accounts payable but would not be reflected on the statement of cash flows until the company actually paid the invoice with cash. Cash flow information is useful to creditors who are interested in determining a company's short-term health, particularly in its ability to pay its bills. In addition, it signals to investors whether the business is generating enough money to buy new inventory and make investments in the business. Accounting personnel, potential employees, or contractors may be interested in cash flow information to determine whether a company will be able to afford salaries and other labor obligations.

Analyzing a Statement of Cash Flows

How is a statement of cash flows analyzed? Each section of the Statement of Cash Flows should be looked at, as well as the summary information at the bottom of the statement.

- The total cash flow from operating activities should be positive. This indicates that a business is generating cash. A negative figure indicates that the company has insufficient funds, which can prove to be problematic and often leads to bankruptcy.

- The investing section of cash flow section shows what the company is doing with the assets, such as buildings and equipment, that are used to run the business. A negative number indicates that the company is using cash to make capital expenditures and is growing. A positive number indicates that the company is receiving cash from the sale of assets, businesses, and investment securities.

- The financing section of the cash flow statement shows what the company has done over the past year to raise money. If stock has been sold or debt issued, then it could indicate that the company is raising money to finance growth. A negative figure could indicate that the company is repurchasing stock, repaying debt, or paying dividends or interest.

- The Net Change in Cash and Cash Equivalents figure at the bottom of the Statement of Cash Flows reflects the overall change in a company's cash position. If it is positive, it means that a company had an overall positive cash flow. If it's negative, a company paid out more cash than it took in.

Recall the balance sheet in Figure 15.13, where the first line item under current assets is cash and cash equivalents. The difference between cash and cash equivalent figures between periods is the same value that appears at the bottom of the cash flow statement for the same period. ■ **FIGURE 15.16** shows a consolidated Statement of Cash Flows from Nike, Inc.

Look at the change in Cash Flows from Operating Activities. Notice that Nike used cash to pay suppliers and employees, as well as to make tax payments and to offset sales returns. The company received cash from changes in depreciation and other operating activities. In the Cash Flows from Investing Activities section, Nike used cash to purchase property, plant, or equipment, as well as to purchase short-term investments. Lastly, the Cash Flows from Financing Activities shows that Nike used cash to buy back some stock as well as to make dividend payments. The 2011 Annual Report notes that Cash Flows from Operating Activities nearly tripled from the previous year, allowing the company to make these dividend payments and stock repurchases. What else does Nike's Statement of Cash Flows say to you about how the company managed its cash flow?

Nike Inc. Summary Statement of Cash Flows as of May 31, 2011 (in millions)		
Cash Flows provided by or used in Operating Activities		
Cash received from sales	$	1,860
Cash paid to suppliers	$	(435)
Cash paid to employees	$	-
Tax payments	$	(76)
Changes in depreciation or amortization	$	358
Changes in other operating activities	$	105
Net Cash provided by operating activities	$	**1,812**
Cash Flows provided by or used in Investing Activities		
Additions or disposal of property, plant, and equipment	$	(461)
Sale or purchase of short-term Investments	$	(560)
Changes in other investing activities	$	57
Net Cash provided by investing activities	$	**(964)**
Cash Flows provided by or used in Financing Activities		
Increase or reduction in long-term debt	$	33
Increase or reduction in common stock	$	(1,450)
Payment of dividends or interest	$	(555)
Net Cash provided by financing activities	$	**(1,972)**
Net Change in cash and equivalents	$	(1,124)
Cash and Equivalents, beginning of year	$	3,079
Cash and Equivalents, end of year	$	1,955

■ FIGURE 15.16
Summary Statement of Cash Flows for Nike, Inc.
Data from Nike, Inc.

Mateo Morales understands that it is important to carefully look at the financial statements for both Nike and Under Armour before he invests in either company. Financial statements, including balance sheets, income statements, and statements of cash flow, reveal a great deal about the health and prospects of a company. Although the abundance of numbers and figures seems a bit overwhelming, Mateo is confident that he'll be able to analyze each company and then make a good decision now that he knows what the statements all mean and how they are calculated. ■

CHAPTER 15
SUMMARY

MyBizLab

Go to **mybizlab.com** to complete the problems marked with this icon ⭐.

1 What is financial management, and how do financial managers fulfill their responsibilities? (pp. 465–466)

- **Financial management** (p. 465) is the strategic planning and budgeting of corporate funds for current and future needs.

- A **financial manager** (p. 466), often the CFO of a corporation, assumes financial management responsibilities. Financial managers generally have an accounting background.

- Financial management includes forecasting short- and long-term needs, developing **budgets** (p. 467) and plans to meet the forecasted needs, and establishing controls to ensure that the budgets and plans are being followed.

2 How do companies finance their short-term business needs? (pp. 470–471)

- It may be necessary to obtain **short-term financing** (p. 470) if cash flow gaps are anticipated.

- **Factoring** (p. 471), selling accounts receivable to a commercial finance company, is an additional way of quickly turning current assets into cash.

3 What kinds of loans and grants are available to finance short-term business needs? (pp. 471–473)

- Suppliers often offer **trade credit** (p. 470), where payment is deferred for usually 30, 60, or 90 days.

- **Commercial banks** (p. 471) are another source of short-term financing and offer services such as **demand deposit** (p. 472) accounts, credit cards, business **lines of credit** (p. 472), or **secured loans** (p. 472).

- **Commercial finance companies** (p. 472) are financial institutions that make loans to companies, but they are not considered banks.

- **Commercial paper** (p. 471), an unsecured short-term debt instrument issued by large, established corporations, is another means of raising funds of $100,000 or more.

- Grants for small businesses are generally targeted for specific research and development or scientific and technical innovation. State and local governments are better sources for business grants, though often these grants are targeted toward specialized businesses that the state or local government are trying to develop, such as child care centers, businesses that improve tourism, or businesses developing an energy efficient solution.

4 What is the purpose of each type of long-term financing? (p. 474)

- Large, capital-intensive projects require a different type of financing. Long-term financing is needed when companies take on expansion projects, such as securing new facilities, developing new products, or buying other companies.

- Venture capitalists, borrowed funds, or raising owners' equity are the primary means of obtaining large amounts of long-term financing.

- **Leverage** (p. 474) is using debt to finance a firm's assets with the intent that the cost of debt will be less than the rate of return on the financed asset. Using leverage can be beneficial unless too much debt is taken on.

5 What are the pros and cons of debt and equity financing? (pp. 474–478)

- Financing with **bonds** (p. 474) allows a company to use money from investors to create or obtain business assets without diluting ownership. If the interest rate of the bond is too high, it can force the cost of the project into something that is not affordable or that just doesn't make economic sense.

- Financing with **equity** (p. 469) allows a company to retain profits and cash rather than to make interest payments and to pay back debt. The biggest disadvantage of equity financing is the dilution of ownership.

6 What are the functions of the different types of accounting? (pp. 479–481)

- **Accounting** (p. 479) tracks a business's income and expenses by recording financial transactions.

- **Corporate accounting** (p. 480) is responsible for gathering and assembling data required for the key financial statements.

- **Managerial accounting** (p. 480) uses accounting information to help make decisions inside a company.

- **Financial accounting** (p. 480) uses accounting information to guide decision makers outside a company, such as investors and lenders.

- **Auditing** (p. 480) reviews and evaluates the accuracy of financial reports.

- **Government and not-for-profit accounting** (p. 481) is required for organizations that are not focused on generating a profit.

- **Tax accounting** (p. 481) involves preparing tax returns and giving advice on tax strategies.

7 How is double entry bookkeeping used to maintain the balance of the fundamental accounting equation? (pp. 483–484)

- **Bookkeeping** (p. 483) is a part of the accounting process that is the precise recording of financial transactions.
- Following the concept of the **fundamental accounting equation** (p. 483), where assets equal the sum of liabilities plus owners' equity, bookkeepers use a **double entry bookkeeping system** (p. 483).
- Double entry bookkeeping assures that the accounts are kept in balance. For every transaction that affects an asset, an equal transaction must also affect a liability or owners' equity.

8 What is the function of balance sheets, income statements, and statement of cash flows? (pp. 485–494)

- The **balance sheet** (p. 485) is a snapshot of a business's financial condition at a specific time. It reflects **assets** (p. 486), **liabilities** (p. 487), and **owners' equity** (p. 487).
- The **income statement** (p. 485) reflects the profitability of a company by showing revenue and operating expenses. The difference between revenue and expense is profit or loss. The income statement highlights management's efficiency at minimizing expenses while maximizing profits.
- A **statement of cash flows** (p. 485) is like a checkbook register and involves cash transactions only. It reveals important information about a company's ability to meet its cash obligations, such as salaries and accounts payable.

Key Terms

accounting (p. 479)
assets (p. 486)
auditing (p. 480)
balance sheet (p. 485)
bonds (p. 474)
bookkeeping (p. 483)
budget (p. 467)
capital budget (p. 467)
cash flow (p. 468)
cash flow budget (p. 468)
Certified Public Accountant (CPA) (p. 480)
collateral (p. 472)
commercial banks (p. 471)
commercial finance companies (p. 472)
commercial paper (p. 471)
corporate accounting (p. 480)
cost of goods sold (COGS) (p. 490)
current assets (p. 486)
current ratio (liquidity ratio) (p. 488)
debt financing (p. 474)
debt-to-equity ratio (p. 488)
demand deposit (p. 472)
depreciation (p. 487)
double entry bookkeeping (p. 483)
earnings per share (EPS) (p. 492)
equity (p. 469)

equity financing (p. 474)
factoring (p. 471)
financial accounting (p. 480)
financial management (p. 465)
financial manager (p. 466)
financial plan (p. 466)
financial statement (p. 485)
fixed assets (p. 486)
fundamental accounting equation (p. 483)
generally acceptable accounting principles (GAAP) (p. 481)
goodwill (p. 487)
government and not-for-profit accounting (p. 481)
gross profit (p. 491)
gross profit margin (p. 492)
income statement (p. 485)
initial public offering (IPO) (p. 476)
intangible assets (p. 487)
inventory (p. 487)
leverage (p. 474)
liabilities (p. 487)
line of credit (p. 472)
liquidity (p. 486)
long-term financing (p. 474)
long-term liability (p. 487)
managerial accounting (p. 480)
microloan (p. 472)

net income (p. 489)
net income after taxes (p. 491)
operating (master) budget (p. 467)
operating expenses (p. 491)
operating profit margin (p. 492)
owners' equity (p. 487)
peer-to-peer lending (p. 472)
private accountant (p. 480)
project budget (p. 468)
public accountant (p. 480)
ratio analysis (p. 488)
retained earnings (p. 487)
revenue (p. 490)
Sarbanes-Oxley Act (p. 481)
secured loan (p. 472)
securities (p. 474)
short-term financing (p. 470)
short-term liability (p. 487)
sinking fund (p. 475)
statement of cash flows (p. 485)
stock (p. 476)
stock certificate (p. 476)
tax accounting (p. 481)
trade credit (p. 470)
unsecured loan (p. 472)
venture capital (p. 476)
working capital (p. 488)

Self-Test

Multiple Choice You can find the answers on the last page of this book.

1. Which formula is the fundamental accounting equation?
   a. Owners' equity = assets + liabilities
   b. Assets = liabilities + owners' equity
   c. Owners' equity = assets ÷ liabilities
   d. Liabilities − assets = owners' equity

2. The role of a financial manager can best be described as
   a. outlining a company's short-term and long-term needs.
   b. identifying the sources and uses of funds for company operations.
   c. monitoring cash flow and investing excess funds.
   d. All of the above

3. Ted White, the owner of an auto parts store, just placed a large order with his oil filters supplier. The supplier has offered Ted the ability to pay 2/10 net 60. If the total purchase costs $500, the discount Ted would receive if he paid early is
   a. $10.
   b. $50.
   c. $60.
   d. $100.

4. Gormley Paper Products, Inc. is a privately held company with no intentions of going public or being managed by an outside group. It is looking to build a new manufacturing facility in another state. It is considering all of its financing options. Which would be a viable possibility for raising the necessary funds for the long-range project?
   a. Issuing bonds
   b. Issuing stock
   c. Seeking venture capital
   d. All of the above

5. Cash flow management is important for which business?
   a. Spring Mountain Ski Shop, which operates between November and March
   b. Lederach Tea Room, which serves breakfast and lunch all year
   c. Tailwinds Airlines, which just had its first stock offering
   d. All of the above

6. Managerial accounting is responsible for
   a. producing budgets and financial documents for corporate management.
   b. producing financial documents for outside investors.
   c. auditing corporate financial statements.
   d. preparing federal tax returns.

7. Which financial statement shows how much the owners own?
   a. Cash flow statement
   b. Profit and loss statement
   c. Balance sheet
   d. Income statement

8. Hunter Wentworth is reviewing last quarter's financial statements and realizes that there has been an increase in working capital. The most likely cause for an increase in working capital is a(n)
   a. decrease in long-term liabilities and an increase in total assets.
   b. increase in current assets and a decrease in current liabilities.
   c. decrease in current assets and an increase in current liabilities.
   d. increase in long-term liabilities and a decrease in total assets.

9. Which ratio tells the portion of a company's profit is allocated to its stockholders?
   a. Gross profit margin
   b. Current ratio
   c. Operating profit margin
   d. Earnings per share

10. Revenue − Expenses = Profits is an equation that can be supported by which financial statement?
    a. The income statement
    b. The cash flow statement
    c. The balance sheet
    d. None of the above

True/False   You can find the answers on the last page of this book.

1. Factoring can be a good source of cash by selling accounts receivable.
   ☐ **True** or ☒ **False**

2. Commercial paper can be a means of short-term financing for companies in need of cash, and, for other companies, commercial paper can be a short-term investment.
   ☒ **True** or ☐ **False**

3. The capital budget includes all the costs necessary to operate an organization, including inventory, sales, manufacturing, marketing, and operating expenses.
   ☐ **True** or ☒ **False**

4. Ratio analysis is conducted to better compare companies of different sizes.
   ☐ **True** or ☒ **False**

5. The income statement is analogous to a checkbook register because it records the cash generated by a business.
   ☒ **True** or ☐ **False**

Critical Thinking Questions

⭐ 1. Jason worked in a deli for five years before starting his own sandwich delivery store. The business has been quite successful for two years. The quality of the service and the sandwiches has caused an increased demand for his products. Jason now thinks he needs to buy more cars to deliver the sandwiches. He is trying to determine the most appropriate way of financing the acquisition of two cars.

   a. What methods of financing should Jason consider?

   b. What information will Jason need to help make his decision?

   c. How might the financing decisions change if Jason also decides to open another store at a new location?

⭐ 2. What are the key financial statements, and what is the importance of financial statements? What information do they contain? Which statement do shareholders typically find most useful? Why? What about independent contractors considering working with a firm?

⭐ 3. The text lists only a few ratios that are used to analyze financial statements. Research three more ratios, and explain how they are calculated and why they are important to financial analysis.

Team Time

INDUSTRY ANALYSIS

Assemble into groups of four or five.

Process

Step 1. As a group, choose an industry and then have each group member pick a company in that industry. The company should be publicly traded so that financial records are easily available.

Step 2. Each group member should review the annual report and the three key financial statements for the chosen company and prepare a brief analysis of the company's financial situation. Then calculate the ratios covered in this chapter and find three other ratios that are meaningful to your analysis.

Step 3. When your report is completed, combine your information with the information from other members of your group into an industry analysis and determine how each company fits into the industry. Would the conclusions from your independent analysis change once you see the analyses of other companies in the industry?

Step 4. As a group, prepare a presentation summarizing your findings for the industry and each company in the industry and present it to the class.

Ethics and Corporate Social Responsibility

GETTING TO THE BOTTOM OF THE SARBANES-OXLEY ACT

In 2002, in the aftermath of some of the largest financial and accounting scandals in recent U.S. history, President George H. W. Bush signed the Sarbanes-Oxley Act into law. The intent of the law is to protect investors from accounting fraud.

Reports indicate that complying with the law's requirements has cost U.S. businesses tens of millions of dollars. In addition, critics state that complying with Sarbanes-Oxley has stripped CEOs of their creativity and is making U.S. companies less competitive internationally,[11] although support for the act's provisions is slowly gaining.

Exercise

Research the history behind the Sarbanes-Oxley Act as well as current compliance with the act's provisions. Then prepare a brief report summarizing your answers to the following questions:

1. What specifically are companies asked to do?

2. How might these requirements affect "CEO creativity" and international competitiveness?

3. What are your thoughts as to the need for and effectiveness of this act? Is it effective, or is it causing more harm than good? Why, and what other measures, if any, do you think should be taken to address these issues?

Web Exercises

1. **Industry Averages**
   Different industries have different standards. Some industries typically have higher debt levels than others or may have greater inventory levels than others. Go to biz.yahoo.com/ic/ and pick five different industries from the Industry List. Then, compare these industries using some of the ratios discussed in the chapter. Write a brief summary that helps to explain the differences and similarities between the industries you chose.

2. **Balancing a Budget**
   Companies are not the only entities that must create budgets. Cities, states, and other governmental agencies must also prepare budgets, but unlike corporations, they can raise or lower taxes to help balance the budget. Raising taxes is not always politically favorable. Lowering taxes helps get the votes, but it is not always fiscally prudent. What would you do if you were just hired to close a $4 billion budget deficit for New York City? Find out by playing Balance: Gotham Gazette's Budget Game (search for it on Google).

3. **Exploring Career Possibilities**
   Visit job search sites, such as Monster, and find postings for financial managers and accountants. What are the job specifications and requirements? What companies are advertising the openings? Are these careers you are interested in pursuing? Why or why not?

4. **Securing Financing**
   Go to the website of a local bank and research its options for short-term business financing. What are the terms of its small-business loans and lines of credit? Does it offer other commercial financing options, such as factoring? If you were going to open a small business, how would you go about financing it, based on what you learned?

5. **Analyzing Current Ratios**
   Using MSN Money (under Guided Research, Research Wizard, Comparison) or Yahoo! Finance (choose specific company, then Competitors), pick an industry (such as telecommunication services) and then two companies within the industry (such as Verizon, AT&T, or Qwest), and do a ratio comparison similar to what was done in the chapter with Nike and Under Armour. Write a summary citing your conclusions from the analysis.

MyBizLab

Go to **mybizlab.com** for Auto-graded writing questions as well as the following Assisted-graded writing questions:

15-1. Discuss the role of independent auditors for a company. Over the past decade, why have independent auditors been under scrutiny by the government?

15-2. Sally owns a small women's apparel design company. Because of the poor economy, her sales have been slow, and she is barely able to make payroll. Last week, she received a surprise order for a large quantity of designs from one of her lines. She'll need to order material and other supplies but doesn't have the cash to pay. What are her options?

15-3. MyBizLab Only - comprehensive writing assignment for this chapter.

Investment Opportunities in the Securities Market

Investment Fundamentals

Lecretia Washington works hard for her money, and she knows she needs to start saving toward big goals, such as buying a new car, taking a vacation, buying a house, and, eventually, retirement. But it seems as if there is never enough money to set aside after paying daily expenses. How can she begin to save toward achieving her long-term goals?

Investing in Stocks

When Gina Smith was young, her grandparents invested money for her in Walt Disney Company stock. Now Gina is older and wants to try her hand at the stock market herself. How does she decide which stocks to buy? How does she buy them?

Investing in Bonds

Dennis Sanchez is starting to think about retirement. He's interested in making some low-risk investments that will also generate income. Dennis believes investing in bonds might be his best option. What type of bonds should he investigate?

Investing in Mutual Funds and Other Opportunities

Keri and Alex Young recently got married and want to start investing in their future immediately. After wedding, honeymoon, and moving expenses, they have only about $3,000 to invest. Why would mutual funds be a good place for them to begin investing?

MyBizLab®

⭐ **Improve Your Grade!**

Over 10 million students improved their results using the Pearson MyLabs.
Visit **mybizlab.com** for simulations, tutorials, and end-of-chapter problems.

Investment Fundamentals pp. 503–507

Lecretia Washington works hard for her money, and every penny she earns has a specific purpose: rent, gas, clothing, food, and entertainment. She is trying to set aside money on a regular basis, but it's difficult. Any extra funds are often set aside to meet short-term goals, such as buying a new car or taking a vacation. Her long-term goals, such as buying a house and saving for retirement, seem a long way off and hard to reach. Why hasn't her savings grown to meet her long-term goals? How can she save toward achieving her long-term goals while not neglecting her current needs and short-term goals? ■

chien321/Shutterstock

The Risks and Rewards of Saving and Investing

Why is it important to put money into a savings account? Although it may not seem like much, putting away a few dollars each week can really add up. Depositing funds into a bank and earning interest is a good way to begin to let money make money. As a young adult, you have time on your side. If you continue to save regularly, your savings will accumulate. How much you end up with depends on three factors: how long you save, how often you add to your savings, and the interest rate. The sooner you begin to save and the more frequently you put money into savings makes a big difference in the amount accumulated in the end. This is the concept of **compound interest:** earned interest is added to the principal investment, which continues to be invested, so that interest also continues to earn interest. To illustrate the power of having your savings work for you, consider the following situation. Imagine that your grandparents began a savings account for you the day you were born. Every month, they deposit $100 so that by your 16th birthday, your grandparents have put aside $19,200. Assuming you haven't touched the account and just let it earn interest, at a 2.5 percent average interest rate the account balance would be $23,578. So after 16 years, you have earned $4,378 by doing nothing more than letting your money sit in a savings account!

Now, you have the choice to take the money and buy a car or continue to save the money. Either way, your grandparents will stop contributing to your savings account. As tempting as it is to buy a new car, your father explains that if you keep the money in the bank, continuing to earn 2.5 percent interest each year, and if you don't touch it until you are 65, you will have $115,192 to contribute to your retirement! So, again, by doing nothing but earning interest, you have grown your money to a substantial amount. But, is this all you can do? There are other alternatives to savings that may make your money grow to even greater amounts.

Why isn't saving enough? While saving is important, it isn't the only way to make money. The Federal Deposit Insurance Corporation (FDIC) insures most savings accounts up to $250,000, so you may be convinced this is a good low-risk strategy since you're guaranteed to receive your money at any time, plus interest earned. However, depending on the amount and timing of your long-term needs, the amount your money will earn in a savings account might not be enough to reach your goals. The interest rates for savings accounts and other short-term, low-risk investments have been at historically low levels over the past decade. In addition, your savings are further compromised by taxes and inflation (see the BizChat box). To reach your long-term financial goals, you'll most likely need to have your money work harder by investing in securities, such as stocks, bonds, or mutual funds.

Continuing the scenario from earlier, now consider that instead of keeping your grandparents' gift in a savings account, you decide to invest the funds in a group of conservative stocks that would earn 8 percent per year on average. When you reach 65, you would have over one million dollars—$1,172,973!

Investment Risk

Isn't investing too risky? As this example illustrates, when you invest money rather than save it in a bank, your money will have the potential to grow even more. **Investing** is using money to buy an asset where there is a chance of losing part or all of your initial investment. Investing and saving are fundamentally different because of the risk involved in each process. Savings has very little, if any, risk, whereas investing has some inherent risk. There is a direct relationship between risk and return for all securities, with the least risky investments offering the lowest amount of return and vice versa. This relationship is known as a **risk-return relationship**. ■ **FIGURE 16.1** shows the risk-return relationships of various investment vehicles. As you can see, the least risky investments offer the least amount of return. If reducing risk is a necessity, then you need to increase the amount of money you invest, increase the length of time to invest, or lower your expectations.

> **1** How do risk-return relationships, risk tolerance, and asset allocation relate to the fundamentals of investments?

Biz CHAT

I Can't Lose Money by Saving, Right?

It's much safer to simply save your money in a bank account than risk losing it in investments, right? Perhaps. But there are two forces beyond your control that you must consider: inflation and taxes. Even after diligent savings, there is still a distinct possibility that you might, over time, lose money due to the effects of inflation and taxes.

Let's say you saved $10 each month for three years in a savings account that earns 3 percent annually (although many savings accounts currently earn far less interest than this). If you didn't withdraw any money, at the end of the three-year period, you would have $377.15. That's pretty good considering that if you had just put the money away under your mattress, at the end of three years, you would have only $360. So, just by putting the money in a savings account, you have earned $17.15. Or have you? Unfortunately, you have to pay taxes on that $17.15. Assuming you're at a 15 percent

income tax bracket, you owe $2.57 to Uncle Sam, reducing your earnings to $14.57. Now, consider that inflation is running at a rate of about 2.5 percent per year. That means that for every dollar you have, you lose two and a half cents every year in buying power. Therefore, had you just put $360 under your mattress, after three years, because of inflation, it would be worth only $351.00 ($9.00 eroded due to loss of purchasing power). The money you have in savings also loses value due to inflation. After deductions for taxes and inflation, your savings would be worth only $365.21. The entire earnings your savings has generated is almost lost because of two things you have no control over: inflation and taxes. In fact, you're almost where you started, earning only $5.21 after three years of saving!

Although savings accounts help offset the effects of inflation, they do not help you build wealth. Savings accounts are great to keep as a "rainy day" account for those unexpected emergencies and short-term cash needs; however, if you are trying to save for a house, college tuition, or retirement, it would be very hard to meet your goals by investing in this type of low-interest account. To achieve big goals, you'll need to make your money work harder.

How do I know my risk tolerance? To determine whether investing is worth the risk, you must know how much risk you can tolerate. The less tolerant you are of risk, the fewer investment chances you can and should take. Most of us have a good idea of how tolerant we are toward risk. Your current behavior with money and other situations are indications of whether you are conservative, moderate, aggressive, or somewhere in between. There are also several tests that you can take online to help quantify your tolerance level. The bottom line to risk tolerance can be determined by answering this question: "Are my investments going to keep me awake at night with worry?" If the answer is "yes," then you need to reduce the risk level of your investments and perhaps lower your expectations accordingly. Over time, your tolerance to risk can change depending on your knowledge level and financial situation. As you become more secure financially, you might be willing to risk losing some money for the possibility of earning more. As you begin to learn more about investing, you may be more comfortable with evaluating some of the risks you will take, thus increasing your risk tolerance.

How do I start investing? Depending on how much money you have to invest, you might start investing by purchasing stock in one or two companies or by investing in a mutual fund. We'll discuss both investment alternatives in more detail later in the chapter. As you invest, you should keep in mind two strategies that help to minimize your risk: *diversification* and *asset allocation*. Both strategies center on the notion of not putting all your eggs in one basket to avoid the possibility of losing everything because of one bad investment.

What is diversification? **Diversification** is having a variety of investments in your portfolio, such as different types of companies in different industries. For example, assume you have $6,000 to invest. You have the option of putting all your money into one company that is strong and has great potential for long-term advancements. You also have the option to diversify your holdings and put $1,500 into four different companies, each in a different industry, and that are deemed great investments.

The first option may be great if the solitary company has unlimited success, but economic factors, consumer demand, competitive advancements, and management performance can combat a company's ability to make money. If you instead invest in several companies that are in different industries, you can insulate yourself from negative influences that affect one company or one industry. You still might experience a loss, but because it's most likely not from all four investments in your portfolio, the loss will not be as significant as it would if it were your only holding. Conventional wisdom, based on these ideas, supports diversification.

What is asset allocation? Similarly, **asset allocation** suggests that you structure your portfolio with different types of assets (stocks, bonds, mutual funds, real estate, etc.) to reduce the risks associated with these broad types of investments—mostly from inflation and changes in interest rates. Studies have shown that most of an investment portfolio's performance is determined by the allocation of its assets, not by individual investment selection or market timing.[1] In addition, asset allocation is important to minimize investment risk in the highly volatile markets that have been common since the new millennium. The allocation of assets in a portfolio depends on your risk tolerance and can change as an investor reaches certain milestones, such as getting married, paying for college tuition, or retiring. ■ **FIGURE 16.2** shows how risk tolerance affects the asset allocation mix in a portfolio.

Are there rules and regulations that govern investing? The Securities and Exchange Commission (SEC) is a U.S. federal agency created to protect investors and maintain a fair and orderly market. It governs the securities exchanges, the people who issue, trade, and deal securities, and those who offer investment advice. The SEC establishes regulations that govern how companies disclose information to the investing public. In addition, the SEC governs how investment information is disclosed to those creating the investment. In doing so, the SEC controls what should be put in the initial documentation (the prospectus) of an initial bond or stock issue.

■ **FIGURE 16.2**
Asset Allocation Mix Based on Risk Tolerance
Based on Your Time Horizon" Graph from "How do LifePath(R) Funds Work?" State Farm Insurance. http://www.statefarm.com/mutual-funds/life-path-funds/how-they-work.asp

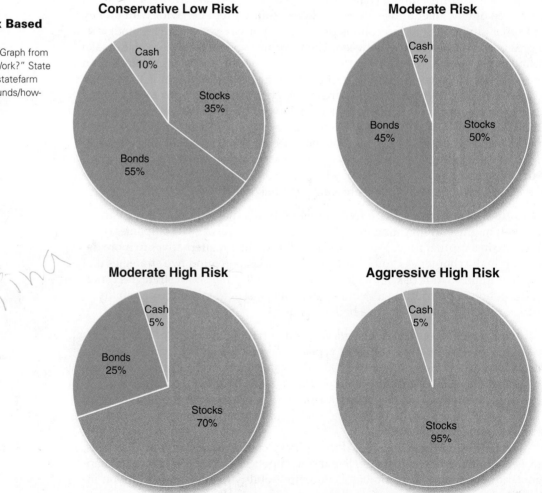

The Madoff Ponzi Scheme

OFF THE MARK

In late 2008, the securities industry was shaken by the incredible fraudulent activities of Bernard Madoff. Madoff, a former NASDAQ (National Association of Securities Dealers Automated Quotations) chairman, and founder of his own investment securities company, was found guilty of running the world's biggest Ponzi scheme. A Ponzi scheme is an illegal financial arrangement in which payments are made to current investors with monies obtained by newer investors. Eventually, the scheme collapses when there are not enough new investors to cover the needs of the current and former investors. Ponzi schemes are named after Charles Ponzi, who used this type of arrangement in the early twentieth century. Madoff's Ponzi scheme is by far the largest— amounting to losses of more than $50 billion.[2] The scam was able to run for many years due to the general increase in overall market gains, which made believable the extraordinarily steady returns the fund was reporting. In addition, Madoff continued to generate interest in his fund and attract new investors by creating a general aura of exclusivity. He often intentionally deferred would-be investors who were anxious to invest after hearing the enthusiastic word-of-mouth reports of financial gains by current investors.

Reports of the investment scam began nearly 10 years prior to Madoff's arrest, when Harry Markopolos informed the SEC of his concern over Madoff's possible illegal behavior. Markopolos had determined that Madoff's remarkable results were mathematically impossible to achieve. The SEC ignored the warnings, including several further attempts in subsequent years.

The fraud impacted thousands of victims who saw their entire life's savings disappear. The list is very diverse, including celebrities, such as talk show host Larry King, and many colleges, private foundations, large investment and money management firms, insurance companies, and not-for-profit organizations lost billions. The scheme also involved many foreign funds from Europe and Latin America.[3] Madoff is currently serving a 150-year prison sentence in a federal correctional facility.

In addition, the SEC prohibits fraudulent activity with regard to the offer, sale, and purchase of securities, such as insider trading. **Insider trading** is the buying and selling of securities based on information that has not been disclosed to the public. For example, suppose you own 1,000 shares of XYZ Corp. stock, and you're on friendly terms with the company's CFO. The CFO tells you the company is going to claim bankruptcy the next week, so you sell all your shares before the information is released so you won't lose your investment. If you do this, you have taken part in illegal insider trading.

One of the most high-profile insider trading cases of the past decade involved the domestic celebrity Martha Stewart. In 2001, Martha Stewart sold almost 4,000 shares of ImClone stock after receiving pertinent information about the company from her friend, ImClone's CEO. Stewart was convicted of insider trading and spent five months in prison and an additional five months under house arrest.

Although there are inherent risks when investing your money in stocks, bonds, or mutual funds, if the investments are within your risk tolerance level, and your portfolio is well diversified with good asset allocation, you can mitigate the risks and allow your money to work harder for you.

Lecretia Washington realizes that building wealth through investments is a process that takes a significant amount of time. She understands that the earlier she begins investing her money, the better. So what did she do? In addition to her traditional savings account, Lecretia decided that establishing separate investment accounts to meet her short-term goals and long-term goals was her best option. She also realized that she needed some professional help, so she is looking into hiring a financial advisor or a brokerage firm. What investment options would work best for you? You'll learn more about how to invest in the next section. ■

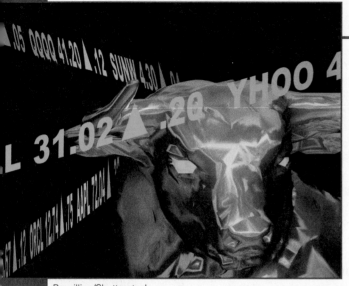

Raxxillion/Shutterstock

Investing in Stocks pp. 508–515

Gina Smith graduated from college last year. She has a great job in a city near to where she grew up, so she is able to live with her parents so she can save a lot of money. Now, after having worked for six months, Gina has accumulated over ten thousand dollars in her savings account, and she wants to do something different with it. She is not interested in buying a house or condominium in the near future and thinks she should invest in the stock market, but she doesn't know where to start. What kind of information should she look at to determine what is a good investment for her? ■

As you read in Chapter 15, companies sometimes issue stock to raise funds for corporate expansion. In this section, you'll learn about how stocks are initially issued, the differences between various types of stocks, how stocks are bought and sold, and the factors that affect stock prices.

2   How do companies issue stocks?

Primary and Secondary Security Markets

How are stocks issued into the primary market? Securities transactions take place in the **capital market**, an arena where companies and governments raise long-term funds by selling stocks and bonds and other securities. The **primary market** is the part of the capital market that deals specifically with new bond and stock issues.

The first sale of stock to the public by a company is called an **initial public offering (IPO)**. A **financial advisory firm** (often referred to as the *underwriter*) serves as an intermediary between a company issuing the stock and the investors who purchase the stock. Before the sale of the stock, the financial advisors prepare the required documents for filing with the SEC. A prospectus is one of the required documents. A **prospectus** is a formal legal document that provides details about an investment. The prospectus helps investors make informed decisions about a new investment. Financial advisors also establish the best timing for the public sale and determine the initial selling price. The advisory firm or bank, along with several other banks, forms a group or syndicate to underwrite the IPO; that is, they take the responsibility and risk of selling their allotment of the issue. The syndicate then purchases the stock and sells it to the public. It can take months or years to successfully structure a stock offering. Financial advisors use that time to generate interest and locate potential buyers for the stocks well ahead of the date of issuance, thus reducing their risk and ensuring the success of the initial issuance.

The initial buyers of an IPO are mostly large institutional buyers, such as insurance companies and large corporate pension plans, and a few high-profile individuals. The underwriters want to sell the issue as quickly as possible to receive a return on their purchase. Because institutional buyers are more likely to buy large quantities of the IPO, it is ultimately more efficient to sell to them than to sell the IPO in little pieces to individual investors. A very small portion of the IPO is actually available to individual investors, but since the quantity is limited, these shares are generally hard to get.

Tale of Two IPOs

ON TARGET

On August 19, 2004, Google sold shares to the public for the first time. At the time, many questioned whether the company was overvalued at $27 billion. Some felt that Google was overhyped, and were resigned to wait and see if the "scrappy" company could surpass its bigger and more established competitors (Yahoo! and Microsoft) and build a superior search engine. Fast forward to the present. Google's stock is above $650 per share, up significantly from the $85/share initial pricing. The company's market capitalization is $188 billion. It is now the biggest search engine company, having surpassed Yahoo! and Microsoft in 2005. It's probably safe to say that the "scrappy" company has done all that it set out to do, and the distraction of being a public company has done little to stop its growth and success. Although Facebook issued its IPO in early 2012, without nearly the skepticism that Google's IPO initially received, the stock was down over 50% within the first year. hat's the difference between the two initial offerings that caused such different reactions by investors?

How are stocks exchanged after they are issued in the secondary market? The **secondary market** refers to the market in which investors purchase securities from other investors rather than directly from an issuing company.

Investing in stocks requires extensive analysis to ensure that you're making the right decision. Stocks that have been on the market for a while are easier to analyze because you can examine their history. IPOs, by their very nature, have no historical information on which to base any analysis.

Types of Stocks

3 What are the different categories of stocks, and how are stocks traded?

Are all stocks the same? There are two main types of stocks that companies issue: *common* and *preferred*. **Common stock** is a class of ownership in which the stockholders have the right to elect a board of directors and vote on corporate policy. They are also entitled to a share of any dividends. A **dividend** is a distribution of a portion of the company's earnings, as determined by the board of directors. However, common stockholders have the least priority as far as ownership and repayment in the event a company goes out of business. **Preferred stock** is a class of ownership in which the preferred stockholders have a claim to assets before common stockholders if a firm goes out of business. In addition, preferred stockholders receive a fixed dividend that must be paid before the payment of any dividends to common stockholders. Preferred shareholders, however, do not have voting privileges.

Stocks can also be categorized based on the type of company and expected growth and return of the investment, as illustrated in ■ **FIGURE 16.3**:

- **Income stocks** are issued by companies that pay large dividends, such as utility companies like Duke Energy, Exelon Corporation, and Exxon Mobil Corporation. Investors who are looking for reliable income from their investments and not appreciation of share value invest in income stocks.

- **Blue chip stocks** are issued by companies that have a long history of consistent growth and stability. Blue chip companies pay regular dividends and maintain a reasonably steady share price. General Electric, IBM, The Walt Disney Company, and 3M are examples of companies that are considered blue chip stocks.

- **Growth stocks** are issued by companies that generate sustained positive cash flow, and have the expectation of revenues and earnings increasing at a faster rate than the average company. These stocks pay little or no dividends so that retained earnings can be reinvested in capital projects that fuel the growth.

■ **FIGURE 16.3**
Types of Stocks
Image Sources, left to right, top to bottom:
Ion Popa/Fotolia; AntonBalazh/Fotolia;
S.John/Fotolia; Kasse Kristensen/Fotolia;
Glacov Vladimir/Fotolia; zero13/Fotolia

Income stocks are issued by companies that pay large dividends, such as utility companies.

Blue chip stocks are issued by companies that have a long history of consistent growth and stability.

Growth stocks are issued by companies that are experiencing rapid growth and expansion.

Value stocks are priced less than what one would expect based on the company's earnings. A good stock at a great price.

Cyclical stocks are issued by companies that produce goods or services that are affected by economic trends.

Defensive stocks usually maintain their value regardless of the state of the economy.

Investment potential is through appreciation in stock value. Growth stocks tend to be riskier than other stocks because entrepreneurial companies do not have a proven track record. Apple, Costco, and Google can be considered growth stocks.

- **Value stocks** are those stocks that are viewed as being priced lower than what they should be based on the company's earnings and financial performance. These stocks have the potential to increase in share price when the market adjusts for the incorrect valuation. These stocks are generally contrasted with growth stocks.

- **Cyclical stocks** are issued by companies that produce goods or services that are affected by economic trends. The prices of these stocks tend to go down when the economy is failing (in a recessionary period) and go up when the economy is healthy. Examples of cyclical stocks include airlines, automobiles, home building, and travel.

- **Defensive stocks** are the opposite of cyclical stocks. Defensive stocks are issued by companies producing staples such as food, drugs, and insurance and usually maintain their value regardless of the state of the economy.

No one type of stock is considered better than another. Investors have to decide for themselves which type of stock fits best with their financial objectives.

How do I choose which stocks to invest in? The answer to this question begins with determining your *investment goals and objectives,* the *time* in which you have to achieve your goals and objectives, and your *risk tolerance,* as shown in ■ **FIGURE 16.4**. Once you know those constraints, you'll be better able to determine what investment strategy best fits your needs.

Many investors begin investing when they form their 401(k) retirement plan at work. This is a good way to start because the 401(k) portfolio manager has narrowed down your investment choices for you. Although there are plenty of professionals to help you, when you start investing on your own, you should research each potential investment for yourself. You should consider the basic stock fundamentals, economic condition, past performance, and published analyses, as described next:

- **Fundamentals.** You can start by evaluating a company's fundamental data, such as earnings, financial statements, and key ratios (discussed in Chapter 15).

■ **FIGURE 16.4**
Things to Consider Before Investing

Time Available to Achieve Goals

Investment Goals and Objectives

Risk Tolerance

- **Economy.** Being aware of current events in the news and changes in economic conditions that could influence a stock's price is also important.

- **Past performance.** Often it's helpful to know how a company and its stock have performed in the past. You can study financial charts to compare the historical performances of multiple companies and observe trends in the data.

- **Published analyses.** Additionally, you might want to consider the opinions of industry analysts who independently research and analyze the investment potential of companies.

All of this information is available in newspapers, on the Internet, or in your public library. Unfortunately, it takes lots of time and research to determine what the right investments are for you. Keep in mind that if the process were easy and straightforward, we'd all be rich! In reality, there is much variability and unpredictability in the market; even with the best analysis, you still might end up with unfavorable results. But, with time on your side, the chance of rebounding from a poor investment outcome is pretty good. Even though the stock market does fluctuate, it has been shown that the stock market has provided a consistent return over a long period of time.

Why is it important to set goals before investing? Assuming you can select companies that you believe will generate a profit based on your research and stock fundamentals, you also need to determine what kind of company meets your investment goals and objectives. Younger investors are investing toward long-term goals such as buying a house or funding a retirement account. Young couples may be investing to fund retirement or college accounts for their children. In these instances, investing in companies that are in their growth phase—where investment gains are made through rapid appreciation in stock value—may be the way to go. Although such companies are more likely to have higher appreciation than more stable companies, they're also more risky and more liable to quickly have their stock lose value, too. However, someone who is 22 and just starting his or her career can "afford" to withstand temporary downfalls.

Someone who is 55 may still be saving for retirement and can't endure the possibility of "starting over" if his portfolio does very poorly. This individual might have a mix of growth companies as well as more stable companies that have a strong history of slow but steady growth. These more stable companies generally do not experience wild swings in stock price and typically offer dividends to their stockholders. Lastly, older investors are investing to preserve their current positions with the intent of earning modest income to help fund their retirement years. Dividends provide another source of income to stockholders beyond appreciation in stock price. A person who is 70 years old, retired, and reliant on income from his or her investments can't afford to lose much money and is thus very risk averse. He or she would be wise to invest mostly in companies that offer high dividends and that will experience only mild swings in stock price. The world of investing is an ongoing experience; if you choose to invest, it is an experience that you should not take lightly. You must be smart about investing and continue to do your research—even if you choose to have someone else guide you in the investment process.

Where are stocks bought and sold? Before the Internet, people could buy stocks only with a **stockbroker** (or broker), a professional who buys and sells securities on behalf of investors. Brokers also provide advice as to which securities to buy and sell and receive a fee for their services. Now, because of the availability of the Internet and electronic trading, individuals have a choice of paying a broker or initiating transactions themselves for a small fee through discount brokers such as E*Trade or Scott Trade. Discount brokers offer limited advice and guidance and are substantially cheaper than financial services firms, such as Bank of America or JP Morgan, which are full-service brokers.

Whether you use a discount broker or full-service broker, the process of buying stock is done through a **stock exchange**, an organization that facilitates the exchange of stocks and other securities between brokers and traders. One of the largest and most dominant stock exchanges is the **New York Stock Exchange (NYSE)**. In 2007, the NYSE merged with the fully electronic stock exchange Euronext, and so is now operated by the combined organization **NYSE Euronext**. In 2008, NYSE Euronext acquired the American Stock Exchange (AMEX), which was formerly another independent U.S. stock exchange. Now, as a part of NYSE Euronext, the exchange deals exclusively with micro- and small-cap companies and is known as **NYSE Amex**. As a combined organization, NYSE Euronext is the global leader in trading, listing nearly 40 percent of the world's trading equities.[4] The **NASDAQ** is the world's second largest stock exchange.[5] It was the world's first electronic stock exchange. Some securities might be too small to meet the requirements to be traded on a formal exchange. Referred to as **over-the-counter (OTC) stocks**, these securities are traded directly between professionals.

How are stocks traded? There are two ways securities are traded: on the exchange floor and electronically. While most trades are done electronically, the process that is depicted in movies and television of a chaotic scene on the exchange floor still exists. A typical trade (purchase or sale of a security) with a broker on the NYSE exchange floor is similar to the process depicted in ■ **FIGURE 16.5**.

Thousands of companies have issued stock and are listed on the NYSE Euronext and NASDAQ exchanges, as well as on many other smaller or international stock

■ **FIGURE 16.5**

Execution of a Simple Stock Trade on the New York Stock Exchange

Image Sources, clockwise from top left: WavebreakmediaMicro/Fotolia; spaxiax/Fotolia; ene/Shutterstock exchanges.[6] Unlike the NYSE, where trades can be made electronically or on the trading floor, the NASDAQ stock exchange has always been completely electronic. Through the NASDAQ system, over two billion shares of stock trade hands every day via a large and immensely reliable coordinated network of computer systems.[7] Trades with the NYSE still require a broker to initiate the order. The broker will place the order electronically into the NASDAQ system, and when the order is received, the electronic exchange tries to match a buy order with a similar sell order. After the order has been executed, the broker notifies the buyer and seller of the successful completion of the trade. ■ **FIGURE 16.6** shows the steps involved with an electronic stock trade.

How is a broker selected? The process of selecting a broker can almost be as complicated as the process of selecting a type of investment. Before you decide on a broker, the SEC suggests you do the following:[8]

• Think about your financial objectives.

• Speak with potential brokers at several firms. Ask each about their education, investment experience, and professional background.

• Inquire about the history of the brokerage firm. You can find out if any disciplinary action has been taken against a firm or a broker online through NASD BrokerCheck. Your state securities regulator can also tell you if a broker is licensed to do business in your state.

• Understand how the brokers are paid. The type of commission a broker receives might affect the advice that is offered. Also, ask what fees or charges you will be required to pay on the account.

• Ask if a brokerage firm is a member of the Securities Investor Protection Corporation (SIPC). The SIPC gives limited customer protection if a firm goes bankrupt.

Although it is ideal to start investing as early as possible, do not rush into the process. Take the time to do the necessary assessment of your own financial goals and consider the risks you're willing to take to meet those goals.

Is investing in foreign companies possible? Investing is not limited to U.S. companies. Investing in foreign companies is a recommended strategy for increasing portfolio diversification and possibly obtaining higher returns. Because of increased communication abilities and the relaxation of legal barriers, investing in almost any foreign or international company is possible. There are a few ways to invest in foreign markets. Some stocks of foreign countries trade directly on the U.S. exchanges, or you can open an online stock brokerage account that allows international stock trading. Mutual funds and exchange traded funds, which will be discussed later in this chapter, are easier and less risky ways to add foreign investments to your portfolio.

Can I buy stocks if I don't have enough cash on hand? Sometimes investors are presented with a great investment opportunity but do not have enough cash on hand to buy the stock. In these cases, the stock can be bought with borrowed funds from a broker. This is referred to as *buying on margin*. Brokers usually use the value of other assets owned by the investor as collateral for the investment. Buying on margin is very risky and is subject to fairly rigid SEC regulations.

Changing Stock Prices

What causes stock prices to change? Stock prices can change rapidly. ■ **FIGURE 16.7** reflects the percent change in closing prices for Citigroup, Gap,

1. You log into your online brokerage account and see that Gap, Inc. is selling for $18.50/share.

2. You place an electronic order with the broker to buy 50 shares of Gap, Inc.

3. Broker receives the order and transmits it electronically to the stock exchange.

4. The order goes to the computer dedicated to handling all orders coming from your broker.

5. The stock exchange tries to match your order electronically with a sell order from someone else.

6. If a match is made, a notification is sent to your broker who then sends you a confirmation.

7. You receive and review the transaction confirmation.

■ **FIGURE 16.6**
Execution of an Electronic Stock Trade
Image Sources: top, iofoto/fotolia; bottom, Scanrail/fotolia

■ **FIGURE 16.7**
**Comparison of Stock
Performance**
Created using Yahoo! Charts with public
stock information on Yahoo! Finance

4 | What is stock performance, and what are the factors that lead to changes in stock price?

Inc., and Philip Morris over a two-year period. What is consistent among all four companies? Their stock prices change daily. There are many reasons why stock prices change, but ultimately it all comes down to the forces of supply and demand. If investors like a stock, they will buy more of it, reducing the supply and pushing up the price. On the other hand, if investors don't like a stock, more investors will sell the stock than buy it, creating a greater supply and causing the price to drop.

What influences investor behavior? There are many influences that causes an investor to favor a stock one day and oppose it another day. In general, most investors will invest if a stock's price reflects what they think a company is worth or will be worth. (Stock price times total number of shares outstanding determines a company's capitalization, or value.)

Often, investors look not only at how a company is currently performing but also consider a company's expected future growth in anticipation of increased earnings or profits. If investors become concerned that something negative will affect a company's value, they will sell their shares and the stock price will fall. For example, ■ **FIGURE 16.8** shows the overall decline in price value of Netflix, Inc. from mid July 2011 to late December 2011. The story of Netflix in 2011 illustrates

■ **FIGURE 16.8**
**Change in Price and
Volume of Netflix Stock
from February 2011 to
February 2012**
Created using Yahoo! Charts with public
stock information

how a company's stock can be affected by news. The company's stock was around $180/share in the beginning of 2011, with a small increase in the spring due to news of a growing subscriber base. Then, in mid-July 2011, Netflix announced that it was increasing the price of its combined renting and streaming services by 60 percent, and the stock price dropped 12 points. In September 2011, the company announced that it expected the third quarter subscription base to decline by nearly 1 million members. This earnings announcement, plus another announcement a week later that Netflix would be splitting the movie streaming business into a separate company named Qwikster, caused the stock to drop nearly 80 points. Later, in October the stock dropped another 35 percent when the company revealed the actual loss in subscribers was 800,000.[9] Notice in the figure how the stock price and the volume of shares traded reacted to these key events.

What else influences stock prices? Stock prices also change in reaction to broader news based on economic forecasts, industry or sector concerns, or global events. In general, financial markets have trends based on investor confidence. A **bull market** indicates increasing investor confidence as the market continues to increase in value. In a bull market, investors are motivated by promises of gains. A **bear market**, however, indicates decreasing investor confidence as the market continues to decline in value.

In addition, industry news can affect the performance of stocks in that industry.

How do you know how the overall market is doing? The *Standard and Poor's 500 Composite Index (S&P 500)*, the *DJIA*, and the *NASDAQ 100* are several benchmarks that indicate the overall health of the U.S. stock market. An **index** represents a collection of stocks based on certain shared characteristics, such as having a similar size, belonging to a common industry, or trading on the same market exchange.

- The *S&P 500* is an index of stocks of the 500 largest companies, most of which are American.
- The *DJIA* is an index of the 30 largest capitalized public companies in the United States. Whereas the DJIA composite index initially included only those companies that had some connection to heavy industry, today that characteristic is not as prevalent. The *S&P 500* and the *DJIA* are the two most widely watched stock indexes. They are important as they often reflect, and sometimes influence, the state of the U.S. economy.
- The *NASDAQ 100* includes 100 of the largest domestic and international non-financial companies listed on NASDAQ. The *NASDAQ 100* is distinguished from the *DJIA* and the *S&P 500* by not including financial institutions in the group and including companies incorporated outside the United States.

How do I make money investing in stocks? There are several ways to earn money investing in stocks. As noted earlier, one of these ways is by collecting dividends. Another way to make money in the stock market is to "buy low and sell high." In other words, you buy a stock at one price, wait for that stock to appreciate, and then sell the stock at the higher price. When this happens, the investor incurs a **capital gain**. If there is a decrease in value between the purchase price and the selling price, the investor incurs a **capital loss**.

Remember Gina Smith? When Gina was researching stocks, she reviewed various financial documents, such as income statements, as well as analyst reports, and company and industry news. When she found a few stocks she was interested in buying, she used a discount broker to help finalize her purchase. By keeping abreast of industry news and monitoring stock indexes, she's able to see how well her stock is doing relative to other stocks. Recently, the price of her portfolio has been going up, and she's hoping that when she sells a holding, it will be at a price higher than which she originally bought the stock. ■

THE List

10 Largest Single-Day Drops in Dow Jones Industrial Average

Rank	Date	Amount	Percent
1.	9/29/2008	$777.68	6.98%
2.	10/15/2008	$733.08	7.87%
3.	9/17/2001	$684.81	7.13%
4.	12/1/2008	$679.95	7.70%
5.	10/9/2008	$678.91	7.30%
6.	8/8/2011	$634.76	5.60%
7.	4/14/2000	$617.78	5.66%
8.	10/27/1997	$554.26	7.18%
9.	8/10/2011	$519.83	4.62%
10.	10/22/2008	$514.45	5.69%

Adapted from data at http://www.djaverages .com/?go=composite-milestones.

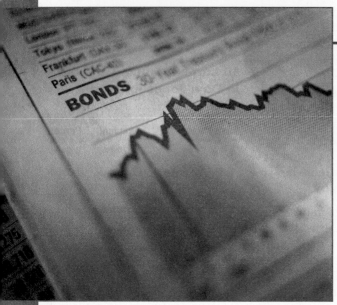

© 24BY36/Alamy

Investing in Bonds pp. 516–520

Dennis Sanchez just turned 55 years old and is starting to think about retirement. He has been investing money in his company's 401(k) plan for many years and wants to do some investing on his own. Now that he is closer to retirement, he would like to receive some income from his investments. He would also like to take a less risky approach to investing his funds by diversifying his portfolio allocation. Dennis decides investing in bonds is the best way to meet both of these goals. How does Dennis know what bonds will meet his financial objectives? ■

We have previously discussed that bonds are like IOUs. As a bond investor, you're lending money to a company for a specific period of time at a specified interest rate. The main reasons you purchase bonds are to add a stream of fixed income or to diversify your portfolio. Bond performance usually reacts counter to that of stocks. When the stock market is performing well, bonds are generally not performing well; conversely, when the stock market is down, bonds are usually up. Because of this contrary relationship, bonds provide great diversification to a stock portfolio. In this section, we'll talk about the different types of bonds and their characteristics, and we'll discuss the risk involved in investing in bonds.

Different Types of Bonds

 How do companies issue bonds?

How do companies issue bonds? If financial managers decide that bonds are the best financing option, they contact a financial advisory firm for expertise. Issuing bonds is a very complex financial and legal process that requires expert advice about the marketplace, the timing of the issue, the issuing price, the structure of the bonds, and other factors. Similar to the initial sale of stocks, a financial advisory firm coordinates the documentation preparation and filing with the SEC. They also consult with rating agencies that assess the issuer's creditworthiness. The resulting credit rating has an impact on the interest rate of the bonds. Financial advisors also help set the price for the bond issue and take the lead in forming and managing a group of financial advisory firms to underwrite, or purchase, the newly issued bonds.

In addition to a managing fee, financial advisors make their money by initially purchasing all the bonds at a discounted price and then quickly selling them to investors at a higher price.

What are the characteristics of a bond? Several characteristics define a bond: par (face) value, coupon (interest rate), maturity, and issuer.

- **Par (face) value** is the amount of money the bondholder will get back once a bond reaches maturity. Most newly issued bonds sell at par value. Treasury bills, discussed later in this section, sell for less than par (face) value.
- The **coupon** is the bond's interest rate. Coupons are a percentage of par (face) value, so a coupon of 10 percent on a bond with $1,000 par

value would generate $100 in interest a year. Although most bonds pay interest twice a year, some bonds offer monthly, quarterly, or annual payments. Originally, bonds had coupons that the investor would tear off and redeem to receive interest. Today, investors do not need to tear off coupons; instead interest payments are transferred electronically to the investor's account.

• The **maturity date** of a bond is the date on which the bond matures and the investor's principal is repaid. Short-term bonds (generally with a maturity of less than five years) have less variability and therefore a lower interest rate than long-term bonds.

Are there different types of bonds? As shown in ■ FIGURE 16.9, bonds are categorized primarily by the type of entity that is issuing the bonds:

• Corporate bonds
• Government bonds
• Municipal bonds

6 What are the different types of bonds, and how is bond risk evaluated?

What are corporate bonds? Corporate bonds are debt securities issued by corporations. There are several types of corporate bonds:

• **Secured bonds** are backed by collateral, which is generally corporate-owned property that will pass to the bondholders (or be sold to reimburse bondholders) if the issuer does not repay the amount borrowed. *Mortgage-backed securities* are special secured bonds that are backed by real property owned by a corporation.

• **Debenture bonds** are unsecured bonds, backed only by a corporation's promise to pay.

• Another modification of a traditional bond is a **convertible bond**, which gives a bondholder the right (but not the obligation) to convert the bond into a predetermined number of shares of the company's stock. Convertible bonds generally carry a lower interest rate because the investor will benefit from investing in the underlying stock.

What are government bonds? Government bonds are debt securities issued by national governments. They are the safest investment because the government backs them, and the risk of default is very low. Government bonds are divided into several categories based on their maturity:

Treasuries
• Deemed safest bonds available.

Treasury Bills
• Sold for terms less than one year. Sold at a discount, redeemed for par value at maturity.

Treasury Notes
• Sold in 5-, 10-, 30-year terms. U.S. mortgage rates often based off of the 10-year Treasury note.

Treasury Inflation-Protected Securities (TIPS)
• Sold in 5-, 10-, 30-year terms. Payments change with inflation.

Treasury Bonds
• Issued for 30-year terms. Pay interest semi-annually.

Municipal Bonds
• Issued by municipalities such as states, cities, and local governments. Sold to cover deficits or to fund specific projects. Investment income exempt from federal taxes.

Corporate Bonds
• Issued by companies. Ranges in degree of riskiness, though generally safer than owning corporate stock.

■ **FIGURE 16.9 Types of Bonds**
Source: http://www.mint.com/blog/investing/what-is-a-bond-02182011/?display=wide

- **Treasury bills** (or **T-bills**) are bonds that mature between 2 weeks and 26 weeks. Instead of paying interest, Treasury bills are sold at a discount, so you are paying less up front. When the bond matures, you receive the full face value of the bond. The difference between the purchase amount and the face value is the interest. For example, to buy a $1,000 T-bill, you might pay $975 up front. When the T-bill matures 26 weeks later, you would receive the face value of $1,000. The $25 difference is interest earned.

- **Treasury notes** (or **T-notes**) are bonds that mature in 2, 5, or 10 years. Interest is paid semiannually. You can hold Treasury notes to maturity, or you can sell them prior to their maturity. When a Treasury note matures, you receive the face value.

- **Treasury Inflation-Protected Securities (TIPS)** provide against inflation, as its name implies. The principal is adjusted to the Consumer Price Index so that when the CPI rises, the principal adjusts upward, and vice versa. Interest is paid semiannually. Although the interest rate remains constant, the interest payment adjusts as the rate is multiplied by the inflation-adjusted principal amount, thus providing the protection against inflation. TIPS are available in 5-, 10- and 30-year maturities.

Treasury bonds are bonds that mature in 30 years and pay interest semiannually. When a Treasury bond matures, you receive the face value.

U.S. Savings bonds are not able to be sold on the secondary market. They have traditionally been given as gifts to babies as a means to help finance education. Savings bonds are issued at face value, and as of January 1, 2012, can be purchased only electronically. There are two types of savings bonds:

- **Series EE bonds** have a 20-year maturity, but will pay interest up to a total of 30 years. Interest accumulates monthly and is paid when the holder redeems the bond.

- **Series I bonds** have an interest rate that is part fixed and part variable that is reset to the inflation rate (similar to TIPS).

What are municipal bonds? **Municipal bonds** (or *munis*) are bonds issued by state or local governments or governmental agencies. There are two varieties of municipal bonds: *general obligation bonds* and *revenue bonds*.

- **General obligation bonds** are supported by the taxing power of the issuer, so they tend to be very safe.

- **Revenue bonds** are supported by the income generated by the project they finance.

The U.S. Treasury debt has always been considered among the safest investments in the world—until August 5, 2011, when the financial rating agency Standard & Poor's downgraded the U.S. Treasury long-term debt from AAA to AA+. Treasury bonds, once indisputably seen as the safest security in the world, were rated lower than bonds issued by countries such as Britain, Germany, France, or Canada. The downgrade reflected S&P's growing concern that Washington's policy makers would not be able to agree to a plan to reduce the huge federal budget deficit. The immediate impact of the downgrade was that the S&P 500 stock index plunged on concerns that the U.S. economy may be heading into another recession, as well as because the European debt crisis has worsened. Typically, a downgrade would cause the interest rates of the debt to rise to compensate for the increased levels of risk. Even a small interest rate increase would have a dramatic impact on the interest payments the government already is making to the investors of Treasury securities. Additionally, at the time of the downgrade, financial experts expressed other concerns, such as the possibility of a "domino effect" of downgrades to state and local debt, a reduction of investments in the Treasury bonds, or even similar downgrades by the other rating agencies. However, to date, none of those concerns have materialized, and the downgrade has seemed to have little impact on investor confidence. In fact, the outlook for U.S. Treasury Bonds seems quite positive. Why do you think the U.S. Treasury offerings are seemingly immune to the effects of a downgrade?

For example, the New Jersey Turnpike Authority may issue $1 billion in municipal revenue bonds to finance the construction and renovation of the I-95 corridor that runs through the state. The tolls collected on that portion of I-95 would be used to pay the interest and principal of the bonds. The advantage of buying municipal bonds and government bonds is that the interest generated from many of them are exempt from federal income tax and, in many cases, state and local income taxes, as well.

What are serial bonds? Municipal bonds, as well as some corporate bonds, are often issued as serial bonds. **Serial bonds** have a series of dates on which portions of the total bond mature, unlike traditional bonds that are paid back to the investor all at once on one date (the *maturity date*). Serial bonds are advantageous to the issuer because they reduce the overall interest expense of the bond issue. Additionally, serial bonds allow the issuer to time the maturity dates to the income from the project financed by the bond proceeds. Thus, for the toll road example above, serial bonds may mature as phases of the toll road are completed and tolls from those portions of the road can be generated.

What are callable bonds? Most corporate and municipal bonds remain outstanding until their maturity date. With **callable bonds**, however, the issuer can either repay investors their initial investment at the maturity date or the issuer can choose to retire the issue early and repay investors at the "callable date." Issuers invoke the call option on callable bonds when interest rates have fallen and the bonds can be refinanced at a lower rate. To the investor, callable bonds present a degree of uncertainty and therefore carry a higher interest rate than similar noncallable bonds.

Are bonds a risky investment? Relative to stocks, bonds are viewed as a conservative investment for several reasons:

- The investor has a promise that his or her initial investment will be returned; stocks offer no such promise.
- The investor has a promise that he or she will receive periodic interest payments at a fixed rate; stocks may pay dividends, but are not obligated to.
- Historically, the bond market overall has been less volatile, thus less variability in the prices of bonds.

However, bonds are not entirely risk free, though some bonds are inherently less risky than others, and those carrying a higher risk will provide a higher return to the investor. There are different types of risk that affect bonds; some are listed in ■ FIGURE 16.10.

■ FIGURE 16.10
Types of Bond Risk

Credit Risk (Default Risk)
- Risk that a borrower will be unable to make interest or principal payments when they are due

Inflation Risk
- Risk that the effects of inflation will reduce the purchasing power of a bond investor's future interest payments and principal

Market Risk
- Similar to stocks, the risk that the effects of the whole market will reduce the value of a bond

Legislative Risk
- Risk that a change in tax code could affect the value of taxable or tax-exempt bonds

Liquidity Risk
- Risk that investors cannot find anyone to buy their bonds in the secondary market if the initial investor does not want to hold the bond to maturity

TABLE 16.1

Bond Rating Scales Used by Moody's and Standard & Poor's

Risk	Bond Rating	
	Moody's	Standard & Poor's
Lowest risk	Aaa	AAA
Low risk	Aa and A	AA and A
Medium risk	Baa	BBB
High risk	Ba and B	BB and B
Highest risk	Caa/Ca/C	CCC/CC/C
In default	C	D

Of all the risks outlined in Figure 16.10, *credit risk*, the risk associated with a bond issuer's ability to meet its financial obligations, can be better assessed at the time of purchase.

How can I tell how safe a bond is before investing? Before a bond is issued, the creditworthiness of the bond issue is evaluated by a rating agency, such as Moody's or Standard & Poor's, the two major rating agencies, and later assigned an investment grade. The higher the rating, the lower the credit risk, which lessens the likelihood of default (or not paying back the investor).

■ **TABLE 16.1** shows the bond rating scales used by both Moody's and Standard & Poor's. To improve their investment grade, many bonds are backed by insurance policies that guarantee repayment to the bondholders in the event the issuer goes into default. Those bonds with the lowest ratings—and the most risk—are known as **junk bonds**. Because of their high risk, junk bonds offer a high interest rate to attract investors. Investors should clearly understand the associated risks of junk bonds before adding them to their portfolios.

Do I have to hold a bond to maturity? Although you certainly can hold a bond to maturity, many investors sell bonds, especially long-term bonds, prior to maturity. Just like stocks, after they are issued, bonds are bought and sold on the secondary market. What makes buying bonds on the secondary market very complicated is that bonds do not trade at par value but at a price higher than par (at a premium) or lower than par (at a discount). Bond prices move in the opposite direction of interest rates. So, if you are trying to sell a bond that has a coupon of 10 percent and current market interest rates are 8 percent, your bond is worth more to investors, so the price of the bond will go up. Conversely, if current interest rates are 12 percent, then demand for your bond is not strong, forcing the price an investor is willing to pay to go down.

Although not completely riskless, bonds are a good investment if you are looking for a relatively conservative investment or a guaranteed stream of income. When it comes to investing in bonds, there are several things to keep in mind, such as the type of bond, the bond's risk rating, the face value of the bond, and the interest rate. Investors can determine a bond's risk based on an issuer's credit rating. One thing Dennis Sanchez could do before he purchases a bond is to review the issuer's credit rating. After doing the necessary research, Dennis would then be able to establish a diversified, less risky portfolio and receive some income. ■

Investing in Mutual Funds and Other Opportunities pp. 520–524

Alex and Keri Young recently got married and want to start saving and investing for a family, traveling, and emergencies. Unfortunately, after their wedding

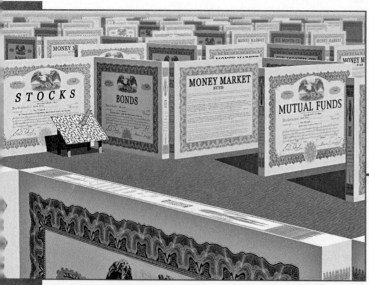

B.A.E./Alamy Images

and honeymoon expenses and buying a condo, they have only $3,000 left in their combined savings. Although Alex and Keri know they should have several different investments for a diversified portfolio, they feel they don't have enough money to do so, and they each have their opinions as to what kind of investments to make. Alex is especially interested in investing in foreign securities but doesn't know if they make sense for them nor specifically which ones to pick. Keri wants to invest in small up-and-coming U.S. companies, but doesn't know which would make the best investment. Fortunately, both Keri and Alex agree that until they know more about investing, they should use a broker or an investment advisor rather than trying to invest themselves. Where should they invest their money? ■

In this section, you'll read about different types of mutual funds, the pros and cons of investing in them, and other investment opportunities.

Mutual Funds

What is a mutual fund? A **mutual fund** is a means by which a group of investors pool money together to invest in a diversified set of investments. Let's say you wanted to invest in the stock market but, like Alex and Keri Young, you had only $3,000 to invest. After looking at possible investments, you realize that with $3,000, you could buy stock in one or two companies only. In talking to several of your friends who are also trying to invest small amounts of money, you realize that they are experiencing the same problem. Then, as a group, you decide to pool your money and hire an expert to buy a portfolio of stocks. With this arrangement, each of you shares a proportional amount of the investment returns, as well as the expenses for the investment advice and other costs of investing. If you were to do that, you would have essentially created a mutual fund.

> **7** What are the different types of mutual fund investments?

Why are mutual funds so popular? Mutual funds are the best kind of investment for those who have little to no experience in investing or who might not have a lot of money to invest. There are many reasons why you should consider investing in mutual funds:

- **Diversification.** The notable advantage to investing in mutual funds is diversification. Mutual funds offer small investors a cost-effective means of purchasing a diversified portfolio. Unless you have a lot of money to invest, it's hard to buy a large variety of securities. Remember, having a portfolio of various types of securities helps to reduce risk without significantly affecting returns.

- **Professional management.** Professional management is another advantage of mutual funds. Someone who has a significant amount of investment experience manages each mutual fund. Additionally, these professionals spend all their time researching, trading, and watching the investments that make up the fund. This is likely more time than you would be able to spend if you created a similar portfolio on your own. The fund managers have great incentive to make sure their funds perform at their best.

- **Liquidity.** It is very easy to buy and sell mutual funds, so you can get to your money quickly—usually within a day. Some mutual funds, primarily money market funds, offer check-writing privileges, so accessing your money is even easier.

- **Cost.** It takes as little as $1,000 to invest in most mutual funds. Some funds charge fees with their purchase or sale, though there are quite a few good "no-load" mutual funds that are virtually free of sales and marketing fees and other charges such as commission fees to enter a mutual fund.

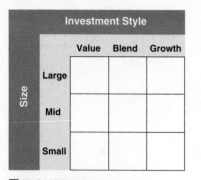

■ FIGURE 16.11
Types of Stock Mutual Funds

Are there different types of mutual funds? Each mutual fund has an investment objective that dictates the types of investments the fund can hold. There are three broad groupings of mutual funds, and then many different subtypes under each grouping. The three main types of mutual funds in order of risk are money market funds, fixed-income funds (bonds), and equity funds (stocks). Additionally, there is a wide assortment of funds that center on international investments, such as global funds, foreign funds, country-specific funds, or emerging market funds. There are also sector funds that invest in companies from a particular industry sector, such as technology, automotive, banking, and health care. Lastly, there are index funds that replicate the performance of some broad market indexes such as the S&P 500 and Dow Jones Industrial Average.

What are money market funds? **Money market funds** are the least risky because they invest in short-term debt obligations, such as Treasury bills and certificates of deposit (CDs). Money market funds are popular because the interest rate is often nearly double that of "regular" interest-bearing checking or savings accounts. In addition, money market funds are very liquid so you have quick access to your money, often simply by writing a check. Perhaps the only drawback of a money market fund over a traditional savings account is that the FDIC does not insure the funds. However, unlike many banks, to date, no money market fund has ever failed. Alternatively, you can invest in a *money market savings account* through a savings bank, and, as with all bank accounts, the money in that account is insured by the FDIC up to $250,000.

What are bond mutual funds? **Bond mutual funds** consist solely of bonds. Some bond funds are categorized by the type of bond, including municipal bond funds, corporate bond funds, and U.S. government bond funds. Alternatively, some bond funds are categorized by maturity, including long-term bond funds, short-term bond funds, and intermediate-term bond funds. **■ TABLE 16.2** summarizes the various types of bond mutual funds.

Are there different types of stock mutual funds? Stock mutual funds, sometimes referred to as **equity funds**, are much more popular than bond or money market funds.[10] Similar to bond funds, stock mutual funds are broken down into various categories as reflected in **■ FIGURE 16.11.**

Some stock funds invest in stocks with a particular strategy in mind, such as growth funds, value funds, and blend funds. Another popular breakdown of stock funds are those that invest in companies defined by their capitalization (cap) or size, such as large-cap funds, mid-cap funds, and small-cap funds. **■ TABLE 16.3** summarizes the various types of stock mutual funds.

How do I make money investing in mutual funds? You can make money investing in mutual funds through dividends, interest, capital gains, and fund

■ TABLE 16.2

Types of Bond Mutual Funds

	Fund Type	Investment Strategy
By Type	Municipal bond funds	Invest in tax-exempt bonds issued by state and local governments. Some municipal bond funds are further specialized in bonds issued by a particular state.
	Corporate bond funds	Invest in debt obligations from U.S. corporations.
	U.S. government bond funds	Invest in U.S. Treasury or government securities.
By Term	Short-term bond funds	Invest in bonds with maturities less than 2 years, including Treasury bills, CDs, and commercial paper.
	Intermediate-term bond funds	Invest in bonds with maturities ranging between 2 and 10 years.
	Long-term bond funds	Invest in bonds with maturities greater than 10 years.

■ **TABLE 16.3**

Stock Mutual Funds

	Fund Type	Investment Strategy
Strategy Types	Growth funds	Invest in stocks of the fastest-growing companies. Often viewed as risky investments. Rarely produce dividend income.
	Value funds	Invest in stocks that are considered to be undervalued. These stocks are thought to be ready for quick appreciation. Some produce dividends.
	Blend (or balanced) funds	Invest in both growth and value companies.
By Size	Large-cap funds	Invest in companies with large (greater than $9 billion) capitalization (price times outstanding shares).
	Medium-cap funds	Invest in companies of medium capitalization—between $1 billion and $9 billion.
	Small-cap funds	Invest in companies with capitalization less than $1 billion. These companies rarely generate dividends.

appreciation. These investment earnings are similar to those generated by individual stock holdings, although they are controlled by the fund manager and distributed to the fund owners periodically. As fund managers adjust the holdings of the fund, they buy some securities and sell others. Capital gains and losses that are incurred through selling securities are passed on to the fund owners. Your mutual fund accumulates any dividends paid by the stocks and interest paid by the bonds held by the mutual fund and periodically distributes the earnings to fund owners. Lastly, mutual funds are measured by the value of the individual holdings. This measure is the **net asset value (NAV)**, which is calculated at the end of each trading day. The end-of-day NAV is the new value of each share of the mutual fund. The NAV increases as the securities held by the fund increase in value. If you sell your mutual fund holding at a higher NAV than when you bought it, you will generate a profit.

What do I need to watch out for when investing in mutual funds?
Although mutual funds are often deemed a great beginner investor's investment because of the advantages listed earlier, like any investment, you still need to do your homework before investing. Some mutual funds, referred to as **load funds**, have additional costs (loads) that are rolled into the overall package to cover marketing and other fund expenses. The ultimate decision in buying a mutual fund should be based on its expected performance and the suitability to your investments needs. If you are given a choice of similar options, try to pick a **no-load fund**, a mutual fund that has little or no additional costs. Load funds have not shown to perform better than no-load funds, so why pay more for little or no extra benefit? It's also important to have a good understanding about who is managing the fund and their success record. The same individual or group of managers often runs a fund for years. However, changes happen, so you want to watch out for that. A change in management could quickly make historical fund performance statistics (what you might be using to evaluate a fund's performance before you buy) less significant.

What are exchange-traded funds? Exchange-traded funds (ETFs) are a pool
of stocks like a mutual fund, but they trade like stocks on the exchange, so their price fluctuates throughout the trading day. Prices of ETFs change throughout the day as they are bought and sold, whereas mutual funds are traded only at the end of the trading day. ETFs incur a fee from a broker; however, the fee is typically lower than mutual fund fees. This makes ETFs a low-cost way to diversify a portfolio as there are a variety of ETFs, similar to the varieties of mutual funds.

8   **What are other investment opportunities besides stocks, bonds, and mutual funds?**

Other Investment Opportunities

Besides stocks, bonds, and mutual funds, what else can I invest in? There are a couple of other types of investments beyond stocks, bonds, and mutual funds. These investments are often complicated and can carry additional risk. Generally only advanced and knowledgeable investors tinker in these alternative investments. *Options* and *futures* fall into this category, as do *commodities, real estate,* and *precious metals.*

What is an option? An **option** is a contract that gives a buyer the right (but not an obligation) to buy (call) or sell (put) a particular security at a specific price on or before a certain date. It's similar to buying an insurance policy. Consider this example: Your uncle is selling a car that you would love to buy but can't quite afford yet. You decide to approach your uncle with a proposal. You would save your money, and at the end of three months, you would have the right to buy the car for $15,000. For accepting this offer, you will give your uncle $250 now. Over the course of the next three months, one of three situations could occur:

1. The car could be ranked one of the best cars on the market, increasing its value from $15,000 to $18,000. You buy the car for the agreed-upon price of $15,000 and then sell the car for $18,000. Taking into consideration the price of the option, you net $2,750 ($18,000 − $15,000 − $250).

2. You find out that a massive recall was just placed on the car. Something to do with the transmission. Now, you really don't want to buy the car. Because you have only an option to buy the car, you're not obligated to purchase the recalled vehicle, but you still lose the $250 for the option.

3. The car value stays at $15,000 and you buy the car for the agreed-upon price of $15,000, plus the initial $250.

Options work similarly in that you aren't buying the underlying asset (in our example, the underlying asset is a car; in reality, it would be a stock). Instead you're paying for the opportunity to buy the asset under certain conditions. If things go wrong, you lose only the cost of the option. If things go right, you could profit. Options are complicated and can be risky. Don't confuse option contracts with stock options your employer may offer as a benefit. The stock option that employers offer gives you the right to buy a specific number of shares of your company's stock at a specific time at a set price. Stock options are used as incentives to retain and motivate employees and were discussed in Chapter 9.

What are futures? A **futures contract** is an agreement between a buyer and a seller to receive (or deliver) an asset sometime in the future at a specific price agreed on today. Usually the underlying asset is a commodity, such as sugar, coffee, or wheat. For these commodities, a price is agreed on before harvest, when the actual goods are bought and sold. Futures markets also include the buying and selling of government bonds, foreign currencies, or stock market indexes. Most holders of futures contracts rarely hold their contracts to expiration. If you hold the futures contract until it expires, you own the commodity. Instead, the contract is traded prior to expiration. If the price of the commodity increases before the contract's expiration date, you make a profit. However, if the price decreases, you may lose money. The difference between a futures contract and an options contract is that an option gives you the *right* to purchase the underlying asset; with a futures contract, you have an *obligation* to purchase the underlying asset.

Alex and Keri Young were glad to learn about mutual funds. Mutual funds allow them to use the limited savings they have and get the diversity they are looking for. There are still things about mutual funds that the couple is unsure about, such as which types of funds will work best for them, so they will continue to take their time, and perhaps consult an investment advisor, before making any final decision. ■

CHAPTER 16
SUMMARY

MyBizLab

Go to **mybizlab.com** to complete the problems marked with this icon ⭐.

1 **How do risk-return relationships, risk tolerance, and asset allocation relate to the fundamentals of investments?** (pp. 504–506)

- Various types of investments have different **risk-return relationships** (p. 504). On one hand, the least risky investments offer the least amount of return. On the other hand, the most risky investments offer the greatest return.

- Investing is not for everyone, and the level and type of investments is very personal and depends on the investor's risk tolerance level.

- Investment portfolios should be allocated or spread out among different types of investments, such as stocks, bonds, and cash, to further reduce investment risk. **Asset allocation** (p. 506) changes as investors reach life milestones; portfolios should be adjusted and rebalanced periodically.

2 **How do companies issue stocks?** (pp. 508–509)

- Stocks are issued in this manner:
  - The first issue of stock is an **initial public offering (IPO)** (p. 508).
  - A financial advisor coordinates the preparation of a **prospectus** (p. 508) and files it with the **Securities and Exchange Commission (SEC)** (p. 506).
  - Financial advisors also establish the best timing for the public sale and determine the initial selling price.
  - Banks form a syndicate to underwrite the IPO. The syndicate then purchases the stock and sells it back to the public.

3 **What are the different categories of stocks, and how are stocks traded?** (pp. 509–513)

- There are two main types of stocks that companies issue: **common** and **preferred** (p. 509). Stocks can be categorized into five categories: **income stocks, blue chip stocks, growth stocks, cyclical stocks**, and **defensive stocks** (pp. 509–510).

- Stocks are purchased through a **stockbroker** (p. 511) who buys and sells stocks on behalf of investors. Brokers also provide advice and receive a fee for their services.

- Stock transactions occur through a **stock exchange** (p. 512) like the **New York Stock Exchange** (**NYSE**) (p. 512) or **NASDAQ** (p. 512).

4 **What is stock performance, and what are the factors that lead to changes in stock price?** (pp. 514–515)

- Stock performance is directly related to changes in stock price.

- Stock prices change in reaction to supply and demand. Other factors that can affect stock prices include economic forecasts, industry or sector concerns, or global events. Stocks also tend to move together as a market. If the market is trending positively, it is a **bull market** (p. 515). A declining market is a **bear market** (p. 515).

5 **How do companies issue bonds?** (p. 516)

- Bonds are issued in the same manner as stock, with a few slight differences:
  - The company's financial manager contacts a financial advisor for advice.
  - Financial advisors prepare documents with the SEC. They also help to set the price of the bond issue and take the lead in forming the group of banks that initially buy the bonds.
  - Financial advisors and bankers generate interest and locate potential buyers for the bonds before issuance.
  - A **financial advisory firm** (p. 508) initially purchases all the bonds at a discount and then quickly sells them in the **primary market** (p. 508) at a higher price.

6 **What are the different types of bonds, and how is bond risk evaluated?** (pp. 517–520)

- Bonds are characterized by their **par** (**face**) **value** (p. 516), which is the money the bondholder will get back once a bond reaches maturity. Most bonds sell at par value. Bonds are also characterized by the **coupon** (p. 516), or interest rate, and **maturity date** (p. 517).

- Bonds are not risk free. The creditworthiness of the issuer is the main factor affecting a bond's risk.

- There are two issuers of bonds: governments and corporations.
  - **Corporate bonds** (p. 517) are issued by corporations and hold the greatest amount of risk. **Secured bonds** (p. 517) are backed by collateral, and **debenture bonds** (p. 517) are unsecured and backed only by a promise to pay.

- **Government bonds** (p. 517) are issued by national governments and are the safest investment.
- **Municipal bonds** (p. 518) are issued by state and local municipalities.

 What are the different types of mutual fund investments? (pp. 521–523)

- **Mutual funds** (p. 521) are popular investments because they provide diversification and professional management. Mutual funds are extremely liquid and fairly cost efficient.
- **Load funds** (p. 523) have additional costs to cover marketing and other fund expenses, whereas **no-load funds** (p. 523) have little or no additional costs.
- **Money market funds** (p. 522) invest in short-term debt obligations. The interest rate for these funds is often nearly double that of "regular" interest-bearing checking or savings accounts. In addition, money market accounts provide check-writing privileges so you have quick access to the money.
- **Bond mutual funds** (p. 522) consist solely of bonds. They can be categorized by the type of bond (municipal bond funds, corporate bond funds, or U.S. government bond funds). Alternatively, some bond funds are categorized by maturity (long-term, short-term, or intermediate-term bond funds).
- **Equity funds** (p. 522) are categorized by investment strategy, such as growth funds, value funds, and blend (or balanced) funds. These funds are also categorized by size of the companies in which they invest, such as large-cap funds, medium-cap funds, and small-cap funds.

8 **What are other investment opportunities besides stocks, bonds, and mutual funds?** (p. 524)

- An **option** (p. 524) is a contract that gives a buyer the right (but not the obligation) to buy or sell a security at a specific price on or before a certain date. Options are complicated and therefore quite risky.
- **Futures contracts** (p. 524) are agreements between a buyer and a seller to receive (or deliver) an asset sometime in the future but at a specific price that is agreed on today.

Key Terms

asset allocation   (p. 506)
bear market   (p. 515)
blue chip stock   (p. 509)
bond mutual fund   (p. 522)
bull market   (p. 515)
callable bond   (p. 519)
capital gain   (p. 515)
capital loss   (p. 515)
capital market   (p. 508)
common stock   (p. 509)
compound interest   (p. 503)
convertible bond   (p. 517)
corporate bond   (p. 517)
coupon   (p. 516)
cyclical stock   (p. 510)
debenture bond   (p. 517)
defensive stock   (p. 510)
diversification   (p. 505)
dividend   (p. 509)
exchange-traded funds (ETFs)   (p. 523)
financial advisory firm   (p. 508)
futures contract   (p. 524)
general obligation bond   (p. 518)

government bond   (p. 517)
growth stock   (p. 509)
income stock   (p. 509)
index   (p. 515)
initial public offering (IPO)   (p. 508)
insider trading   (p. 507)
investing   (p. 504)
junk bond   (p. 520)
load fund   (p. 523)
maturity date   (p. 517)
money market fund   (p. 522)
municipal bond   (p. 518)
mutual fund   (p. 521)
NASDAQ   (p. 512)
net asset value (NAV)   (p. 523)
New York Stock Exchange (NYSE)   (p. 512)
NYSE Euronext   (p. 512)
NYSE Amex   (p. 512)
no-load fund   (p. 523)
option   (p. 524)
over-the-counter (OTC) stock   (p. 512)
par (face) value   (p. 516)

preferred stock   (p. 509)
primary market   (p. 508)
prospectus   (p. 508)
revenue bond   (p. 518)
risk-return relationship   (p. 504)
secondary market   (p. 509)
secured bond   (p. 517)
Securities and Exchange Commission (SEC)   (p. 506)
serial bond   (p. 519)
Series EE bond   (p. 518)
Series I bond   (p. 518)
stockbroker   (p. 511)
stock exchange   (p. 512)
stock mutual fund (equity fund) (p. 522)
Treasury bill (T-bill)   (p. 518)
Treasury bond   (p. 518)
Treasury Inflation-Protected Securities (TIPS)   (p. 518)
Treasury note (T-note)   (p. 518)
U.S. Savings Bond   (p. 518)
value stock   (p. 510)

Self-Test

Multiple Choice   You can find the answers on the last page of this book.

1. Mason recently bought a $1,000 Government bond with a 3.5% interest rate. For the first two years, his semiannual interest payments were $175, $175, $200, $200. What kind of government bond would Mason most likely have purchased?
   a. Treasury bill
   b. Treasury note
   c. TIPS
   d. Treasury bond

2. Which of the following could cause a stock price to change for Sunny Orange Growers, Inc.?
   a. More investors dislike the stock and sell it than those who like the stock and buy it.
   b. An unexpected freeze ruins the Florida orange crop for the year.
   c. The government establishes a tax incentive for all U.S. agricultural companies that will help boost net income.
   d. All of the above

3. What document must companies prepare and make available to investors when issuing stocks?
   a. A prospectus
   b. An initial public offering
   c. Proprietary underwriting
   d. Investor guideline sheets

4. Tracy Quinn feels she has a great investment portfolio. She has investments in technology stocks, banking stocks, consumer goods stocks, and foreign stock mutual funds. Which best reflects her investment strategy?
   a. Portfolio diversification
   b. Asset allocation
   c. Both A and B
   d. Neither A nor B

5. Jose Fernandez is saving toward retirement and has an investment portfolio that is reflective of Jose's risk tolerance. It was carefully put together by a trusted investment advisor. Unfortunately, the returns on the portfolio are not projected to generate the type of savings Jose desires. What should Jose do?
   a. Invest in riskier stocks that have a higher return.
   b. Lower his retirement expectations.
   c. Increase his risk tolerance.
   d. Change employers.

6. When interest earnings are added to principal and continue to earn interest, this is known as
   a. mutual fund earnings.
   b. capital gains.
   c. compound interest.
   d. net asset value.

7. Which of the following describes a security issued by a local government agency?
   a. Acme, Inc. debenture bond
   b. Souderton County Water Authority bond
   c. Treasury bond
   d. Fidelity bond fund

8. If you owned a $10,000 bond that had a coupon of 4.5 percent and paid interest semiannually, how much interest would you receive?
   a. $450 every six months
   b. $225 every six months
   c. $4,500 once a year
   d. $2,250 once a year

9. Which is *not* an advantage of investing in mutual funds?
   a. Mutual funds are less risky than investing in stocks or bonds.
   b. Mutual funds provide immediate diversification.
   c. Mutual fund investments are managed by a professional.
   d. All of the above

10. Which describes a pool of stocks traded on the stock exchange throughout the day?
    a. A mutual fund
    b. An ETF
    c. Futures contracts
    d. A stock option

Self-Test (continued)

True/False You can find the answers on the last page of this book.

1. A person's risk tolerance might change with more investment knowledge or greater wealth.
   ☐ True or ☐ False

2. Five years ago, Jerome bought 100 shares of Kodak at $40 per share. Last month, he sold the 100 shares at $55 per share. Jerome has a capital loss from the sale.
   ☐ True or ☐ False

3. Short-term government bonds are considered low-risk investments.
   ☐ True or ☐ False

4. Common stockholders get paid before preferred stockholders if a firm goes out of business.
   ☐ True or ☐ False

5. Because mutual funds are professionally managed, you do not need to worry about which mutual fund you invest in.
   ☐ True or ☐ False

Critical Thinking Questions

⭐ 1. Before investing, you should determine your risk level. How would you define risk tolerance? What, if anything, might change your risk tolerance?

2. Discuss your life goals and how much time you have to accomplish the goals. What kind of savings and investment strategy might you need to pursue to ensure that you meet your goals?

⭐ 3. The term *blue chip* applies to stocks issued by a company in excellent financial standing with a record of producing earnings and paying dividends. Stocks in companies such as GE and Chrysler were initially considered blue chip stocks. Today, stocks in companies that were not in existence when the term was coined, such as Intel and Walmart, are considered blue chip stocks. What other companies might you consider blue chip stocks and why?

Team Time

TAKE THIS $50,000 AND INVEST IT!

Assemble in teams of four or five students. Suppose your team is given a theoretical $50,000 that you need to invest. Your team must assemble a portfolio by selecting a minimum of five investments but no more than ten investments. The portfolios should be well diversified and include different types of assets or stocks from different industries or sectors.

Process

Step 1. Your team should fill out the following charts as you conduct your research:

Name of Investment	Type of Investment	Industry/Sector

Name of Investment	Purchase Price	# Shares	Initial Value	% of Total Portfolio

Step 2. Your team should prepare a presentation outlining your investment choices. The presentation should include reasons why you included each investment choice in the portfolio. In addition, the presentation should discuss the diversification strategies you took.

Step 3. Optional ongoing exercise. Teams should monitor their portfolios on a weekly basis. At the end of the specified period of time, teams should determine which team portfolio has the highest value.

Ethics and Corporate Social Responsibility

CAN INVESTMENTS BE SOCIALLY RESPONSIBLE *AND* LUCRATIVE?

Socially responsible investing describes an investment strategy that invests in companies that offer the potential for maximized gains and businesses that favor practices that are environmentally responsible, support workplace diversity, and increase product safety and quality. Some socially responsible investments also avoid businesses involved in alcohol, tobacco, gambling, weapons, other military industries, and/or abortion.

Process

Step 1. On your own or with a partner, research several individual companies and mutual funds that would qualify as socially responsible investments.

Step 2. In one to two paragraphs, comment on whether this type of investment strategy is a sound investment strategy.

Web Exercises

1. **Tracking an IPO**
   Go to the MSN Money website and find a company that recently created an IPO. Research the method of IPO allocation the company used and track its performance from the day the company went public until now. How have the stock prices changed? Was it a good decision to go public?

2. **Getting the Most for Your Savings**
   At this stage in your life, putting your money in a savings account may be the most you can do. Savings rates are at historically low levels, so it is even more important that you find the most advantageous interest rate for your savings account. Go to Bankrate.com, where you can search and compare interest rates on checking and savings accounts in your local area and nationally. What is the best rate you can find in your local area? How does that compare to nationally available rates?

3. **Dogs of the Dow**
   Several investment strategies help investors select stocks. Dogs of the Dow is one of the most publicized strategies.

   Research Dogs of the Dow and describe the strategy. Would this be a good investment strategy for you?

4. **Dollar Cost Averaging**
   It is very difficult to perfectly time your investments so that you purchase when a stock is at its lowest point or sell when a stock is at its highest point. Research the investment strategy of dollar cost averaging. In a paragraph, describe what this strategy is, why it is used, and the advantages and disadvantages it has over other investment strategies.

5. **Municipal Bonds: Paving Roads and Building Schools**
   Municipal bonds are issued by local and state governments and other municipal organizations, such as school districts and toll road authorities. Conduct online research to determine the municipal bonds that the state in which you live has issued. What was the purpose behind the bond issues?

MyBizLab

Go to **mybizlab.com** for Auto-graded writing questions as well as the following Assisted-graded writing questions:

16-1. Facebook finally entered the public market in 2012. Mark Zuckerberg, Facebook's CEO, was reluctant to enter the public market, stating that he wanted his employees to focus on making great products, not the stock price.[11] What does he mean by that?

16-2. Mutual funds often compare their performance to that of the S&P 500 with the goal of "beating" it. Is this a fair comparison? Why or why not?

16-3. MyBizLab Only – comprehensive writing assignment for this chapter.

Personal Finance

Garry L./Fotolia

People often associate discussing personal finances with calamity—trying to cover expenses after losing a job or managing a household because of an illness or becoming unable to work because of an injury. But personal finance is a set of decisions that lets people achieve their dreams and goals—owning a home, affording college for their children, and so on.

You should begin to think seriously about your personal finances when you get your first job, if not earlier. It is most prudent to begin personal finance management from the day you receive your first allowance! The sooner you think seriously about personal finance, the easier it is to direct your earnings toward achieving your goals in life.

When an individual or a family applies financial principles in managing the ways money is budgeted, saved, invested, preserved for future life events, and protected against risks, it's called **personal finance**. In its simplest form, personal finance is about setting goals, making choices, and following through. Ultimately, as shown in ■ **FIGURE 1**, you need to have a plan for reducing expenses and increasing income and assets so they begin to work for you. **Money management** is a key component of personal finance and generally includes the following:

- Determining what you have
- Setting goals for what you want or need
- Planning how to achieve your goals

There are several different aspects to effective money management. We begin by exploring how to create a financial plan.

Do You Need Tools to Help Manage Your Money?

Many online resources and software tools can help you manage your money. A spreadsheet program, such as Microsoft Excel, can handle simple financial worksheets and budgets, and Intuit's Quicken is a popular software tool that offers more features specifically tailored to money-management capabilities. Many websites, such as Mint.com and MoneyStrands.com, also offer free online tools to help you track and manage your finances.

■ **FIGURE 1**
Basic Personal Finance
Adapted from Peter Milner, "Personal Finance 101: An Introduction." From Plan Your Escape.com http://www.planyourescape.ca/personal-finance-101-an-introduction-11

Creating a Financial Plan

Let's walk through the steps involved in creating a financial plan.

Step 1: Take a Financial Inventory

The first thing you need to do when beginning a financial plan is to *take a financial inventory*. List everything of value that you own (your assets) and then subtract from that total everything that you owe in loans and credit card balances. These are your liabilities. The remaining amount is your net worth. As shown in ■ **TABLE 1**, determining your net worth is similar to a company preparing a balance sheet; it is just arranged somewhat differently. If you're young and just starting out, there might not be much to write down at first. But it's still a useful exercise. As time passes, you'll have more to add to this statement. The discipline and practice of recording where you are, even if done only once per year, will help you become more able to define your goals.

Step 2: Set Financial Goals

Next you can begin to *set financial goals*. These can be both short-term and long-term goals. Short-term goals should be measurable and realistic to complete in a time frame of less than a year, such as, "I need to replace my car next year." Long-term goals can be more motivational, such as, "I would like to have $250,000 in investment assets before I turn 40." Now break down the long-term goals into smaller, more manageable short-term goals. This increases the chance of achieving the long-term goals. For example, "I would like to have $250,000 in investment assets before I turn 40" could be broken down as follows: "I would like to save $5,000 each year and invest it in a money market fund that's earning 8 percent interest."

Finally, prioritize your goals by identifying them as wants and needs. Organize needs above wants and short-term goals above long-term goals. Assign short-term needs (buying a new car) as a top priority and long-term wants (a swimming pool in the backyard) as a lower priority. Choose goals that you're excited about and are determined to see come to fruition. Write these goals down in a place that you can refer to periodically to remind yourself of what you're working toward.

■ TABLE 1

Net Worth Worksheet

Assets: What You Own	Value
Cash	
Savings	
Checking account	
Certificates of deposit (CDs)	
Investments	
Mutual funds	
Stocks	
Bonds	
Retirement accounts (IRA, 401[k], pension)	
Automobile	
Personal property (electronics, jewelry, etc.)	
Cash value life insurance	
Real estate (owned)	
Total Assets	
Liabilities: What You Owe	**Value**
Student loan(s)	
Automobile loan(s)	
Credit card balance(s)	
Other loans	
Mortgage balance	
Other	
Total Liabilities	
Total Net Worth = Total Assets − Total Liabilities	

Step 3: Know Where Your Money Goes

You've figured out what you have and what you owe, and you've set financial goals. Now you need to know what you're currently spending. To start, list all the expenses you incur in a month, similar to the list shown in ■ **TABLE 2**. It's easy to figure out the *fixed expenses*—expenditures that don't change from month to month, such as rent and car payments. The harder part is tracking *variable expenses*—monthly payments you have to make that may change from month to month. Gas, food, clothing, entertainment, utility, and cell phone charges are variable expenses.

You'll also need to include *periodic expenses*—items such as taxes or donations that you make but not on a monthly basis. Also, note the category of *unexpected expenses* in Table 2. Although you can't determine the exact amount to fill in for this category—will you get a speeding ticket this year?—it is important to remember that the unexpected can happen any time, and when it does, it can throw a monkey wrench into the best-laid plans unless modestly planned for.

■ TABLE 2

Monthly Expenses

Fixed Expenses	Amount	Need or Want?
Housing (mortgage/rent)		
Car payment		
Insurance premiums (health, car, renter's)		
Internet/cable/cell phone		
Savings		
Other		
Variable Expenses	**Amount**	**Need or Want?**
Electricity		
Gas/heating/oil		
Water		
Phone		
Food		
Gas		
Transportation (bus or subway fare)		
Child care		
Clothing		
Entertainment		
Other		
Periodic Expenses	**Amount**	**Need or Want?**
Taxes		
Donations		
Union/professional dues		
Unexpected Expenses	**Amount**	**Need or Want?**
Car/home repairs		
Speeding tickets		
Medical bills		
Other		

As you create your list, you may need to track "invisible" expenses—items you don't realize you buy, such as daily lattes, chips from the vending machine, or gadgets for your car. The best way to determine your invisible expenses is to create a "penny journal" that tracks your daily spending habits to the last penny. The penny journal will also help you define your variable expenses. As you continue to work with your plan, you'll be able to refine these numbers, as well as establish limits for some of the expenses.

Analyze the penny journal and expense list and identify the expenses you must cover (fixed expenses) and those that you might be able to cut back on (variable and invisible expenses). Now you're ready to develop a budget.

Step 4: Create a Budget

A budget, or a spending plan, tells you where money goes each month. The budget should be realistic in terms of the expenses you must pay. It should also include savings as a regular fixed expense. Every month, whether you think you can afford to or not, *you need to pay yourself first*. Don't fall into the trap of depositing into your savings account whatever is left over. Instead, make a conscious effort to pay yourself. Initially, your savings should accumulate so that you have a "rainy day fund" that is equal to at least one month's worth of bills. Eventually, this fund should be built up to cover three to six months of fixed expenses. This fund will cover your expenses should the unexpected happen, such as a job loss or an injury. Once you've established a rainy day fund, your savings should go into an interest-bearing account—whether it is a certificate of deposit (CD), a money market fund, a mutual fund, or stocks and bonds.

Many financial planning experts suggest setting aside at least 10 percent of every paycheck. No matter what, you should not miss making the payment to yourself. The secret to success is not so much the amount of money you save, but the persistence with which you do it.

So You Want to Be a Millionaire?

Which of the following individuals will save enough to be a millionaire by the time he or she is 60 years old?

  a. A 10-year-old who puts $25 in the bank every week for 50 years

  b. A 22-year-old who puts $68 in the bank every week for 38 years

  c. A 40-year-old who puts $370 in the bank every week for 20 years

  d. All of the above

If you chose *d,* you're right—all of these individuals with the prescribed savings plans will become millionaires before they reach 60. Notice the difference time makes in the amount each individual must contribute. The longer you have to save, the less you need to set aside. Similarly, if payment periods were less frequent (monthly instead of weekly), you would need to deposit larger amounts. The 22-year-old, for example, would need to set aside $300 (= 4 × $75) every month instead of $68 every week. What makes the difference? Compound interest. **Compound interest** is interest that is earned not only on principal but also on any interest earned previously. In a savings account, as long as you leave your money in the account and don't take out the interest you've earned, you'll benefit from the compounding effect. The moral of the story is to start saving early, save often, and don't withdraw the interest earnings!

Step 5: Execute the Plan

Tracking your expenses and setting up a budget can be tedious and time-consuming. Software packages are available to help you, such as the one shown in ■ **FIGURE 2**. The real challenge is sticking to your plan, which requires discipline and perseverance. Just cutting out one cup of designer coffee a week saves over $200 a year. Here are a few other tips for plugging leaks in your budget:

• **Pay off all unpaid credit card debt.** Carrying a balance on your credit cards is financial suicide. Most credit card companies charge more than 18 percent on unpaid balances. Therefore, pay down your credit card debt before depositing money into a savings or investment account. Also, pay your credit card bill on time. Late fees are a waste of money!

Monthly Budget

	Projected Monthly	Actual Monthly
Income 1		$4,000
Income 2	$1,300	$1,300
Extra income	$300	$300
Total monthly income	**$5,600**	**$5,600**

Total Projected Cost	Total Actual Cost	Total Difference
$1,195	$1,236	($41)
Projected balance (Projected income minus projected costs)	**Actual balance** (Actual income minus actual costs)	**Difference** (Actual minus projected)
$4,405	$4,364	($41)

Housing	Projected Cost	Actual Cost	Difference
Mortgage or rent	$1,000	$1,000	$0
Phone	$54	$100	($46)
Electricity	$44	$56	($12)
Gas	$22	$28	($6)
Water and sewer	$8	$8	$0
Cable	$34	$34	$0
Waste removal	$10	$10	$0
Maintenance or repairs	$23	$0	$23
Supplies	$0	$0	$0
Other	$0	$0	$0
Subtotals	$1,195	$1,236	($41)

Transportation	Projected Cost	Actual Cost	Difference
Vehicle 1 payment			$0
Vehicle 2 payment			$0
Bus/taxi fare			$0
Insurance			$0
Licensing			$0
Fuel			$0
Maintenance			$0
Other			$0
Subtotals	$0	$0	$0

Insurance	Projected Cost	Actual Cost	Difference
Home			$0
Health			$0
Life			$0
Other			$0
Subtotals	$0	$0	$0

Food	Projected Cost	Actual Cost	Difference
Groceries			$0
Dining out			$0
Other			$0
Subtotals	$0	$0	$0

Savings or Investments	Projected Cost	Actual Cost	Difference
Retirement account			$0
Investment account			$0
College			$0
Other			$0
Subtotals	$0	$0	$0

Personal Care	Projected Cost	Actual Cost	Difference
Medical			$0
Hair/nails			$0
Clothing			$0
Dry cleaning			$0
Health club			$0
Organization dues or fees			$0
Other			$0
Subtotals	$0	$0	$0

Loans	Projected Cost	Actual Cost	Difference
Personal			$0
Student			$0
Credit card			$0
Credit card			$0
Other			$0
Subtotals	$0	$0	$0

Children	Projected Cost	Actual Cost	Difference
Medical			$0
Clothing			$0
School tuition			$0
School supplies			$0
Organization dues of fees			$0
Lunch money			$0
Child care			$0
Toys/games			$0
Other			$0
Subtotals	$0	$0	$0

Taxes	Projected Cost	Actual Cost	Difference
Federal			$0
State			$0
Local			$0
Other			$0
Subtotals	$0	$0	$0

Gifts and Donations	Projected Cost	Actual Cost	Difference
Charity 1			$0
Charity 2			$0
Charity 3			$0
Subtotals	$0	$0	$0

Legal	Projected Cost	Actual Cost	Difference
Attorney			$0
Alimony			$0
Other			$0
Subtotals	$0	$0	$0

Pets	Projected Cost	Actual Cost	Difference
Food			$0
Medical			$0
Grooming			$0
Toys			$0
Other			$0
Subtotals	$0	$0	$0

Entertainment	Projected Cost	Actual Cost	Difference
Video/DVD			$0
CDs			$0
Movies			$0
Concerts			$0
Sporting events			$0
Live theater			$0
Other			$0
Subtotals	$0	$0	$0

■ **FIGURE 2**
Sample Budget Template
Budget templates like this one can help you set up your spending plan.

- **If you have outstanding loans, see if you can reduce the interest rate or consolidate into a more manageable payment.** Call your bank and ask! You might be surprised at the response you get.
- **To reduce impulse buying, try using cash only.** When you use cash instead of credit, you immediately see the effects of your spending.

Step 6: Monitor and Assess Your Plan

Revisit your plan periodically and make adjustments as necessary. Look at your budget every month and make adjustments every year.

Managing Personal Credit

Credit is your ability to buy things now and pay for them later. When used responsibly, credit cards can be good things. Showing future lenders that you have a good history with credit will help you when you apply for car loans or a mortgage. But abusing credit can quickly add up to serious problems. Consider this: It might not take you very long to accumulate $3,000 on your credit card, but it will take you nearly 15 years paying $50 a month to pay it off completely! And that's if you never charge another cent! Here are a few tips to help you manage your personal credit.

iceteastock/Fotolia

Using credit cards wisely can help you secure a car or home loan later down the road. However, reckless spending with credit cards can lead to financial disaster.

Tip #1: Check the Interest Rate and the Annual Fee.

Credit is not free, so check the fine print on your credit card contract. Even if the initial offer is a zero or very low percentage interest rate, that interest rate will change when the promotional period ends. Make sure you understand what the new interest rate will be. Also try to find a credit card company that does not charge an annual fee. If there is an annual fee, call to find out if the issuing company will waive it. Be sure to carefully evaluate credit cards that offer airline miles or other incentives. Often, these cards charge higher interest rates and annual fees.

Tip #2: Don't Charge If You Can't Pay.

Don't look at your credit card as a means of financial freedom. If you can't afford to pay cash for an item, then don't use a credit card. Think of a credit card as a short-term loan that needs to be paid back in 30 days or less. To use credit wisely, pay off the balance in full every month. Doing so allows you to keep your money earning interest longer (assuming you have an interest-bearing checking or savings account), thus making your money work for you. Some cards are beginning to encourage on-time payments. Discover's Motiva card, for example, pays you back for paying on time. Plus, like other Discover cards, it gives you a cash-back bonus on your purchases.

Tip #3: Establish a Credit History in Another Way.

Although establishing a good credit history is important, you don't need to begin with a national credit card if you feel the temptation is too great to charge more than you can afford. Another way to establish credit is to begin with a single store credit card or a single-purpose credit card, such as a gas card. Using these cards responsibly by making occasional purchases and paying your bill in full every month demonstrates your ability to use credit wisely.

Know Your Credit Score

If you've been using credit, then you've established a credit record. Lenders convert your credit history into a numeric score that they use when qualifying an applicant for a loan. There is no absolute number that guarantees your chances of qualifying for credit or lower interest rates, but a higher score is better. You can find out your number by obtaining a credit report from one of the three credit bureaus: Equifax, Experian, and TransUnion. Every individual is entitled to one free credit report each year from each bureau. Go to the Annual Credit Report website for more information. If possible, several months before applying for a big loan, obtain your credit report to make sure all the information listed is accurate. If there are errors in your credit report (which occasionally happen), you will have some time to fix them.

Car Considerations

Having a car is a top financial priority for many people. Let's look at the financial decisions and considerations involved in owning a car.

Getting Wheels

Whether you're replacing your current car or are buying one for the first time, you'll need to make several decisions. The first is whether you're buying a new car or a used car. New cars have warranties, so the manufacturer covers virtually all repairs. However, the value of a new car depreciates 20–30 percent almost as soon as you

■ TABLE 3

Buying Versus Leasing a Car

Buying a Car	Leasing a Car
Pay for the entire cost of car.	Pay for only a portion of the car's cost.
You need to make a down payment and pay sales tax on the entire cost of the car.	You sometimes have the option to not make a down payment and pay the sales tax on your monthly payments.
You make the first loan payment a month after you buy the car.	You make the first lease payment when you sign the contract.
When you sell the car, it's at the depreciated value. Your outstanding loan obligation may be more than the depreciated value.	When you terminate the lease, you may either return the vehicle or purchase it for its depreciated value.
There are no use restrictions on mileage and no specified maintenance requirements.	Usually there are mileage restrictions (12,000 miles a year) and maintenance requirements. Turning the car in with stained carpets, dents, and dings brings on extra fees. Going over the mileage limit will mean paying extra fees.

drive the car off the dealer's lot.[1] Your car loan might already be more than the car is worth before there are even 50 miles showing on the odometer! Used cars have depreciated already, so your loan is probably less and closer to the current value of the car. Don't forget that you'll need to pay for maintenance (whether the car is used or new), and depending on the age and condition of the car, the maintenance might be costly. Consider buying a "new used car," which is a car that is only a few years old, has been well maintained, and has low mileage. Sometimes, initial warranties extend to used cars, as well. In many ways a new used car is like new, although you have not had to pay for the immediate depreciation.

If you decide to get a new car, you have another decision: to buy or lease. ■ **TABLE 3** outlines some of the considerations in buying or leasing a new car. Many people lease cars because they can get a more expensive car for less up-front cash. However, if you finance a car with a loan, at the end of the loan, you still own your car. If you continue to drive that car, you then have the money you used to spend on the loan payments to put to other uses, such as paying off debt.

Buying a car requires that you make a number of decisions.

Insurance and Investments

Taking care of yourself now and in the future constitutes another area of financial planning. Buying insurance and making investments are two ways you can accomplish these goals.

Insuring Your Present and Your Future

When something goes wrong, you need help to cover the costs so you can recover quickly. Fortunately, insurance is available for a variety of risks so you don't have to bear the burden of covering these costs alone.

1. **Health insurance.** Health insurance is a must. No matter how healthy you are today, a serious illness or an injury, plus

Monkey Business/Fotolia

any rehabilitation expenses, can be astronomically expensive. If your employer offers health insurance coverage, take it. You might have to contribute some of the cost yourself, but it's well worth it. If you're self-employed, unemployed, or not covered by your employer, investigate what affordable options you have for coverage. If you are even a part-time student, you might be eligible for a college subsidized group health plan. If you are self-employed, you may qualify for a group plan through associations and organizations you have joined.

2. **Disability insurance.** Disability insurance pays you benefits should you become disabled and are no longer able to earn a living. Many employers offer disability insurance coverage along with their health insurance coverage. If yours does not, determine how your expenses would be met should something permanently disabling happen.

3. **Car insurance.** Most states require car insurance. There are three types of car insurance coverage: liability, collision, and comprehensive. *Liability* covers damage or injury you have caused to someone else. You should always have liability coverage. *Collision* covers damage to your vehicle from a collision with a moving or stationary object. *Comprehensive* covers damage to your car from theft, fire, or other non–collision-related accidents. If you're insuring an older car, it might not be worth carrying the cost of collision and comprehensive coverage.

4. **Homeowner's and renter's insurance.** These types of insurance protect your home and the contents inside. Homeowner's insurance also has liability coverage to protect you if someone is injured while on your property. If you have a mortgage on your home, the bank usually requires insurance. Many landlords require their tenants to demonstrate proof that they have renter's insurance. If your landlord does not, still consider it because it is affordable and will protect your assets in cases of fire or theft.

5. **Life insurance.** Life insurance helps replace income lost due to your death to those who are dependent on you, such as a spouse, children, parents, or other family members. When you purchase a life insurance policy, you name the person(s) who receive your life insurance benefits as your beneficiaries. Some types of life insurance policies can act as long-term savings plans, whereas other types are strictly for protection. You might not need life insurance if you're single, with no one depending on you or your income, or if you're married, without children, and your spouse is capable of working.

Consulting an insurance professional will help you determine your needs for many types of insurance. It pays to shop around and compare rates. Often, you can receive discounts if you carry several types of insurance (such as homeowner's and automobile) with the same company. Moreover, you should review and compare your rates every few years to make sure the rates you are paying are still competitive and your coverage is adequate.

Insurance policies cover natural disasters to varying degrees. Make sure you read the fine print so you know exactly what is protected in your insurance plan.

Mary Hobbs/Alamy

Investing Now and for the Future

Investing your money is not without risk, although there are strategies you can pursue to help reduce these risks. Learning as much as you can about the various investment opportunities that are available to you is a useful part of your financial planning. As we discussed in Chapter 16, many types of investments exist. As you begin to build up your savings, you might choose to invest your savings in CDs or money market accounts. As your knowledge of and comfort level with investments increase, and your amount of discretionary income builds, you might consider investing in mutual funds, stocks, or bonds.

How Fast Can Your Investment Double in Value?

The **rule of 72** is an easy way to figure out how long it will take to double your money at a given interest rate. All you have to do is divide the investment's interest rate into 72. For example, if you want to know how long it will take to double your money at 6 percent interest, divide 6 into 72 and get 12 years. The rule of 72 works well as long as the interest rate is less than 20 percent. You can also use the rule of 72 to determine the interest rate needed to double your money in a certain amount of time. If you wanted to double your money in three years, you would divide 3 into 72. Now you know you would need an interest rate of about 24 percent.[2]

Investing for Retirement

At this point in your life, retirement probably seems a very long way off. Unfortunately, Social Security is no longer something you can rely on to fully meet your financial needs after you retire. Therefore, it is very important that you take responsibility for planning to meet your financial needs during retirement. It's best to accumulate savings for retirement by starting early and investing regularly, but other mechanisms are available to help. If you work, your employer may have a retirement plan that you can join. If you're self-employed or your employer does not offer retirement benefits, you can set up your own retirement program. Funds specifically designated for retirement, such as Individual Retirement Accounts (IRAs), Roth IRAs, and 401(k) programs, offer tax advantages to encourage you to save for retirement.

Individual Retirement Accounts

Individual retirement accounts (IRAs) are special savings accounts created by the government. The benefit of putting your retirement savings into an IRA is that you put pretax money into an IRA, thus reducing your current taxable income. You don't pay tax on money in the account until after you have retired and withdrawn the money. (The idea here is that after you retire, you will be in a lower income tax bracket and pay less tax.) You cannot begin to withdraw money without penalty from your IRA until after you have reached the age of $59\frac{1}{2}$. You must begin to withdraw from your IRA when you are $70\frac{1}{2}$. Despite these restrictions, you should strongly consider contributing the maximum amount you are allowed every year.

Roth IRAs

A **Roth IRA** is another type of retirement account, but it differs from a traditional IRA in several ways. Contributions to a Roth IRA are not made with pretax dollars. However, withdrawals are usually tax free, and there are fewer restrictions on when and how you can withdraw your money. Roth IRAs are restricted to individuals whose income falls below a certain level specified by guidelines established by the IRS.

Pension Plans

Pension plans are retirement plans established by your employer. There are two kinds of pension plans: defined benefit and defined contribution. In the past, most companies offered **defined benefit plans** in which you were paid a certain percentage of your salary after you had retired. To qualify, you had to work for the company for a certain amount of time. The problem with defined benefit plans is that the companies bore the risk and responsibility of having sufficient funds to meet their pension obligations.

When this became too difficult and costly, many companies switched to offering defined contribution plans. **Defined contribution plans** are the most common retirement benefit offered today. In this type of plan, your employer contributes a percentage of each paycheck that you have specified into your account. To encourage you to contribute to the plan, many companies will match your investment—in essence giving you money when you save. The money in your account is invested for you in stocks, bonds, mutual funds, annuities, or company stock. You often have the opportunity to select the investments from a menu of choices and direct the proportion of your contributions going into each investment. Should you change jobs or leave a company before you retire, you may rollover the proceeds of your defined contribution plan into your new plan or an IRA.

401(k), 403(b), and 457 Plans

These plans are forms of defined contribution plans. For-profit companies offer 401(k) plans, non-for-profit organizations offer 403(b) plans, and government entities offer the 457 plan. (The numbers of the plans refer to the sections in the federal tax law that authorizes the plans.)

Taxes

Everyone who earns income is required to file an income tax return. Even if you owe no taxes, you must file a return. Failure to do so will result in fines and penalties. When you get your paycheck, an estimate of the taxes you owe has already been taken out. Your tax return calculates the exact amount you owe. If not enough has been deducted from your paycheck, you pay the remainder of what you owe when you file your return. If you have had too much deducted from your paycheck, the IRS will refund the difference.

The IRS offers every taxpayer a standard deduction that reduces the amount of taxable income. You have a choice to either take this standard deduction or itemize your own deductions. Deductions include interest paid on mortgages, contributions to a tax-deferred retirement plan, contributions to charity, and a certain amount of medical expenses, to name a few. You should itemize your deductions if they're greater than the standard deduction. Generally, if you don't own your own home, you're better off taking the standard deduction. In addition, completing the tax return is much easier when you take the standard deduction!

How Much Tax Are You Paying?

Income taxes are computed on a marginal tax rate. This means that tax rates progressively increase as your income increases, and the tax rate applies to only the income in each bracket range. Remember that not all income is taxable income. Standard deductions and personal exemptions can be subtracted from what you make. These will vary depending on your personal situation. ■ **TABLE 4** summarizes the tax rates for single people.

If you want to know your tax bill, you can quickly estimate with these formulas. Try out an interactive website like MoneyChimp.com to show you the detailed calculation for your salary.

Knowing your tax bracket is important in financial planning to determine how much tax you might pay on extra income you earn or, conversely, how much tax you will save by increasing your deductions.

TABLE 4

Personal Income Tax Rates[3]

If Taxable Income Is at Least . . .	But Not More Than . . .	Your Highest Tax Rate Is
$ 0	$ 8,700	10%
$ 8,700	$ 35,350	15%
$ 35,350	$ 85,650	25%
$ 85,650	$178,650	28%
$178,650	$388,350	33%
$388,350	No limit	35%

Managing your personal finances may sound tedious and time-consuming, but it has rewards. Remember the following tips:

- Set your financial goals.
- Make a plan to achieve these goals and stick to it.
- Pay yourself first, start early, and pay often.
- Use debt wisely and establish good credit.
- Make sure you and your assets are insured.

Soon enough you'll be on the road to financial success.

Business Plan Project Appendix

Part 1. Introduction

Business Name
What is the name of your business?

Hint: When choosing a name for your business, make sure it captures the spirit of the business you're creating. Also refer to the BizChat in Chapter 5 for tips on naming your business.

Description of Business
What will your business do?

Hint: Imagine that you're explaining your business to a family member or a friend. It should be easy to explain, using 30 words or less.

Form of Business Ownership
What form of business ownership (sole proprietorship, partnership, LLC, or corporation) will your business take? Why did you choose this form?

Hint: For more information on forms of business ownership, refer to Chapter 6.

Ideal Customers
Describe your ideal customers. What are they like in terms of age, income level, and so on?

Hint: You don't have to go into too much detail in this part of the plan; you'll provide more details about customers and marketing in later parts. For now, simply outline the kind of customers your product or service will best fit.

Company Advantages
Why will customers choose to buy from your business instead of your competition?

Hint: Describe what will be unique about your business. For example, is your product special, will customer service be exceptional, or will your price be lower?

Part 2. The Company and Management Team

THE MISSION STATEMENT

Mission Statement
Write a brief mission statement for your business.

Hint: Refer to the discussion of mission statements in Chapter 7. Be sure to include how you will stand out from your competition and why customers will buy from you.

Ethical Issues

All businesses must deal with ethical issues. One way to address these issues is to create a code of ethics. List three core (unchanging) principles that your business will follow.

Hint: To help you consider the ethical issues your business might face, refer to Chapter 3.

Social Responsibility

A business shows social responsibility by respecting all its stakeholders. What steps will you take to create a socially responsible business?

Hint: To help you consider the issues of social responsibility, refer to the discussion in Chapter 3. Consider how you may need to be socially responsible toward your customers and, if applicable, investors, employees, and suppliers.

INDUSTRY PROFILE

Industry Description

Describe the industry and sector in which your company operates.

Hint: Industries are broad categories, such as financial, technology, services, or health care. Sectors are more specific categories within an industry, such as a sporting goods store in the services industry or computer peripherals in the technology industry. In your description of the industry and sector, discuss economic trends as well as the current outlook for the industry, including growth potential.

Opportunities and Threats

Describe the opportunities and threats that face your company.

Hint: For this section, refer to the discussion of the economy in Chapter 2. Consider external factors, such as macroeconomic matters, technological changes, legislation, and sociocultural changes that may affect the industry as well as your company. This typically is done as part of a SWOT analysis, which is discussed in Chapter 7.

COMPANY PROFILE AND STRATEGY

Business Goals

What are three business goals you want to achieve in the first year? What are two intermediate to long-term goals you want to achieve in the next three to five years?

Hint: Refer to the discussion of goal setting in Chapter 7. Be as specific and realistic as possible with the goals you set. Remember the SMARTER acronym; goals should be specific, measurable, acceptable, realistic, timely, extending, and rewarding. For example, if you are selling a service, how many customers do you want by the end of the first year and how much do you want each customer to spend? If you are selling a good, what volume of sales do you hope to achieve?

Company Strengths

Describe the strengths of your company.

Hint: In evaluating a company's strengths, analyze its internal resources, including finances, human resources, marketing, operations, and technological resources. A company's strength might be its strong marketing department or a favorable location.

Raw Materials and Supplies
Explain what raw materials and supplies you will need to run your business. How will you produce your good? What equipment do you need? What hours will you operate?

Hint: Refer to Chapter 11 for information to get you started.

ANTICIPATED CHALLENGES AND PLANNED RESPONSES

Anticipated Challenges
Describe any weaknesses or potential challenges that face your company.

Hint: Consider any potential vulnerability from the competition, problems with suppliers or resources, or any legal factors that might affect the business, such as pending lawsuits or patent or copyright issues.

Planned Responses
Describe any plans you have to address these weaknesses and anticipated challenges.

Hint: Consider any resources your company can make available to address these challenges.

THE MANAGEMENT TEAM

Management
Who are the key individuals that will manage the business?

Hint: Refer to the discussion of managers in Chapter 7. Think about how *many levels* of management as well as what *kinds* of managers your business needs. In addition, outline how each manager's contribution will positively impact the business. What is it about that particular manager that will help the business succeed?

Organization Chart
Show how the "team" fits together by creating a simple organizational chart for your business. Make sure the organizational chart indicates who will work for each manager as well as each person's job title.

Hint: Most businesses start quite small. However, as you create your organizational chart, consider what your business will look like in the future. What different tasks are involved in the business? Who will each person report to in the organizational structure? Refer to the discussions of organizational structure in Chapters 6 and 7 for information to get you started.

Part 3. Marketing

MARKET ANALYSIS

Market Research
Describe your target market in terms of age, education level, income, and other demographic variables.

Hint: Refer to Chapter 12 for more information on the aspects of target marketing and market segmentation that you may want to consider. Be as detailed as possible about who you think your customers will be.

Assessment of the Competition
Describe three companies that you see as your main competitors.

Hint: For each company, describe the company's perceived strengths and weaknesses. How do you intend to take advantage of each weakness and respond to each strength?

THE PRODUCT OR SERVICE

Product Features and Benefits
Describe the features and benefits of your product or service.

Hint: As you learned in Chapter 13, a product has tangible and intangible benefits that create a *total product offer*. Describe your product on three levels, as outlined in Chapter 13—the *core product* (What basic needs or wants does this product or service satisfy?), the *actual product* (What are the tangible aspects of the product that you can taste, see, smell, touch, and hear?), and the *augmented product* (What are the perceived benefits that provide additional value to a customer's purchase?).

Product Differentiation
How will you make your product(s) stand out in the crowd?

Hint: There are many ways to stand out in the crowd, such as a unique product, outstanding service, or a great location. What makes your product special? Does it fill an unmet need in the marketplace? How will you differentiate your product to make sure that it succeeds?

Pricing
What pricing strategy will you choose for your product(s), and why did you choose this strategy?

Hint: Refer to Chapter 13 for more information on pricing strategies and tactics. Because your business is new, so is the product. Therefore, you will probably want to choose between price skimming and penetration pricing. Which will you choose and why?

SALES AND PROMOTION

Place (Distribution) Issues
Where will customers find your product or service? (That is, what distribution channels should you consider?)

Hint: If your business will sell its product directly to consumers, what types of stores will sell your product? If your product will be sold to another business, which channel of distribution will you use? Refer to Chapter 14 for more information on aspects of distribution you may want to consider.

Advertising
How will you advertise to your target market? Why have you chosen these forms of advertisement?

Hint: Marketers use several different advertising media—specific communication devices for carrying a seller's message to potential customers; each form has advantages and drawbacks. Refer to Chapter 14 for a discussion of the types of advertising media you may wish to consider.

Promotions
What other methods of promotion will you use and why?

Hint: There's more to promotion than simple advertising. Other methods include *personal selling, sales promotions,* and *publicity and public relations.* Refer to the discussion of promotion in Chapter 14 for ideas on how to promote your product that go beyond just advertising.

Part 4. The Financials

Expected Revenue
How much will you charge for your product? How many products do you believe you can sell in one year (or how many customers do you think your business will attract)? Multiply the price that you will charge by the number of products that you hope to sell or the amount you hope each customer will spend. This will give you an estimate of your *revenues* for one year.

Hint: You will use the amounts you calculate in the costs and revenues questions in this section in the accounting statements, so be as realistic as you can.

Cost of Doing Business
What are the costs of doing business? Equipment, supplies, salaries, rent, utilities, and insurance are just some of these expenses. Estimate what it will cost to do business for one year. Include any assumptions you use in generating cost estimates.

Hint: Insert the costs associated with doing business in the table on the following page. The following list provides some hints as to where you can get this information. Note that these are estimates; try your best to include accurate costs for the expenses you think will be a part of doing business.

Hints for each expense in the following table:
- **Rent:** What is the "going rate" per square foot for office space in your community? A real estate agent or a local SBA representative (www.sba.gov) can also be helpful in answering this question.
- **Salaries and Wages:** Refer to the organizational chart. How much will each employee earn? How many hours will each employee be needed on a weekly basis? Once you've determined the weekly cost, then expand it to a monthly cost and a yearly cost.
- **Supplies:** How much will all the computers, equipment, and furniture cost? What kinds of general office supplies will you need? Most prices for this information can be found on an office supply Web site, such as Staples.com.
- **Advertising and Other Promotions:** Refer to your marketing section. You have described how you wish to reach your customers; now you need to decide how much it will cost. If you're using television, contact the sales department at a local station. If you're using newspapers, contact their advertising department. Salespeople are usually happy to answer your questions.
- **Utilities:** These amounts will vary depending on your business and what utilities you will pay. If your business looks like an office, this cost may be similar to what a homeowner pays. However, if your business involves making a product, then the costs will be significant. An SBA representative can be a good resource.
- **Insurance:** This value will be affected by the nature of the business. More equipment will usually mean higher insurance costs. Again, contact an SBA representative for feedback.

Expenses	Expected Monthly Cost	Expected Yearly Cost
Rent		
Salaries and Wages		
Supplies: technological, equipment, furniture, other (computers, software, copy machine, desks, chairs, etc.)		
Advertising and Other Promotions		
Utilities: heat, electricity, etc.		
Utilities: telephone, Internet		
Insurance		
Other (specify)		
Other (specify)		

Start-up Costs
How much money will you need to get your business started?

Hint: Refer back to where you analyzed the costs involved in running your business. Approximately how much will you need to get your business started?

Financing
How will you finance your business? For example, will you seek out a bank loan? Borrow from friends? Try crowdfunding? Sell stocks or bonds initially or as your business grows?

Hint: Refer to Chapter 15 for information on sources of short-term and long-term funds. Refer to Chapter 16 for information on securities, such as stocks and bonds.

Income Statement and Balance Sheet
Create a balance sheet and an income statement for your business.

Hint: You have **two** options for creating these reports. The first option is to create your own financial statements using the guides provided on the next pages.

The second option is to use the specific Microsoft Word or Excel templates created for each statement. You'll find these templates online in this text's MyBizLab. The Excel files are handy because all the calculations are preset; all you have to do is "plug in" the numbers. The calculations are performed automatically. If you make adjustments to the values in the Excel worksheets, you'll automatically see how changes to expenses, for example, can improve the "bottom line."

Twelve-Month Income Statement (Profit & Loss Statement)

	June	July	Aug.	Sept.	Oct.	Nov.	Dec.	Jan.	Feb.	March	April	May	YEARLY
Revenue (Sales)													
Category 1													
Category 2													
Total Revenue (Sales)													
Cost of Goods Sold													
Category 1													
Category 2													
Total Cost of Goods Sold													
Gross Profit													
Operating Expenses													
Rent Expense													
Salary/Wage Expenses													
Supplies Expense													
Advertising Expense													
Utilities Expense													
Telephone/Internet Expense													
Insurance Expense													
Interest from Loans (if applicable)													
Other Expenses (specify)													
Total Expenses													
Net Profit													

Balance Sheet

Assets	
Current Assets	
Cash in Bank	
Cash Value of Inventory	
Prepaid Expenses (insurance)	
Total Current Assets	
Fixed Assets	
Machinery & Equipment	
Furniture & Fixtures	
Real Estate/Buildings	
Total Fixed Assets	
Total Assets	
Liabilities & Net Worth	
Current Liabilities	
Accounts Payable	
Taxes Payable	
Notes Payable (due within 12 months)	
Total Current Liabilities	
Long-Term Liabilities	
Bank Loans Payable (greater than 12 months)	
Less: Short-Term Portion	
Total Long-Term Liabilities	
Total Liabilities	
Owners' Equity (Net Worth)	
Total Liabilities & Net Worth	

Part 5. The Finishing Touches

COVER SHEET AND TABLE OF CONTENTS

Cover Sheet
Create a cover sheet for your business plan.

Hint: The cover sheet should include the following:

- Basic company information (name, address, phone number, and web address)
- The company logo
- Contact information of the owner(s) and any officers (names, titles, addresses, phone numbers, and e-mail addresses)
- The date the business plan was created
- The name(s) of those who prepared the plan

Table of Contents
Create a table of contents for the plan so a reader can quickly find information.

Hint: The table of contents should include the headings of each section and the page number of the first page of each section. All pages in the document should be numbered.

Executive Summary
After you've finished your business plan, write an executive summary that contains the key points of the business plan. The summary should be brief—no more than two pages—and cover the following points:

- The name of your business
- Where your business will be located
- The mission of your business
- The product or service you are selling
- Who your ideal customers are
- How your product or business will stand out in the crowd
- Who the owners of the business are and what experience they have
- An overview of the future prospects for your business and industry
- An overview of the amount and uses of required initial financing

Hint: You've already answered these questions, so what you need to do is put the ideas together into a "snapshot" format. The executive summary is a sales pitch; it's an investor's first impression of your idea. Ultimately, you're enticing a reader to want to read more. If investors don't get excited about your business and the prospects of success from reading the executive summary, they'll stop reading and most likely not consider the plan. Therefore, as with all parts of the plan, write in a clear and professional way but be compelling about your business.

Note: Once you have created the cover sheet, the table of contents, and the executive summary, move these sections to the beginning of your business plan, with the cover sheet as the very first element.

Reference Notes

Chapter 1

1. Shontell, Alyson. "The Youngest, Most Successful Tech Founders," Business Insider, 23 Sept. 2011. Retrieved from http://www.businessinsider.com/young-successful-entrepreneur-world-digital-100-2011-9

2. Barret, Victoria. "Dropbox: The Inside Story of Tech's Hottest Startup," *Forbes*, 18 Oct. 2011.

3. "Nantucket Nectars from the Beginning," *Nantucket Allserve, Inc*. Retrieved from www.nantucketnectars.com/fullstory .php?PHPSESSID=996c6c936ce6351082022525b73e9fce

4. Ostrow, Adam. "LinkedIn's IPO," Featured Articles from CNN, 20 May 2011. Retrieved from http://articles.cnn .com/2011-05-20/tech/linked.in.ostrow_1_linkedin-s-ipo-social-media-web-companies?_s=PM:TECH

5. Wilcox, Joe. "Microsoft, Apple Alliance at Key Juncture," *CNETNew.com*, 22 Feb. 2002. Retrieved from http://news .cnet.com/2100-1040-843145.html

6. "Bing-O: Potential Microsoft Apple Alliance," *InvestorGuide*, 20 Jan. 2010. Retrieved from www.investorguide.com/ article/5675/bing-o-potential-microsoft-apple-alliance-msft/

7. O'Brien, Sharon. "Fun Facts About the Senior Population: Demographics," *About.com*. Retrieved from http:// seniorliving.about.com/od/lawpolitics/a/senior_pop_ demo.htm

8. "100 Best Companies to Work for 2010: Top Companies: Most Diverse," *Fortune*. Retrieved from http://money .cnn.com/magazines/fortune/bestcompanies/2010/ minorities/

9. Cooper, Andrea. "The Influencers," *Entrepreneur.com*, 11 Mar. 2008. Retrieved from http://www.usnews.com/ articles/business/small-business-entrepreneurs/2008/03/11/ the-influencers_print.htm

10. "About Us," *FedEx*. Retrieved from http://about.fedex .designcdt.com/our_company/company_information

11. Green, Robert. "This Old Computer: Upgrade or Replace?" *Robert Green's DIY*, 17 Mar. 2009. Retrieved from www.rbgrn .net/content/212-old-computer-upgrade-or-replace

12. Azzarello, Patty. "How to Overcome IT's Credibility Challenges," *CIO Update*, 25 Sept. 2007. Retrieved from http:// cioupdate.com//article.php/3701571

13. "Mobile Worker Population to Reach 1.3 Billion by 2015," Business Wire, IDC, 5 Jan. 2012. Retrieved from http:// www.businesswire.com/news/home/20120105005455/en/ Mobile-Worker-Population-Reach-1.3-Billion-2015

14. Neff, Jack. "Beyond Online Ads: P&G Sets $4 Bil E-commerce Goal," *Advertising Age* 80, no. 29, pp. 3–25.

15. Dolan, Pamela Lewis. "Amednews: Medical Identity Theft a Growing Problem. Oct. 17, 2011. American Medical News," American Medical Association, American Medical News, 17 Oct. 2011. Retrieved from http://www.ama-assn .org/amednews/2011/10/17/bisa1017.htm

16. "The Wawa Story." Retrieved from www.wawa.com/ WawaWeb/pdfs/theWawaStory.pdf

17. "History," *CVS Caremark*. Retrieved from http://info .cvscaremark.com/our-company/history

18. "Temporary Disability Insurance," *Rhode Island Department of Labor and Training*. Retrieved from www.dlt.ri.gov/tdi/

19. "About Us," *McDonald's*. Retrieved from www.mcdonalds .ca/en/aboutus/faq.aspx

20. "Strange International Foods: Our Top Seven," *Independent Traveler.com*. Retrieved from www.independenttraveler .com/resources/article.cfm?AID=860&category=43; Erin Petrun. "Where's the Beef?" Retrieved from www.cbsnews .com/stories/2007/04/02/asia_letter/main2640540.shtml

21. Wolcott, Robert. "Building a Business within Wawa," Kellogg School of Management. Retrieved from http://hbr.org/ product/wawa-building-a-new-business-within-an-established/an/KEL240-PDF-ENG

Chapter 2

1. "Taxes and Other Revenues." *CIA World Fact Book*. Central Intelligence Agency, February 2, 2012. Retrieved from https://www.cia.gov/library/publications/the-world-factbook/fields/2221.html

2. "The Education System in Demark," *UNI•C*. Retrieved from http://tilgaengelighed.emu.dk/tilgaengelighed/ English/info.html

3. Veenhoven, Ruut. "World Database of Happiness," *Erasmus University Rotterdam*. Retrieved from http:// worlddatabaseofhappiness.eur.nl

4. "Country Rankings," *Index of Economic Freedom*, The Heritage Foundation, 02 Feb. 2012. Retrieved from http:// www.heritage.org/index/ranking.

5. Pontz, Zach. "A Year Later, Amazon's Kindle Finds a Niche, *CNN.com*, 4 Dec. 2008. Retrieved from www.cnn.com/2008/ TECH/12/03/kindle.electronic.reader/index.html

6. "Microsoft Corporation," *Encyclopædia Britannica*. Retrieved from www.britannica.com/EBchecked/topic/380624/ Microsoft-Corporation

7. Data from "The World Factbook: Country Comparison: GDP (Purchasing Power Parity)," *Central Intelligence Agency*. Retrieved from https://www.cia.gov/

8. "Frequently Asked Questions, Question 6," *Bureau of Labor Statistics*. Retrieved from www.bls.gov/cpi/cpifaq .htm#Question_6

9. "Table 1: Relative Importance of Components in the Consumer Price Indexes: U.S. City Average," December 2010. *Bureau of Labor Statistics*. Retrieved from www.bls .gov/cpi/cpiri2010.pdf

10. "Historical Inflation." *InflationData.com*. Retrieved from http://www.inflationdata.com/Inflation/Inflation_Rate/ HistoricalInflation.aspx

11. "The U.S. Inflation Rate—1948–2007," *The U.S. Misery Index*, 24 Feb. 24. Retrieved from www.miseryindex.us/ irbyyear.asp

12. Mamudi, Sam. "Lehman Folds with Record $613 Billion Debt – MarketWatch," *MarketWatch*, The Wall Street Journal, 15 Sept. 2008. Retrieved from http://www.marketwatch.com/story/ lehman-folds-with-record-613-billion-debt?siteid=rss

13. "Humbled GM Files for Bankruptcy Protection - Business - Autos - Msnbc.com," Msnbc.com. MSN, 1 June 2009. Retrieved from http://www.msnbc

.msn.com/id/31030038/ns/business-autos/t/
humbled-gm-files-bankruptcy-protection/

14 Sullivan, Dr. Teresa. *"Bankruptcy Statistics 1980–2010,"*
BankruptcyAction.com. Retrieved from http://www
.bankruptcyaction.com/USbankstats.htm

15 Reprinted with permission from the Federal Reserve Bank
of New York. Retrieved from http://www.newyorkfed
.org/markets/statistics/dlyrates/fedrate.html

Chapter 3

1 "Ethics," *The American Heritage® Dictionary of the English
Language*, 4th ed. (Boston: Houghton Mifflin Company,
2004). Retrieved from http://dictionary.reference.com/
browse/ethics

2 Pomeroy, Ann. "The Ethics Squeeze," *HR Magazine*, March
2006, p. 53.

3 "Authentic Happiness," *University of Pennsylvania Positive
Psychology Center*. Retrieved from www.authentichappiness
.sas.upenn.edu/Default.aspx

4 Merle, Renae. "Boeing CEO Resigns over Affair with Subordinate," *Washington Post*, 08 Mar. 2005. Retrieved from www
.washingtonpost.com/wp-dyn/articles/A13173-2005Mar7
.html?nav=rss_topnews

5 From Anne Pomeroy, "The Ethics Squeeze," *HR Magazine*.
Vol. 51, No. 3, p. 53.

6 Ibid.

7 Abkowitz, Alyssa. "The Informant: I Thought I Was
Bulletproof," *Fortune*, 25 Sept. 2009. Retrieved from http://
money.cnn.com/2009/09/24/news/companies/the_
informant_mark_whitacre.fortune/index.htm

8 *Fetzer Vineyards Philosophy*, Retrieved from www.fetzer
.com/philosophy.aspx (February 10, 2012). Reprinted with
permission of Fetzer Vineyards.

9 *Boston College Center for Corporate Citizenship*, (April 24,
2010).

10 Young, Mark. "HR as the Guardian of Corporate Values at
Cadbury Schweppes," *Strategic HR Review* 10 (Jan/
Feb 2006), pp. 10–11.

11 "Indian Government Must Stop Refinery Expansion Until
Human Rights Are Addressed," *Amnesty International*. Retrieved from www.amnesty.org/en/news-and-updates/
report/vedanta

12 Alsever, Jennifer. "Chiquita Cleans Up Its Act," *Money.com*.
Retrieved from http://money.cnn.com/magazines/business2/
business2_archive/2006/08/01/8382241/index.htm

13 "Citations of Statistics Used in the Film," *BraveNew Films*.
Retrieved from www.walmartmovie.com/facts.php

14 "Who's Who," *The Corporation*. The Big Picture Media
Corporation. Retrieved from www.thecorporation.com

15 "Building a Quantitative Business Case" By Chris Tuppen.
From Corporate Social Responsibility. *European Business
Forum Ltd.*, Summer 2004. Retrieved from www
.johnelkington.com/ebf_CSR_report.pdf

16 "Chroma Wins Worldwide Award for Democracy in the
Workplace," *Chroma Technology Group*. Retrieved from
www.chroma.com/newsevents/articles/chroma-wins-
worldwide-award-democracy-workplace

17 "Being Their Own Bosses," *Chroma technology Group*.
Retrieved from www.chroma.com/newsevents/articles/
being-their-own-bosses

18 "Citizenship," *Time Warner*. Retrieved from www.timewarner
.com/corp/citizenship/index.html

19 "Community Outreach," *Target.com*. Retrieved from http://
sites.target.com/site/en/company/page.jsp?contentId=
WCMP04-031700&ref=sr_shorturl_community

20 Vranica, Suzanne. "Twitter Crowns Wendy's Promo As
'Most Retweeted'" WSJ Blogs - WSJ. 8 Dec. 2011. Retrieved from http://blogs.wsj.com/digits/2011/12/08/
twitter-crowns-wendys-promo-as-most-retweeted/

21 "Global HIV/AIDS estimates, end of 2008," *Avert.org*.
Retrieved from www.avert.org/worldstats.htm

22 "HIV/AIDS, TB and Malaria," *DATA (debt AIDS
trade Africa)*. Retrieved from http://www.one.org/
blog/2010/04/22/africas-progress-in-fighting-malaria/

23 "Corporate Responsibility Report," *Intel*. Retrieved from
www.intel.com/intel/corpresponsibility/awards.htm

24 Sparks, John. "Try Being Nice," *Newsweek*, 26 June 2006.
Retrieved from www.newsweek.com/2006/06/25/try-
being-nice.html; "About Us," *Kaplan Thaler Group*. Retrieved
from www.kaplanthaler.com/#/about

25 Kaplan, Linda and Robin Koval. *The Power of Nice: How to
Conquer the World with Kindness*. Crows Nest, N.S.W.: Allen &
Unwin, 2007.

26 Ibid.

27 Lush, Val. "Consumer Bill of Rights," *BookRags*. Retrieved
from www.bookrags.com/research/consumer-bill-of-
rights-ebf-01/

28 "BP Establishes $20 Billion Claims Fund for Deepwater
Horizon Spill and Outlines Dividend Decisions," BP. British
Petroleum, 16 June 2010. Retrieved from http://www.bp.com/
genericarticle.do?categoryId=2012968&contentId=7062966

29 Data from Enron's *Corporate Responsibility Annual Report*,
2000. Retrieved from http://www.corporateregister
.com/a10723/enr00-cr-usa.pdf.

30 "Ponzi Scheme," *Merriam-Webster Online*. Retrieved from
www.merriam-webster.com/dictionary/ponzi%20scheme

31 "GreenStop," *Topia Energy*. Retrieved from www
.topiagreenstop.com/

32 "Malaria Prevention," *The Medical News*. © 2007, 2012
Interface Inc. All rights reserved. Used with permission.

33 Adams, Patrick. "The Sanaria *PfSPZ* Malaria Vaccine, Until
Recently Considered Impossible, Is Entering Phase II Trials,"
TropIKA.net, 15 Dec. 2009. Retrieved from www.tropika
.net/svc/interview/Adams-20091216-Interview-

34 Musil, Steven. "Week in Review: Google Slams China
Censorship," *CNET.com*. Retrieved from http://news.cnet
.com/8301-1001_3-10435702-92.html

35 Bill Xia quoted in Ben Elgin and Bruce Einhorn, "Outrun-
ning China's Web Cops," *BusinessWeek*, February 20, 2006.
Retrieved from www.businessweek.com

36 Daigle, Katy. "Google India Bars Offensive Content."
Featured Articles from Philly.com. 07 Feb. 2012. Web.
14 Feb. 2012. Retrieved from http://articles.philly.com

37 "Our Progress," *Interface, Inc*. Retrieved from www
.interfaceglobal.com/Sustainability/Sustainability-in-
Action.aspx

38 "What Is Sustainability?" *Interface, Inc*. Retrieved from
www.interfacesustainability.com/whatis.html

39 "Interface's Values Are Our Guiding Principles,":
© 2007, 2012 *Interface Inc*. All rights reserved. Used with
permission.

40 "Groups," *Interface, Inc*. Retrieved from http://missionzero
.org/groups

41 Musil, Steven. "Week in Review: Google Slams China
Censorship."

42 "Being a Responsible Company," *Starbucks*. Retrieved from
www.starbucks.com/responsibility

43 "CTCA Quality Story" Cancer Treatment Centers of
America. Retrieved from http://www.cancercenter.com

44 Young, Mark. "HR as the Guardian of Corporate Values
at Cadbury Schweppes," *Strategic HR Review*, 2006, Vol. 5
Iss. 2, pp. 10–11.

45 "Lockheed Martin Gray Matters Ethics Game,"*e-businessethics.com*. Retrieved from www.e-businessethics.com/Game.htm

46 "Employers Find Maintaining an Ethical Workplace Is Paramount, Especially in Tough Ethical Times," Business Wire, 6 Apr. 2010. Retrieved from http://www.businesswire.com/portal/site/home/permalink/?ndmViewId=news_view&newsId=20100406005609&newsLang=en

47 "Ethics Training in Law Enforcement," *International Association of Chiefs of Police*. Retrieved from www.theiacp.org/PoliceServices/ExecutiveServices/ProfessionalAssistance/Ethics/ReportsResources/EthicsTraininginLawEnforcement/tabid/194/Default.aspx

48 Carpenter, Megan. "Judge Overturns Corporate Patent on Human DNA," *Washington Independent*. Retrieved from http://washingtonindependent.com/80919/judge-overturns-corporate-patent-on-human-dna

Chapter 4

1 President Bill Clinton, "Remarks by the President to Vietnam National University," *Embassy of the United States*, Hanoi, Vietnam, November 17, 2000.

2 Hill, Charles W. L. *International Business: Competing in the Global Marketplace*, 8th ed. (Burr Ridge, IL: Irwin/McGraw-Hill Publishing Co., 2010), pp. 6–8.

3 Ibid.

4 Pierson, David. "Ford Plays Catch-up in China's Growing Auto Market," Los Angeles Times, February 25, 2012. Retrieved from http://articles.latimes.com/2012/feb/25/business/la-fi-china-ford-20120225

5 Seshan, Govindkrishna. "Fruit Punch," *Business Standard*, February 26, 2008. Retrieved from www.business-standard.com/india/storypage.php?autono=

6 Charles W. L. Hill, *International Business: Competing in the Global Marketplace*, 8th ed. (Burr Ridge, IL: Irwin/McGraw-Hill Publishing Co., 2010), pp. 6–8.

7 "Economy Rankings." *Ranking of Economies*. The World Bank, June 1, 2011. Retrieved from http://www.doingbusiness.org/rankings

8 Hill, Charles W. L. *International Business: Competing in the Global Marketplace*, pp. 18–24.

9 Holstein, William. "ChiefExecutive.net," *Secrets of Mini-Multinationals*, Chief Executive.net, 2012. Retrieved from http://chiefexecutive.net/secrets-of-mini-multinationals

10 McGeehan, Patrick. "Foreign Investment in City Is Growing, Report Finds," *MitchellMoss.com*. Retrieved from www.mitchellmoss.com/mentions/NYTimes-27-June-08.pdf

11 "A Massive Investment in Education to Give Queensland Kids a Flying Start," *mysunshinecoast.com.au*. Retrieved from www.mysunshinecoast.com.au/articles/article-display/a-massive-investment-in-education-to-give-queensland-kids-a-flying-start,17463

12 Pines, Ayala, Miri Lerner, and Dafna Schwartz. "Gender Differences Among Social vs. Business Entrepreneurs." Retrieved from http://cdn.intechopen.com/pdfs/31886/InTech-Gender_differences_among_social_vs_business_entrepreneurs.pdf

13 "Promoting Entrepreneurialship," *Ministry of Trade and Industry*. Retrieved from www.regjeringen.no/en/dep/nhd/selected-topics/innovation/promoting-entrepreneurship.html?id=582899

14 "Background Note: Cuba," *U.S. Department of State*. Retrieved from www.state.gov/r/pa/ei/bgn/2886.htm

15 "The GATT Years: From Havana to Marrakesh," *World Trade Organization*. Retrieved from www.wto.org/english/thewto_e/whatis_e/tif_e/fact4_e.htm

16 "Understanding the WTO," *World Trade Organization*. Retrieved from www.wto.org/english/thewto_e/whatis_e/tif_e/tif_e.htm

17 "Doha Development Agenda: Negotiations, Implementation, and Development," *World Trade Organization*. Retrieved from www.wto.org/english/tratop_e/dda_e/dda_e.htm

18 "Rank Order: Exports," *CIA: The World Factbook*. Retrieved from https://www.cia.gov/library/publications/the-world-factbook/rankorder/2078rank.html; "Rank Order: Imports," *CIA: The World Factbook*. Retrieved from https://www.cia.gov/library/publications/the-world-factbook/rankorder/2087rank

19 Rosenberg, Matt. "Euro Countries," *About.com*. Retrieved from http://geography.about.com/od/lists/a/euro.htm

20 "Microsoft Loses Anti-Trust Appeal," *BBC News*, September 17, 2007. Retrieved from http://news.bbc.co.uk/1/hi/business/6998272.stm; "Microsoft Hit by Record EU Fine," *BBC News*, March 24, 2004. Retrieved from http://news.bbc.co.uk/1/hi/business/3563697.stm

21 Rosenberg, Matt. "Euro Countries."

22 "About APEC," *Asian-Pacific Economic Cooperation*. Retrieved from http://www.apec.org/FAQ.aspx

23 "MO China Profile." *Mobility China*. Siemens, July 5, 2011. Retrieved from http://cn.siemens.com/cms/cn/English/TS/Mobility/About%20us/MOChinaProfile/Pages/Default.aspx

24 "Subway Sandwiches Franchise Opportunity," *Franchise International*. Retrieved from www.franchise-international.net/show/subway-sandwiches/198

25 "Disney Signs India Master," *Franchise International*. Retrieved from www.franchise-international.net/franchise/Walt-Disney-Company/Disney-signs-India-Master/1554

26 "Intellectual Property and Licensing," *SRI International*. Retrieved from www.sri.com/rd/hot.html

27 Bajaj, Vikas. "Wal-Mart Debate Rages in India," *The New York Times*, December 6, 2011. Retrieved from http://www.nytimes.com/2011/12/06/business/global/wal-mart-hears-a-familiar-complaint-in-india.html?pagewanted=all

28 Cellan-Jones, Rory. "Nokia and Microsoft Form Partnership," BBC News, BBC, November 2, 2011. Retrieved from http://www.bbc.co.uk/news/business-12427680

29 Chen, Tain-Jy. "The Development of Taiwan's Personal Computer Industry," *Department of Economics, National Taiwan University, Chung-Hua Institution for Economic Research*, Working Paper Series Vol. 2002–15.

30 Kavilanz, Parija B. "Mattel Fined $2.3 Million over Lead in Toys." CNNMoney. Cable News Network, 5 June 2009. Retrieved from http://money.cnn.com/2009/06/05/news/companies/cpsc/

31 "Hyundai Is First Foreign Automaker to Install a Stamping Shop in Russia," *Infibeam.com*. Retrieved from http://news.infibeam.com/blog/news/2010/05/20/hyundai_is_first_foreign_automaker_to_install_a_stamping_shop_in_russia.html

32 "Foreign Trade." - U.S. Top Trading Partners. U. S., Department of Commerce, April 1, 2012. Retrieved from http://www.census.gov/foreign-trade/statistics/highlights/topcurmon.html

33 "Fund Rankings | Sovereign Wealth Fund Institute," *Fund Rankings, Sovereign Wealth Fund Institute*, SWF Institute, May 1, 2012. Retrieved from http://www.swfinstitute.org/fund-rankings/

34 Logutenkova, Elena, and Yalman Onaran. "Singapore, Abu Dhabi Face Losses on UBS, Citigroup (Update2)," *Business-Week*, March 2, 2010. Retrieved from http://www.bloomberg.com/apps/news?pid=newsarchive&sid=aeS1DdEYqj_Q

35 Alex, C. G., and Barbara Bowers. "The American Way to Countertrade," *BarterNews* 17 (1988). Retrieved from www.barternews.com/american_way.htm

36 Black, George. "India Calling: How the Cell Phone Revolution Can Raise Millions Out of Poverty and Help Fix the Climate," *ThinkProgress*, OnEarth Magazine, March 18, 2012. Retrieved from http://thinkprogress.org/climate/2012/03/18/442167/india-cell-phone-revolution-poverty-help-fix-the-climate/?mobile=nc

37 "Results of Poor Cross Cultural Awareness," *Kwintessential*. Retrieved from http://www.kwintessential.co.uk/cultural-services/articles/Results%20of%20Poor%20Cross%20Cultural%20Awareness.html

38 Quoted in "Cross Cultural Business Blunders," *Kwintessential*. Retrieved from www.kwintessential.co.uk/cultural-services/articles/crosscultural-blunders.html

39 Taylor, Chris. "There's More Vacation Time on Tap for You," *CNN Money*, August 3, 2006. Retrieved from http://money.cnn.com/2006/08/03/technology/fbvacations0803.biz2/index.htm

40 Ibid.

41 Ibid.

42 "Foreign Corrupt Practices Act," *U.S. Department of Justice*. Retrieved from www.justice.gov/criminal/fraud/fcpa/

Mini Chapter 1

1 Rappa, Michael. "Managing the Digital Enterprise: Intellectual Property," Digital Enterprise.org, 31 May 2009. Retrieved from http://digitalenterprise.org/ip/ip.html

2 "FTC Rejects Proposed Settlement in Staples/Office Depot Merger," FTC.gov, 4 April 1997. Retrieved from http://www.ftc.gov/opa/1997/04/stapdep.shtm

3 "Music groups settle on CD price-fixing." BBC News. 30 Sept. 2002. Retrieved from http://news.bbc.co.uk/2/hi/business/2289224.stm

4 "Landmark Study: The Economic Impact of Advertising Expenditures in the U.S," ANA, 14 Oct. 2010. Retrieved from https://www.ana.net/miccontent/show/id/economic-impact-advertising-stud

Chapter 5

1 From "Small Business Size Standards," *U.S. Small Business Administration*. Retrieved from www.sba.gov/size/

2 "Statistics about Small Business from the Census Bureau," *U.S. Census Bureau*. Retrieved from http://www.census.gov/econ/smallbus.html

3 "Small Business Size Standards," *SBA.gov*, The U.S. Small Business Administration.Retrieved from http://www.sba.gov/content/table-small-business-size-standards

4 "NFIB's Small Business Growth Agenda for the 112th Congress | NFIB," *NIFB.com*, National Federation of Independent Business. Retrieved from http://www.nfib.com/issues-elections/issues-elections-item?cmsid=56420

5 Ibid.

6 "World Economic Outlook Database September 2011," *IMF.com*, International Monetary Fund. Retrieved from http://www.imf.org/external/pubs/ft/weo/2011/02/weodata/index.aspx

7 "Profile of U.S. Exporting Companies: 2008–2009," *U.S. Census Bureau*, 12 Apr. 2011. Retrieved from http://www.census.gov/foreign-trade/Press-Release/edb/2009/index.html

8 Breitzman, Anthony, and Diana Hicks. "An Analysis of Small Business Patents by Industry and Firm Size," *Sba.gov*, Small Business Association, November 2008. Retrieved from http://archive.sba.gov/advo/research/rs335tot.pdf

9 "About Omnipod," *myomnipod.com*. Retrieved from www.myomnipod.com

10 "Fabric: Recycled Polyester," *Patagonia.com*. Retrieved from http://www.patagonia.com/us/patagonia.go?assetid=2791

11 Giard, Keith. "GM Bankruptcy Spells Disaster for Small Suppliers," *Washington Post*, 28 May 2009. Retrieved from http://allbusiness.washingtonpost.com/government/elections-politics-campaigns/12344120-1.html

12 Klier, Thomas H., and James M. Rubenstein. "The U.S. Auto Supplier Industry in Transition—The New Geography of Auto Production," *chicagofed.org*, May 2006. Retrieved from www.chicagofed.org/digital_assets/publications/chicago_fed_letter/2006/cflmay2006_226.pdf

13 "SBA Frequently Asked Questions," *Sba.gov*, Small Business Administration, Jan. 2011. Retrieved from http://www.sba.gov/sites/default/files/sbfaq.pdf

14 Ibid.

15 "Economy: A Report to the President, *Small Business Administration, Office of Advocacy*. Retrieved from http://www.sba.gov/sites/default/files/sb_econ2010.pdf

16 Del Ray, Jason. War Zone Start-up, *Inc. Magazine*, Apr. 2010. Retrieved from www.inc.com/magazine/20100401/war-zone-start-up.html

17 Lesonsky, Rieva. "Customers Say Small Business Social Media Efforts Failing: Survey Says," *Huff Post News and Trends*, The Huffington Post, 6 Feb. 2012. Retrieved from http://www.huffingtonpost.com/2012/02/06/social-media-efforts-fail_n_1210447.html

18 "The ASC Story," *animatedspeech.com*. Retrieved from www.animatedspeech.com/Story/story_founders.html

19 Freeman, Bruce. "Fired? Start a Business!" *ProLine Communications*. Retrieved from http://www.prolinepr.com/Fired.html

20 Tynan, Dan. "The 25 Worst Tech Products of All Time," *pcworld.com*, 26 May 2006. Retrieved from www.pcworld.com/article/id,125772-page,6/article.html

21 Kilroy, Jake. "Wahoo's Has a Birthday Party (And I Get Invited)," *Entrepreneur Daily Dose*, February 27, 2009. Retrieved from http://blog.entrepreneur.com/2009/02/wahoos-has-a-birthday-party-and-i-get-invited.php

22 "McDonald's Corp." Retrieved from http://finance.yahoo.com/q/pr?s=MCD+Profile

23 "Citizen Wayne—The Unauthorized Biography," *Miami New Times* 9, no. 33 (December 1–7, 1994). Retrieved from www.corporations.org/wmi/huizenga.html

24 "Quotations from Famous Entrepreneurs on Entrepreneurship: Inspiring Words from the Best of the Best," Peter Drucker, *Innovation and Entrepreneurship*. Harper & Row, 1985, p. 19.

25 "Henry Ford," *About.com*. Retrieved from http://inventors.about.com/library/inventors/blford.htm

26 Adapted from Jack Kaplan and Anthony Warren, *Patterns of Entrepreneurship*, 2nd ed. (John Wiley & Sons, Inc.), p. 27; "The State of Small Business: A Report of the President," *U.S. Small Business Administration* (Washington, D.C.: U.S. Government Printing Office, 1995), p. 114.

27 "Nimble and Quick: Entrepreneurs That Move, Adapt and Change Are Winners," *Nesheim OnLine*, February 3, 2010. Retrieved from http://nesheimgroup.typepad.com

28 "Pete's Wicked." Retrieved from www.petes.com/

29 "Lifestyle Entrepreneurs: RV-Based Businesses Can Be Going Concerns," *Entrepreneur.com*. Retrieved from www.entrepreneur.com/franchises/franchisezone/startupjournal/article64548.html

30 Sheena Edwards in "About Us," LizzieLou Shoes (Feb. 15, 2012). Retrieved from http://lizzieloushoes.com Reprinted by permission of Sheena Edwards.

31 Ray, Leena. "Facebook for Latinos Quepasa Buys MyYearbook for $100 Million in Cash and Stock." *TechCrunch*, 20 July 2011. Retrieved from http://techcrunch.com/2011/07/20/facebook-for-latinos-quepasa-buys-myyearbook-for-100-million-in-cash-and-stock/

32 Helft, Miguel. "The Class That Built Apps, and Fortunes," *Nytimes.com*, The New York Times, 7 May 2011. Retrieved from http://www.nytimes.com/2011/05/08/technology/08class.html?_r=1&pagewanted=all

33 Case, John. "The Gazelle Theory," *Inc. Magazine*, May 2001. Retrieved from www.inc.com/magazine/20010515/22613.html

34 Rosen, James. "Economists Credit Small Business 'Gazelles' With Job Creation," *Foxnews.com*, Fox News, 25 Apr. 2011. Retrieved from http://www.foxnews.com/us/2011/04/25/economists-credit-small-business-gazelles-job-creation.

35 "Creativity Overflowing," *Bloomberg Businessweek*. Retrieved from www.businessweek.com/magazine/content/06_19/b3983061.htm?chan=searchand

36 "How Whirlpool Defines Innovation," *Bloomberg Businessweek*. Retrieved from www.businessweek.com/innovate/content/mar2006/id20060306_287425.htm?chan=search

37 Swearingen, Jake. "Great Intrapreneurs in Business History," *CBS Business Network*. Retrieved from www.bnet.com/2403-13070_23-196888.html?tag=content;col1

38 Dees, J. Gregory. "The Meaning of Social Entrepreneurship," *Kauffman Foundation*. Retrieved from www.caseatduke.org/documents/dees_sedef.pdf

39 "Meet the New Heroes: Mimi Silbert," *The New Heroes*. Retrieved from www.pbs.org/opb/thenewheroes/meet/silbert.html

40 Jablow, Ashley. "2010 Conference: The Business of Corporate Citizenship: Becoming a Social Intrapreneur," *Boston College Center for Corporate Citizenship*. Retrieved from http://blogs.bcccc.net/2010/04/the-business-of-corporate-citizenship-becoming-a-social-intrapreneur/

41 Josh Cleveland, "Creating a Company Culture That Engages Social Intrapreneurs," *Green-Biz.com*, June 29, 2009. Retrieved from www.greenbiz.com

42 Joel Holland, "From College Students to Million-Dollar Partners." *Entrepreneur.com*. January 18, 2010

43 "Big Bang! UC Davis Business Plan Competition," *University of California, Davis, Graduate School of Management*. Retrieved from http://bigbang.gsm.ucdavis.edu/

44 "Franchise Law: What Is a Franchise Business?" *freeadvice.com*. Copyright by and used with permission of Freeadvice.com

45 "Franchise Business Economic Outlook: 2011," PriceWaterhouseCoopers, 3 Jan. 2011. Retrieved from http://www.franchise.org/uploadedFiles/Franchise%20Business%20Outlook%20Report%202011%20final.pdf

46 Ibid.

47 "Home Based Franchise Business Opportunities | *Entrepreneur.com*," Entrepreneur.com. Retrieved from http://www.entrepreneur.com/franchises/homebased/index.html

48 "Franchise Statistics for the European Union," *Franchise Europe*. Retrieved from www.franchiseeurope.com/top500/article/franchisestatisticsfortheeuropeanunion/4/

49 "2010 Low Cost Franchises," *Entrepreneur.com*. Retrieved from www.entrepreneur.com/franchises/lowcost/index.html

50 "BDS Database List," *U.S. Census Bureau*. Retrieved from http://webserver03.ces.census.gov/index.php/bds/bds_database_list

51 Perman, Stacy, Jeffrey Gangemi, and Douglas MacMillan. "Entrepreneurs' Favorite Mistakes," *BusinessWeek*. Retrieved from http://images.businessweek.com/ss/06/09/favorite_mistake/index_01.htm

52 *National Business Incubator Association*. Retrieved from www.nbia.org

53 "About Us: History," *Subway.com*. Retrieved from www.subway.com/subwayroot/AboutSubway/history/subwayHistory.aspx

54 "Financing Options for a Small Business: Finding the Right Funding," *StartupNation.com*. Retrieved from www.startupnation.com/articles/890/1/AT_Finding-FundingThatsRight.asp

Chapter 6

1 Mooney, Nan. "When Good Friends Make Poor Colleagues," *Inc. Magazine*, September 2006. Retrieved from www.inc.com/resources/women/articles/20060901/nmooney.html/

2 From "Corporation." Ambrose Bierce. The Devil's Dictionary. New York, NY: Neale Publishing Company, 1911.

3 "Tax Facts for Individuals—2010," *A/N Group Inc.* Retrieved from www.smbiz.com/sbrl001.html#pis10

4 © Maureen Priest, Moyo Toga LLC.

5 "S Corporations." *S Corporations*. Internal Revenue Service, n.d. Retrieved from http://www.irs.gov/businesses/small/article/0,,id=98263,00.html

6 "Our Story," *KaBoom!* Retrieved from http://kaboom.org/about_kaboom/our_story

7 From "Top 25 Most Successful Non-Profit Organizations in the World." *Masters in Nonprofit Management Online Programs: MS, MPA, MPP.* 9 Mar. 2011. www.mastersinnonprofitmanagement.com

8 Frederick, Donald A. "Co-ops 101 – An Introduction to Cooperatives," *Rural Development*, U.S. Department of Agriculture, Apr. 1997. Retrieved from http://www.rurdev.usda.gov/rbs/pub/cir55/cir55rpt.htm

9 "About Co-ops," *National Cooperative Business Association*. Retrieved from www.ncba.coop/abcoop.cfm

10 "Florida's Natural." Retrieved from www.floridasnatural.com/

11 "Intology – Intelligent Technology NewsComputers Technology Internet Arts Business Science Sports," *Intology*, 29 Apr. 2008. Retrieved from http://www.intology.com/business-finance/microsoft-vs-yahoo-hostile-take-over-explained/

12 Ross, Andrew, and Jeff Wilson. "Pfizer Agrees to Pay $68 Billion for Rival Drug Maker Wyeth," The New York Times, 25 Jan. 2009. Retrieved from http://www.nytimes.com/2009/01/26/business/26drug.html?pagewanted=all

13 Gerald Levin quoted in Press Release, "AOL & Time Warner Will Merge To Create the World's First Internet-Age Media & Communications Company." January 10, 2000. Retrieved from www.timewarner.com

14 Stephen Case quoted in Press Release, "AOL & Time Warner Will Merge To Create the World's First Internet-Age Media & Communications Company." January 10, 2000. Retrieved from www.timewarner.com

15 Ted Leoniss, quoted in Tim Arango, "How the AOL-Time Warner Merger Went So Wrong" *New York Times*, Jan 11, 2010. Retrieved from http://www.nytimes.com

16 Rosoff, Matt. "Google's 15 Biggest Acquisitions and What Happened to Them," *Business Insider*, 14 Mar. 2011. Retrieved from http://www.businessinsider.com/googles-15-biggest-acquisitions-and-what-happened-to-them-2011-3?op=1

17 Cartwright, Susan. Why Mergers Fail and How to Prevent It, *QFinance.com*. Retrieved from www.qfinance.com/mergers-and-acquisitions-best-practice/why-mergers-fail-and-how-to-prevent-it?page=1

Mini Chapter 2

1 "Pizza Hut Inc.," *Funding Universe*. Retrieved from www .fundinguniverse.com/company-histories/Pizza-Hut-Inc-Company-History.html

2 "Our History," *Pizza Hut Online*. Retrieved from www .pizzahut.co.uk/restaurants/our-history.aspx; David Gumpert, *How to Really Create a Successful Business Plan* (Inc. Publishing, 1990), p. 17.

3 Berry, Tim. "Business Plan Contests Grow Up and Mean Business," *Bplans.com*. Retrieved from http://timberry .bplans.com/2010/04/business-plan-contests-growing-up-and-meaning-business.html

4 "C-Crete Technologies Wins the MIT $100K Business Plan Contest," *$100K MIT Entrepreneurship Competition*. Retrieved from www.mit100k.org/home/mit-100k-finale-is-upon-us-may-12-7pm-kresge/

Chapter 7

1 "At a Glance: Ursula Burns," *Forbes*, Forbes Magazine, August 2011. Retrieved from http://www.forbes.com/profile/ursula-burns/

2 Williams, Carol J. "LA Times: California Physician Assistant Wins $168 Million in Harassment Suit," *Los Angeles Times*, 2 Mar. 2012. Retrieved from http://www.workplacebullying .org/2012/03/02/168mil/

3 "Vision Statement" from Widimedia Foundation, Retrieved from http://wikimediafoundation.org

4 Chen, Ting. "Wikimedia Blog," Wikimedia Presents Its Five-year Strategic Plan, Wikimedia Foundation, 25 Feb. 2011. Retrieved from http://blog.wikimedia.org/2011/02/25/wikimedia-presents-its-five-year-strategic-plan/

5 Quoted in Pete Johnson, "Best Vision Statement," *Nerd Guru Wordpress Blog*. September 25, 2008. Retrieved from http://blog.nerdguru.net

6 "Our History: Our Company : GE." GE Past Leaders: John F. Welch Jr., Biography. General Electric, n.d. Retrieved from http://www.ge.com/company/history/bios/john_welch.html

7 From "Hometown Hospitality" on www.culvers.com

8 From "About the American Cancer Society," American Cancer Society. (June 16, 2012). Retrieved from www.cancer .org/AboutUs/WhoWeAre/acsmissionstatements

9 McNamara, Carter. "Strategic Planning (in Nonprofit or For-Profit Organizations)," *Free Management Library*. Retrieved from www.managementhelp.org/plan_dec/str_plan/str_plan.htm

10 Ishiguro, Rie, and Shinji Kitamura. "Japan Quake's Economic Impact Worse Than First Feared," Reuters. Thomson Reuters, 12 Apr. 2011. Retrieved from http://www.reuters.com/article/2011/04/12/us-japan-economy-idUSTRE73B0O320110412

11 "Business Contingency Planning and Disaster Recovery Programs at Vanguard," *The Vanguard Group*. Retrieved from www.vanguard.com/pdf/ccri.pdf

12 Ostroff, Frank. *The Horizontal Organization* (Oxford: Oxford University Press, 1999), pp. 25–57 and pp. 102–150.

13 Paul Allaire, quoted in Thomas A. Stewart, "The Search for the Organization of Tomorrow," *Fortune*, May 18, 1992. Retrieved from http://money.cnn.com

14 "Vineet Nayar's Scrapbook: In Search of New Leaders: Interview with Fox News," 23 June 2010. Retrieved from www.vineetnayar.com/interview-with-fox-news/

15 Arakali, Harichandan. "HCL Tech Exceeds Expectations, Records 29% Jump in Net Profit - Corporate News - Livemint .com," Reuters, 2012. Retrieved from http://www.livemint .com/2012/04/18085442/HCL-Tech-exceeds-expectations .html

16 From Vineet Nayar, "A Maverick CEO Explains How He Persuaded His Team to Leap into the Future." *Harvard Business Reivew*. June 2010. Reprint ID: R1006J. Retrieved from http://www.hcl.in/files/a-maverick-ceo-explains.pdf

17 Nayar, Vineet. "How I Did It: A Maverick CEO Explains How He Persuaded His Team to Leap into the Future," *Harvard Business Review*, June 2010. Retrieved from http://hbr.org/2010/06/how-i-did-it-a-maverick-ceo-explains-how-he-persuaded-his-team-to-leap-into-the-future/ar/1

18 "Pest Control Company Exterminates Business Problem," *Anchor Pest Control*. Retrieved from www.carchip.com/Product_Docs/CS_PestControl.pdf

19 "Six Sigma: So Yesterday?" *Bloomberg Businessweek*. Retrieved from www.businessweek.com/magazine/content/07_24/b4038409.htm

Chapter 8

1 Csikszentmihalyi, Mihaly. *Flow* (New York: HarperCollins, 1990).

2 "Employee Engagemen,." *Employee Engagement*, Gallup, 25 June 2012. Retrieved from http://www.gallup.com/consulting/52/employee-engagement.aspx

3 Tan, Ian. "Why Work for SAS." *SAS*. Retrieved from http://www.sas.com/offices/asiapacific/singapore/press/why-sas.html

4 Brown, Beverly. "SAS Achieves Double-digit Growth, Rockets 12 Percent to Record $2.725 Billion," *SAS*, 19 Jan. 2012. Retrieved from http://www.sas.com/news/preleases/2011financials.html

5 James Goodnight, quoted in James Goodnight and Richard Florida, "Managing for Creativity," *Harvard Business Review*, Jul/Aug2005, Vol. 83 Issue 7/8, pp. 124–131.

6 Goodnight, Jim, and Richard Florida. "Managing for Creativity," *Harvard Business Review*, July 2005, pp. 124–131.

7 "Employee Engagement," *Employee Engagement*, Gallup, 25 June 2012. Retrieved from http://www.gallup.com/consulting/52/employee-engagement.aspx

8 Slide, Casey. "9 Leadership Lessons & Quotes from Truett Cathy, Founder of Chick-fil-A," 9 Leadership Lessons & Quotes from Truett Cathy of Chick-fil-A, n.d. Retrieved from http://www.moneycrashers.com/leadership-lessons-from-truett-cathy-founder-of-chick-fil-a/

9 "Chick-fil-A: Company Fact Sheet," Chick-fil-A: Company Fact Sheet. Retrieved from http://www.chick-fil-a.com/Company/Highlights-Fact-Sheets

10 Polman E., and K. J. Emich (2011). Decisions for Others Are More Creative Than Decisions for the Self. *Personality and social psychology bulletin* PMID: 21317316.

11 "Strengths Based Performance Management," StrengthsManagement.com. Retrieved from www .strengthsmanagement.com

12 Buckingham, Marcus. *Now, Discover Your Strengths* (New York: Free Press, 2001).

13 Pink, Daniel. *Drive* (New York: Riverhead Books, 2009).

14 Pink, Daniel H. *Drive: The Surprising Truth about What Motivates Us*. (New York: Riverhead, 2009). Print.

15 Drucker, Peter. "Quotation Details," *The Quotations Page*. Retrieved from http://quotationspage.com/quote/26536.html

16 *Black Friday*, a 7-minute video on the *Toy Story* Blu-Ray DVD. Retrieved from Youtube. http://www.youtube.com/watch?v=bk8a_C0ao9Y

17 Kouzes, James M., and Barry Z. Posner. *The Leadership Challenge*, 4th ed. (San Francisco: Jossey-Bass, 2008).

18 Sheldrick, Aaron. "Former Tepco Chief to Be Grilled over Fukushima Disaster," *Chicago Tribune*, 07 June 2012. Retrieved from http://articles.chicagotribune.com/2012-06-07/news/sns-rt-us-japan-nuclear-shimizubre85703w-20120607_1_fukushima-plant-masataka-shimizu-tepco-executives

19 Neilson, April. "Is Chest Beating as Good for People as It Is for Primates? Stanford Knowledgebase, Stanford Graduate School of Business, 15 Mar. 2007. Retrieved from http://www.stanford.edu/group/knowledgebase/cgi-bin/2007/03/15/is-chest-beating-as-good-for-people-as-it-is-for-primates/

20 Hsieh, Tony. *Delivering Happiness: A Path to Profits, Passion, and Purpose*, Business Plus, 2010.

21 From "Introducing Core Values Frog!" Zappos.com

22 Based on "Our Unique Culture" and various blogs, Zappos.com

23 Tony Hsieh, quoted in Venuri Siriwardane, "Zappos CEO adds happiness to corporate culture," Zappos.com. www.nj.com/business/index.ssf/2010/06/zappos_ceo_adds_happiness_to_c.html (July 7, 2010).

24 "Fact Sheet,." Southwest Airlines, 1 Feb. 2012. Retrieved from http://www.southwest.com/html/about-southwest/history/fact-sheet.html

25 Based on "About Southwest; Our Culture" -Southwest Airlines, 1 Jan. 2012. Web. 26 June 2012. Retrieved from http://www.southwest.com/html/about-southwest/index.html

26 Milo, Moryt. "Executive of the Year," Teslamotors.com. *San Jose Business Journal*, 24 Dec. 2010. Retrieved from http://www.teslamotors.com/sites/default/files/blog_attachments/elon_musk_ceo_of_the_year.pdf

27 Katzenbach, John R., and Douglas K. Smith, *The Wisdom of Teams* (Cambridge, Massachusetts: Harvard University Press, 1993).

28 Rosoff, Matt. "The Story Behind Kinect, Microsoft's Newest Billion Dollar Business," *Business Insider*, 19 Jan. 2011. Retrieved from http://www.businessinsider.com/the-story-behind-microsofts-hot-selling-kinect-2011-1?op=1

29 "Teamwork Concept Questioned," *National Association of College Stores*, 11 Aug. 2006. Retrieved from www.nacs.org/news/081106-teamwork.asp?id=cm

30 Howe, Neil, and William Strauss. *Millennials Rising: The Next Great Generation* (Vintage, 2000).

31 Armour, Stephanie "Generation Y: They've Arrived at Work with a New Attitude," *USA Today*, 6 Nov. 2005. Retrieved from www.usatoday.com/money/workplace/2005-11-06-gen-y_x.htm

32 William Strauss, quoted in Matt Ehlers, "What's Up with Gen Y?" The News & Observer, February 5, 2006. Retrieved from www.newsobserver.com

33 Bob Topping, quoted in Anna Mulrine, "The Army Trains a Skeptics Corps to Battle Groupthink," US News and World Report 144, no. 15 (May 26, 2008), pp. 30–32.

34 Anders, George. "Jeff Bezos Gets It." Forbes. Forbes Magazine, 25 Apr. 2012. Retrieved from http://www.forbes.com/global/2012/0507/global-2000-12-amazon-jeff-bezos-gets-it.html

35 Robertson, David, and Per Hjuler. "Innovating a Turnaround at LEGO," *Harvard Business Review*, September 2009. Retrieved from http://hbr.org/2009/09/innovating-a-turnaround-at-lego/ar/1

36 Lurey, J. S., and M. S. Raisinghani. "An Empirical Study of Best Practices in Virtual Teams," *Information & Management*, 38, no. 8, 2001, pp. 523–544.

37 Based on Covey, Stephen R.. *The 7 Habits of Highly Effective People* (New York: Free Press, 1989).

Chapter 9

1 "About Us," LinkedIn.com. Retrieved from http://press.linkedin.com/about

2 Adler, Lou. "Hiring and Recruiting Challenges Survey 2008 Preliminary Results," *ere.net*. Retrieved from www.ere.net/2007/11/09/hiring-and-recruiting-challenges-survey-2008-preliminary-results/

3 "Cisco's Internet Postings Policy," *Blogs@Cisco*, Cisco, 24 Mar. 2008. Retrieved from http://blogs.cisco.com/news/ciscos_internet_postings_policy

4 Cappelli, Peter. "How to Get a Job? Beat the Machines," *TIME.com*, Time Moneyland, 11 June 2012. Retrieved from http://moneyland.time.com/2012/06/11/how-to-get-a-job-beat-the-machines/

5 O'Connell, Vanessa. "Test for Dwindling Retail Jobs Spawns a Culture of Cheating," *Wall Street Journal*, 7 Jan. 2009. Retrieved from http://online.wsj.com/article_email/SB123129220146959621-lMyQjAxMDI5MzAxNzIwOTcyWj.html

6 Zupek, Rachel. "Infamous Resume Lies," MSN Careers, CareerBuilder.com, 7 July 2010. Retrieved from http://msn.careerbuilder.com/Article/MSN-1154-Cover-Letters-Resumes-Infamous-R%C3%A9sum%C3%A9-Lies/

7 "About EEOC," *U.S. Equal Employment Opportunity Commission*. Retrieved from www.eeoc.gov

8 "Facts About the Americans with Disabilities Act," *U.S. Equal Employment Opportunity Commission*. Retrieved from www.eeoc.gov/facts/fs-ada.html

9 "Age Discrimination," *U.S. Equal Employment Opportunity Commission*. Retrieved from www.eeoc.gov/laws/types/age.cfm

10 Adapted from McNamara, Carter. "Employee Training and Development: Reasons and Benefits," © Copyright *Authenticity Consulting, LLC*. www.managementhelp.org/trng_dev/basics/reasons.htm (July 1, 2012)

11 "Nuclear Pharmacy Opportunities with Cardinal Health," *RXInsider*. Retrieved from www.allpharmacyjobs.com/nuclear_pharmacy_cardinal_health_nuclear.htm

12 Steinberg, Scott. "Video Games Are Tomorrow's Answer to Executive Training, FastCompany.com, 14 Mar. 2012. Retrieved from http://www.fastcompany.com/1824740/video-games-are-tomorrows-answer-to-executive-training

13 Lanese, L., and F. Nguyen. "The Journey from Formal Learning to Performance Support," Performance Improvement, 11 May 2012. Retrieved from http://frankn.net/Publications/PI2012-JourneyFormal2Ps.pdf

14 Banks, Shannon, Matthew Farmer, and Luke Sandelands. "Microsoft Leaders Excel through Action Learning," *Training and Management Development Methods* 25 (2011): 23–26.

15 "Our Curriculum" McDonald's. Retrieved from http://www.aboutmcdonalds.com/mcd/corporate_careers/training_and_development/hamburger_university/our_curriculum.html

16 Reuters, Alexei Oreskovic, and Sarah McBride. "Facebook IPO Sparks Dreams of Riches, Adventure," Reuters, 9 Dec. 2011. Retrieved from http://www.reuters.com/article/2011/12/09/us-facebook-millionaires-idUSTRE7B72NK20111209

17 Menke, John D., and Dickson C. Buxton. "The Origin and History of the ESOP and Its Future Role as a Business Succession Tool," *Journal of Financial Service Professionals*, May 2010, p. 61. Retrieved from http://www.menke.com/esop-information/articles/pdf/origin-history-of-esops.pdf

18 "Why Work for SAS, SAS.com. Retrieved from http://www.sas.com/offices/asiapacific/singapore/press/why-sas.html

19 "The Domestic Partnership Benefits and Obligations Act," *Human Rights Campaign*. Human Rights Campaign, 18 Nov. 2011. Retrieved from http://www.hrc.org/laws-and-legislation/federal-legislation/the-domestic-partnership-benefits-and-obligations-act

20 Pender, Kathleen. "Who Pays Tax on Domestic Partner Benefits?" *SFGate*, San Francisco Chronicle, 24 June 2012. Retrieved from http://www.sfgate.com/business/networth/article/Who-pays-tax-on-domestic-partner-benefits-3259655.php

21 "US: Lack of Paid Leave Harms Workers, Children | Human Rights Watch." *US: Lack of Paid Leave Harms Workers, Children | Human Rights Watch*. Human Rights Watch, 23 Feb. 2011. Retrieved from http://www.hrw.org/news/2011/02/23/us-lack-paid-leave-harms-workers-children

22 "Flex-Time Workers Add Two Days to Their Workweek," *GreenBiz.com*, 4 June 2010. Retrieved from www.greenbiz.com/news/2010/06/04/flex-time-workers-add-two-days-their-workweek

23 "Transforming Employee Engagement," Cisco. Retrieved from http://www.cisco.com/en/US/solutions/collateral/ns340/ns1176/business-of-it/Cisco_IT_Trends_in_IT_Article_Employee_Engagement_V2.html

24 "Cisco's Telecommuting Program Boosts Productivity, Cuts Costs and Emissions," *GreenBiz.com*, 26 June 2009. Retrieved from www.greenbiz.com/news/2009/06/26/ciscos-telecommuting-program-boosts-productivity-cuts-costs-and-emissions?src=int

25 Reuters, and Nick Zieminski. "More Temporary Workers Earn Permanent Positions, as Economy Improves," *The Huffington Post*, 9 Mar. 2012. Retrieved from http://www.huffingtonpost.com/2012/03/09/temporary-workers-permanent-positions_n_1335238.html

26 "Canadian Employment Law Today Article—Medical Practice Messes Up Secretary's Termination," Canadian Employment Law Today Article—Medical Practice Messes up Secretary's Termination, N.p., 23 May 2012. Retrieved from http://www.employmentlawtoday.com/articleprint.aspx?articleid=2731

27 Nyce, Steve. "Towers Watson," Employee Retirement Planning in a Post-Crisis Economy. Towers Watson, 1 Jan. 2012. Retrieved from http://www.towerswatson.com/united-states/newsletters/insider/6214

28 Stephenson, Emily. "U.S. Postal Service Offers Buyouts to 45,000 Workers," Yahoo! News. Yahoo!, 25 May 2012. Retrieved from http://news.yahoo.com/u-postal-offers-buyouts-45-000-workers-223341169--sector.html

29 McCutcheon, Duff. "Hireimmigrants.ca." *HR 101: Creating Diversity Plans*, N.p., 22 June 2012. Retrieved from http://www.hireimmigrants.ca/2012/06/22/hr-101-diversity-plans/

30 "Ask DiversityInc: How Does Your Company Handle Religious Holidays?" Corporate Diversity, Diversity Inc., Jan. 2012. Retrieved from http://diversityinc.com/diversity-and-inclusion/ask-diversityinc-how-does-your-company-handle-religious-holidays/

31 Cullen, Lisa Takeuchi. "Employee Diversity Training Doesn't Work," *Time*, 26 April 2007. Retrieved from www.time.com/time/magazine/article/0,9171,1615183,00.html

32 Based on Governor Scott Walker (R), Wisconsin. From speech delivered at a Milwaukee Press Luncheon on Dec 7, 2010.

33 Reported in "'General Strike!' Thousands Storm, Reoccupy Wisconsin Capitol in Response to Legislative Votes" Common Dreams. Wisconsin State Journal, 10 Mar. 2011.

34 "Union Members Summary, *U.S. Bureau of Labor and Statistics*, 27 Jan. 2012. Retrieved from www.bls.gov/news.release/union2.nr0.htm

35 York, Monica Davey, and Jeff Zeleny, authors; Steven Yaccino, contributor; Marjorie Connelly, Dalia Sussman, and Allison Kopicki research contributors. "Governor Wins Wisconsin Vote in Recall Drive," *New York Times*, 6 June 2012. Retrieved from http://www.nytimes.com/2012/06/06/us/politics/walker-survives-wisconsin-recall-effort.html?pagewanted=all

36 HR World Editors, "30 Interview Questions You Can't Ask and 30 Sneaky, Legal Alternatives to Get the Same Info," *HRWorld.com*, 15 Nov. 2007. Retrieved from www.hrworld.com/features/30-interview-questions-111507/

37 Quast, Lisa. "How Your Social Media Profile Could Make or Break Your Next Job Opportunity," Forbes, 23 Apr. 2012. Retrieved from http://www.forbes.com/sites/lisaquast/2012/04/23/your-social-media-profile-could-make-or-break-your-next-job-opportunity/

Chapter 10

1 Duffy, Brian. "E-Commerce Growth—How Online Business Has Grown," Ebusinessmatters.com, EBusiness Matters, 25 July 2011. Retrieved from http://www.ebusinessmatters.com/e-commerce-growth-infographic/

2 Jackson, Eric M. "Why 'The PayPal Mafia' Is Killing It," Breaking News and Opinion on The Huffington Post, Huffington Post, 1 Dec. 2011. Retrieved from http://www.huffingtonpost.com/eric-m-jackson/why-the-paypal-mafia-is-k_b_1121899.html

3 Hanna, Julia. "Broadband: Remaking the Advertising Industry," *Harvard Business School, Working Knowledge*, 17 Sept. 2007. Retrieved from http://hbswk.hbs.edu/item/5652.html

4 Apple Introduces iAds: "Mobile Ads with Emotion," Mashable.com. Retrieved from http://mashable.com/2010/04/08/apple-iads/

5 Marshall, Jack. "Budweiser's Global World Cup Campaign Rooted in Social Media," *ClickZ.com*. Retrieved from www.clickz.com/3640608

6 "Web 2.0," *Proquest Discovery Guides*. Retrieved from www.csa.com/discoveryguides/scholarship/gloss.php

7 Lee, Chris, "'Alien' Bus-Stop Ads Create a Stir," *Los Angeles Times*, 19 June 2009. Retrieved from http://articles.latimes.com/2009/jun/19/entertainment/et-district19

8 "District 9," *The Internet Movie Database*. Retrieved from www.imdb.com/title/tt1136608/business

9 "Welcome to eProcurement.ky.gov," *Kentucky eProcurement*. Retrieved from http://eprocurement.ky.gov/

10 "Welcome to TheMedica.com," TheMedica.com. Retrieved from www.themedica.com/

11 "B2B B2C Web Portals," *Dream Designers*. Retrieved from www.dreamdesigners.co.in/b2c-web-portals.html

12 "Robert Purchese, 'Eurogamer,'" 18 Oct. 2010. Retrieved from http://www.eurogamer.net/articles/2010-10-18-steam-has-over-30-million-accounts

13 "What Online Sales Are Subject to Sales Tax?" AllBusiness.com. Retrieved from www.allbusiness.com/sales/internet-e-commerce/2652-1.html

14 Ibid.

15 Connolly, Chris, and Peter van Dijk. "What Is E-Commerce Legal Infrastructure?," *Galexia*. Retrieved from www.galexia.com/public/research/articles/research_articles-pa04.html#Heading296

16 "Daily Policy Digest: Legal Jurisdiction over the Internet," *National Center for Policy Analysis*, 29 Apr. 2003. Retrieved from www.ncpa.org/sub/dpd/index.php?Article_ID=5250

[17] Worthen, Ben. "Mid-Market: The Big Upgrade to Microsoft Vista," *CIO.com*, 16 Nov. 2006. Retrieved from www.cio .com/article/26664/Mid_Market_The_Big_Upgrade_ to_Microsoft_Vista

[18] Gottlieb, Karen. "Using Court Record Information for Marketing in the United States: It's Public Information, What's the Problem?" *Privacy Rights Clearinghouse*, January 2004. Retrieved from www.privacyrights.org/ar/courtmarketing.htm

[19] "How Much Is a Petabyte?" Online Backup, Mozy, 2 July 2009. Retrieved from http://mozy.com/blog/misc/how-much-is-a-petabyte/

[20] "Cognos Supply Chain Analytics," IBM. Retrieved from www-01.ibm.com/software/data/cognos/products/performance-applications/supply-chain-analytics/capabilities.html

[21] "Adware," SearchCIO-MidMarket.com, 6 Jan. 2007. Retrieved from http://searchcio-midmarket.techtarget .com/sDefinition/0,id183_gci521293,00.html

[22] "Spyware," SearchSecurity.com. Retrieved from http://searchsecurity.techtarget.com/sDefinition/0,sid14_gci214518,00.html

[23] Porter, Rebecca. "Who's Watching Your PC?" *Trial*, 1 Aug. 2004. Retrieved from http://goliath.ecnext.com/coms2/gi_0199-107385/Who-s-watching-your-PC.html

[24] "Phishing," *OnGuard OnLine*. Retrieved from http://onguardonline.gov/phishing.html

[25] "Marketplace Safety Tips," *eBay*. Retrieved from http://pages.ebay.com/securitycenter/

[26] Elfrink, Tim. "The Biggest Identity Theft Case Ever. Right Here in Miami," *Hack Pack, Miami New Times*, 20 May 2010. Retrieved from www.miaminewtimes.com/content/printVersion/2270696

[27] Potter, Ned. "Sony PlayStation Network Hacked Again," ABC News blog, 12 Oct. 2011. Retrieved from http://abcnews .go.com/blogs/technology/2011/10/sony-playstation-network-hacked-again-closes-93000-accounts/

[28] Nakaso, Dan. "$1 Tickets Crash Airline's Website," *USA Today*, 12 June 2007. Retrieved from www.usatoday.com/travel/flights/2007-06-12-one-dollar-tickets-crash-web_N.htm

[29] McCue, Andy. "IT Failure Remains Top Cause of Business Disaster," *Silicon.com*, 11 Mar. 2005. Retrieved from http://hardware.silicon.com/storage/0,39024649,39128617,00.htm

[30] "About Us," wikiLeaks.org. Retrieved from www .wikileaks.org

[31] Chuchmach, Megan. "WikiLeaks Preparing to Release Video of Alleged U.S. 'Massacre' in Afghanistan," *ABC News*, 18 June 2010. Retrieved from http://abcnews.go.com/Blotter/wikileaks-preparing-release-video-alleged-us-massacre-afghanistan/story?id=10954929

[32] Heathfield, Susan. "Listen with Your Eyes: Tips for Understanding Nonverbal Communication," About.com. Retrieved from http://humanresources.about.com/od/interpersonalcommunicatio1/a/nonverbal_com.htm

[33] "Electronic Eavesdropping," *Encyclopædia Britannica*. Retrieved from www.britannica.com/EBchecked/topic/183788/electronic-eavesdropping

[34] DiTecco, D., G. Cwitco, A. Arsenault, and M. Andre. "Operator Stress and Monitoring Practices," *Applied Ergonomics* 23, no. 1 (February 1992), pp. 29–34.

[35] Espen. "Dell's Hell – Looking Back with Jeff Jarvis." Blogcampaigning. 25 Oct. 2007. Retrieved from http://blogcampaigning.com/2007/10/dells-hell-looking-back-with-jeff-jarvis/

[36] Lau, Adaline. "Dell Expands Listening Center to Asia," ClickZ, 22 Sept. 2011. Retrieved from http://www.clickz.com/clickz/news/2111465/dell-expands-listening-center-asia

[37] Menchaca, Lionel. "Dell's Next Step: The Social Media Listening Command Center," Dell Community. Dell, 8 Dec. 2010. Retrieved from http://en.community.dell.com/dell-blogs/direct2dell/b/direct2dell/archive/2010/12/08/dell-s-next-step-the-social-media-listening-command-center.aspx

[38] Li, Shan. "Social Media Jobs Getting More Plentiful," *The Los Angeles Times*, 28 Sept. 2011. Retrieved from http://articles.latimes.com/2011/sep/28/business/la-fi-social-media-jobs-20110929

[39] Tweet from unknown user. Quoted in Smith, Cooper. "Microsoft Sorry For 'Insensitive' Amy Winehouse Tweet." The Huffington Post. 26 July 2011. www.huffingtonpost.com

Chapter 11

[1] "National Data," U.S. Bureau of Economic Analysis (BEA). Retrieved from http://bea.gov/iTable/iTable.cfm?ReqID=9

[2] Ibid.

[3] Ibid.

[4] Cleveland, Douglas B. "The Role of Services in the Modern U.S. Economy," U.S. Department of Commerce. Retrieved from http://trade.gov/td/sif/PDF/ROLSERV199.PDF

[5] United States Economy. "CIA World Factbook." Central Intelligence Agency. Web. 7 May 2012. https://www.cia.gov/library/publications/the-world-factbook/geos/us.html

[6] Ibid.

[7] Ibid.

[8] Data from World Economic Outlook Database April 2012. Web. (07 June 2012.) http://www.imf.org/external/pubs/ft/weo/2012/01/weodata/index.aspx.

[9] Van Dusen, Steven. "The Manufacturing Practices of Nike and Its Competitors." Retrieved from http://www.unc .edu/~andrewsr/ints092/vandu.html

[10] Feemster, Tim. "A Step-by-Step Guide to Choosing the Right Site," Area Development Online, November 2007. Retrieved from www.areadevelopment.com/Print/siteSelection/nov07/stepByStep.shtml

[11] "Tata Steel Ranked World's Best Steel Maker by World Steel Dynamics," *Tata*, 22 June 2005. Retrieved from www.tata .com/media/releases/inside.aspx?artid=nAIH2iibp8Q=

[12] "Does Your Business Produce Hazardous Waste?" Local Hazardous Waste Management Program in King County. Retrieved from www.lhwmp.org/home/BHW/index.

[13] Graham, Paul. "How to Be Silicon Valley," May 2006. Retrieved from http://www.paulgraham.com/siliconvalley .html

[14] Shivapriya, N. "India Remains World's Top Outsourcing Destination," *Bloomberg Businessweek*, 10 July 2009. Retrieved from www.businessweek.com/globalbiz/content/jul2009/gb20090710_974200.htm

[15] Kerr, Jennifer C.. "Mattel Fined $2.3M for Lead Paint on Toys," *USA Today*, 5 June 2009. Retrieved from www .usatoday.com/money/industries/retail/2009-06-05-mattel-fine_N.htm

[16] "The Gartner Supply Chain Top 25 for 2012 | 2021615." The Gartner Supply Chain Top 25 for 2012 | 2021615. Web. 06 June 2012. http://www.gartner.com

[17] "Reducing Costs through Production and Supply Chain Management," *QFINANCE*. Retrieved from http://www .qfinance.com/operations-management-best-practice/reducing-costs-through-production-and-supply-chain-management?page=1

[18] "Automation," *Encyclopædia Britannica*. Retrieved from www.britannica.com/eb/article-24854/automation

19 Hart, Christopher W. "Creating Competitive Advantage through Mass Customization," Spire Group. Retrieved from http://www.spiregroup.biz/pdfs/06-04-07%20 Creating%20Competitive%20Advantage%20through%20 Mass%20Customization.pdf

20 "Robot," *Merriam-Webster Online Dictionary*. Retrieved from www.merriam-webster.com/dictionary/robot

21 Kucera, David. "Computer-Aided Design (CAD) and Computer-Aided Manufacturing (CAM)," *Encyclopedia of Business*, 2nd ed. Retrieved from www.referenceforbusiness .com/encyclopedia/Clo-Con/Computer-Aided-Design-CAD-and-Computer-Aided-Manufacturing-CAM.html

22 Ibid.

23 Mullaney, Tim. "An IPO That Might Print You Some Money," *BusinessWeek.com*, 9 Nov. 2005. Retrieved from www.businessweek.com/the_thread/dealflow/ archives/2005/11/vistaprint.html?chan=search

24 "Customer-Made," trendwatching.com. http:// trendwatching.com/trends/CUSTOMER-MADE.htm (May 31, 2012). Reprinted with permission.

25 "Inventory Control," SCORE (Counselors to America's Small Business). Retrieved from www.ct-clic.com/ Newsletters/customer-files/inventory0602.pdf

26 Bymes, Jonathan. "Dell Manages Profitability, Not Inventory," *Working Knowledge for Business Leaders*, Harvard Business School. Retrieved from http://hbswk.hbs.edu/ archive/3497.html

27 "What Is ERP?" techFAQ. Retrieved from www.tech-faq .com/erp.html

28 "The History of Quality—Total Quality," American Society for Quality. Retrieved from www.asq.org/learn-about-quality/history-of-quality/overview/total-quality.html

29 "Continuous Improvement," American Society for Quality. Retrieved from www.asq.org/learn-about-quality/ continuous-improvement/overview/overview.html

30 "Motorola University: Six Sigma in Action," Motorola, Inc. Retrieved from www.motorola.com/Business/US-EN/ Motorola+University

31 Crocket, Roger O., and Jena McGregor. "Six Sigma Still Pays Off at Motorola," *Bloomberg Businessweek*, 4 Dec. 2006. Retrieved from www.businessweek.com/magazine/ content/06_49/b4012069.htm

32 "ISO Standards," International Organization for Standardization. Retrieved from www.iso.org/iso/iso_catalogue.htm

33 "Discover ISO: ISO's Mame," International Organization for Standardization. Retrieved from www.iso.org/iso/ about/discover-iso_isos-name.htm

34 Fielding, Stanley. "ISO 14001 Brings Change and Delivers Profits," *Quality Digest*. Retrieved from www.qualitydigest .com/nov00/html/iso14000.html

Mini Chapter 3

1 Westheim, Edward G. "The Importance of Effective Communication," *Northeastern University, College of Business Administration*. Retrieved from http://windward.hawaii .edu/facstaff/dagrossa-p/ssci193v/articles/Effective Communication.pdf

2 Chapman, Alan. "Mehrabian's Communication Research," *Businessballs.com*. Retrieved from www.businessballs .com/mehrabiancommunications.htm

3 "E-mail Privacy," Nolo.com. Retrieved from www.nolo .com/legal-encyclopedia/article-29610.html

4 Horng, Eric. "No-E-mail Fridays Transform Office," *ABC News*, 7 Apr. 2007. Retrieved from http://abcnews.go.com/ WNT/Story?id=2939232&page=1

5 Hansen, Evan. "Google Blogger: 'I Was Terminated,'" *CNET News.com*, 11 Feb. 2005. Retrieved from http://news.cnet .com/Google-blogger-I-was-terminated/2100-1038_ 3-5572936.html

6 Sutter, John D. "The Coming-Out Stories of Anonymous Bloggers," *CNN.com*. Retrieved from www.cnn.com/2009/ TECH/08/21/outing.anonymous.bloggers/

7 "1 in 3 Fortune 500 Companies Have Branded Twitter Profiles," *Corporate Eye*. Retrieved from www.corporate-eye .com/blog/2010/03/1-in-3-fortune-500-companies-have-branded-twitter-profiles/

8 Ibid.

Chapter 12

1 From "Vehicle History." Ford Motor Company, n.d. Web. (01 June 2012.) http://corporate.ford.com

2 From "Community: AMA Definition of Marketing." American Marketing Association. Resource Library Dictionary. N.p., n.d. Web. 12 June 2012. http://www.marketingpower .com/_layouts/Dictionary.aspx?dLetter=M Reprinted with permission.

3 Henry Ford, quoted in "Showroom of Automotive History: The Model T." Henry Ford Museum and Greenfield Village. p., n.d. Web. 18 June 2012. N.p., n.d. Web. (18 June 2012.) www.hfmgv.org

4 From General Electric 1952 Annual Report, p. 21, as quoted in Rom Zemke and John A. Woods, *Best Practices in Customer Service* (Amherst, MA: HRD Press, 1998), p. 3.

5 "About Us," *TheBodyShop.com*, n.d. Retrieved from http:// www.thebodyshop-usa.com/about-us/aboutus.aspx?cm_ re=Tyra_CrueltyFreeMakeup2012-_-Navigation-_-about-us

6 "About Buzzed Driving." Ad Council. http://adcouncil.org/

7 *L.L. Bean*, Retrieved from www.llbean.com/

8 Lamb, Charles W., Jr., Joseph F. Hair, and Carl McDaniel. *Marketing*, 7th ed. (Stamford, CT: Thomson Publishing Company, 2004), p. 33.

9 *John Deere*. Retrieved from www.deere.com

10 *High Beam Research*. Retrieved from www.omniglot.com/ language/articles/spanishtranslation.htm

11 "Will Harley-Davidson Hit the Wall? It Redefined the Motorcycle Industry as It Roared through 16 Years of Growth. But as Its Customers Age--and the Stock Market Slides--the Ride Could Get Uneasy," *CNNMoney*, Cable News Network, 12 Aug. 2002. Retrieved from http://money.cnn.com/magazines/fortune/ fortune_archive/2002/08/12/327029/index.htm

12 Kotler, Philip, and Gary Armstrong. *Principles of Marketing*, 12th ed. (Upper Saddle River, NJ: Pearson/Prentice Hall, 2008), pp. 131–147.

13 "Sales Savvy Series for Women Entrepreneurs: #6—Gender Differences in Buying Habits," *Women's Enterprise Centre*. Retrieved from www.womensenterprise.ca/enews/articles/ Microsoft%20Word%20-%206%20-%20Gender% 20Differences%20_2_.pdf

Chapter 13

1 "Most Frequently Asked Questions," *SC Johnson and Son, Inc.* Retrieved from www.oust.com/faq.aspx?oust=airSanitizer

2 "Honda Products Web Sites—Honda Autos, Motorcycles, Services Links," *Honda Products Web Sites—Honda Autos, Motorcycles, Services Links*. Retrieved from http://corporate .honda.com/products_services/details.aspx?id=sites

3 "Growth, Leadership, Sustainability," *Coca-Cola Company Information: The Coca-Cola Company*. Retrieved from http:// www.thecoca-colacompany.com/ourcompany/index.html

4 "Product List," *List of Coca-Cola Products: Comprehensive Coca-Cola Brand List.* Retrieved from http://www.thecoca-colacompany.com/brands/brandlist.html

5 "GE," *Products & Services Overview: Introduction, Businesses, Categories.* Retrieved from http://www.ge.com/products_services/index.html

6 Howard, Theresa. "Coke Finally Scores Another Winner," *USA Today*, 28 Oct. 2007. Retrieved from www.usatoday.com/money/advertising/adtrack/2007-10-28-coke-zero_N.htm

7 "The NRF Top 100 Retailers Are Private Brand Stars," *My Private Brand*, 1 July 2010. Retrieved from http://mypbrand.com/2010/07/01/the-nrf-top-100-retailers-are-private-brand-stars/. Copyrighted 2010 NRF Enterprises Inc. 69694-12mcd.

8 Tom Peters, "The Brand Called You," Fast Company, August 31, 1997. Retrieved from www.fastcompany.com

9 "Welcome to Tiffany & Co." *Tiffany & Co.* Retrieved from http://www.tiffany.com/About/Default.aspx

10 Harsh, Paul. "Puma Gives Up Wasteful Packaging in Favor of Eco-friendly Packages," *Greenpacks.org*, 13 Apr. 2010. Retrieved from www.greenpacks.org/2010/04/13/puma-gives-up-wasteful-packaging-in-favor-of-eco-friendly-packages/

11 "Kimpton Hotels: Boutique Hotels, Luxury Travel and Chef-Driven Gourmet Restaurants," *Kimpton Hotels: Boutique Hotels, Luxury Travel and Chef-Driven Gourmet Restaurants.* Retrieved from http://www.kimptonhotels.com/kimpton-cares/earthcare.aspx

12 "FDA Takes Issue with Cheerios Health Claims," *MSNBC*, 13 May 2009. Retrieved from www.msnbc.msn.com/id/30701291/

13 Ackerman, Alliston. "P&G Shapes the Store." *CGT.* Consumer Goods Technology, 16 Sept. 2011. Retrieved from http://consumergoods.edgl.com/case-studies/P-G-Shapes-the-Store75556

14 Toor, Amar. "Peapod brings 'virtual grocery stores to Chicago's 'L' stations," *The Verge*, 8 May 2012. Retrieved from http://www.theverge.com/2012/5/8/3006535/peapod-virtual-grocery-store-chicago-qr-code-shopping

15 Ross, Michael E. "It Seemed Like a Good Idea at the Time," *MSNBC*, 22 Apr. 2005. Retrieved from www.msnbc.msn.com/id/7209828

16 Cannon, Robert E. "A Tutorial on Product Life Cycle." Retrieved from www.mrotoday.com/progressive/online%20exclusives/productlifecycle.htm

17 Swenson, Dan, Shahid Ansari, Jan Bell, and Il-Woon Kim, "Best Practices in Target Costing," *Management Accounting Quarterly*, Winter 2003, p. 13.

Chapter 14

1 Blum, Steven. "Google Quadruples Their Advertising Budget ," " Here Are Our Fave Ads," *AndroidPit*, 29 Mar. 2012. Retrieved from http://www.androidpit.com/Google-ads

2 "Super Bowl Ads Cost Average Of $3.5M," *ESPN*, ESPN Internet Ventures, 6 Feb. 2012. Retrieved from http://espn.go.com/nfl/playoffs/2011/story/_/id/7544243/super-bowl-2012-commercials-cost-average-35m

3 "7 Awesomely Amazing Examples of Success Through YouTube," *Social Maximizer*, 3 June 2010. Retrieved from http://blog.socialmaximizer.com/

4 Ritkes, Gary. "Direct Mail Statistics Show Effectiveness," *SproutLoud's Marketing & Technology Blog*, 23 June 2012. Retrieved from http://blog.sproutloud.com/index.php/2012/06/direct-mail-statistics-show-effectiveness/

5 Mamutov, Tilek. "More People Have a Mobile Phone than a Toothbrush..." *Tilek Mamutov Blog*, 3 June 2012. Retrieved

from https://plus.google.com/117523780312701271966/posts/J1EhzETRUQp

6 Kats, Rimma. "Universal Pictures Relies on Mobile Advertising to Drive New Film Awareness," *Mobile Marketer*, 26 June 2012. Retrieved from http://www.mobilemarketer.com/cms/news/advertising/13182.html

7 Dukcevich, Davide. "TV's Most Successful Products," *Forbes.com*, 13 Nov. 2002. Retrieved from www.forbes.com/home/2002/11/13/cx_dd_1113products.html

8 Cutlip, Scott M., Allen H. Center, and Glen M. Broom. *Effective Public Relations*, 9th ed. (Upper Saddle River, NJ: Pearson Prentice Hall, 2009), pp. 1, 321.

9 Moriarty, Sandra, Nancy Mitchell, and William Wells. *Advertising, Principles and Practices*, 8th ed. (Upper Saddle River, NJ: Pearson Prentice Hall, 2009), pp. 517–526.

10 Moriarty, Sandra, Nancy Mitchell, and William Wells. *Advertising, Principles and Practices*, p. 528.

11 "Welcome to the A+ School Rewards Program!" *Giant Food Giant*. Retrieved from http://www.giantfood.com/aplus/

12 Kotler, Philip, and Gary Armstrong. *Principles of Marketing*, 12th ed. (Upper Saddle River, NJ: Pearson Prentice Hall, 2008), p. 386.

13 United States Census Bureau, *2007 Census*. U.S. Census Bureau, Table 1042. Wholesale and Retail Trade – Establishments, Sales, Payroll, and Employees: 2002 and 2007. Retrieved from http://www.census.gov/compendia/statab/2012/tables/12s1043.pdf

14 "Table 1.52: Freight Activity in the United States 2007," *Research and Innovative Technology Administration, Bureau of Transportation Statistics*. Retrieved from www.bts.gov/publications/national_transportation_statistics/html/table_01_52.html

15 Donohue, Julie M., Marisa Cevasco, and Meredith B. Rosenthal. "A Decade of Direct-to-Consumer Advertising of Prescription Drugs," *New England Journal of Medicine*, 16 Aug. 2007. Retrieved from www.nejm.org/doi/full/10.1056/NEJMsa070502

Mini Chapter 4

1 "Economic News Release, Employment Situation Summary," *U.S. Bureau of Labor Statistics*. Retrieved from www.bls.gov/news.release/empsit.nr0.htm

2 Pender, Kathleen. "Job Seeker to Job Ratio a Stat Mashup," *San Francisco Chronicle*, 15 July 2010. Retrieved from www.sfgate.com/cgi-bin/article.cgi?f=/c/a/2010/07/14/BUQU1EDVF0.DTL

3 "Résumé Development," *Ball State University Career Center*. Retrieved from http://cms.bsu.edu/About/Administrative-Offices/CareerCenter/MyCareerPlan/JobSearchDocs/Resumes.aspx

4 Doyle, Allison. "Cover Letters," About.com. Retrieved from http://jobsearch.about.com/od/coverletters/a/aa030401a.htm

5 Kendall, Pat. "Cover Letter Tips," *Advanced Resume Concepts*. Retrieved from www.reslady.com/coverletters.html

6 Ibid.

7 Hoffman, Allan. "Seven Tips for Marketing Yourself," *Monster Career Advice*. Retrieved from http://content.comcast.monster.com/job-search-essentials/technology/Seven-Tips-for-Marketing-Yourself/home.aspx

8 Jansen, Randall S. "15 Myths and Misconceptions About Job-Hunting," *Quintessential Careers*. Retrieved from www.quintcareers.com/job-hunting_myths.html

9 Schlegel, Johanna, and Brian Braiker. "Inappropriate Questions," Salary.com. Retrieved from http://www.salary.com/Articles/ArticleDetail.asp?part=par284

10 Della Monaca, Christine F. "Interview Take-Along Checklist," *Monster Career Advice*. Retrieved from http://career-advice.monster.com/interview-preparation/interview-take-along-checklist/article.aspx

Chapter 15

1 *Apple Inc. – Overview*, 14 Oct. 2011. Retrieved from http://investor.apple.com/

2 "Barnes & Noble Booksellers," *Barnes & Noble, Inc.* Retrieved from http://www.barnesandnobleinc.com/for_investors/annual_reports/annual_reports.html

3 "6 Sources of Bootstrap Financing," *Entrepreneur.com*. Retrieved from http://www.entrepreneur.com/money/financing/selffinancingandbootstrapping/article80204.html

4 "Small Business Lending on the Rise According to Recent Surveys," *Reuters.com*, 30 June 2011. Retrieved from http://www.reuters.com/article/2011/06/30/idUS257727+30-Jun-2011+MW20110630

5 "Dallas Keeps on Truckin' with GE Capital," *GE Reports.com*, General Electric, 21 May 2009. Retrieved from www.gereports.com/dallas-keeps-on-truckin-with-ge-capital

6 "Microloan Program," *SBA.gov*, U.S. Small Business Administration. Retrieved from http://sba.gov

7 Johnson, Drew. "BMW Announces $900M Spartanburg Expansion, Confirms X4 Production," *Left Lane News*, 12 Jan. 2012. Retrieved from http://www.leftlanenews.com/bmw-announces-900m-spartanburg-expansion-confirms-x4-production.html

8 Estrada, Herón Márquez. "Carver County Contrite About Tax Goof, but Residents Fuming," *Minneapolis-St. Paul Star Tribune*, 12 Dec. 2007. Retrieved from www.startribune.com/local/west/12448481.html

9 "The Biggest Accounting Scandals of All Time (Photos)," *Huffington Post*, 9 Aug. 2010. Retrieved from www.huffingtonpost.com/2010/03/17/biggest-accounting-scanda_n_502181.html#s74418. Reprinted with permission of the Huffington Post.

10 "Nike Inc 2011 Annual Report," *NIKE, Inc.*

11 Stone, Amey. "SOX: Not So Bad After All?" *Bloomberg Businessweek*, 1 Aug. 2005. Retrieved from www.businessweek.com/bwdaily/dnflash/aug2005/nf2005081_7739_db016.htm

Chapter 16

1 Brinson, Gary P., Brian D. Singer, and Gilbert L. Beebower. "Determinants of Portfolio Performance II: An Update," *Financial Analysts Journal*, May/June 1991, pp. 40–48.

2 Barr, Alistair, and Ronald Orol. "Madoff Arrested in Alleged Ponzi Scheme," *MarketWatch*, 11 Dec. 2008. Retrieved from www.marketwatch.com/story/madoff-arrested-charged-may-be-facing-50-bln-in-losses-fbi

3 "Bernie Madoff Scandal: Where Are They Now?" *Time Magazine*, March 2010. Retrieved from www.time.com/time/specials/packages/completelist/0,29569,1971588,00.html

4 Quick Facts | NYSE Euronext," *NYSE Euronext*, 27 Jan. 2012. Retrieved from http://corporate.nyx.com/en/who-we-are/quick-facts

5 "WFE – Statistics," *WFE – World Federation of Exchanges*, 30 Jan. 2012. Retrieved from http://www.world-exchanges.org/statistics

6 "Listings," *NYSE Euronext*. Retrieved from www.nyse.com/about/listed/1170350259411.html

7 Witkowski, Wallace. "Nasdaq-listed Share Volume Reaches Six-day High – MarketWatch," *MarketWatch*, Wall Street Journal, 11 Aug. 2011. Retrieved from http://www.marketwatch.com/story/nasdaq-listed-share-volume-reaches-six-day-high-2011-08-11

8 "Invest Wisely: Advice from Your Securities Industry Regulators," *SEC*. Retrieved from www.sec.gov/investor/pubs/inws.htm

9 "BBC News – Netflix Splits DVD and Streaming Service," *BBC*, 19 Sept. 2011. Retrieved from http://www.bbc.co.uk/news/technology-14973753

10 "Trends in Mutual Fund Investing, November 2011," *ICI.org*, National Association of U.S. Investment Companies, 29 Dec. 2011. Retrieved from http://ici.org/research/stats/trends/trends_11_11

11 Raice, Shayndi, and Randall Smith. "Facebook Readies IPO Filing," *Wsj.com*, Wall Street Journal, 28 Jan. 2012. Retrieved from http://online.wsj.com/article/SB10001424052970204573704577187062821038498.html

Mini Chapter 5

1 Orman, Suze. "Buy 'New Used' Instead," *Yahoo! Finance*. Retrieved from http://biz.yahoo.com/pfg/e16buylease/art021.html

2 "Compound Interest . . . The 8th Wonder!" *GreekShares.com*. Retrieved from www.greekshares.com/8th.php

3 "Federal Tax Brackets," *MoneyChimp.com*. Retrieved from www.moneychimp.com/features/tax_brackets.htm

Glindex

Page numbers followed by an *f* indicate figures, page numbers followed by a *t* indicate tables.

A

Absolute advantage is the ability to produce more of a good or a service than any other country, 92

Absolute liability is the legal responsibility for damages or injury, 122

Abu Dhabi, 107

Abu Ghraib prison, 73

Accountants, 482*t*

Accounting involves tracking a business's income and expenses by recording its financial transactions, 479

audits of, 480–481

corporate, 480

errors, 479

financial, 480, 480*f*

fraud, 481

fundamentals of, 479

government and not-for-profit, 481

managerial, 480, 480*f*

process of, 483, 483*f*, 484*f*

scandals, 481

software for, 478

standards for, 481–484

tax, 481

types of, 479–481, 480*f*

Accounts payable, 487, 494

Accrued expenses, 487

Accumulated profits, 475

Achievement, need for, 232

Acquisitions occur when one company completely buys out another company, 183

advantages of, 184

and mergers compared, 183–184

Action learning, 266

Actual product is the tangible aspect of the purchase that you can touch, see, hear, smell, or taste, 386

ADA (Americans with Disabilities Act), 62, 72, 262–263

Ad Council, 357

Adidas, 327

ADM (Archer Daniels Midland), 62

Administrative laws are rules and regulations passed by regulatory bodies, 120

Administrative trade barriers, 95

Adornment Expressive Accessories, 152

AdSense, 423

Advanced Enological Closures, 142

Advantage

absolute, 92

comparative, 92

Advertising-based models, 291

Advertising is paid, impersonal mass communication from an identified sponsor to persuade or influence a targeted audience, 419

advantages and disadvantages of, 421, 422*t*

advocacy, 421

AdWare, 298

AdWords, 288, 423

B2B, 421

comparative, 421

corporate (institutional), 421

direct mail, 421, 422

economic impact of, 420

globalization of, 425

high traffic, 291

iAds, 288

infomercials, 424

interactive, 421

Internet (online), 421, 423

media, 420–421, 422

mobile, 421

mobile marketing, 424

nonprofit, 421

online, 288

pay-per-click (PPC), 288

product, 421

product placement, 424

public service, 357, 421

recent developments in, 423–425

retail (local), 421

role of, 419–420

social media and, 424

types of, 420, 421*f*

Advertising laws, 127–128

Advisory boards are a group of individuals who offer guidance to the new business owner, 153

Advocacy advertising promotes an organization's position on a public issue, such as global warming or immigration, 421

Adware is any software application that displays banner ads or pop-up ads while a program is running, 298

AdWords, 288, 423

Aesthetics, 110

Affiliated Computer Services, 203

Affiliation, need for, 232

Affiliative (laissez-faire) leaders are advisory in style, encouraging employees to contribute ideas rather than specifically directing their tasks, 238–239, 238*t*

Affirmative action, 275

Affordability, pricing and, 405

Affordable labor, 317

AFL-CIO, 278

African Americans, 133

Age Discrimination in Employment Act (ADEA), 263

Agents-brokers are intermediaries that facilitate negotiations between buyers and sellers of goods and services but never take title (ownership) of the products traded, 435, 439, 439*f*

Aging population, 8–9, 8*f*

Airlines. *See* specific airlines

Allaire, Paul, 216

Alliances, strategic, 103, 104

Alternative scheduling plans, 271

Amazon.com, 36, 141, 245–246, 356

American Cancer Society, 210

American Civil Liberties Union (ACLU), 299

American Customer Satisfaction Index, 221

American Express, 314

American Federation of Labor (AFL) was founded in 1886 to protect skilled workers, 278

American Franchisee Association, 144

American Indians, 133–134

American Recovery and Reinvestment Act, 45

American Stock Exchange (AMEX) is a stock exchange where stocks are bought and sold on a trading floor or via an electronic market, 512

Americans with Disabilities Act (ADA), 62, 72, 262–263

America Online (AOL), 186

Component parts, 390–391

Compound interest is earned interest that is added to the principal investment, which continues to be invested so that the interest also continues to earn interest, 503

Compressed workweek allows employees to work four 10-hour days each week, or 9 days instead of 10 in a two-week schedule for 80 hours, 271

Computer-aided design (CAD) refers to using a computer and software to create two-dimensional or three-dimensional models of physical parts, 326

Computer-aided manufacturing (CAM) uses the design data to control the machinery used in the manufacturing process, 327

Computer-integrated manufacturing (CIM) systems combine design and manufacturing functions with other automated functions, such as order taking, shipment, and billing for the complete automation of a manufacturing plant, 327

Concept development and testing, 400

Conceptual skills are the ability to think abstractly to picture an organization as a whole and understand its relationship to the remainder of the business community, 205–206

Conglomeration, 186, 187

Congress of Industrial Organizations (CIO) was formed in 1935 to represent entire industries rather than specific workers' groups, 278

Consequences of purchase, 359

Constitutional law is the written text of the U.S. Constitution and the Bill of Rights, 120

Consultants are contingent workers who are generally self-employed and who companies hire on a temporary basis to perform specific tasks, 272

Consumer behavior refers to the ways individuals or organizations search for, evaluate, purchase, use, and dispose of goods and services, 373–377
  consumer markets, 374–376
  influences on buying decisions, 375f

Consumer Bill of Rights, 72

Consumer debt, 45

Consumer issues, marketing and, 64, 66

Consumer markets are markets where individuals purchase goods and services for personal consumption, 374, 376–377, 377t

Consumer preferences, 34

Consumer price index (CPI) tracks changes in prices over time by measuring changes in the prices of goods and services that represent the average buying pattern of urban households, 40–41, 41f

Consumer product classifications, 388–389

Consumer Product Safety Commission, 104, 367

Consumer products are convenience goods and services, shopping goods and services, specialty goods and services, and unsought goods and services, 388, 388f
  classifications of, 388–389, 389f

Consumer sales promotions are incentives designed to increase final consumer demand for a product, 432

Consumer to consumer (C2C) transactions refers to consumers selling goods and services to other consumers, sometimes with the involvement of a third party, 290

Contextual advertising refers to online ads automatically generated by the content on a specific site, 288

Contingency planning is a set of plans that ensures that an organization will run as smoothly as possible during an unexpected disruption, 212–213, 212f

Contingent workers are people who are hired on an as-needed basis and lack status as regular, full-time employees, 272

Contract is an agreement between two parties, 121–122, 122f

Contract law, 121–122

Contract manufacturing occurs when a firm subcontracts part or all of its goods to an outside firm as an alternative to owning and operating its own production facility, 103, 104

Control charts, 219, 220f

Controlled messages, 426

Controlling (monitoring) is the process by which managers measure performance and make sure the company's plans and strategies are being or have been properly carried out, 218–221, 219f

Convenience goods and services are those products that customers purchase frequently, immediately, and effortlessly

Converse, 327

Convertible bonds give a bondholder the right (but not the obligation) to convert the bond into a predetermined number of shares of the company's stock, 517

Cook, Catherine, 141

Cook, David, 141

Cook, Geoff, 141

Cool Carpet, 76–77

Cooperatives are businesses that are owned and governed by members who use its products or services, not by outside investors, 182–183, 440

Copyright, 124

Core product provides the core benefit or service that satisfies the basic need or want that motivates a consumer's purchase, 386

Cornell University, 233

Corporate accounting is the part of an organization's finance department that is responsible for gathering and assembling data required for key financial statements, 480

Corporate advertising (institutional advertising) focuses on creating a positive image toward an organization or an entire industry as opposed to a specific product, 421

Corporate bonds are debt securities issued by corporations, 517

Corporate chain stores are two or more retail outlets owned by a single corporation, 440

Corporate culture is a collection of values, norms, and behavior shared by management and workers that defines the character of an organization, 241
  ethical focus and, 78–79
  leadership and, 241–242

Corporate philanthropy is when a company donates some of

challenges of, 292–293
consumer-to-consumer, 12
Economic effects, of corporate social responsibility, 70
Economic environment, 364–365
Economic indicators, 38–43
Economic policy, international business and, 108–109
Economics is the study of how individuals and businesses make decisions to best satisfy wants, needs, and desires with limited resources and how efficiently and equitably resources are allocated, 25–28
competition and, 35–38
economic indicators, 38–43
price determination factors, 31–35
Economic systems, 26–28, 27t
degree of government control, 28f
types of, 26–27, 27t
Economy is a system that tries to balance the available resources of a country, such as land, capital, and labor, against the wants and needs of consumers
business and, 28
free-market, 91, 108
global, 314–315
government and, 43–49
green, 9–10
market, 27
service-based, 314
stock prices and, 511
supply and demand, 29–31
types of, 26–28, 27t
unemployment and, 26, 41–42, 365
EDLP (Everyday low pricing), 407
Edwards, Sheena, 140
Efficiency, production and, 325
Egozy, Eran, 196
Electronic monitoring is commonly used to track employees' keystrokes and e-mails, examine their Internet browsing histories, and even monitor their cell phone and instant messaging usage, 301
Electronic Performance Support Systems (EPSSs), 265
Electronic retailing is the selling of consumer goods and services over the Internet, 441. *See also* E-commerce
Electronic trading, 511
Elevator pitch a brief statement that clearly summarizes your skills and what you can offer, 456
E-mail, 346–348

Embargoes are a total restriction on an import or an export, 95
Emich, Kyle, 233
Emotional intelligence is the ability to understand both one's own and others' emotions, 240
Employee benefits are indirect financial and nonfinancial payments an employer offers that supplement cash compensation, 270–271
noncash forms of, 270
trends in, 270–271
Employee empowerment, 7–8
Employee laws ensure that all workers and employees are treated fairly, 128
Employee morale, corporate social responsibility and, 70
Employees
alternative scheduling and work arrangements, 271–272
benefits (compensation), 270–271
compensation of, 269–270
contingent workers, 272
empowerment of, 7–8
evaluation of, 266–268
hiring, 261–262
job analysis for, 258
job description for, 258–259
monitoring, 219
moral of, 70
motivation of, 231, 230t
new employee orientation, 264, 264t
permanent part-time, 271
personal ethics of, 61–62
privacy of, 300–301
promotion of, 272–273
recruitment of, 260, 260f, 261
retirement and, 274
termination of, 273
training methods and requirements, 264–266
Employees First, Customers Second (Nayar), 217
Employee stock ownership plans (ESOPs) use a company's pension plan for employees to invest in company stock, effectively giving employees significant ownership in a company, 270
Employee stock purchase plans allow employees to buy company stock at a discount, 270
Employment, finding. *See* Finding a job
Employment at will is a legal doctrine that states that an employer can fire an employee for any reason at any time, 273
Employment laws mandate that companies do not discriminate in their hiring practices, 128

Employment standards, 64–65
Empowerment, of employees, 7–8
Engadget, 328
Enron, 72–73, 74
Enterprise resource planning (ERP) is a system that can do the same inventory control and process scheduling that MRP can do, but that integrates these functions with all the other aspects business management would like to tie together, such as finance and human resources, 332
Enterprise social networking refers to the application of products like Facebook in a corporate setting, 302
Enterprise zones are geographic areas targeted for economic revitalizing, 153
Entrepreneur, 4
Entrepreneurial teams are groups of qualified individuals with varied experiences and skills that come together to form a new venture, 142–143
Entrepreneurs assume the risk of creating, organizing, and operating a business and direct all of a business's resources, 137–143
growth, 141
home-based, 140
innovation and, 138, 138f, 143
Internet, 141
lifestyle, 140
micropreneurs, 140
social, 142
traits of, 138–140
types of, 140–142
Entrepreneurs Organization (EO), 152
Environment. *See also* Workplace environment
corporate social responsibility and, 69–70
ethical, 77–79
packaging and, 397
Environmental concerns, and corporate social responsibility, 64, 69–70
Environmental laws, 127
Environmental Protection Agency (EPA), 127, 367
Environmental scanning is the process of surveying the marketing environment to assess external threats and opportunities, 364
EPA, 127
E-procurement, 290
Equal Employment Opportunity Commission (EEOC), 72

and the investors who purchase the bonds, 508

Financial capital is money used to facilitate a business enterprise, 4

Financial management involves the strategic planning and budgeting of short- and long-term funds for current and future needs, 465–469, 466*f*

addressing cash flow and budget, 468–469

planning for financial needs, 466–468

small business management, 469–473

Financial managers (or chief financial officers (CFOs)) oversee the financial operations of a company, 465–466

Financial plan, personal, 533–537, 533*f*, 534*t*, 535*t*

Financial planning, 466–468, 467*f*

Financial section, of business plan, 200

Financial statements are formal reports of a business's financial transactions that accountants prepare periodically, 485, 485*f*

balance sheets, 485–487

income statements, 489–491

statement of cash flows, 493–494

Financing

angel investors, 156

bootstrap, 155

crowdfunding, 154–155

loans and grants, 471–473

long-term, 474–478

partnerships, 170, 171

short-term, 470–471

for small businesses, 154–157

sole proprietorships, 168

venture capitalists, 156–157

Financing activities, 493

Finding a job, 450–462

interviewing and negotiating, 459–462

marketing yourself, 450–456

search strategies, 456–459

Finley, Matt, 221

Firing. *See* Termination

First, Tom, 6

First-line managers fill a supervisory role over those employees who carry out the day-to-day operations of a company, 206

Fiscal policy determines the appropriate level of taxes and government spending, 44–45

Fishbone diagram. *See* Cause-and-effect diagrams

501(c)(3) status. *See* Tax-exempt status

Fixed assets are assets that have long-term use, such as real estate, buildings, machinery, and equipment, 486–487

Fixed costs, 408

Fixed exchange rate system, 107

Fixed position layouts are used for manufacturing large items; the product stays in one place, and the workers move around the product to complete its assembly, 319

Flat organization, 215

Fletcher, Joseph, 58

Flexibility, small business owners and, 136

Flexible benefit plans (cafeteria plans) permit an employee to pick from a menu of several choices of taxable and nontaxable forms of compensation, 270

Flexible manufacturing, 324

Flexible manufacturing system (FMS) is a system in which machines are programmed to process different part types simultaneously—allowing a manufacturer to mass-produce customized products, 322

Flextime is an alternative scheduling practice in which management defines a total number of required hours as a core workday and is flexible with starting and ending hours, 271

Florida's Natural Grower Cooperative, 182

Flow is a state of feeling completely involved and focused on a task, 230, 245

FMS. *See* Flexible manufacturing system (FMS)

Focus groups are typically groups of 8–10 potential customers who are asked for feedback on a good or a service, an advertisement, an idea, or packaging style, 369

Food and Drug Administration (FDA), 120, 367

Ford, Henry, 138, 354

Ford Explorers, 123

Ford Motor Company, 88, 88*f*, 89*f*, 335, 353, 359

Forecasting is the process through which future demand for employees is determined, 268, 297

Foreign direct investment is the purchasing of property

and businesses in a foreign nation, 90

Foreign markets. *See also* International business

advantages/disadvantages of entry modes, 104–105, 104*t*

entrance into, 101–104

Forest, Bruce, 62

Form utility is satisfaction derived from the shape of a good or presentation of a service, 358

Forward scheduling, 329

Fossbenner, Kevin, 297

457 plans, 542

401(k) plans are defined contribution plans in which pretax dollars are invested in a bundle of investments that are generally managed by an outside investment company, 259, 542

403(b) plans, 542

Four Seasons (hotels), 9

Foursquare, 135, 398

Fractional pricing, 408

Franchisees are the independent third-party operators of a franchise, 102, 144, 440

Franchiser, 440

Franchises, 440

Franchise Zone, 144

Franchising involves selling a well-known brand name or a proven method of doing business to an investor in exchange for a fee and a percentage of sales or profits, 102, 104

buying an existing business, 146–148

considerations, 146–149, 147*t*, 148*t*

in foreign markets, 144

opportunities, 144

pros and cons of, 145, 145*f*, 146*f*

Web-based resources for, 144*t*

Franchisors are businesses that sell their product or service and its method of doing business to independent third-part operators, 102, 144

FranNet, 144

Fraud

accounting, 481

click, 288

securities investments, 73, 507

spyware and, 298

Freely floating (flexible) exchange rate system, 107

Freeman, Bruce, 136

Free trade refers to the unencumbered flow of goods and services across national borders, 94

environmental effects of, 69–70

international organizations promoting, 96–98

Grants are financial awards that are offered by federal and state governments and some private organizations, 155–156

Grapevine Mall (Grapevine, Texas), 135

Graphical user interface (GUI), 7

"Gray Matters" (game), 78

Green, Robin, 391

Green businesses, 76–77

Green-collar workers, 9

Green economy factors ecological concerns into business decisions, 9–10

GreenStop, 75

Greenwald, Robert, 66

Gross domestic product (GDP) measures the overall market value of final goods and services produced in a country in a year, 39–40
by country, 39
debt-to-GDP of world economies, 40f
industrial production and, 315f

Gross national product (GNP) attributes earnings to the country where the company was owned, not where the product was manufactured, 39

Gross profit tells how much money a company makes just from its products and how efficiently management controls costs in the production process, 491

Gross profit margin determines a company's profitability of production, 491, 492

Group flow occurs when a group knows how to work together so that each individual member can achieve flow, 245

Groupon, 361, 425

Groupthink is the practice of thinking or making decisions as a group in a way that discourages individual ideas or responsibilities, 244

Growth entrepreneurs strive to create fast-growing businesses and look forward to expansion, 141

Growth stocks are issued by young entrepreneurial companies that are experiencing rapid growth and expansion, 509–510

GUI (Graphical user interface), 7

Gutierrez, Ana, 229, 236

H

Hackers are individuals who gain unauthorized entry into a computer system, 299

Happiness, 60

Harley-Davidson, 372

Harmonix, 196

Hawthorne effect states that when workers feel important, productivity increases, 235

Hazardous waste, 317

HCL Technologies, 217

Health, corporate social responsibility and, 64, 66

Health insurance, 539

Healy, Mark, 213, 218

Hensel, George, 263

Herbalife health products, 441

Hertz Corporation, 184

Herzberg, Frederick, 232

Hewlett-Packard (HP), 103
spying scandal, 300

Hidden fees and charges, 358

Hierarchy of needs describes motivation as a response to a progressive set of needs for physiology, safety, belonging, esteem, and self-actualization, 231–232, 231f

High motivation, 234

Hiring, 261–263, 262f. See also Human resource management (HRM)

Hispanics, 133–134

Histograms, 220, 220f

Hoffman, Aaron, 359

Hoffman, Reid, 288

Hoffman, Stephen, 75–76

Hogan Personality Inventory, 70

Hogg, Jason, 139

Home-based entrepreneurs are entrepreneurs who run their businesses out of their homes, 140–141

Home Depot, 221, 403

Homeowners insurance, 540

Honda, 9, 387

Horizontal mergers occur when two companies that share the same product lines and markets and are in direct competition with each other merge, 186, 187

Horizontal organizations are flattened organizations where the management layer is collapsed and the majority of the employees are in working teams or groups, 215, 215f, 216

Hostile takeovers, 184

Houston, Drew, 2, 3

Howe, Neil, 244–245

Hoyt, Ted, 322

HP (Hewlett-Packard), 103, 300

H&R Block, 424

HRM. See Human resource management (HRM)

Hsieh, Tony, 134, 241–243

Huizenga, Wayne, 138

Human resource management (HRM) is the organizational function that deals with the people in the business: executives and managers plus frontline production, sales, and administrative staff, 257–263. See also Employees; Workforce
alternative scheduling, 271–272
functions of, 258f
hiring process, 261–263, 262f
labor unions and, 277–278
managing staffing needs, 257–261
social media risks, 261
software for, 262
workplace diversity and, 274–277

Human rights, 64–65

Hurley, Chad, 288

Hybrid vehicles, 9

Hygiene factors are factors such as safe working environment, proper pay and benefits, and positive relationships with coworkers, 232

I

Iacocca, Lee, 110

iAds, 288

Idea generation, 399

Idea screening, 399

Identity theft is the illegal gain and use of personal information, 13

IKEA, 320–321, 322

Image, pricing and, 405

ImClone, 507

Importing is buying products from other countries, 87

Incentive-based payment structures have a lower base salary enhanced with commissions, compensation based directly on an employee's performance, 269

Income
effect of business loss on personal, 167
net, 489
operating, 491

Income statements show how much money is coming into a company and how much money a company is spending over a period, 467, 485, 489–491
analysis of, 491–493, 492t
cost of goods sold, 490–491
operating expenses, 491
revenue, 490

Income stocks are issued by companies that pay large dividends, such as utility companies, 509, 510

Permanent part-time employees are hired on a permanent basis to work a part-time week, 271

Personal brand, 395

Personal ethics are the principles that guide the decisions you make in your life, 58–60
  business ethics and, 60–63
  determining code of, 59t

Personal finance, 532–543, 533f
  buying or leasing a car, 538–539
  financial plan for, 533–537, 537f
  insurance, 539–540
  investments, 540–541
  managing credit, 537–538
  retirement planning, 541–542
  software for, 532
  taxes and, 542–543

Personal influences, on buyer consumption, 375

Personal information, misuse of, 358

Personality assessments, 241

Personal liability, 165

Personal liability, S corporations and, 178

Personal selling is direct communication between a firm's sales force and potential buyers to make a sale and build good customer relations, 428–431, 430f
  sales force advantages and disadvantages, 428–429
  salesperson roles, 429–430
  selling process, 430

PERT Charts, 329, 330f

Per unit variable cost, 408

Peters, Tom, 395

Pete's Brewing Company, 140

Pettingill, Sonja, 287

Pfizer, 184

P&G (Procter & Gamble), 110

Philanthropy, corporate, 427

Phillips, Lana, 71, 74

Phishing is a common way to trick online users into sending their personal information, like credit card numbers, straight to hackers, 298–299

Phoenix Textile Corp., 156

Physical distribution is a system that involves getting products to customers when and where they want them, 442

Physiological needs are basic needs such as water, food, sleep, and reproduction, 231

Picketing is a form of protest during a strike when workers walk around company entrances carrying signs and distributing pamphlets that display the nature of their grievances, 279

PittGirl blog, 350

Pixar, 239

Pizza Hut, 194

Place (distribution) component of the marketing mix refers to all the methods involved in getting a product into the hands of customers, 361

Place utility is the satisfaction derived from obtaining a product where it is desired, 358

Planned economy is an economic system in which the government has more control over what is produced, the resources to produce the goods and services, and the distribution of the goods and services, 26, 27

Planned responses, in business plan, 198

Planning is the process of establishing goals and objectives and determining the best ways to accomplish them, 208
  contingency, 212–213, 212f, 213f
  strategic, 208–209, 208f

Plans
  contingency, 212–213, 212f, 213f
  marketing, 370–371
  operational, 212, 213f
  production, 323
  retirement, 541–542
  strategic, 208–209, 208f
  tactical, 211–212, 213f

Playground design, 245

Podcasts, 350–351

Political action committees (PACs), 367

Political candidates, marketing of, 357

Political environment, marketing and, 367

Polman, Evan, 233

Ponzi, Charles, 507

Ponzi scheme, 73, 507

Population, as determinant of demand, 34

Pop-up ads, 423

Positioning is the process of developing a unique marketing mix that best satisfies a target market, 372

Power, need for, 232

Power of Nice, The (Thaler and Koval), 70

PowerPoint, 342, 343

PPC (pay-per-click) advertising, 288

Prada, 66

Preferred stock is a class of ownership in which the preferred stockholders have a claim to assets before common stockholders if a firm goes out of business, 509

Premium pricing, 408

Prestige pricing (premium pricing) is the practice of charging a high price to invoke perceptions of high quality and privilege, 408

Price collusion, 126–127

Price discrimination is charging different prices to different customers when these price differences are not a reflection of cost differences, 406–407

Price expectations, 32–33

Price fixing occurs when a group of companies agree among themselves to set a product's prices, independent of market demand or supply, 62

Price indices, 40–41

Price sensitivity, 373

Price skimming involves charging a high price for a product initially and then lowering the price over time, 407

Price-takers, 404

Pricing, 361
  adjustments, 409, 409f
  as component in marketing mix, 404–405
  dynamic, 409
  everyday low, 407
  factors determining, 31
  goods and services, 403–409
  loss leaders, 408
  objectives for, 404
  penetration, 407–408
  prestige (premium), 408
  price skimming, 407
  psychological (odd or fractional), 408
  reference, 408
  status quo, 405
  strategies for, 405–408, 406f
  value-based, 404

Priest, Maureen, 176

Primary data is raw data collected by a researcher, 369, 369t

Primary markets are a part of the capital markets that deal with new bond and stock issues, 508

Principles of Scientific Management, The (Taylor), 235

Privacy, 13, 300–301

Private accountants, 480

Private brands are brands created by a distributor, or a middleman, 394

Privately held (closed) corporations are owned, in most cases, by the company's founders, a management team, or a group of private investors, 175

ethics, 79
for managers, 265–266
off-the-job, 264
online, 265
on-the-job, 264
simulation (vestibule), 265
for small business owners,
    152–153
technology for, 265
teletraining, 265
Transnational strategy offers a
    customized product while
    simultaneously selling
    it at the lowest possible
    price, 101
Transportation, 442–443, 443*t*
Treasury bills (or T-bills) are bonds
    that mature between 2 and
    26 weeks, 517, 518
Treasury bonds are bonds that
    mature in 30 years and pay
    interest, 518
**Treasury Inflation-Protected Securities
    (TIPS)** are bonds whose
    principal is adjusted to the
    CPI, 517, 518
Treasury notes (T-notes) are bonds
    that mature in 2, 5, or 10
    years and pay interest
    semiannually, 517, 518
Trends, marketing and, 366
Trendwatching, 327
Trough, 44
Truck wholesalers (or truck jobbers)
    sell and deliver directly from
    their trucks, 438
Trump, Donald, 395
Trunk shows, 375
Truth-in-advertising rules, 127, 128
Turnkey projects occur when firms
    export their technological
    know-how in exchange for a
    fee, 102, 104
Twitter, 7, 11, 135, 424
Two factor theory, 232
Tyco International, 73–74

U

Under Armour, 489
Undercapitalization occurs when
    a business owner cannot
    gain access to adequate
    funding, 14
Understanding, 249
Understudy programs, 266
\nemployment, 136
  \clical, 42
  omy and, 26, 42, 43, 365
  al, 42
  Depression, 355

Unemployment rate measures the
    number of workers who are
    at least 16 years old, who
    are not working, and who
    have been trying to find a job
    within the past four weeks
    and still haven't found one,
    41–43
Unethical behavior is defined as
    behavior that does not
    conform to a set of approved
    standards of social or
    professional behavior, 58
Unicru, 262
Uniform Commercial Code (UCC) is
    a set of model laws that
    govern businesses selling
    goods within the U.S.
    and its territories, 125,
    126, 126*t*
Unions. *See* Labor unions
United Airlines, 326
Universal Pictures, 424
Universal product codes, 443
Unlimited liability means that if
    business assets are not
    enough to pay business
    debts, then personal
    assets, such as the sole
    proprietor's house, personal
    investments, or retirement
    funds, can be used to pay the
    balance, 168
Unprocessed materials, 390
Unsecured bonds are bonds that are
    issued with no collateral; it
    is also called a debenture
    bond, 517
Unsecured loans are loans that do
    not require collateral
    to guarantee the debt
    obligation, 472
Unsought goods and services are
    products buyers don't
    usually think about buying,
    don't know exist, or buy
    only when a specific problem
    arises, 389
Unspoken language, 111
Uruguay Round, 97
U.S. Department of Agriculture
    (USDA), 72
U.S. Savings bonds are issued at face
    value, given at maturity, 518
U.S. Treasury debt, 518
Utility is the production of value by
    satisfying consumers' wants
    or needs, 323
Utility supply is the availability
    of public infrastructure
    services, such as electricity,
    natural gas, water, and
    communications, 316

V

Vaccines, 75–76
Vadanta Resources, 65
Valence is the importance that the
    individual places on the
    expected outcome of a
    situation, 234
Value of a product equals the ratio of
    a product's benefits to its
    costs, 358
Value stocks are viewed as being
    priced lower than what
    they should be based on the
    company's earnings and
    financial performance, 510
Vanguard Group, 213
Variable costs, 408
Venture capital is an investment in the
    form of money that includes
    a substantial amount of risk
    for investors, 156–157, 476
Venture capitalists contribute money
    to a business in return for
    some form of equity—a piece
    of ownership, 476
Verizon Communications, 184
Versace, 66
Vertical merger, 186, 187
Vertical mergers occur when two
    companies that have
    a company/customer
    relationship or a company/
    supplier relationship
    merge, 186
Vertical organizations are organized
    by specific function, such
    as marketing, finance,
    purchasing, information
    technology, and human
    resources, 215–216, 215*f*
Vertical portals, 291
Veterans Affairs data breach, 300
Videoconferencing, 265, 349
Village Voice, 270
Viral marketing is a practice that
    involves using social
    networks, e-mail, and
    websites to spread the
    awareness of a particular
    brand, 289–290, 366
Virtual team members are located in
    different physical locations
    but work together to achieve
    a goal, 247
Virtual teams, 247
Visionary leaders are able to inspire
    others, believe in their own
    vision, and move people
    toward a shared dream,
    238*t*, 239
Vision identifies what the business
    wants to be in the future,
    209, 210, 403

Answer Key

CHAPTER 1
Business Basics

Self-Test Multiple Choice
(Answers): 1. a; 2. b; 3. d; 4. b; 5. b; 6. d; 7. a; 8. b; 9. a; 10. c

Self-Test True False
(Answers): 1. True; 2. False; 3. True; 4. True; 5. False

CHAPTER 2
Economics and Banking

Self-Test Multiple Choice
(Answers): 1. a; 2. c; 3. a; 4. b; 5. b; 6. c; 7. b; 8. a; 9. d; 10. c

Self-Test True False
(Answers): 1. True; 2. False; 3. False; 4. True; 5. False

CHAPTER 3
Ethics in Business

Self-Test Multiple Choice
(Answers): 1. b; 2. d; 3. b; 4. b; 5. c; 6. d; 7. d; 8. c; 9. a; 10. b

Self-Test True False
(Answers): 1. False; 2. False; 3. True; 4. False; 5. False

CHAPTER 4
Business in a Global Economy

Self-Test Multiple Choice
(Answers): 1. a; 2. d; 3. a; 4. d; 5. a; 6. a; 7. d; 8. b; 9. d; 10. b

Self-Test True False
(Answers): 1. True; 2. True; 3. False; 4. False; 5. True

CHAPTER 5
Small Business and the Entrepreneur

Self-Test Multiple Choice
(Answers): 1. d; 2. d; 3. a; 4. a; 5. b; 6. a; 7. c; 8. c; 9. d; 10. c

Self-Test True False
(Answers): 1. True; 2. False; 3. False; 4. False; 5. True

CHAPTER 6
Forms of Business Ownership

Self-Test Multiple Choice
(Answers): 1. d; 2. d; 3. c; 4. a; 5. d; 6. b; 7. d; 8. a; 9. a; 10. b

Self-Test True False
(Answers): 1. False; 2. False; 3. True; 4. False; 5. True

CHAPTER 7
Business Management and Organization

Self-Test Multiple Choice
(Answers): 1. b; 2. a; 3. b; 4. b; 5. a; 6. c; 7. a; 8. b; 9. b; 10. d

Self-Test True False
(Answers): 1. False; 2. True; 3. True; 4. True; 5. False

CHAPTER 8
Motivation, Leadership, and Teamwork

Self-Test Multiple Choice
(Answers): 1. b; 2. d; 3. a; 4. b; 5. c; 6. c; 7. a; 8. d; 9. a; 10. c

Self-Test True False
(Answers): 1. False; 2. False; 3. True; 4. True; 5. False

CHAPTER 9
Human Resource Management

Self-Test Multiple Choice
(Answers): 1. d; 2. a; 3. d; 4. a; 5. a; 6. b; 7. b; 8. d; 9. b; 10. c

Self-Test True False
(Answers): 1. True; 2. True; 3. True; 4. True; 5. True

CHAPTER 10
Online Business and Technology

Self-Test Multiple Choice
(Answers): 1. d; 2. a; 3. a; 4. a; 5. d; 6. d; 7. c; 8. b; 9. d; 10. a

Self-Test True False
(Answers): 1. False; 2. True; 3. False; 4. True; 5. True

CHAPTER 11
Production, Operations, and the Supply Chain

Self-Test Multiple Choice
(Answers): 1. b; 2. a; 3. c; 4. a; 5. b; 6. d; 7. c; 8. a; 9. a; 10. b

Self-Test True False
(Answers): 1. True; 2. True; 3. False; 4. False; 5. False

CHAPTER 12
Marketing and Consumer Behavior

Self-Test Multiple Choice
(Answers): 1. b; 2. b; 3. c; 4. d; 5. b; 6. a; 7. c; 8. d; 9. d; 10. a

Self-Test True False
(Answers): 1. False; 2. True; 3. True; 4. True; 5. False

CHAPTER 13
Product Development and Pricing Strategies

Self-Test Multiple Choice
(Answers): 1. d; 2. c; 3. a; 4. c; 5. b; 6. d; 7. d ; 8. a ; 9. b; 10. d

Self-Test True False
(Answers): 1. True; 2. True; 3. False; 4. True; 5. False

CHAPTER 14
Promotion and Distribution

Self-Test Multiple Choice
(Answers): 1. b; 2. d; 3. b; 4. b; 5. a; 6. a; 7. c; 8. a; 9. d; 10. c

Self-Test True False
(Answers): 1. True; 2. True; 3. True; 4. False; 5. False

CHAPTER 15
Financing and Tracking Business Operations

Self-Test Multiple Choice
(Answers): 1. b; 2. d; 3. a; 4. a; 5. d; 6. a; 7. c; 8. b; 9. d; 10. a

Self-Test True False
(Answers): 1. True; 2. True; 3. False; 4. True; 5. False

CHAPTER 16
Investment Opportunities in the Securities Market

Self-Test Multiple Choice
(Answers): 1. c; 2. d; 3. a; 4. a; 5. b; 6. c; 7. b; 8. b; 9. a; 10. b

Self-Test True False
(Answers): 1. True; 2. False; 3. True; 4. False; 5. False